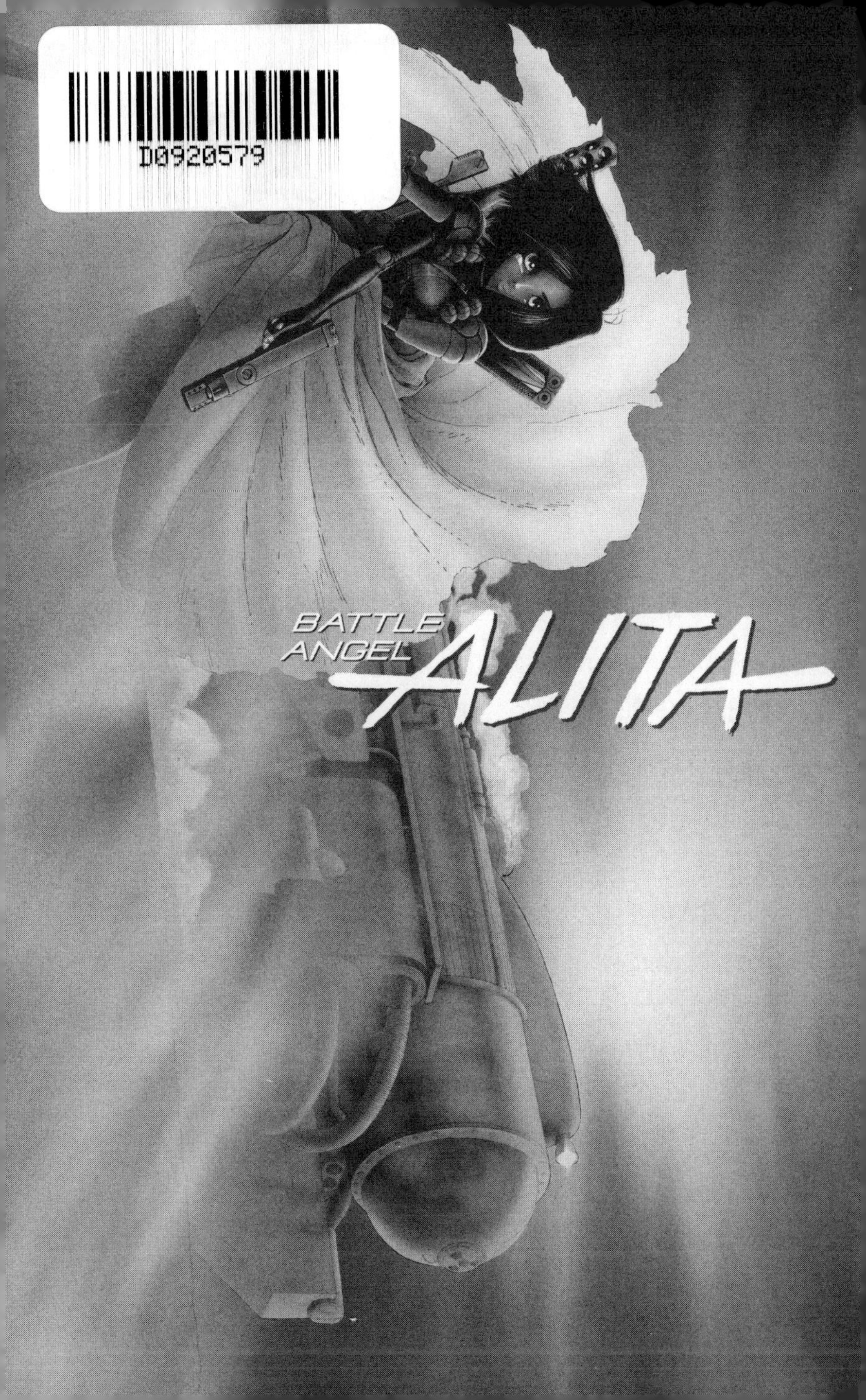
BATTLE ANGEL
ALITA

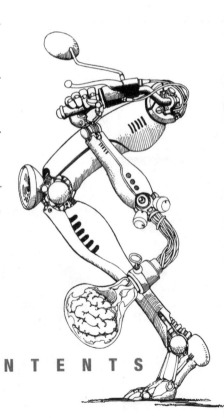

C O N T E N T S

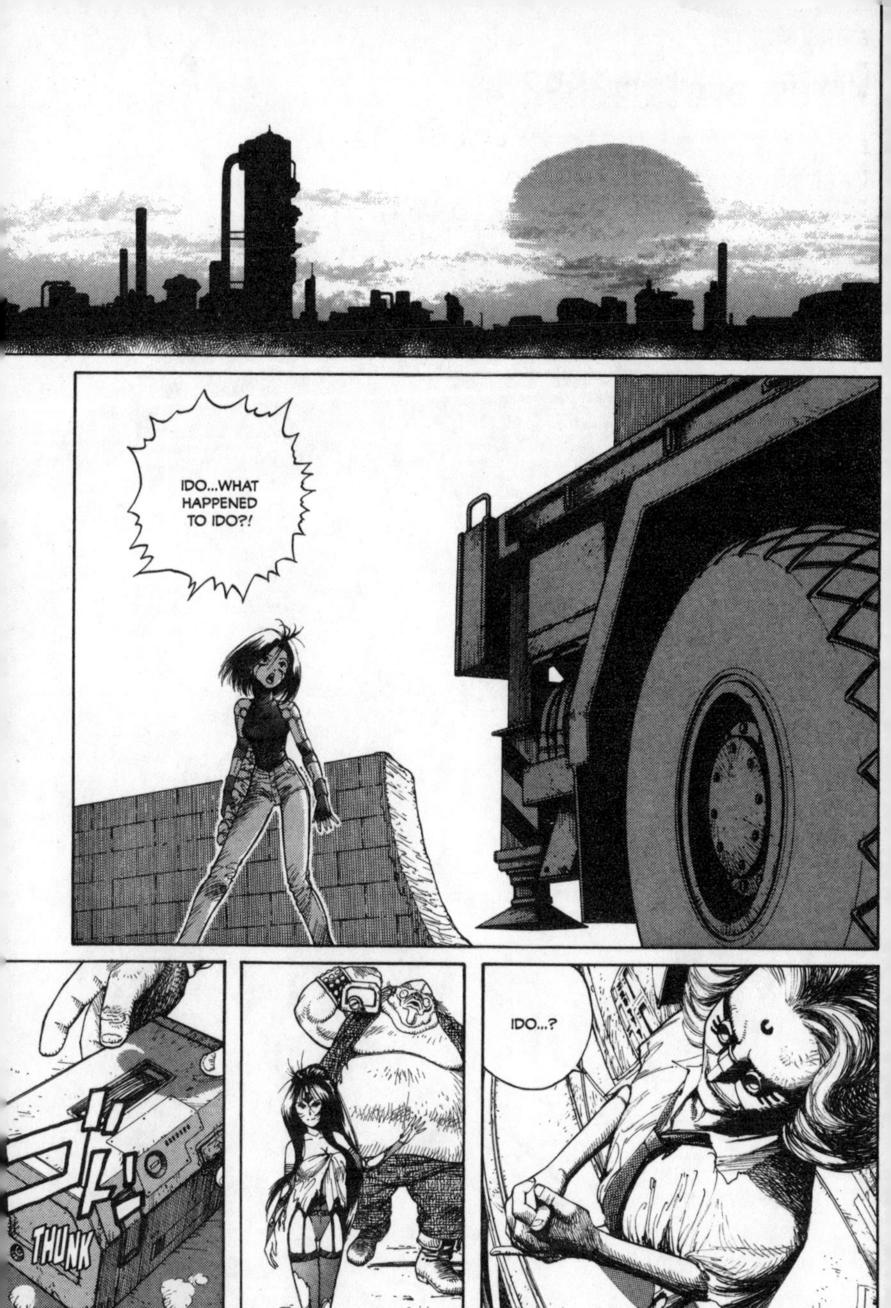
IDO...WHAT HAPPENED TO IDO?!
IDO...?
THUNK

FIGHT_026 Collapse

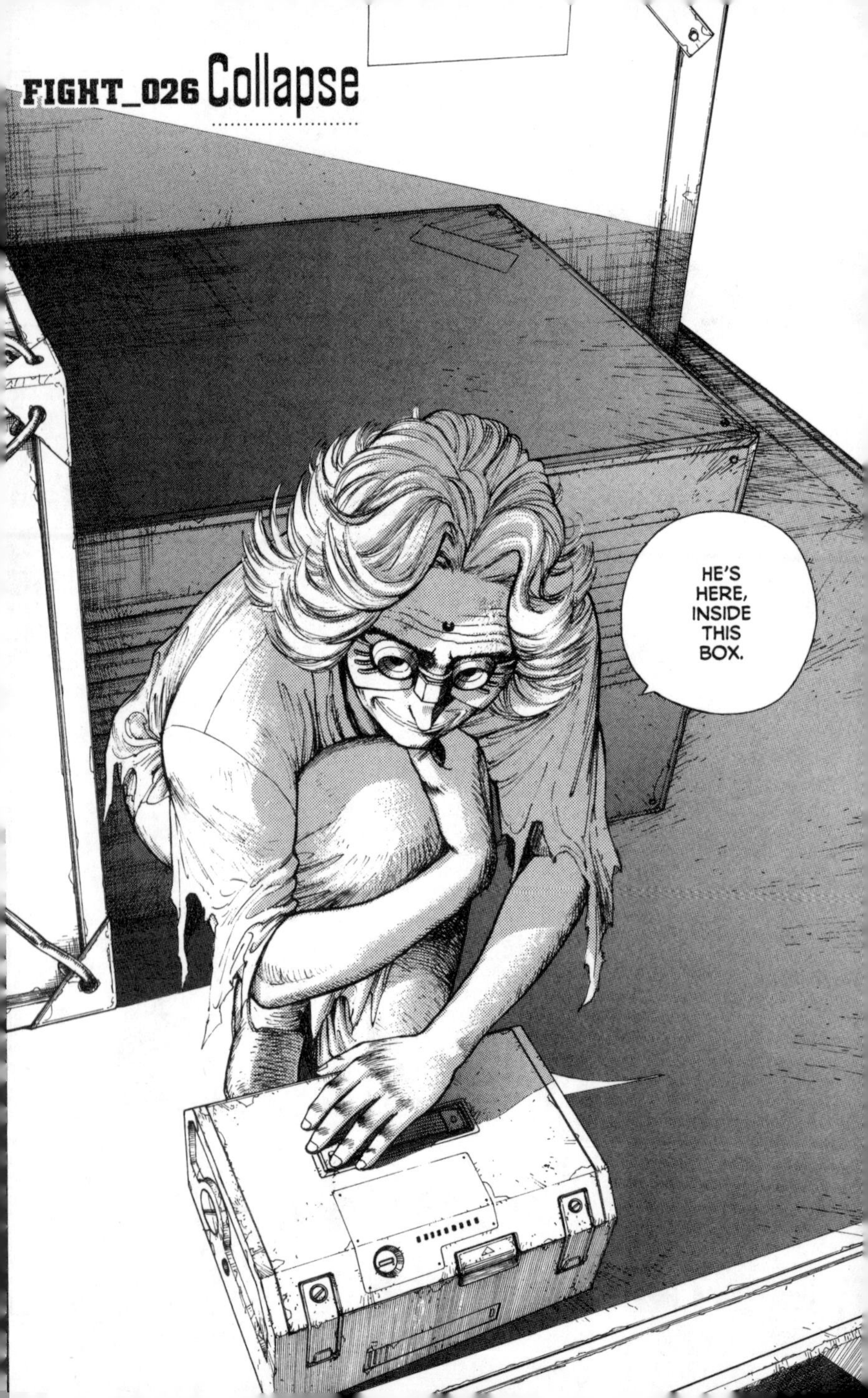
FIGHT_026 Collapse
HE'S HERE, INSIDE THIS BOX.

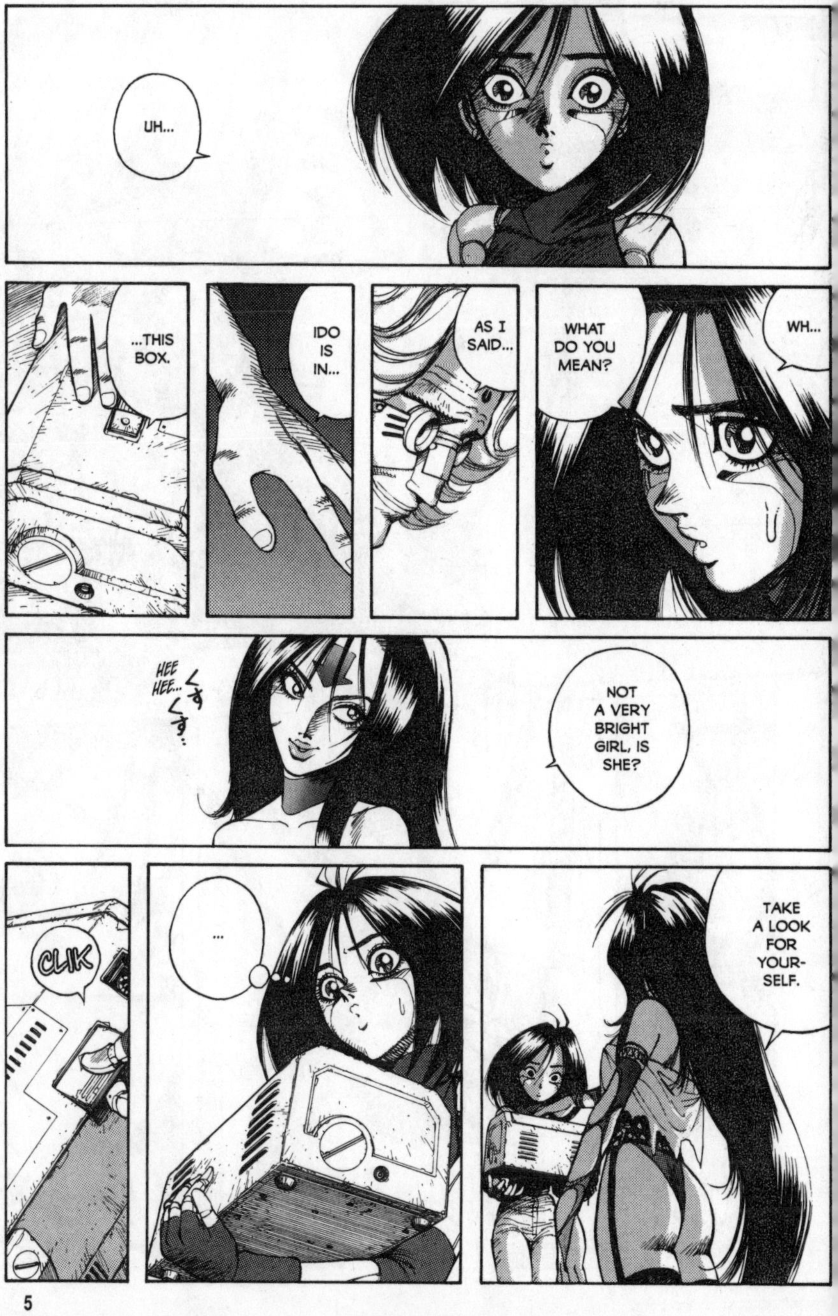
UH...
WH...
WHAT DO YOU MEAN?
AS I SAID...
IDO IS IN...
...THIS BOX.
NOT A VERY BRIGHT GIRL, IS SHE?
HEE HEE... くす くす‥
TAKE A LOOK FOR YOUR-SELF.
...
CLIK

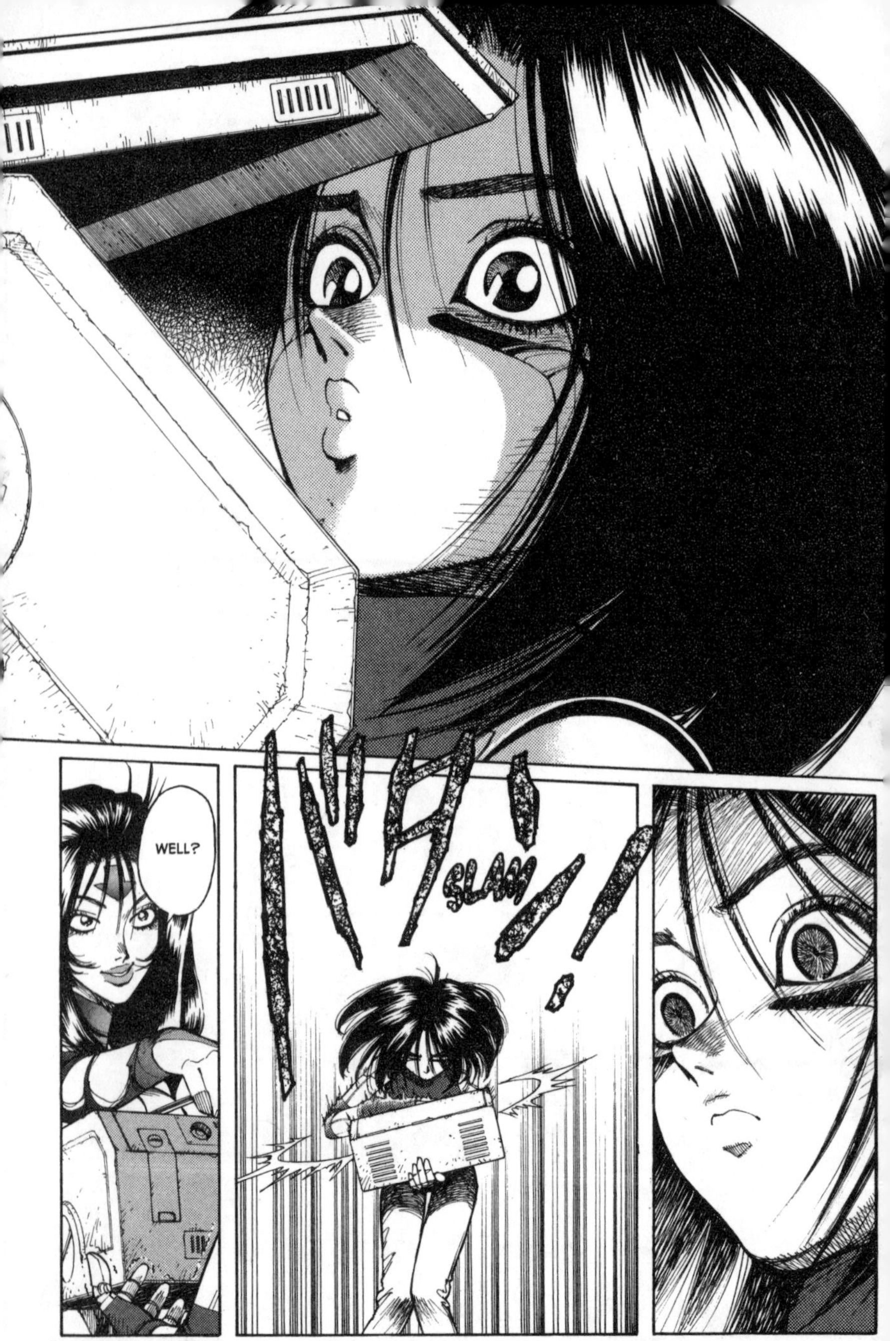
SLAM
WELL?

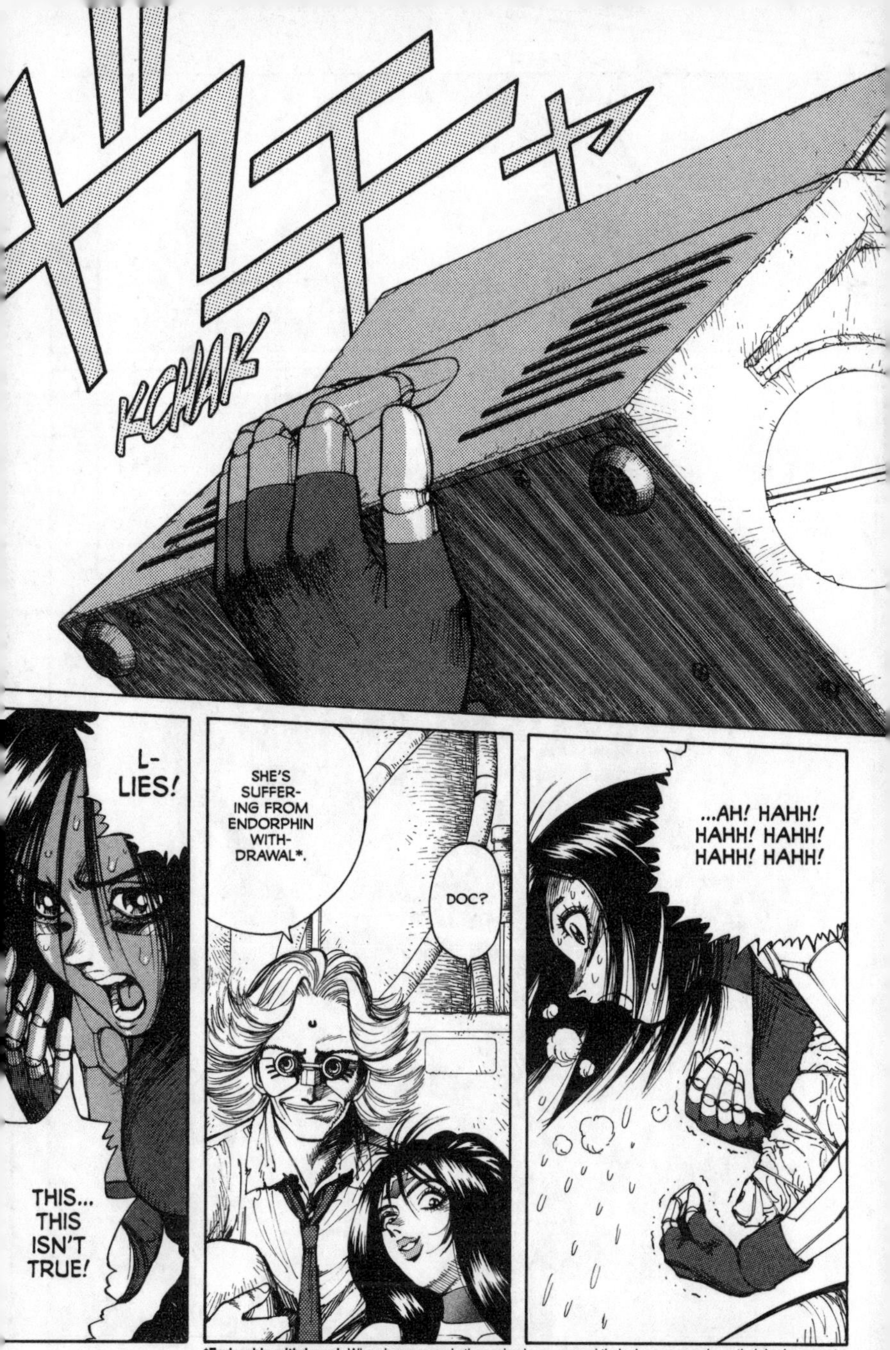
KCHAK
...AH! HAHH! HAHH! HAHH! HAHH! HAHH!
SHE'S SUFFERING FROM ENDORPHIN WITHDRAWAL*.
DOC?
L- LIES!
THIS... THIS ISN'T TRUE!

*Endorphin withdrawal:** When humans and other animals are around their close companions, their brains secrete endorphins that ease anxiety and produce happiness. When they feel separation from those companions, the brain stops producing endorphins, leading to a kind of chemical withdrawal. Some call this "love withdrawal."

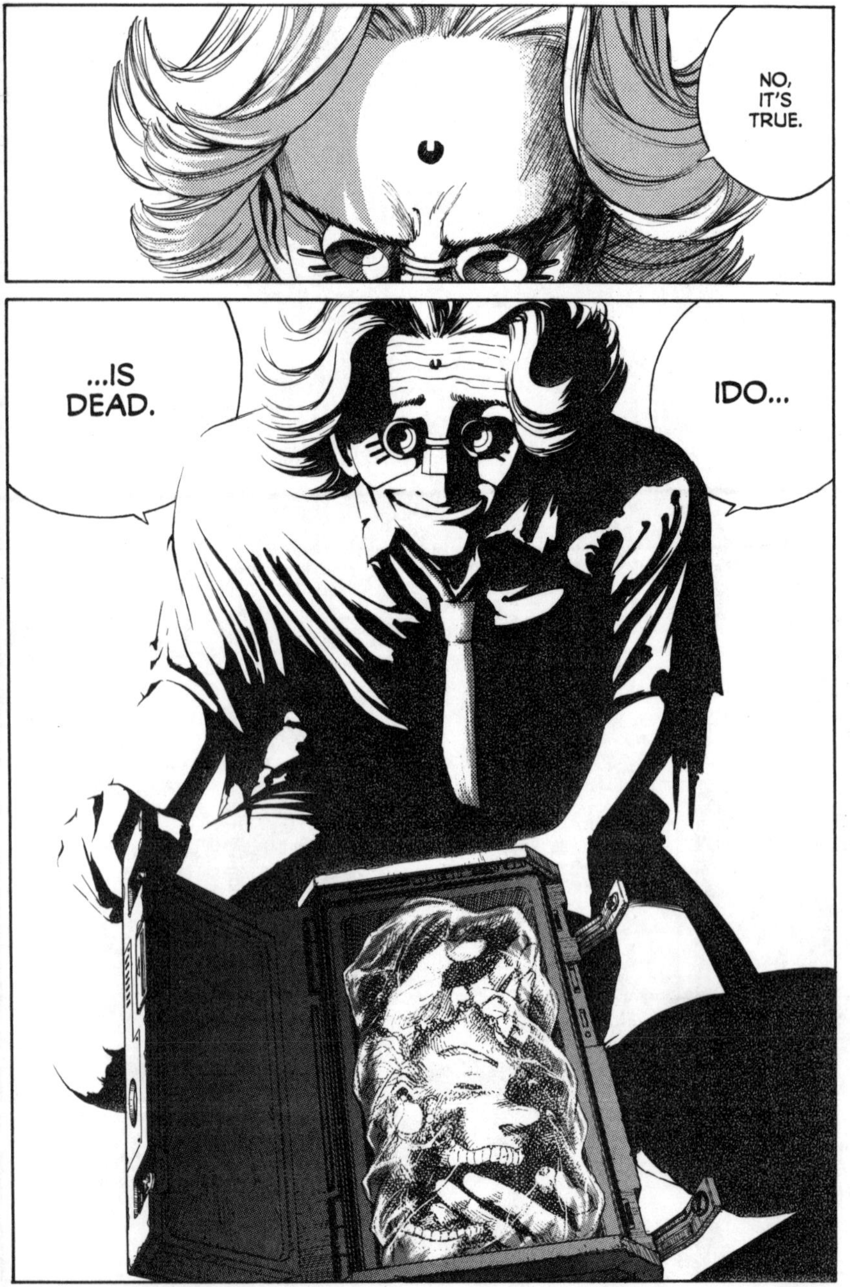
NO, IT'S TRUE.
IDO...
...IS DEAD.

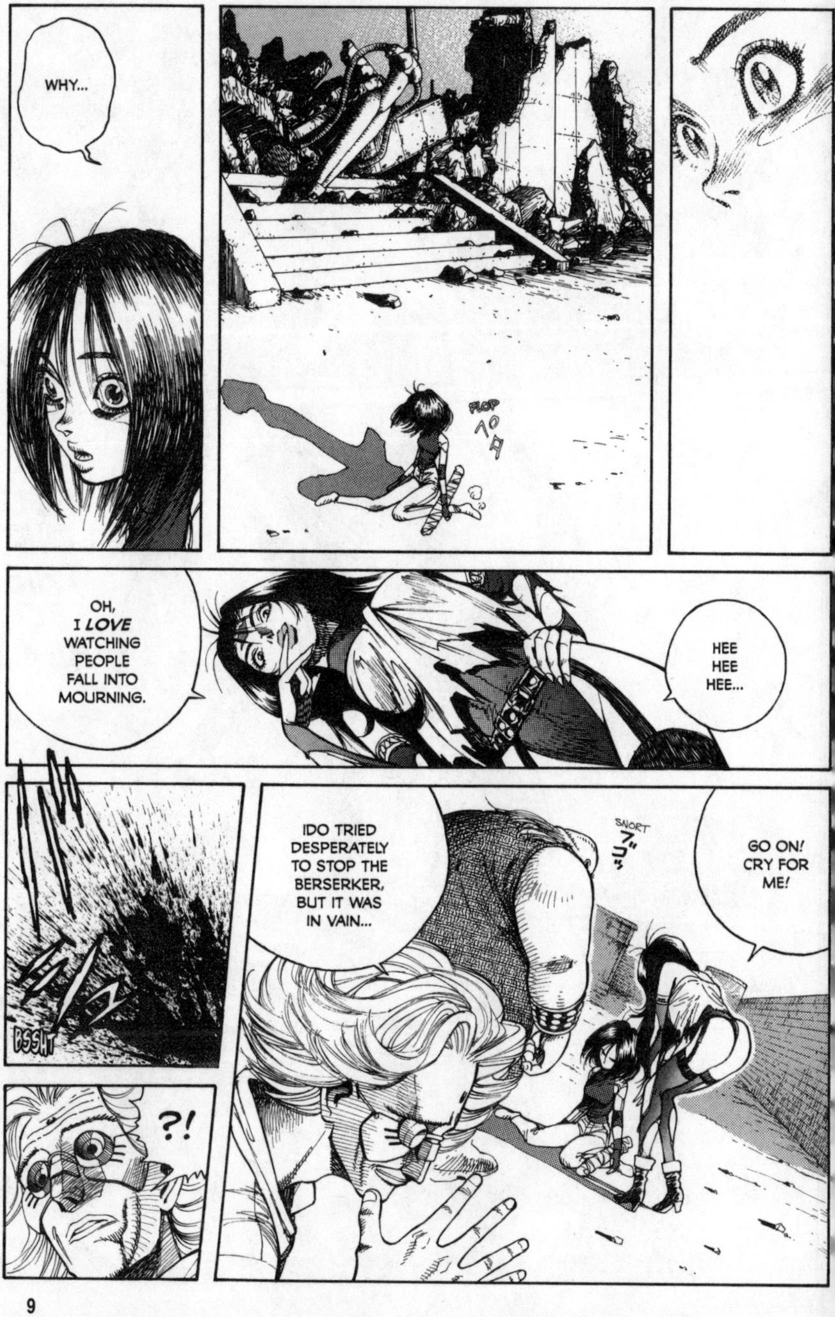
FLOP
WHY...
HEE HEE HEE...
OH, I *LOVE* WATCHING PEOPLE FALL INTO MOURNING.
GO ON! CRY FOR ME!
SNORT
IDO TRIED DESPERATELY TO STOP THE BERSERKER, BUT IT WAS IN VAIN...
BSSHT
?!

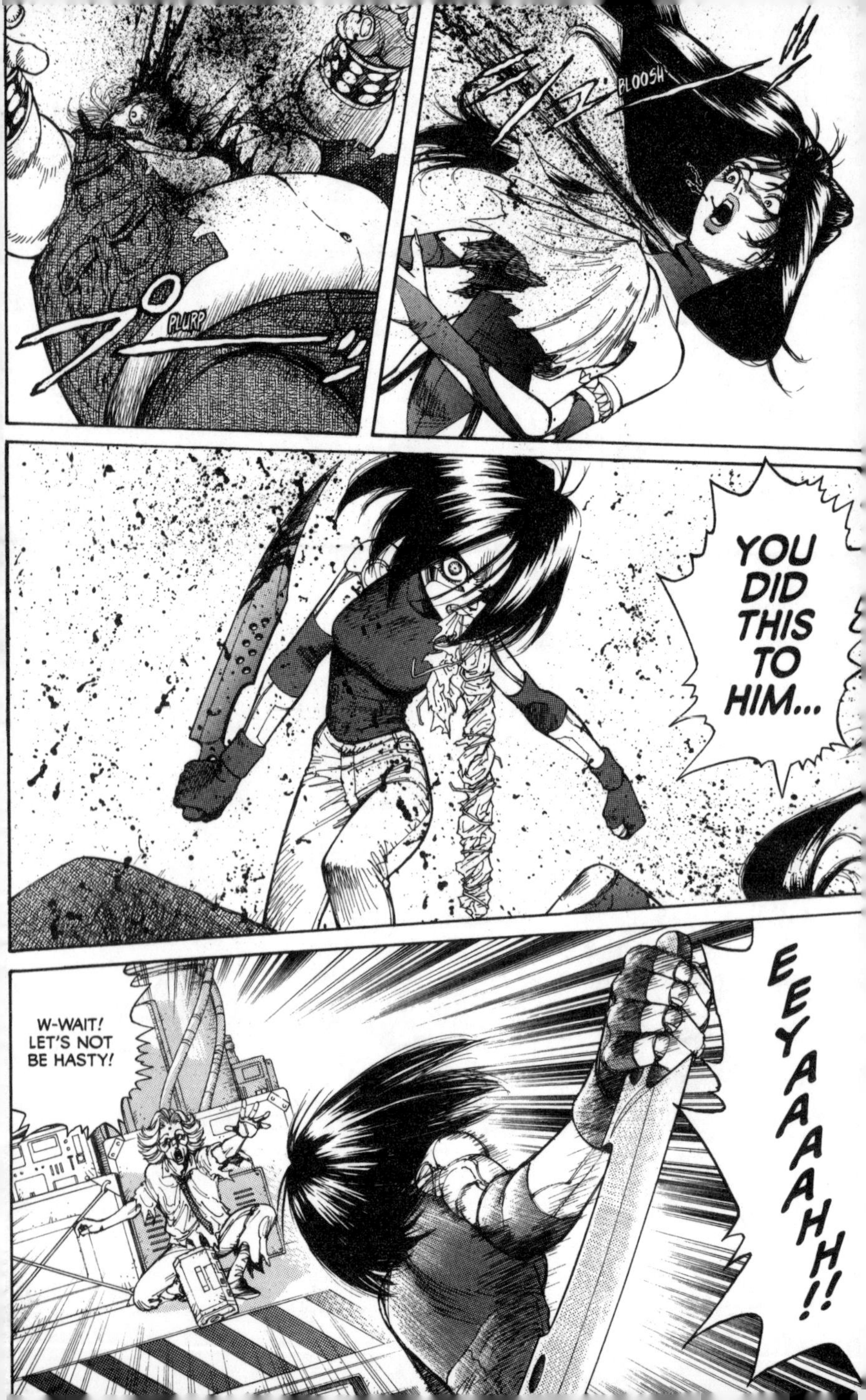
BLOOSH
PLURP
YOU DID THIS TO HIM...
EEYAAAAAHH!!
W-WAIT! LET'S NOT BE HASTY!

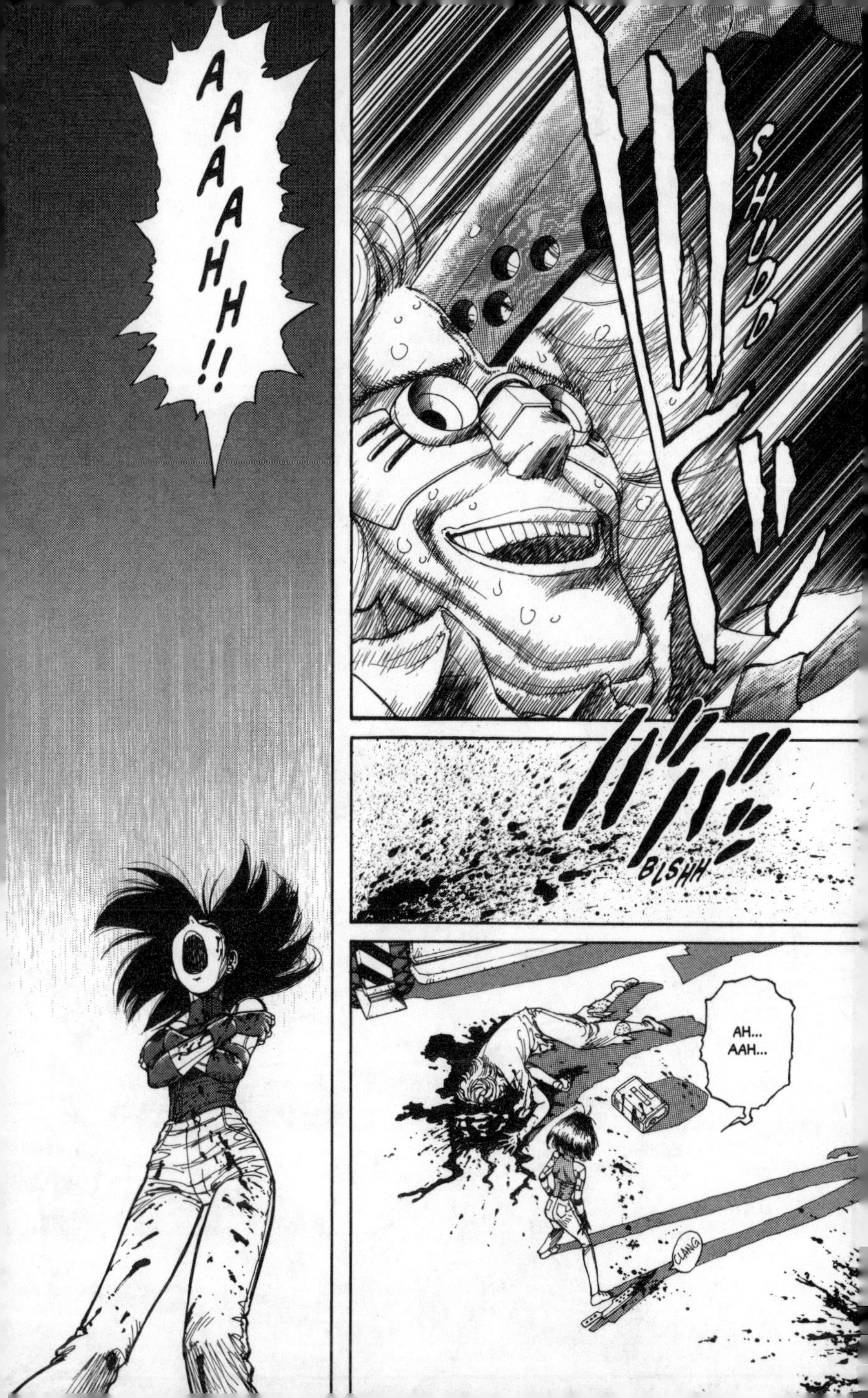
SHUDD
BLSHH
AH...
AAH...
CLANG
AAAAHH!!

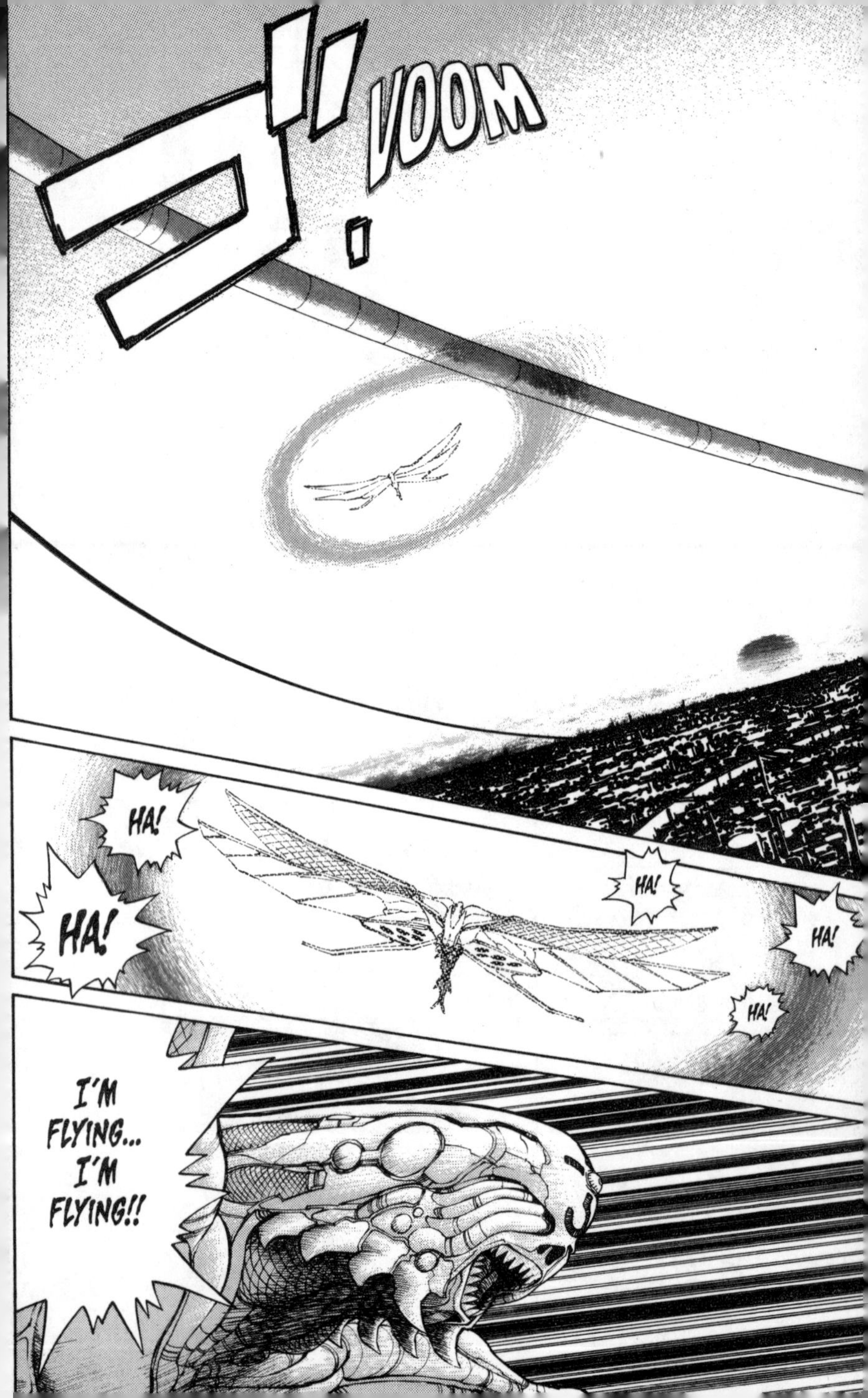
VOOM
HA!
HA!
HA!
HA!
HA!
I'M FLYING... I'M FLYING!!

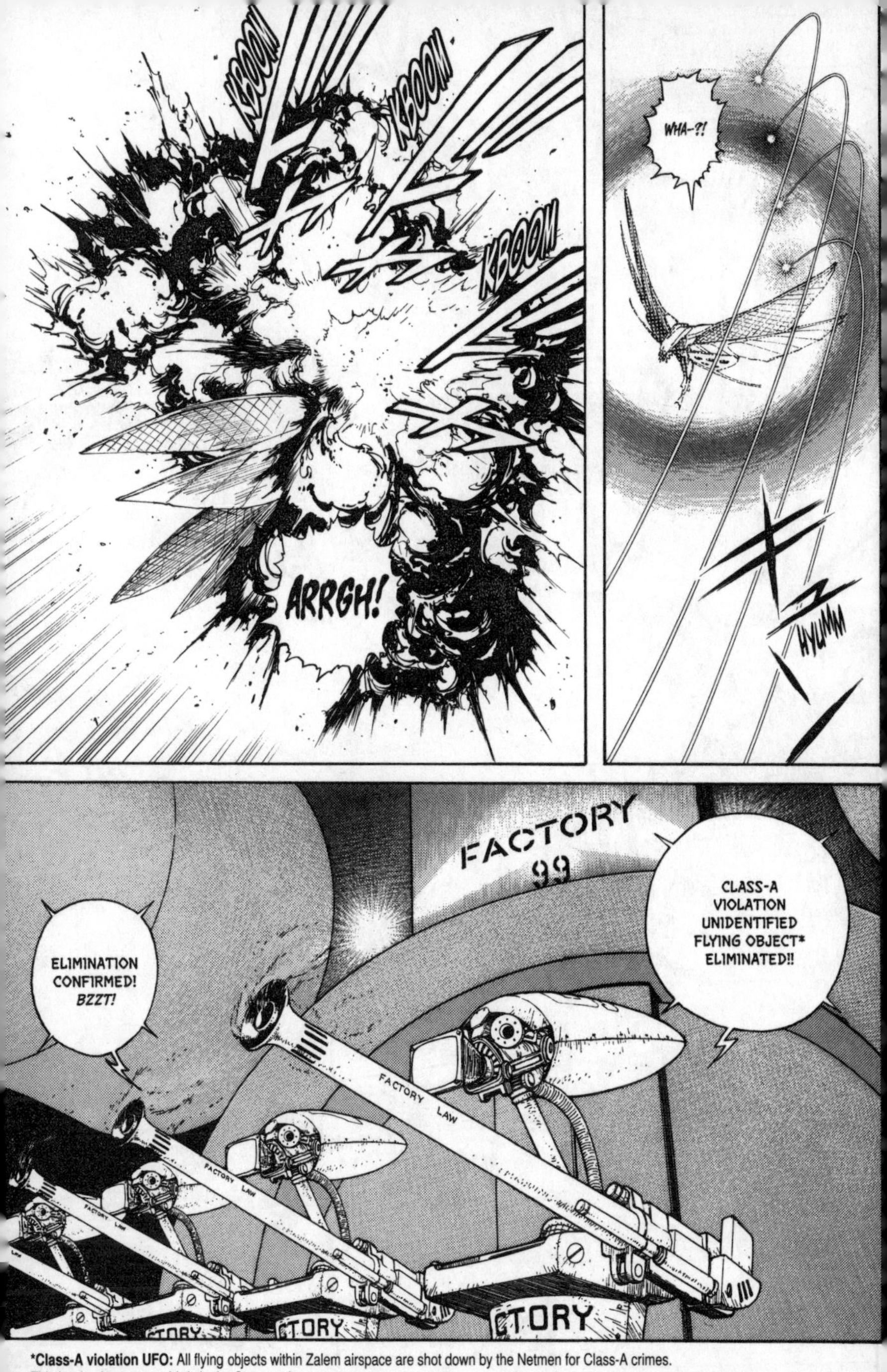
WHA-?!
HYUMM
KBOOM
KBOOM
KBOOM
ARRGH!
FACTORY 99
CLASS-A VIOLATION UNIDENTIFIED FLYING OBJECT* ELIMINATED!!
ELIMINATION CONFIRMED! BZZT!
FACTORY LAW
FACTORY LAW
CTORY

***Class-A violation UFO:** All flying objects within Zalem airspace are shot down by the Netmen for Class-A crimes. This is why there are no birds in the Scrapyard.

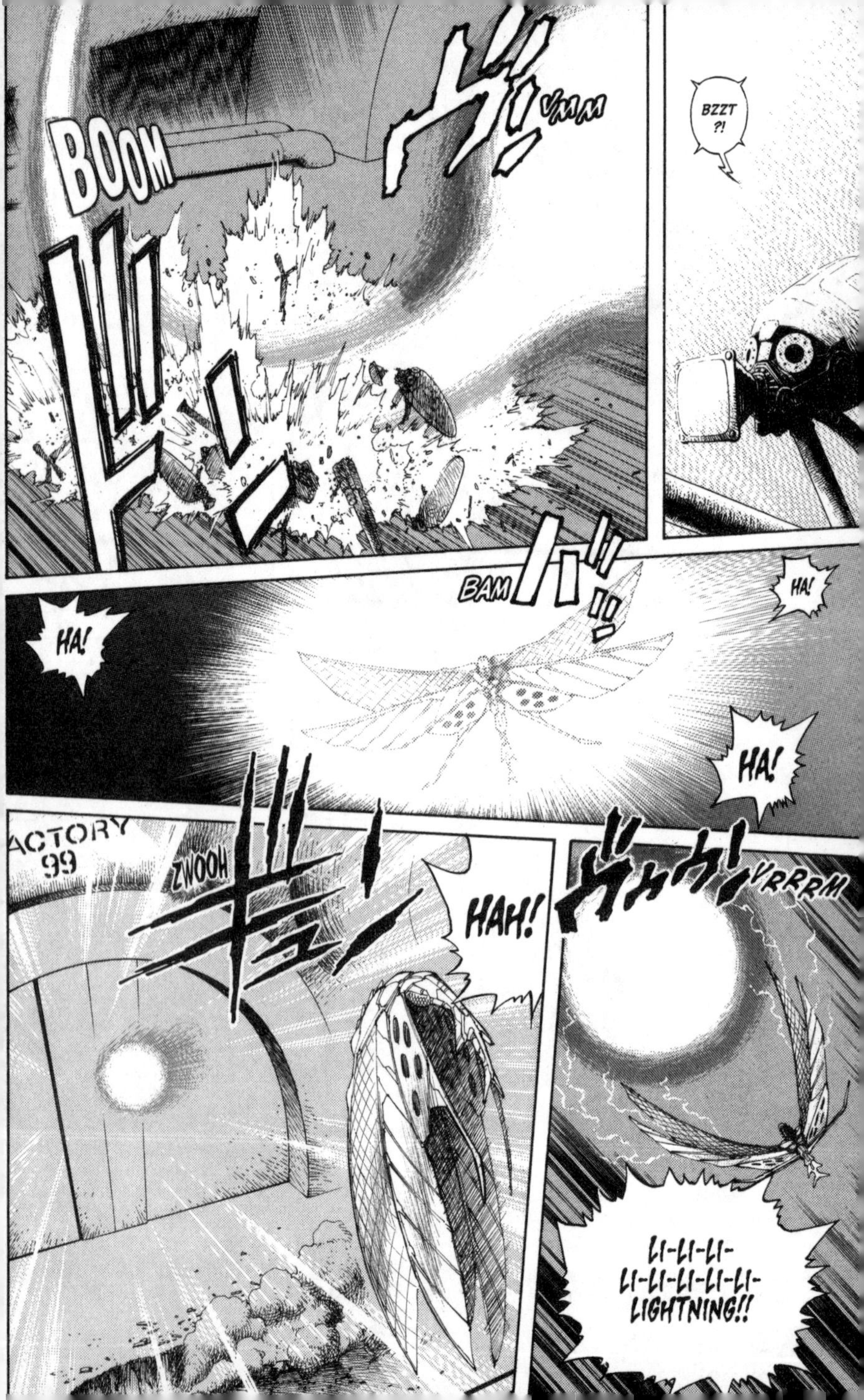
BZZT ?!
VMMM
BOOM
HA!
BAM
HA!
HA!
VRRRM
LI-LI-LI-
LI-LI-LI-LI-LI-
LIGHTNING!!
ACTORY
99
ZWOOH
HAH!

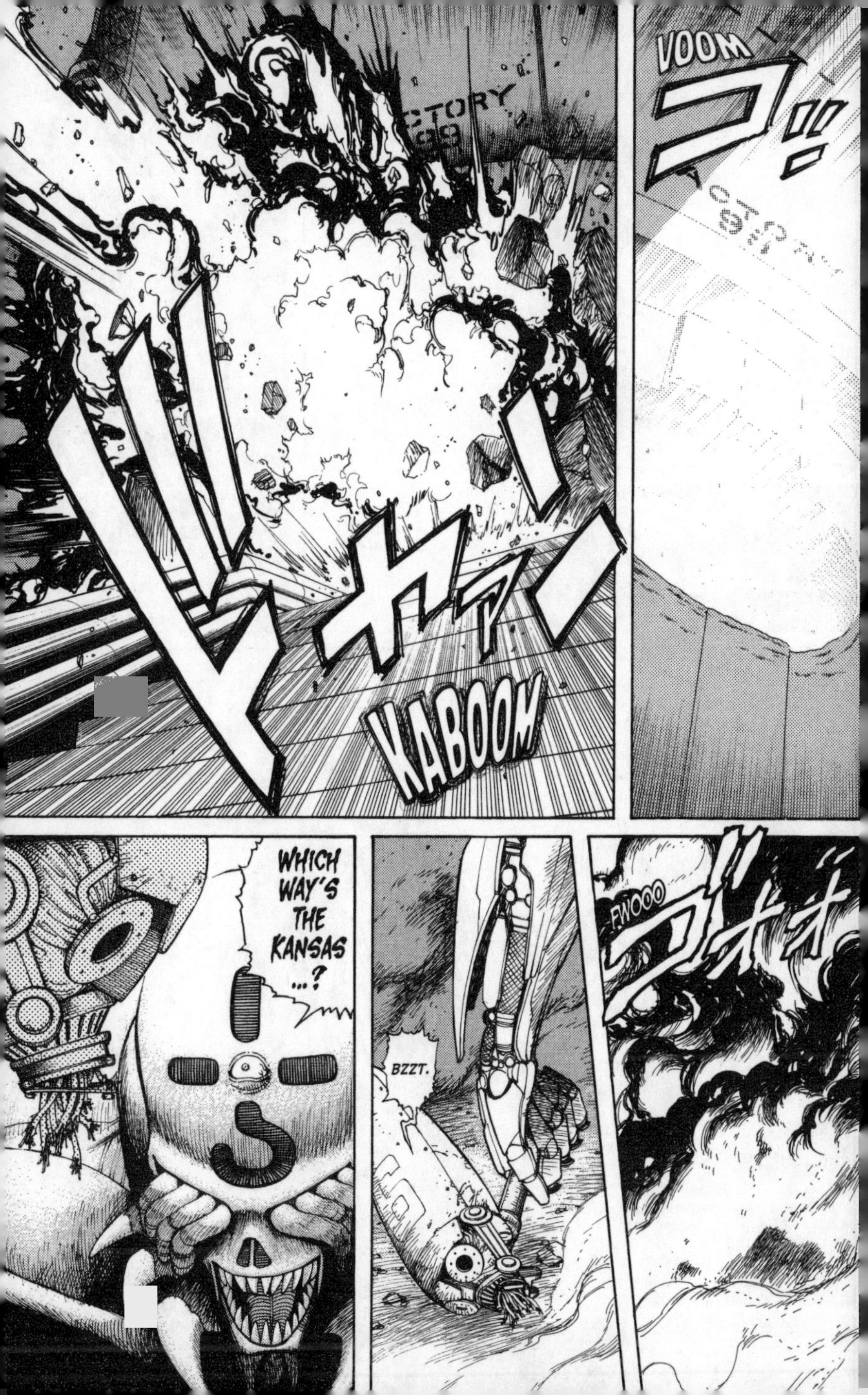
VOOM
KABOOM
FWOOO
BZZT.
WHICH WAY'S THE KANSAS ...?

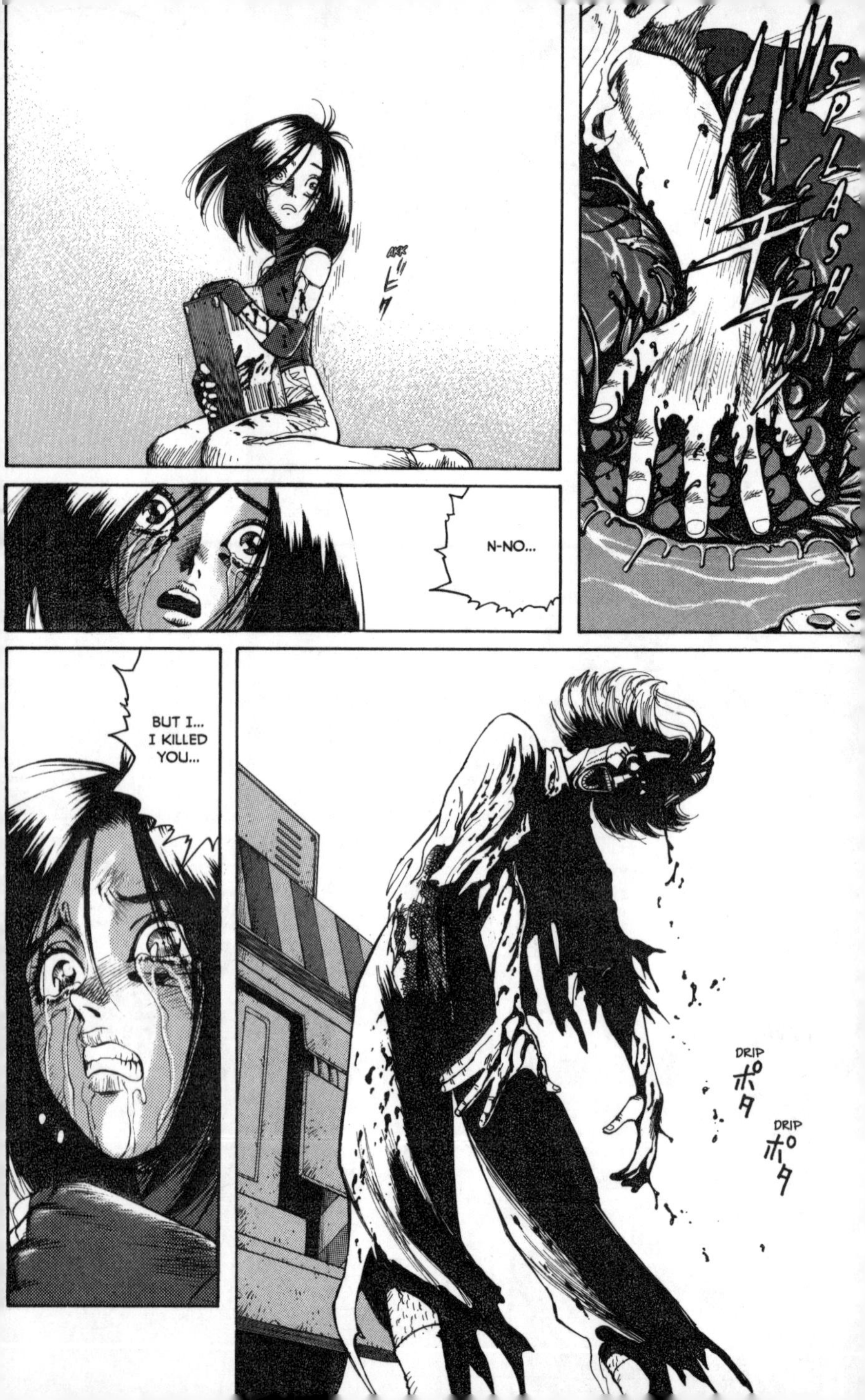
SPLASH
AKK
N-NO...
DRIP
ポタ
DRIP
ポタ
BUT I...
I KILLED
YOU...

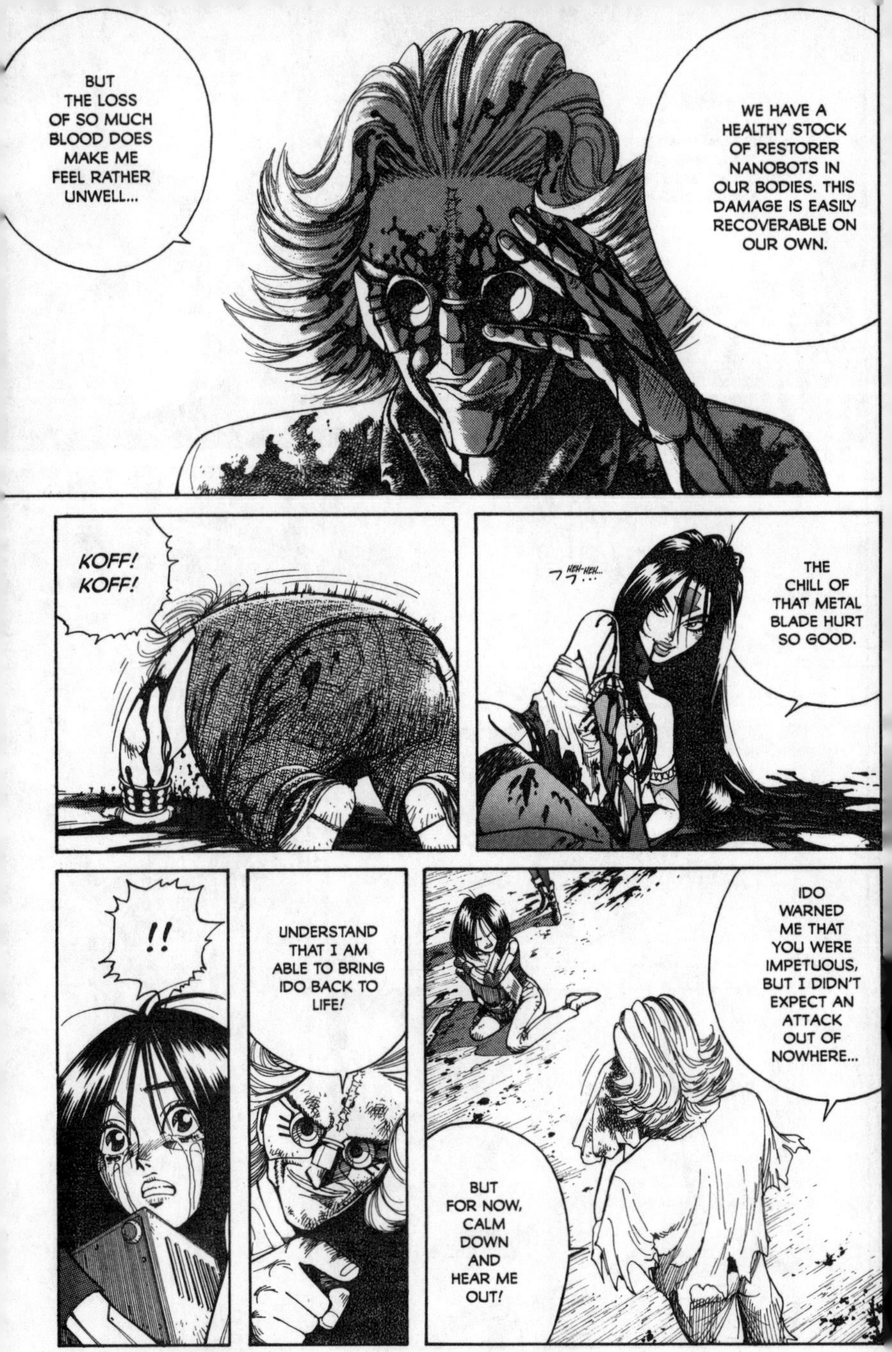
WE HAVE A HEALTHY STOCK OF RESTORER NANOBOTS IN OUR BODIES. THIS DAMAGE IS EASILY RECOVERABLE ON OUR OWN.
BUT THE LOSS OF SO MUCH BLOOD DOES MAKE ME FEEL RATHER UNWELL...
HEH-HEH...
THE CHILL OF THAT METAL BLADE HURT SO GOOD.
KOFF! KOFF!
IDO WARNED ME THAT YOU WERE IMPETUOUS, BUT I DIDN'T EXPECT AN ATTACK OUT OF NOWHERE...
BUT FOR NOW, CALM DOWN AND HEAR ME OUT!
UNDERSTAND THAT I AM ABLE TO BRING IDO BACK TO LIFE!
!!

IDO DIED WHEN HE ATTEMPTED TO STOP THE MAN NAMED ZAPAN*, WHO WAS BROUGHT BACK AS A BERSERKER.

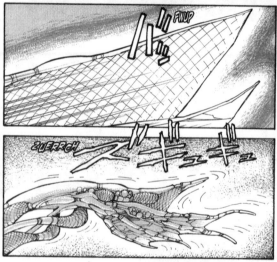

FNUP

ZUERRCH

WhOoooSR

ZAP

ZAP

AAAAH!

*Zapan: One of the names of the seven kings (Bael, Pursan, Beleth, Paimon, Belial, Asmoday, Zapan) who rule the four directions of Hell, according to the demonologist Johann Weyer (1516-1588).

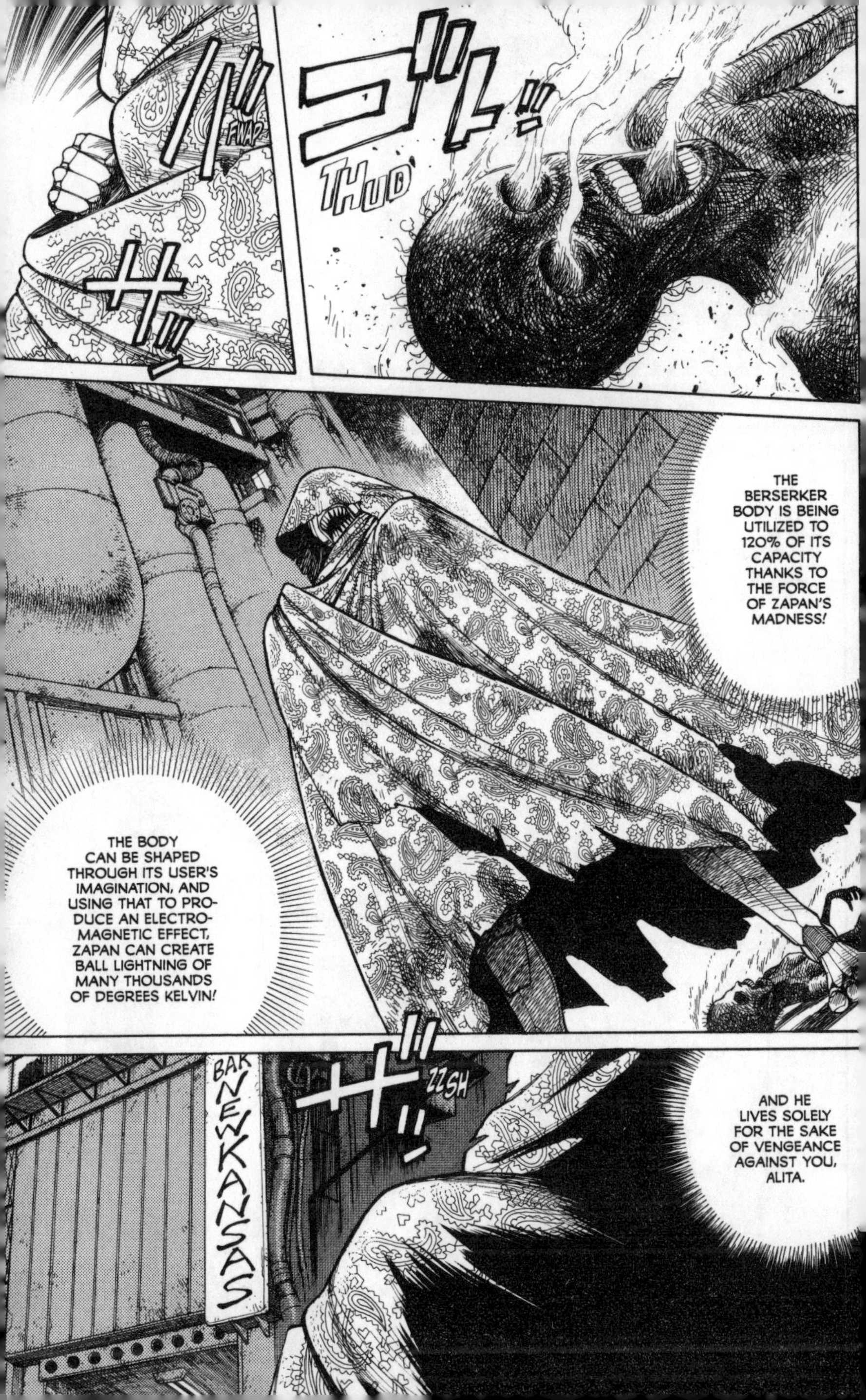
THUD
FWAP
THE BERSERKER BODY IS BEING UTILIZED TO 120% OF ITS CAPACITY THANKS TO THE FORCE OF ZAPAN'S MADNESS!
THE BODY CAN BE SHAPED THROUGH ITS USER'S IMAGINATION, AND USING THAT TO PRODUCE AN ELECTROMAGNETIC EFFECT, ZAPAN CAN CREATE BALL LIGHTNING OF MANY THOUSANDS OF DEGREES KELVIN!
AND HE LIVES SOLELY FOR THE SAKE OF VENGEANCE AGAINST YOU, ALITA.
ZZSH
BAK
NEWKANSAS

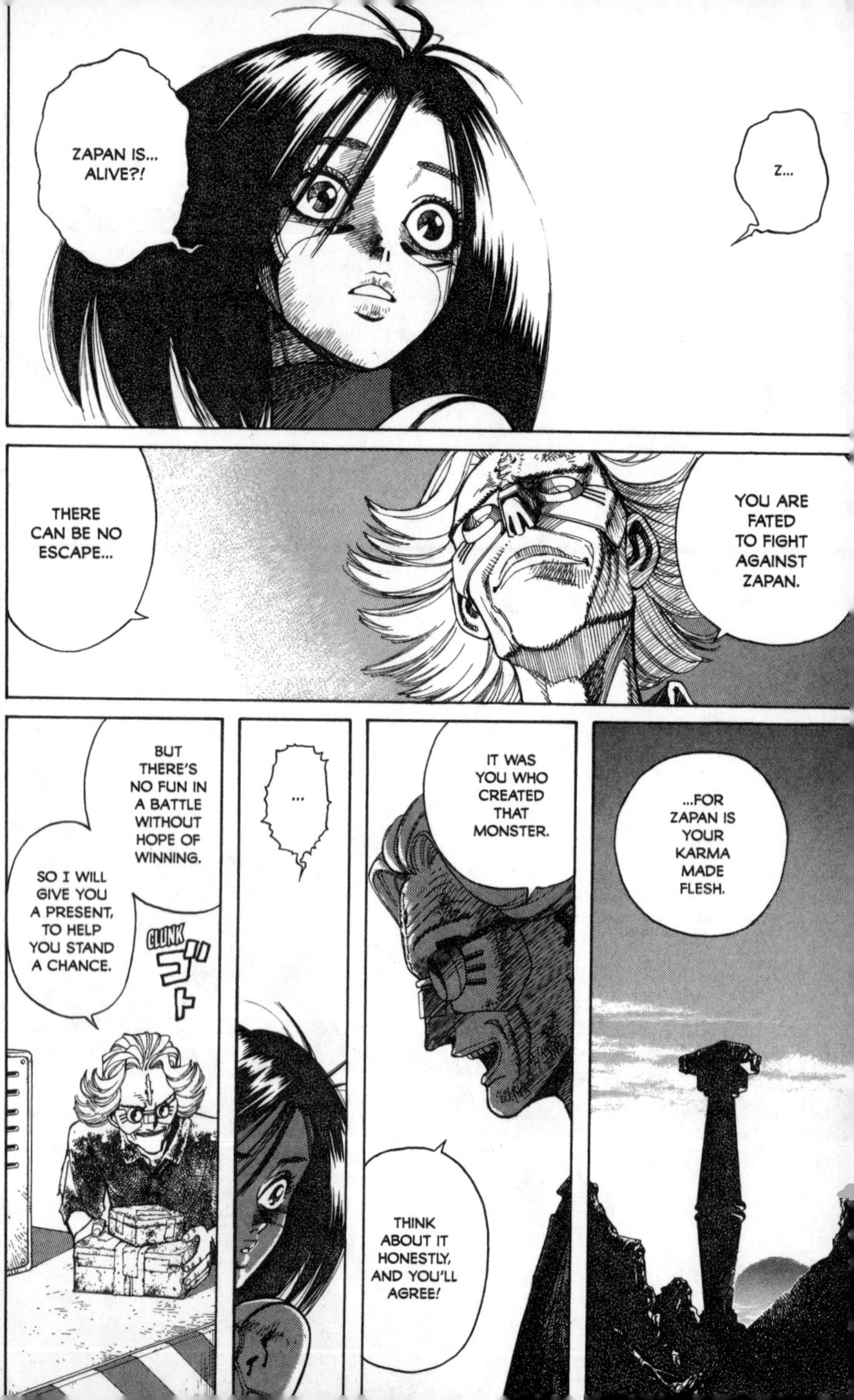
Z...
ZAPAN IS... ALIVE?!
YOU ARE FATED TO FIGHT AGAINST ZAPAN.
THERE CAN BE NO ESCAPE...
...FOR ZAPAN IS YOUR KARMA MADE FLESH.
IT WAS YOU WHO CREATED THAT MONSTER.
THINK ABOUT IT HONESTLY, AND YOU'LL AGREE!
...
BUT THERE'S NO FUN IN A BATTLE WITHOUT HOPE OF WINNING.
SO I WILL GIVE YOU A PRESENT, TO HELP YOU STAND A CHANCE.
CLUNK

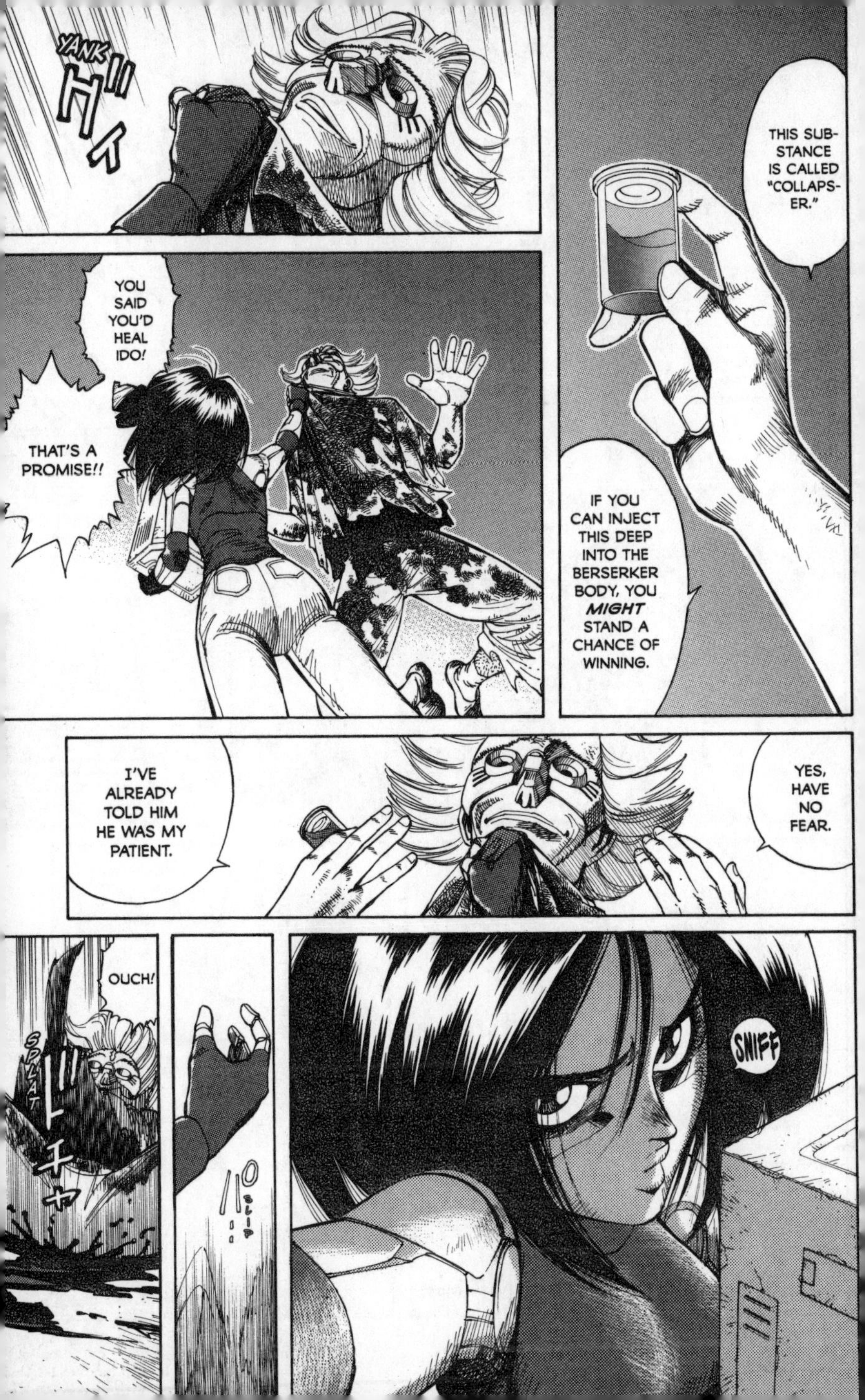

THIS SUBSTANCE IS CALLED "COLLAPSER."
IF YOU CAN INJECT THIS DEEP INTO THE BERSERKER BODY, YOU *MIGHT* STAND A CHANCE OF WINNING.
YANK
YOU SAID YOU'D HEAL IDO!
THAT'S A PROMISE!!
YES, HAVE NO FEAR.
I'VE ALREADY TOLD HIM HE WAS MY PATIENT.
SNIFF
SLIP
OUCH!
SPLAT

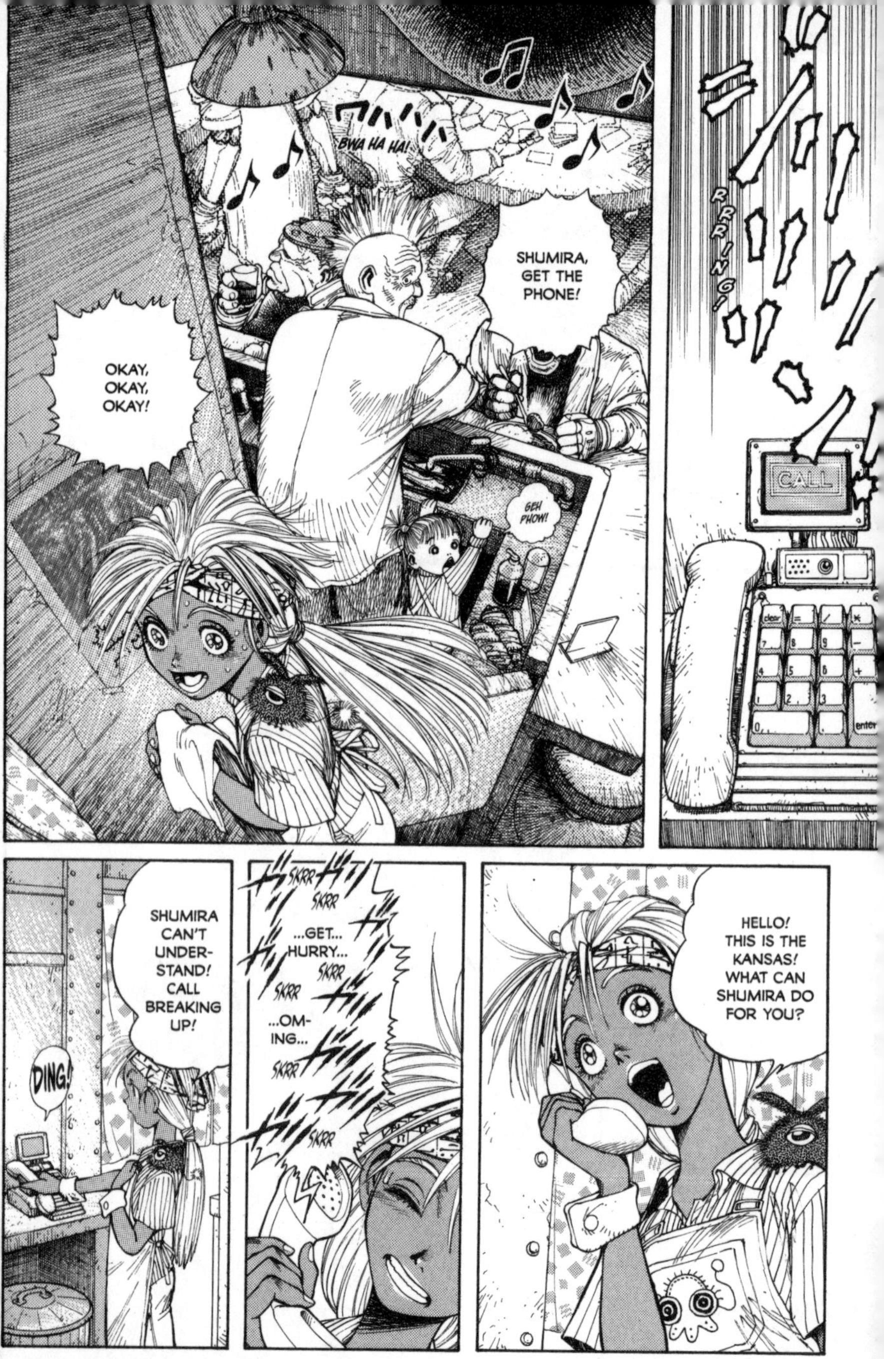
RRRING!
CALL
BWA HA HA!
SHUMIRA, GET THE PHONE!
OKAY, OKAY, OKAY!
GEH PHOW!
HELLO! THIS IS THE KANSAS! WHAT CAN SHUMIRA DO FOR YOU?
SKRR
...GET... HURRY...
SKRR
...OM-ING...
SKRR
SKRR
SHUMIRA CAN'T UNDER-STAND! CALL BREAKING UP!
DING!

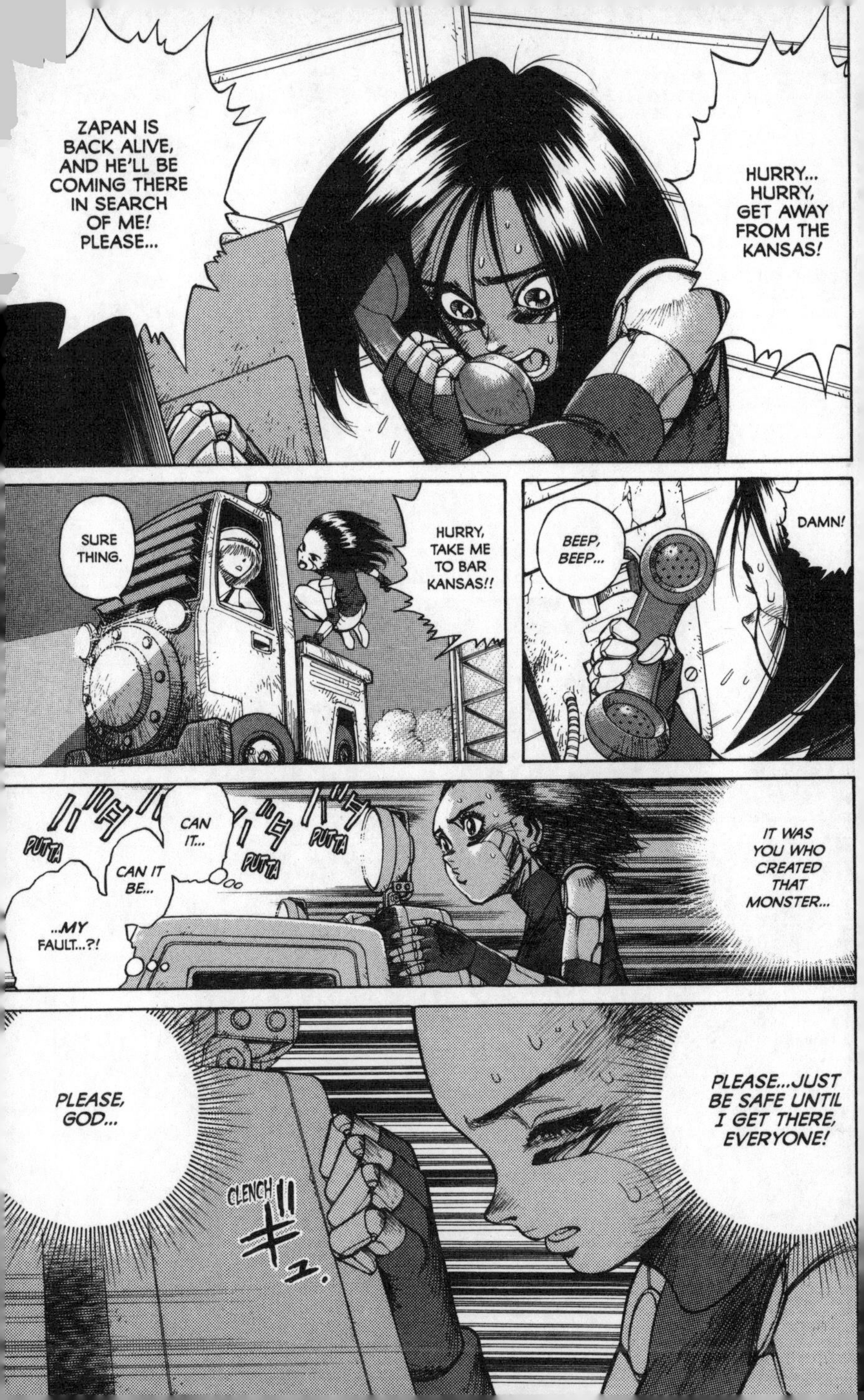
HURRY... HURRY, GET AWAY FROM THE KANSAS!
ZAPAN IS BACK ALIVE, AND HE'LL BE COMING THERE IN SEARCH OF ME! PLEASE...
DAMN!
BEEP, BEEP...
HURRY, TAKE ME TO BAR KANSAS!!
SURE THING.
IT WAS YOU WHO CREATED THAT MONSTER...
PUTTA
PUTTA
CAN IT...
PUTTA
CAN IT BE...
...MY FAULT...?!
PLEASE...JUST BE SAFE UNTIL I GET THERE, EVERYONE!
PLEASE, GOD...
CLENCH!!

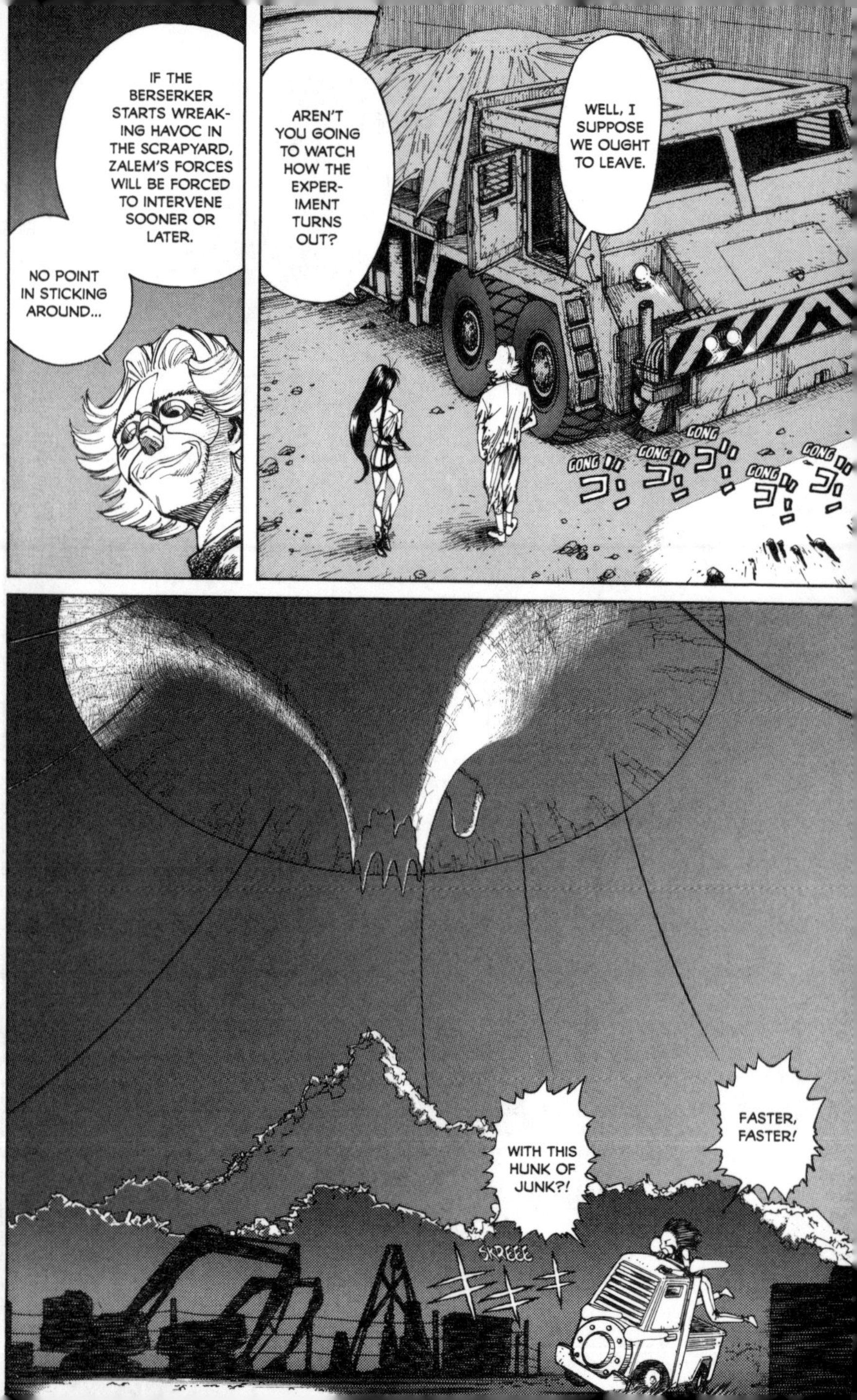
WELL, I SUPPOSE WE OUGHT TO LEAVE.
AREN'T YOU GOING TO WATCH HOW THE EXPER-IMENT TURNS OUT?
GONG GONG GONG GONG GONG
IF THE BERSERKER STARTS WREAK-ING HAVOC IN THE SCRAPYARD, ZALEM'S FORCES WILL BE FORCED TO INTERVENE SOONER OR LATER.
NO POINT IN STICKING AROUND...
FASTER, FASTER!
WITH THIS HUNK OF JUNK?!
SKREEE

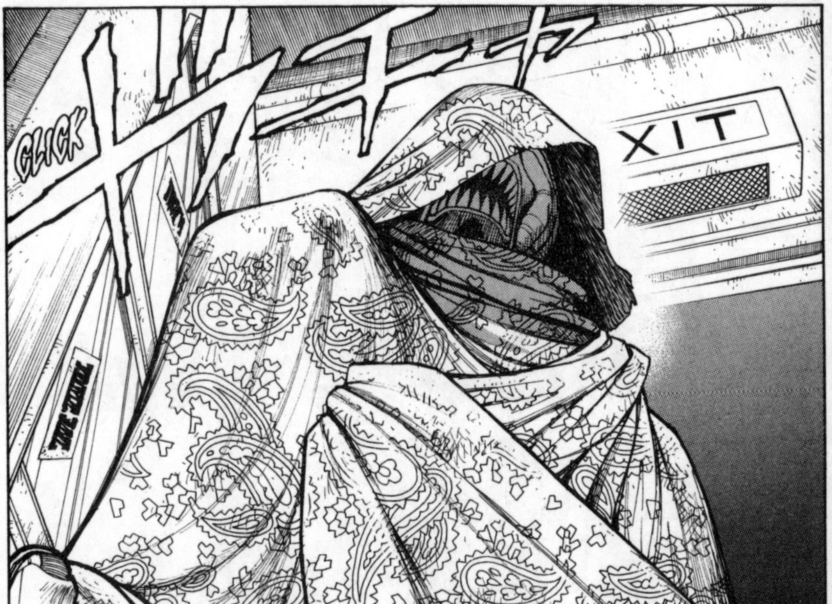
CLICK
XIT

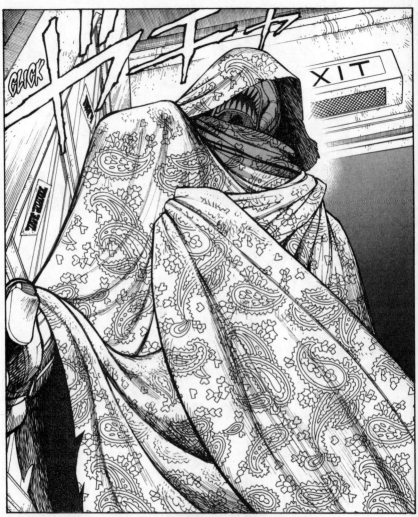

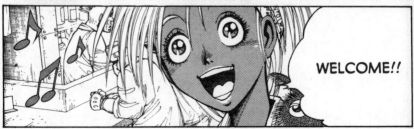

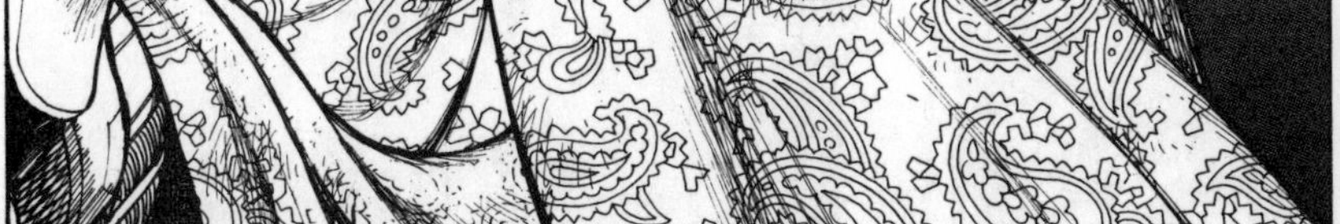
WELCOME!!

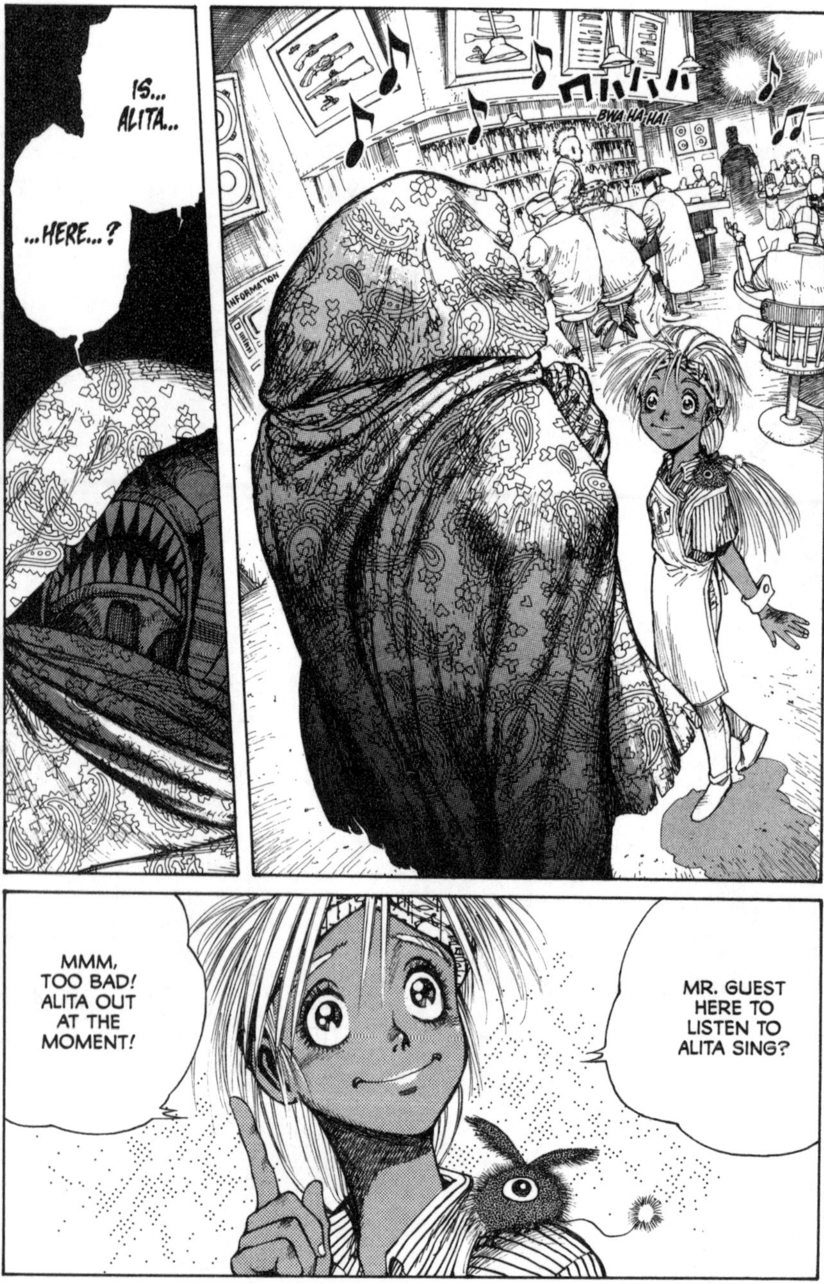
BWA HA HA!
INFORMATION
IS... ALITA...
...HERE...?
MR. GUEST HERE TO LISTEN TO ALITA SING?
MMM, TOO BAD! ALITA OUT AT THE MOMENT!

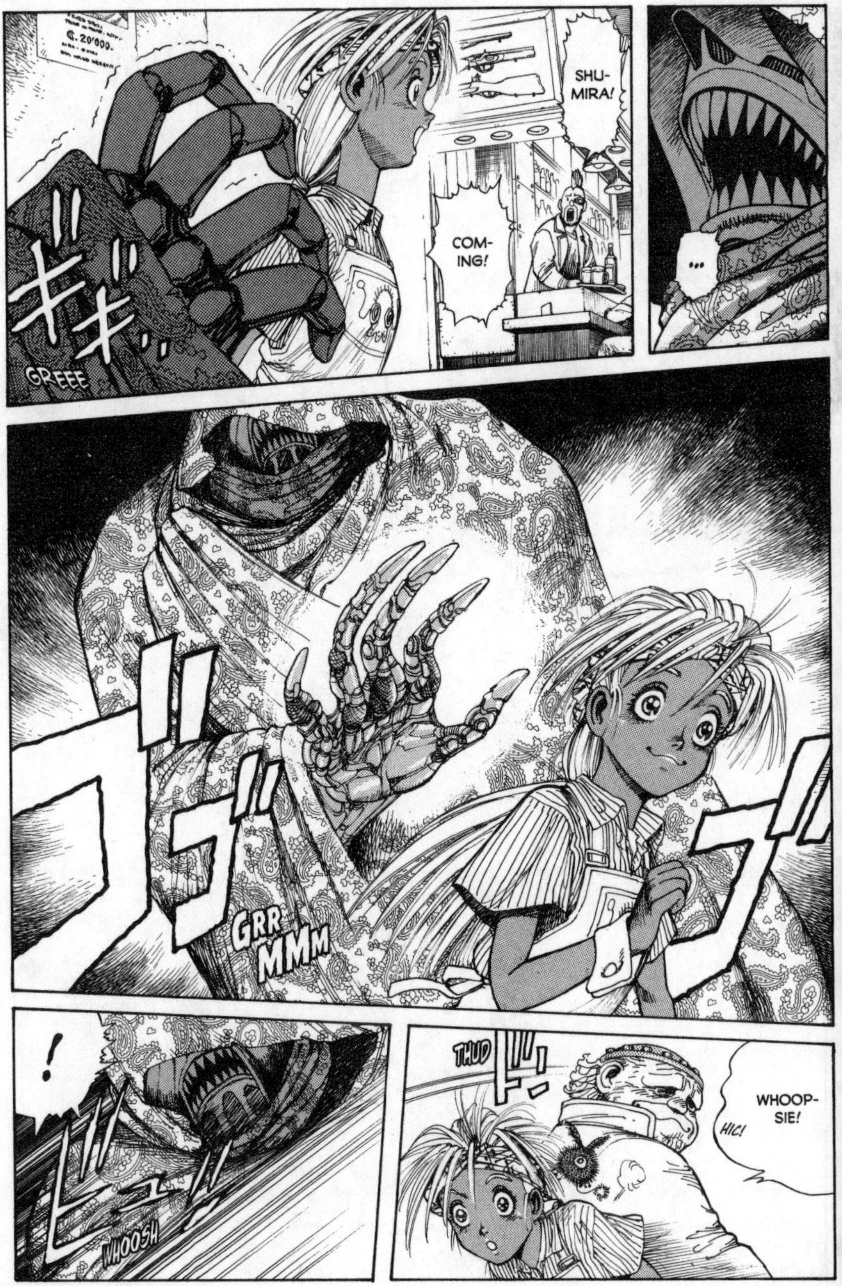
...
SHU-MIRA!
COMING!
GREEE
GRR MMM
WHOOP-SIE!
HIC!
THUD
!
WHOOSH

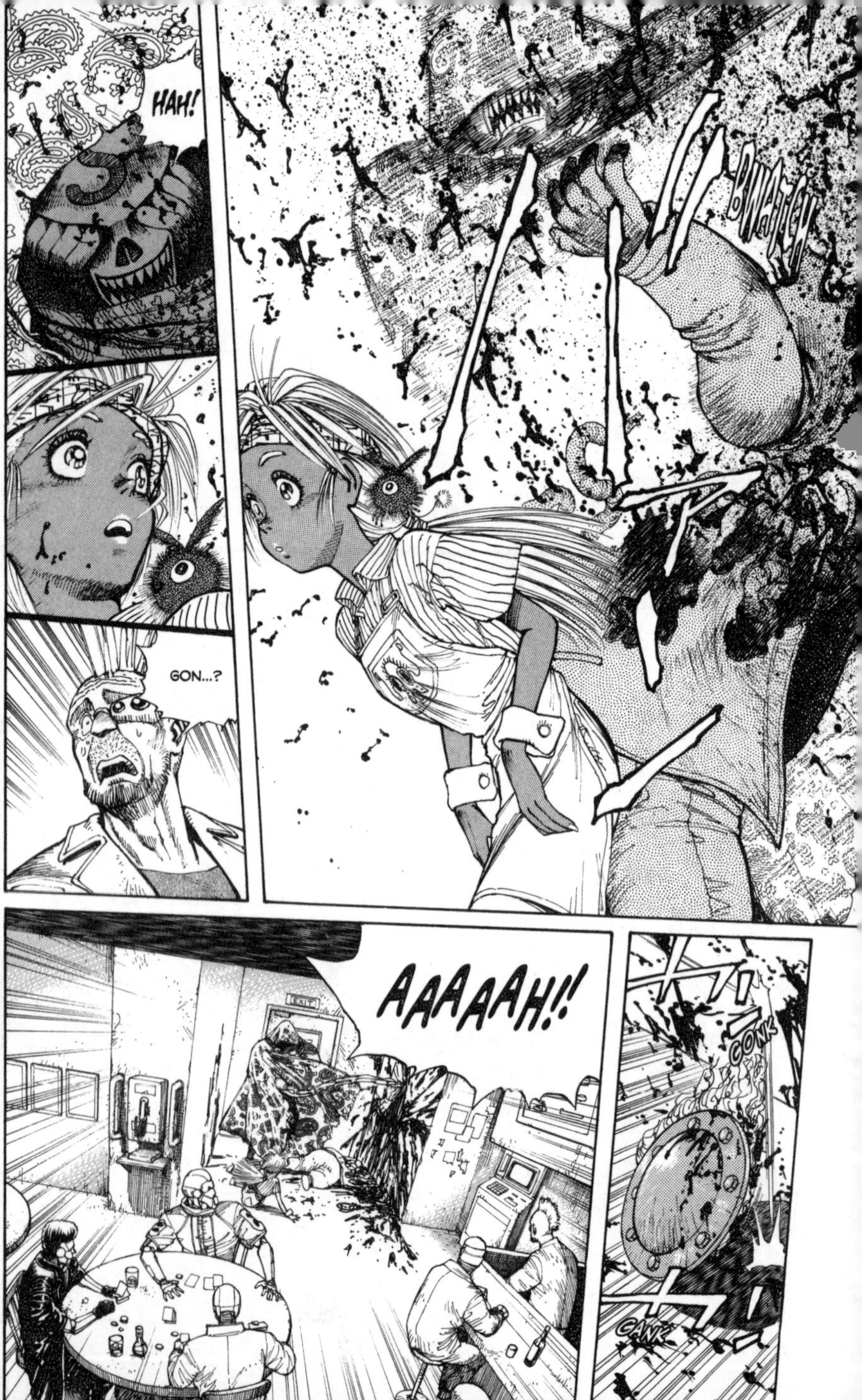
BWATCH
HAH!
GON...?
CONK
CANK
AAAAAH!!

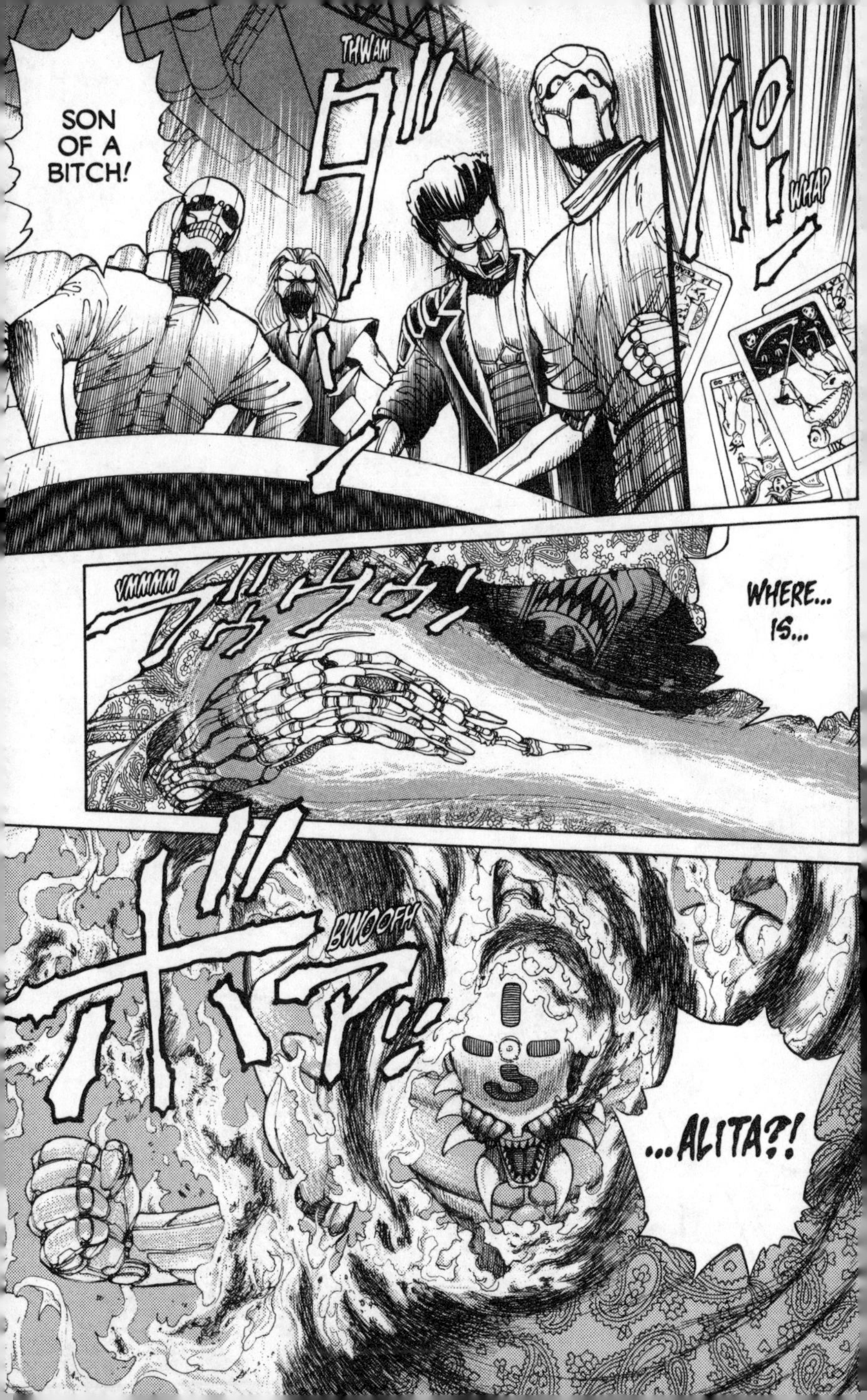
WHAP
THWAM
SON OF A BITCH!
WHERE... IS...
VMMMM
...ALITA?!
BWOOFH

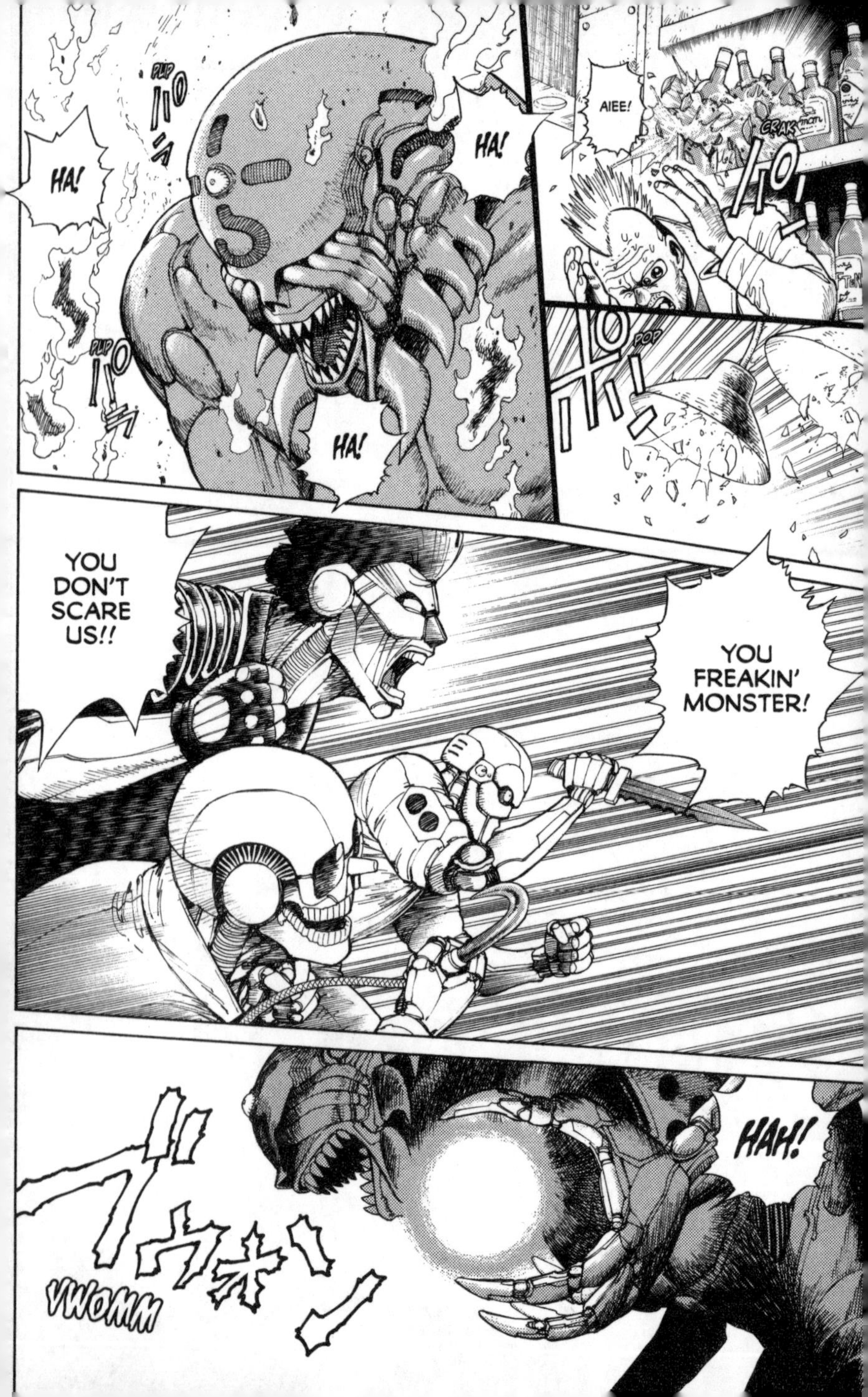
AIEE!
CRAK
POP
HA!
PLIP
HA!
PLIP
HA!
YOU FREAKIN' MONSTER!
YOU DON'T SCARE US!!
HAH!
VWOMM

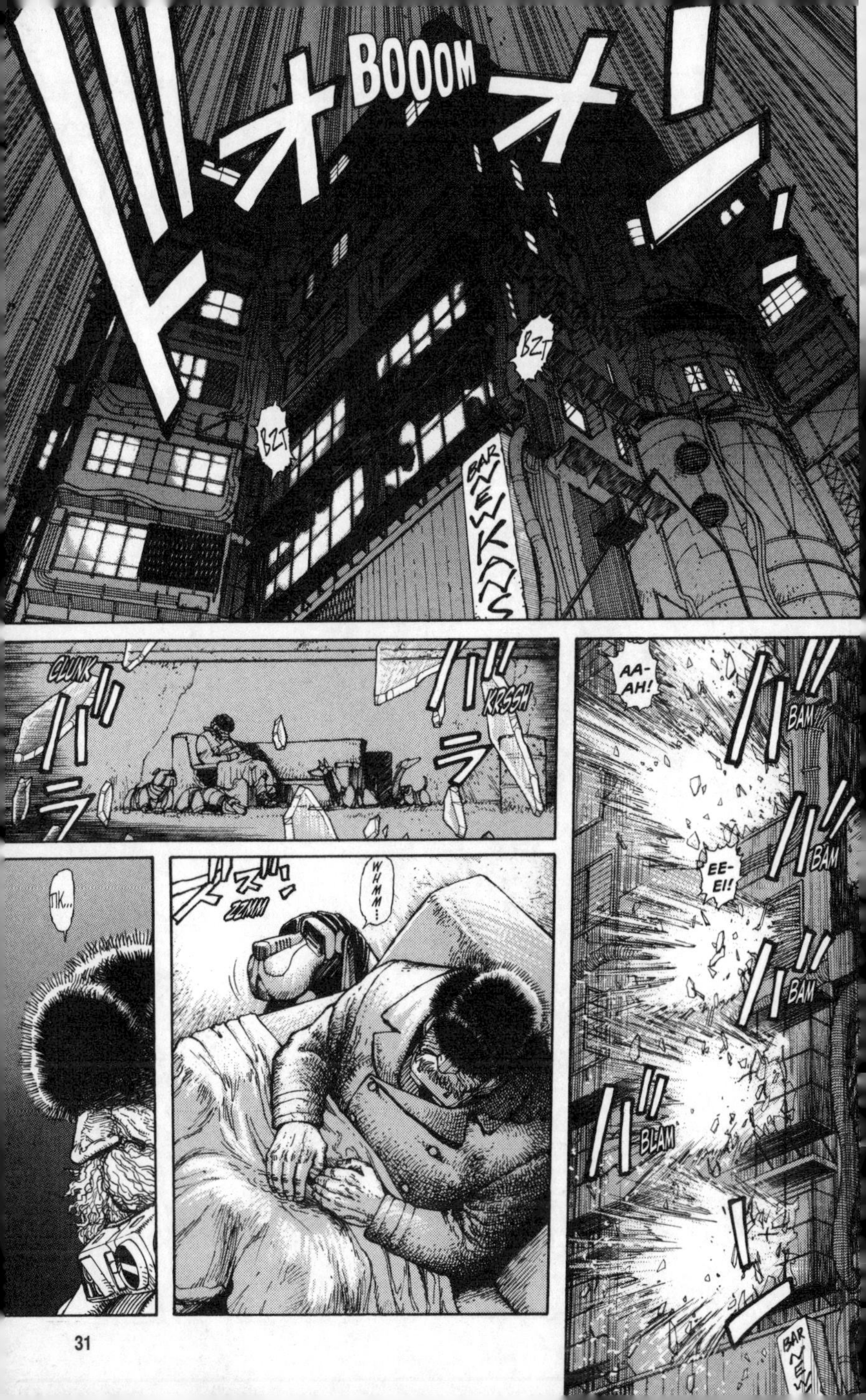
BOOOM
BZT
BZT
BAR
AA-AH!
BAM
EE-EI!
BAM
BAM
BLAM
BAR
CLUNK
KRSSH
WHMMM...
ZZMM
TIK...

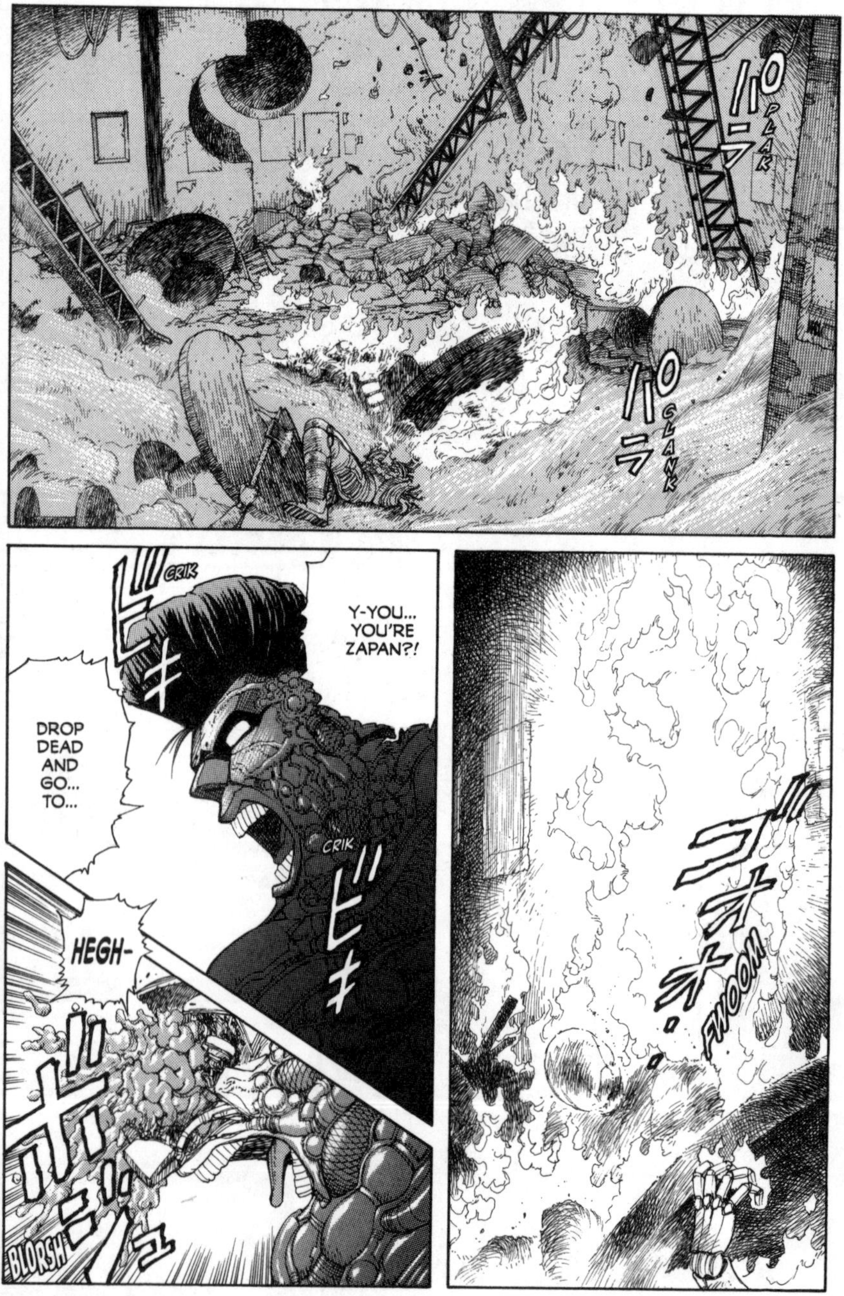
PLAK
GLANK
FWOOM
CRIK
Y-YOU... YOU'RE ZAPAN?!
DROP DEAD AND GO... TO...
CRIK
HEGH-
BLORSH

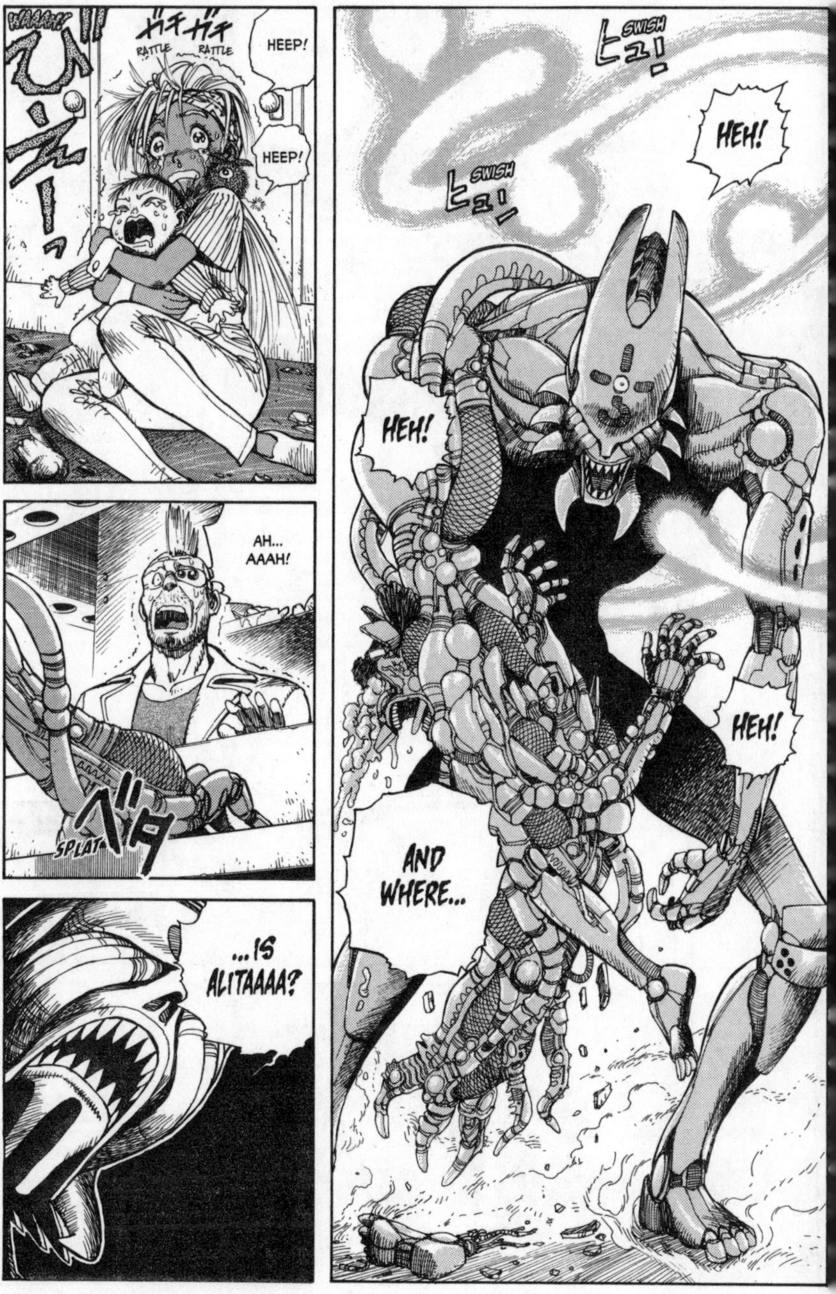
SWISH
HEH!
SWISH
HEH!
HEH!
AND WHERE...
HEEP!
HEEP!
RATTLE RATTLE
WAAAH!
AH... AAAH!
SPLAT
...IS ALITAAAA?

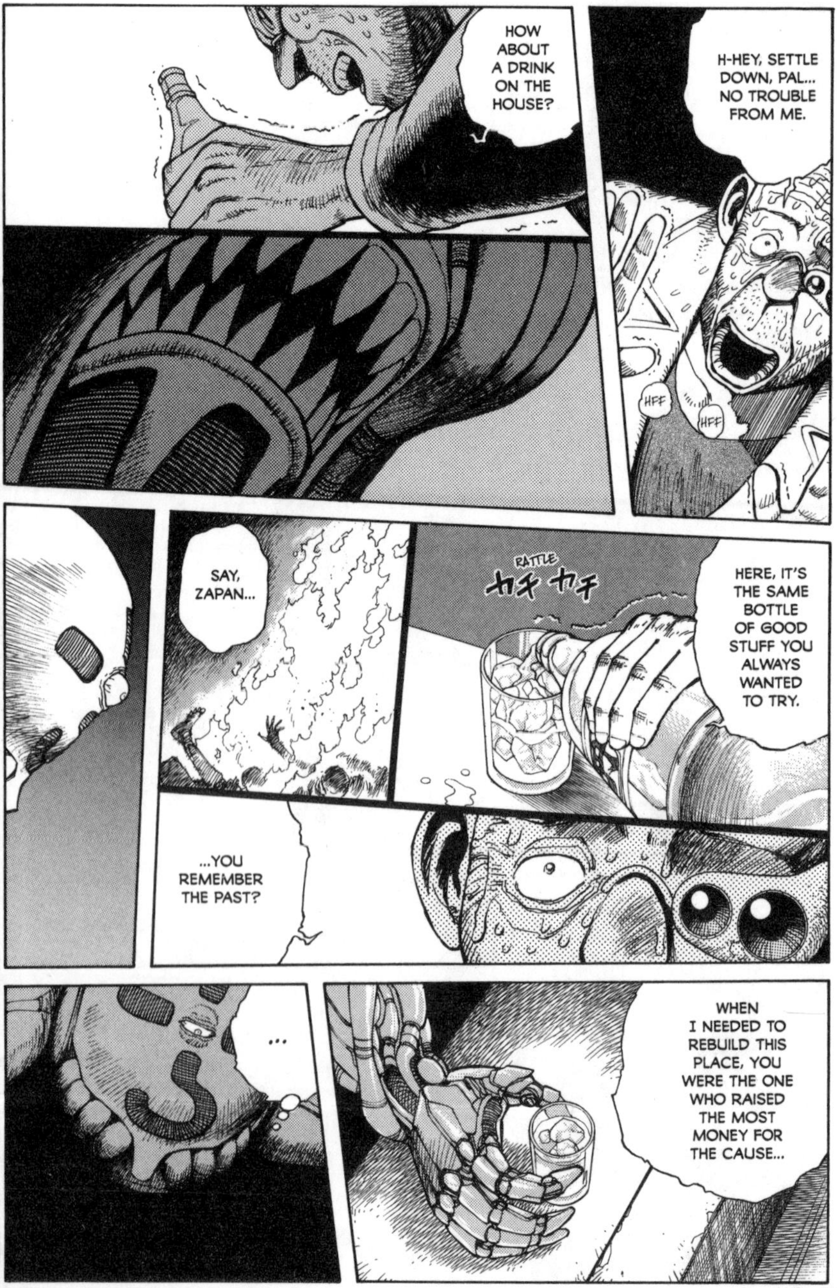

H-HEY, SETTLE DOWN, PAL... NO TROUBLE FROM ME.
HFF
HFF
HOW ABOUT A DRINK ON THE HOUSE?
RATTLE
カチ カチ
HERE, IT'S THE SAME BOTTLE OF GOOD STUFF YOU ALWAYS WANTED TO TRY.
SAY, ZAPAN...
...YOU REMEMBER THE PAST?
WHEN I NEEDED TO REBUILD THIS PLACE, YOU WERE THE ONE WHO RAISED THE MOST MONEY FOR THE CAUSE...
...

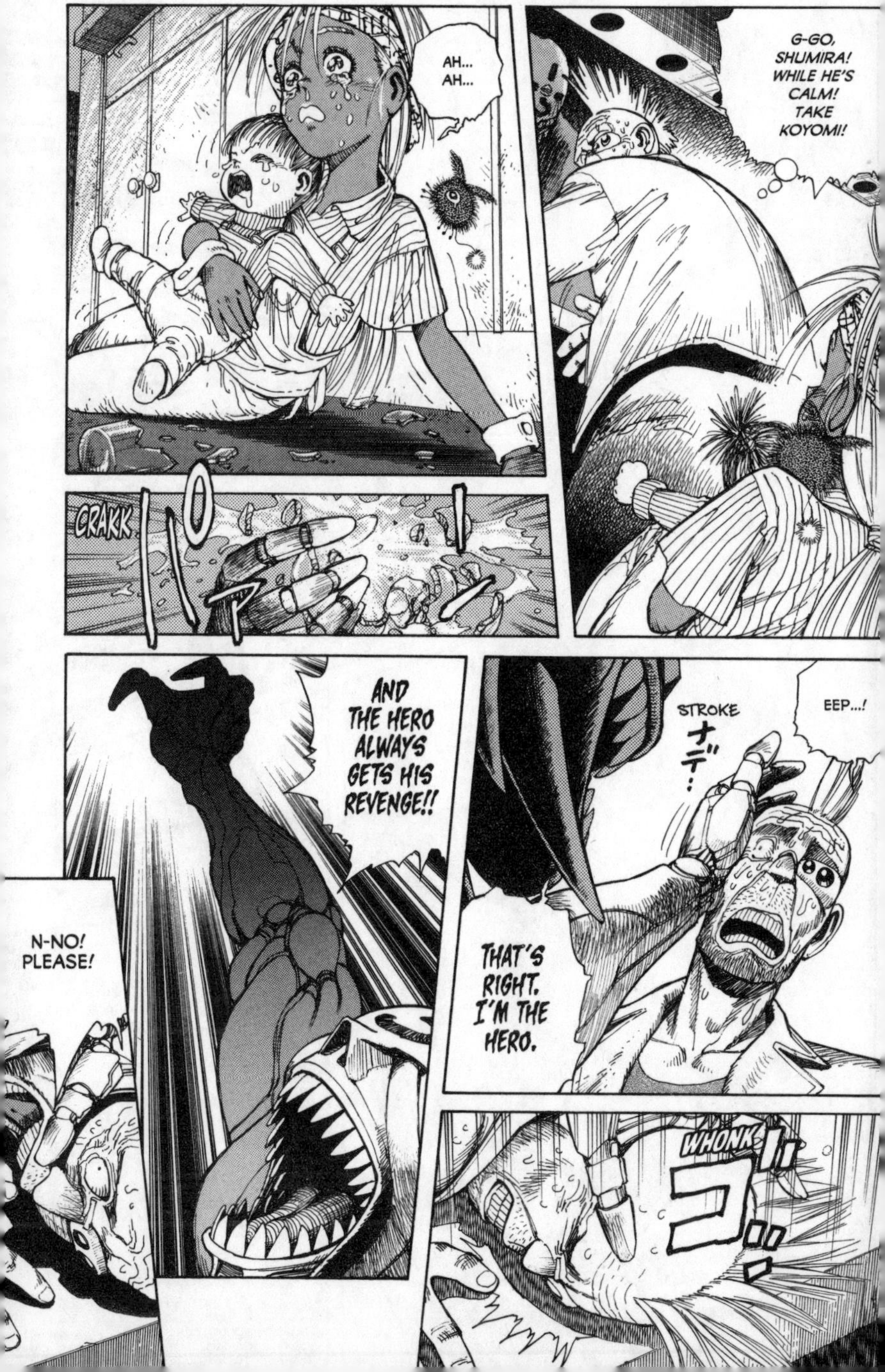
G-GO, SHUMIRA! WHILE HE'S CALM! TAKE KOYOMI!
AH... AH...
CRAKK
EEP...!
STROKE
ナデ
THAT'S RIGHT. I'M THE HERO.
AND THE HERO ALWAYS GETS HIS REVENGE!!
N-NO! PLEASE!
WHONK

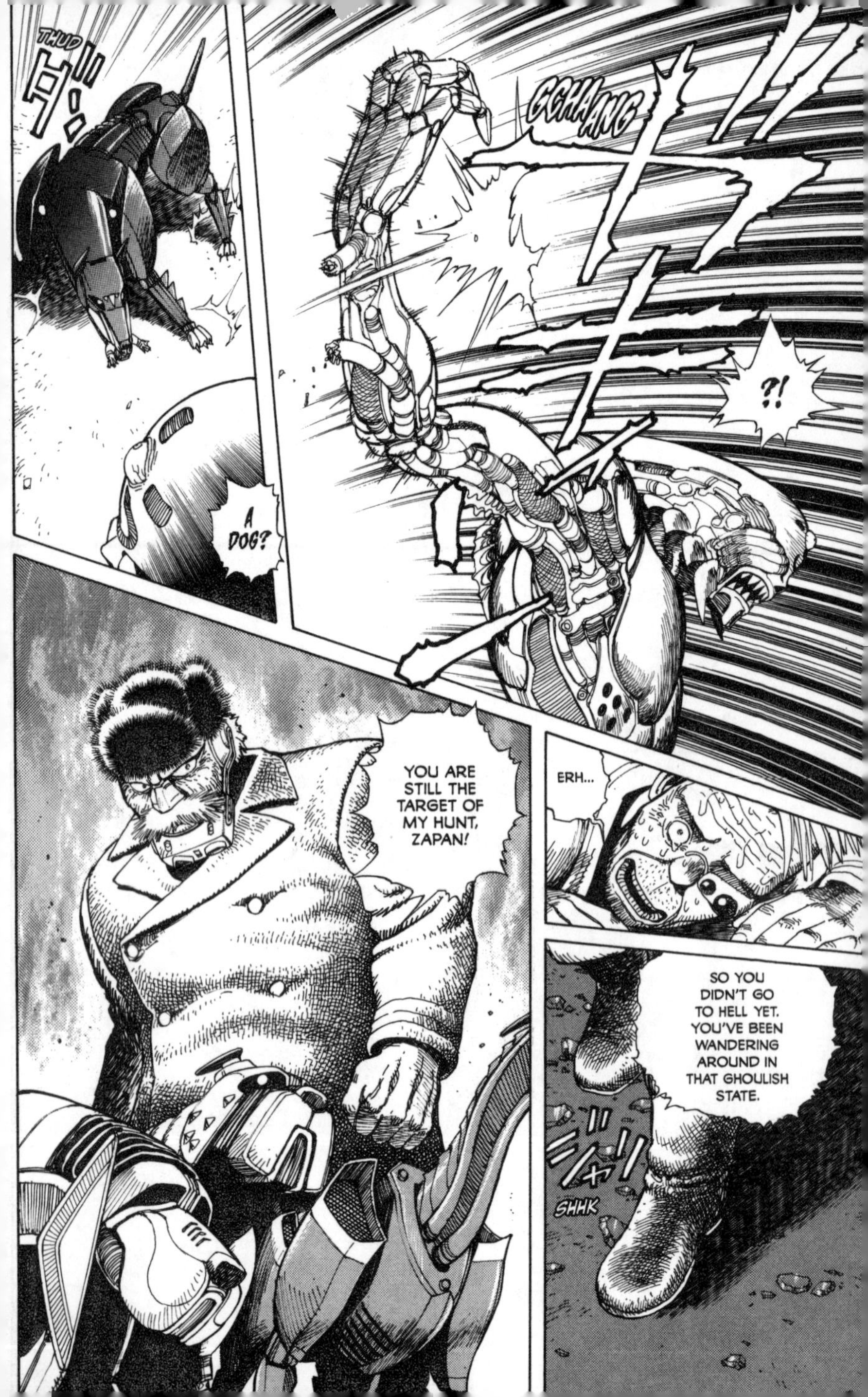
GCHANG
?!
THUD
A DOG?
ERH...
SO YOU DIDN'T GO TO HELL YET. YOU'VE BEEN WANDERING AROUND IN THAT GHOULISH STATE.
SHHK
YOU ARE STILL THE TARGET OF MY HUNT, ZAPAN!

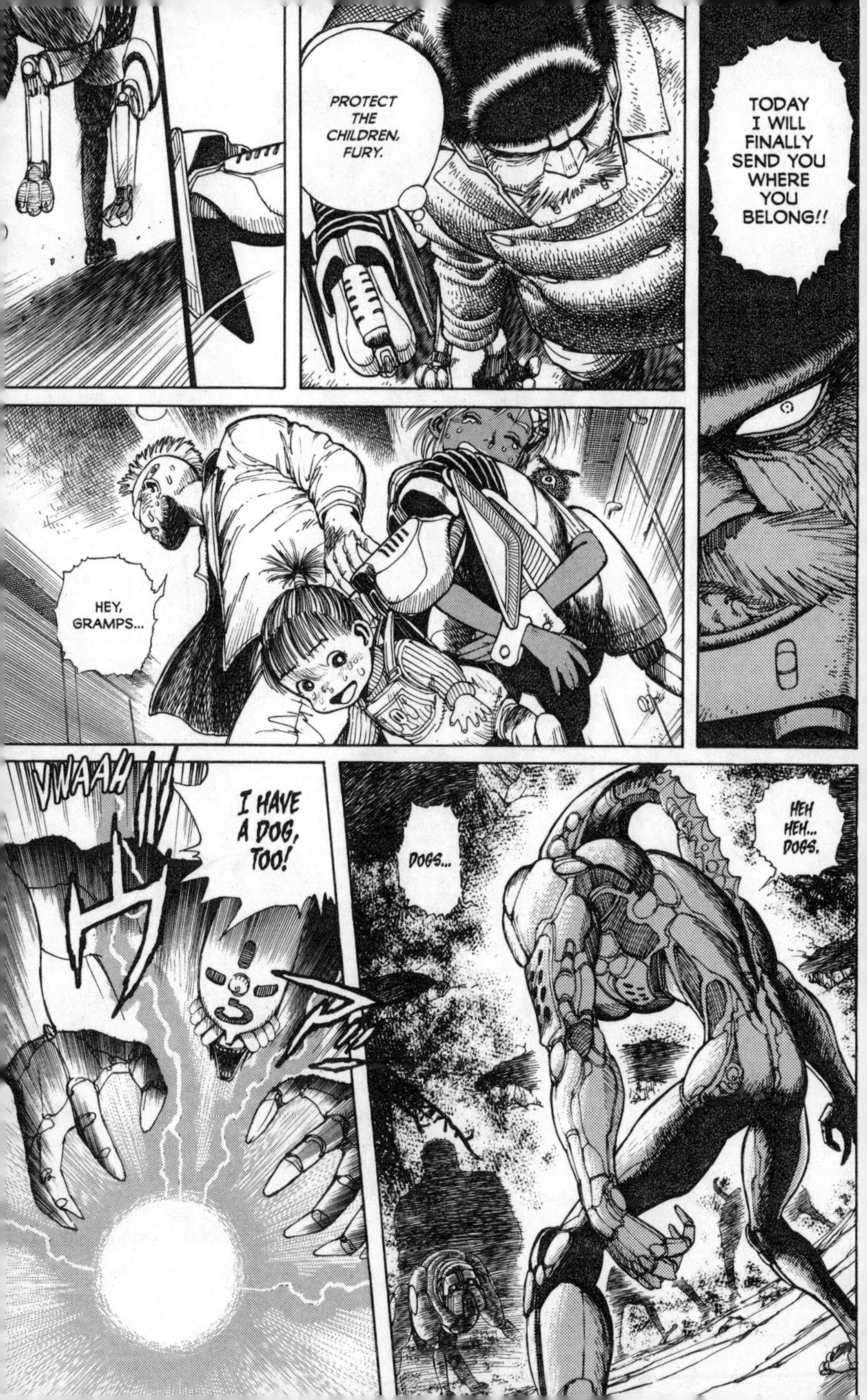
TODAY I WILL FINALLY SEND YOU WHERE YOU BELONG!!
PROTECT THE CHILDREN, FURY.
HEY, GRAMPS...
HEH HEH... DOGS.
DOGS...
I HAVE A DOG, TOO!
VWAAH

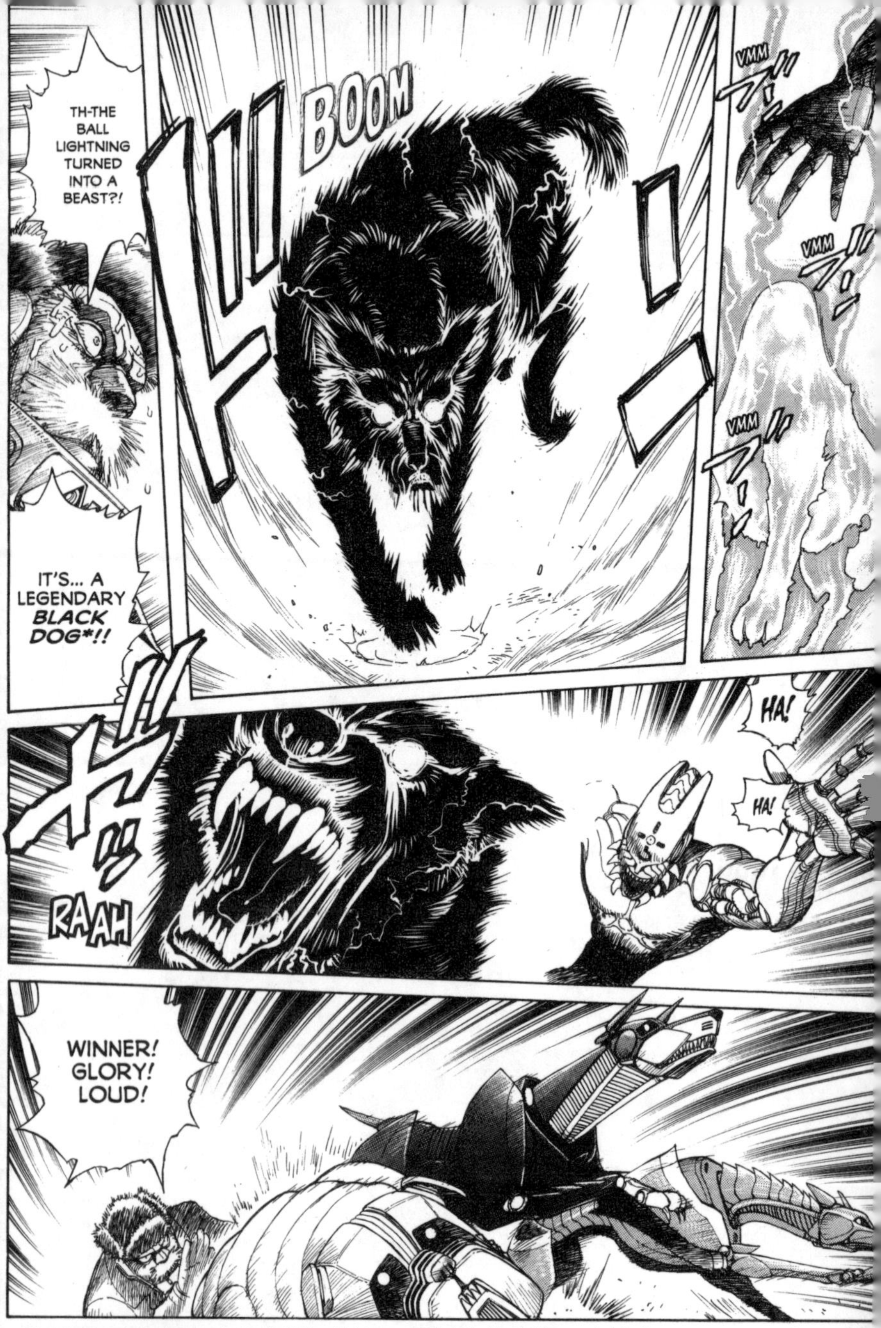
VMM
VMM
VMM
BOOM
TH-THE BALL LIGHTNING TURNED INTO A BEAST?!
IT'S... A LEGENDARY *BLACK DOG**!!
HA!
HA!
RAAH
WINNER! GLORY! LOUD!

***Black dog:** A supernatural monster from English folklore. It's known as the Black Shuck in Norfolk, a puca in Ireland, and the Gurt Dog in Somerset. It appears along with a bolt of lightning, kills people, then disappears in an explosion of light. It also leaves behind the stench of sulfur.

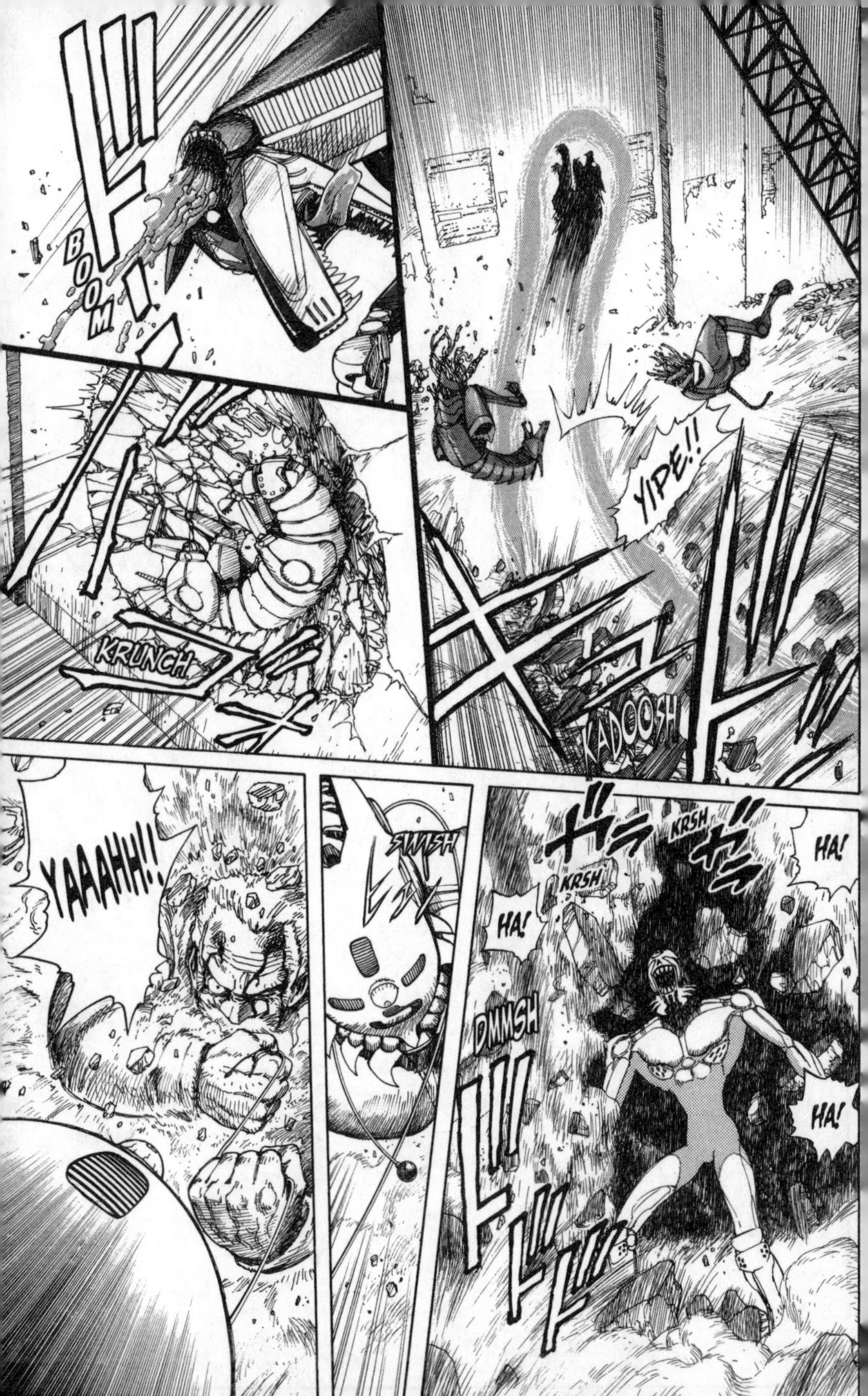
YIPE!!
KADOOSH
BOOM!!
KRUNCH
HA!
KRSH
KRSH
HA!
HA!
DMMSH
SWISH
YAAAHH!!

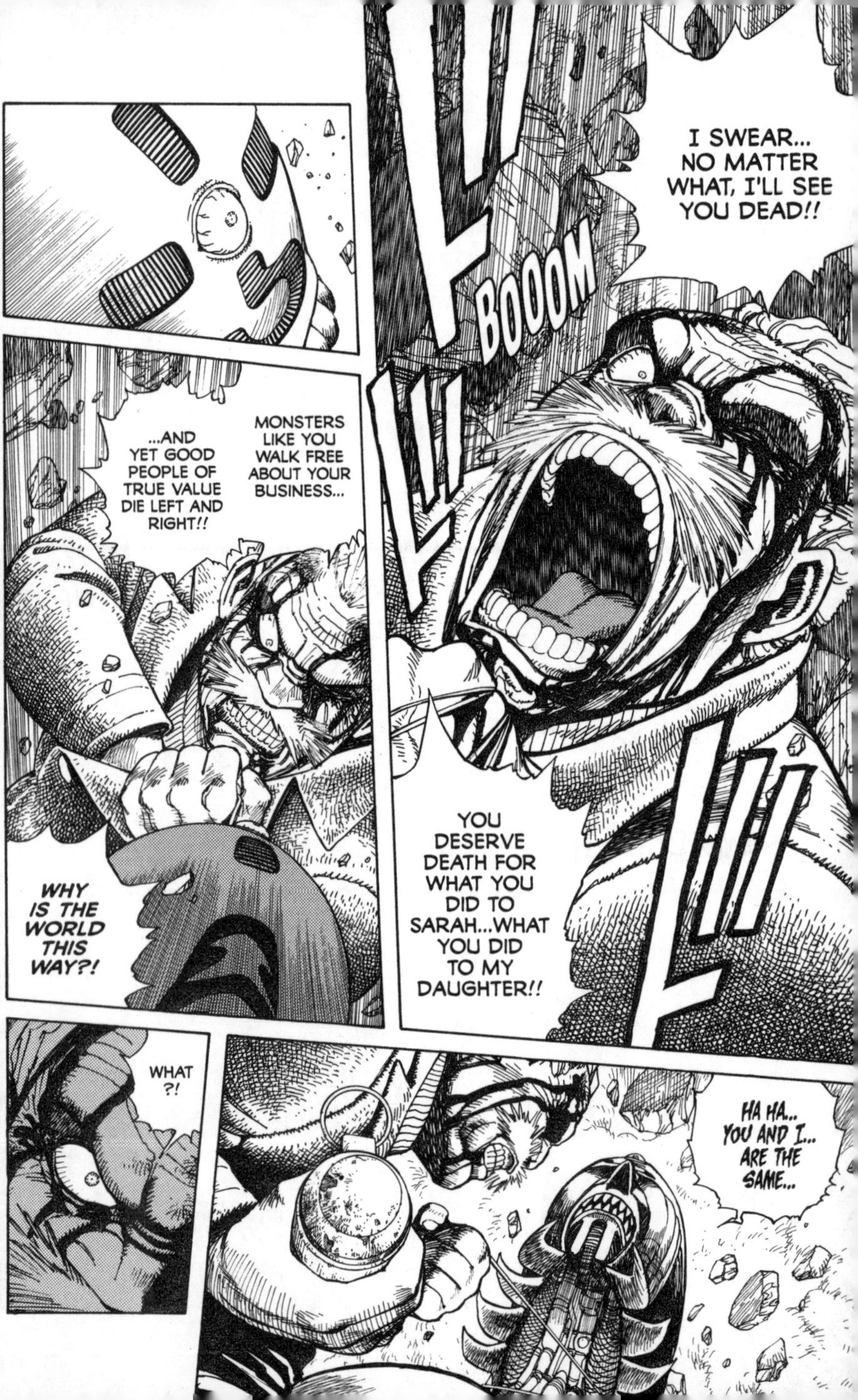
I SWEAR... NO MATTER WHAT, I'LL SEE YOU DEAD!!
BOOOM
YOU DESERVE DEATH FOR WHAT YOU DID TO SARAH...WHAT YOU DID TO MY DAUGHTER!!
MONSTERS LIKE YOU WALK FREE ABOUT YOUR BUSINESS...
...AND YET GOOD PEOPLE OF TRUE VALUE DIE LEFT AND RIGHT!!
WHY IS THE WORLD THIS WAY?!
HA HA... YOU AND I... ARE THE SAME...
WHAT?!

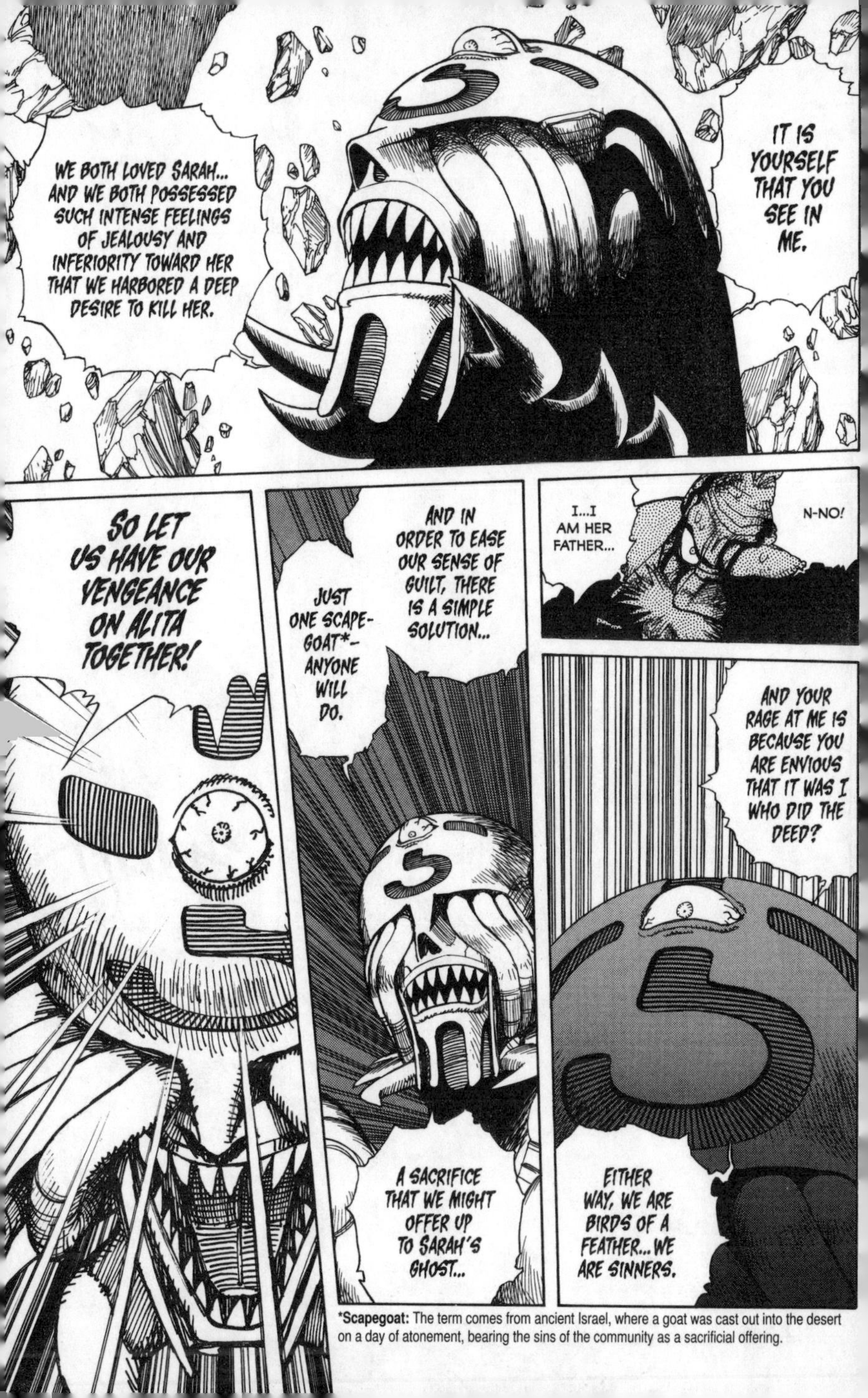
IT IS YOURSELF THAT YOU SEE IN ME.
WE BOTH LOVED SARAH... AND WE BOTH POSSESSED SUCH INTENSE FEELINGS OF JEALOUSY AND INFERIORITY TOWARD HER THAT WE HARBORED A DEEP DESIRE TO KILL HER.
N-NO!
I...I AM HER FATHER...
AND YOUR RAGE AT ME IS BECAUSE YOU ARE ENVIOUS THAT IT WAS I WHO DID THE DEED?
EITHER WAY, WE ARE BIRDS OF A FEATHER... WE ARE SINNERS.
AND IN ORDER TO EASE OUR SENSE OF GUILT, THERE IS A SIMPLE SOLUTION...
JUST ONE SCAPE-GOAT*- ANYONE WILL DO.
A SACRIFICE THAT WE MIGHT OFFER UP TO SARAH'S GHOST...
SO LET US HAVE OUR VENGEANCE ON ALITA TOGETHER!

***Scapegoat:** The term comes from ancient Israel, where a goat was cast out into the desert on a day of atonement, bearing the sins of the community as a sacrificial offering.

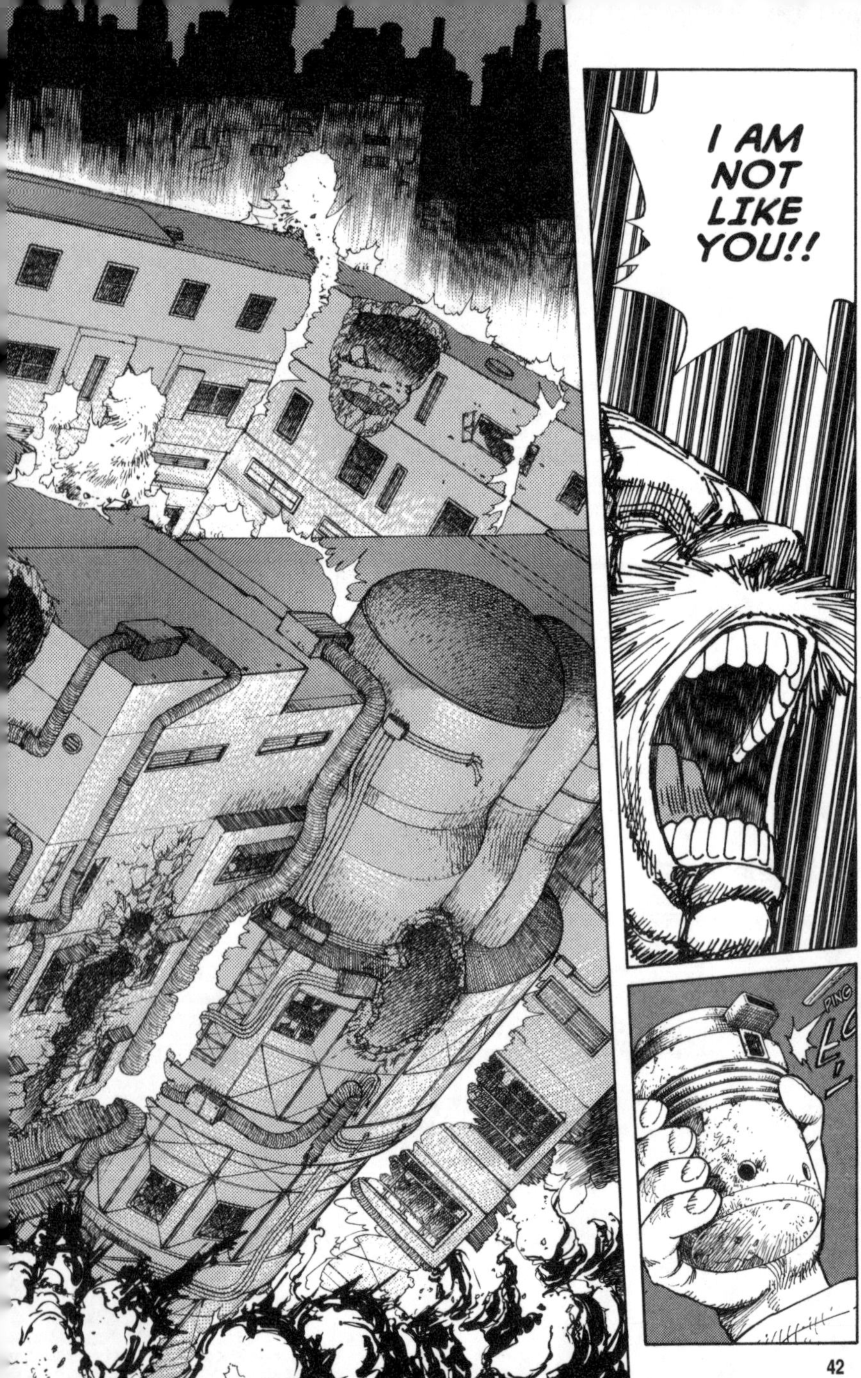
I AM NOT LIKE YOU!!
PING

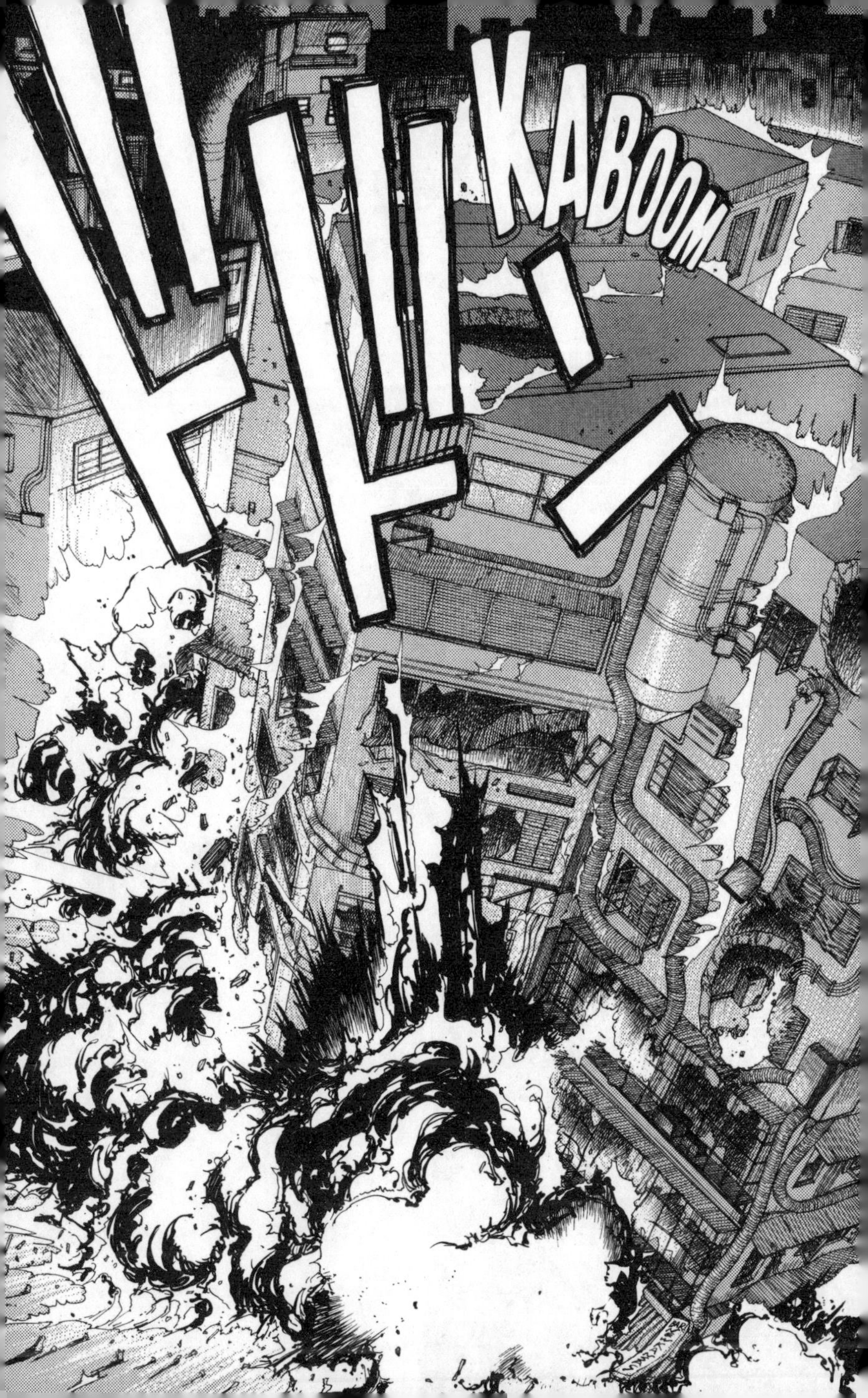
KABOOM

Marker: Fang **Sign:** Don't step on the flowers!

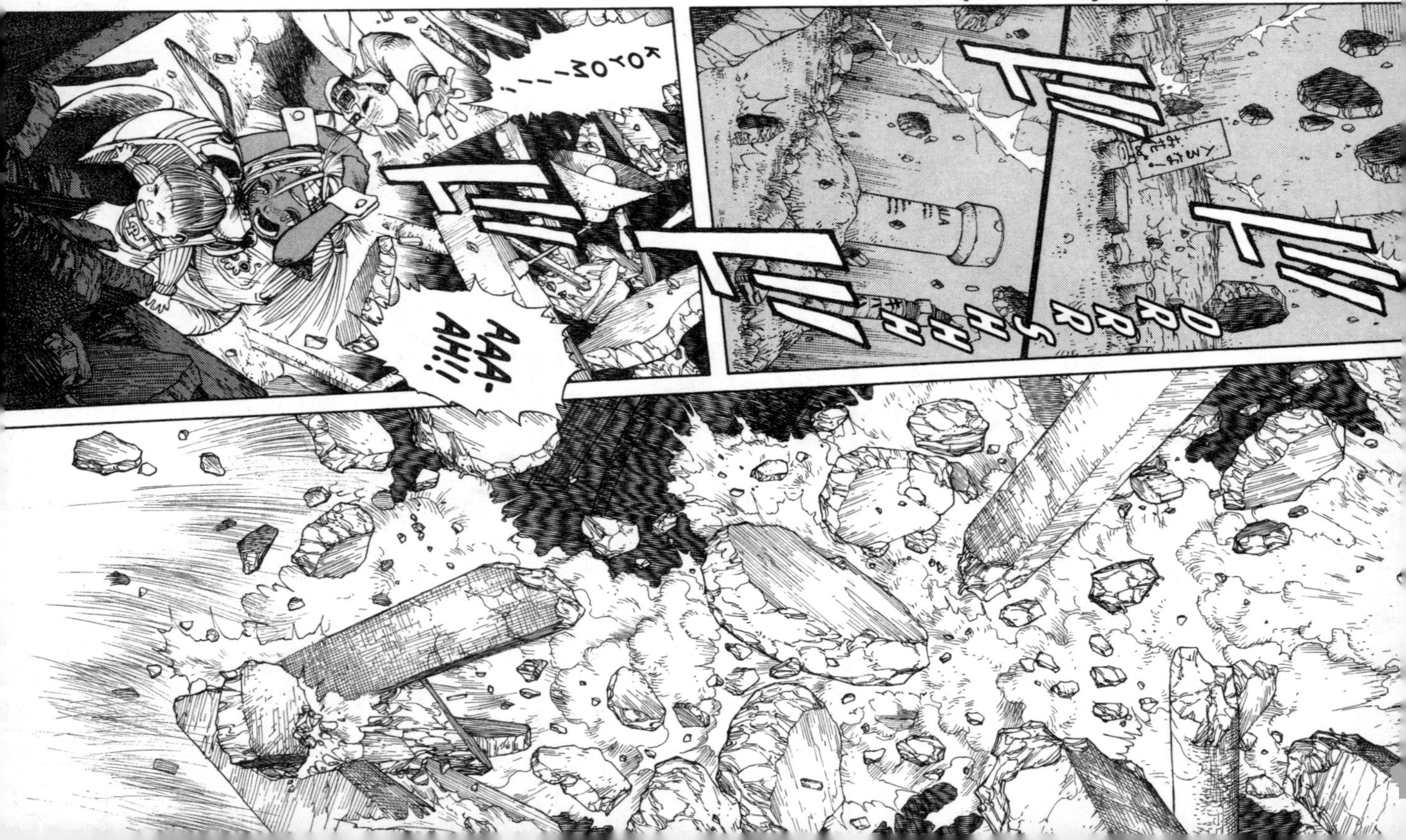
DRRRSHHH
KOYOMI!!!
AAA-AH!!

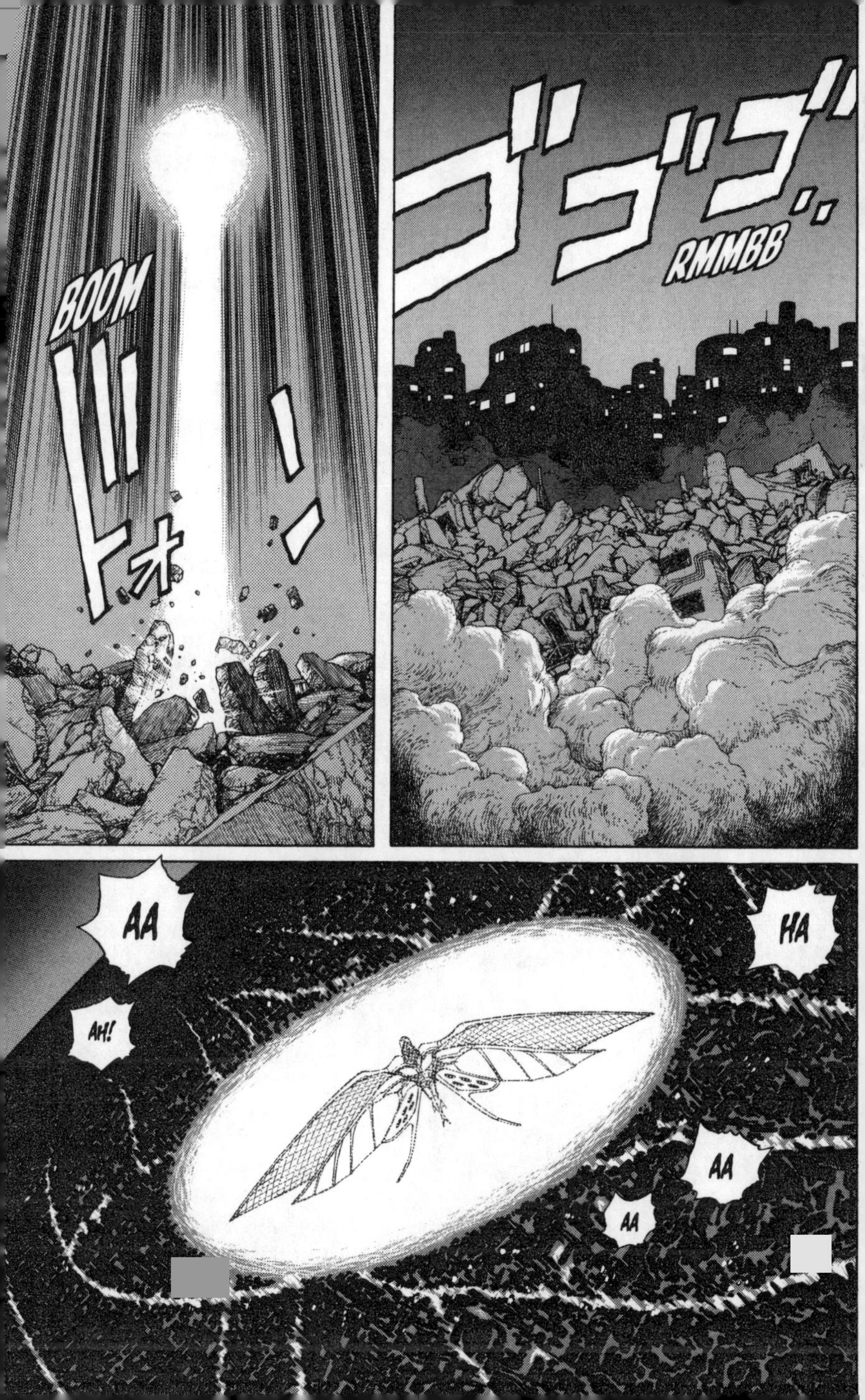
ゴゴ
RMMBB
BOOM
ドォーン
HA
AA
AA
AA
AH!

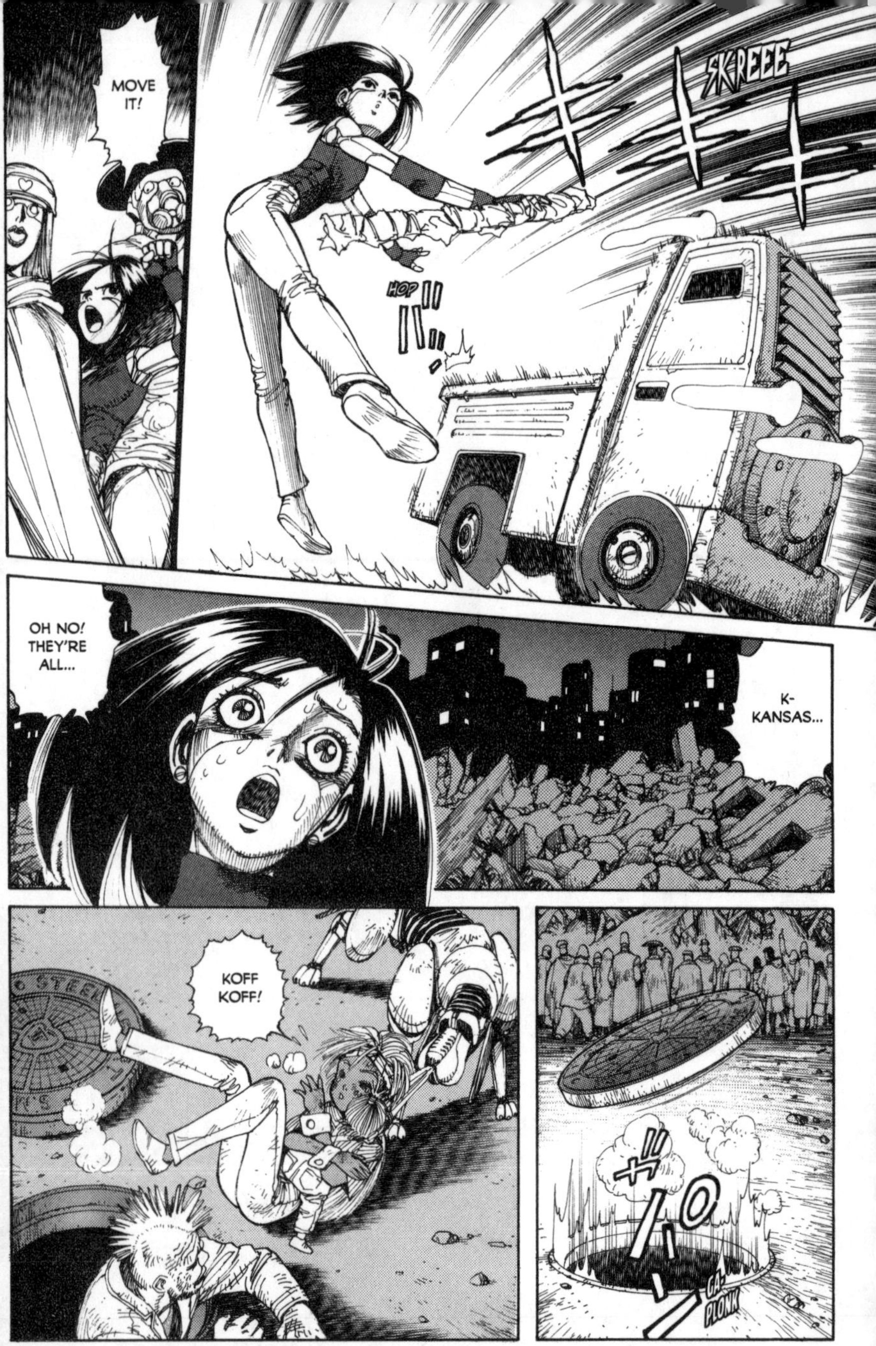

SKREEE
HOP
MOVE IT!
OH NO! THEY'RE ALL...
K-KANSAS...
GA-PLONK
KOFF KOFF!

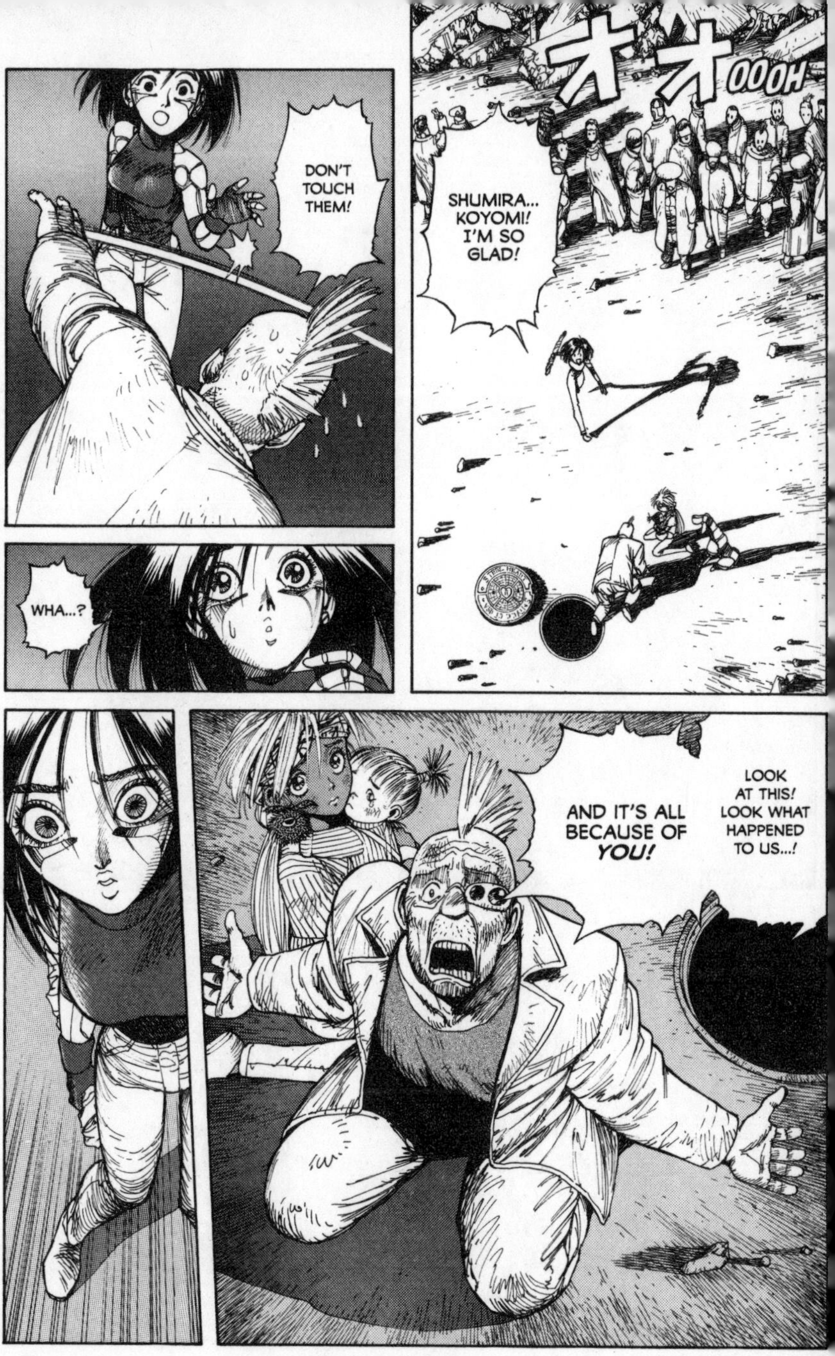
オオ OOOH
SHUMIRA... KOYOMI! I'M SO GLAD!
DON'T TOUCH THEM!
WHA...?
LOOK AT THIS! LOOK WHAT HAPPENED TO US...!
AND IT'S ALL BECAUSE OF *YOU!*

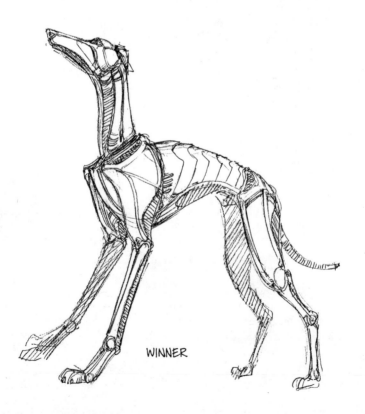

WINNER

FIGHT_027 Scapegoat

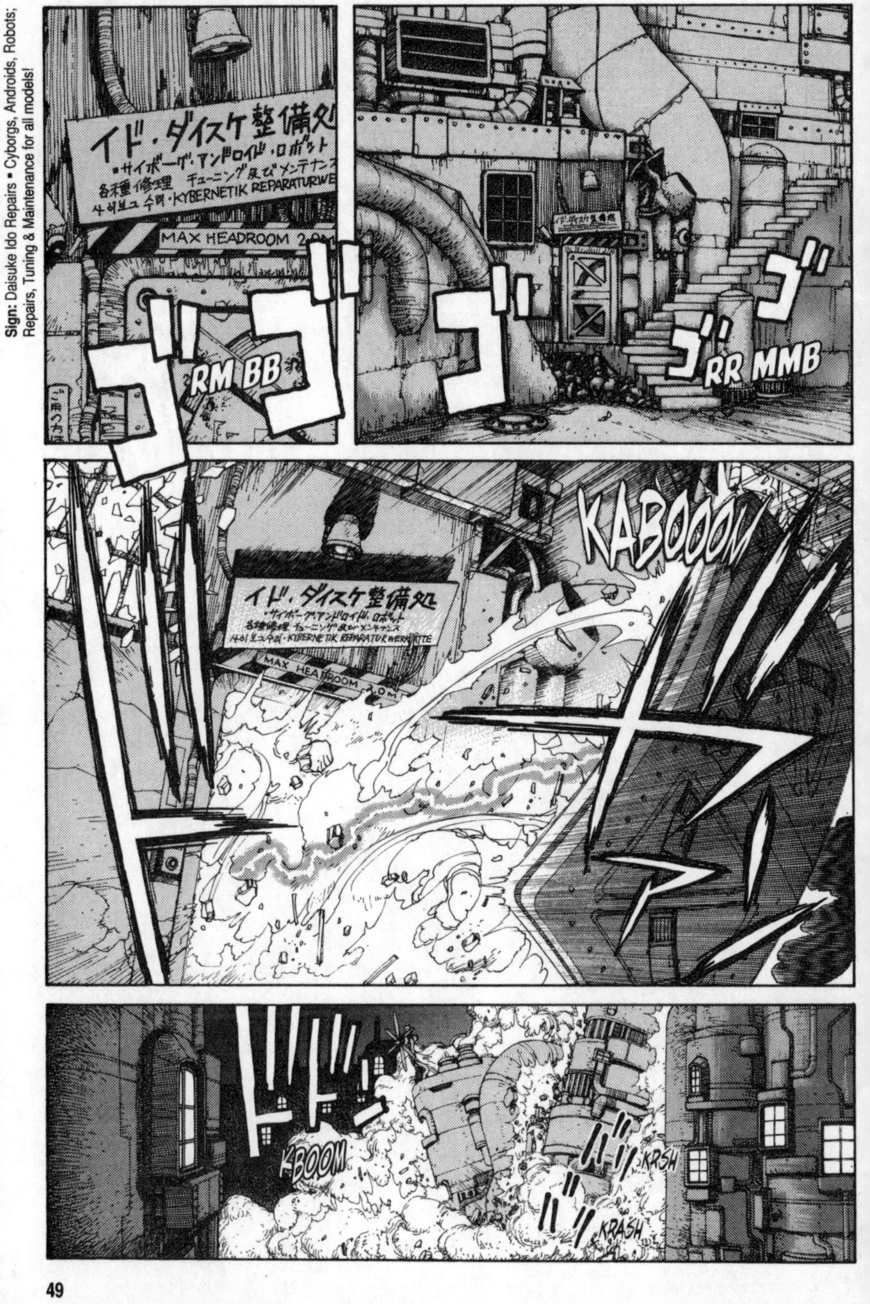
RR MMB
イド・ダイスケ整備処
MAX HEADROOM 2.0M
RM BB
KABOOOM
KBOOM
KRSH
KRASH

Sign: Daisuke Ido Repairs • Cyborgs, Androids, Robots; Repairs, Tuning & Maintenance for all models!

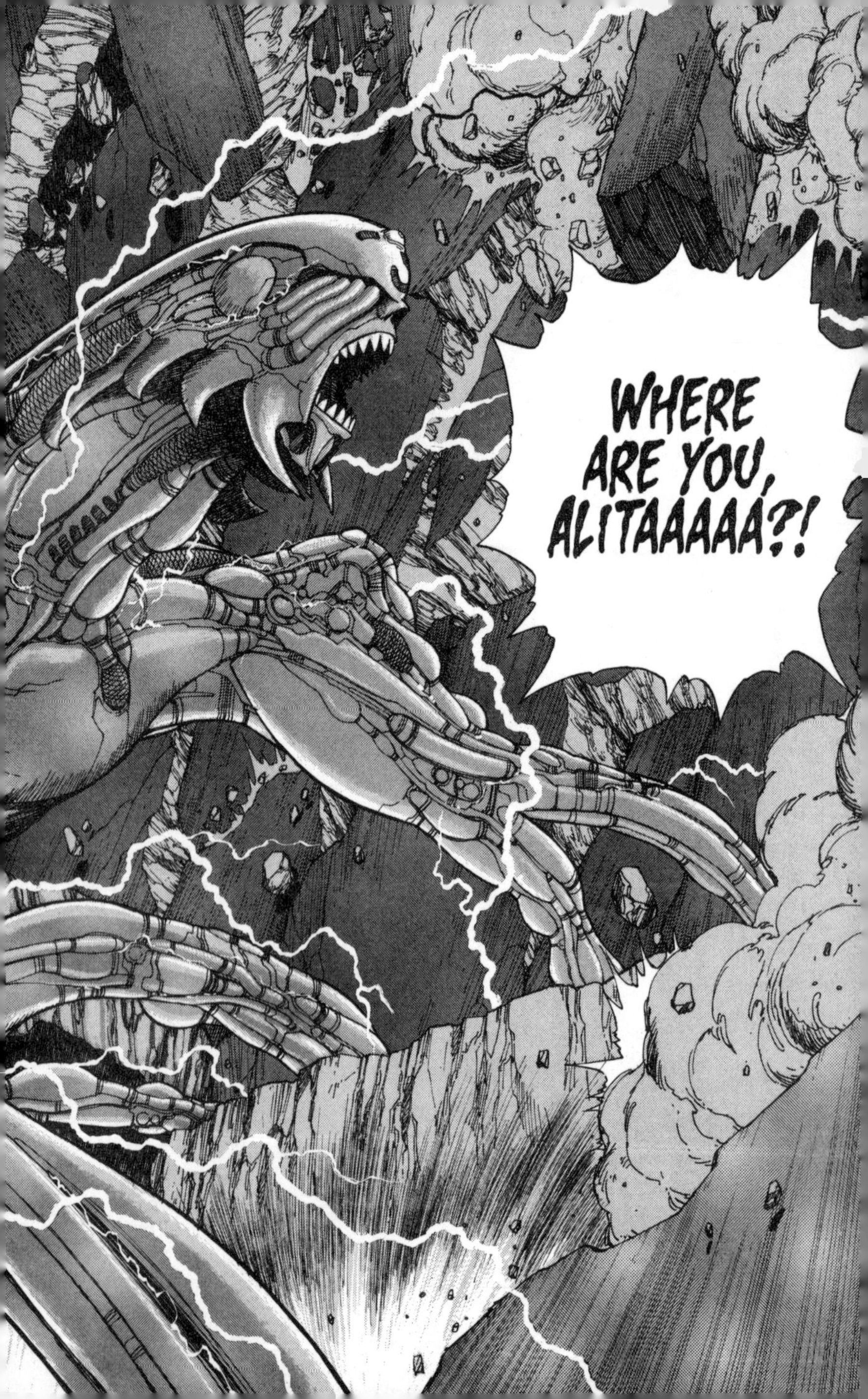
WHERE ARE YOU, ALITAAAAA?!

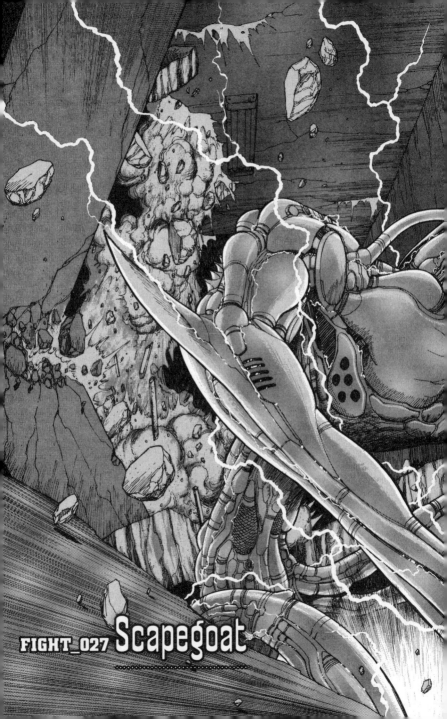

FIGHT_027 Scapegoat

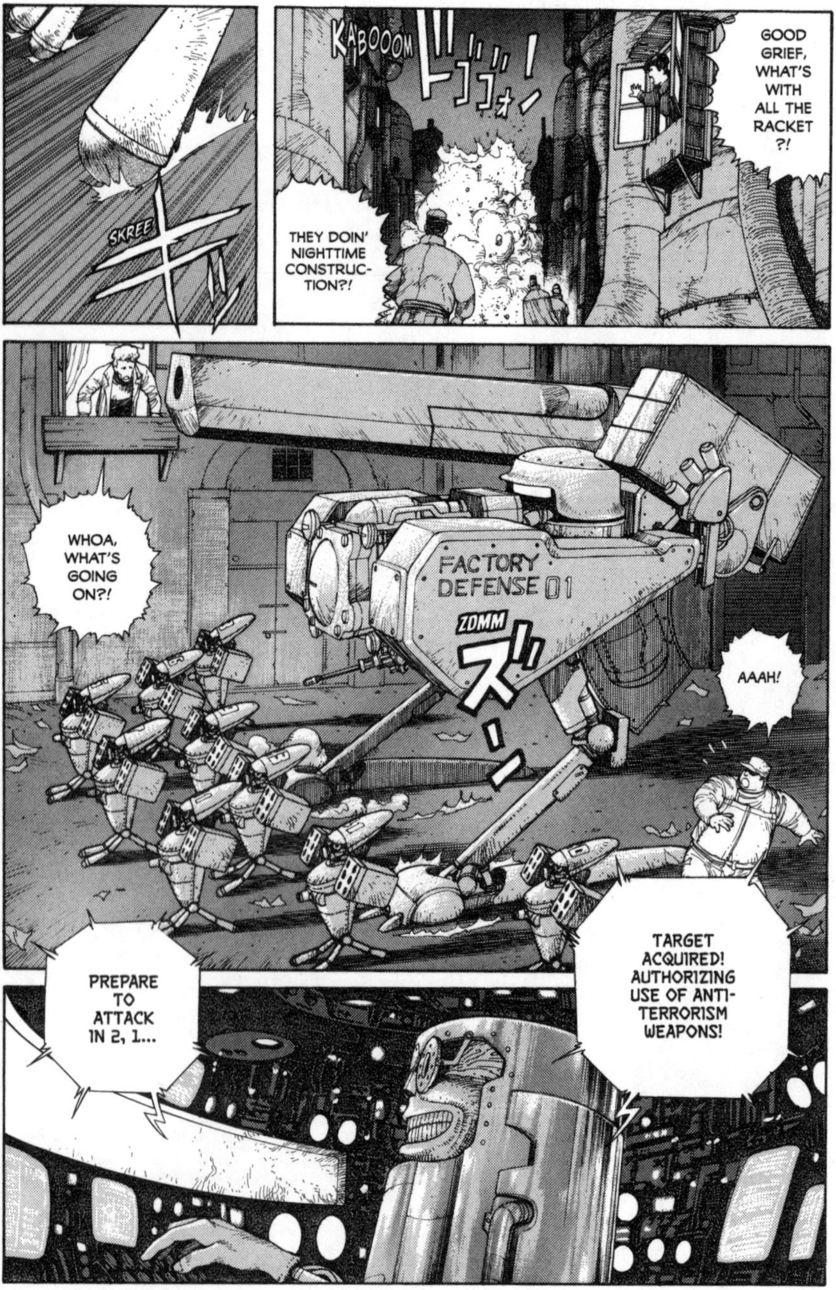
KABOOOM
GOOD GRIEF, WHAT'S WITH ALL THE RACKET ?!
THEY DOIN' NIGHTTIME CONSTRUC-TION?!
SKREE
AAAH!
FACTORY DEFENSE 01
ZDMM
WHOA, WHAT'S GOING ON?!
TARGET ACQUIRED! AUTHORIZING USE OF ANTI-TERRORISM WEAPONS!
PREPARE TO ATTACK IN 2, 1...

BOOM
BOOM
BOOM
PSH
PSH
BABOOMF

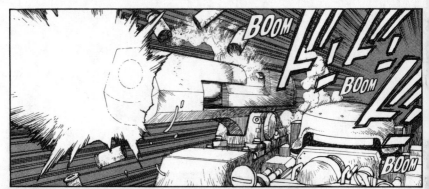

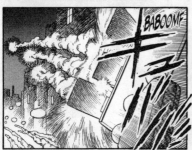

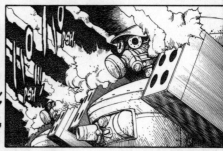

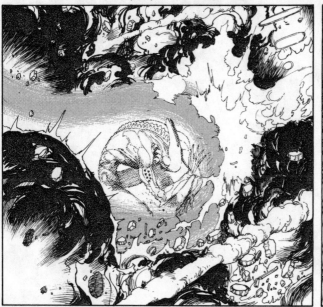

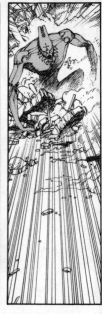

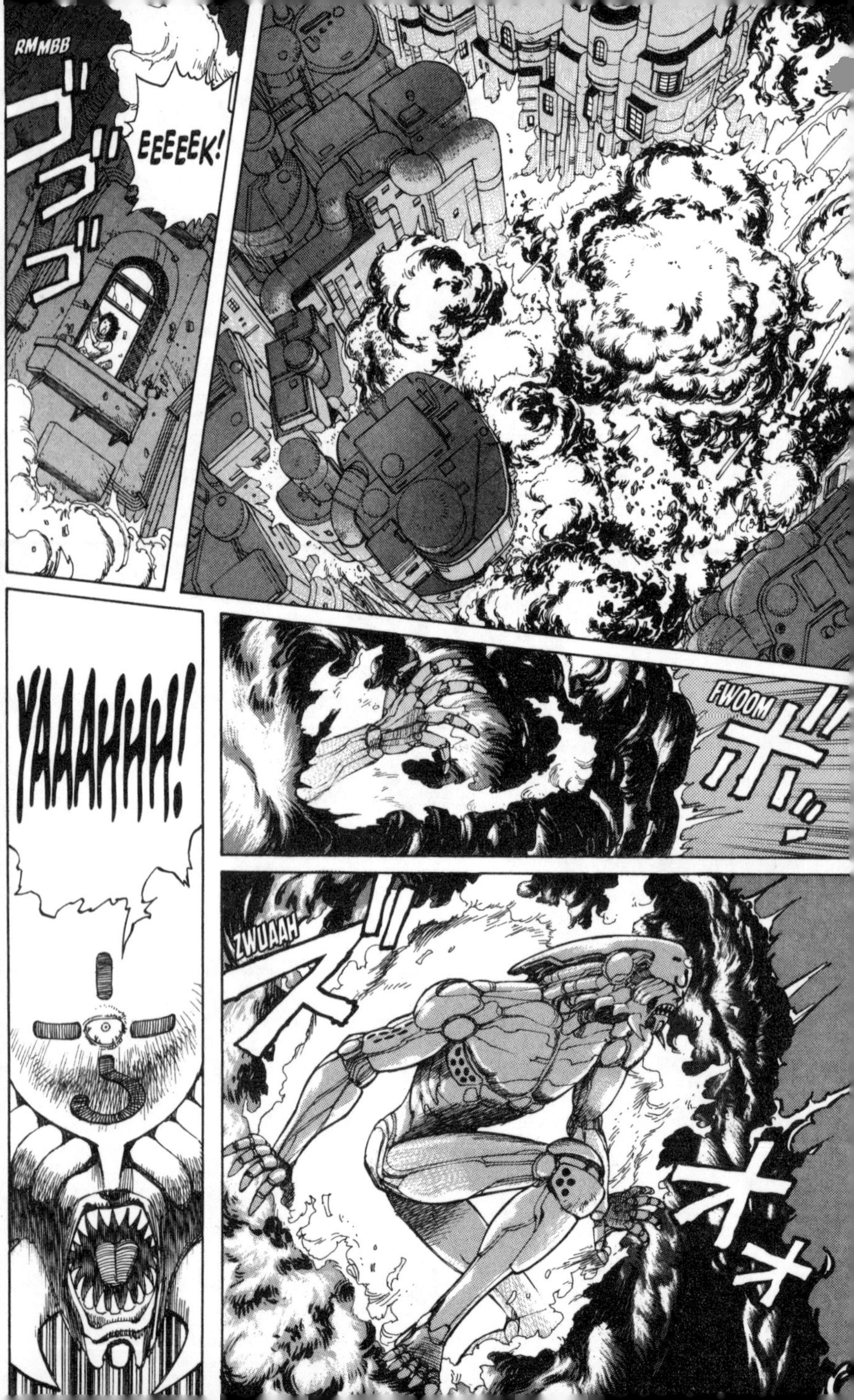
RMMBB
EEEEEK!
FWOOM
ZWUAAH
YAAAHHH!

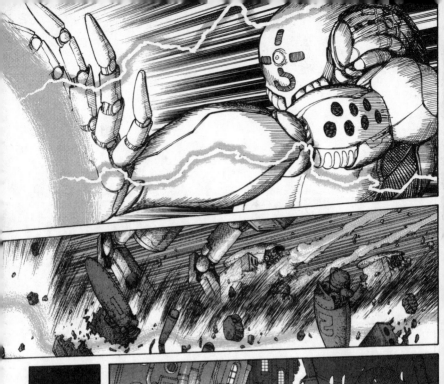

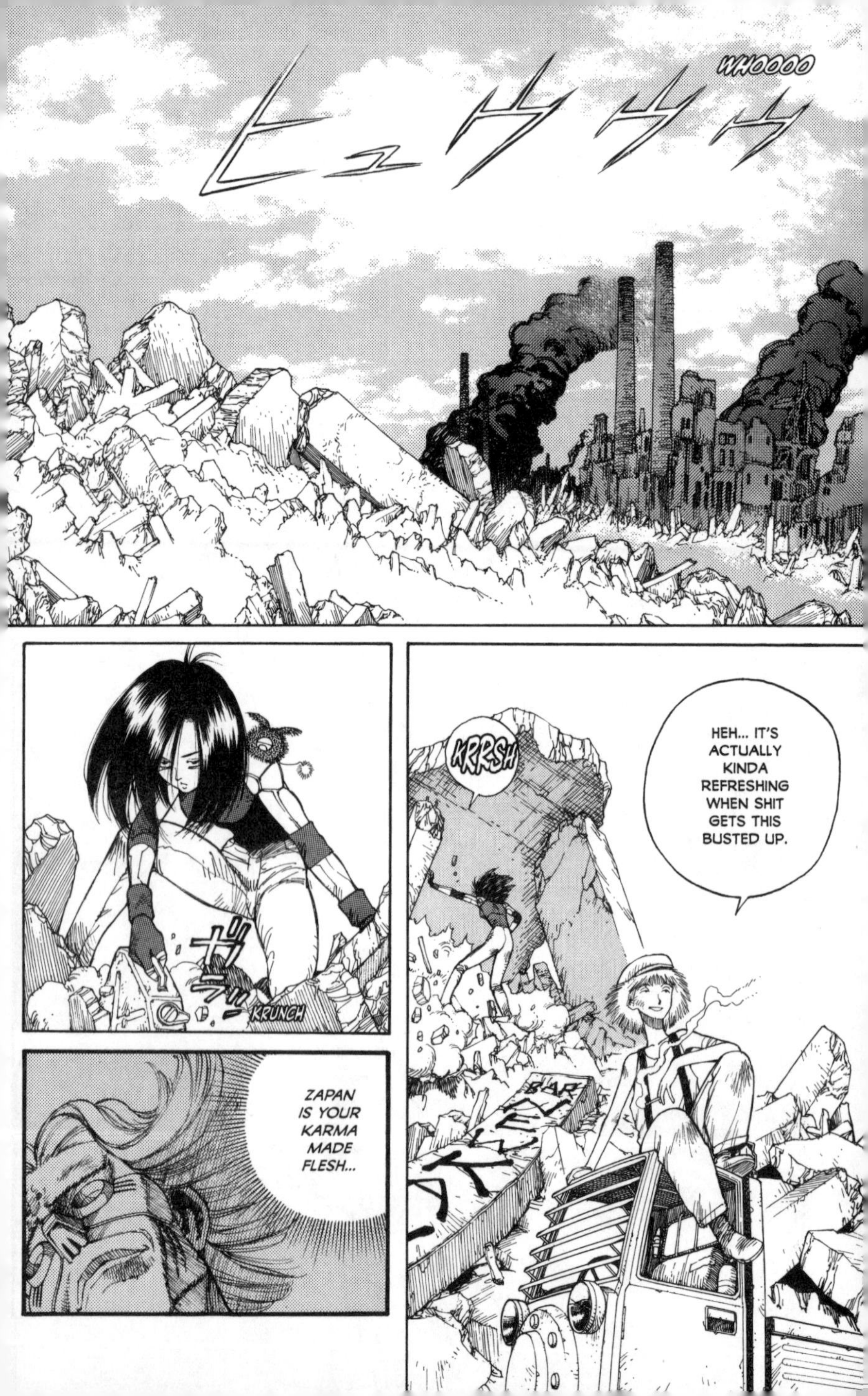
WHOOOO
ヒュウウウ
KRRSH
HEH... IT'S ACTUALLY KINDA REFRESHING WHEN SHIT GETS THIS BUSTED UP.
BAR
KRUNCH
ZAPAN IS YOUR KARMA MADE FLESH...

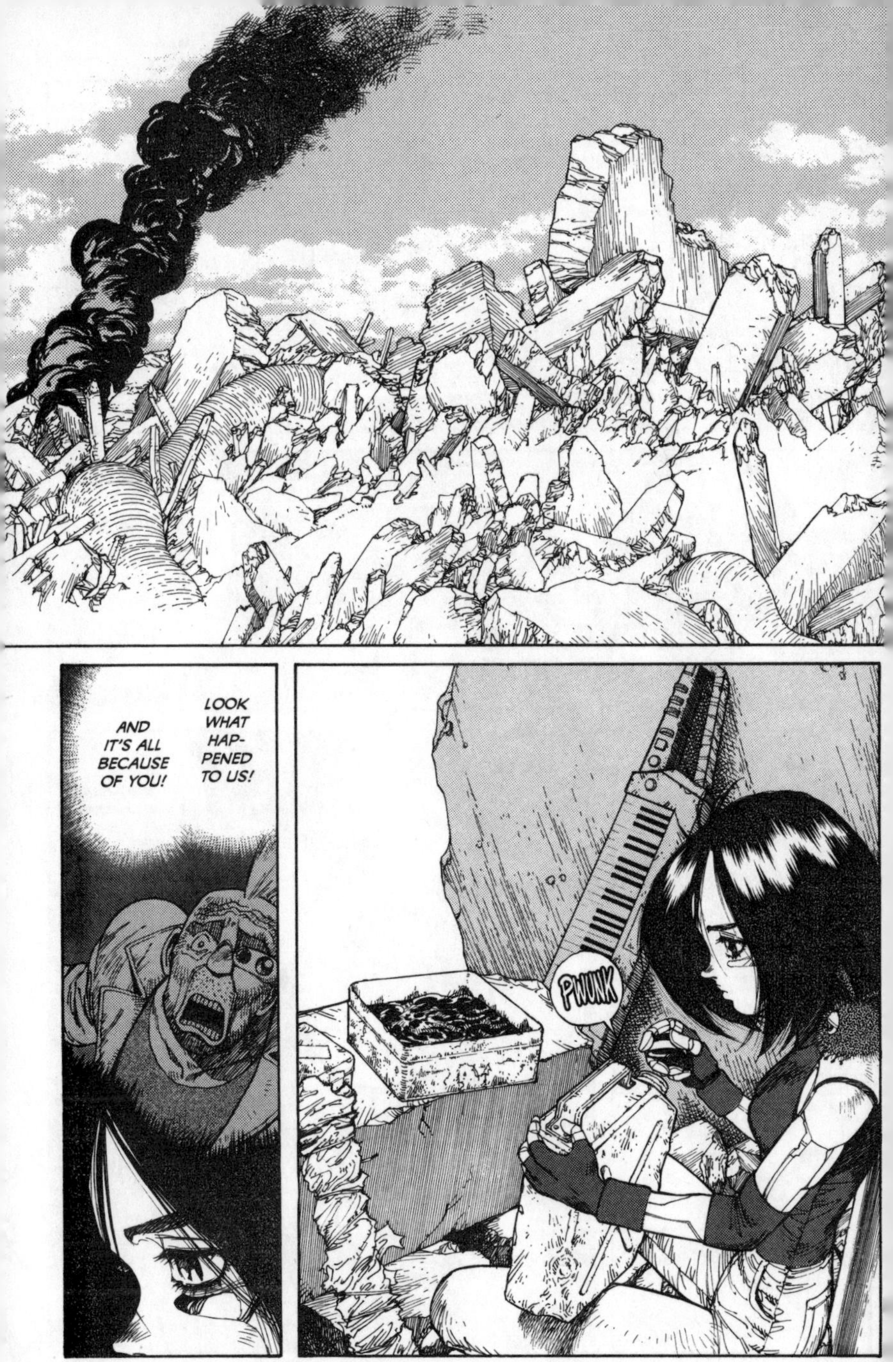
PWUNK
LOOK WHAT HAP-PENED TO US!
AND IT'S ALL BECAUSE OF YOU!

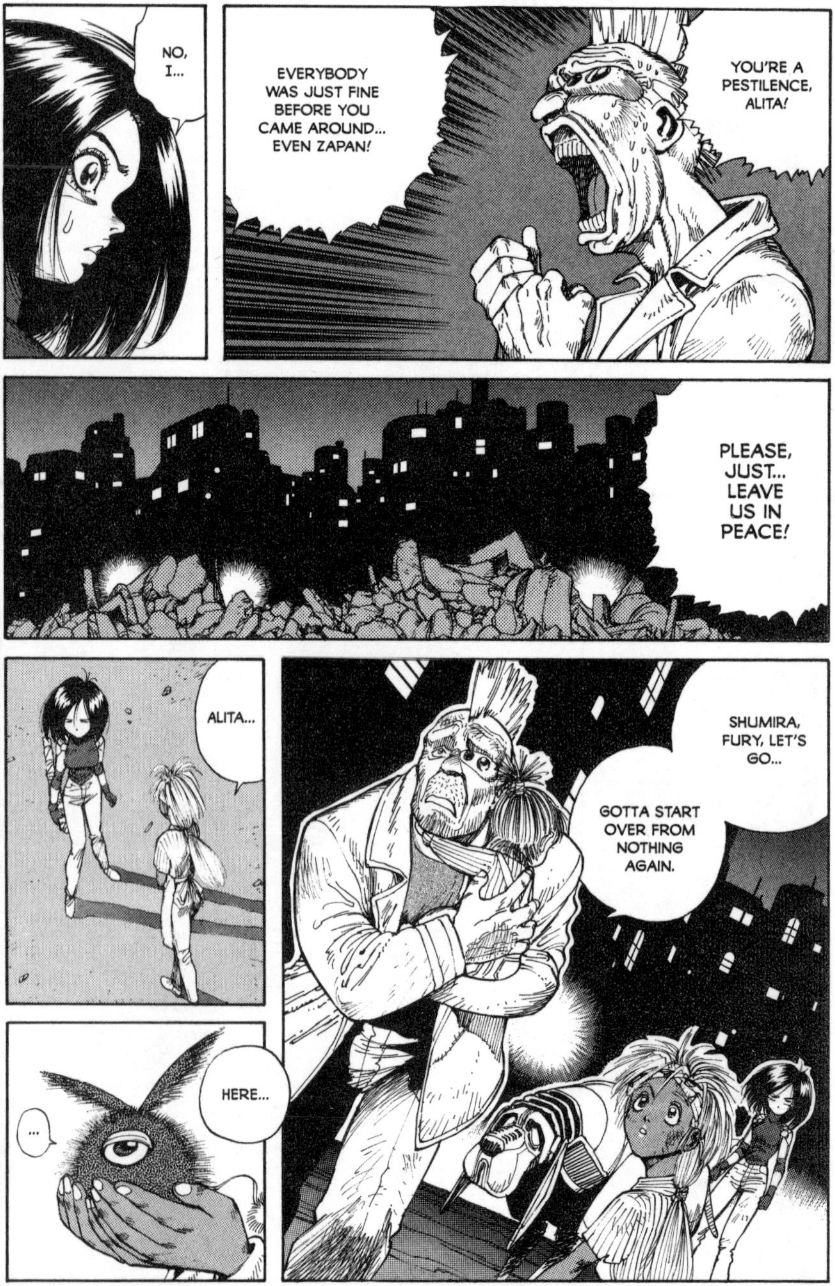
YOU'RE A PESTILENCE, ALITA!
EVERYBODY WAS JUST FINE BEFORE YOU CAME AROUND... EVEN ZAPAN!
NO, I...
PLEASE, JUST... LEAVE US IN PEACE!
SHUMIRA, FURY, LET'S GO...
GOTTA START OVER FROM NOTHING AGAIN.
ALITA...
HERE...
...

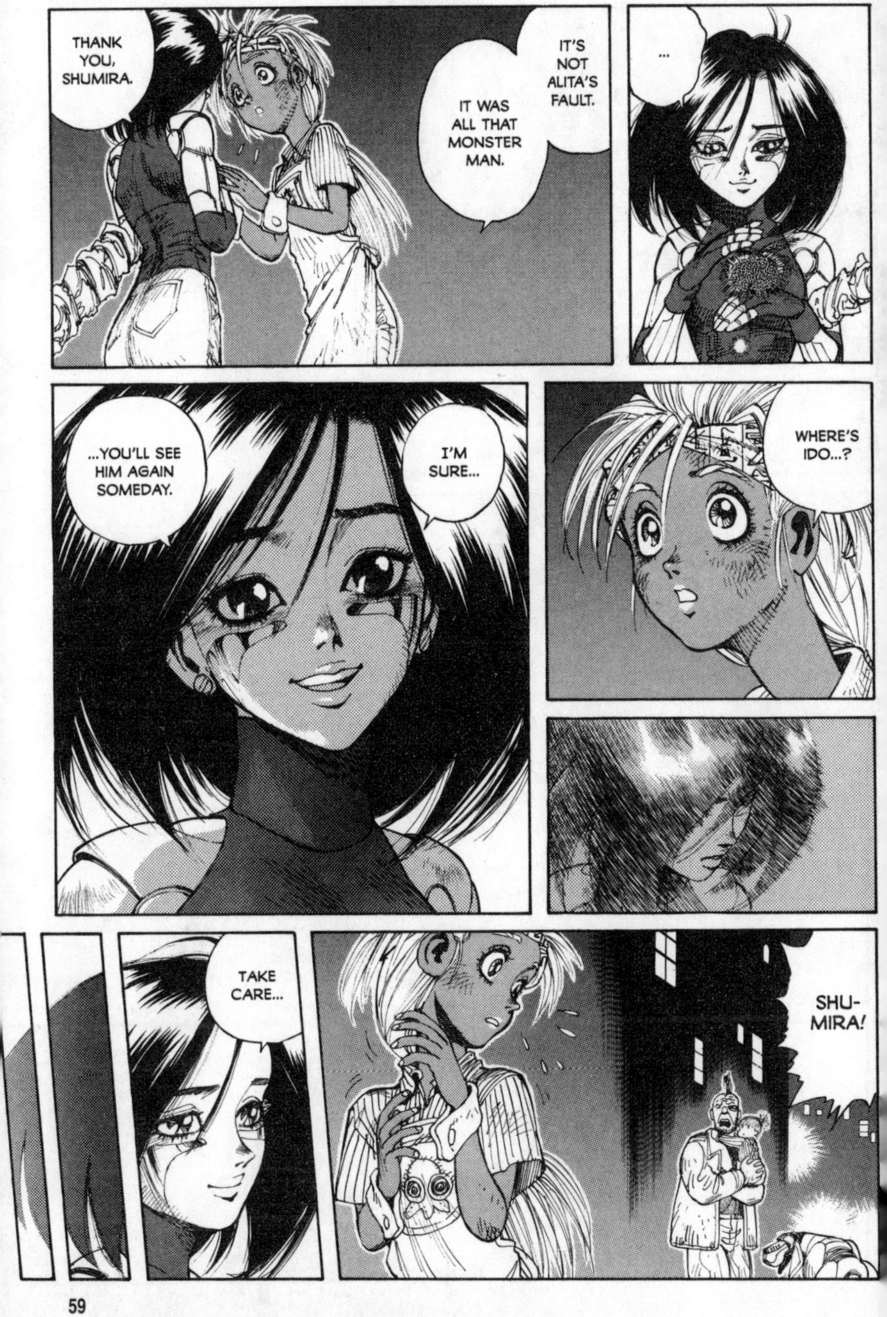
...
IT'S NOT ALITA'S FAULT.
IT WAS ALL THAT MONSTER MAN.
THANK YOU, SHUMIRA.
WHERE'S IDO...?
I'M SURE...
...YOU'LL SEE HIM AGAIN SOMEDAY.
SHU-MIRA!
TAKE CARE...

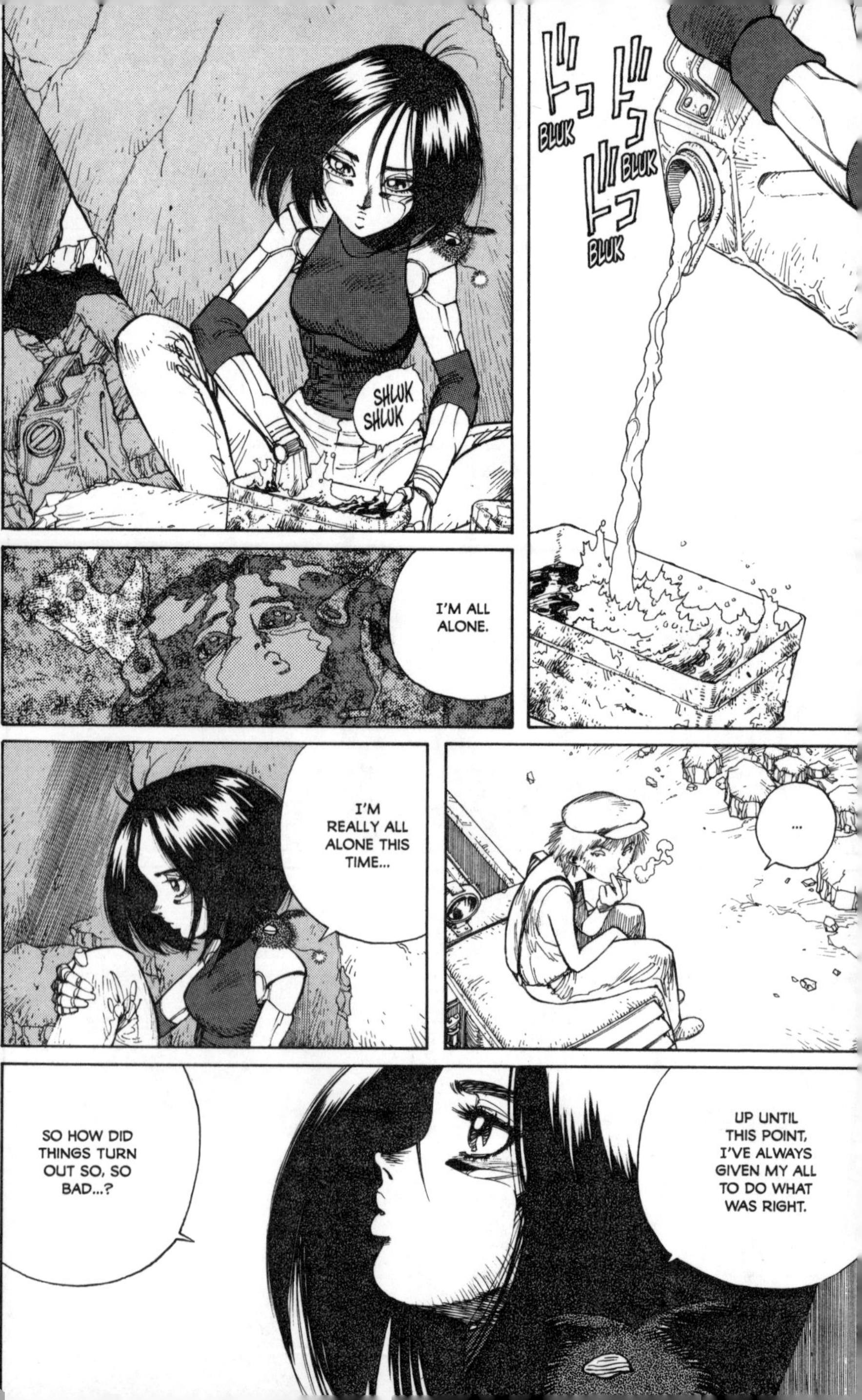
ドッ
BLUK
ドッ
BLUK
ドッ
BLUK
SHLUK SHLUK
I'M ALL ALONE.
...
I'M REALLY ALL ALONE THIS TIME...
UP UNTIL THIS POINT, I'VE ALWAYS GIVEN MY ALL TO DO WHAT WAS RIGHT.
SO HOW DID THINGS TURN OUT SO, SO BAD...?

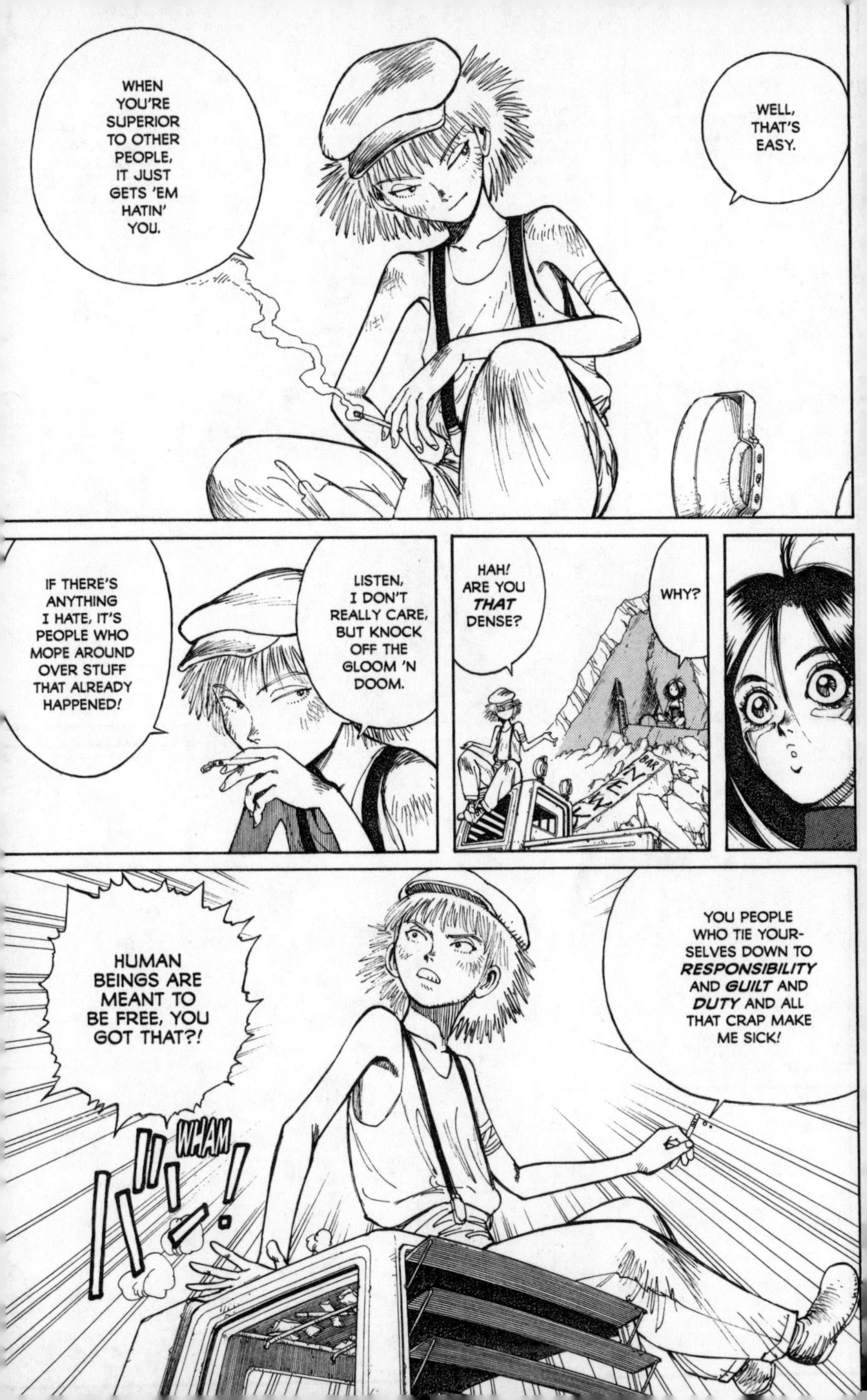
WELL, THAT'S EASY.
WHEN YOU'RE SUPERIOR TO OTHER PEOPLE, IT JUST GETS 'EM HATIN' YOU.
WHY?
HAH! ARE YOU *THAT* DENSE?
BAR
LISTEN, I DON'T REALLY CARE, BUT KNOCK OFF THE GLOOM 'N DOOM.
IF THERE'S ANYTHING I HATE, IT'S PEOPLE WHO MOPE AROUND OVER STUFF THAT ALREADY HAPPENED!
YOU PEOPLE WHO TIE YOURSELVES DOWN TO ***RESPONSIBILITY*** AND ***GUILT*** AND ***DUTY*** AND ALL THAT CRAP MAKE ME SICK!
HUMAN BEINGS ARE MEANT TO BE FREE, YOU GOT THAT?!
WHAM

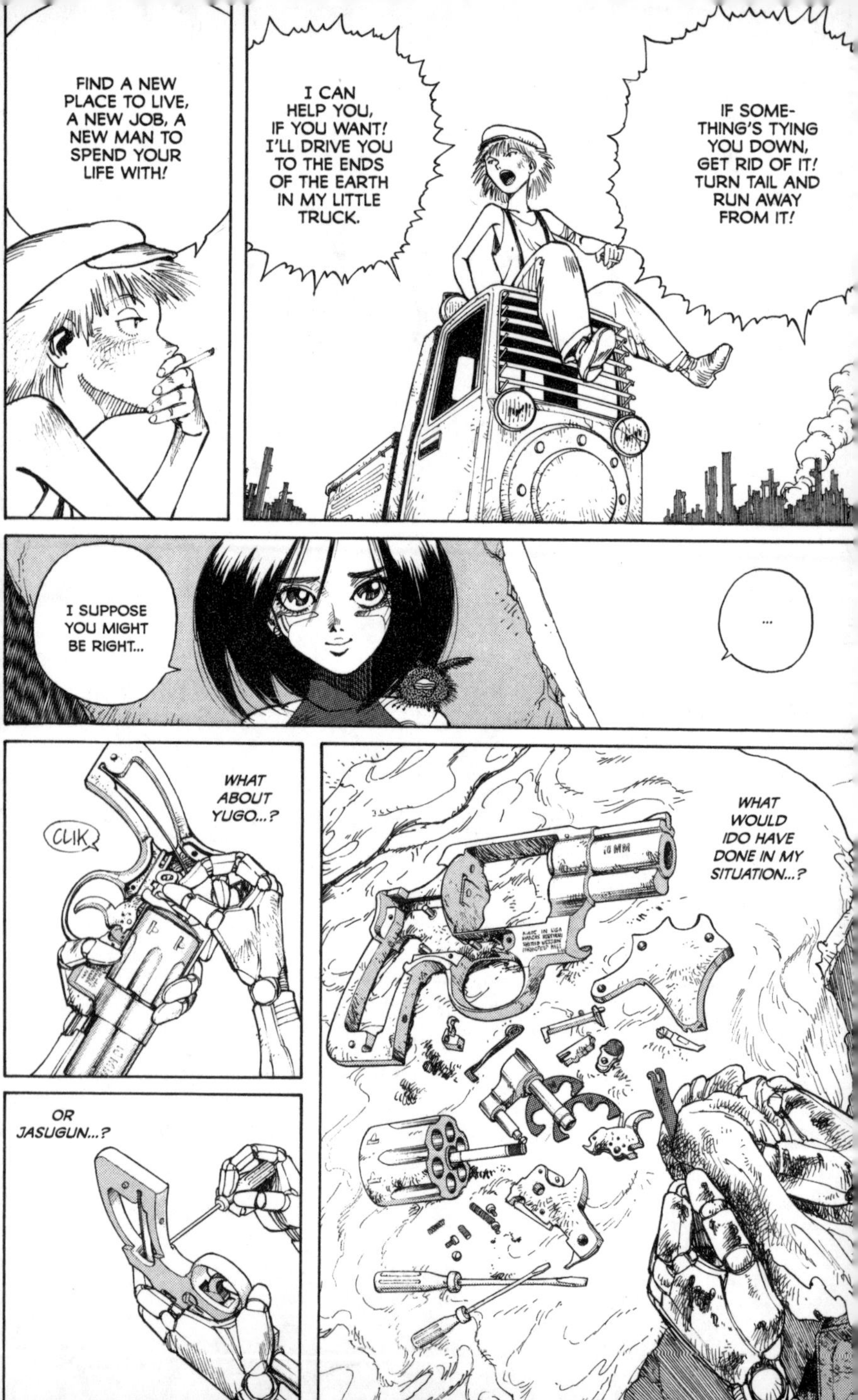
IF SOME-
THING'S TYING
YOU DOWN,
GET RID OF IT!
TURN TAIL AND
RUN AWAY
FROM IT!
I CAN
HELP YOU,
IF YOU WANT!
I'LL DRIVE YOU
TO THE ENDS
OF THE EARTH
IN MY LITTLE
TRUCK.
FIND A NEW
PLACE TO LIVE,
A NEW JOB, A
NEW MAN TO
SPEND YOUR
LIFE WITH!
...
I SUPPOSE
YOU MIGHT
BE RIGHT...
WHAT
WOULD
IDO HAVE
DONE IN MY
SITUATION...?
WHAT
ABOUT
YUGO...?
CLIK
OR
JASUGUN...?

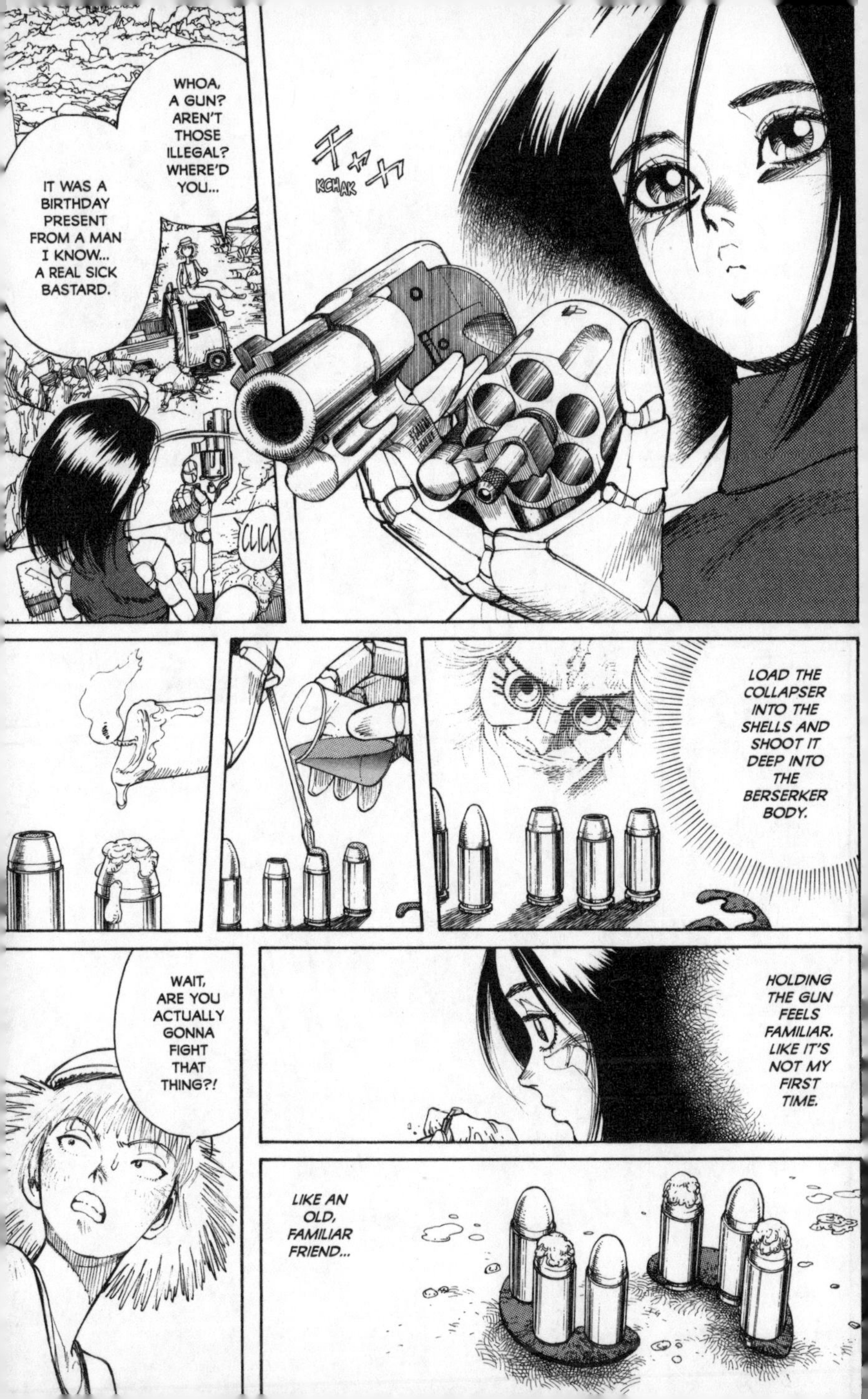

チャカ
KCHAK
WHOA, A GUN? AREN'T THOSE ILLEGAL? WHERE'D YOU...
IT WAS A BIRTHDAY PRESENT FROM A MAN I KNOW... A REAL SICK BASTARD.
CLICK
LOAD THE COLLAPSER INTO THE SHELLS AND SHOOT IT DEEP INTO THE BERSERKER BODY.
HOLDING THE GUN FEELS FAMILIAR. LIKE IT'S NOT MY FIRST TIME.
LIKE AN OLD, FAMILIAR FRIEND...
WAIT, ARE YOU ACTUALLY GONNA FIGHT THAT THING?!

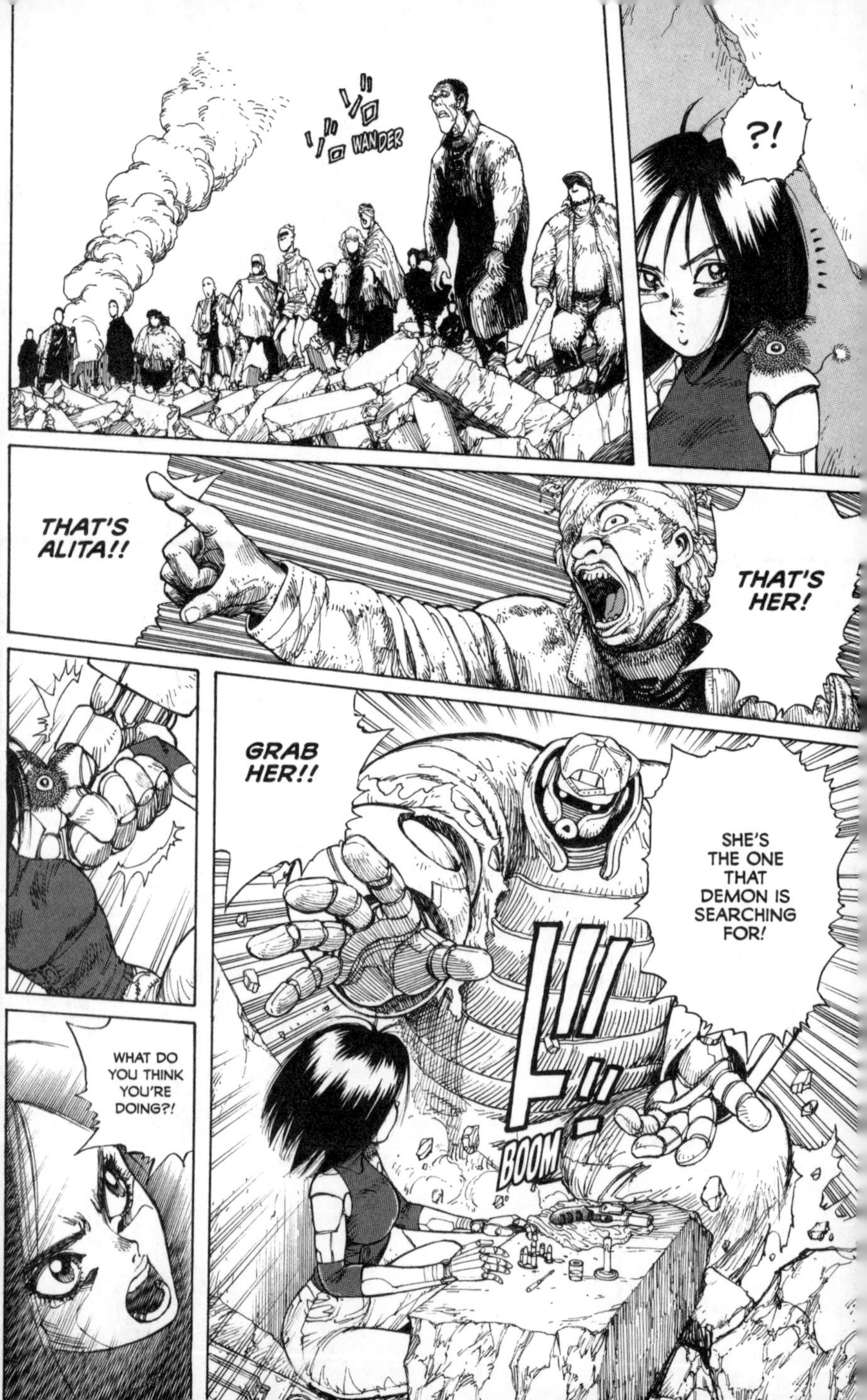
?!
WANDER
THAT'S HER!
THAT'S ALITA!!
SHE'S THE ONE THAT DEMON IS SEARCHING FOR!
GRAB HER!!
BOOM
WHAT DO YOU THINK YOU'RE DOING?!

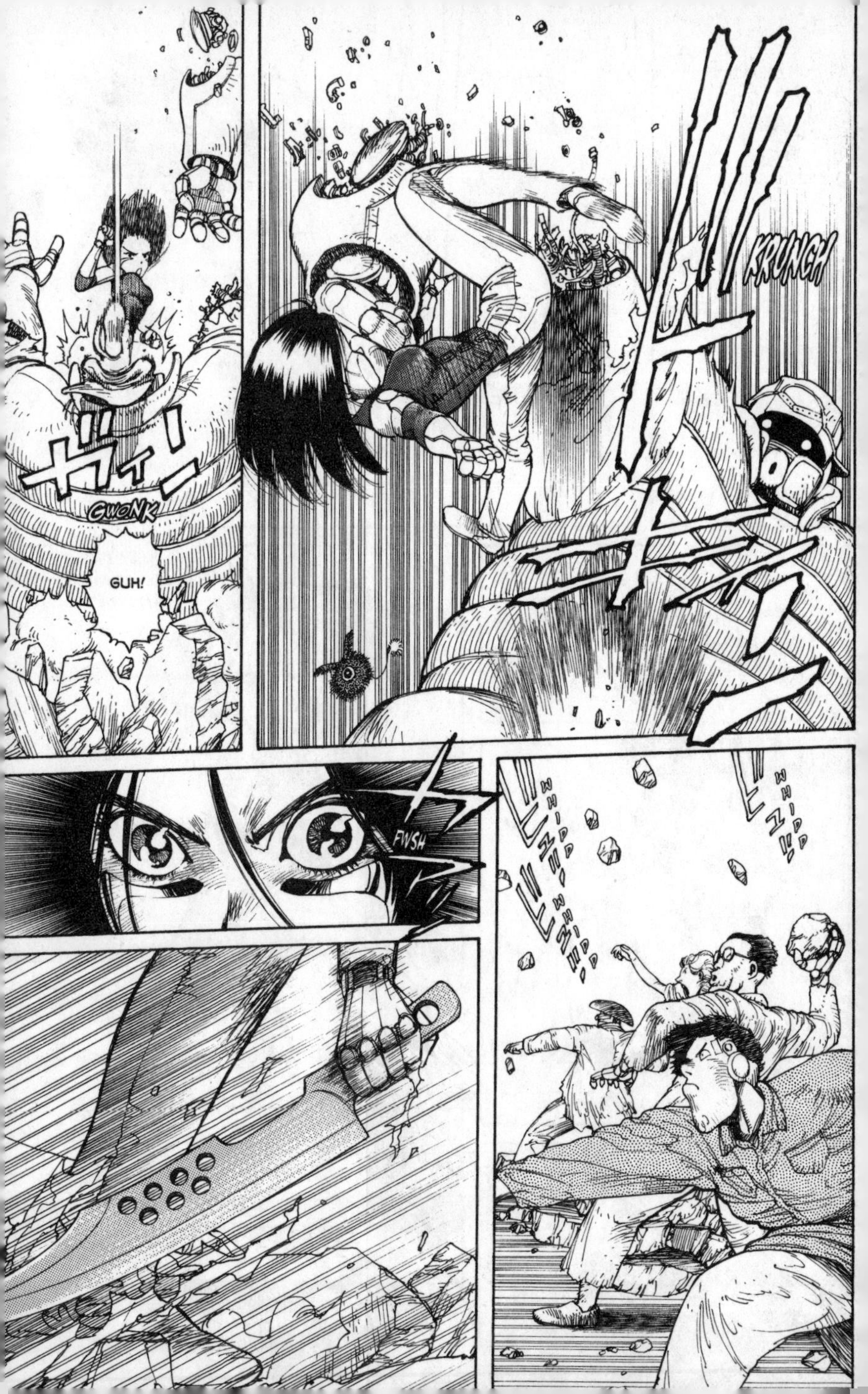
KRUNCH
ヴィー
GWONK
GUH!
WHIDD
WHIDD
WHIDD
FWSH

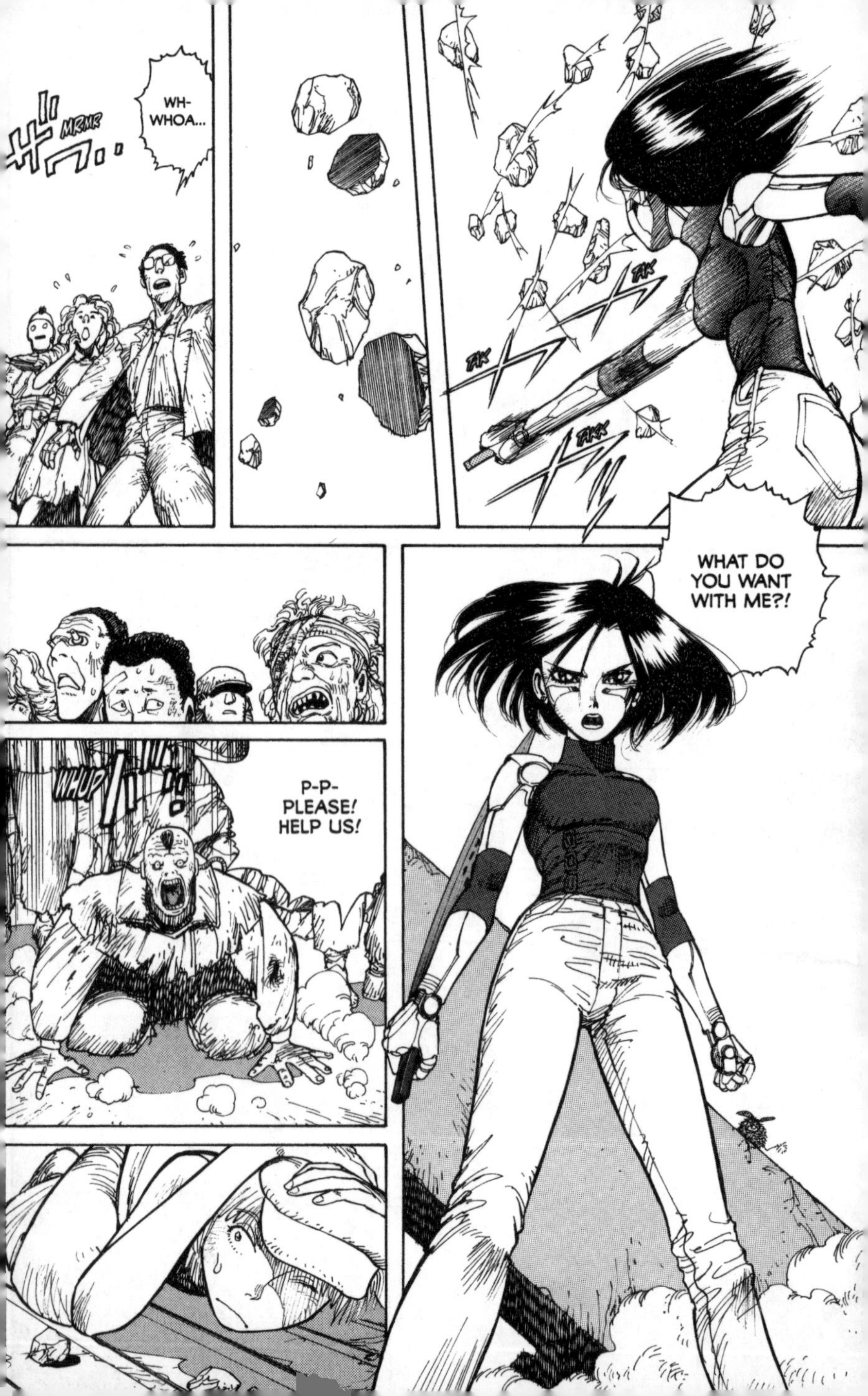

TAK
TAK
TAKK
WH- WHOA...
MRMR
WHAT DO YOU WANT WITH ME?!
WHUP
P-P- PLEASE! HELP US!

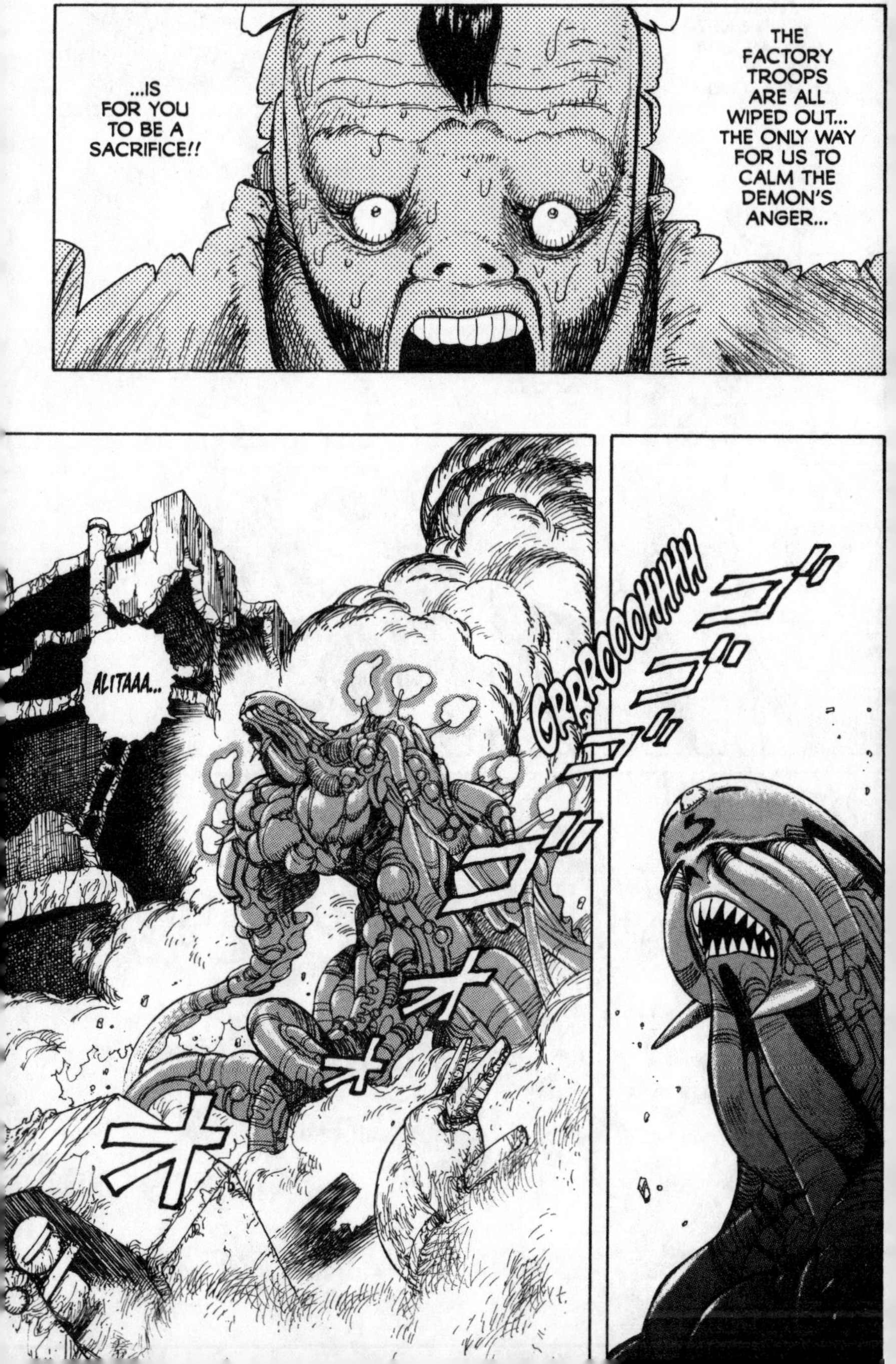

THE FACTORY TROOPS ARE ALL WIPED OUT... THE ONLY WAY FOR US TO CALM THE DEMON'S ANGER...
...IS FOR YOU TO BE A SACRIFICE!!
ゴゴ
GRRROOOHHHH
ゴゴゴ
ALITAAA...
オオオ

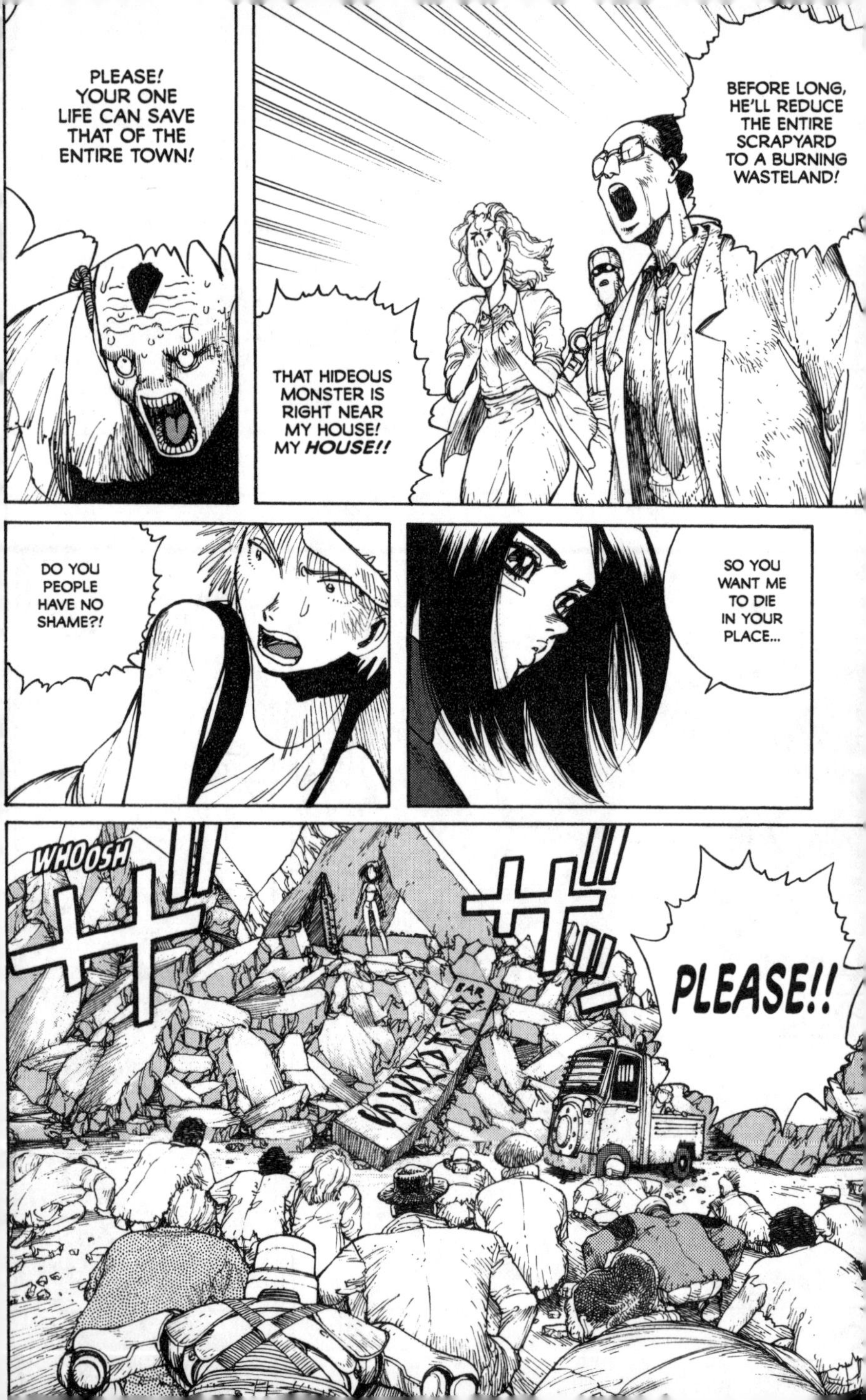
BEFORE LONG, HE'LL REDUCE THE ENTIRE SCRAPYARD TO A BURNING WASTELAND!
THAT HIDEOUS MONSTER IS RIGHT NEAR MY HOUSE! MY *HOUSE!!*
PLEASE! YOUR ONE LIFE CAN SAVE THAT OF THE ENTIRE TOWN!
SO YOU WANT ME TO DIE IN YOUR PLACE...
DO YOU PEOPLE HAVE NO SHAME?!
PLEASE!!
WHOOSH

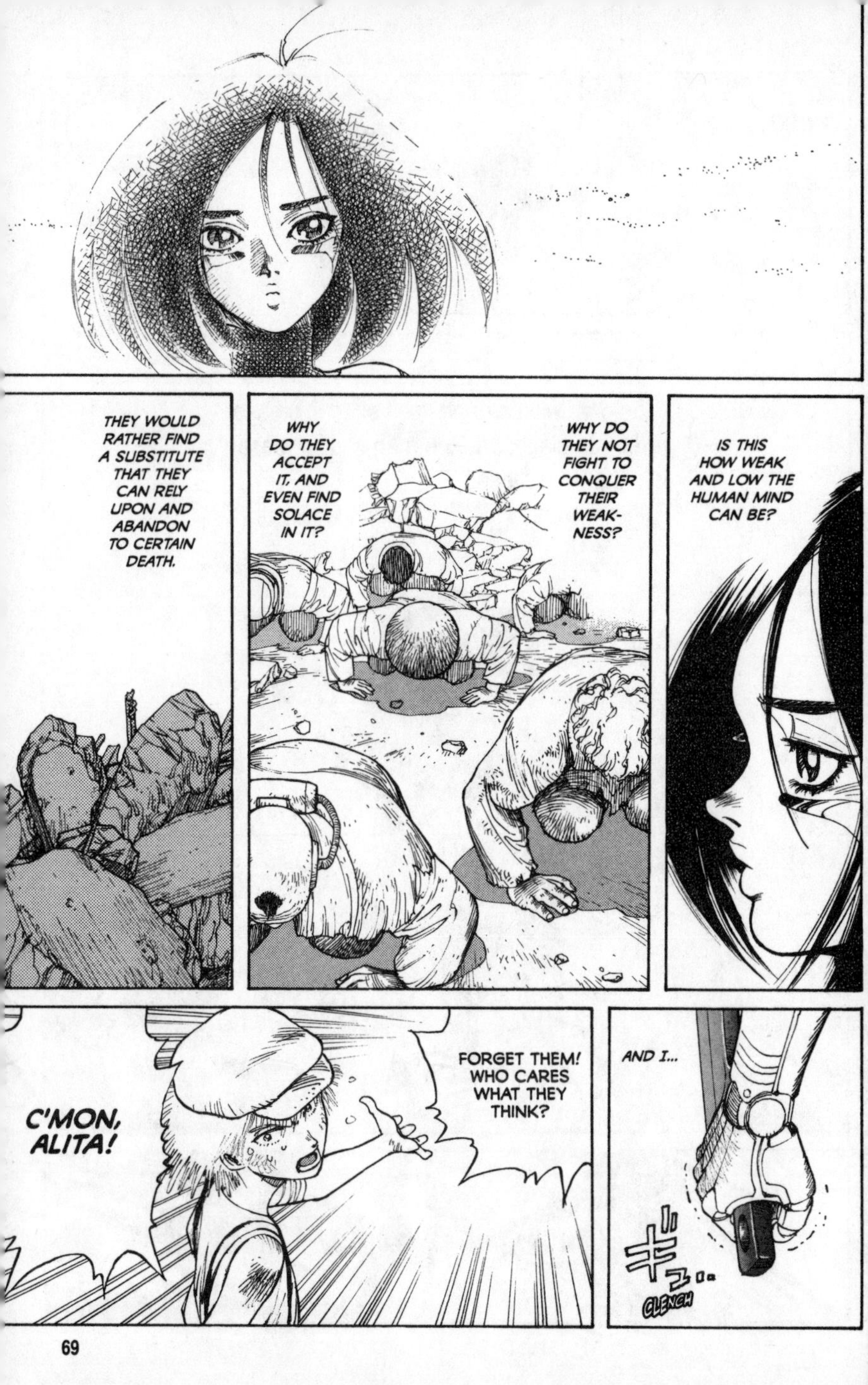
IS THIS HOW WEAK AND LOW THE HUMAN MIND CAN BE?
WHY DO THEY NOT FIGHT TO CONQUER THEIR WEAKNESS?
WHY DO THEY ACCEPT IT, AND EVEN FIND SOLACE IN IT?
THEY WOULD RATHER FIND A SUBSTITUTE THAT THEY CAN RELY UPON AND ABANDON TO CERTAIN DEATH.
AND I...
CLENCH
FORGET THEM! WHO CARES WHAT THEY THINK?
C'MON, ALITA!

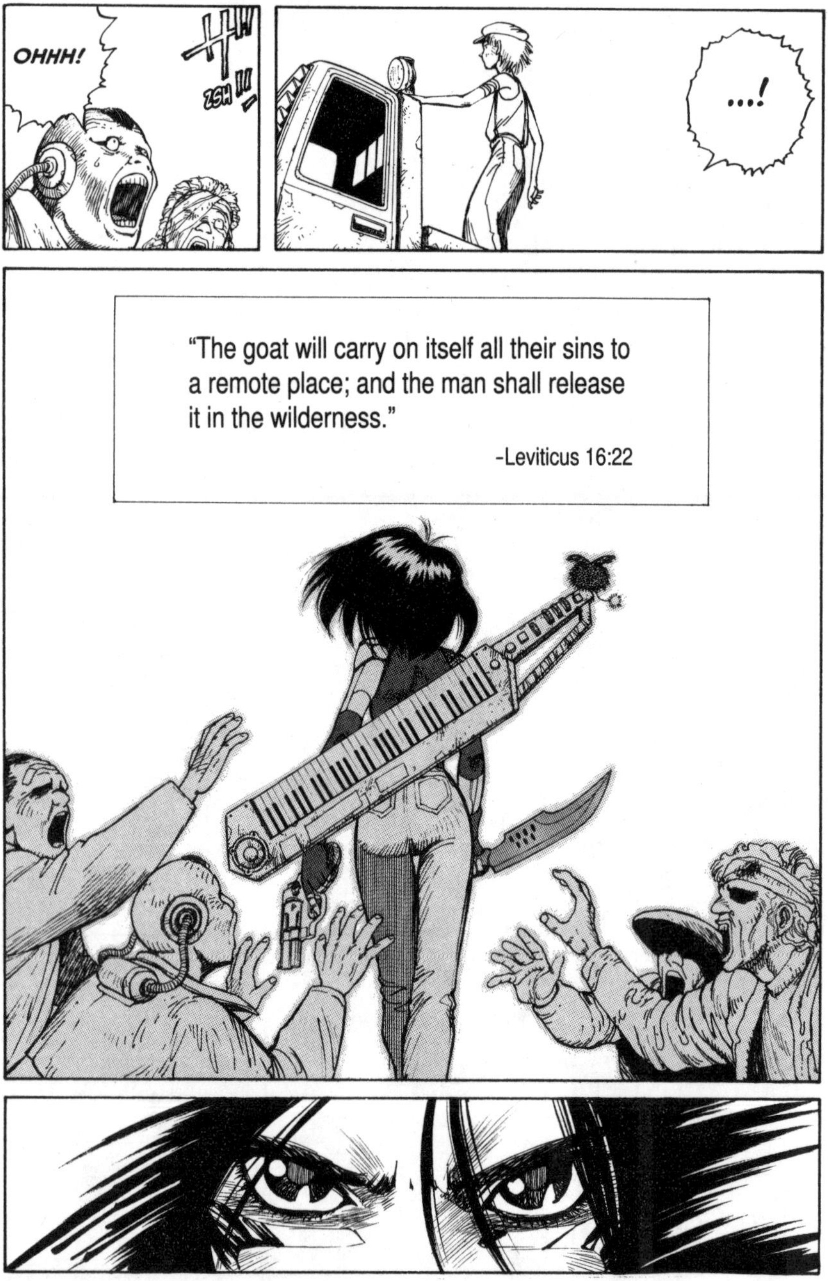
...!
OHHH!
ZSH!!!
"The goat will carry on itself all their sins to a remote place; and the man shall release it in the wilderness."
-Leviticus 16:22

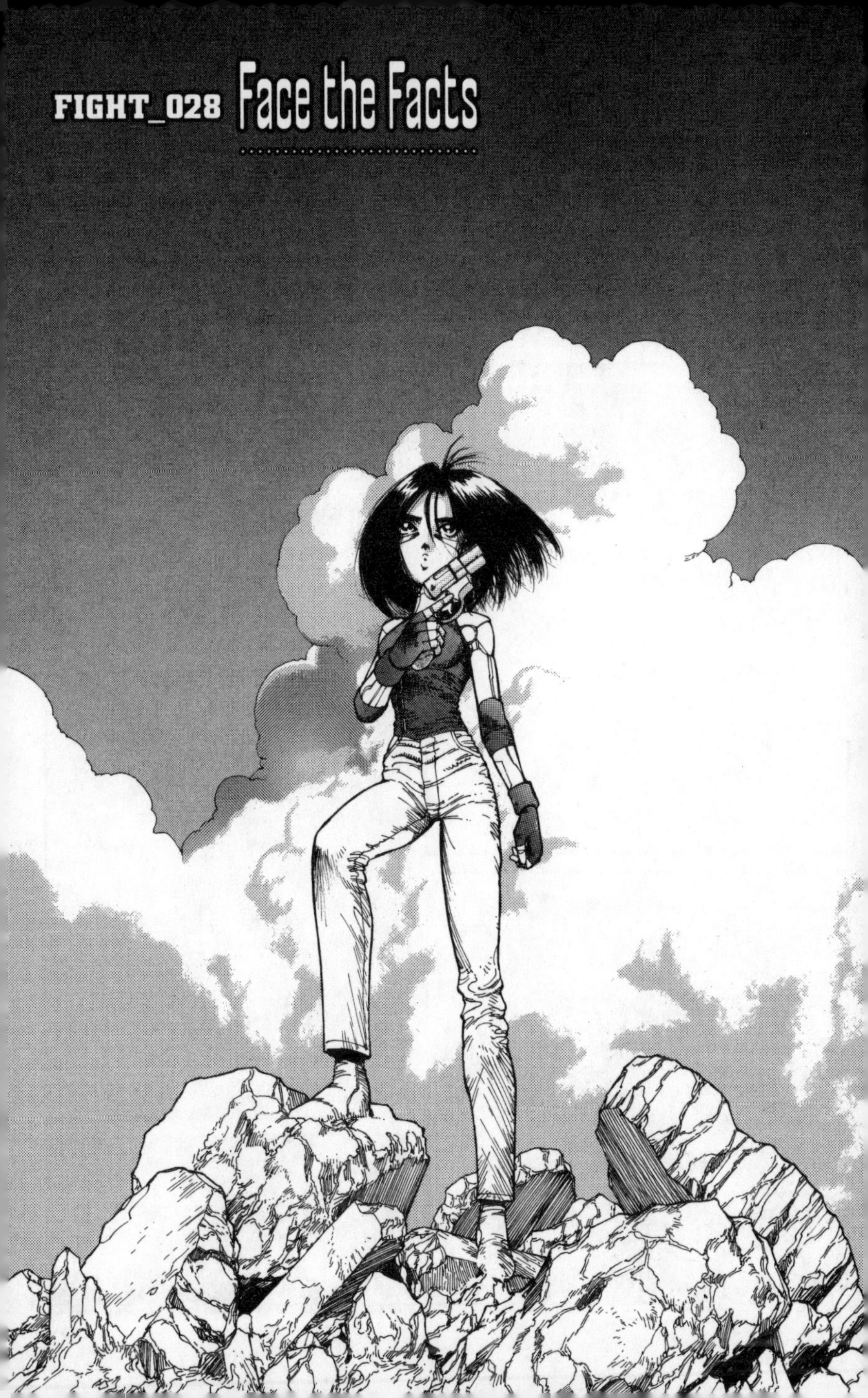
FIGHT_028 Face the Facts

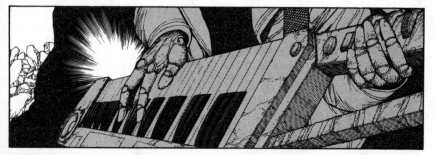

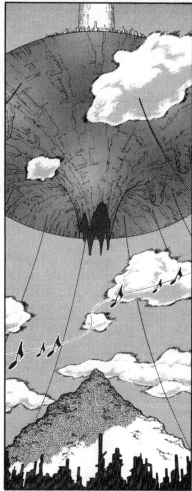

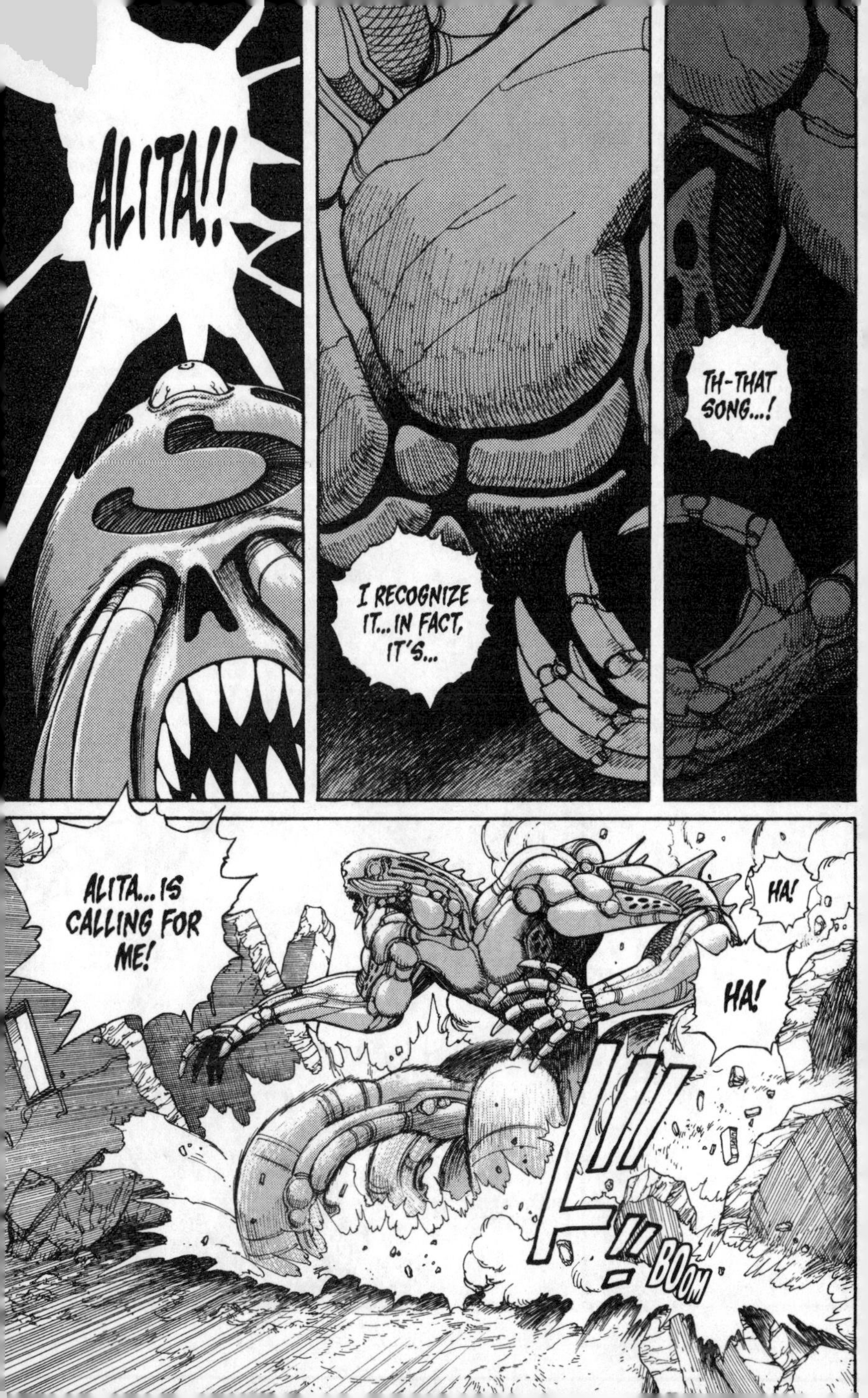
TH-THAT SONG...!
I RECOGNIZE IT...IN FACT, IT'S...
ALITA!!
ALITA...IS CALLING FOR ME!
HA!
HA!
BOOM

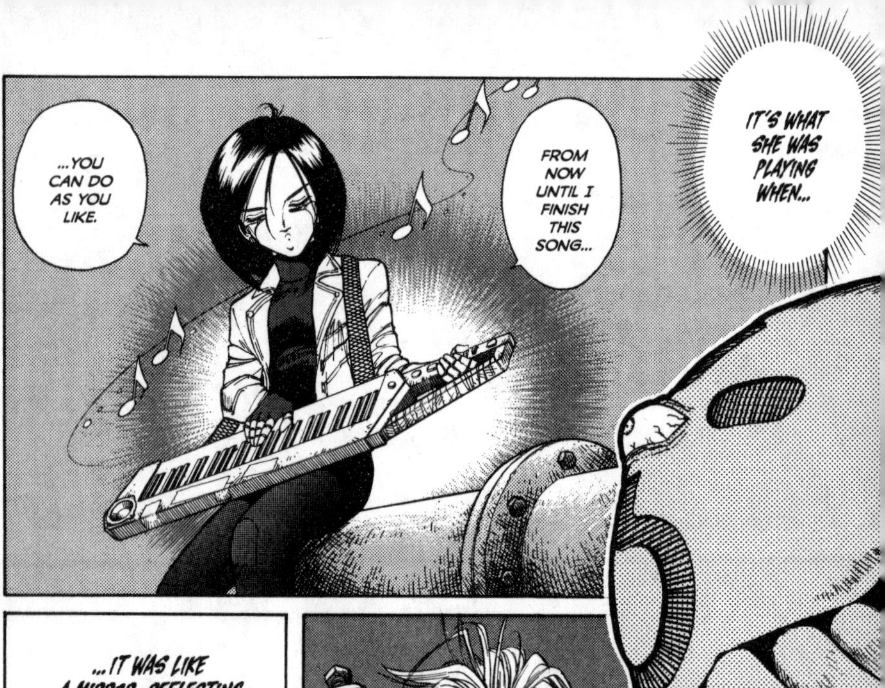
FROM NOW UNTIL I FINISH THIS SONG...
...YOU CAN DO AS YOU LIKE.
IT'S WHAT SHE WAS PLAYING WHEN...
WHEN I DESCENDED UPON HER DEFENSELESS BACK...
...IT WAS LIKE A MIRROR, REFLECTING THAT HIDEOUS VISAGE OF MINE BACK AT ME- THE VERY LAST THING I WANTED TO FACE!

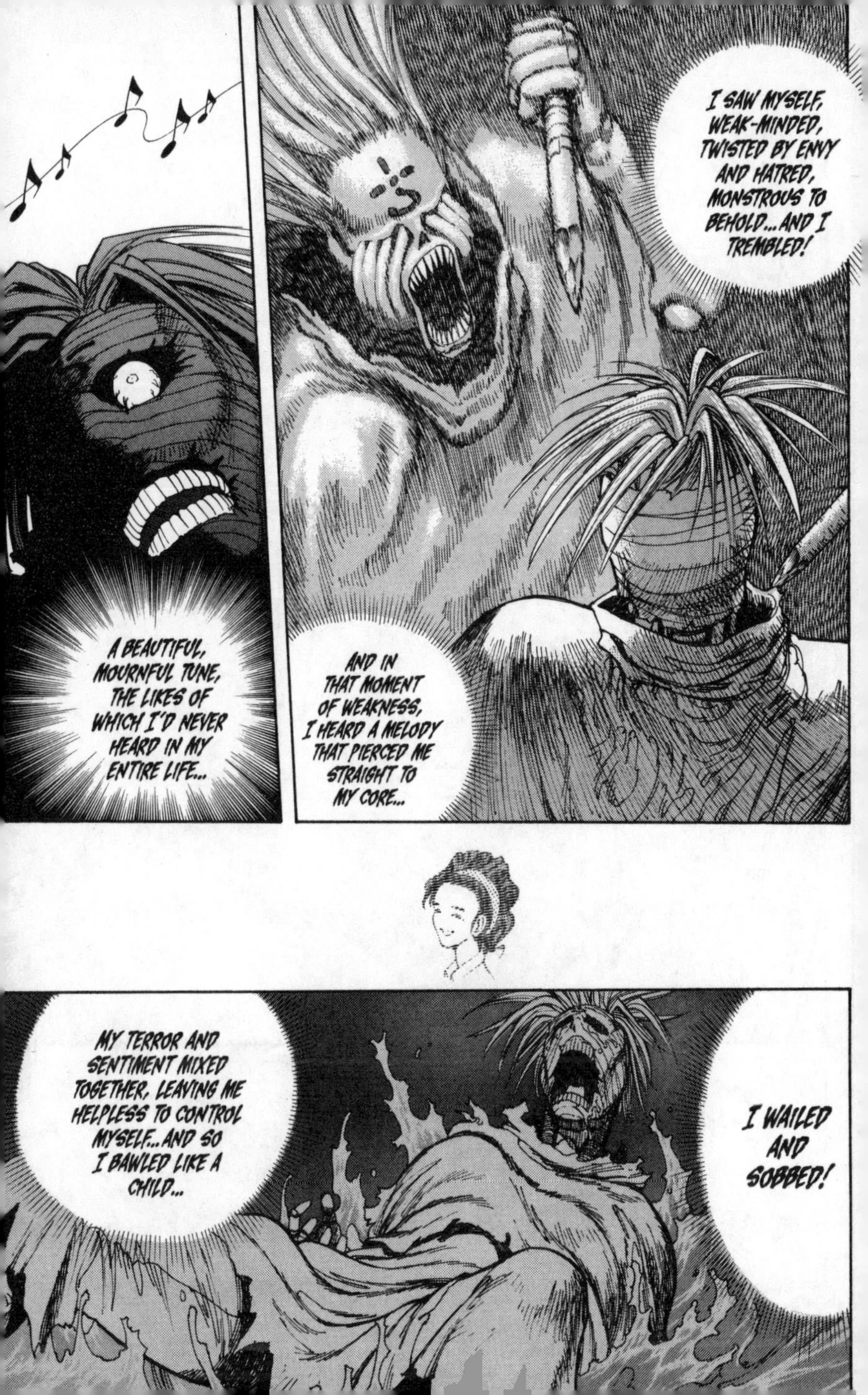
I SAW MYSELF, WEAK-MINDED, TWISTED BY ENVY AND HATRED, MONSTROUS TO BEHOLD... AND I TREMBLED!
AND IN THAT MOMENT OF WEAKNESS, I HEARD A MELODY THAT PIERCED ME STRAIGHT TO MY CORE...
A BEAUTIFUL, MOURNFUL TUNE, THE LIKES OF WHICH I'D NEVER HEARD IN MY ENTIRE LIFE...
I WAILED AND SOBBED!
MY TERROR AND SENTIMENT MIXED TOGETHER, LEAVING ME HELPLESS TO CONTROL MYSELF... AND SO I BAWLED LIKE A CHILD...

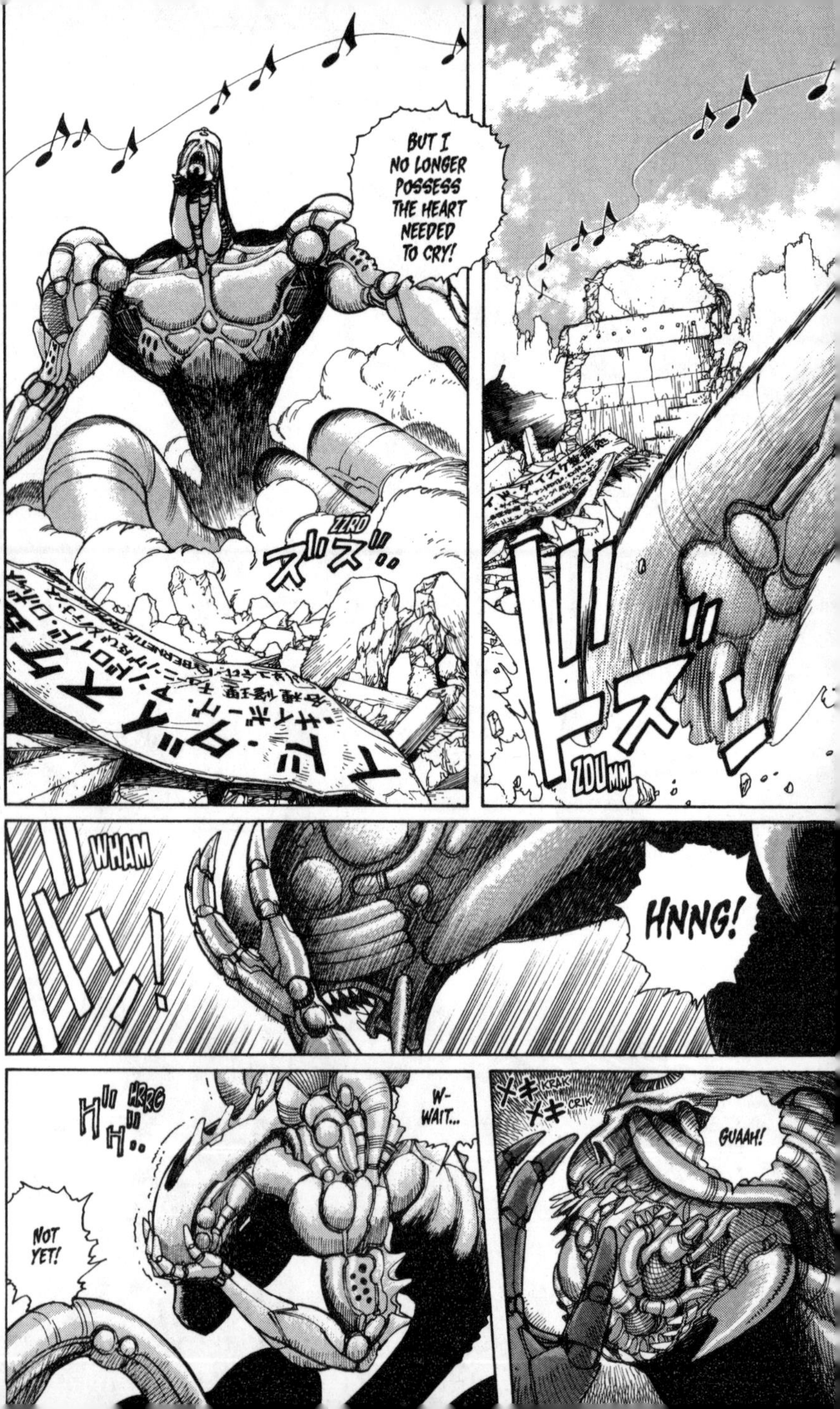

ZDUMM
BUT I NO LONGER POSSESS THE HEART NEEDED TO CRY!
ZZRO
HNNG!
WHAM
KRAK
CRIK
GUAAH!
W-WAIT...
HRRG
NOT YET!

Sign: Daisuke Ido Repairs • Cyborgs, Androids, Robots; Repairs, Tuning & Maintenance for all models!

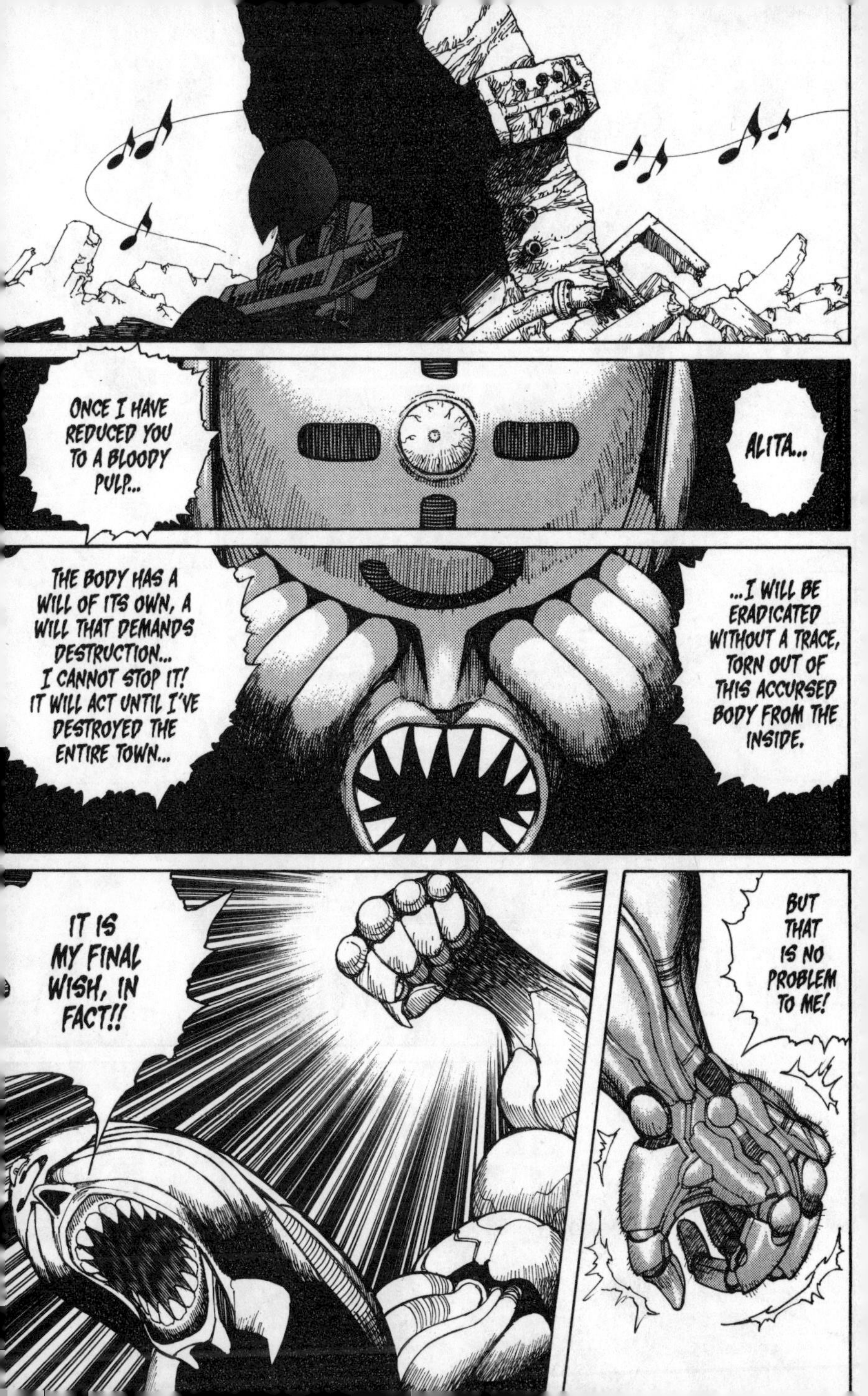
ALITA...
ONCE I HAVE REDUCED YOU TO A BLOODY PULP...
...I WILL BE ERADICATED WITHOUT A TRACE, TORN OUT OF THIS ACCURSED BODY FROM THE INSIDE.
THE BODY HAS A WILL OF ITS OWN, A WILL THAT DEMANDS DESTRUCTION... I CANNOT STOP IT! IT WILL ACT UNTIL I'VE DESTROYED THE ENTIRE TOWN...
BUT THAT IS NO PROBLEM TO ME!
IT IS MY FINAL WISH, IN FACT!!

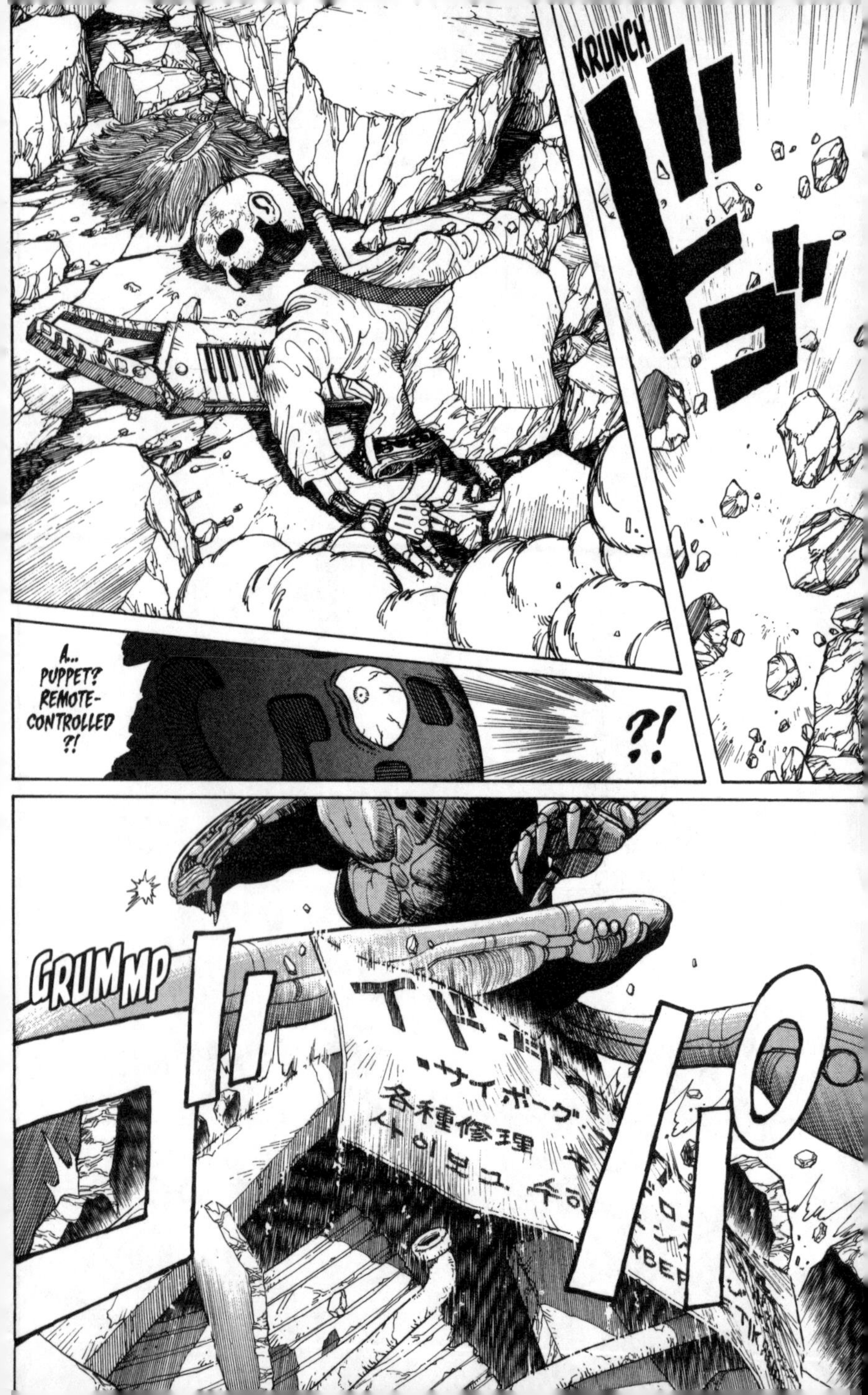
KRUNCH
?!
A... PUPPET? REMOTE-CONTROLLED ?!
GRUMMP
サイボーグ
各種修理

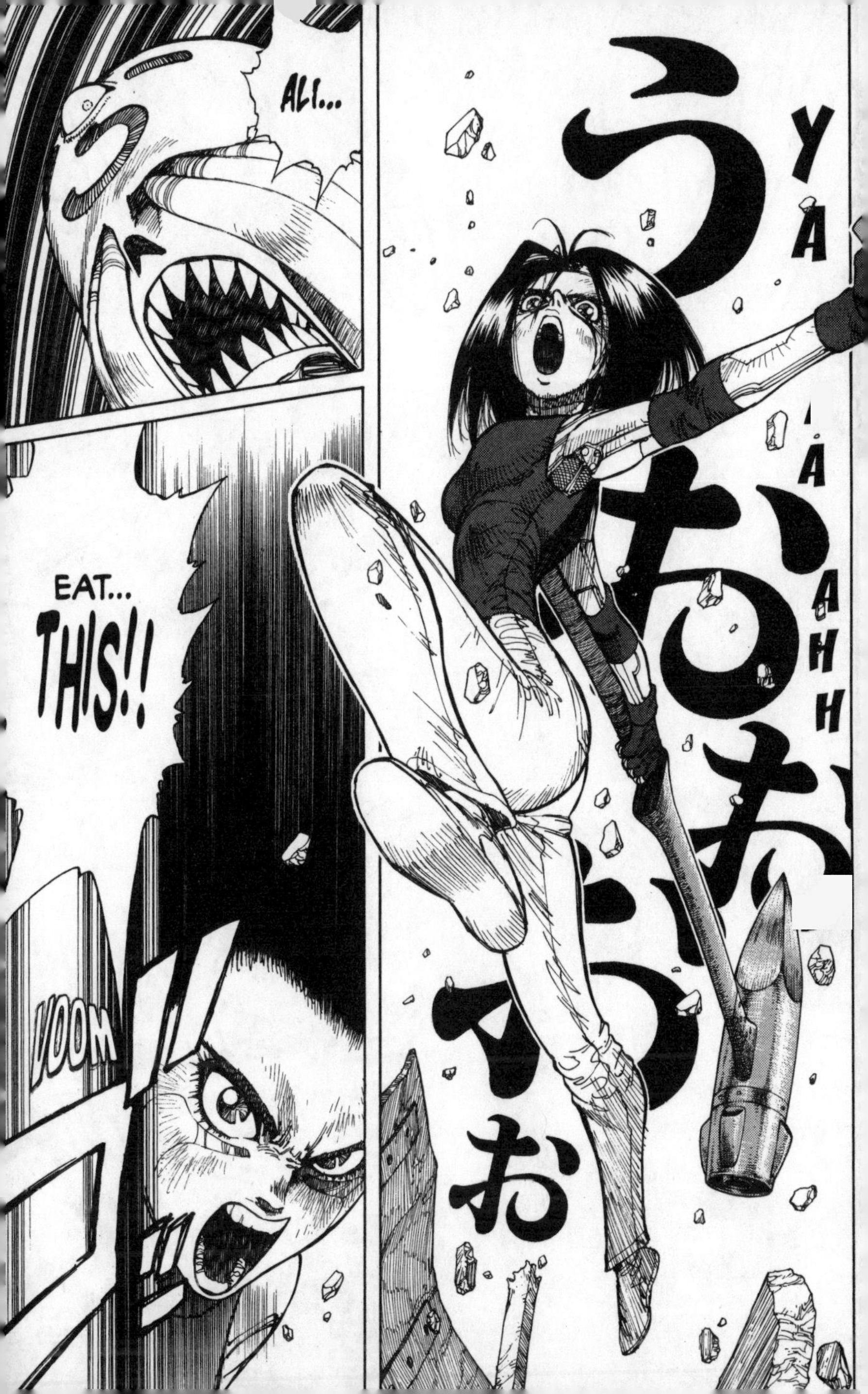
YAAAAHHH
ALI...
EAT...
THIS!!
VOOM

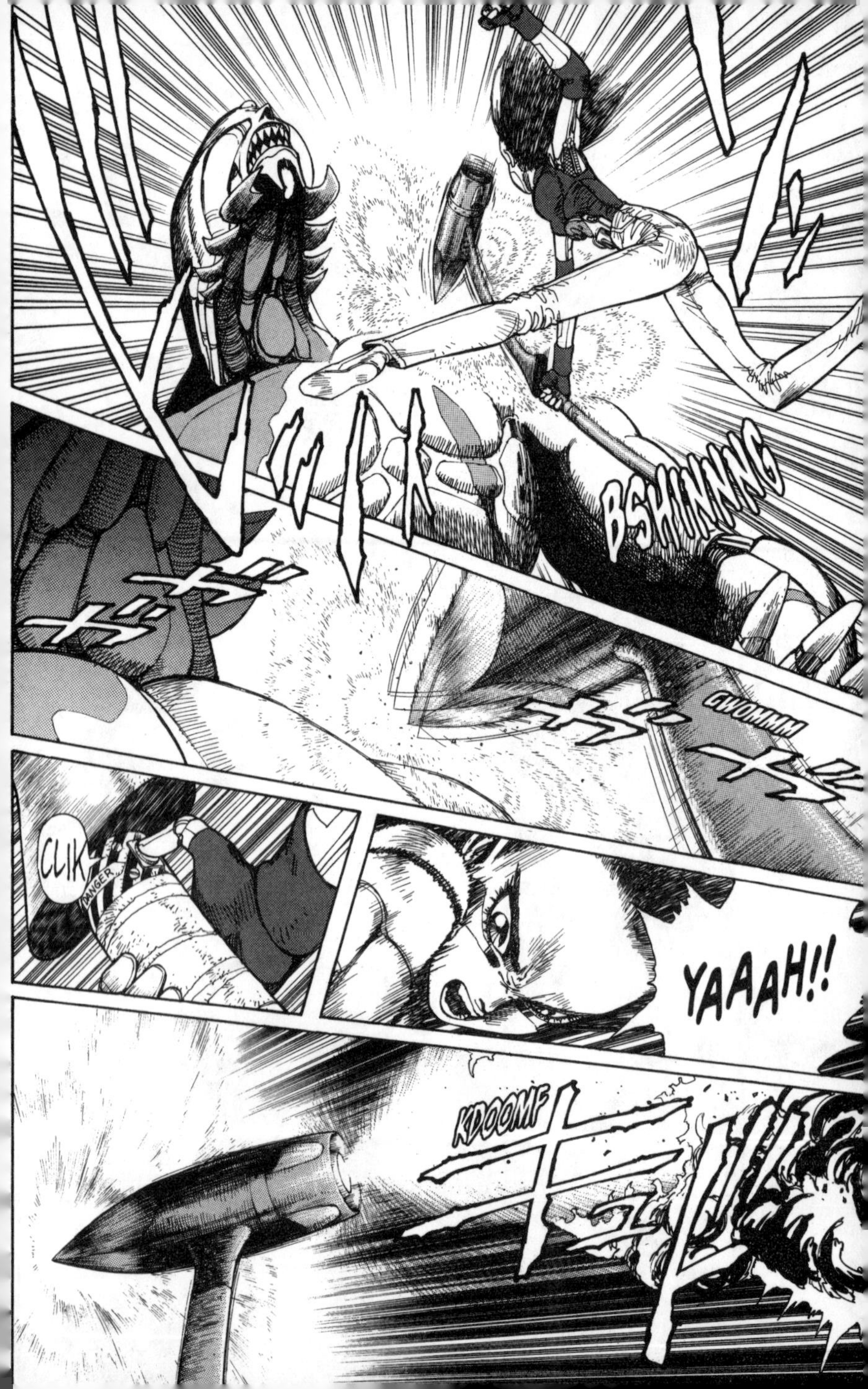
BSHINNNG
GWOMMM
YAAAH!!
CLIK
DANGER
KDOOMF

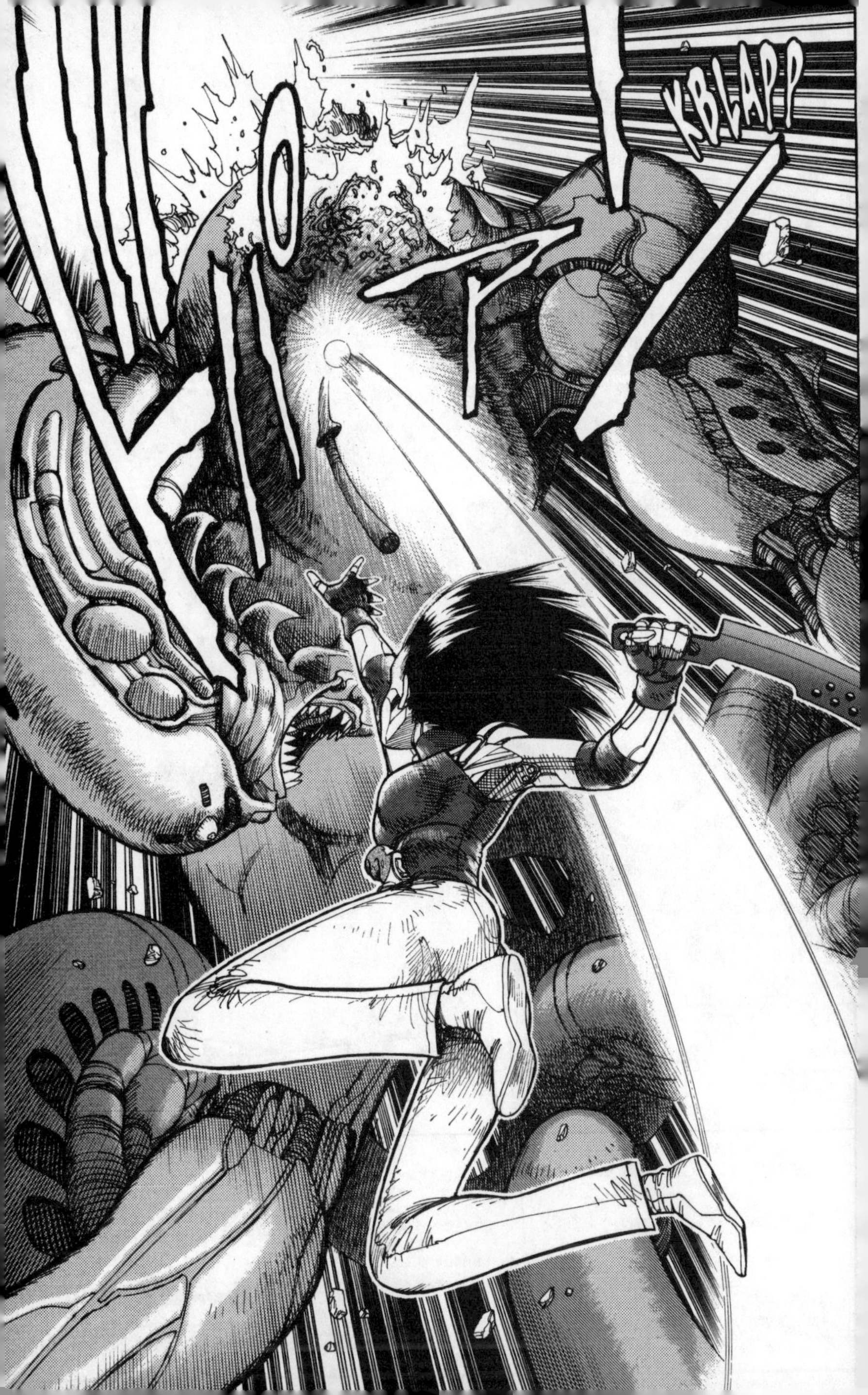
KBLAPP

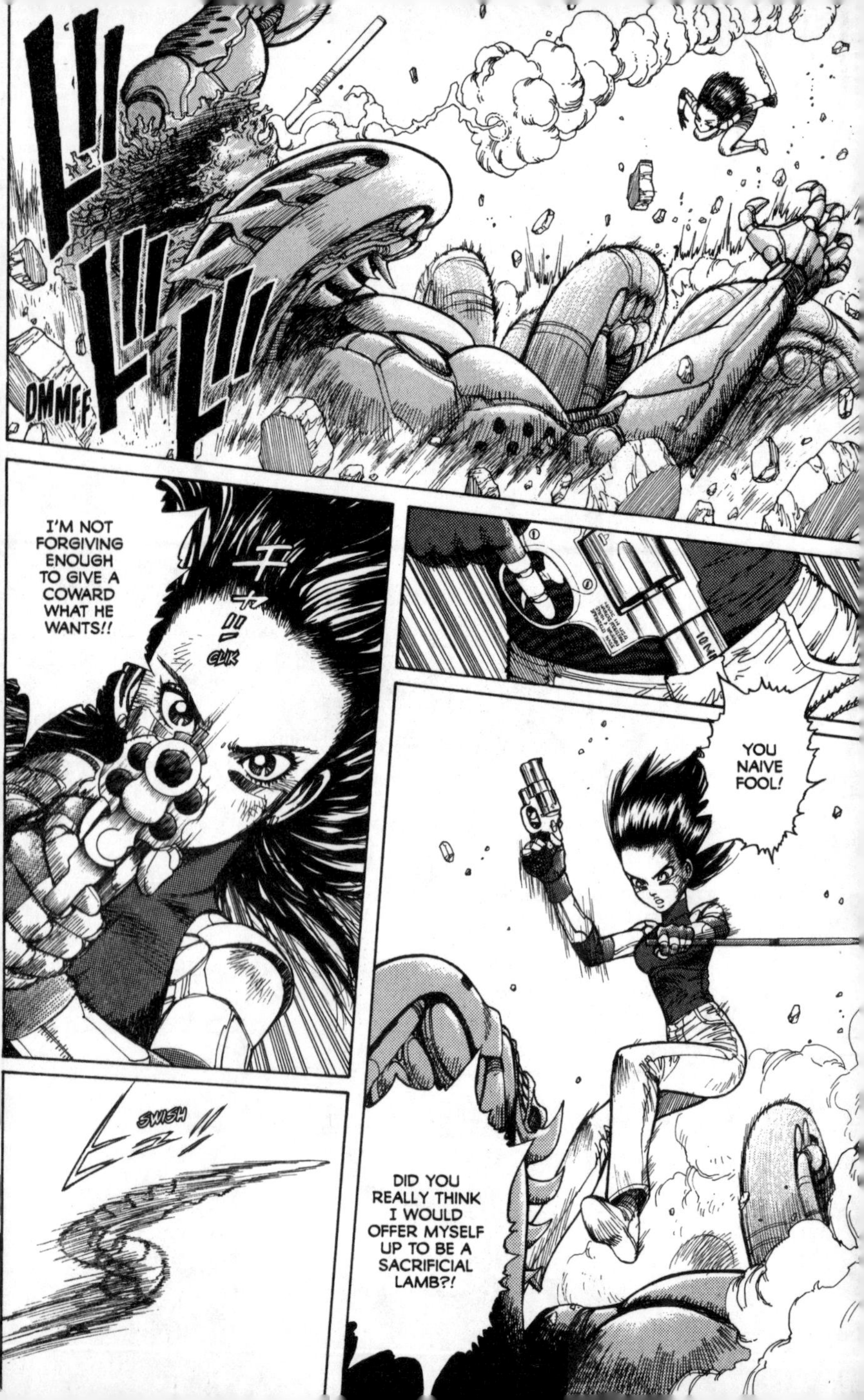
DMMFF
CLIK
I'M NOT FORGIVING ENOUGH TO GIVE A COWARD WHAT HE WANTS!!
YOU NAIVE FOOL!
DID YOU REALLY THINK I WOULD OFFER MYSELF UP TO BE A SACRIFICIAL LAMB?!
SWISH

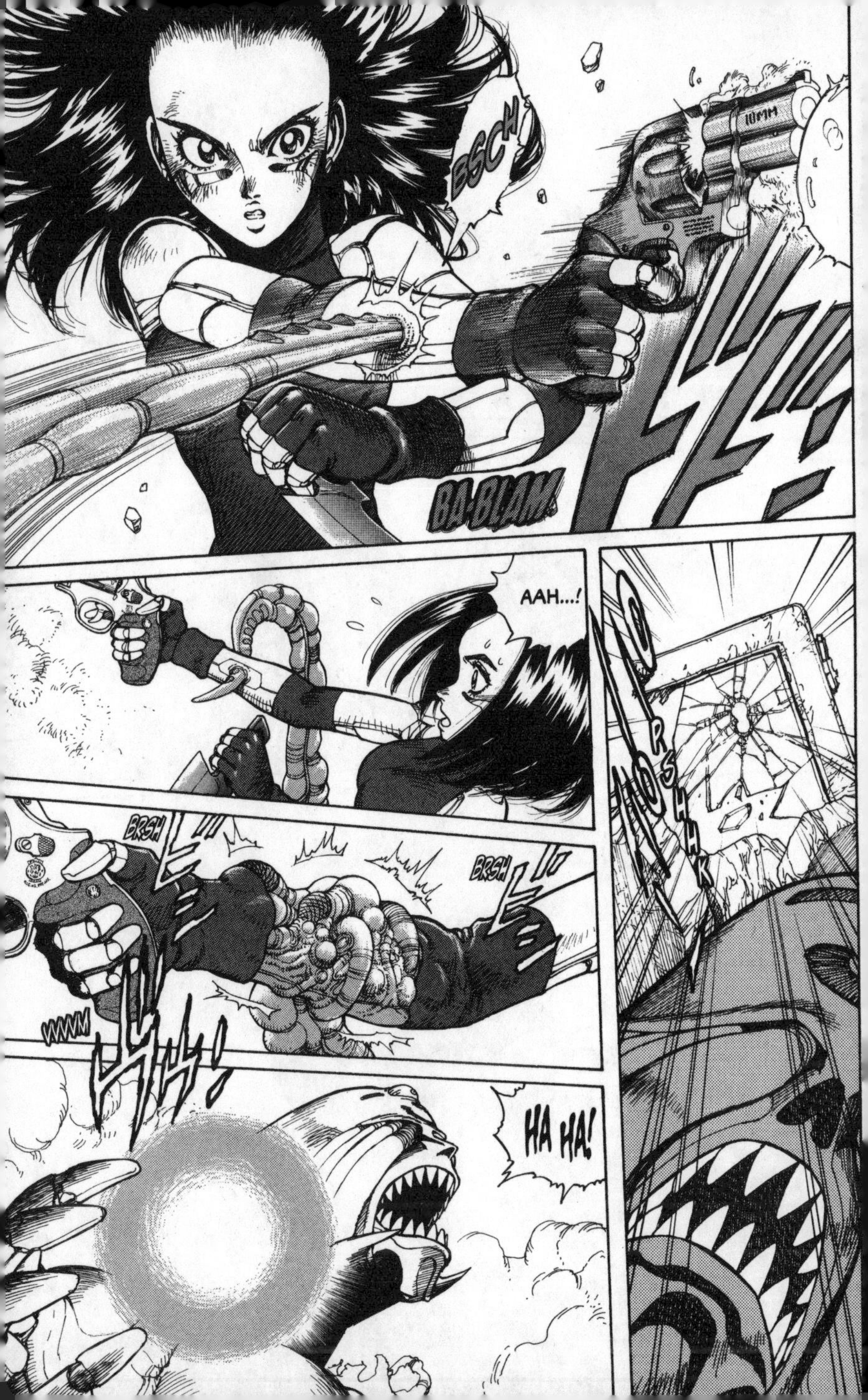
BSCH
10MM
BA-BLAM
PRSHHK
AAH...!
BRSH
BRSH
HA HA!

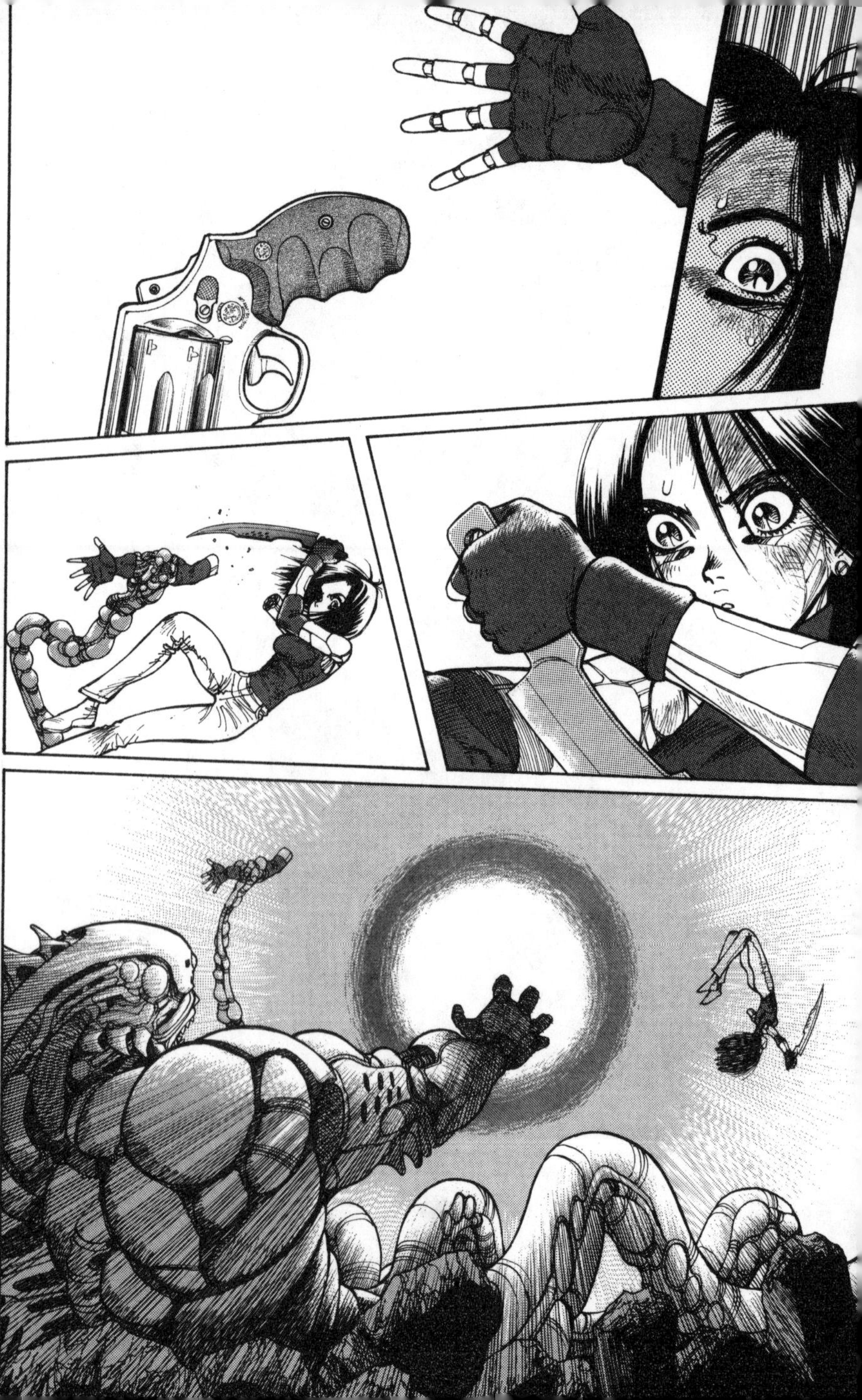

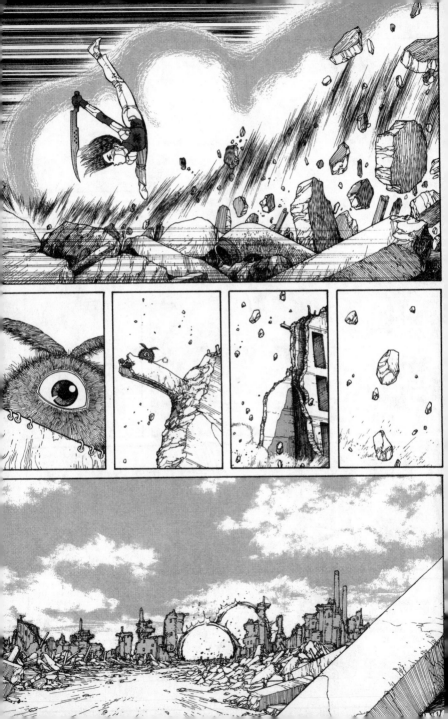

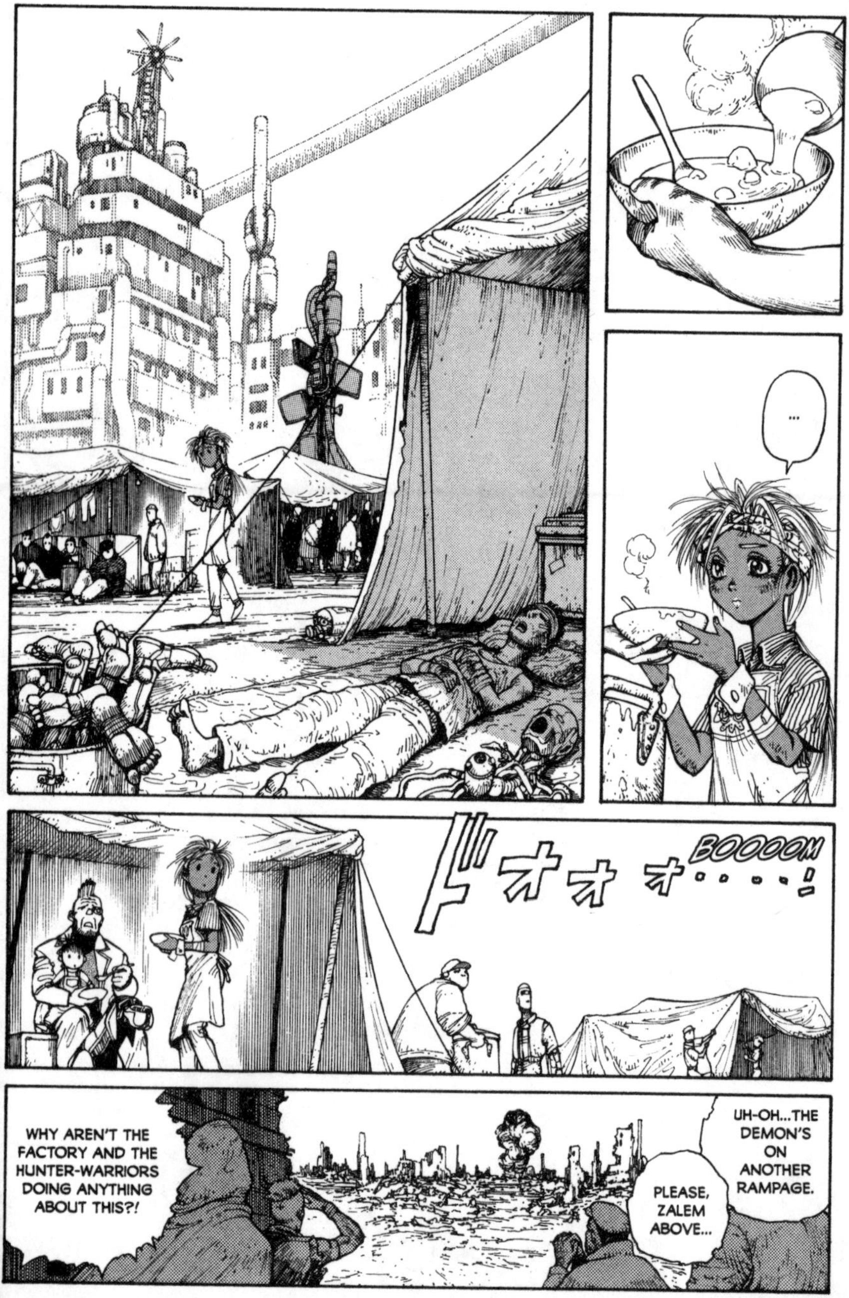
...
ドオオオ......!
BOOOOM
UH-OH...THE DEMON'S ON ANOTHER RAMPAGE.
PLEASE, ZALEM ABOVE...
WHY AREN'T THE FACTORY AND THE HUNTER-WARRIORS DOING ANYTHING ABOUT THIS?!

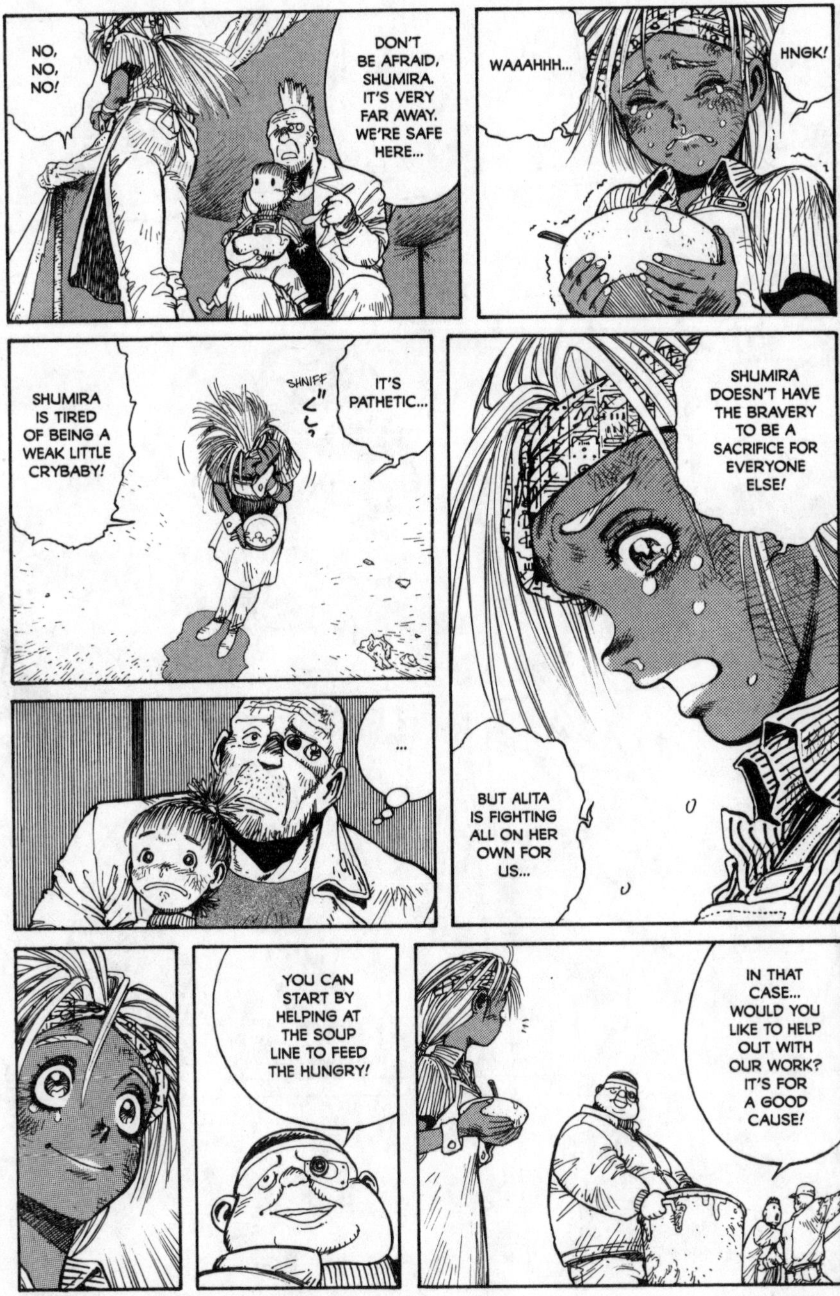
HNGK!
WAAAHHH...
DON'T BE AFRAID, SHUMIRA. IT'S VERY FAR AWAY. WE'RE SAFE HERE...
NO, NO, NO!
SHUMIRA DOESN'T HAVE THE BRAVERY TO BE A SACRIFICE FOR EVERYONE ELSE!
BUT ALITA IS FIGHTING ALL ON HER OWN FOR US...
IT'S PATHETIC...
SHNIFF
SHUMIRA IS TIRED OF BEING A WEAK LITTLE CRYBABY!
...
IN THAT CASE... WOULD YOU LIKE TO HELP OUT WITH OUR WORK? IT'S FOR A GOOD CAUSE!
YOU CAN START BY HELPING AT THE SOUP LINE TO FEED THE HUNGRY!

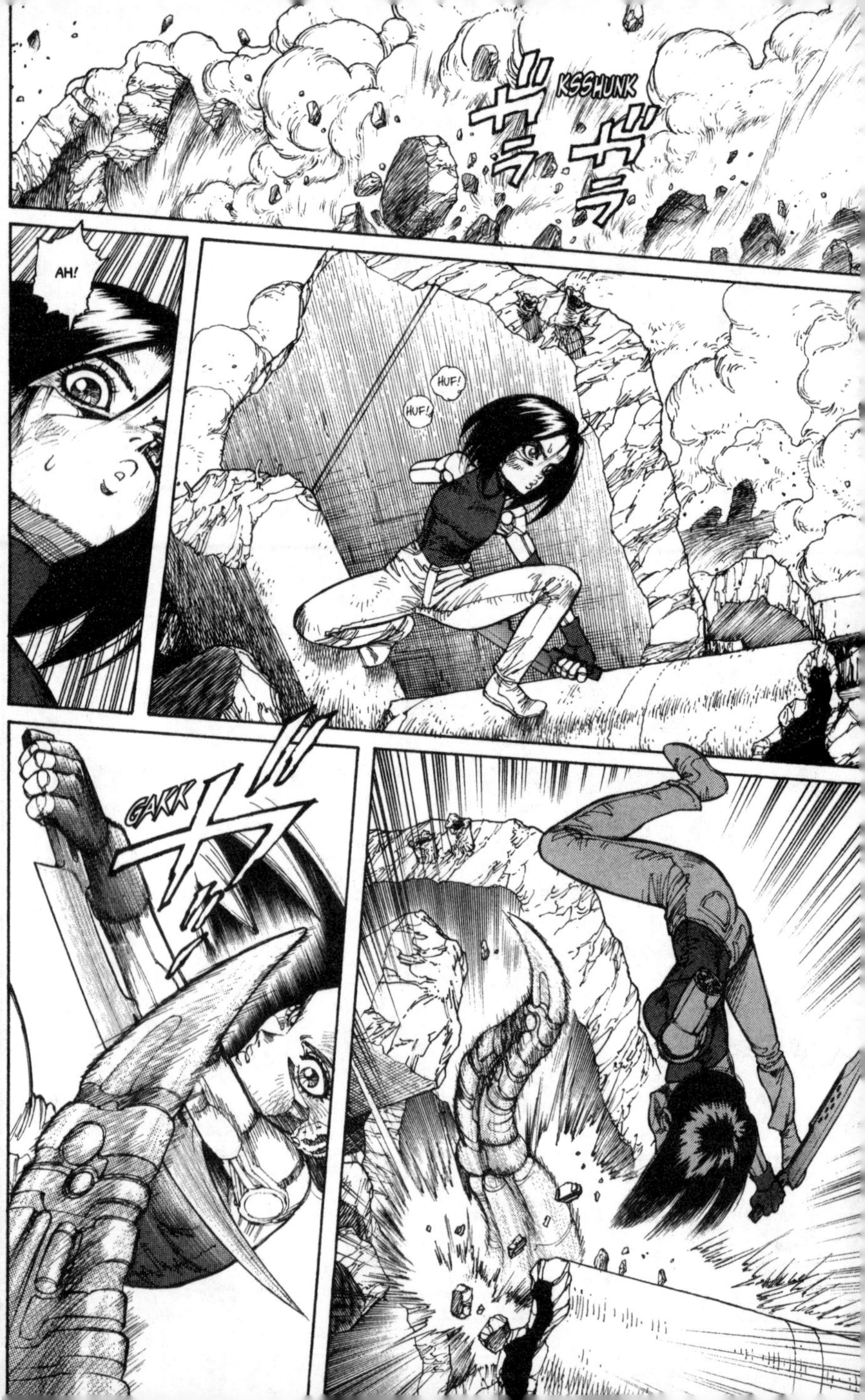
KSSHUNK
ガラガラ
HUF!
HUF!
AH!
GARK

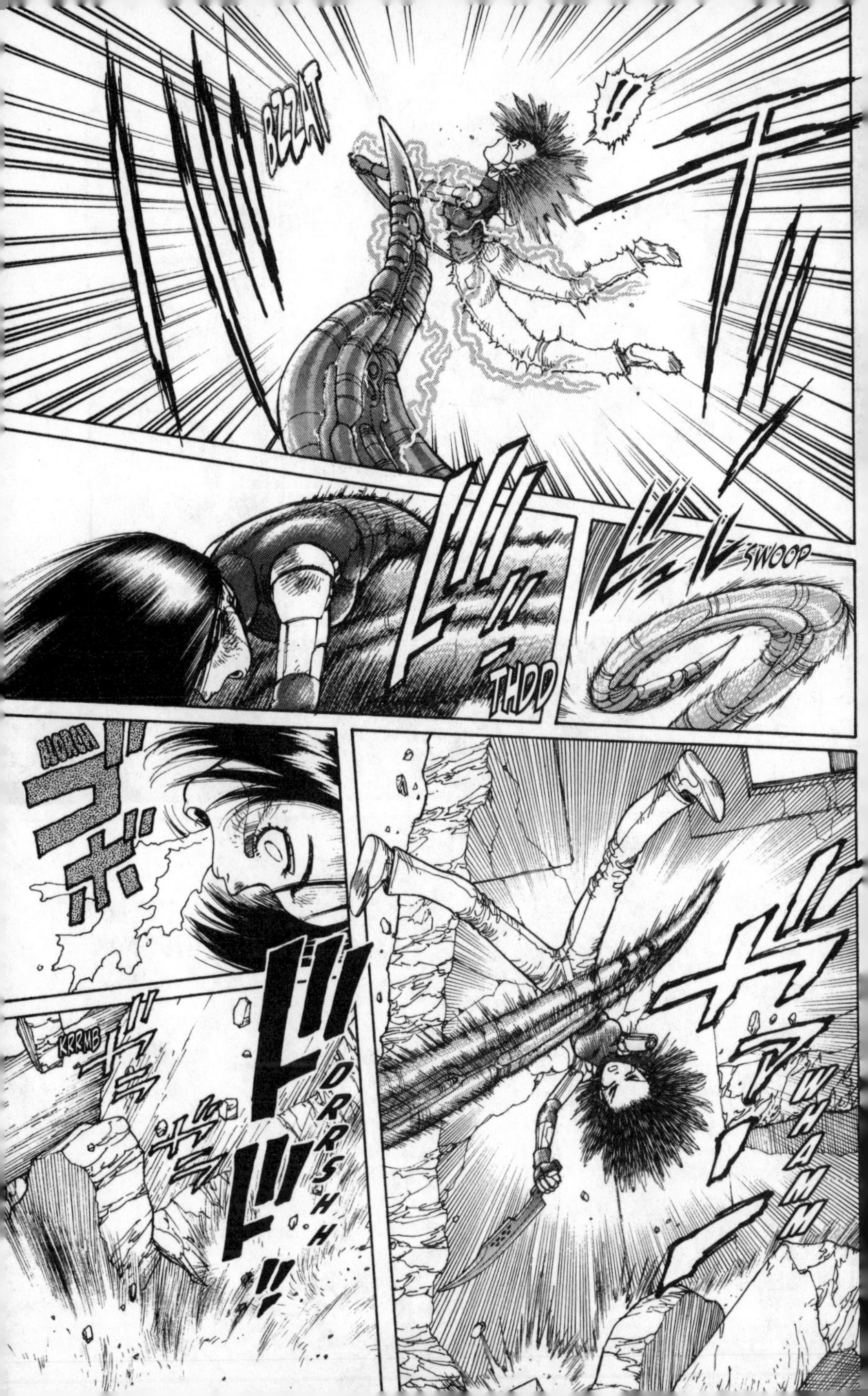

!!
BZZAT
SWOOP
THDD
WHAMMM
KRRMB
DRRSHHH!!

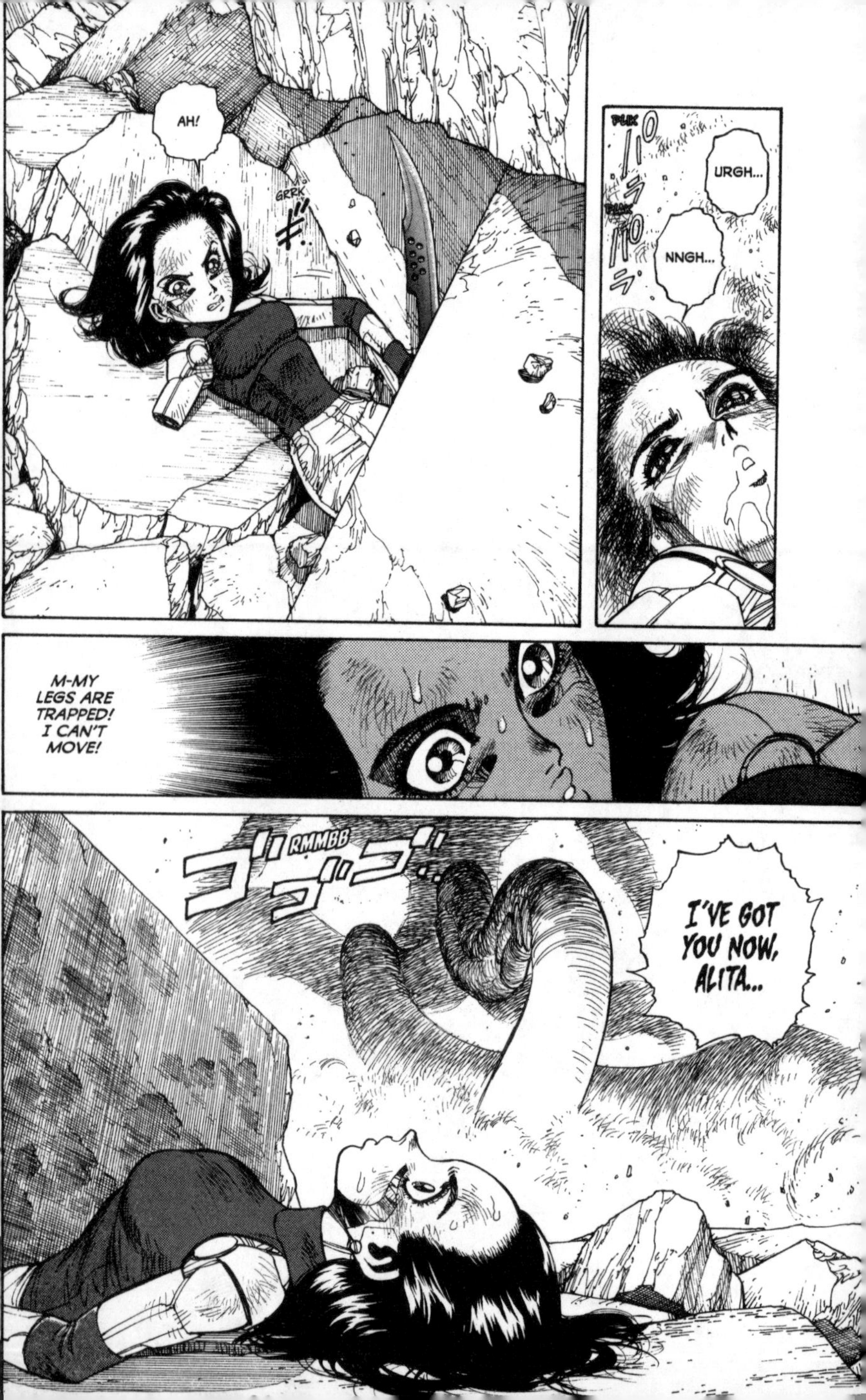
PUK
URGH...
PUK
NNGH...
AH!
GRRK
M-MY LEGS ARE TRAPPED! I CAN'T MOVE!
RMMBB
I'VE GOT YOU NOW, ALITA...

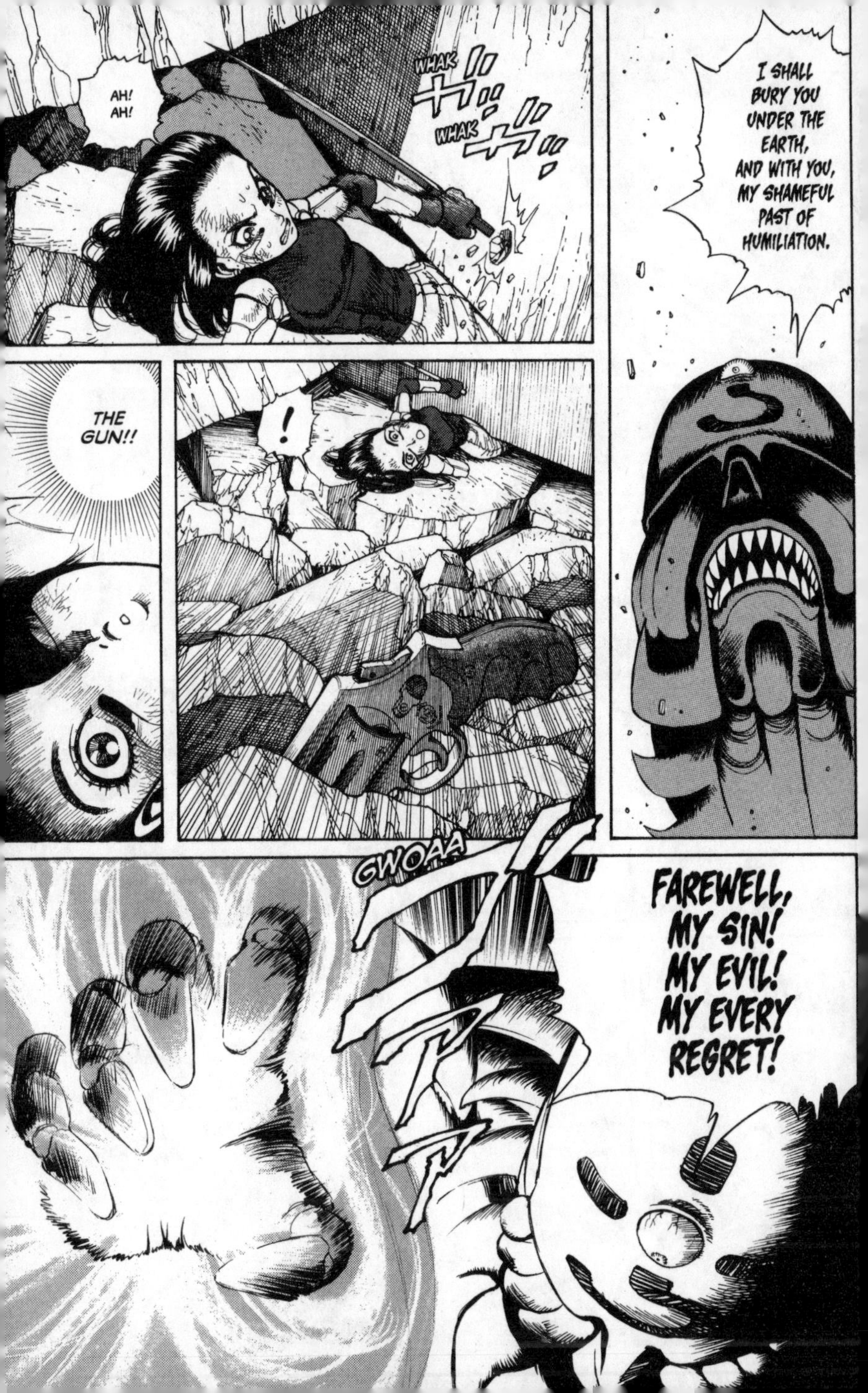
I SHALL BURY YOU UNDER THE EARTH, AND WITH YOU, MY SHAMEFUL PAST OF HUMILIATION.
WHAK
WHAK
AH! AH!
!
THE GUN!!
GWOAA
FAREWELL, MY SIN! MY EVIL! MY EVERY REGRET!

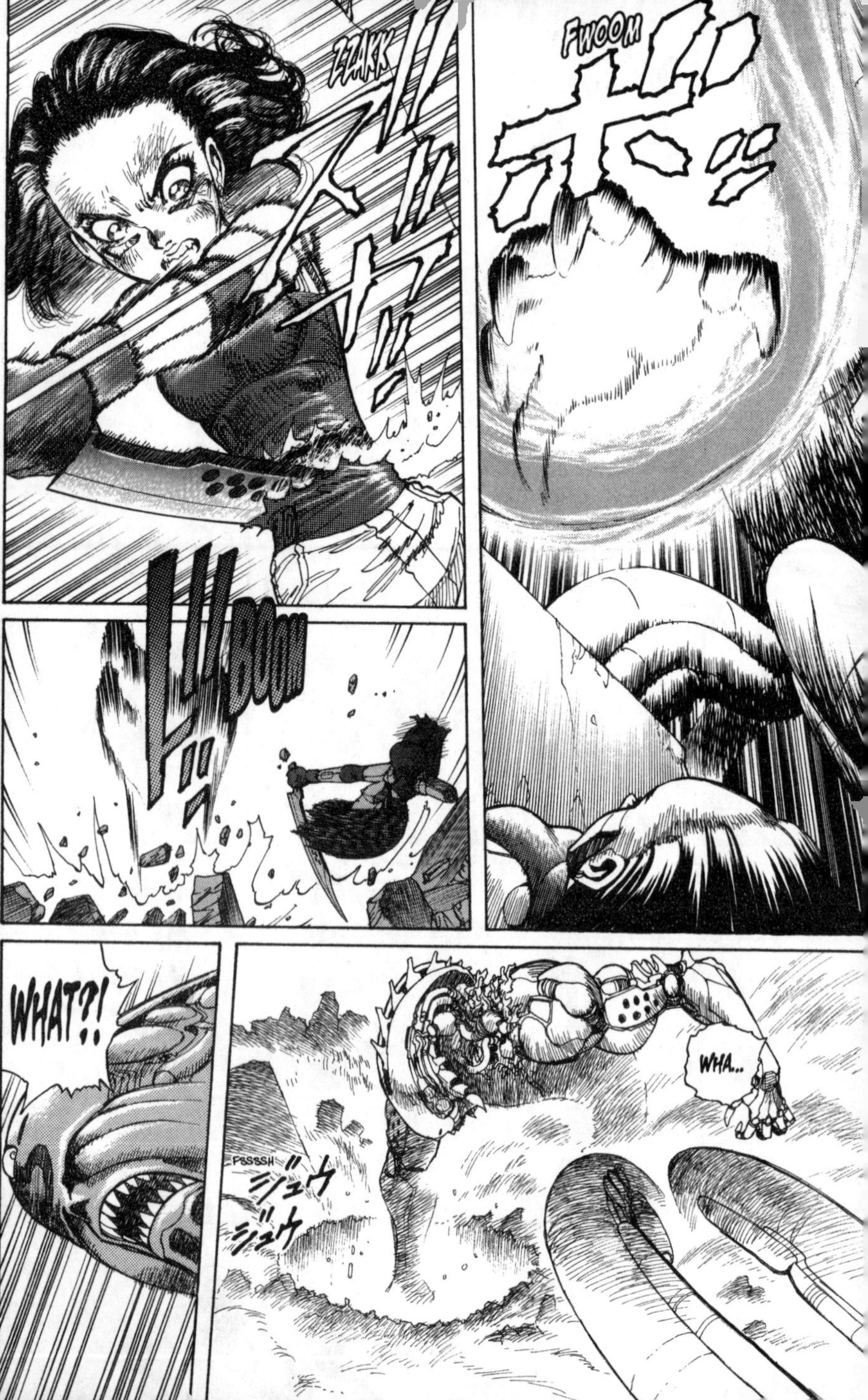
FWOOM
ZZAKK
BOOM
WHA...
FSSSSH
ジュウ
ジュウ
WHAT?!

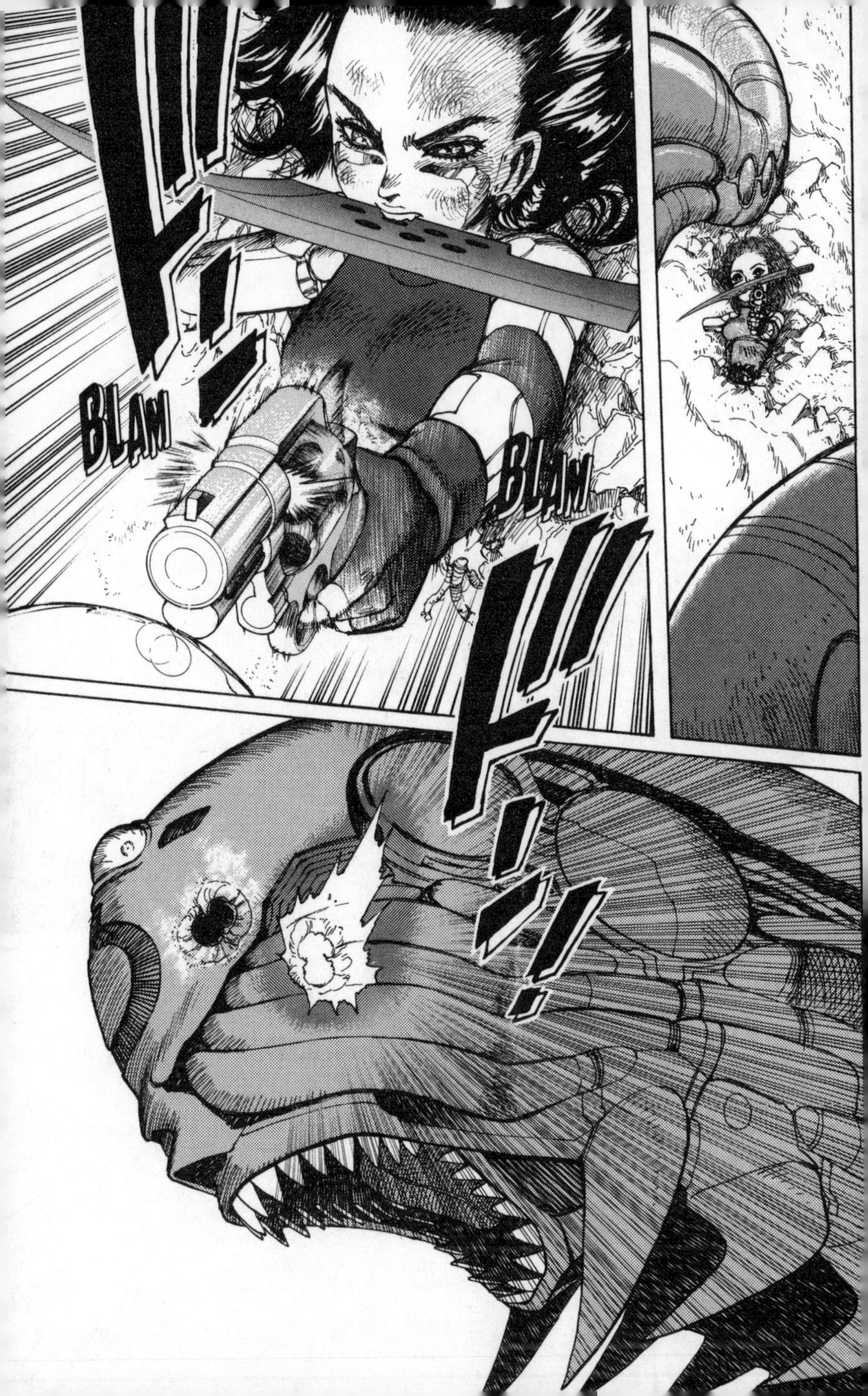
BLAM
BLAM

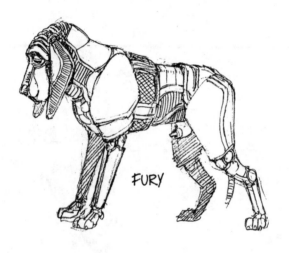

FURY

カク...
TIK
CLIK...
FFFH!
FFFH!
FIGHT_029
Lion and the Lamb

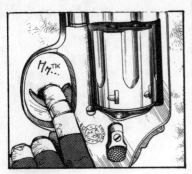

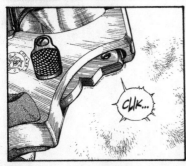

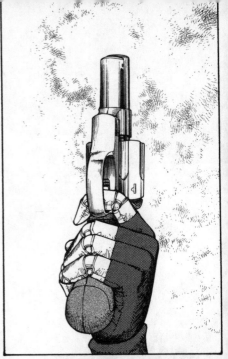

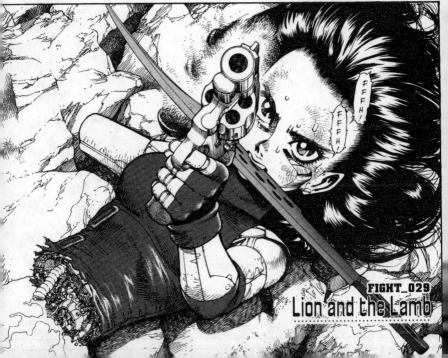

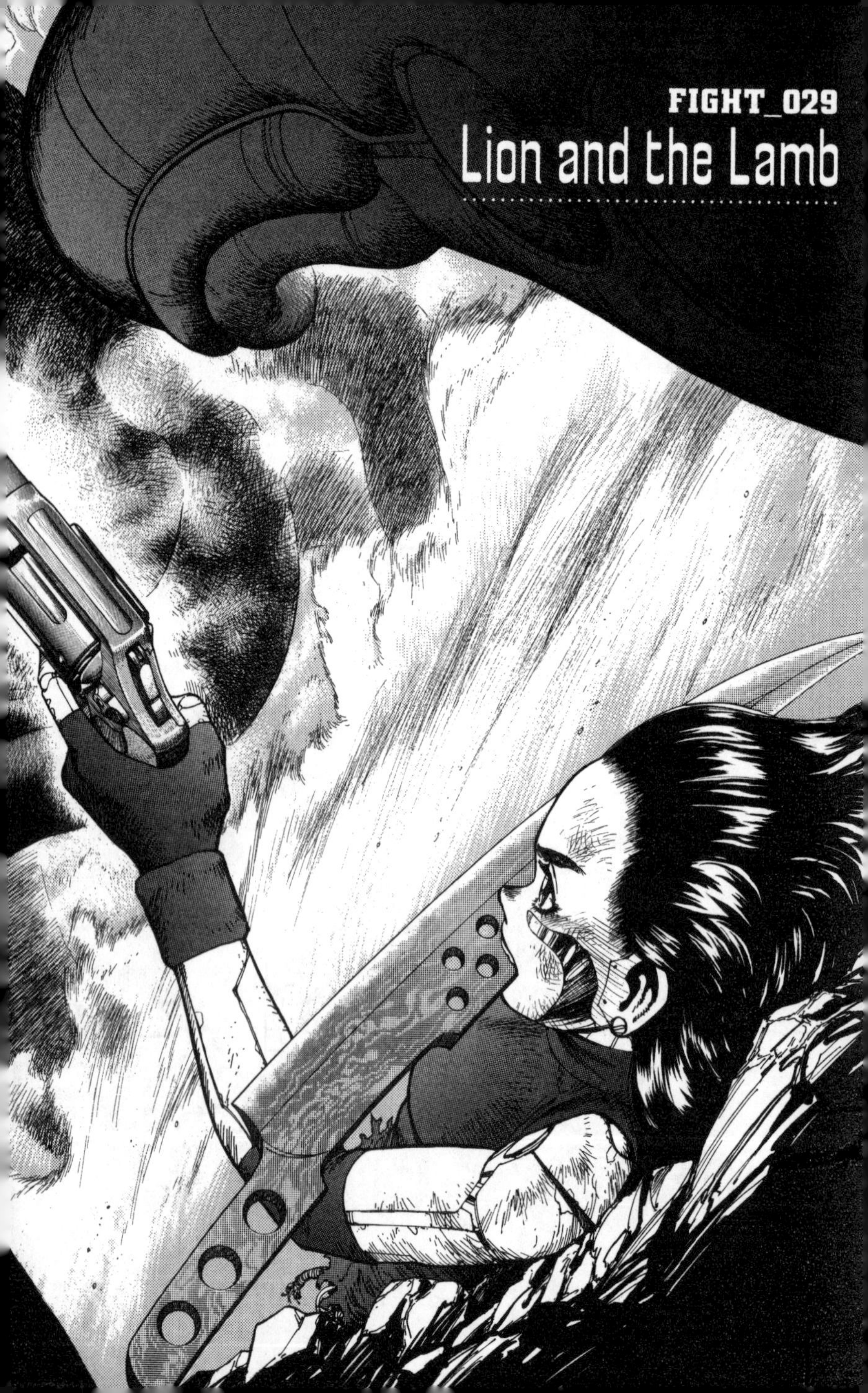
FIGHT_029
Lion and the Lamb

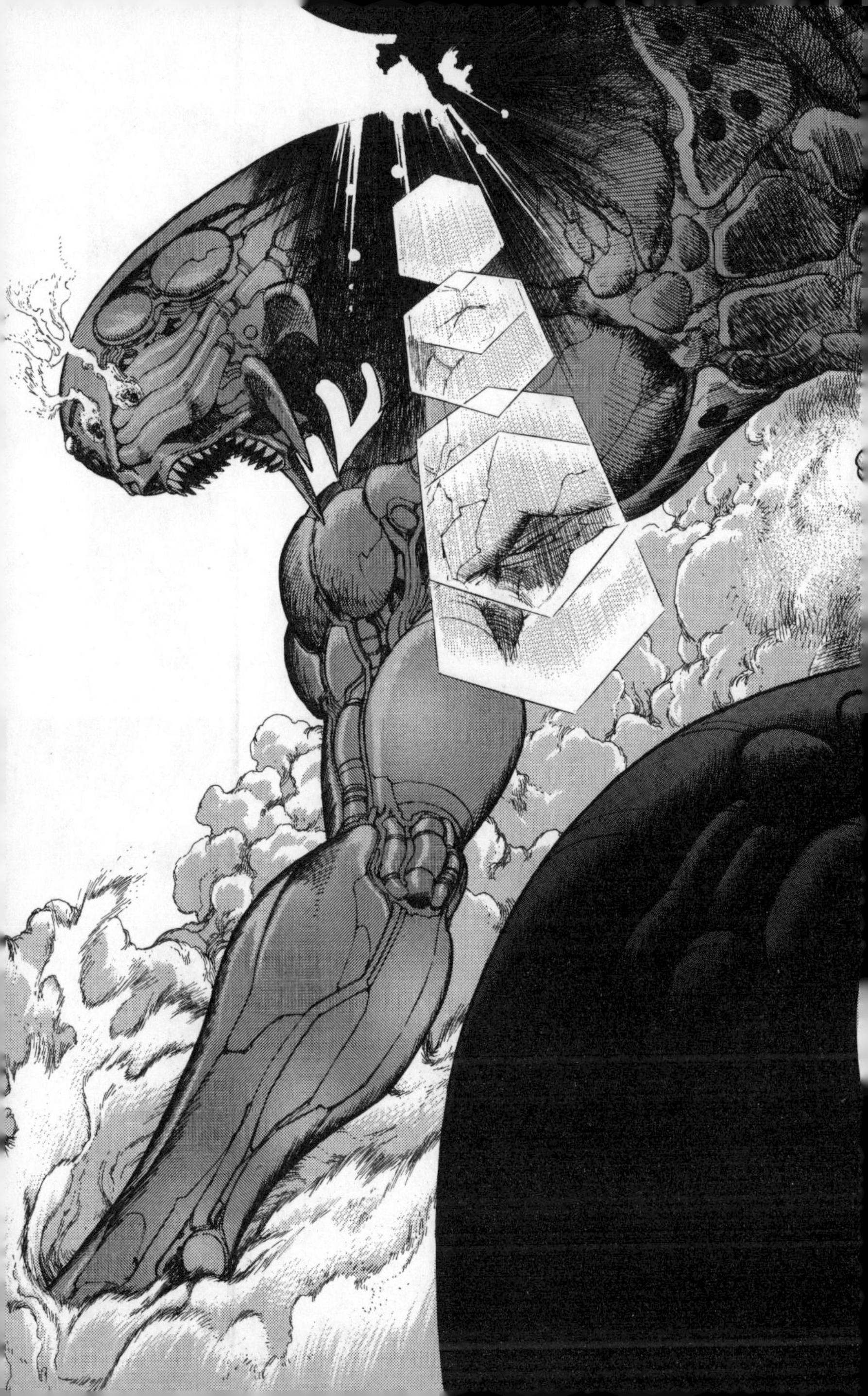

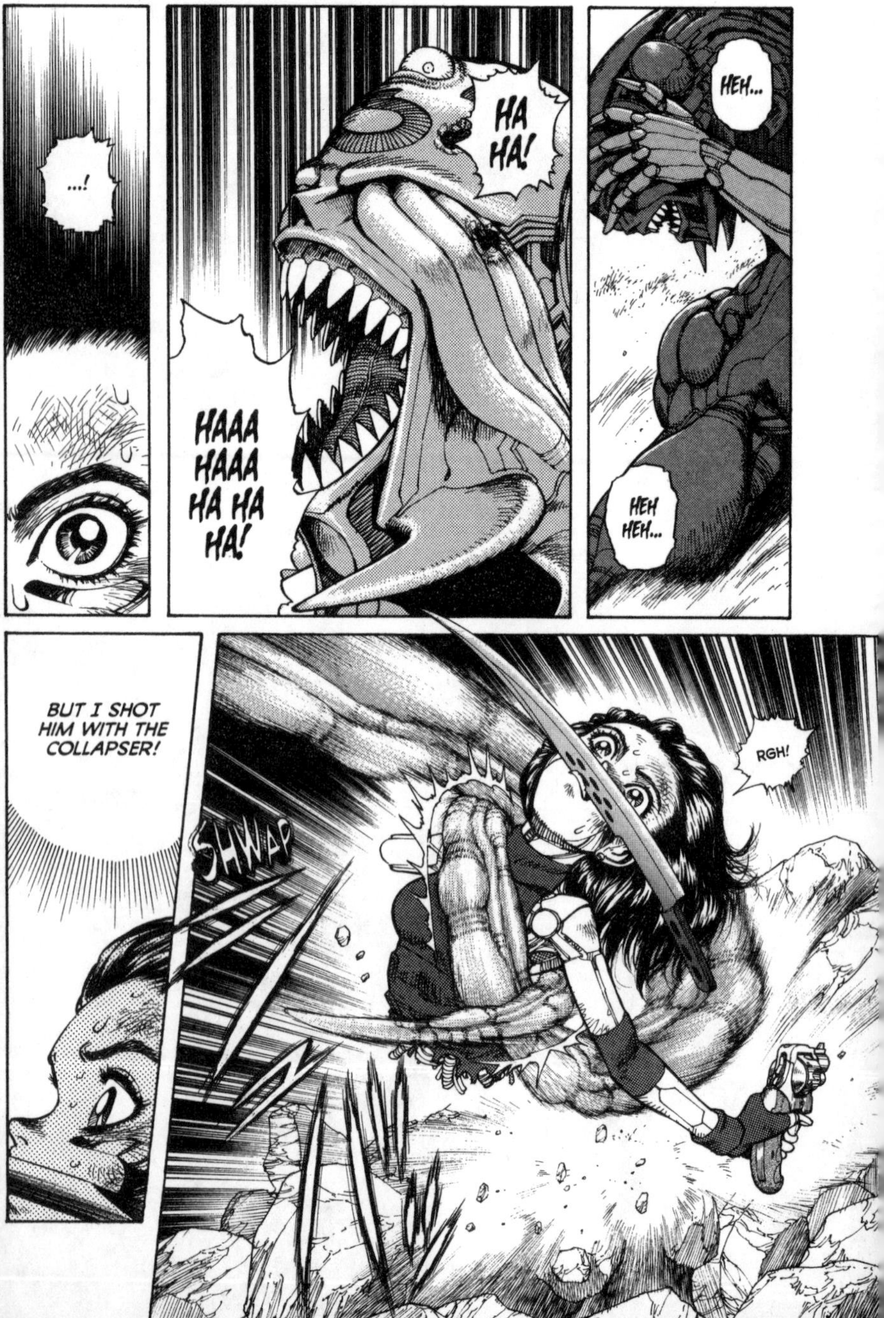
HEH...
HEH HEH...
HA HA!
HAAA HAAA HA HA HA!
...!
RGH!
SHWAP
BUT I SHOT HIM WITH THE COLLAPSER!

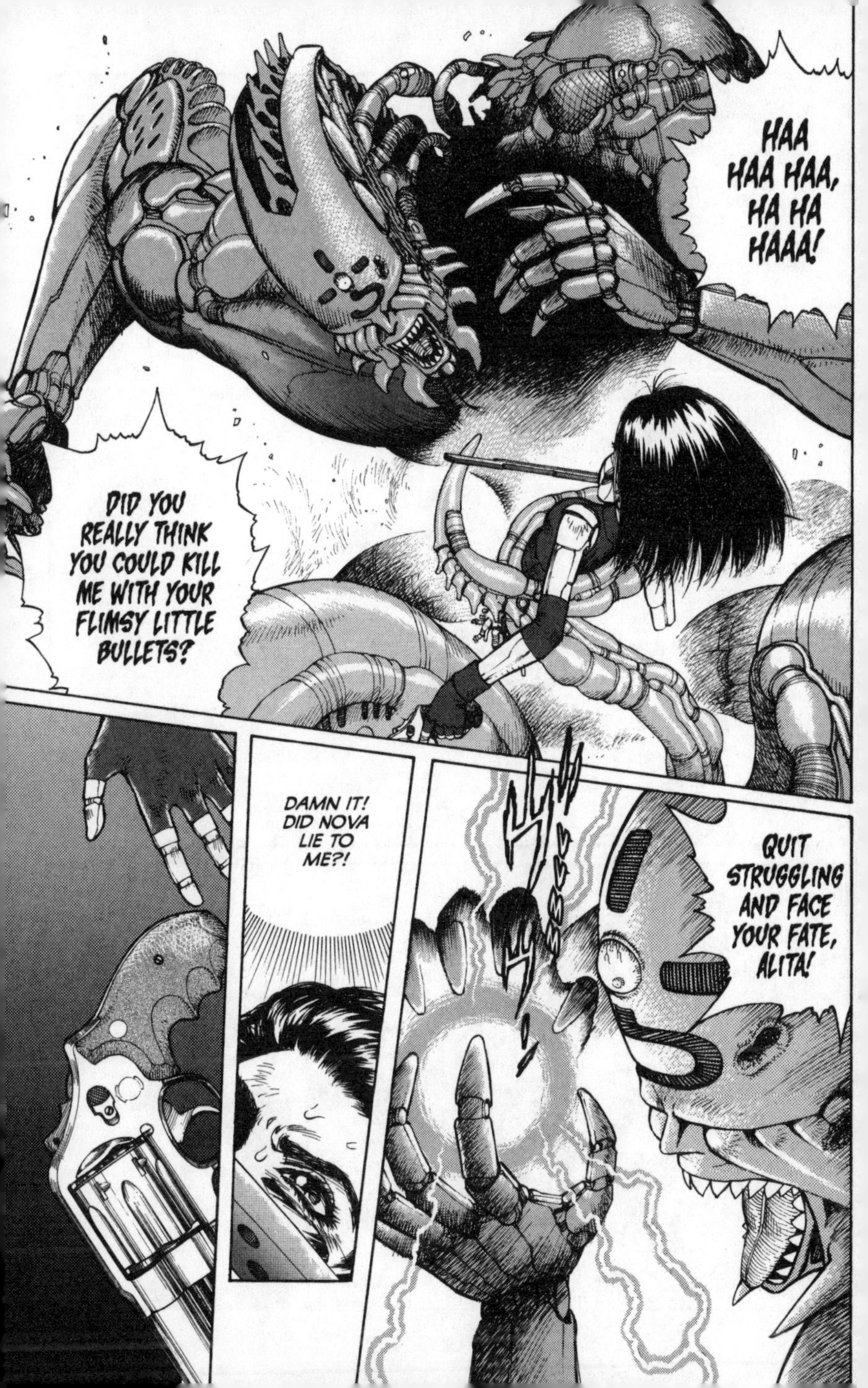
HAA HAA HAA, HA HA HAAA!
DID YOU REALLY THINK YOU COULD KILL ME WITH YOUR FLIMSY LITTLE BULLETS?
QUIT STRUGGLING AND FACE YOUR FATE, ALITA!
DAMN IT! DID NOVA LIE TO ME?!

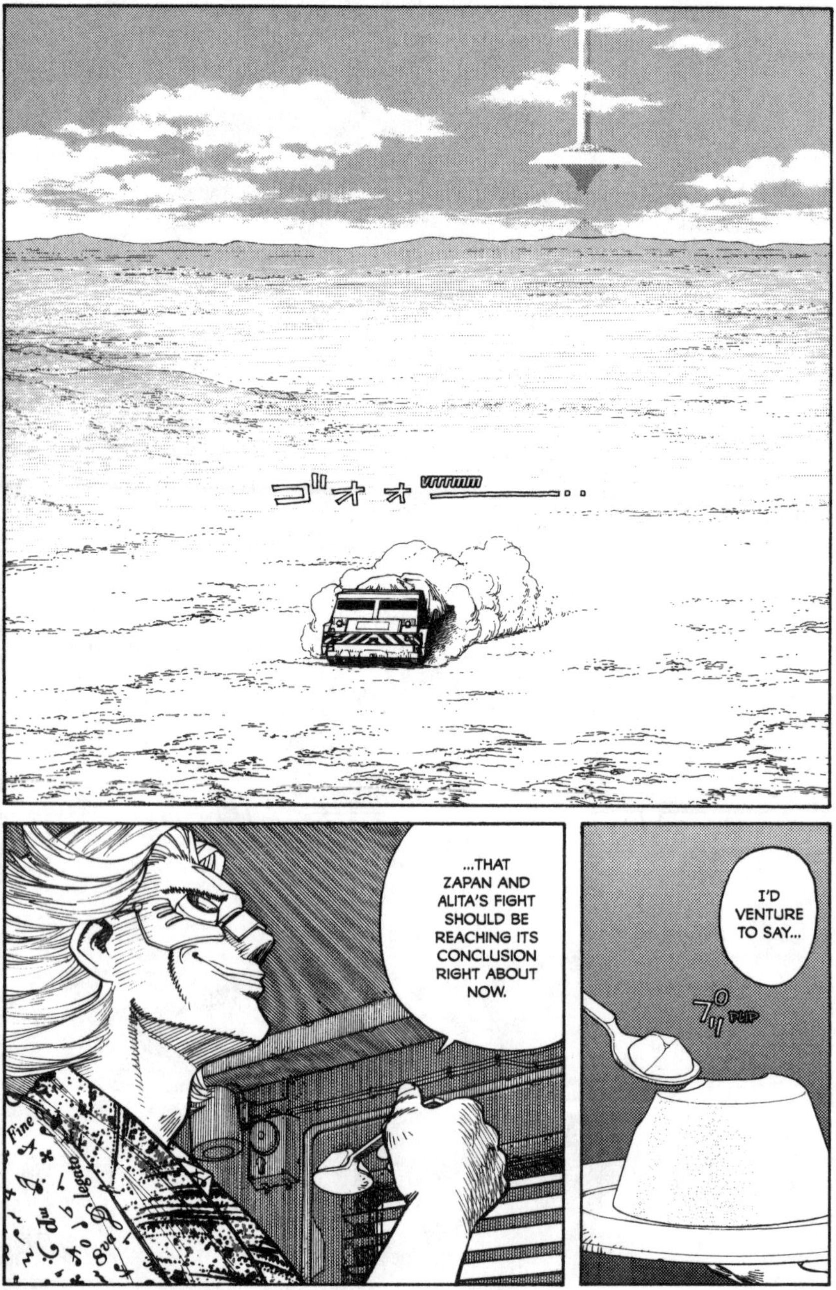
ゴオォーー・・
VRRRMM
I'D VENTURE TO SAY...
プッ
PUP
...THAT ZAPAN AND ALITA'S FIGHT SHOULD BE REACHING ITS CONCLUSION RIGHT ABOUT NOW.

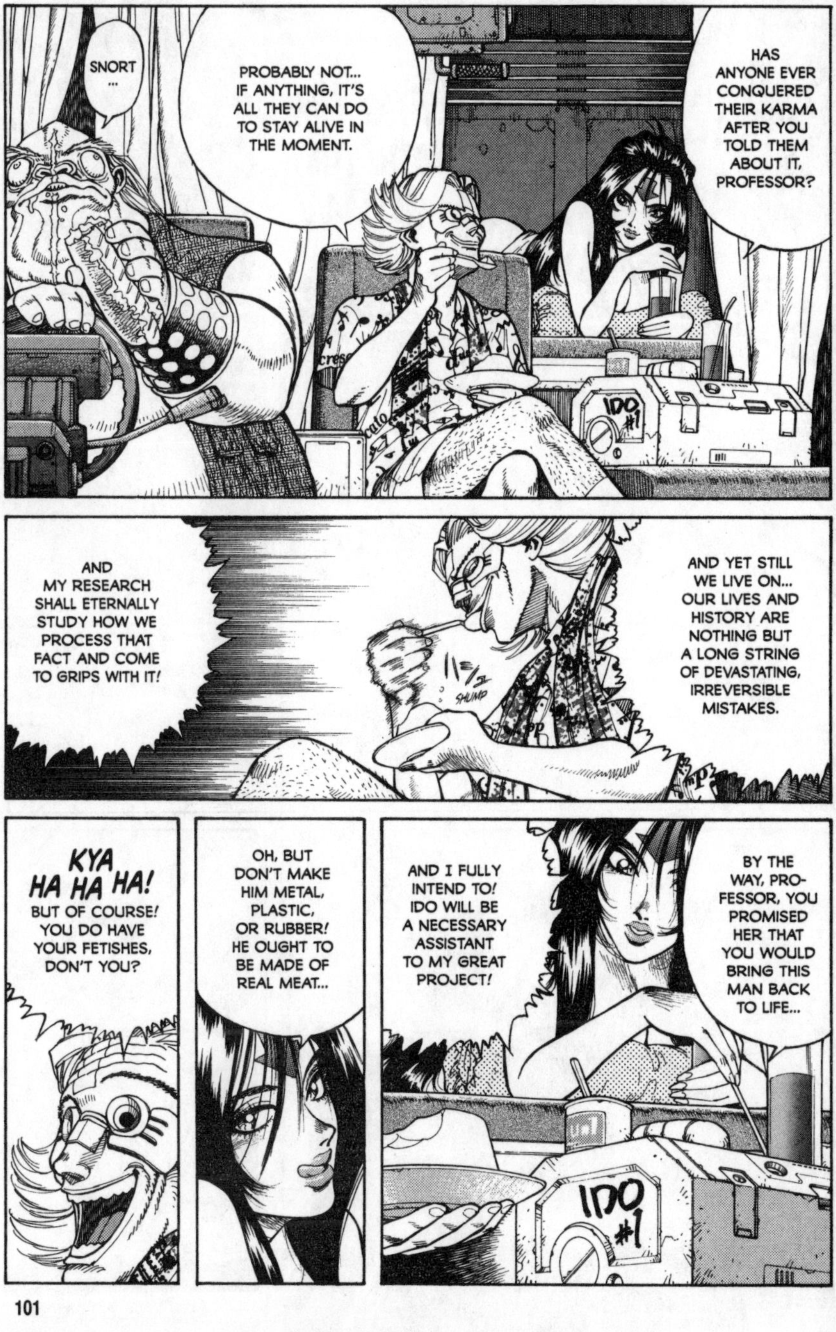
HAS ANYONE EVER CONQUERED THEIR KARMA AFTER YOU TOLD THEM ABOUT IT, PROFESSOR?
PROBABLY NOT... IF ANYTHING, IT'S ALL THEY CAN DO TO STAY ALIVE IN THE MOMENT.
SNORT ...
IDO #1
AND YET STILL WE LIVE ON... OUR LIVES AND HISTORY ARE NOTHING BUT A LONG STRING OF DEVASTATING, IRREVERSIBLE MISTAKES.
SHUMP
AND MY RESEARCH SHALL ETERNALLY STUDY HOW WE PROCESS THAT FACT AND COME TO GRIPS WITH IT!
BY THE WAY, PRO-FESSOR, YOU PROMISED HER THAT YOU WOULD BRING THIS MAN BACK TO LIFE...
AND I FULLY INTEND TO! IDO WILL BE A NECESSARY ASSISTANT TO MY GREAT PROJECT!
IDO #1
OH, BUT DON'T MAKE HIM METAL, PLASTIC, OR RUBBER! HE OUGHT TO BE MADE OF REAL MEAT...
KYA HA HA HA! BUT OF COURSE! YOU DO HAVE YOUR FETISHES, DON'T YOU?

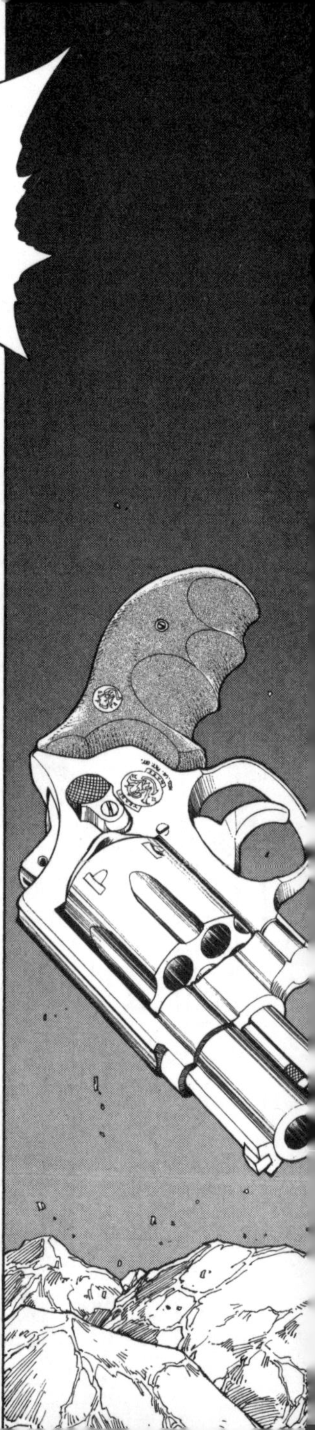

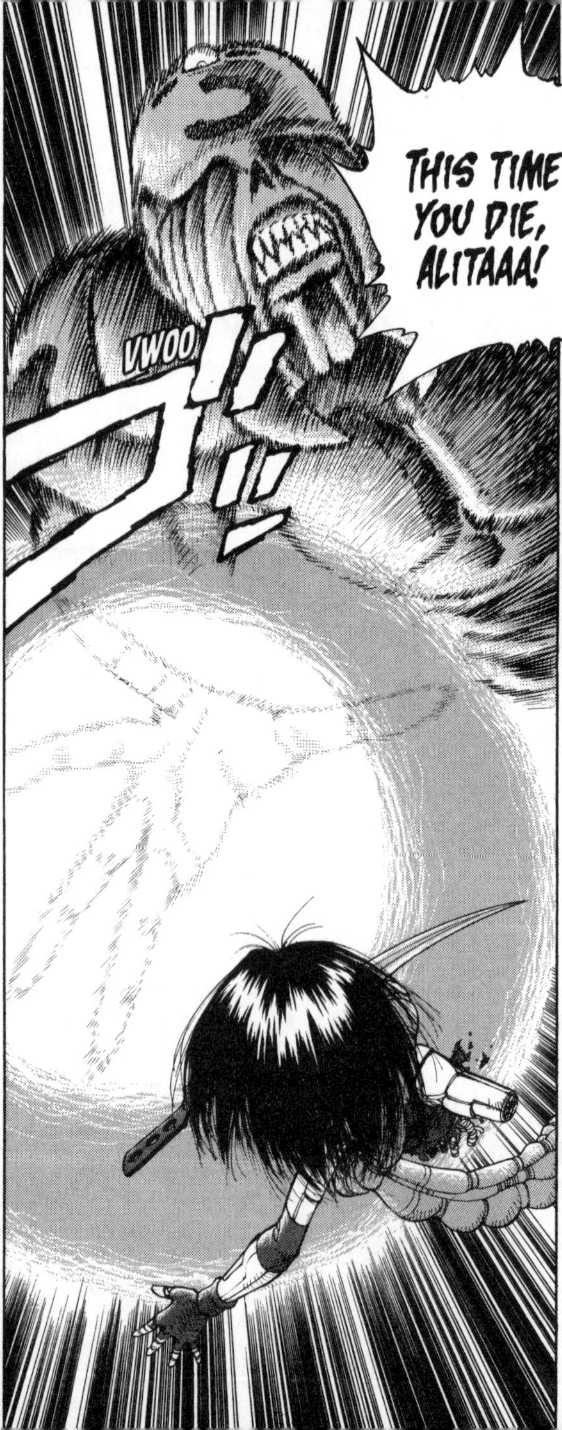
THIS TIME YOU DIE, ALITAAA!
VWOO

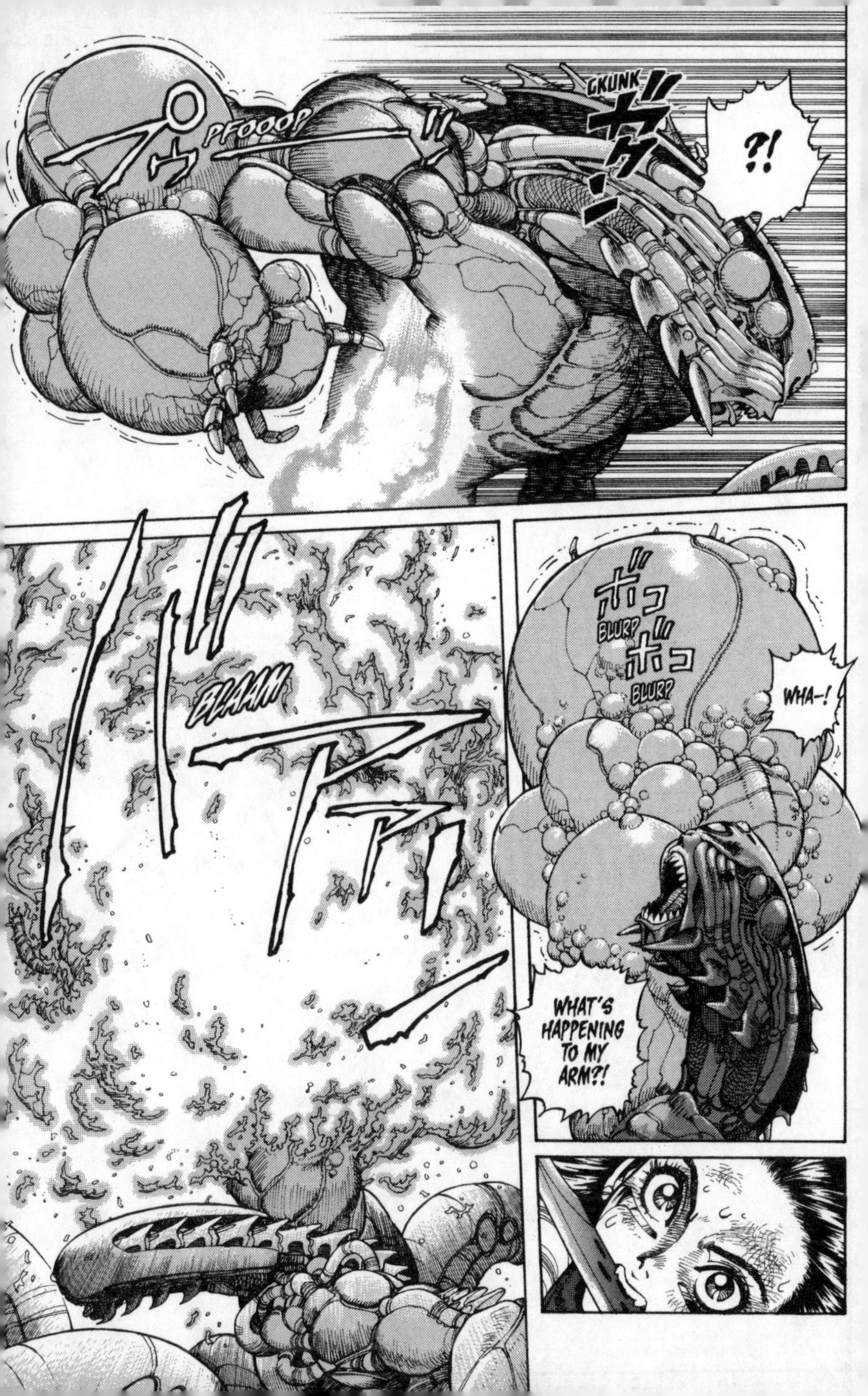

?!
GKUNK
PFOOOP
ボコ
BLURP
ボコ
BLURP
WHA-!
WHAT'S HAPPENING TO MY ARM?!
BLAAM

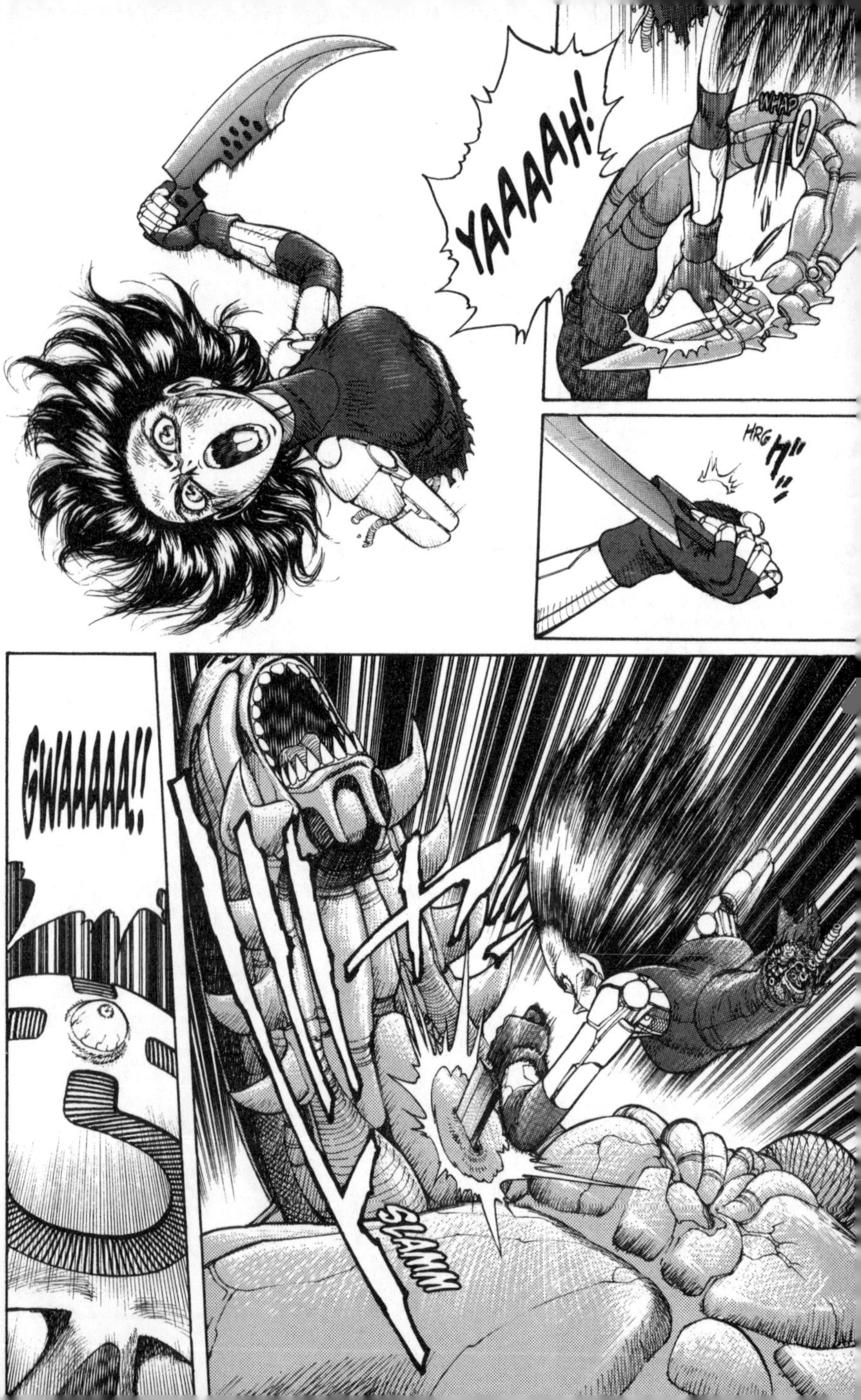
YAAAAH!
WHAP
HRG H""
SLAMM
GWAAAAA!!

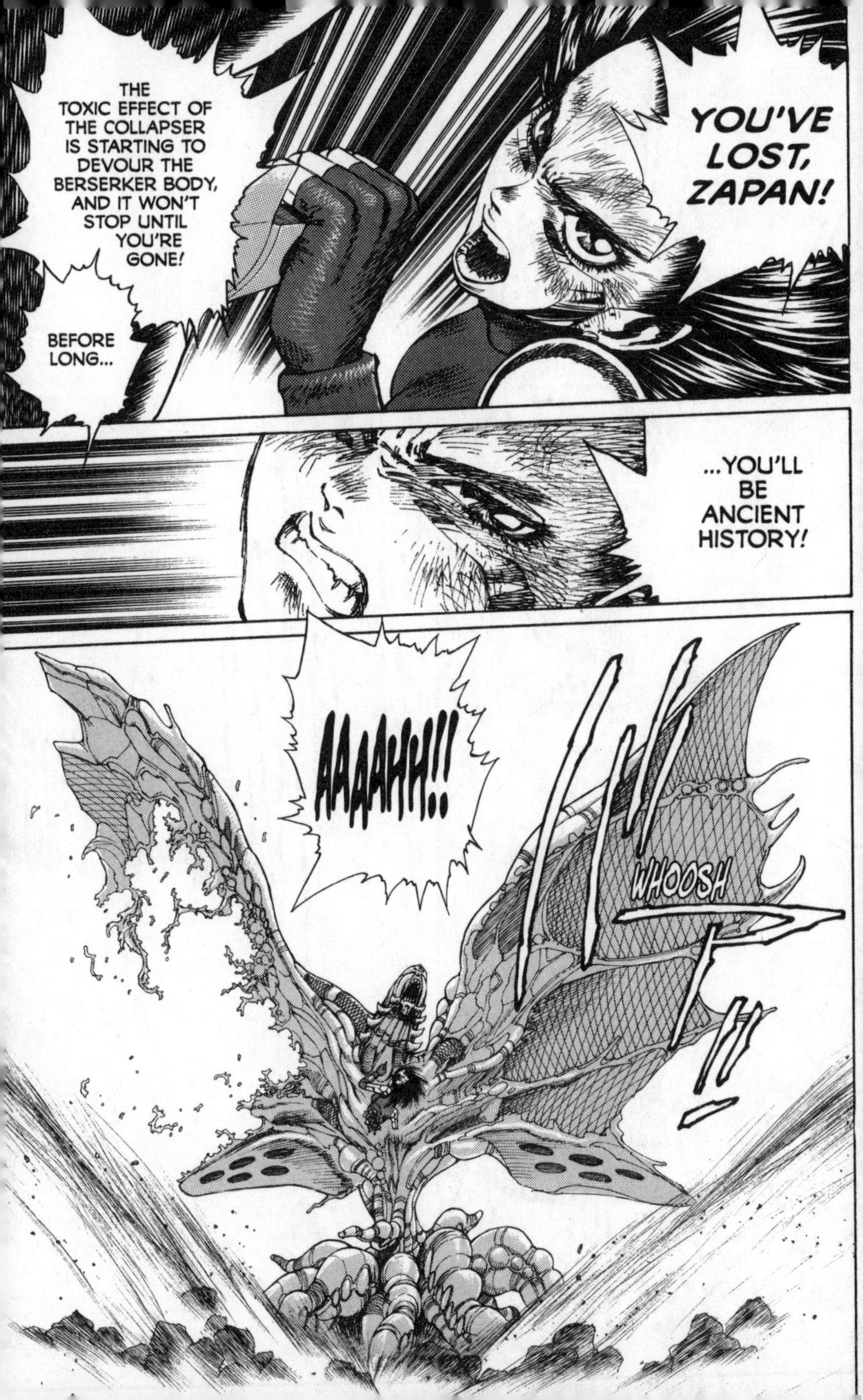
YOU'VE LOST, ZAPAN!
THE TOXIC EFFECT OF THE COLLAPSER IS STARTING TO DEVOUR THE BERSERKER BODY, AND IT WON'T STOP UNTIL YOU'RE GONE!
BEFORE LONG...
...YOU'LL BE ANCIENT HISTORY!
WHOOSH
AAAAHH!!

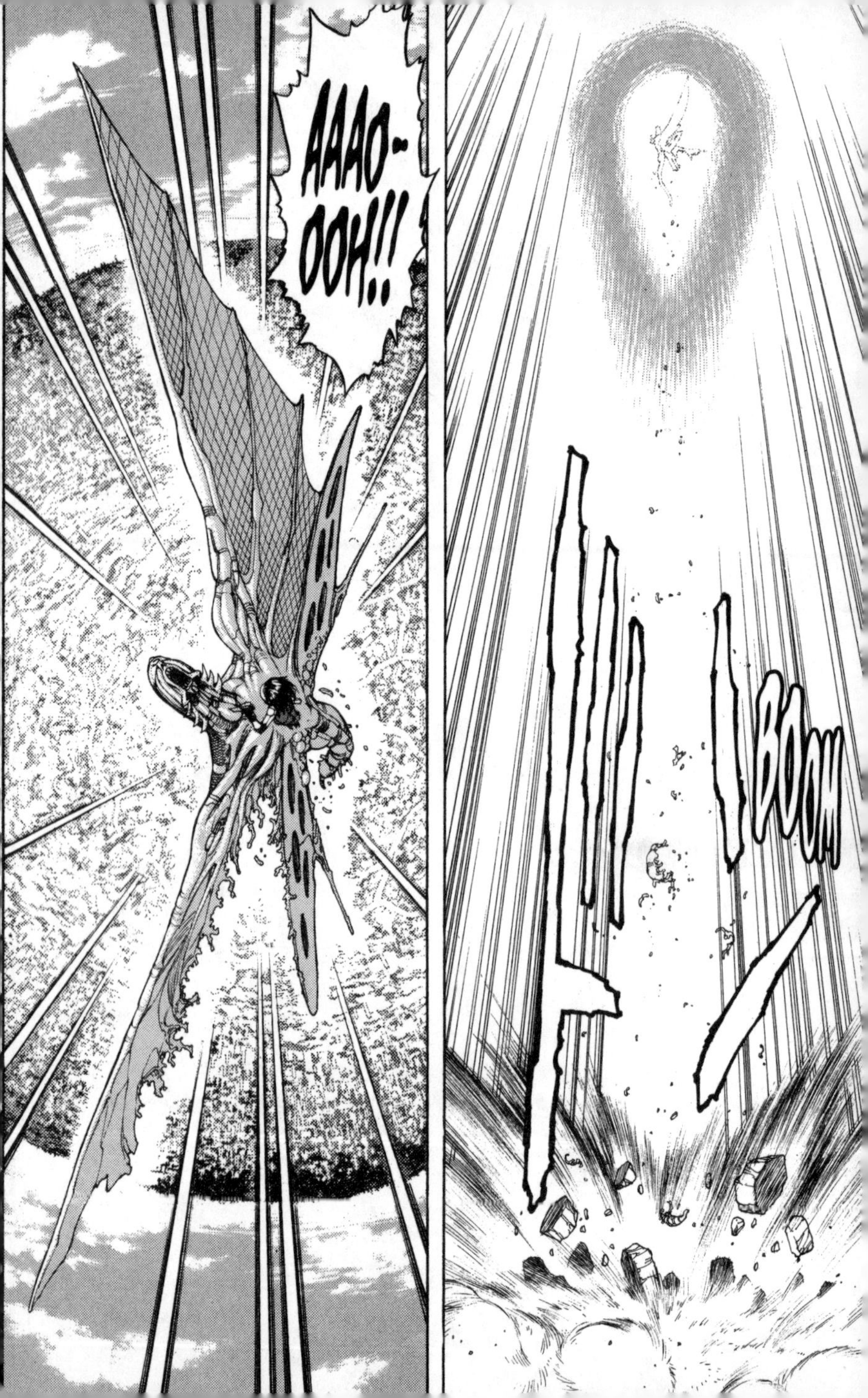
BOOM
AAAO-OOH!!

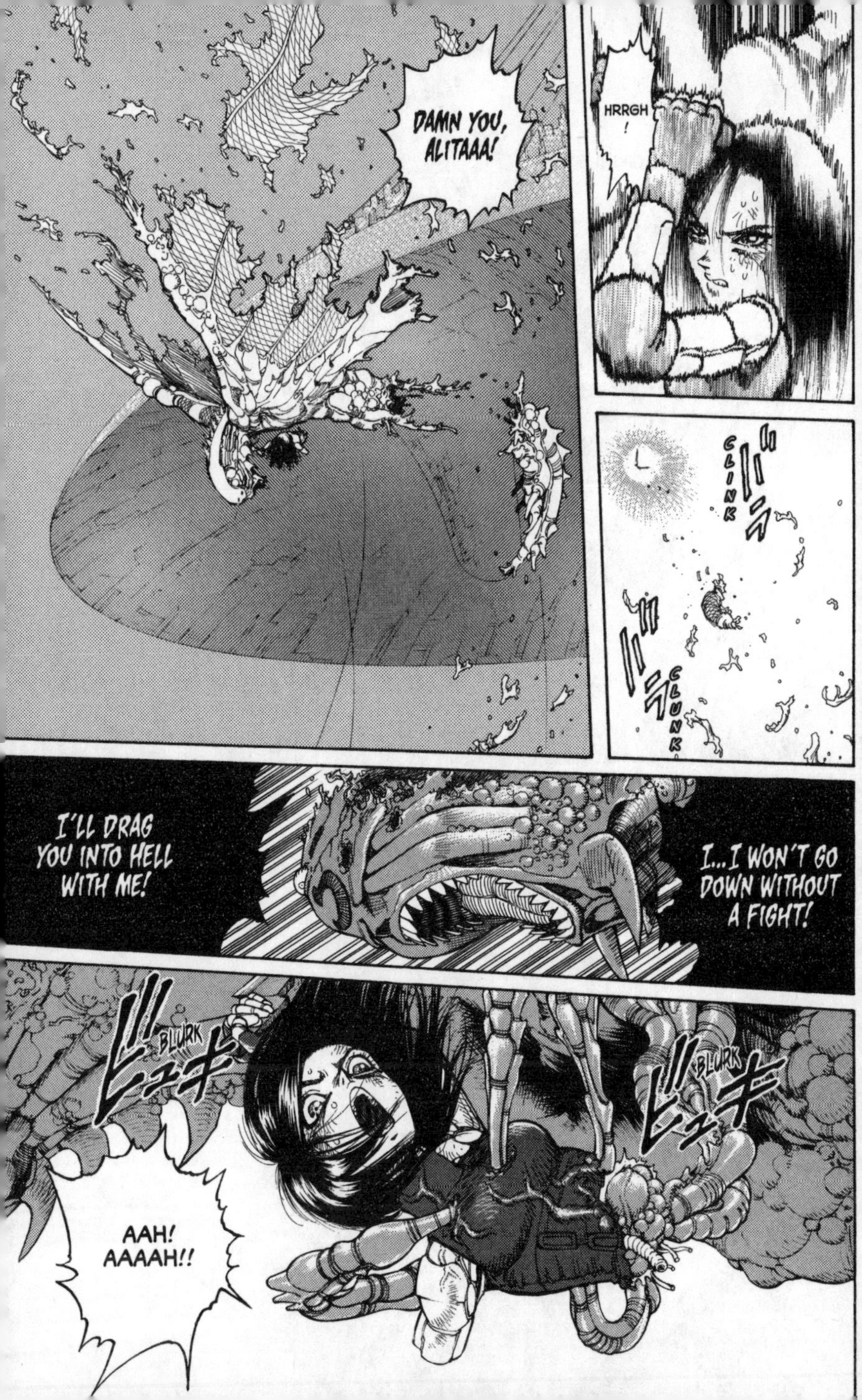
HRRGH!
CLINK
CLUNK
DAMN YOU, ALITAAA!
I...I WON'T GO DOWN WITHOUT A FIGHT!
I'LL DRAG YOU INTO HELL WITH ME!
BLURK
BLURK
AAH! AAAAH!!

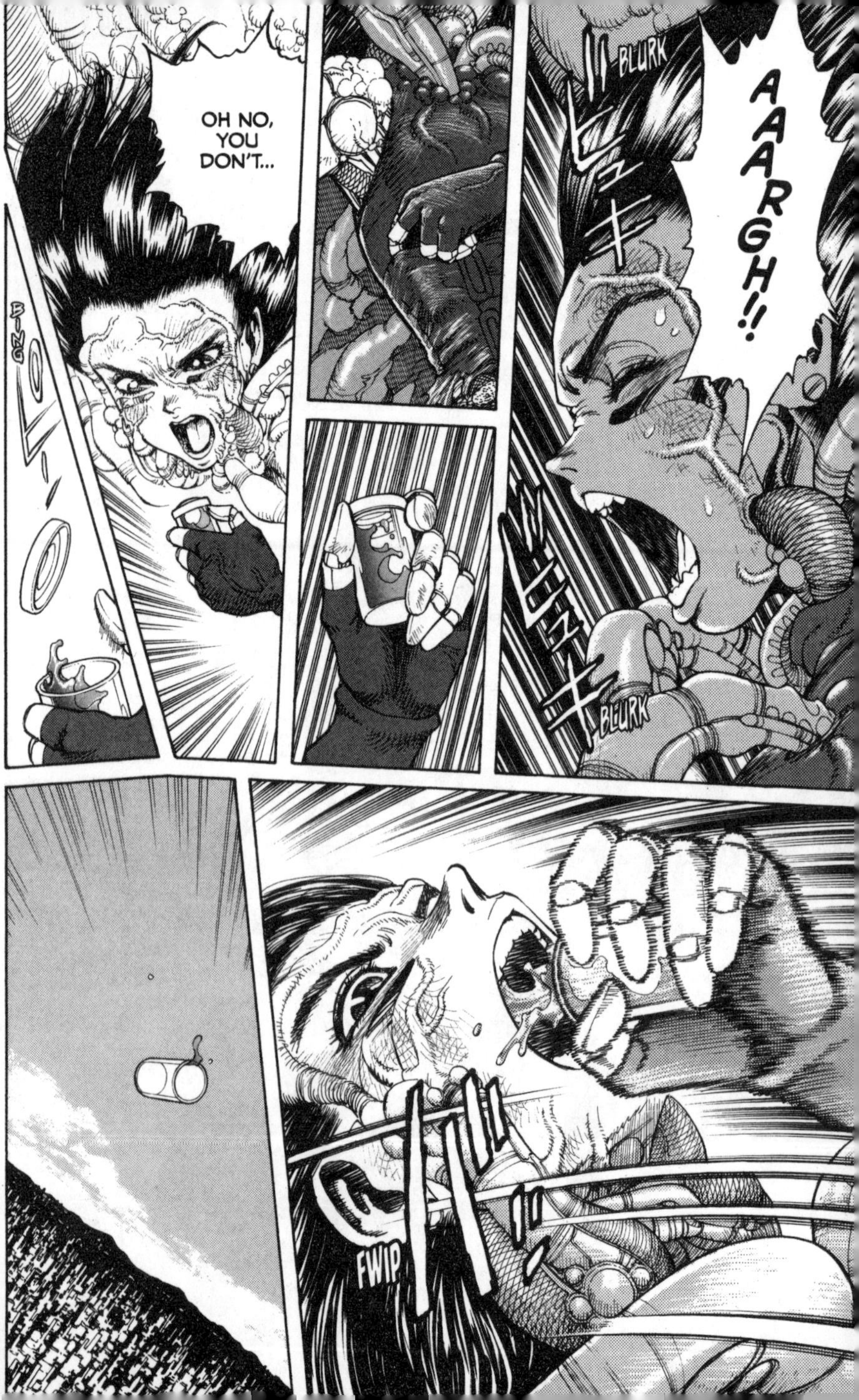
BLURK
AAARGH!!
BLURK
OH NO, YOU DON'T...
BING
FWIP

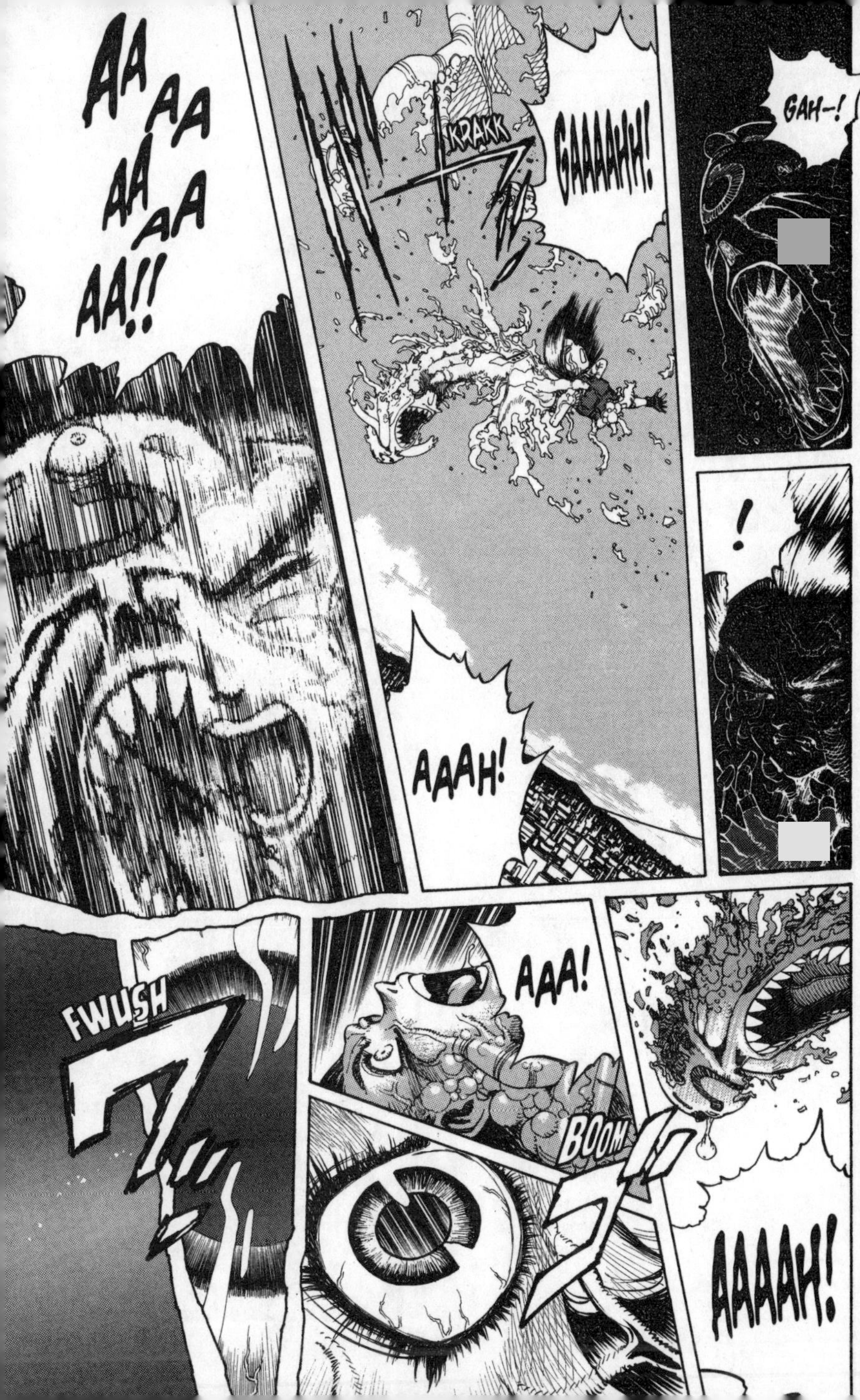
GAH—!
!
KRAKK
GAAAAHH!
AAAH!
AA AA AA AA AA AA!!
AAAAH!
AAA!
BOOM
FWUSH

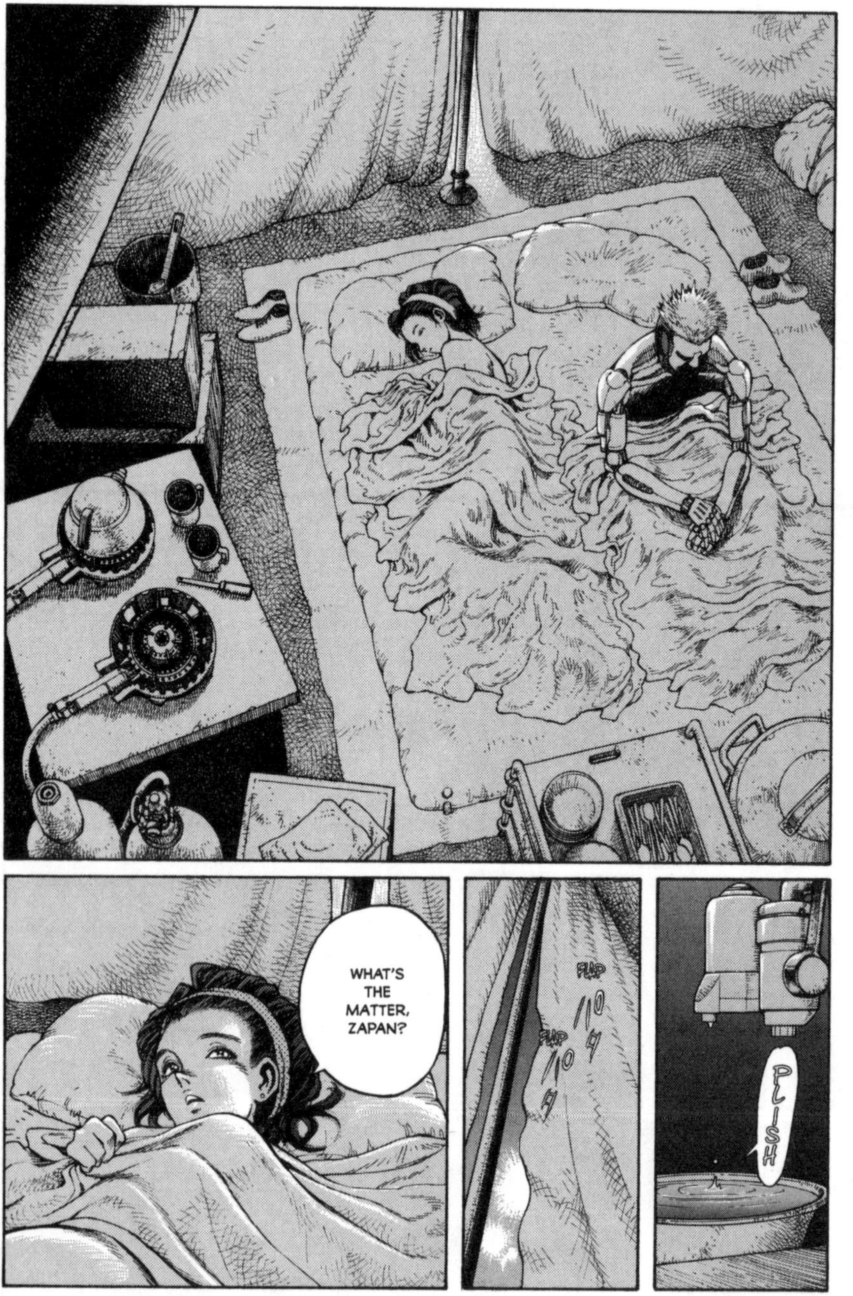
PLISH
FLAP
FLAP
WHAT'S THE MATTER, ZAPAN?

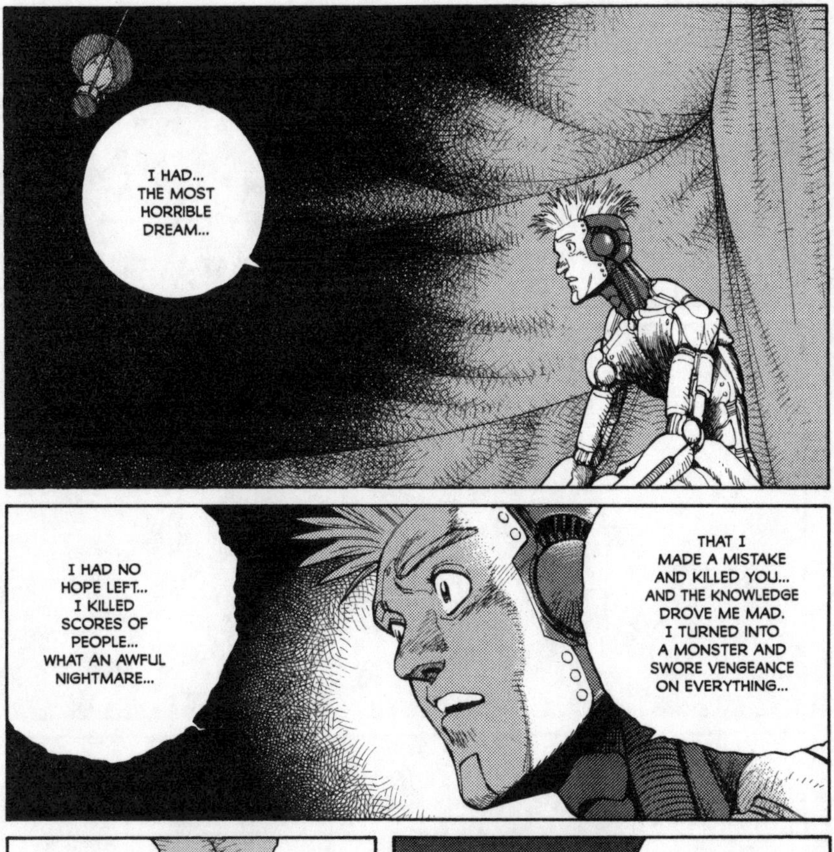
I HAD... THE MOST HORRIBLE DREAM...
THAT I MADE A MISTAKE AND KILLED YOU... AND THE KNOWLEDGE DROVE ME MAD. I TURNED INTO A MONSTER AND SWORE VENGEANCE ON EVERYTHING...
I HAD NO HOPE LEFT... I KILLED SCORES OF PEOPLE... WHAT AN AWFUL NIGHTMARE...
YOU'RE FINE... IT WAS JUST A DREAM. THAT'S NOT THE KIND OF PERSON YOU ARE.
SARAH... I'M WORRIED.
I'M SO, SO TERRIFIED. WHAT IF... WHAT IF I *LOST* YOU...?

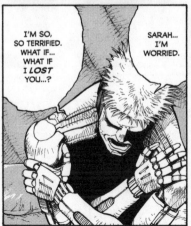

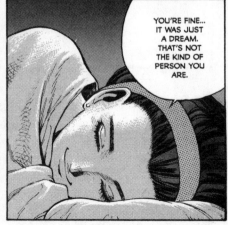

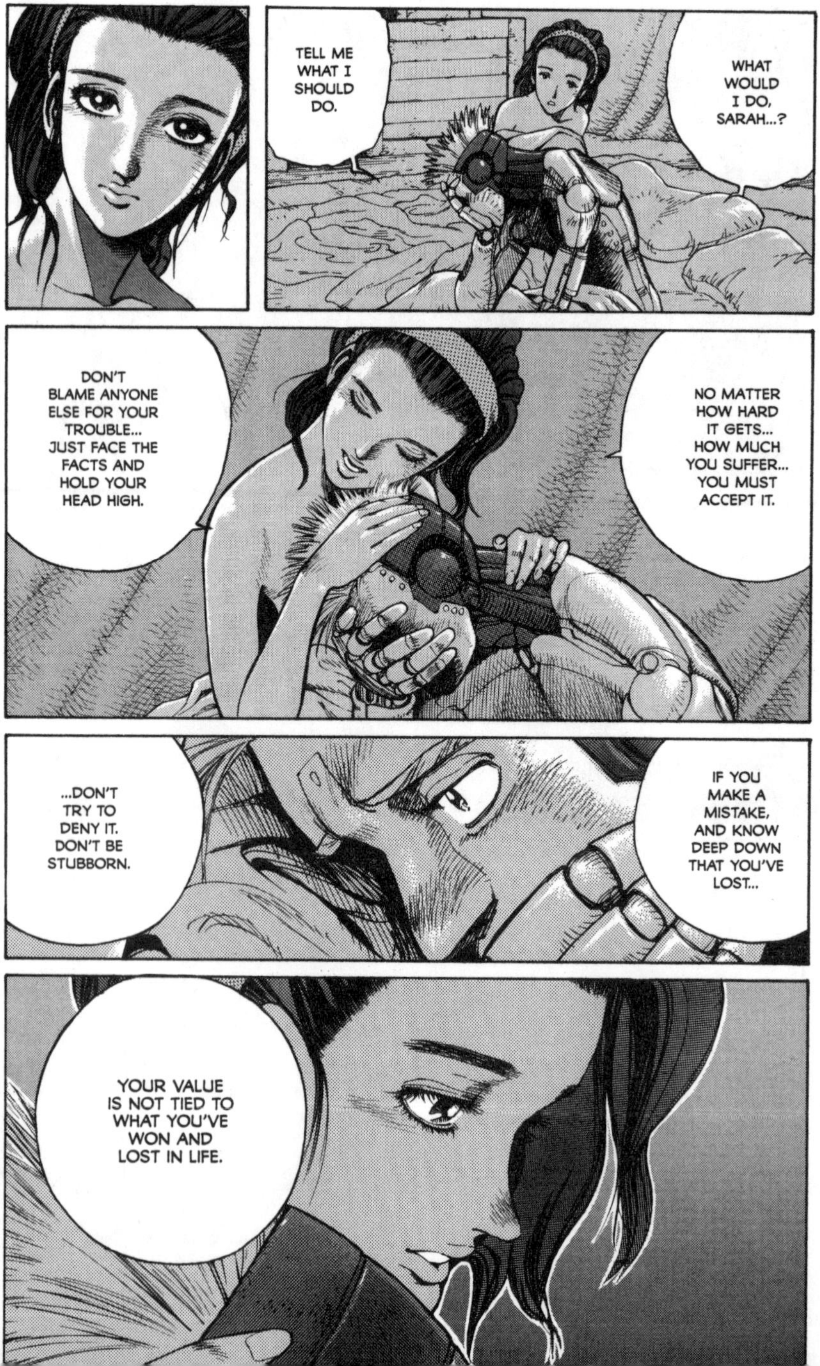
WHAT WOULD I DO, SARAH...?
TELL ME WHAT I SHOULD DO.
NO MATTER HOW HARD IT GETS... HOW MUCH YOU SUFFER... YOU MUST ACCEPT IT.
DON'T BLAME ANYONE ELSE FOR YOUR TROUBLE... JUST FACE THE FACTS AND HOLD YOUR HEAD HIGH.
IF YOU MAKE A MISTAKE, AND KNOW DEEP DOWN THAT YOU'VE LOST...
...DON'T TRY TO DENY IT. DON'T BE STUBBORN.
YOUR VALUE IS NOT TIED TO WHAT YOU'VE WON AND LOST IN LIFE.

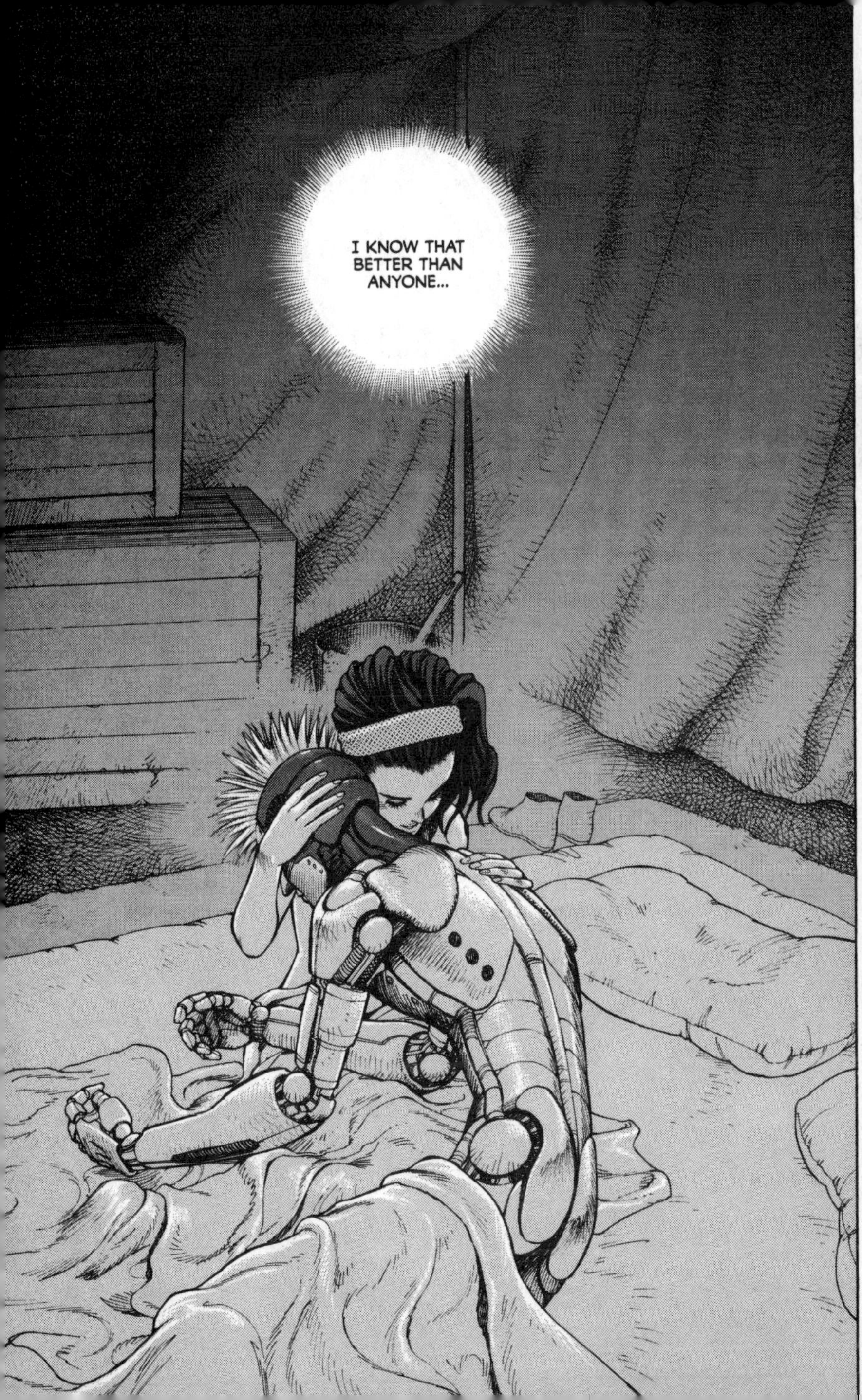
I KNOW THAT BETTER THAN ANYONE...

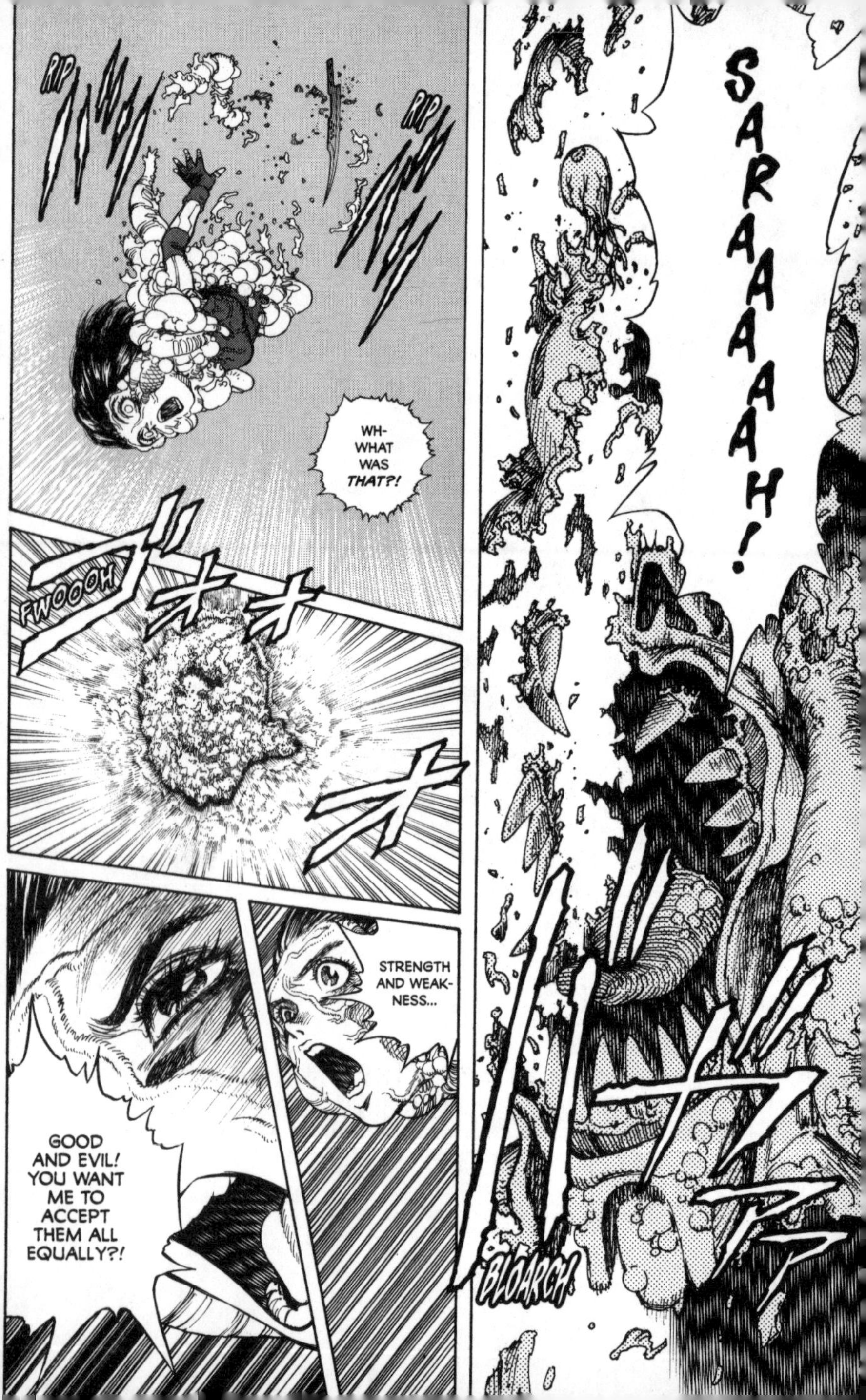
SARAAAAAH!
BLOARCH
RIP
RIP
WH-WHAT WAS *THAT?!*
FWOOOH
STRENGTH AND WEAK-NESS...
GOOD AND EVIL! YOU WANT ME TO ACCEPT THEM ALL EQUALLY?!

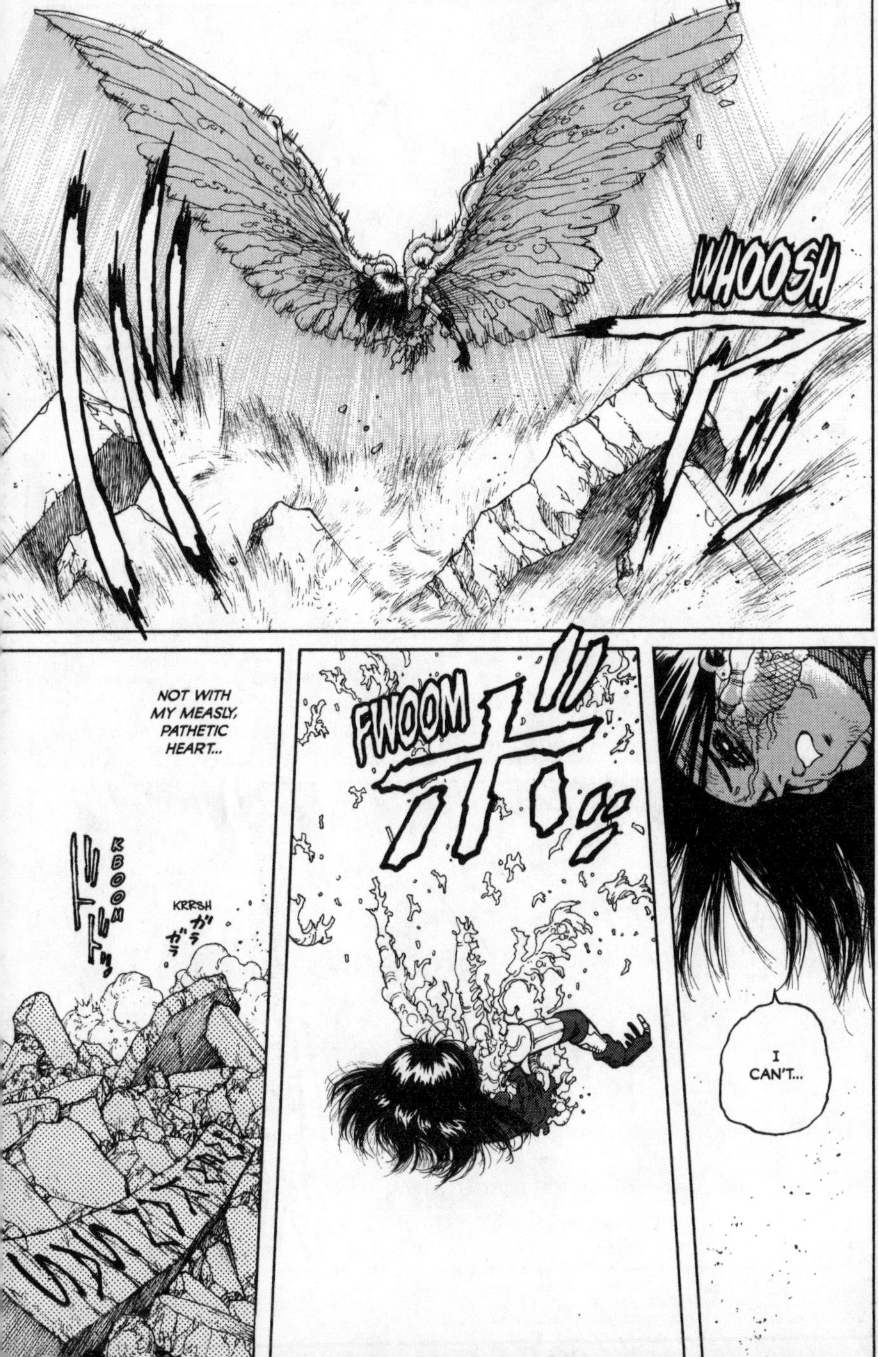
WHOOSH
I CAN'T...
FWOOM
NOT WITH MY MEASLY, PATHETIC HEART...
KBOOM
KRRSH
ガラ
ガラ

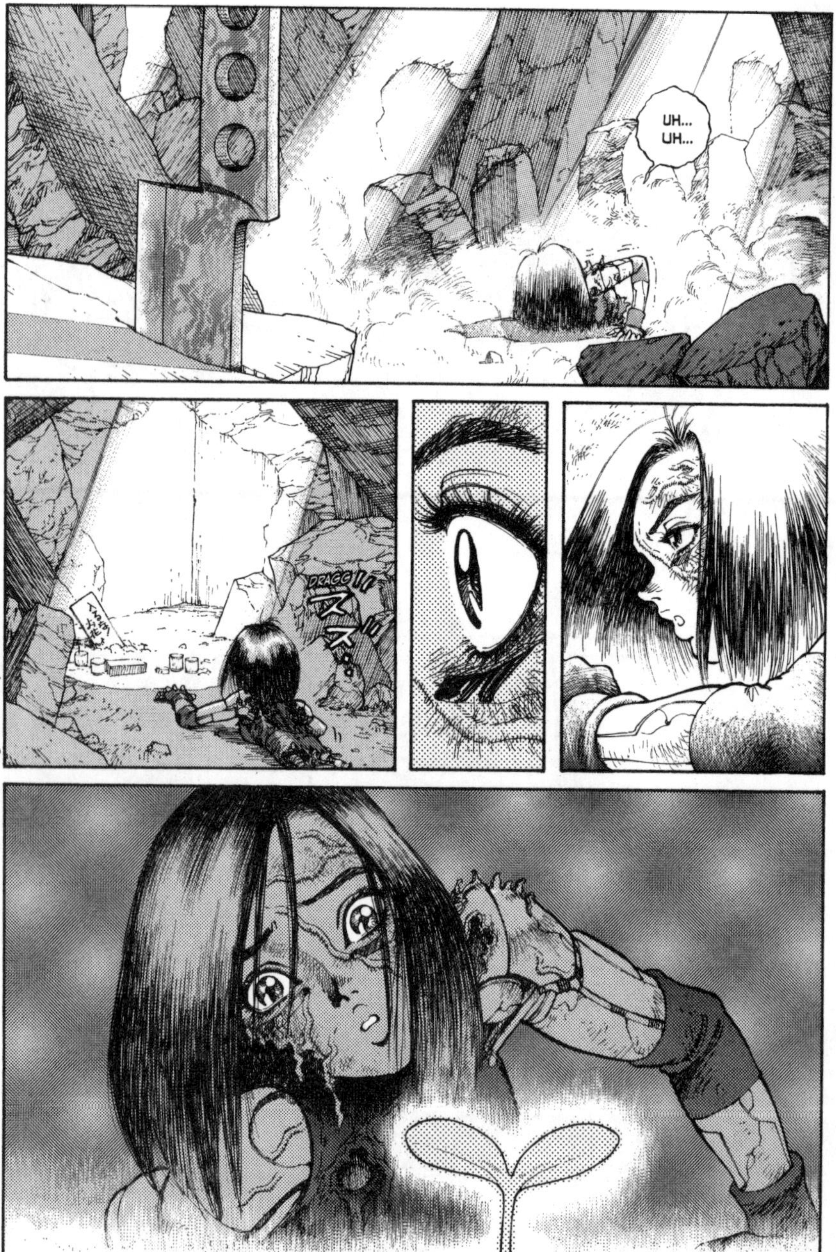
UH...
UH...
DRAGG
ズズ…

Sign: Don't step on the flowers!

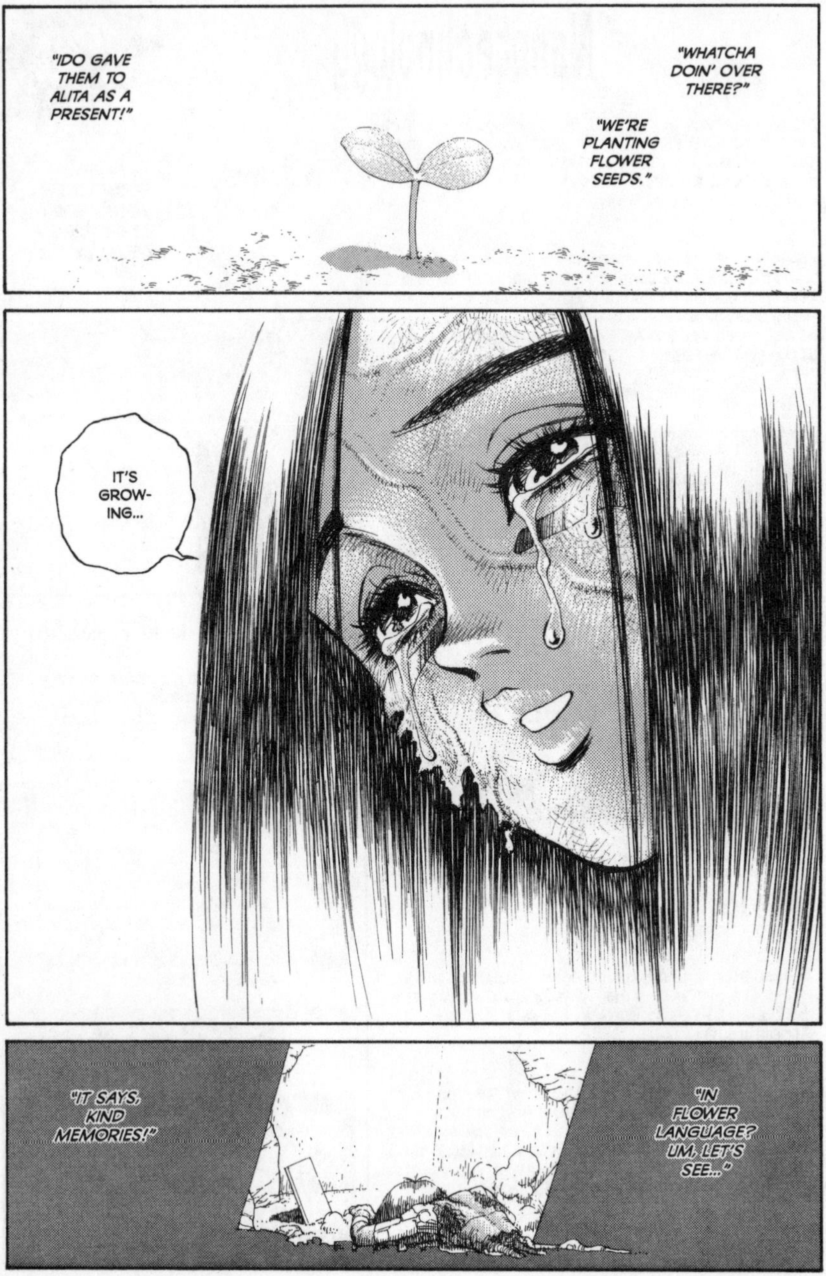
"WHATCHA DOIN' OVER THERE?"
"WE'RE PLANTING FLOWER SEEDS."
"IDO GAVE THEM TO ALITA AS A PRESENT!"
IT'S GROWING...
"IN FLOWER LANGUAGE? UM, LET'S SEE..."
"IT SAYS, KIND MEMORIES!"

Nanotechnology

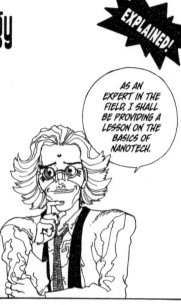

EXPLAINED!

ONE NANOMETER IS 10^{-9} METERS, OR 1/1,000,000,000TH OF A METER. "NANO" COMES FROM THE GREEK ROOT NANOS, MEANING "DWARF." INCIDENTALLY, THE KANJI CORRESPONDING TO ONE NANO IS JIN, MEANING "DUST."

AS AN EXPERT IN THE FIELD, I SHALL BE PROVIDING A LESSON ON THE BASICS OF NANOTECH.

A NANOMACHINE IS A MICROSCOPIC ROBOT CONSISTING OF GEARS, BEARINGS, AND MOTORS CONSTRUCTED AT THE INDIVIDUAL MOLECULAR LEVEL. IT'S POWERED BY STATIC ELECTRICITY AND, DUE TO THE PROPERTIES OF MOLECULAR BONDS, IS VERY HARDY. IT RUNS OFF OF PRELOADED PROGRAMMING. THESE MOLECULAR ROBOTS ARE CALLED "ASSEMBLERS."

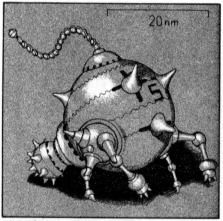

20nm

NOVA'S ASSEMBLER DESIGN. 20 NANOMETERS IS THE SIZE OF THE WORLD'S SMALLEST VIRUSES.

AN ASSEMBLER CAN GRAB AND PLACE MOLECULES AND ATOMS AT A SPEED OF A MILLION PER SECOND, MEANING THAT IT CAN CREATE A PERFECT REPLICA OF ITSELF IN ABOUT FIFTEEN MINUTES.

WHEN EACH COPY THEN REPEATS THE REPLICATION PROCESS, THEIR NUMBERS GROW EXPONENTIALLY. WITHIN TEN HOURS YOU'D HAVE 68 BILLION NANOMACHINES. IN LESS THAN A DAY, THEY'D WEIGH AN ACTUAL TON. BY THE END OF TWO DAYS, THEY COULD WEIGH MORE THAN THE ACTUAL EARTH. NATURALLY, THERE WILL BE MULTIPLE LAYERS OF PROGRAMMING AND FAILSAFE MECHANISMS DESIGNED TO AVOID SUCH A DISASTER.

THE ROOTS OF NANOTECHNOLOGY

1942: THE FIRST PIECE OF SCI-FI WRITING INVOLVING NANOTECH: ROBERT A. HEINLEIN'S SHORT STORY "WALDO."

1959: RICHARD FEYNMAN GIVES A LECTURE TITLED "THERE'S PLENTY OF ROOM AT THE BOTTOM."

1976: ERIC DREXLER FIRST PROPOSES THE CONCEPT OF THE "ASSEMBLER."

1981: THE STM (SCANNING TUNNELING MICROSCOPE) IS DEVELOPED BY DRS. ROHRER AND BINNIG AT IBM ZURICH RESEARCH LABORATORY.

1986: ERIC DREXLER'S BIBLE OF NANOTECHNOLOGY: *ENGINES OF CREATION*.

1990: IBM SCIENTISTS USE THEIR STM TO CREATE THE IBM LOGO USING ATOMS (VISUALIZED BELOW).

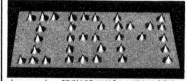

5 nm

SPELLED USING 35 XENON ATOMS.

IN THEORY, ASSEMBLERS CAN ESSENTIALLY CREATE ANYTHING THAT IS PHYSICALLY POSSIBLE TO EXIST. THEIR INDUSTRIAL POWER IS BASICALLY LIMITLESS.

IN PRACTICE

- BRAIN RECONSTRUCTION........(BRAIN AUGMENTATION)
- BERSERKER BODY..........................(MECHANICAL LIFE)
- ARTIFICIAL SPINE..............(ARTIFICIAL STRUCTURES)
- RESTORERS...(IMMORTALITY)

(OTHER USES)

- SYTHESIZING FOOD FROM INORGANIC MATTER
- AUTO-GROWTH/COMPLETION OF ALL KINDS OF MECHANICAL DEVICES
- DEVELOPMENT OF NEW MATERIALS
- MOLECULAR COMPUTING
- PLANET TERRAFORMING
- ETC.

ACCORDING TO THE THEORY, THIS TECHNOLOGY OFFERS ABSOLUTE CONTROL OVER THE STRUCTURE OF ALL MATTER!!
KYA HA HA!

THE CREATION OF FLAN!

HEH HEH... WITNESS THE BRILLIANCE OF MY FLAN MACHINE!
YOU JUST SHOVEL IN WATER, MUD, FISH BONES, AND WHATEVER ELSE YOU HAVE ON HAND, AND...
ザザザ
SHLOP
秘
Machine: Top Secret
IT'S A NANO-MIRACLE! THE BIRTH OF GLORIOUS FLAN!
JIGGLE
プリン
YAY!
NUMMY!!

THEN THE MACHINE WENT ON THE FRITZ.

THE ASSEMBLERS WENT COMPLETELY OUT OF CONTROL AND TRANSFORMED NOVA'S ENTIRE LAB INTO A GIANT MASS OF FLANS.
JIGGLE
プリン
JIGGLE
プリン
JIGGLE
プリン
AAAH!
RMMBB
ゴゴゴ

THE END.

YUKITO.
1993. 8. 12.

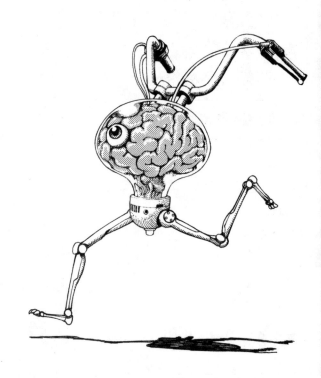

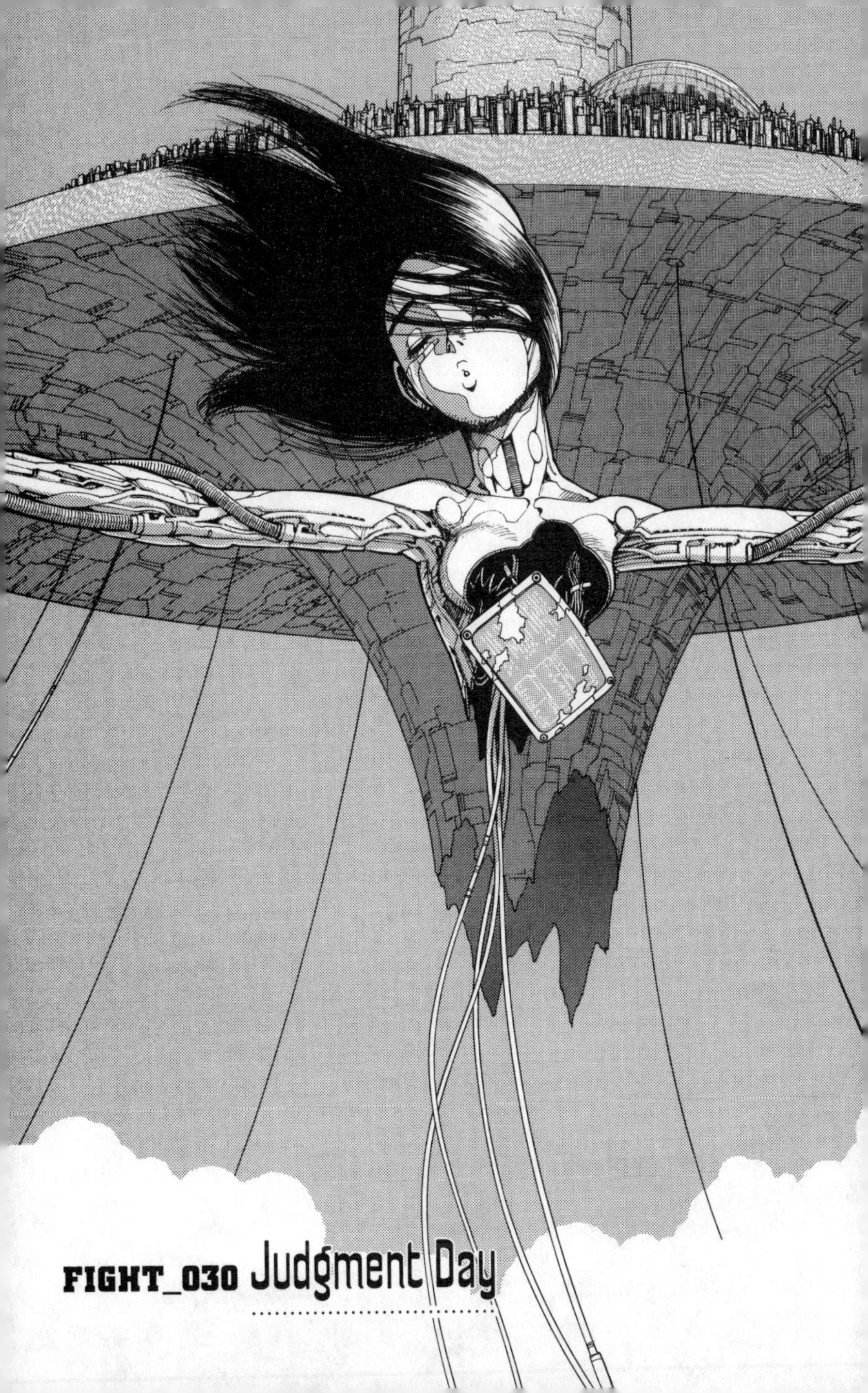
FIGHT_030 Judgment Day

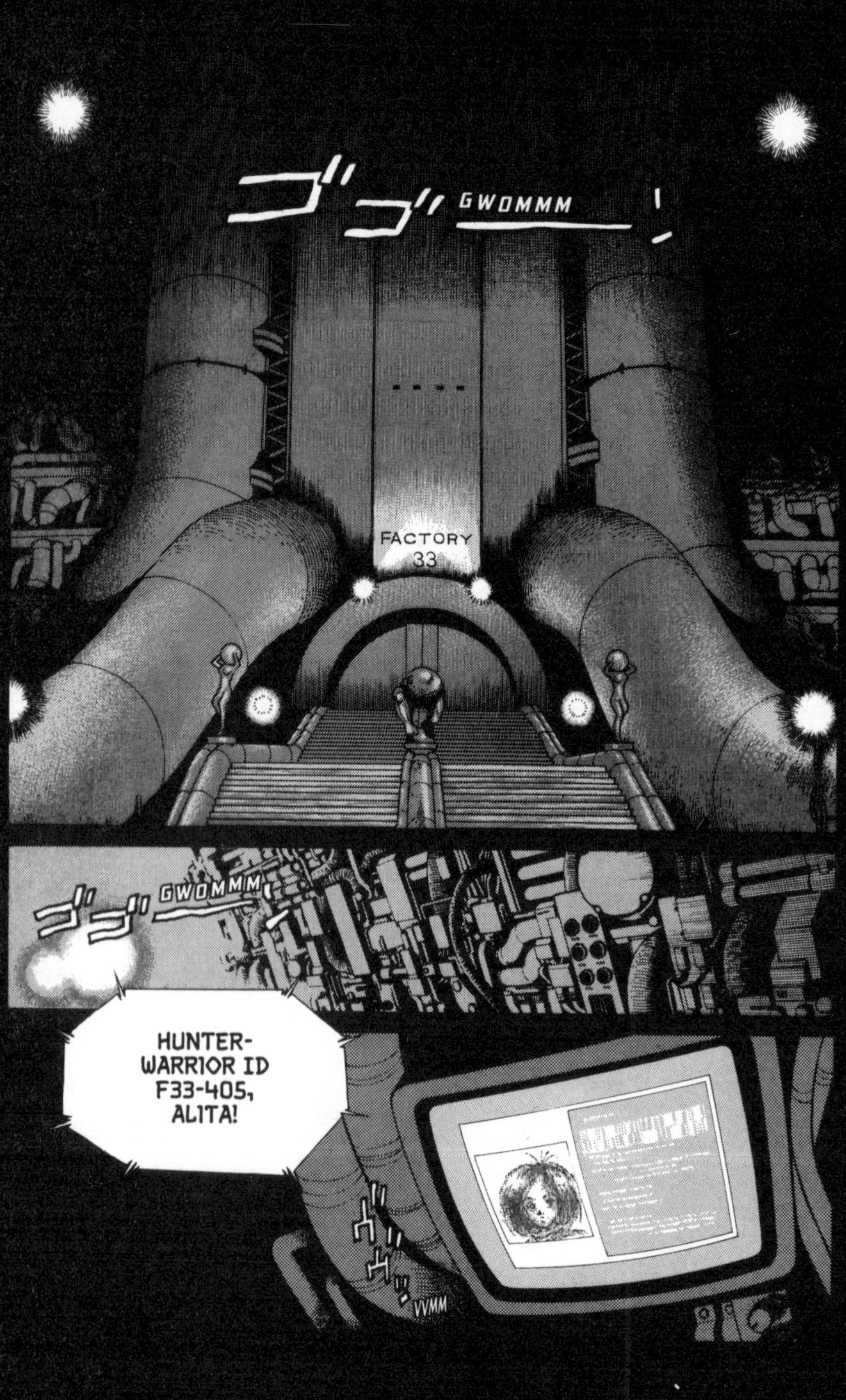
ゴゴ GWOMMM
....
FACTORY 33
ゴゴ GWOMMM
HUNTER-WARRIOR ID F33-405, ALITA!
ヴヴ VVMM

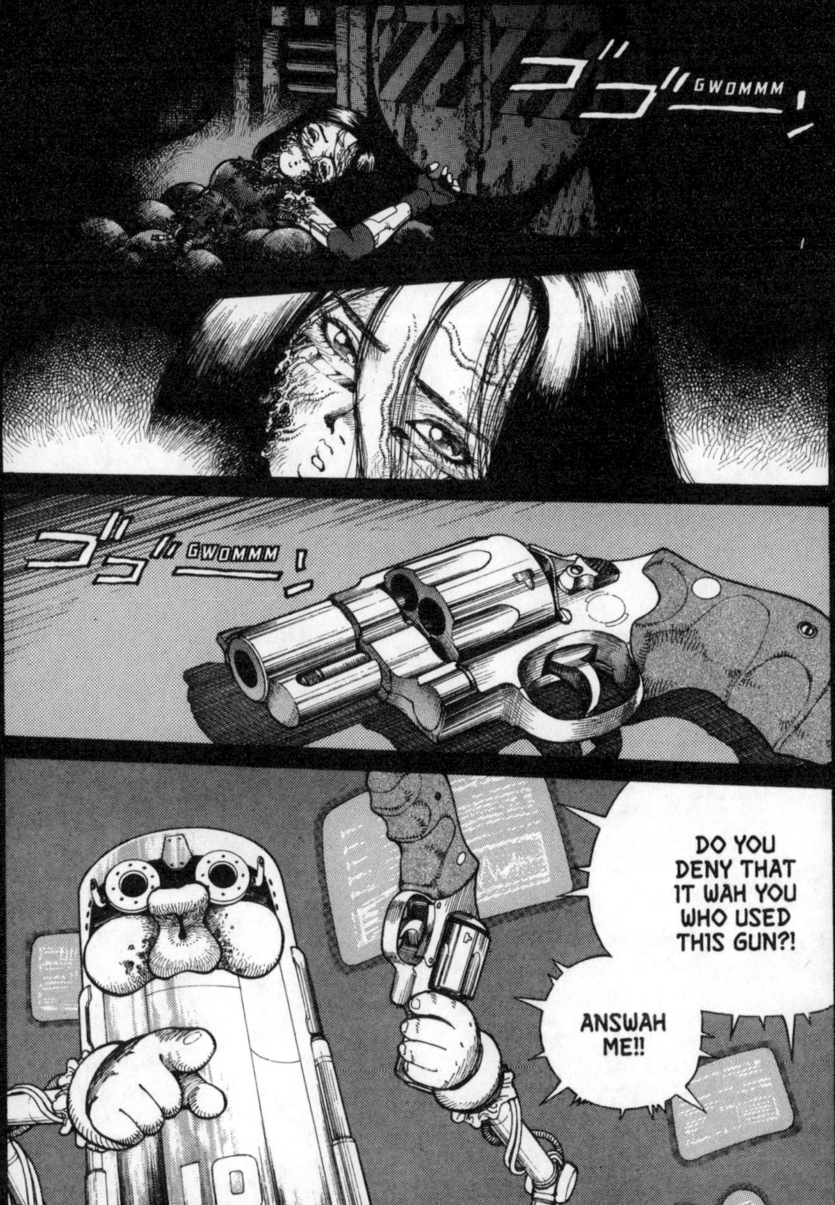
GWOMMM
GWOMMM
DO YOU DENY THAT IT WAH YOU WHO USED THIS GUN?!
ANSWAH ME!!

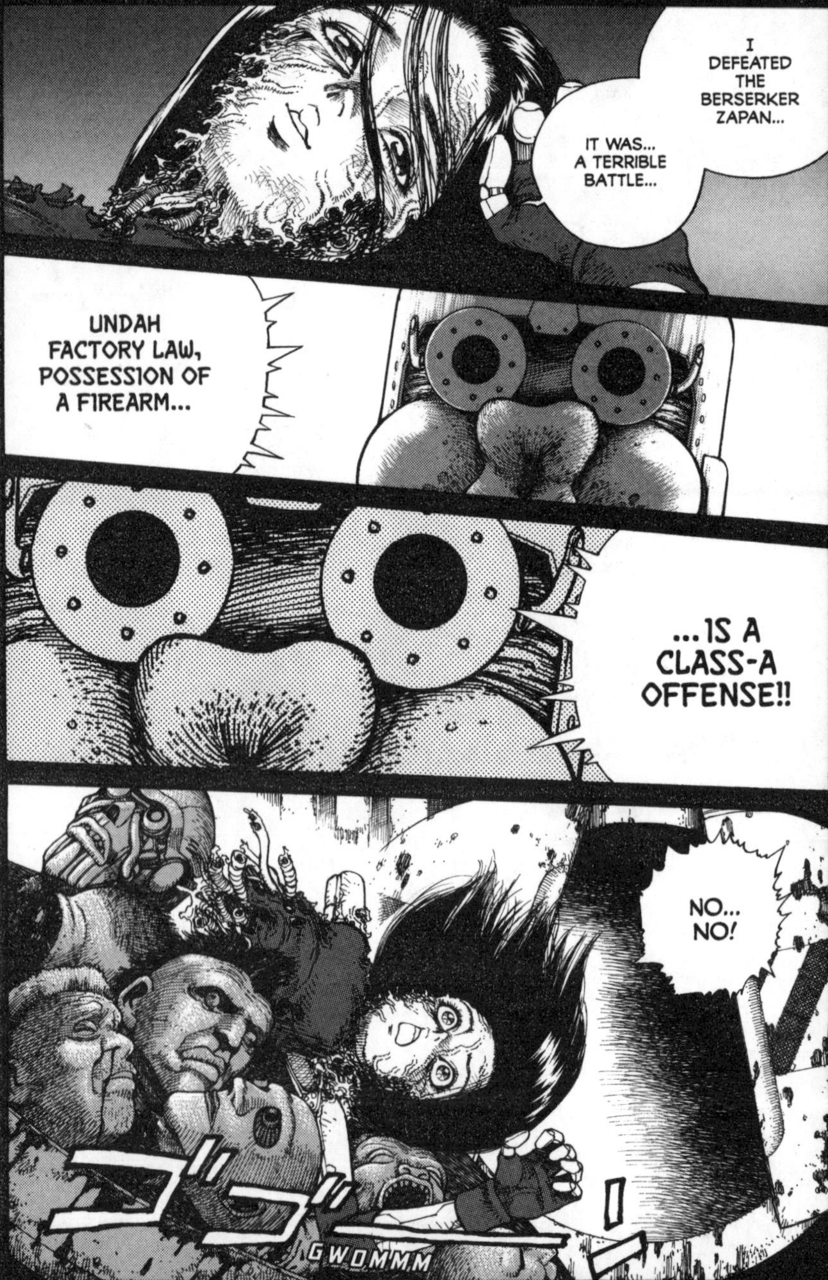
I DEFEATED THE BERSERKER ZAPAN...
IT WAS... A TERRIBLE BATTLE...
UNDAH FACTORY LAW, POSSESSION OF A FIREARM...
...IS A CLASS-A OFFENSE!!
NO... NO!
ゴゴー
GWOMMM

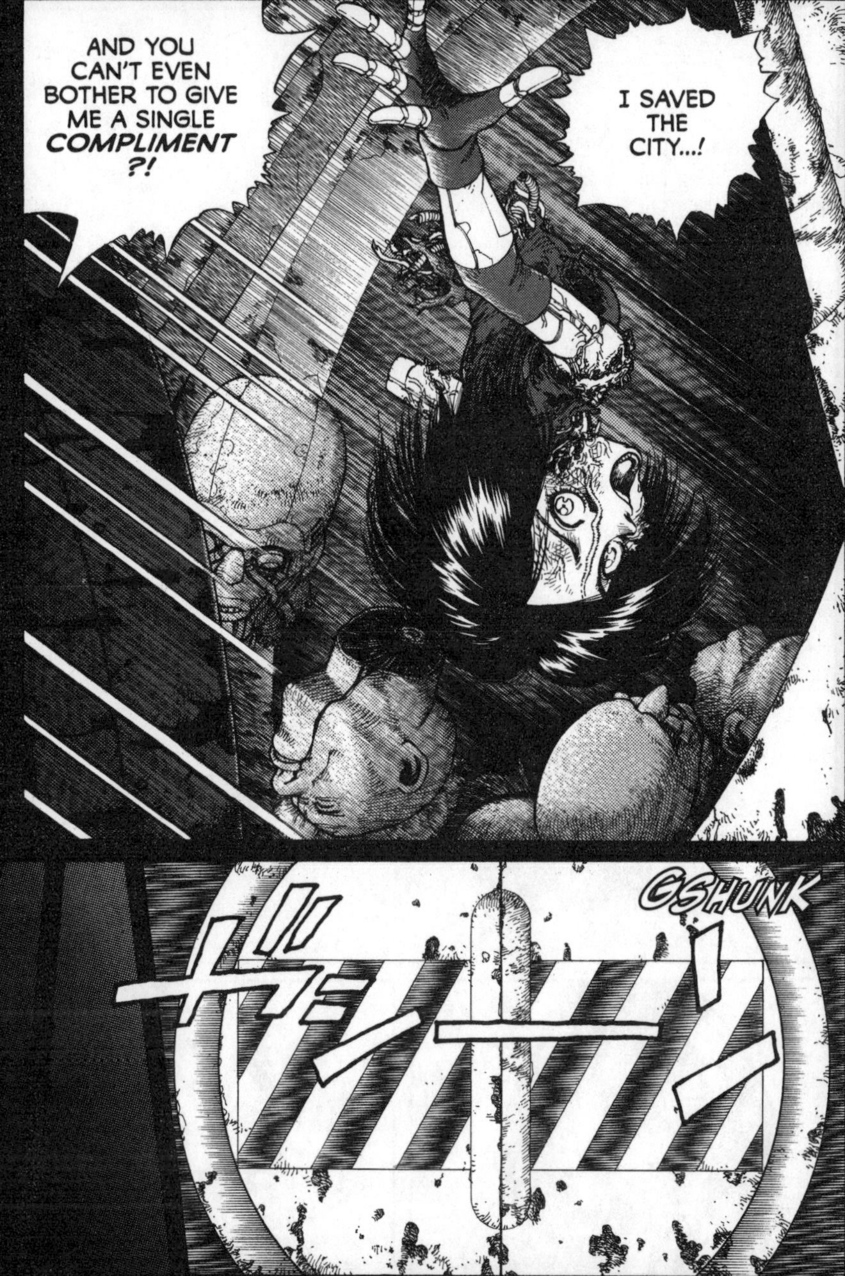
I SAVED THE CITY...!
AND YOU CAN'T EVEN BOTHER TO GIVE ME A SINGLE *COMPLIMENT* ?!
GSHUNK

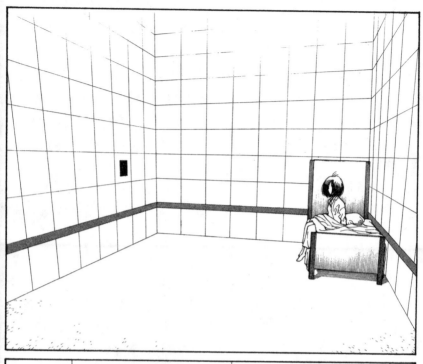

HUH...?

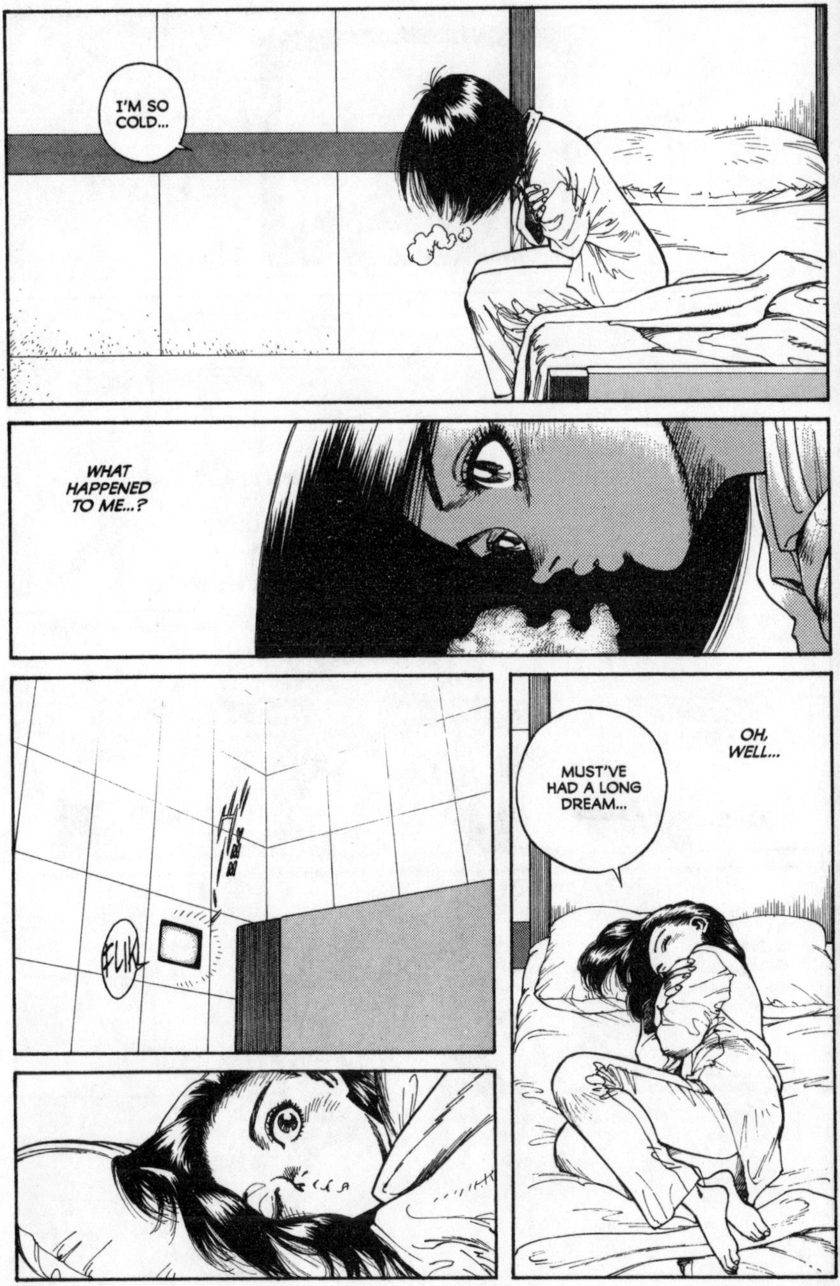
I'M SO COLD...
WHAT HAPPENED TO ME...?
OH, WELL...
MUST'VE HAD A LONG DREAM...
FLIK

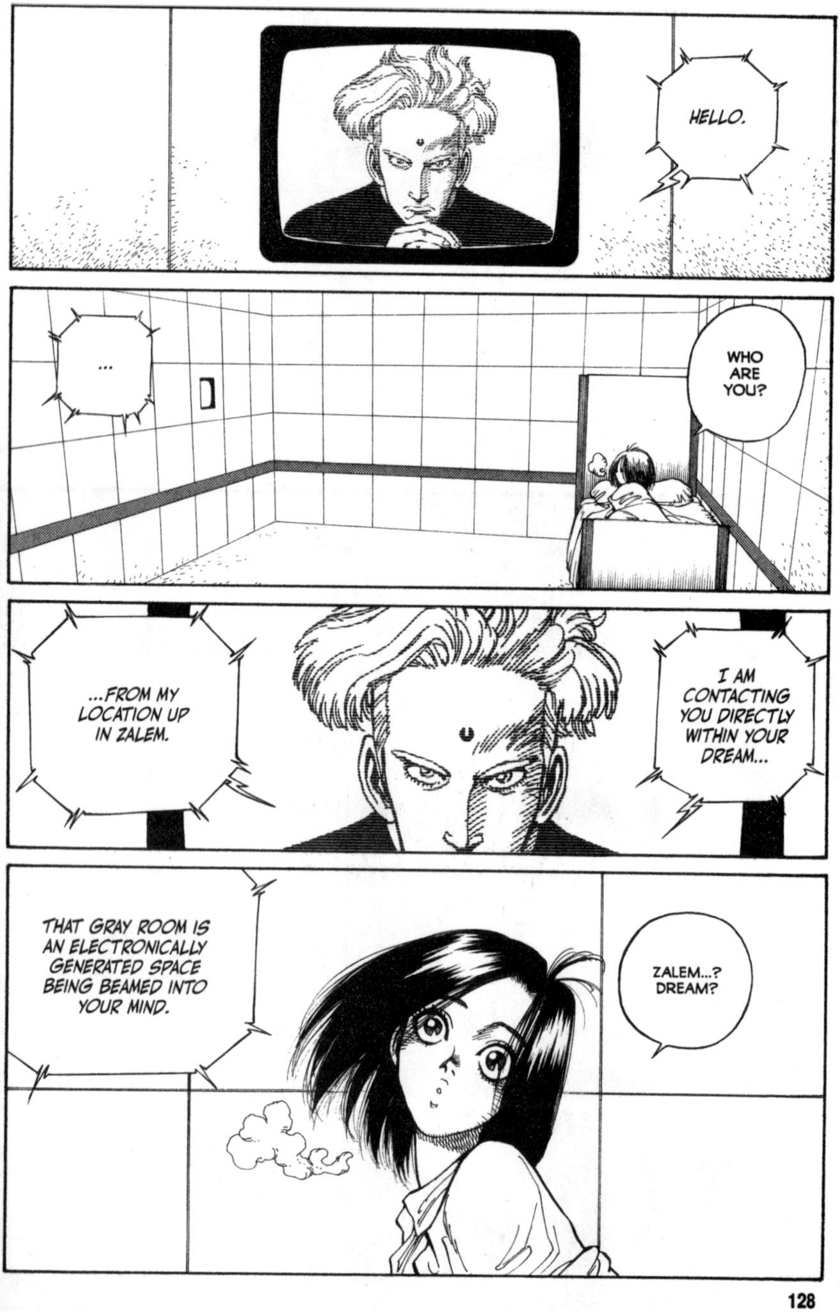
HELLO.
WHO ARE YOU?
...
I AM CONTACTING YOU DIRECTLY WITHIN YOUR DREAM...
...FROM MY LOCATION UP IN ZALEM.
ZALEM...? DREAM?
THAT GRAY ROOM IS AN ELECTRONICALLY GENERATED SPACE BEING BEAMED INTO YOUR MIND.

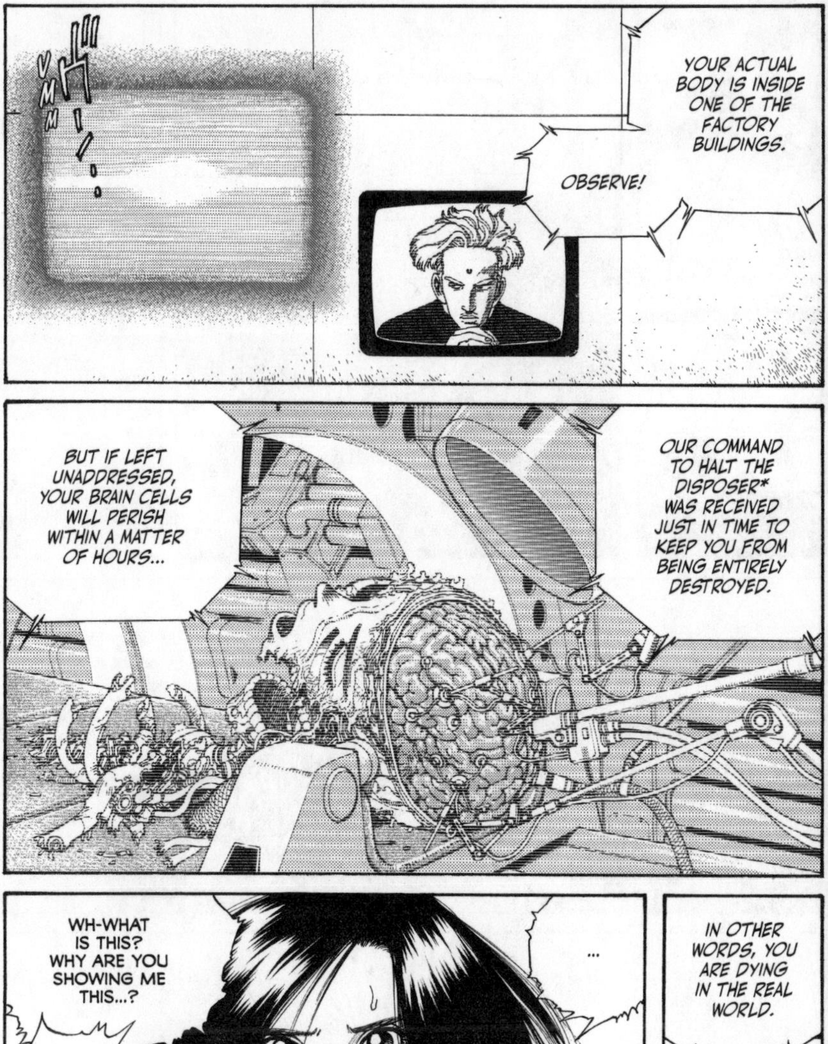
YOUR ACTUAL BODY IS INSIDE ONE OF THE FACTORY BUILDINGS.
OBSERVE!
OUR COMMAND TO HALT THE DISPOSER* WAS RECEIVED JUST IN TIME TO KEEP YOU FROM BEING ENTIRELY DESTROYED.
BUT IF LEFT UNADDRESSED, YOUR BRAIN CELLS WILL PERISH WITHIN A MATTER OF HOURS...
IN OTHER WORDS, YOU ARE DYING IN THE REAL WORLD.
...
WH-WHAT IS THIS? WHY ARE YOU SHOWING ME THIS...?
WHAT DO YOU WANT?!

***Disposer:** An electric waste-disposal machine that crushes garbage and flushes it into the sewers.

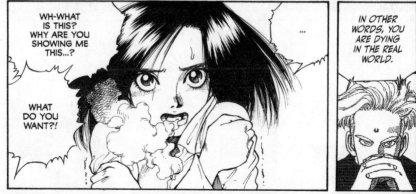

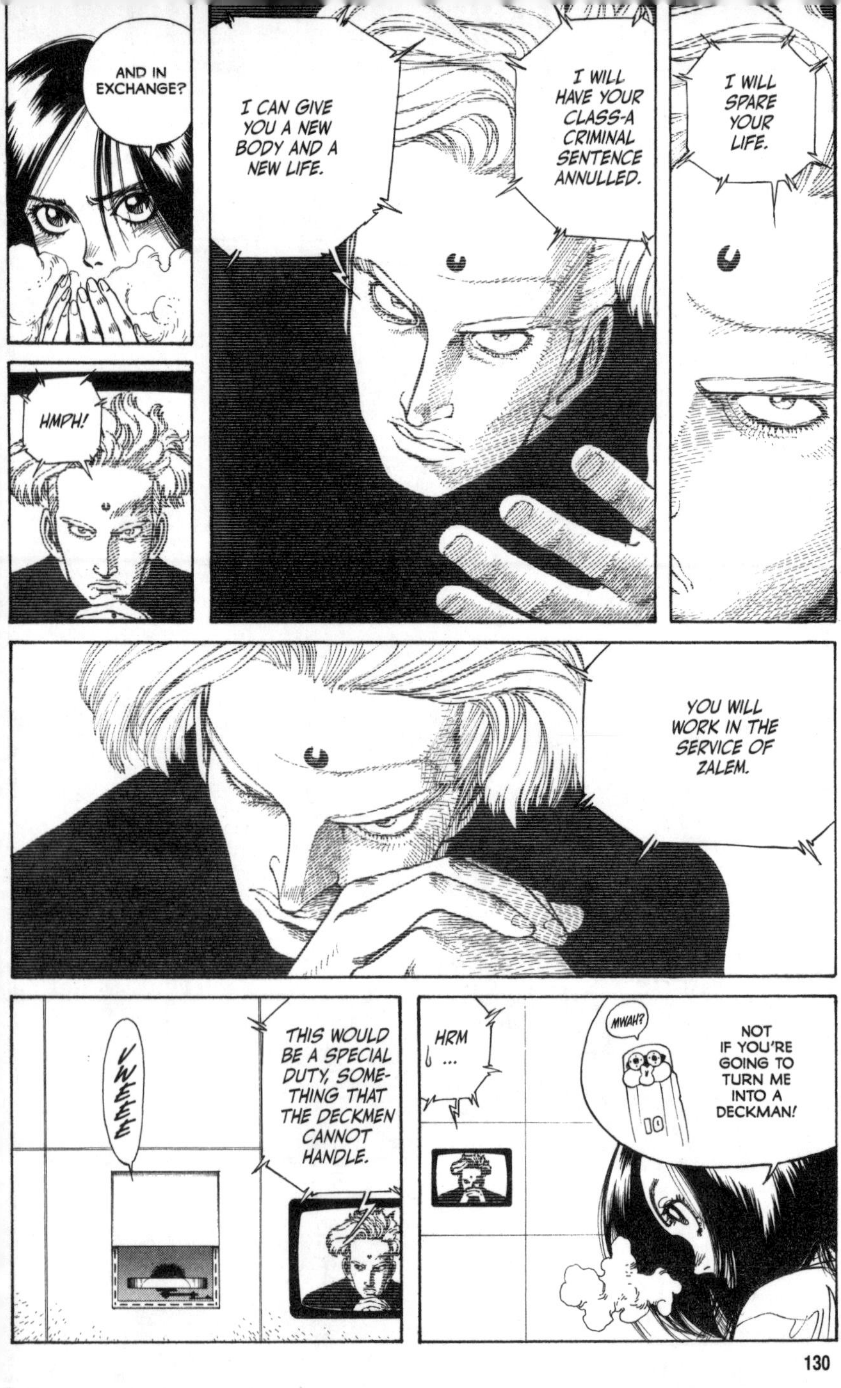
I WILL SPARE YOUR LIFE.
I WILL HAVE YOUR CLASS-A CRIMINAL SENTENCE ANNULLED.
I CAN GIVE YOU A NEW BODY AND A NEW LIFE.
AND IN EXCHANGE?
HMPH!
YOU WILL WORK IN THE SERVICE OF ZALEM.
NOT IF YOU'RE GOING TO TURN ME INTO A DECKMAN!
MWAH?
HRM ...
THIS WOULD BE A SPECIAL DUTY, SOMETHING THAT THE DECKMEN CANNOT HANDLE.
VWEEE

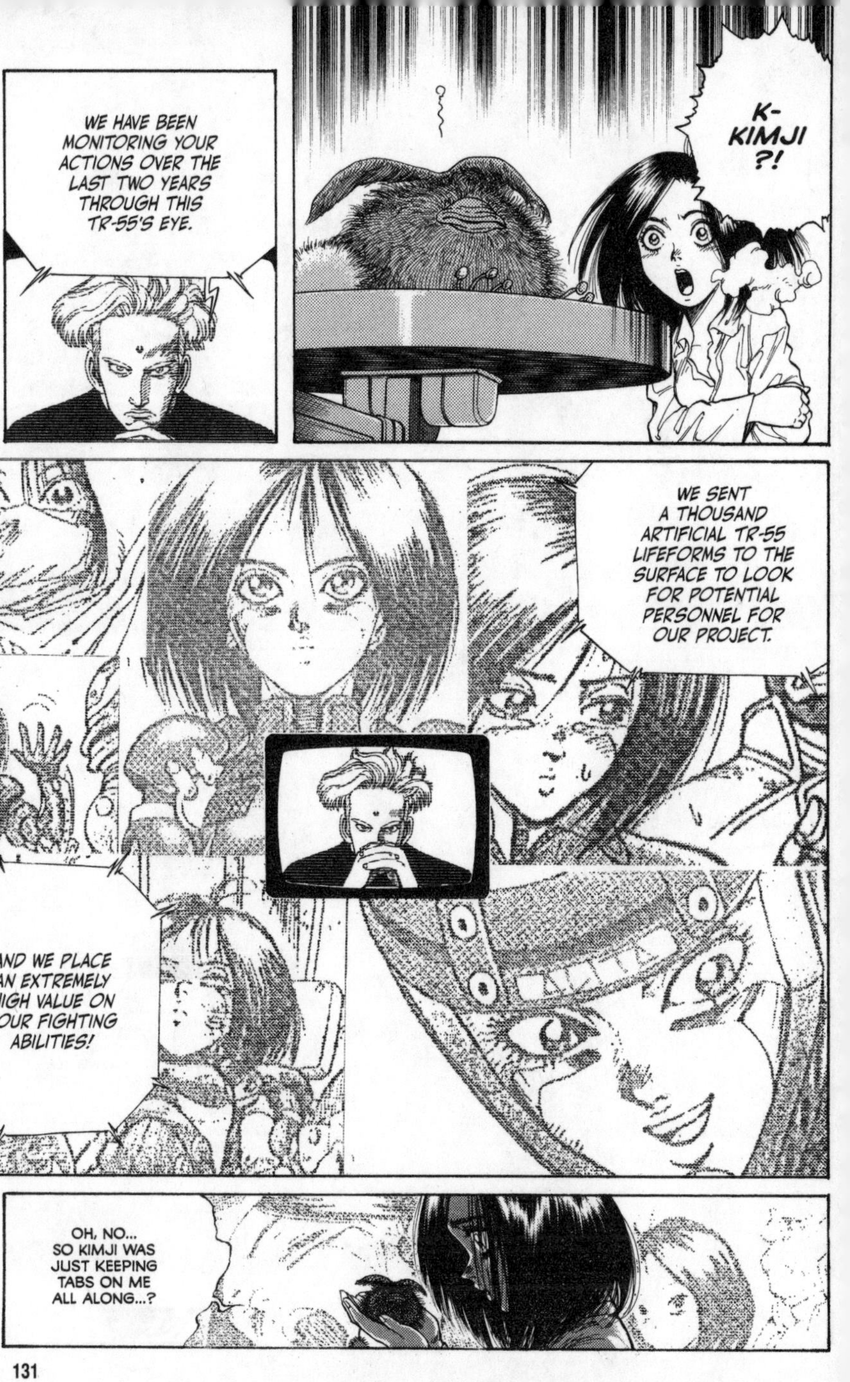

K-KIMJI ?!
WE HAVE BEEN MONITORING YOUR ACTIONS OVER THE LAST TWO YEARS THROUGH THIS TR-55'S EYE.
WE SENT A THOUSAND ARTIFICIAL TR-55 LIFEFORMS TO THE SURFACE TO LOOK FOR POTENTIAL PERSONNEL FOR OUR PROJECT.
AND WE PLACE AN EXTREMELY HIGH VALUE ON YOUR FIGHTING ABILITIES!
OH, NO... SO KIMJI WAS JUST KEEPING TABS ON ME ALL ALONG...?

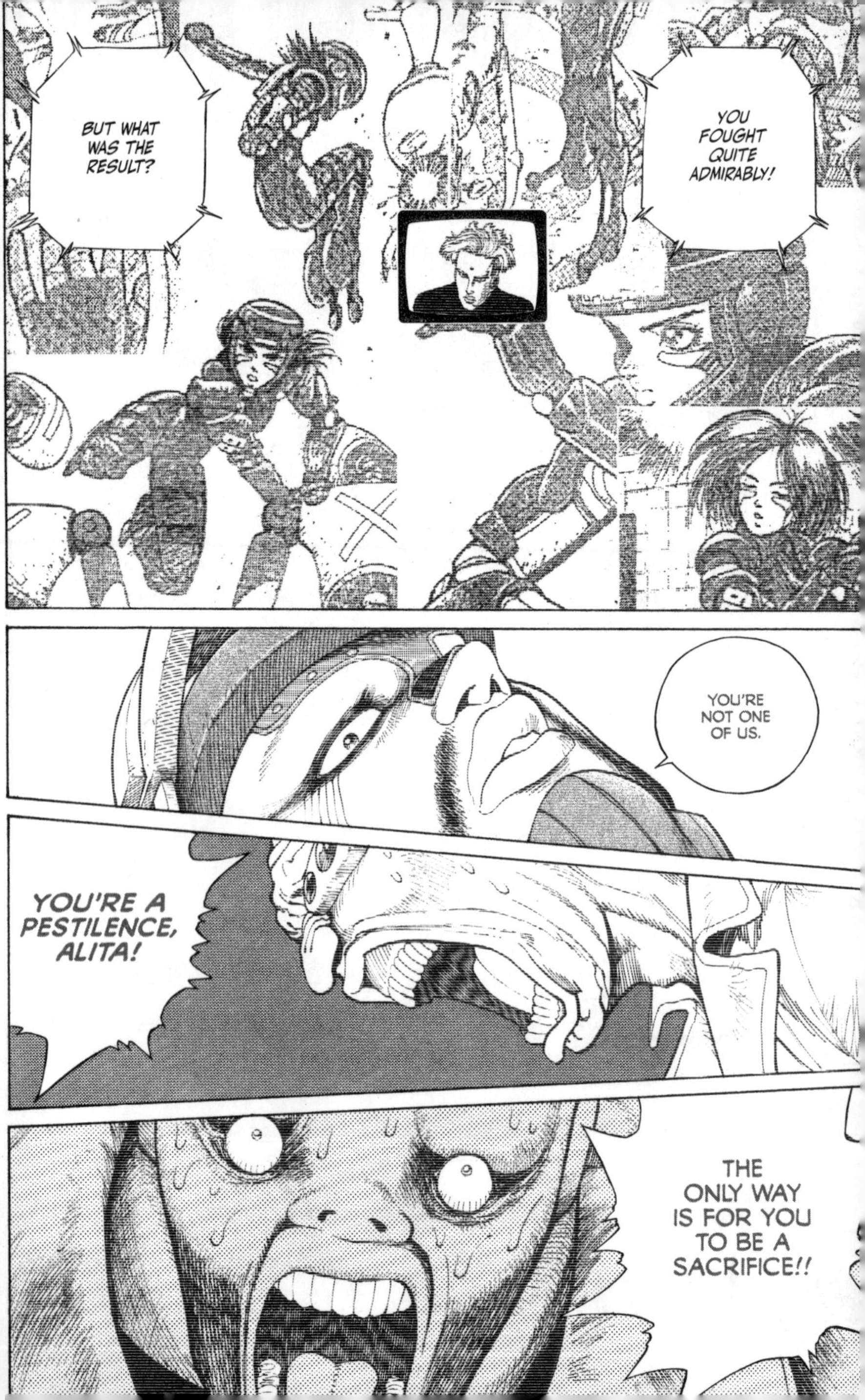
YOU FOUGHT QUITE ADMIRABLY!
BUT WHAT WAS THE RESULT?
YOU'RE NOT ONE OF US.
YOU'RE A PESTILENCE, ALITA!
THE ONLY WAY IS FOR YOU TO BE A SACRIFICE!!

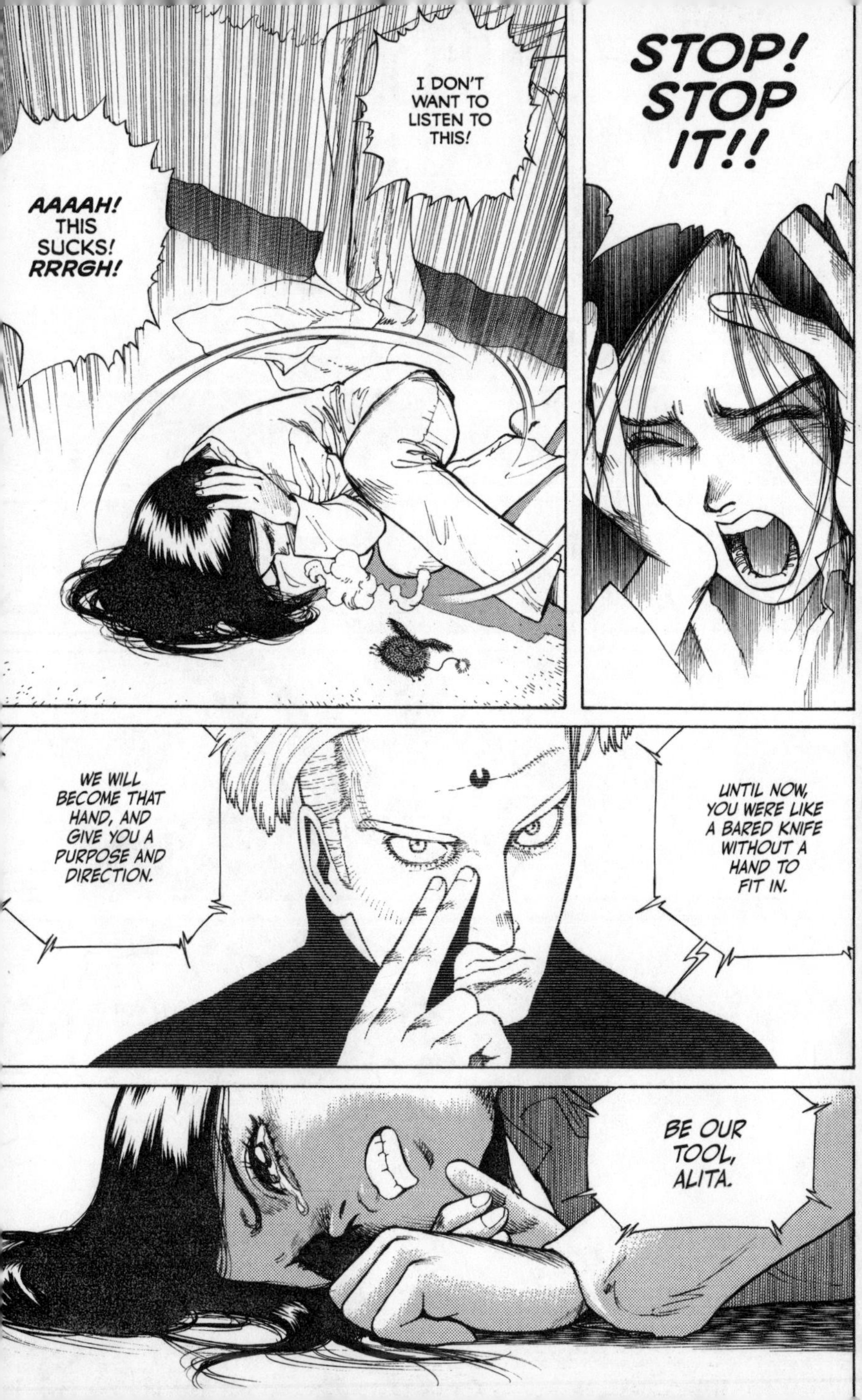
STOP! STOP IT!!
I DON'T WANT TO LISTEN TO THIS!
AAAAH! THIS SUCKS! RRRGH!
UNTIL NOW, YOU WERE LIKE A BARED KNIFE WITHOUT A HAND TO FIT IN.
WE WILL BECOME THAT HAND, AND GIVE YOU A PURPOSE AND DIRECTION.
BE OUR TOOL, ALITA.

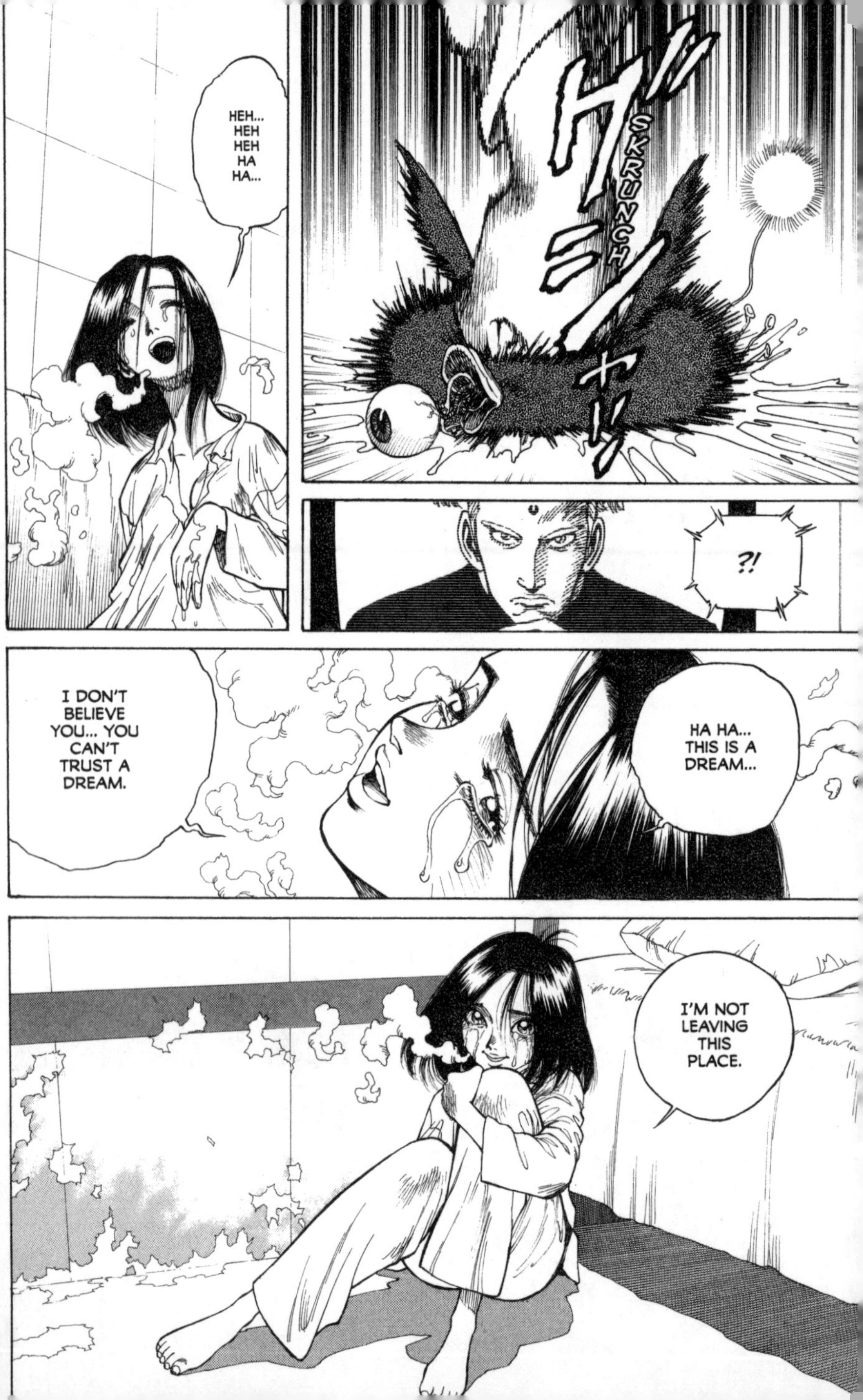
SKRUNCH
?!
HEH... HEH HEH HA HA...
HA HA... THIS IS A DREAM...
I DON'T BELIEVE YOU... YOU CAN'T TRUST A DREAM.
I'M NOT LEAVING THIS PLACE.

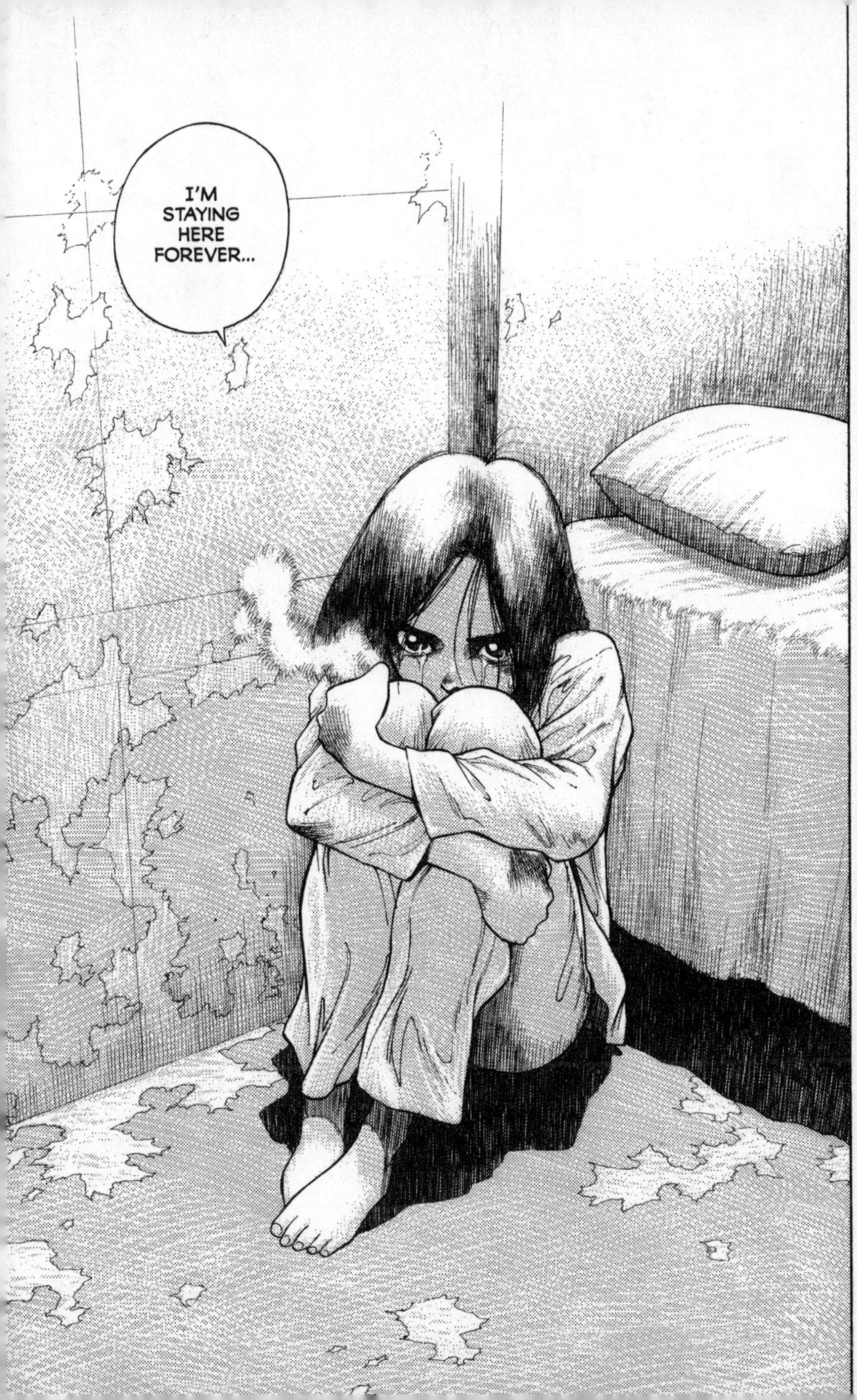
I'M STAYING HERE FOREVER...

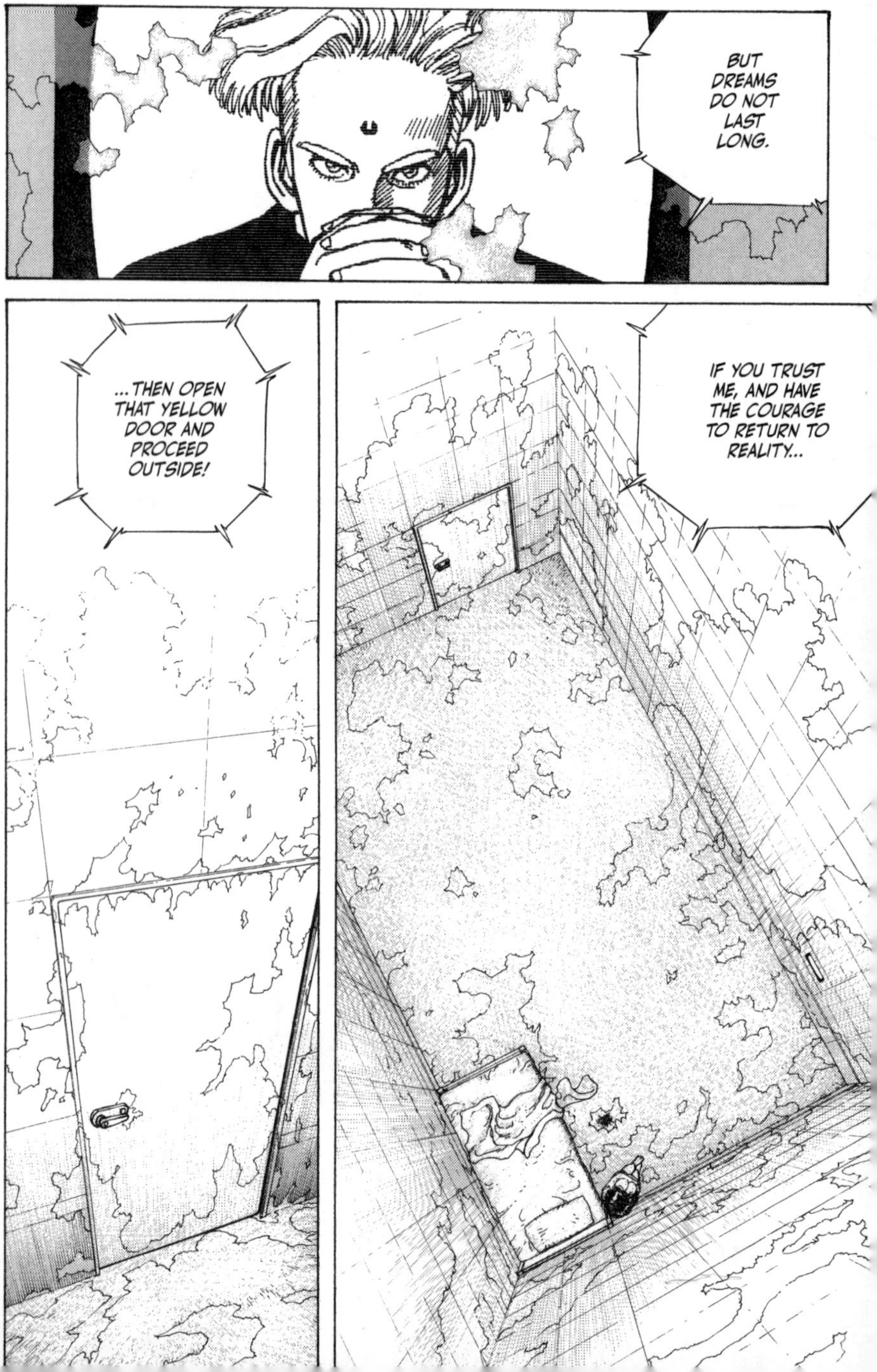
BUT DREAMS DO NOT LAST LONG.
IF YOU TRUST ME, AND HAVE THE COURAGE TO RETURN TO REALITY...
...THEN OPEN THAT YELLOW DOOR AND PROCEED OUTSIDE!

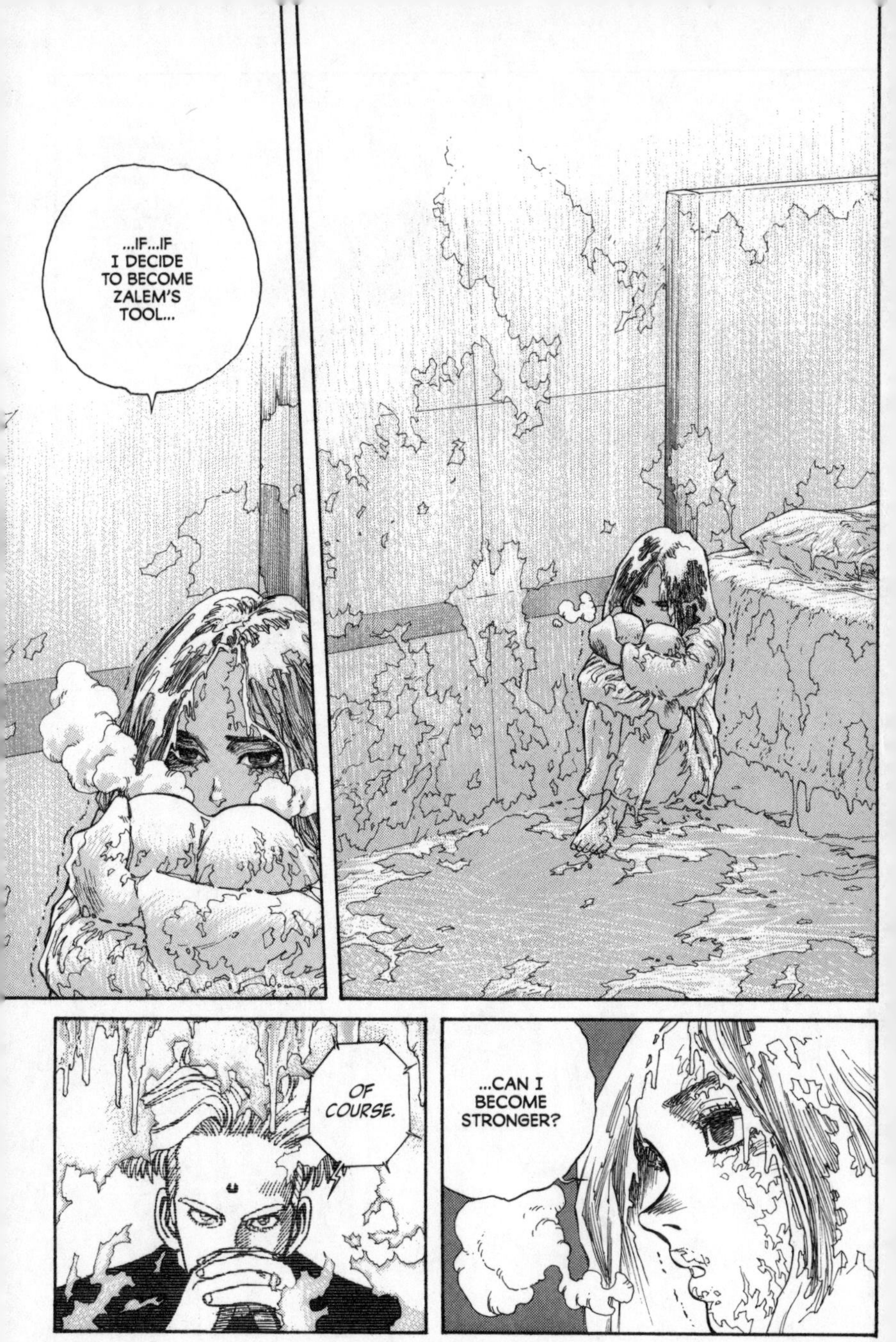
...IF...IF I DECIDE TO BECOME ZALEM'S TOOL...
...CAN I BECOME STRONGER?
OF COURSE.

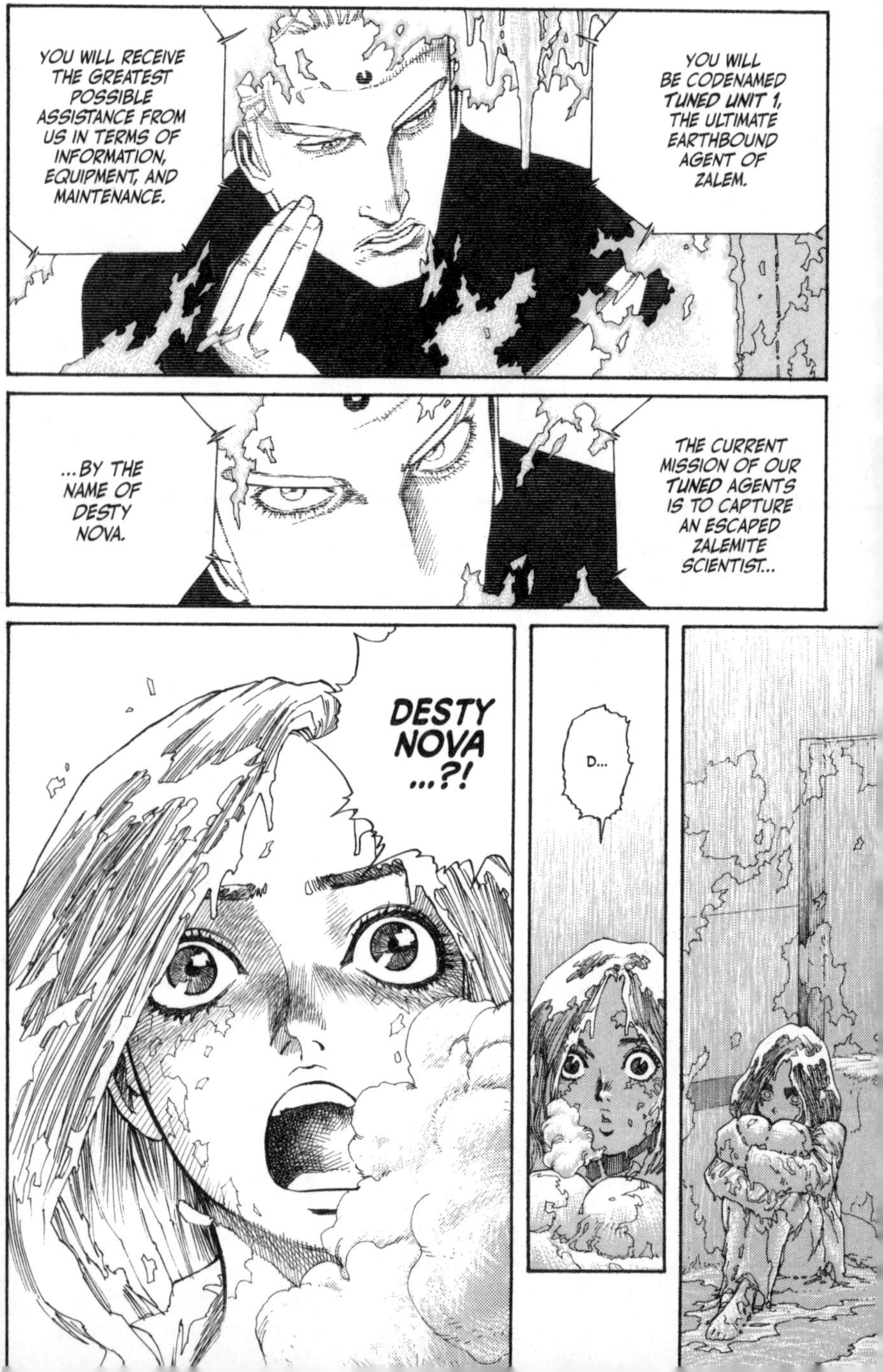
YOU WILL BE CODENAMED TUNED UNIT 1, THE ULTIMATE EARTHBOUND AGENT OF ZALEM.
YOU WILL RECEIVE THE GREATEST POSSIBLE ASSISTANCE FROM US IN TERMS OF INFORMATION, EQUIPMENT, AND MAINTENANCE.
THE CURRENT MISSION OF OUR TUNED AGENTS IS TO CAPTURE AN ESCAPED ZALEMITE SCIENTIST...
...BY THE NAME OF DESTY NOVA.
D...
DESTY NOVA ...?!

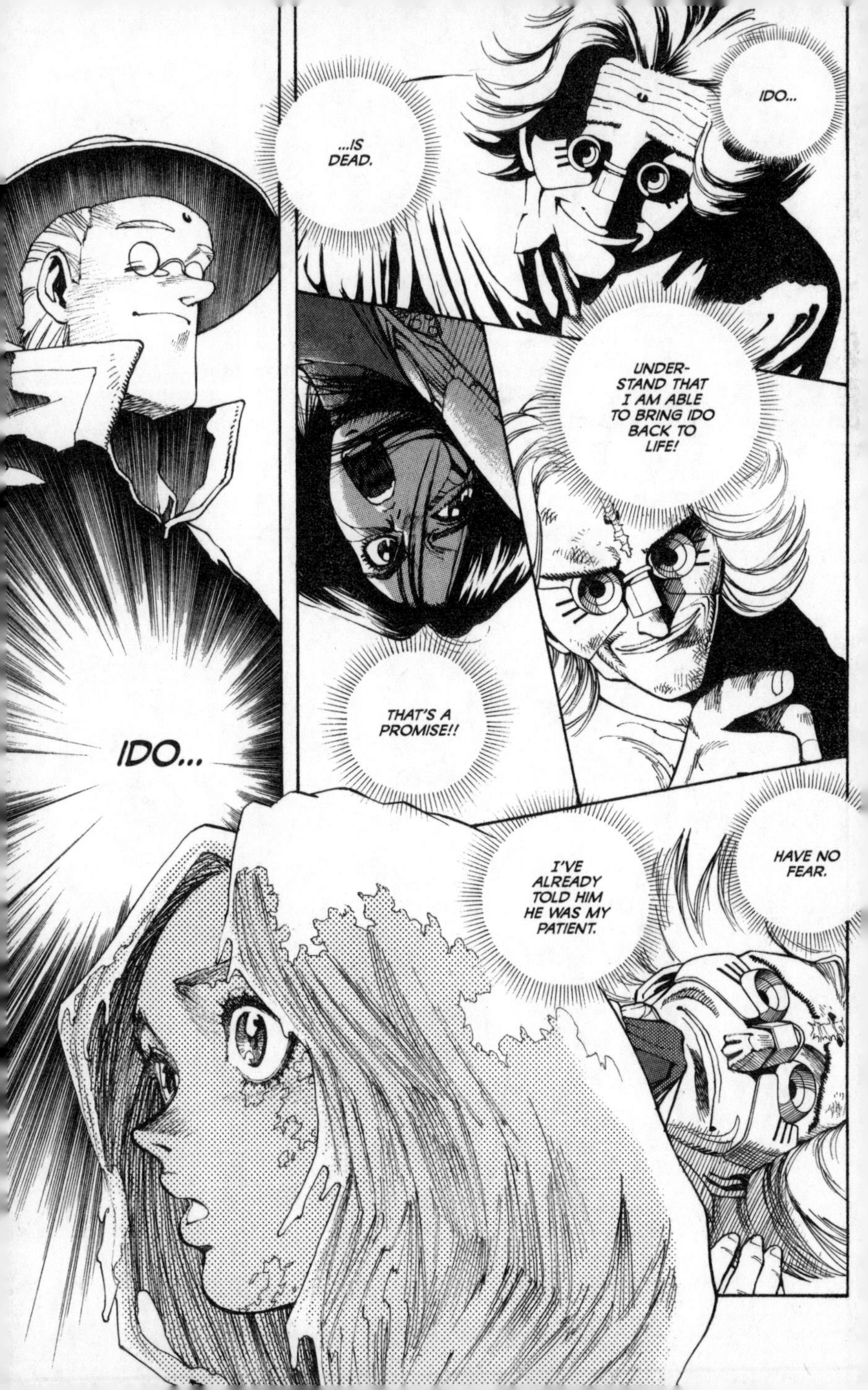
IDO...
...IS DEAD.
UNDER-STAND THAT I AM ABLE TO BRING IDO BACK TO LIFE!
THAT'S A PROMISE!!
IDO...
HAVE NO FEAR.
I'VE ALREADY TOLD HIM HE WAS MY PATIENT.

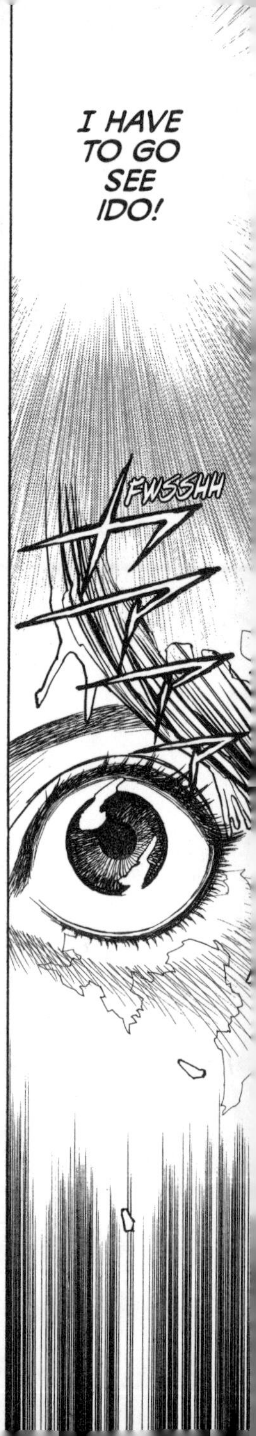
I HAVE TO GO SEE IDO!
FWSSHH
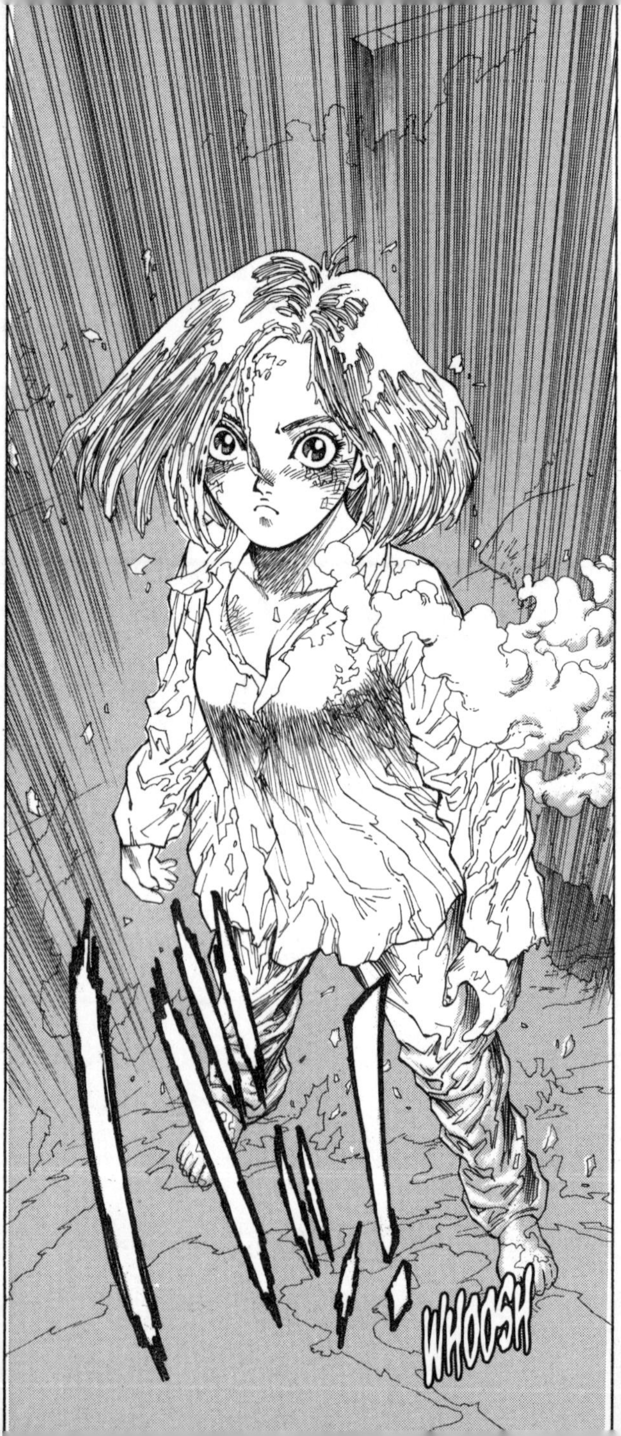
WHOOSH

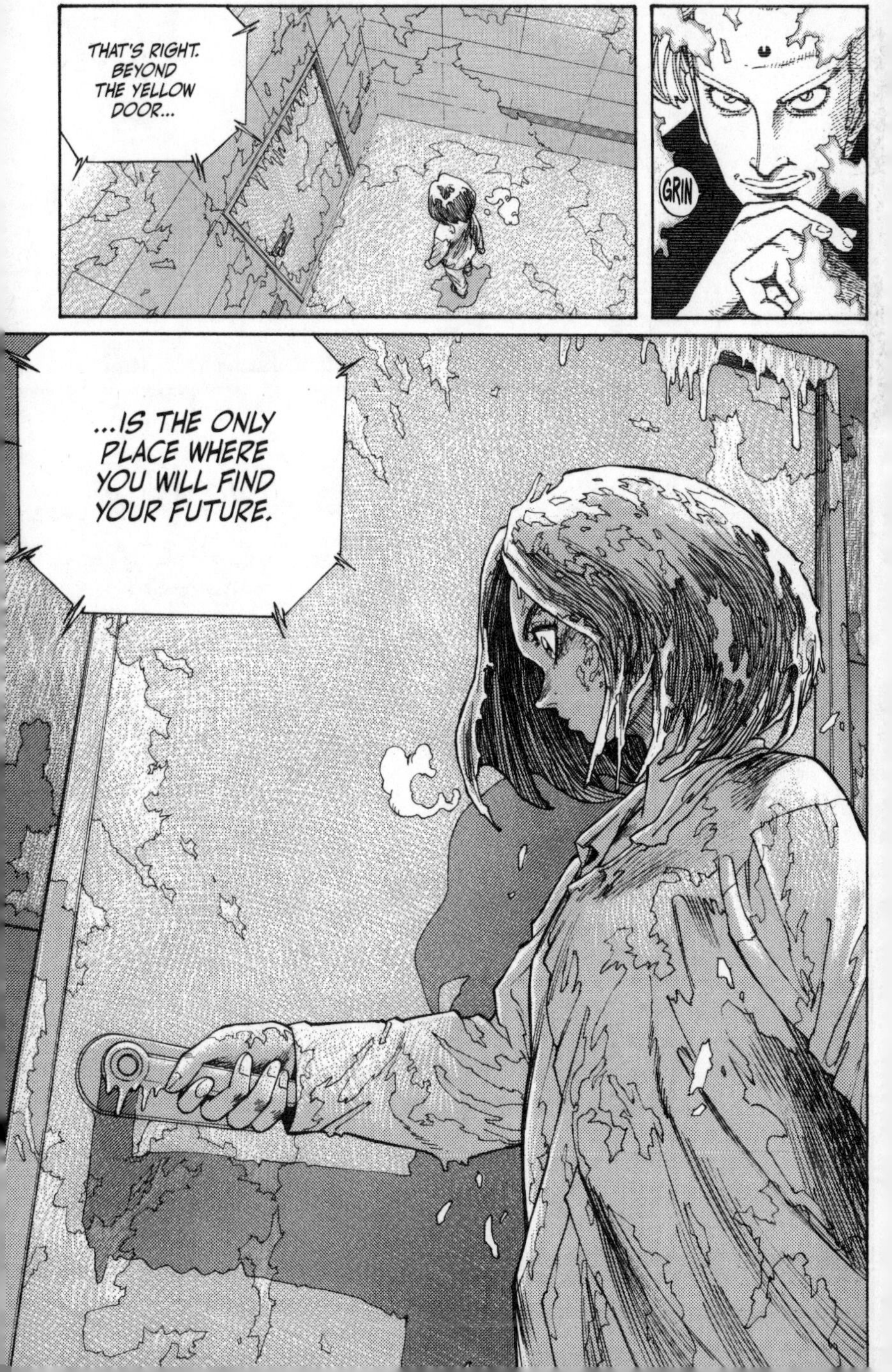
GRIN
THAT'S RIGHT. BEYOND THE YELLOW DOOR...
...IS THE ONLY PLACE WHERE YOU WILL FIND YOUR FUTURE.

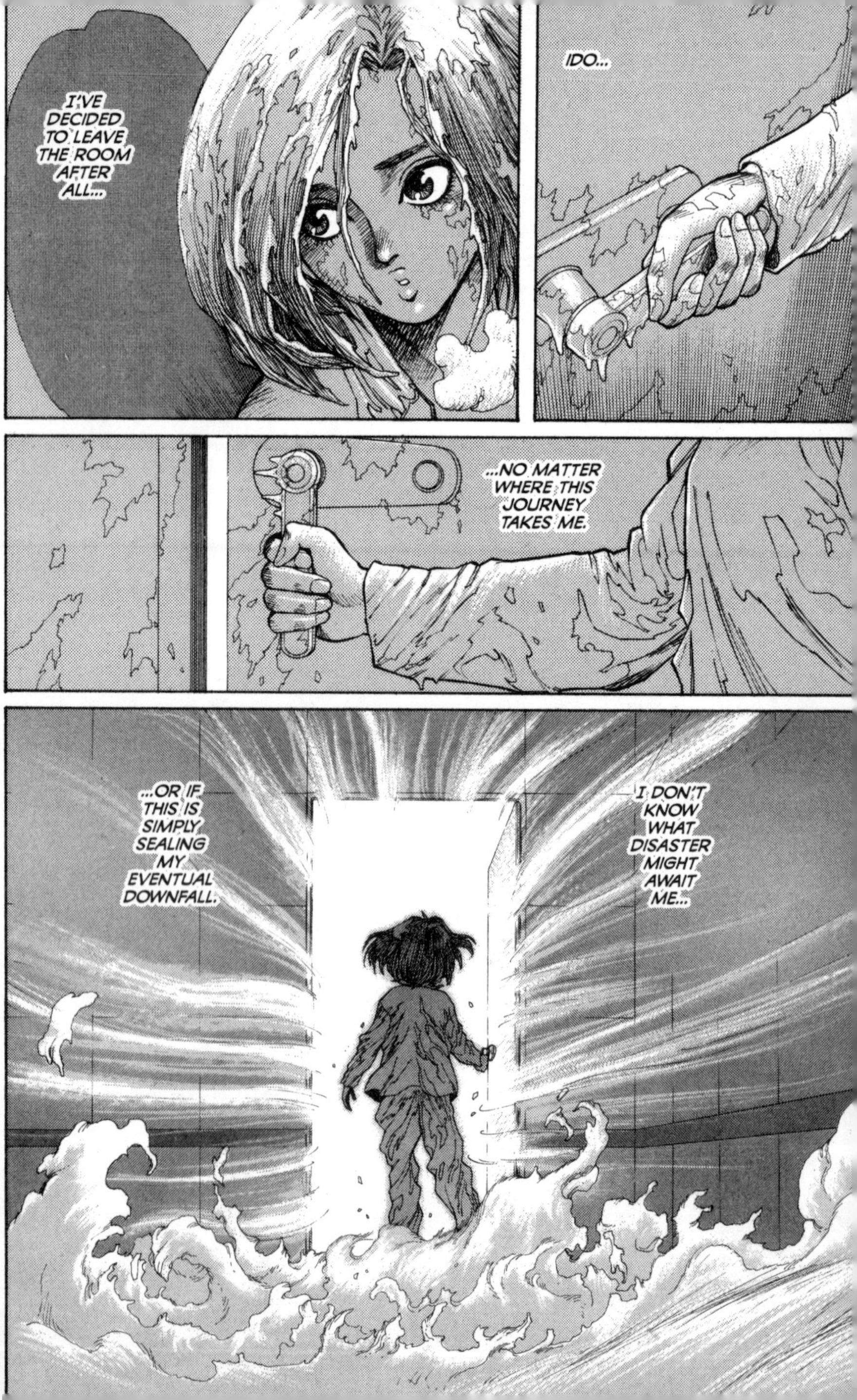
IDO...
I'VE DECIDED TO LEAVE THE ROOM AFTER ALL...
...NO MATTER WHERE THIS JOURNEY TAKES ME.
I DON'T KNOW WHAT DISASTER MIGHT AWAIT ME...
...OR IF THIS IS SIMPLY SEALING MY EVENTUAL DOWNFALL.

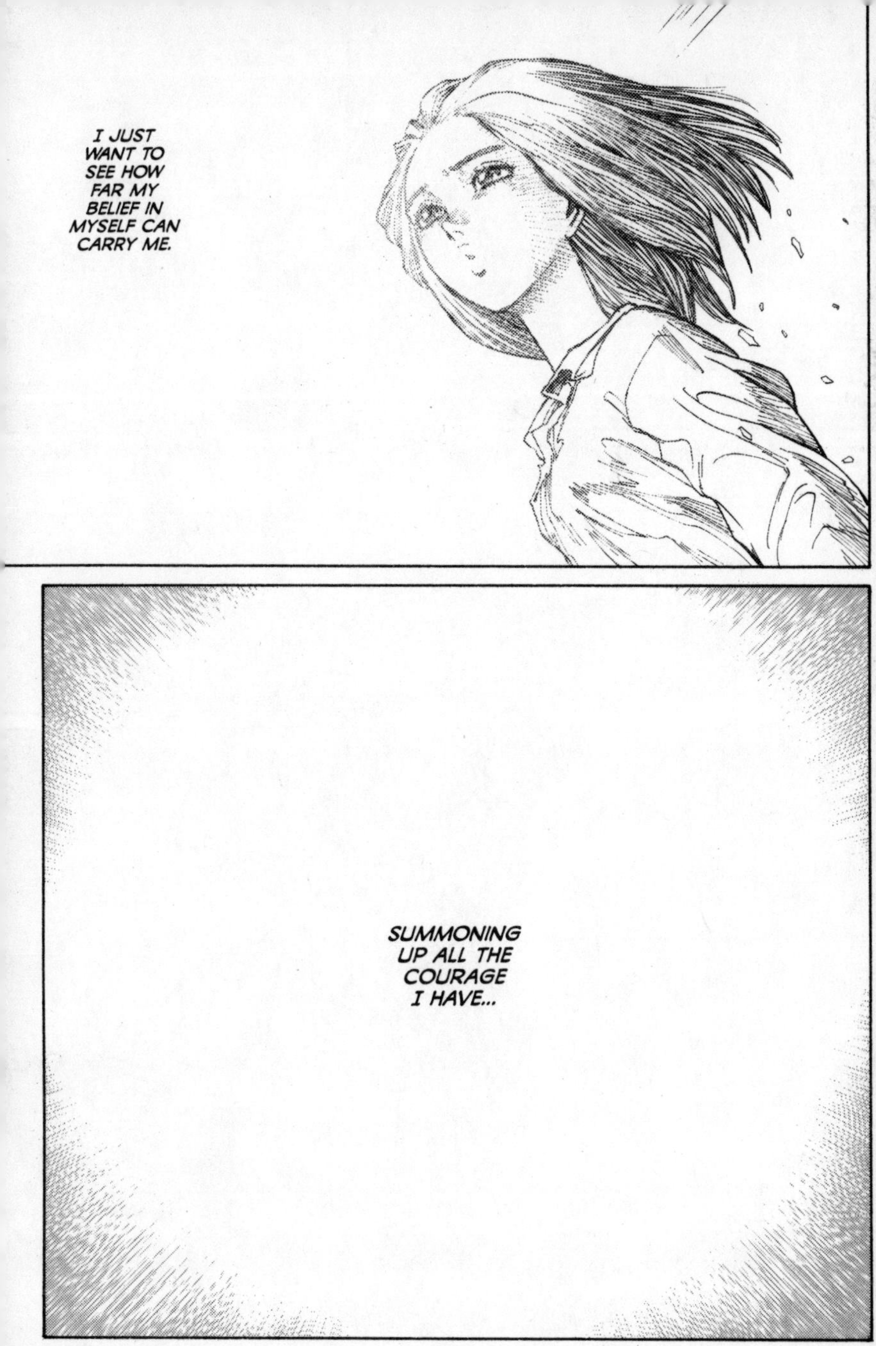
I JUST WANT TO SEE HOW FAR MY BELIEF IN MYSELF CAN CARRY ME.
SUMMONING UP ALL THE COURAGE I HAVE...

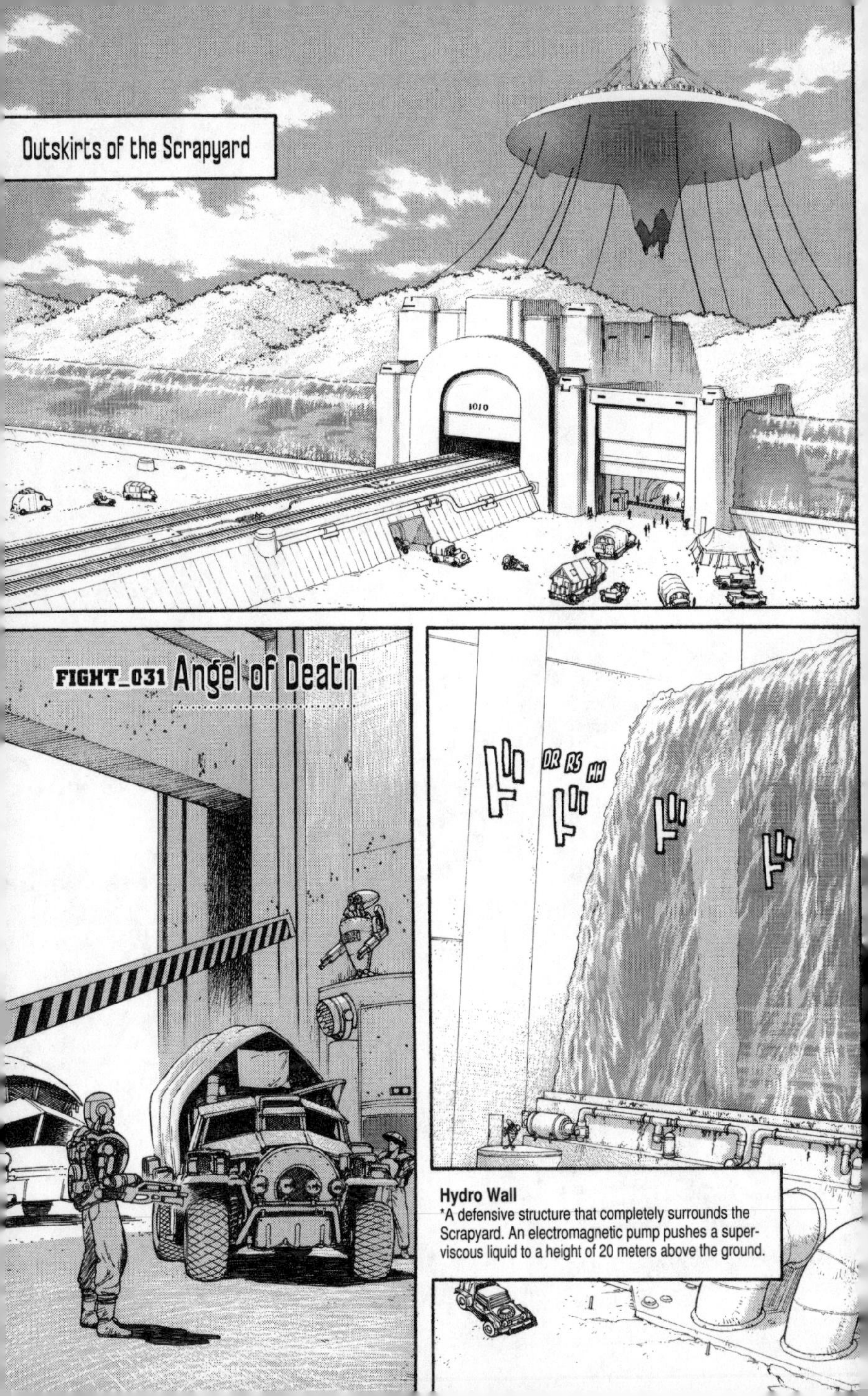
Outskirts of the Scrapyard
1010
ド
ド
DRRSHH
ド
ド
Hydro Wall
*A defensive structure that completely surrounds the Scrapyard. An electromagnetic pump pushes a super-viscous liquid to a height of 20 meters above the ground.
FIGHT_031 Angel of Death

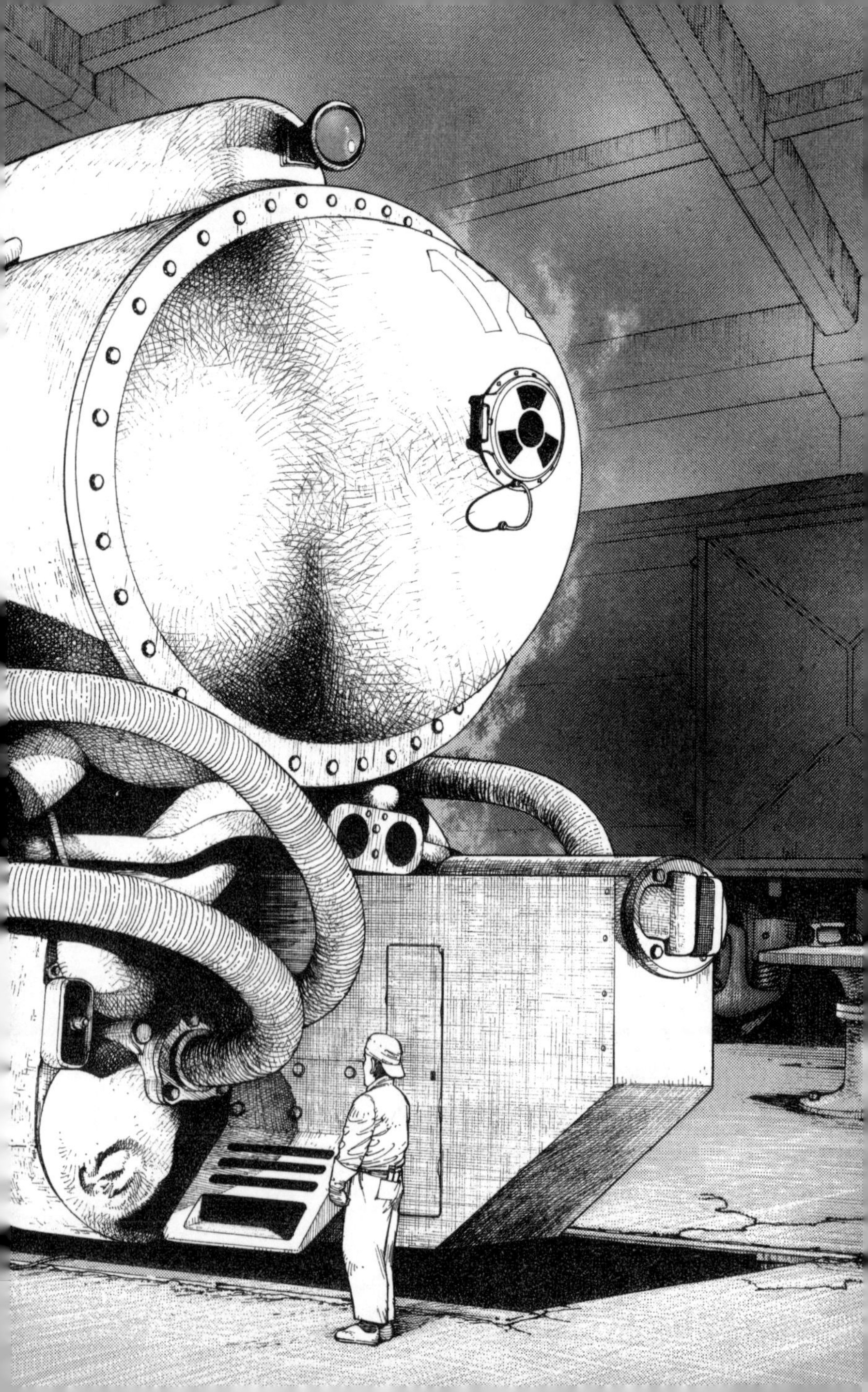

FIGHT_031 Angel of Death

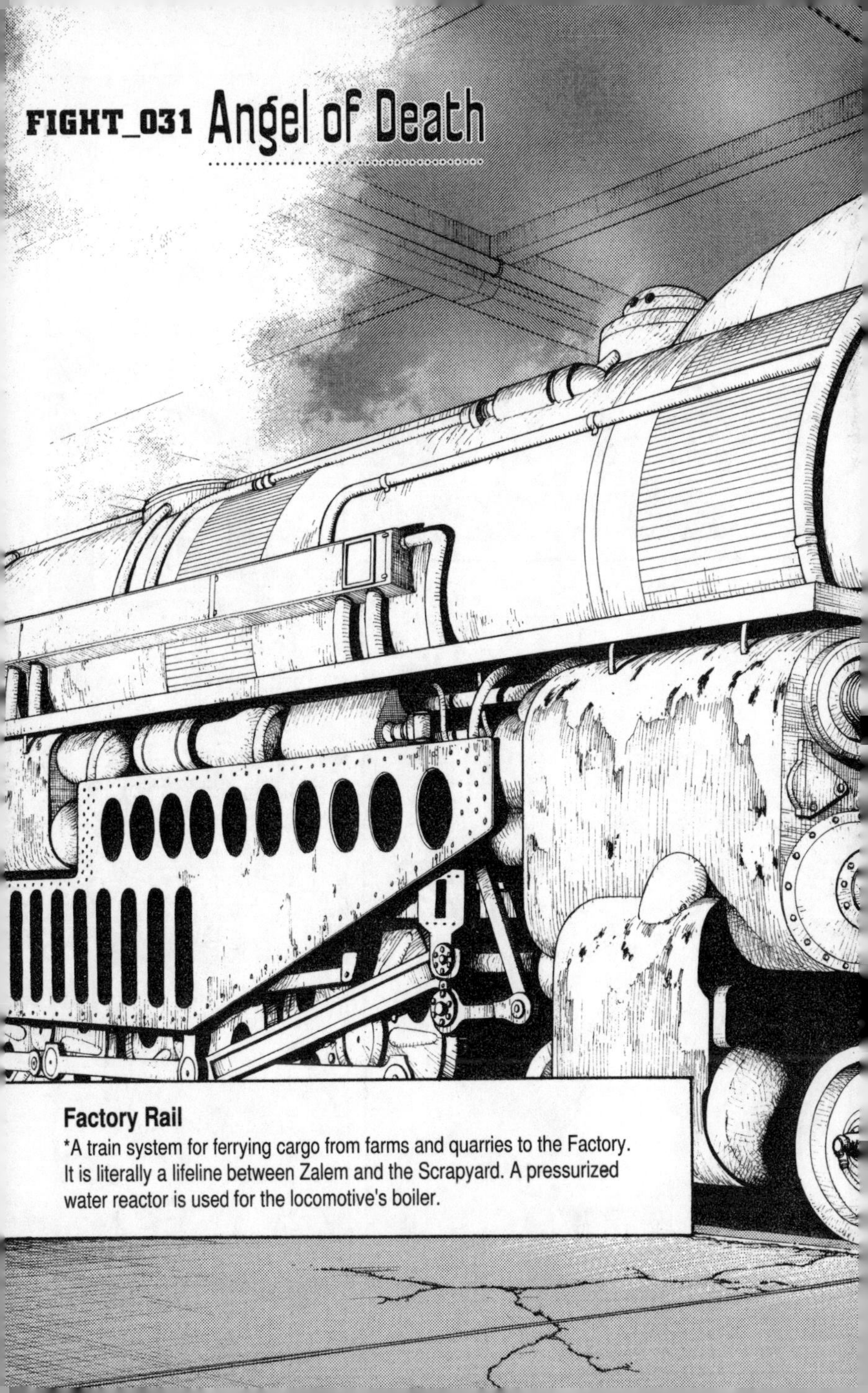
Factory Rail
*A train system for ferrying cargo from farms and quarries to the Factory. It is literally a lifeline between Zalem and the Scrapyard. A pressurized water reactor is used for the locomotive's boiler.

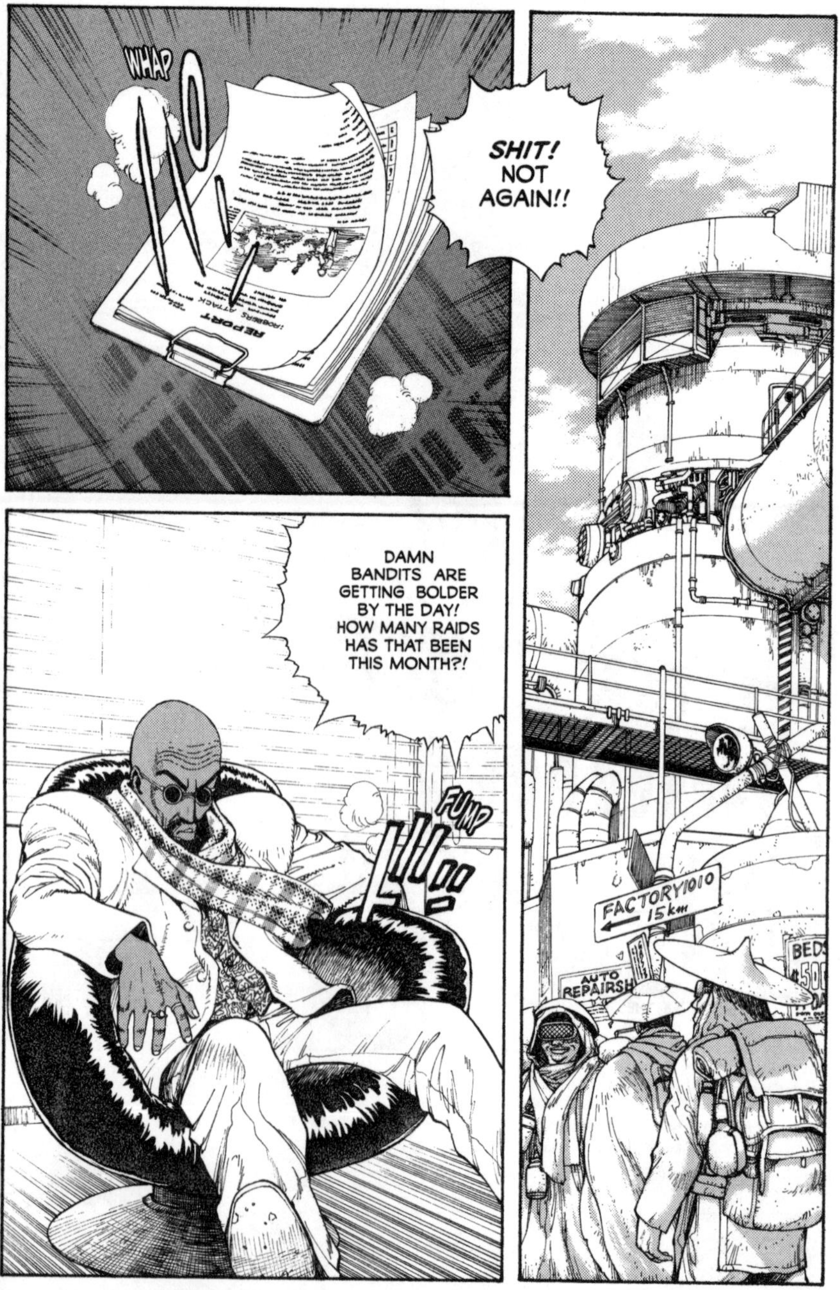

SHIT! NOT AGAIN!!
FACTORY1010
15km
WHAP
DAMN BANDITS ARE GETTING BOLDER BY THE DAY! HOW MANY RAIDS HAS THAT BEEN THIS MONTH?!
FUMP

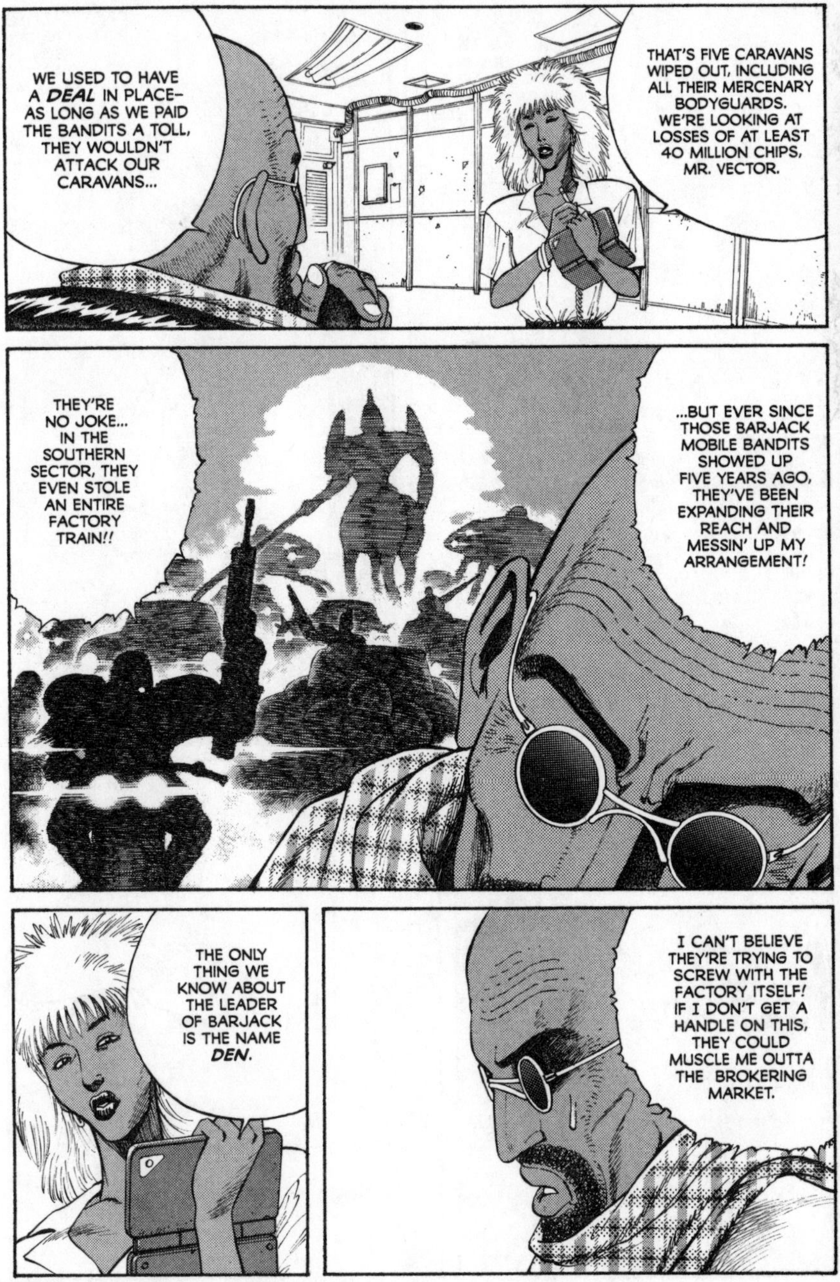
THAT'S FIVE CARAVANS WIPED OUT, INCLUDING ALL THEIR MERCENARY BODYGUARDS. WE'RE LOOKING AT LOSSES OF AT LEAST 40 MILLION CHIPS, MR. VECTOR.
WE USED TO HAVE A *DEAL* IN PLACE– AS LONG AS WE PAID THE BANDITS A TOLL, THEY WOULDN'T ATTACK OUR CARAVANS...
...BUT EVER SINCE THOSE BARJACK MOBILE BANDITS SHOWED UP FIVE YEARS AGO, THEY'VE BEEN EXPANDING THEIR REACH AND MESSIN' UP MY ARRANGEMENT!
THEY'RE NO JOKE... IN THE SOUTHERN SECTOR, THEY EVEN STOLE AN ENTIRE FACTORY TRAIN!!
I CAN'T BELIEVE THEY'RE TRYING TO SCREW WITH THE FACTORY ITSELF! IF I DON'T GET A HANDLE ON THIS, THEY COULD MUSCLE ME OUTTA THE BROKERING MARKET.
THE ONLY THING WE KNOW ABOUT THE LEADER OF BARJACK IS THE NAME ***DEN***.

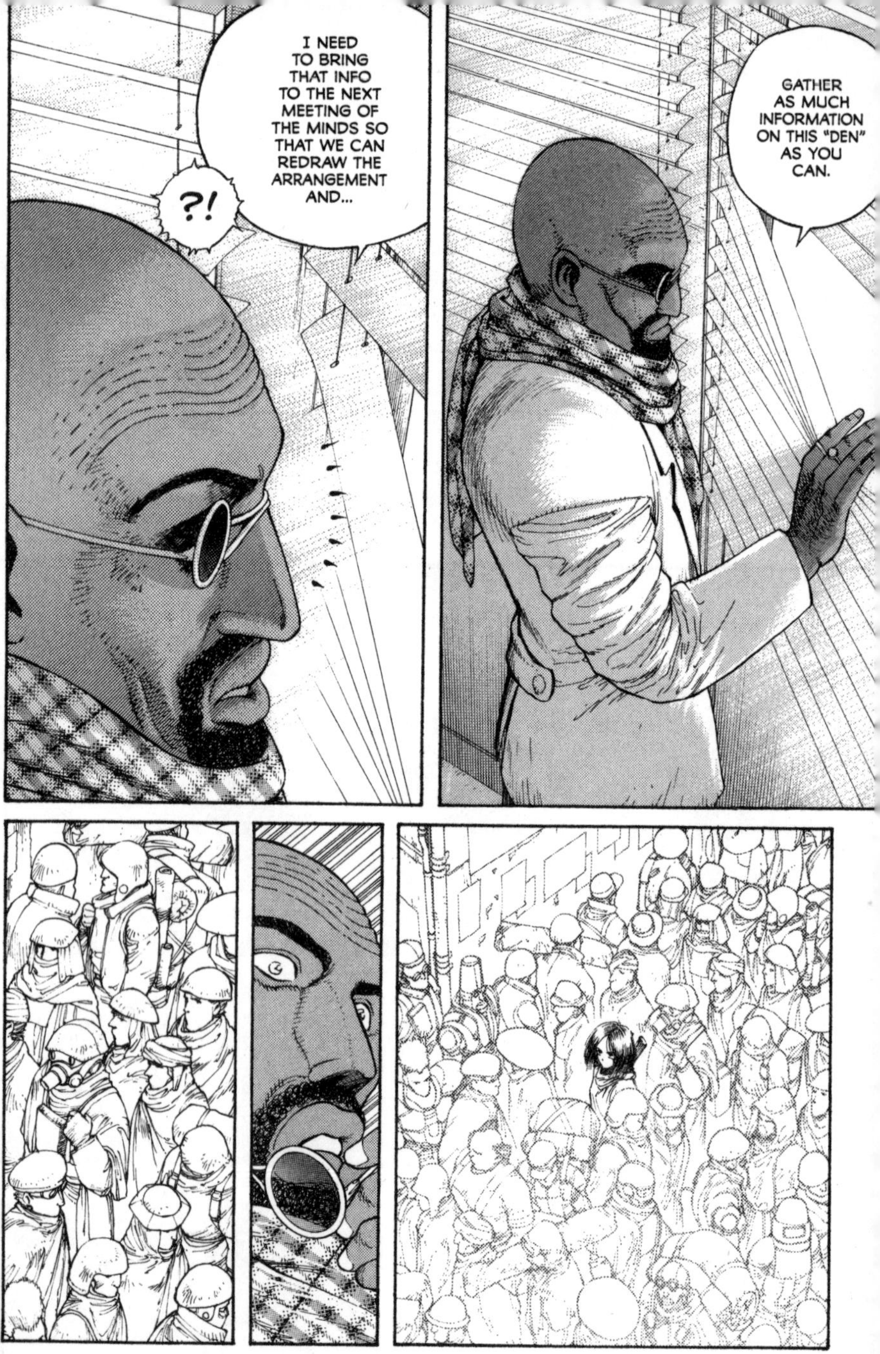
GATHER AS MUCH INFORMATION ON THIS "DEN" AS YOU CAN.
I NEED TO BRING THAT INFO TO THE NEXT MEETING OF THE MINDS SO THAT WE CAN REDRAW THE ARRANGEMENT AND...
?!

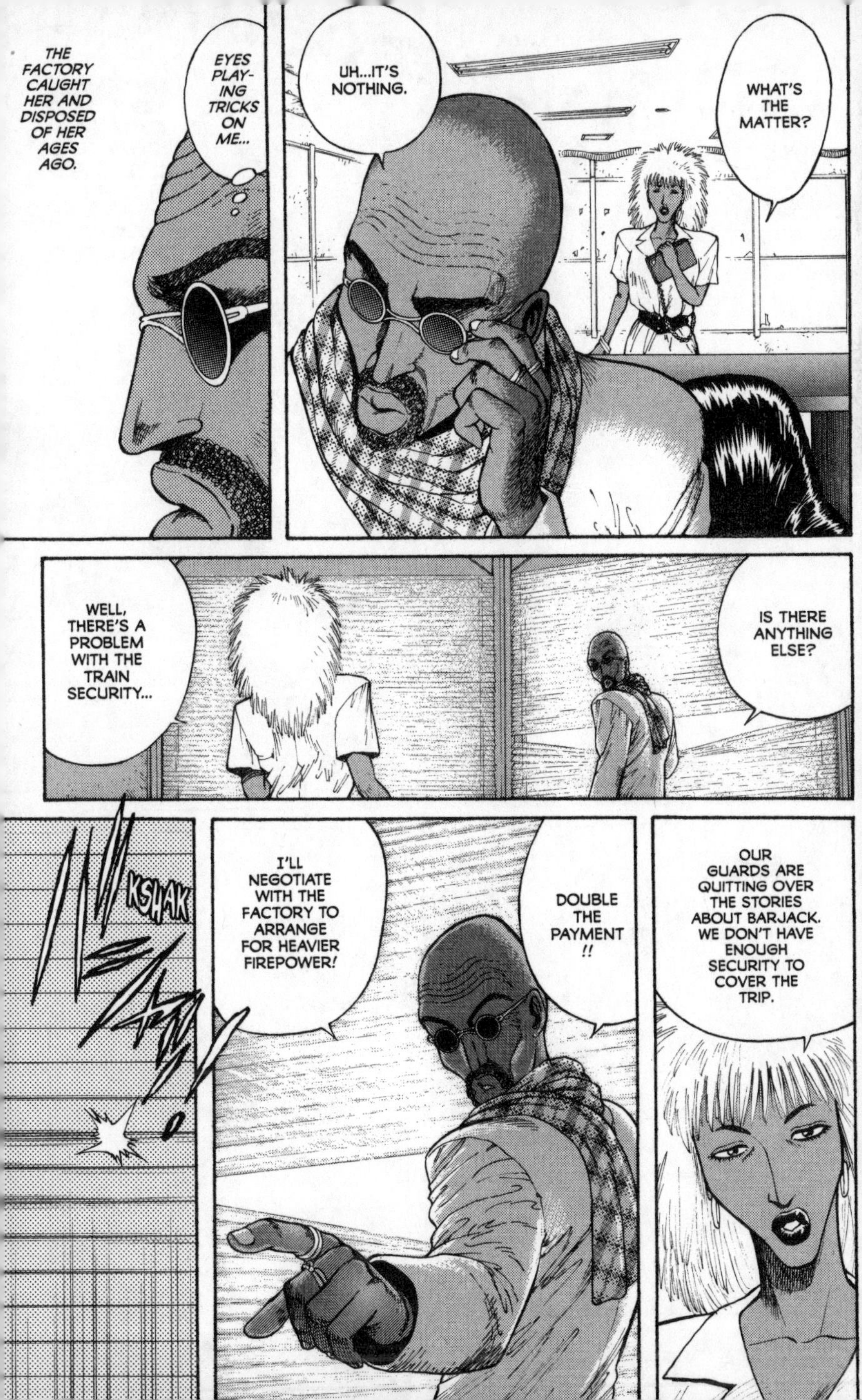
WHAT'S THE MATTER?
UH...IT'S NOTHING.
EYES PLAYING-ING TRICKS ON ME...
THE FACTORY CAUGHT HER AND DISPOSED OF HER AGES AGO.
IS THERE ANYTHING ELSE?
WELL, THERE'S A PROBLEM WITH THE TRAIN SECURITY...
OUR GUARDS ARE QUITTING OVER THE STORIES ABOUT BARJACK. WE DON'T HAVE ENOUGH SECURITY TO COVER THE TRIP.
DOUBLE THE PAYMENT!!
I'LL NEGOTIATE WITH THE FACTORY TO ARRANGE FOR HEAVIER FIREPOWER!
KSHAK

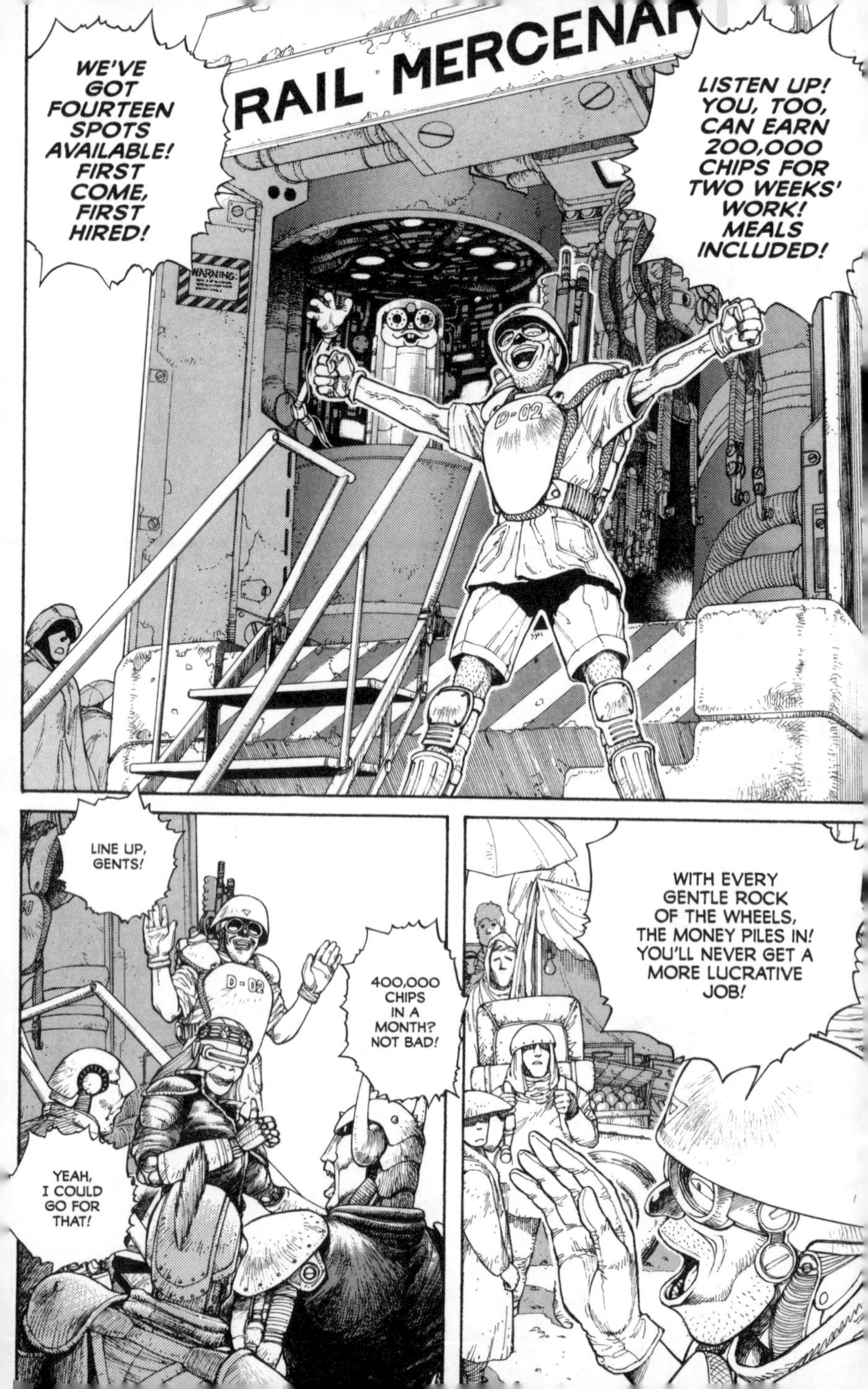
RAIL MERCENAR
LISTEN UP! YOU, TOO, CAN EARN 200,000 CHIPS FOR TWO WEEKS' WORK! MEALS INCLUDED!
WE'VE GOT FOURTEEN SPOTS AVAILABLE! FIRST COME, FIRST HIRED!
WARNING:
WITH EVERY GENTLE ROCK OF THE WHEELS, THE MONEY PILES IN! YOU'LL NEVER GET A MORE LUCRATIVE JOB!
LINE UP, GENTS!
400,000 CHIPS IN A MONTH? NOT BAD!
YEAH, I COULD GO FOR THAT!

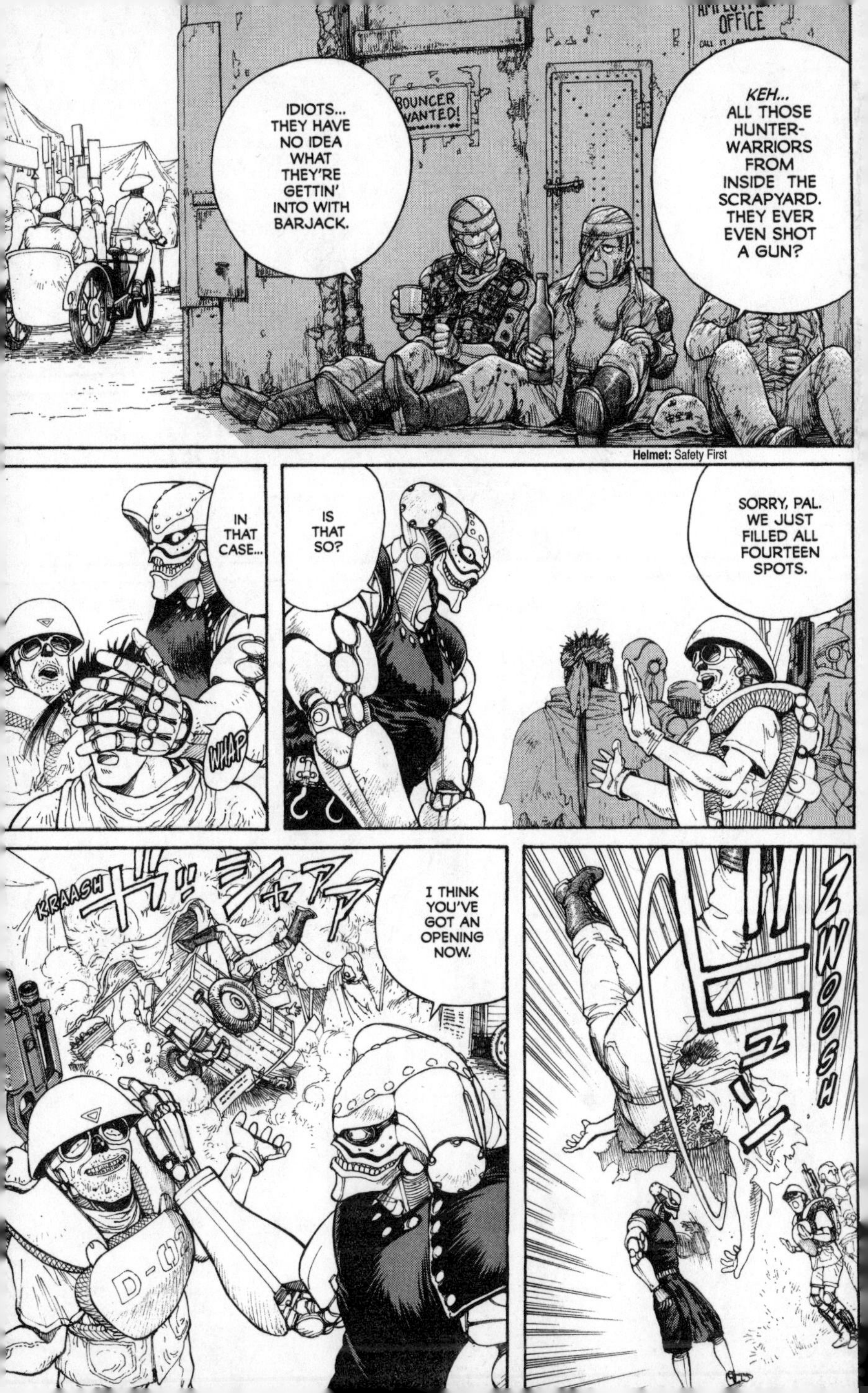
OFFICE
KEH... ALL THOSE HUNTER-WARRIORS FROM INSIDE THE SCRAPYARD. THEY EVER EVEN SHOT A GUN?
BOUNCER WANTED!
IDIOTS... THEY HAVE NO IDEA WHAT THEY'RE GETTIN' INTO WITH BARJACK.
SORRY, PAL. WE JUST FILLED ALL FOURTEEN SPOTS.
IS THAT SO?
IN THAT CASE...
WHAP
ZWOOSH
I THINK YOU'VE GOT AN OPENING NOW.
KRAASH
Helmet: Safety First

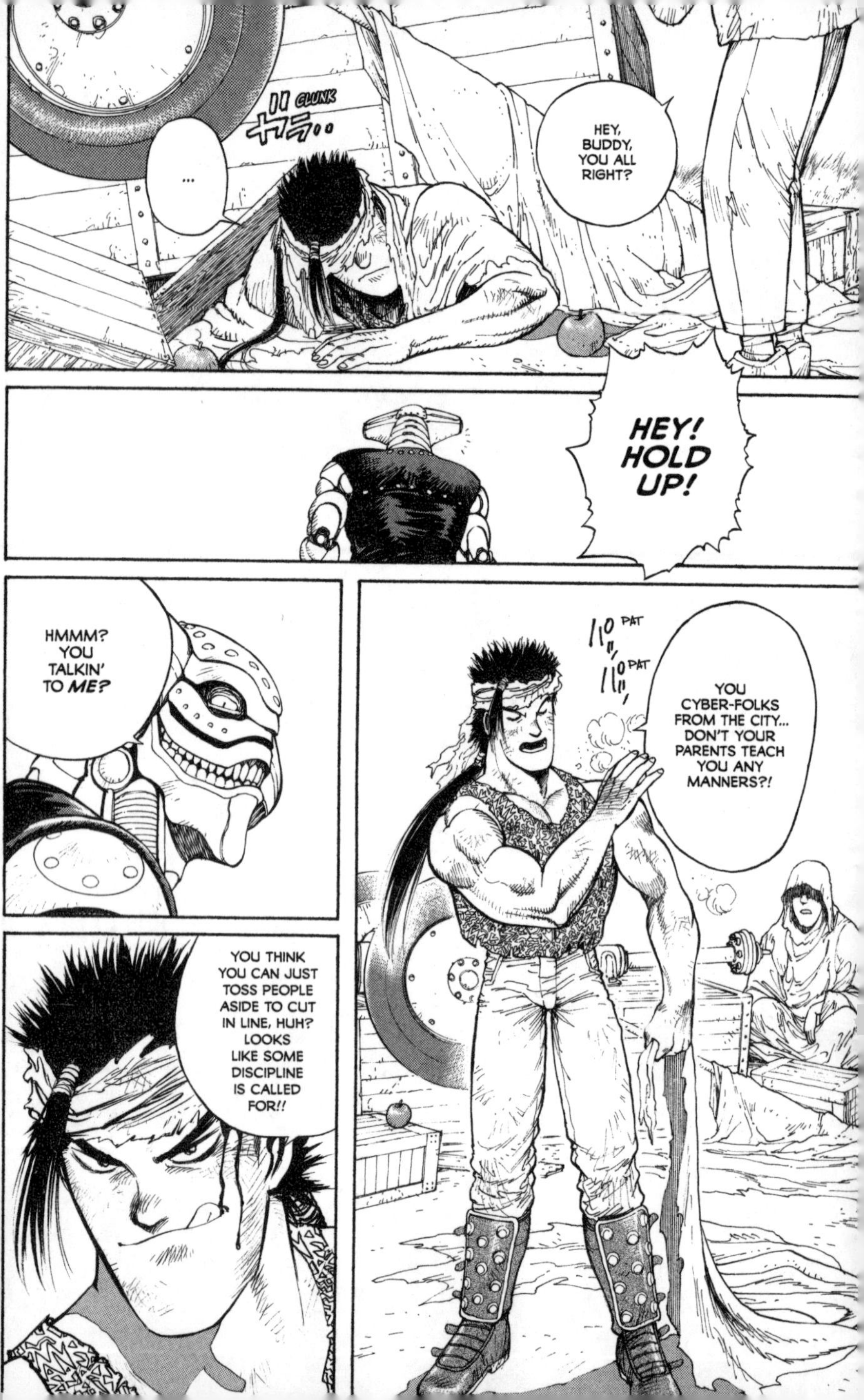
HEY, BUDDY, YOU ALL RIGHT?
CLUNK
...
HEY! HOLD UP!
PAT
PAT
YOU CYBER-FOLKS FROM THE CITY... DON'T YOUR PARENTS TEACH YOU ANY MANNERS?!
HMMM? YOU TALKIN' TO *ME?*
YOU THINK YOU CAN JUST TOSS PEOPLE ASIDE TO CUT IN LINE, HUH? LOOKS LIKE SOME DISCIPLINE IS CALLED FOR!!

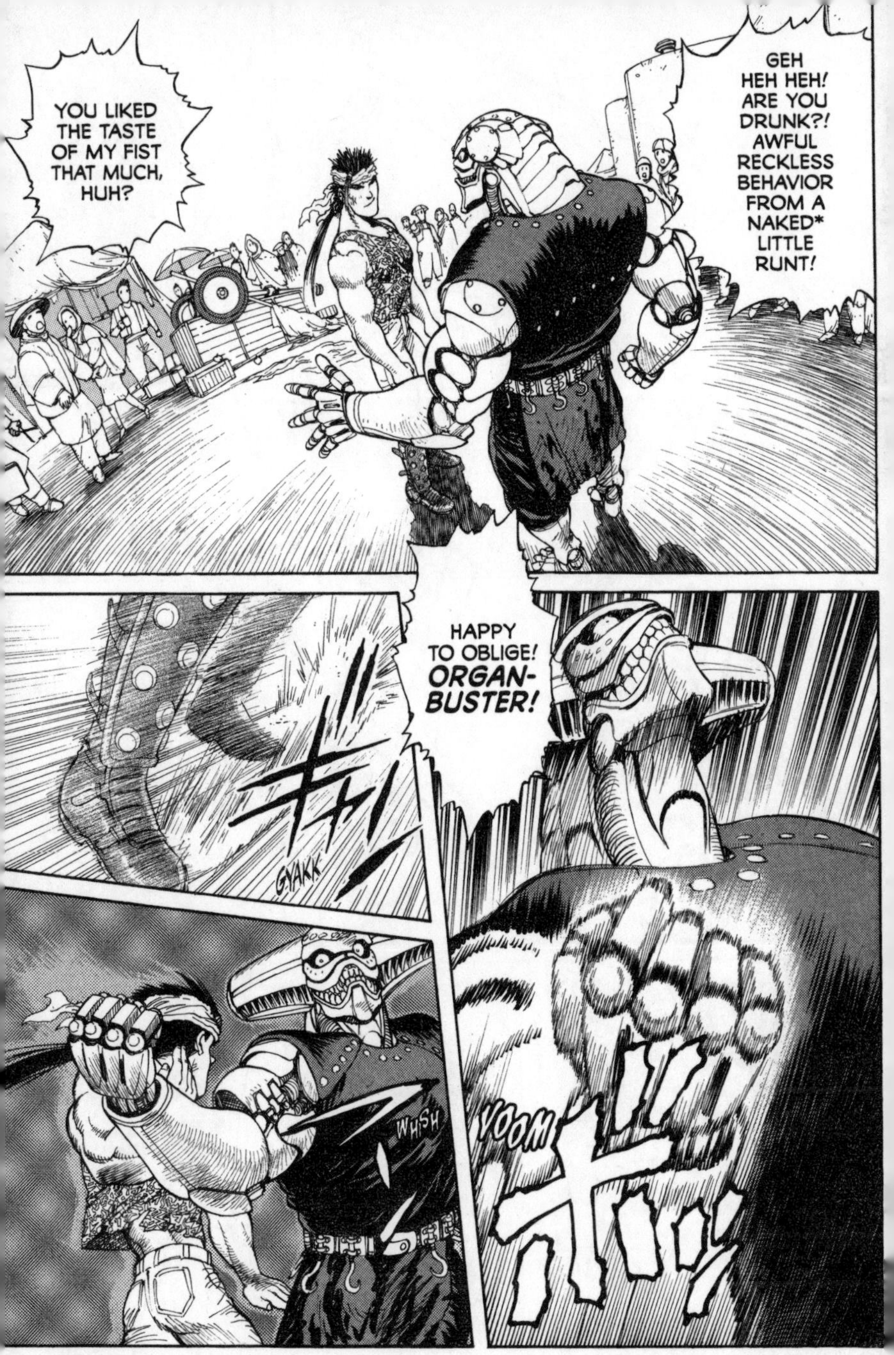
GEH HEH HEH! ARE YOU DRUNK?! AWFUL RECKLESS BEHAVIOR FROM A NAKED* LITTLE RUNT!
YOU LIKED THE TASTE OF MY FIST THAT MUCH, HUH?
HAPPY TO OBLIGE! *ORGAN-BUSTER!*
GYAKK
VOOM
WHISH

*Naked: When used in this sense, a slang term that refers to being biological or unarmed; without cybernetic enhancements or weapons.

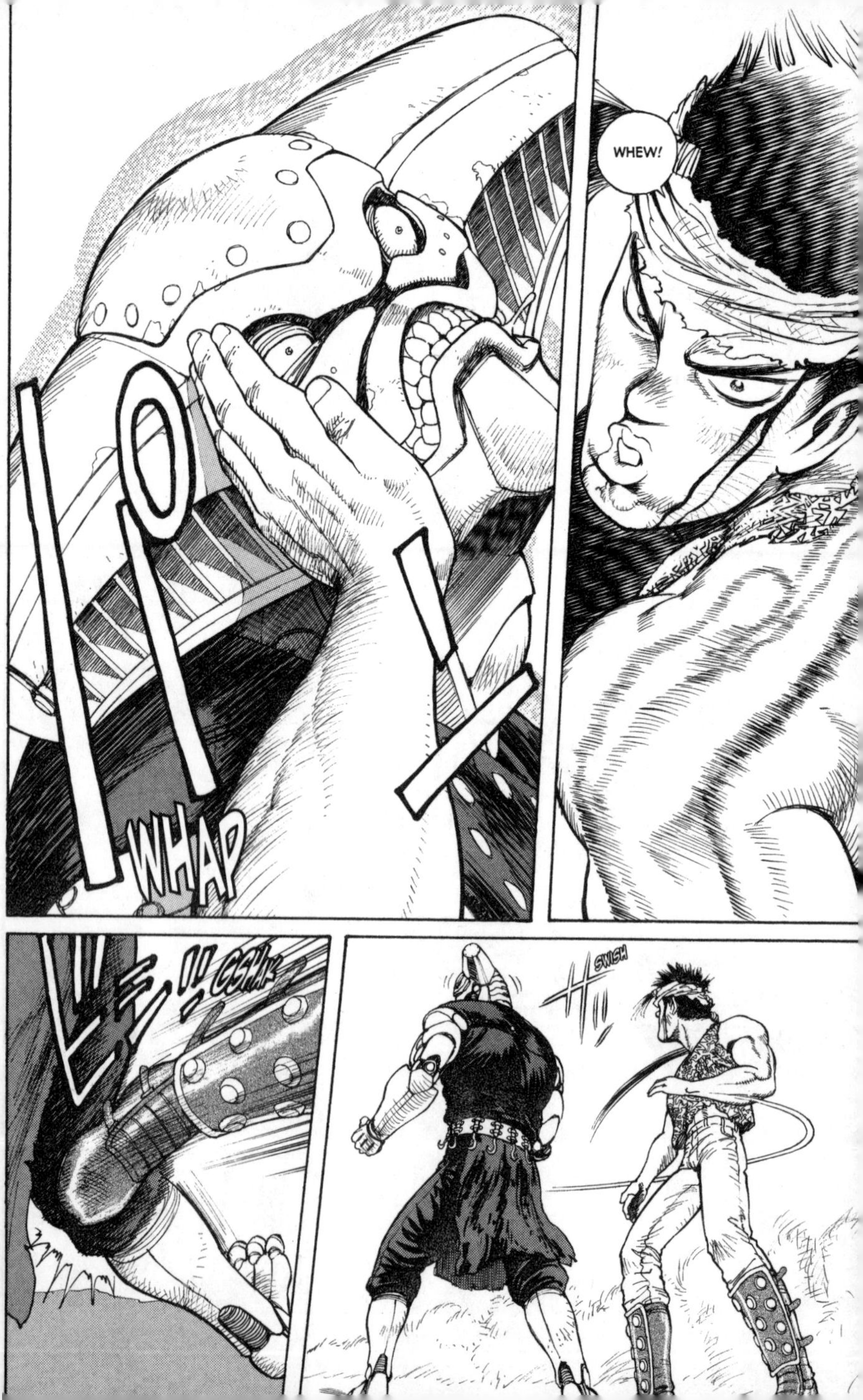
WHEW!
WHAP
SWISH
GSHK

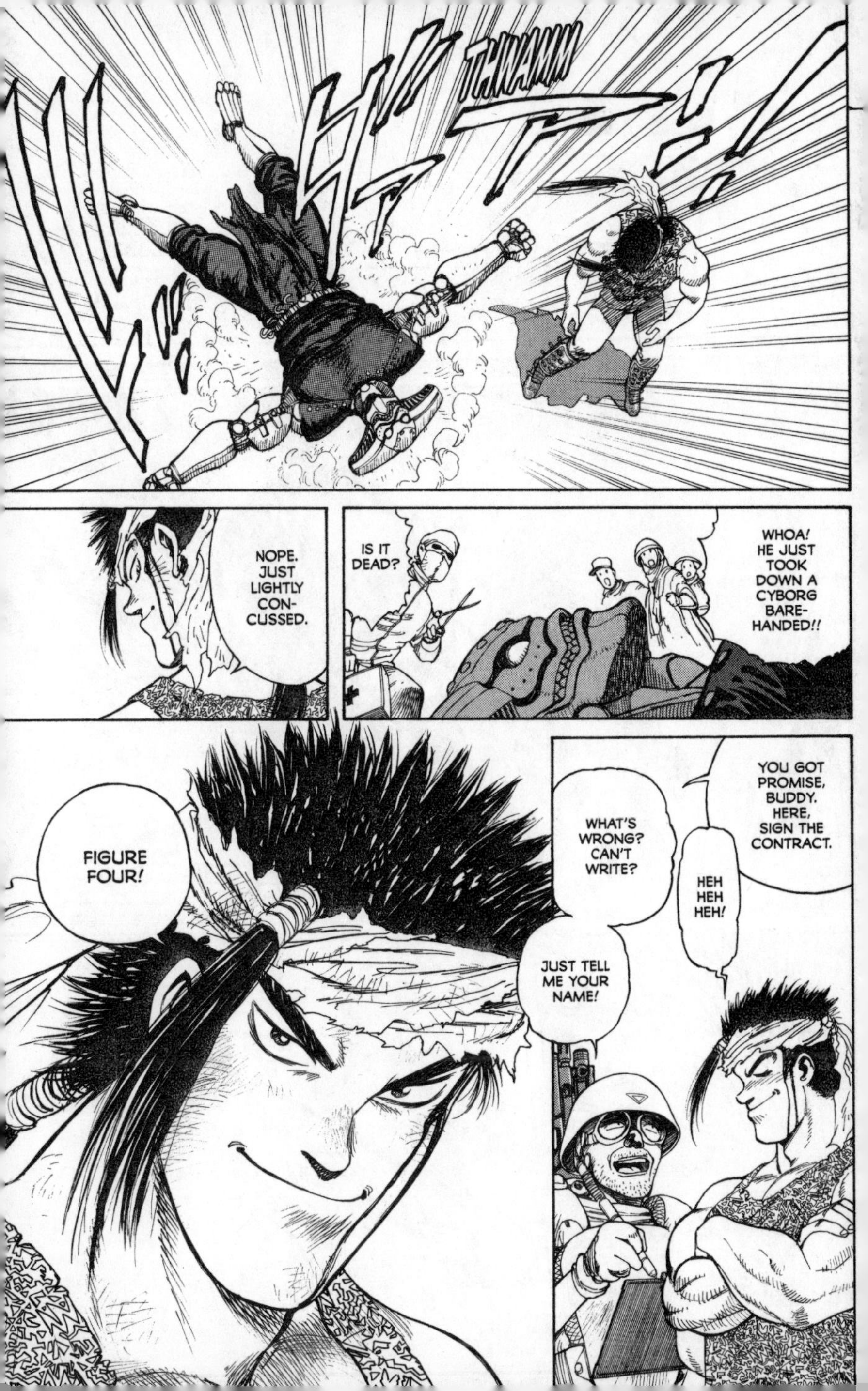
THWAMM
WHOA! HE JUST TOOK DOWN A CYBORG BARE-HANDED!!
IS IT DEAD?
NOPE. JUST LIGHTLY CON-CUSSED.
YOU GOT PROMISE, BUDDY. HERE, SIGN THE CONTRACT.
HEH HEH HEH!
WHAT'S WRONG? CAN'T WRITE?
JUST TELL ME YOUR NAME!
FIGURE FOUR!

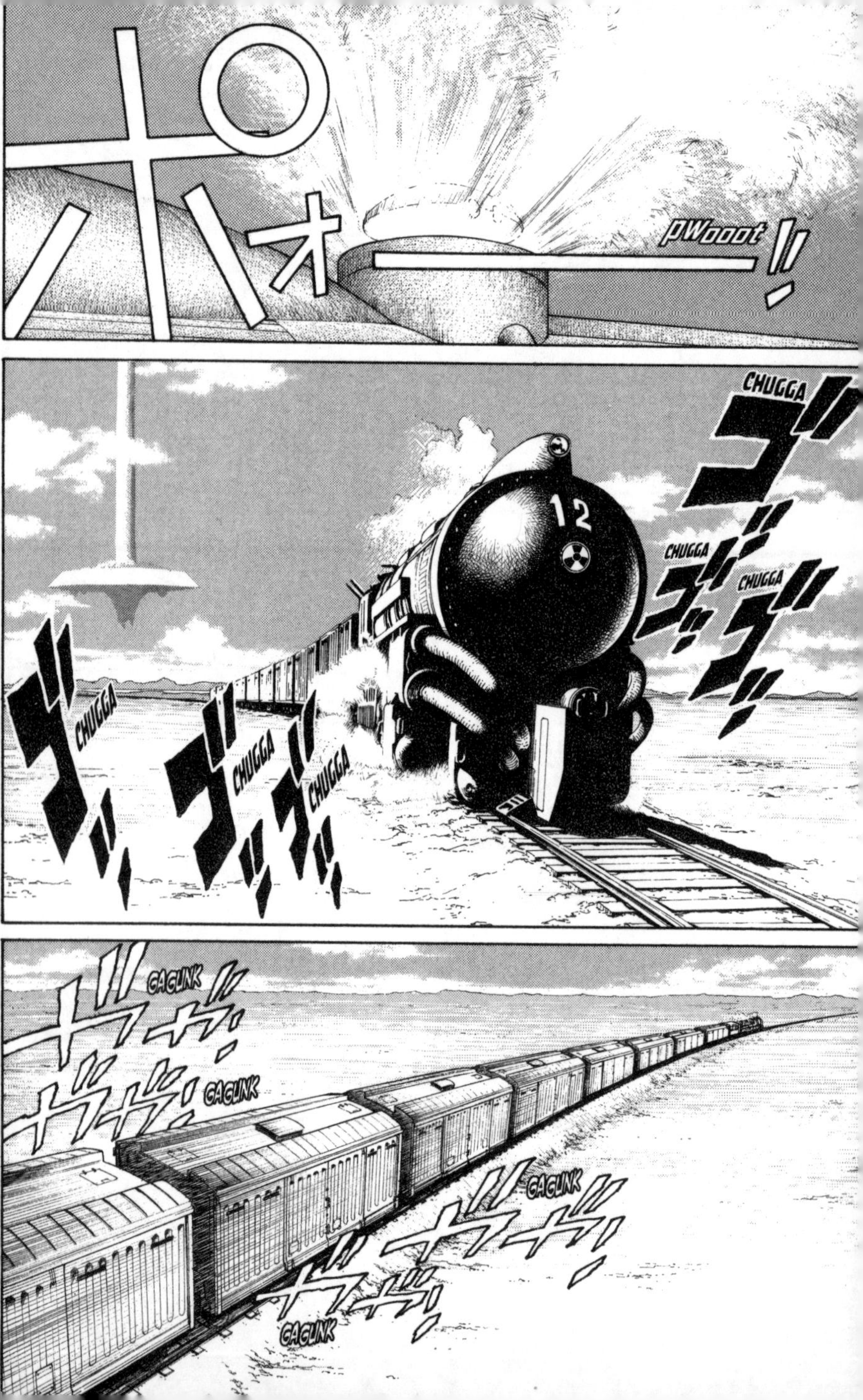
pWooot!!
CHUGGA
CHUGGA
CHUGGA
CHUGGA
CHUGGA
CHUGGA
GAGUNK
GAGUNK
GAGUNK
GAGUNK

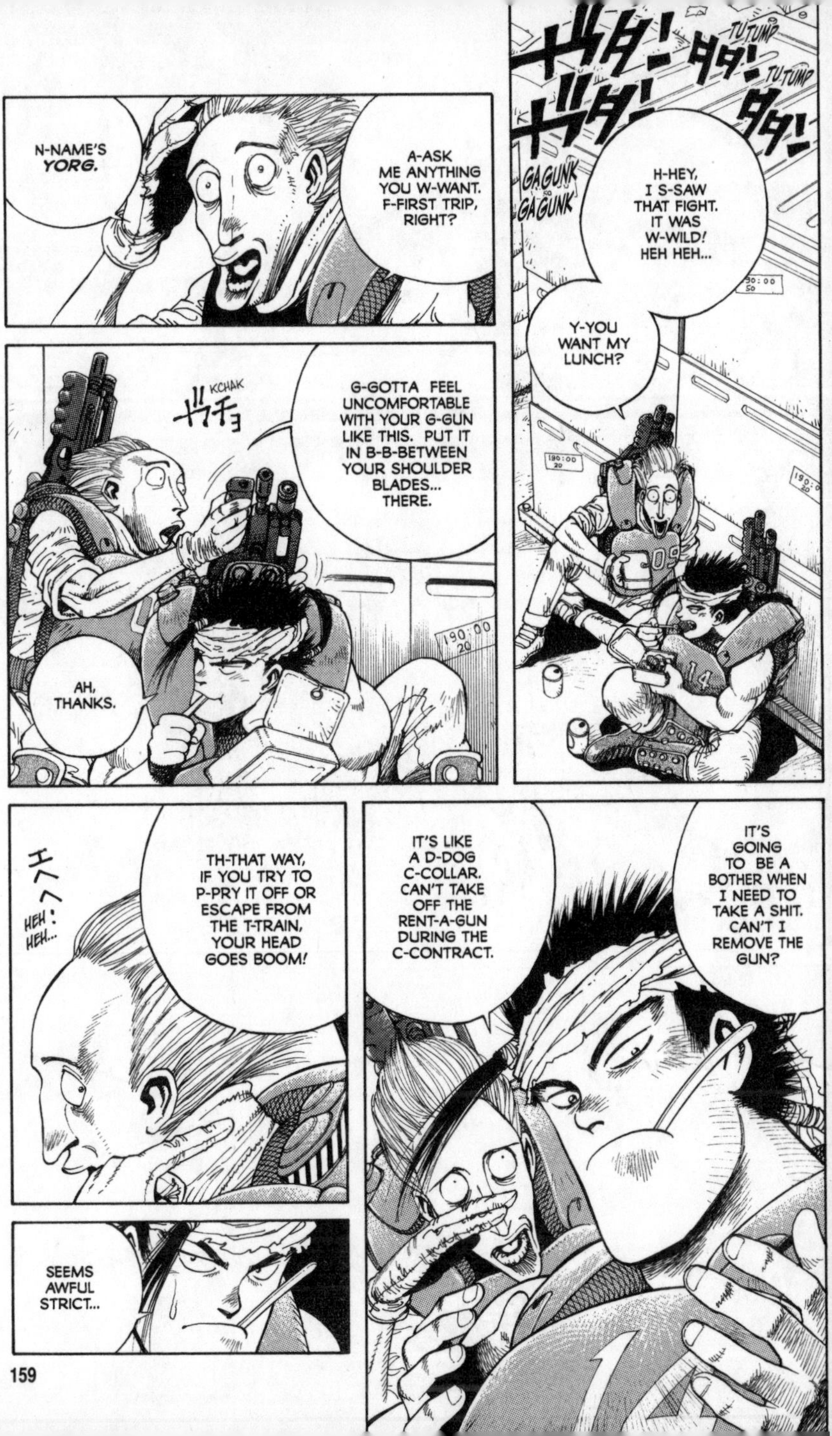
TU TUMP
TU TUMP
GA GUNK GA GUNK
H-HEY, I S-SAW THAT FIGHT. IT WAS W-WILD! HEH HEH...
Y-YOU WANT MY LUNCH?
A-ASK ME ANYTHING YOU W-WANT. F-FIRST TRIP, RIGHT?
N-NAME'S *YORG.*
G-GOTTA FEEL UNCOMFORTABLE WITH YOUR G-GUN LIKE THIS. PUT IT IN B-B-BETWEEN YOUR SHOULDER BLADES... THERE.
KCHAK
AH, THANKS.
IT'S GOING TO BE A BOTHER WHEN I NEED TO TAKE A SHIT. CAN'T I REMOVE THE GUN?
IT'S LIKE A D-DOG C-COLLAR. CAN'T TAKE OFF THE RENT-A-GUN DURING THE C-CONTRACT.
TH-THAT WAY, IF YOU TRY TO P-PRY IT OFF OR ESCAPE FROM THE T-TRAIN, YOUR HEAD GOES BOOM!
HEH HEH...
SEEMS AWFUL STRICT...

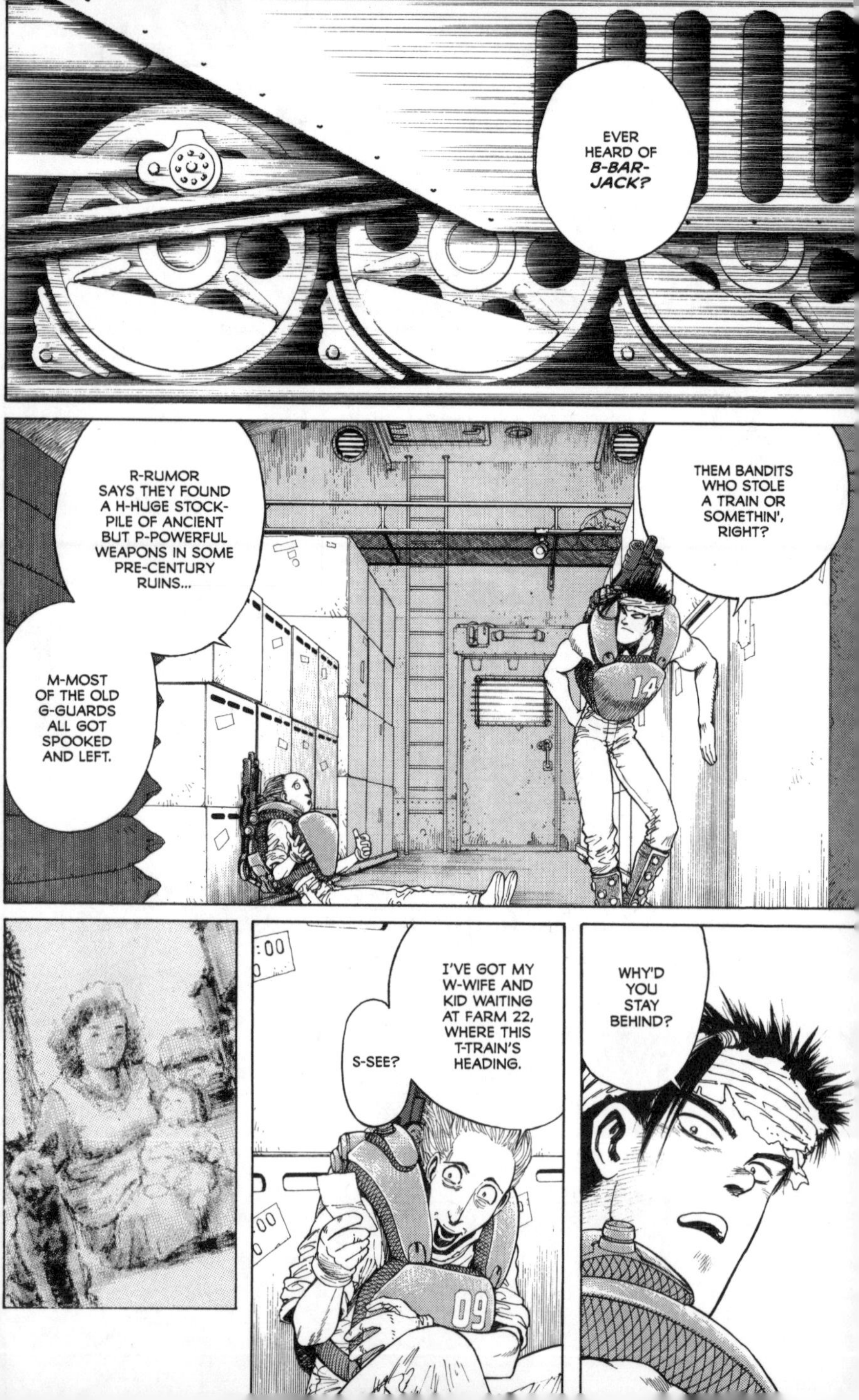
EVER HEARD OF B-BAR-JACK?
THEM BANDITS WHO STOLE A TRAIN OR SOMETHIN', RIGHT?
R-RUMOR SAYS THEY FOUND A H-HUGE STOCK-PILE OF ANCIENT BUT P-POWERFUL WEAPONS IN SOME PRE-CENTURY RUINS...
M-MOST OF THE OLD G-GUARDS ALL GOT SPOOKED AND LEFT.
WHY'D YOU STAY BEHIND?
I'VE GOT MY W-WIFE AND KID WAITING AT FARM 22, WHERE THIS T-TRAIN'S HEADING.
S-SEE?

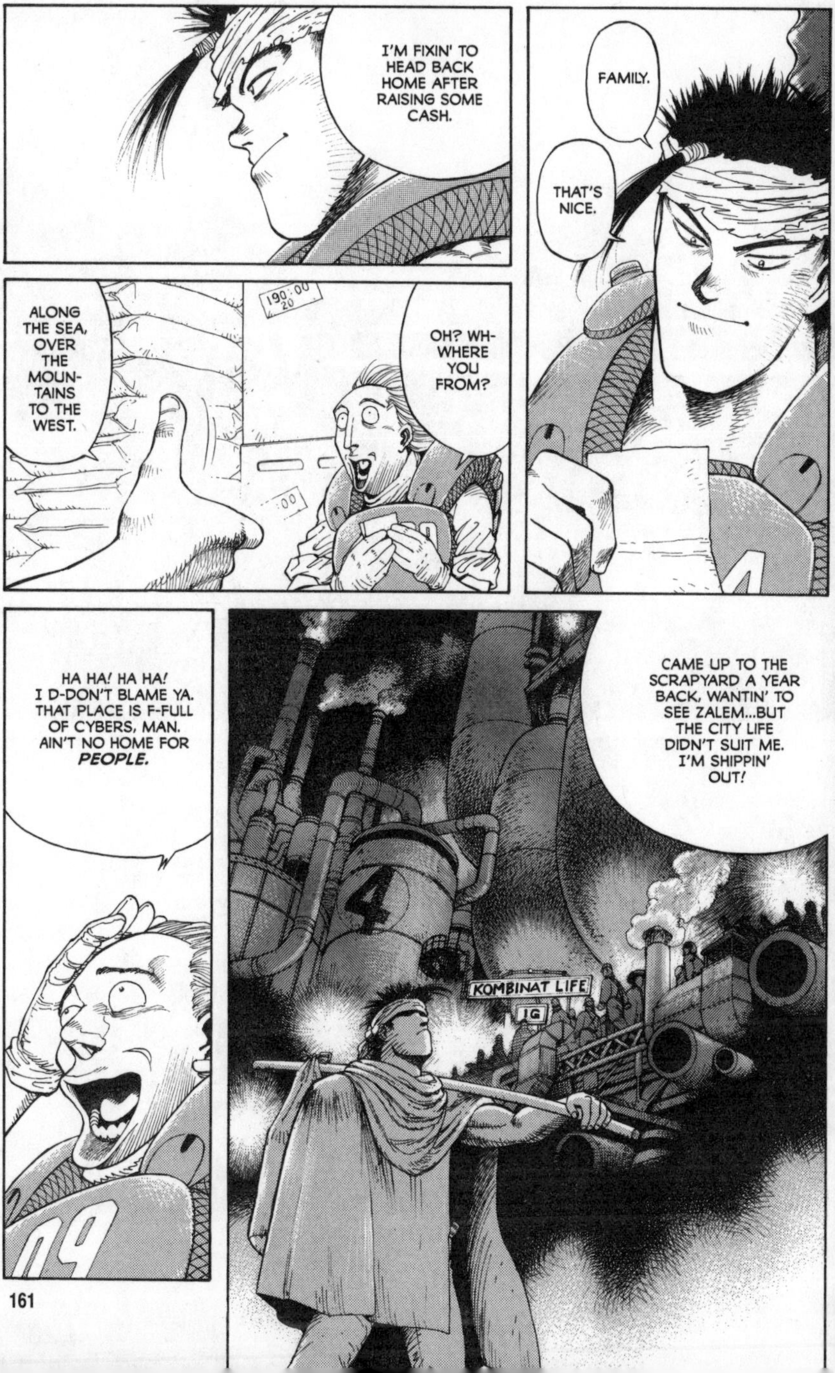
FAMILY.
THAT'S NICE.
I'M FIXIN' TO HEAD BACK HOME AFTER RAISING SOME CASH.
190:00 20
OH? WH-WHERE YOU FROM?
ALONG THE SEA, OVER THE MOUNTAINS TO THE WEST.
CAME UP TO THE SCRAPYARD A YEAR BACK, WANTIN' TO SEE ZALEM...BUT THE CITY LIFE DIDN'T SUIT ME. I'M SHIPPIN' OUT!
KOMBINAT LIFE
IG
HA HA! HA HA! I D-DON'T BLAME YA. THAT PLACE IS F-FULL OF CYBERS, MAN. AIN'T NO HOME FOR ***PEOPLE.***

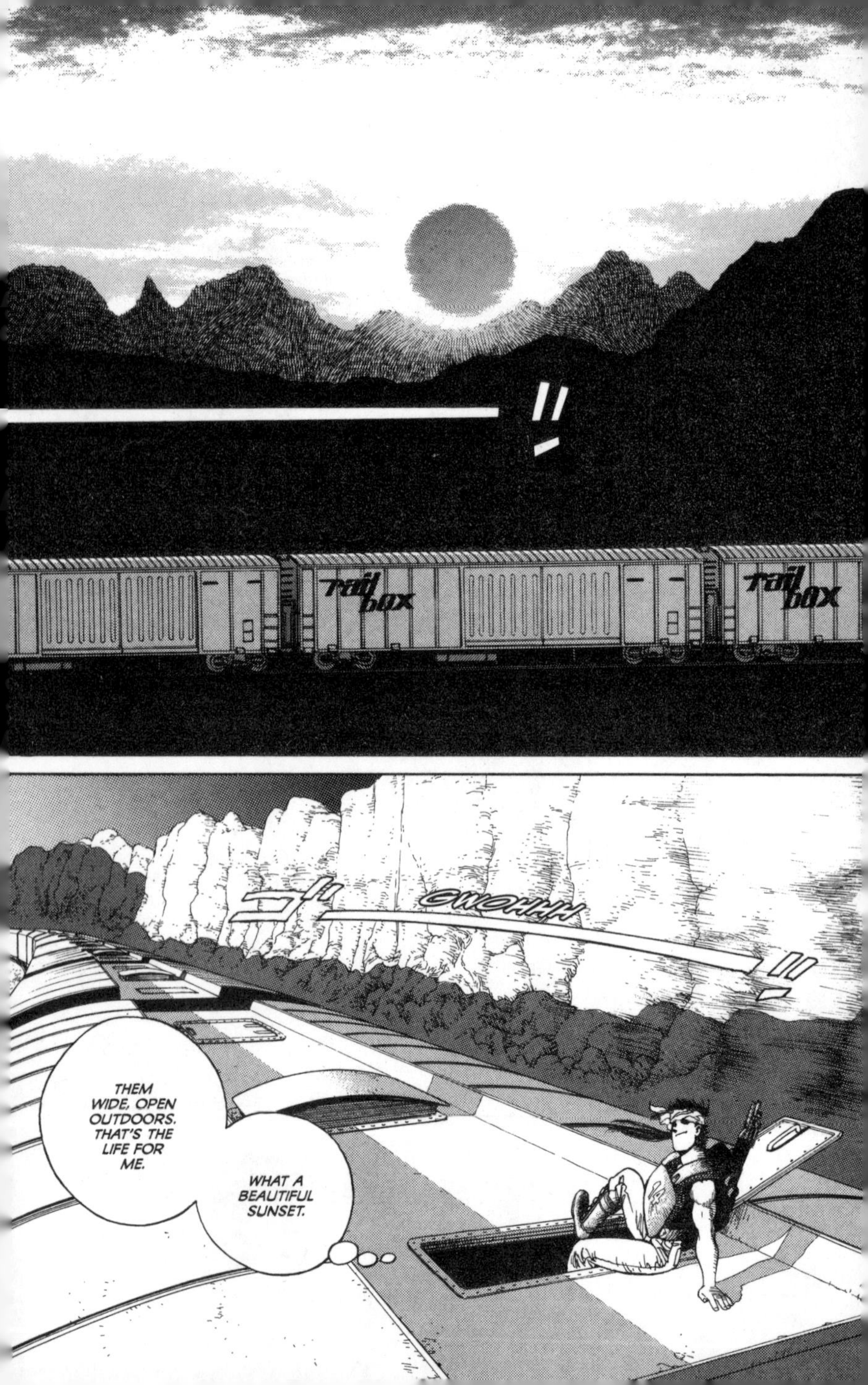
GWOHHH
WHAT A BEAUTIFUL SUNSET.
THEM WIDE, OPEN OUTDOORS. THAT'S THE LIFE FOR ME.

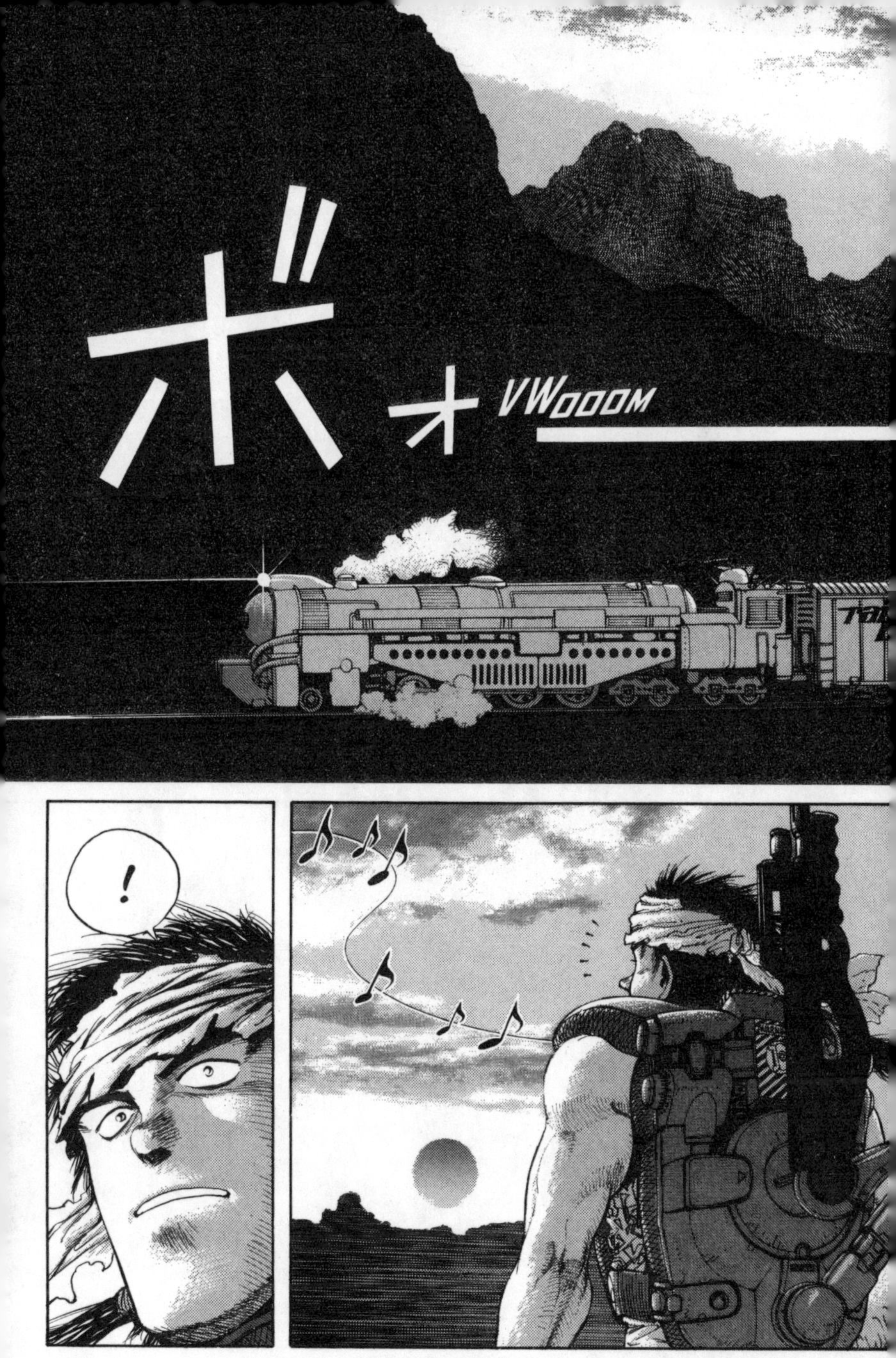
ボォ
VWOOOM
!

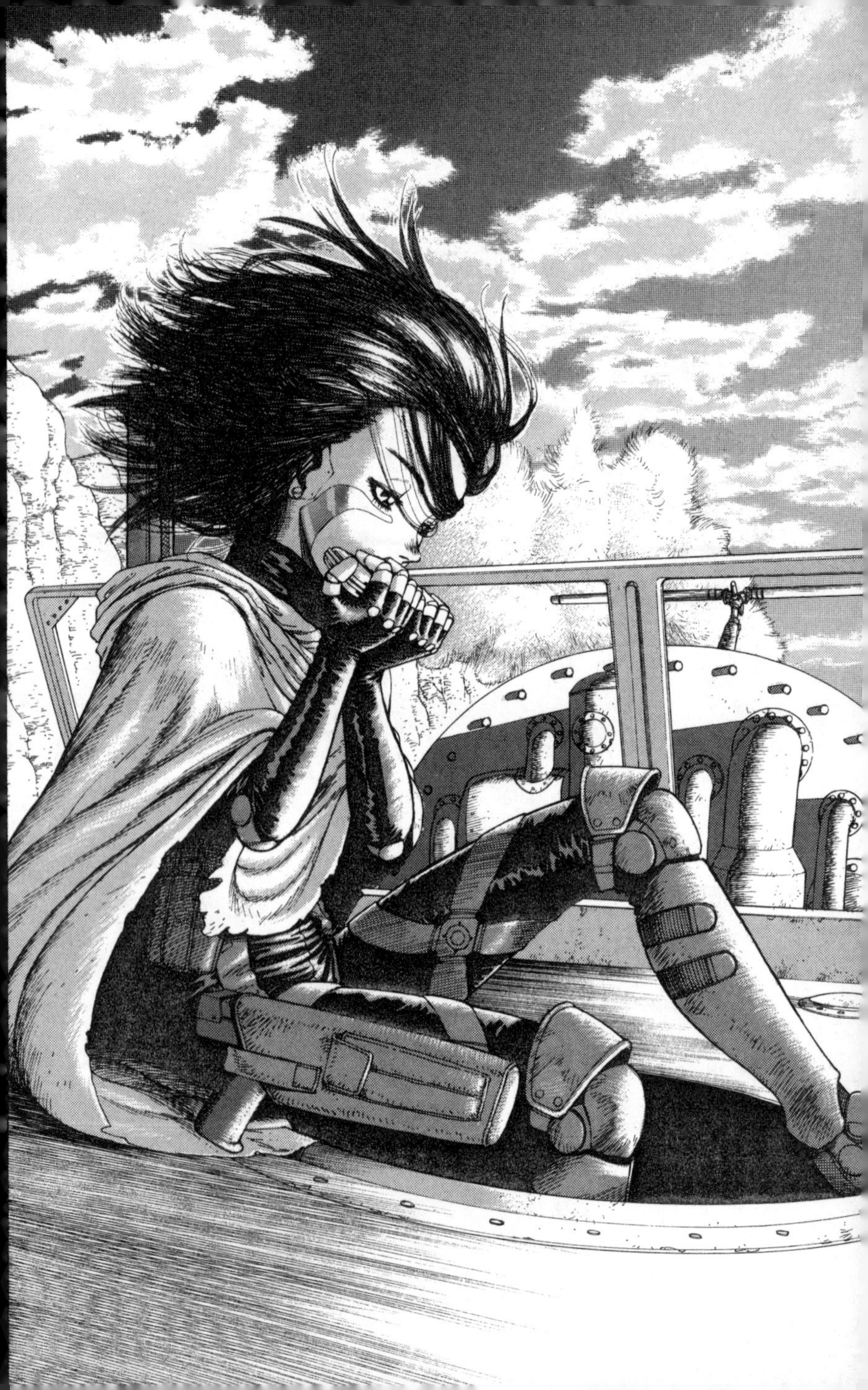

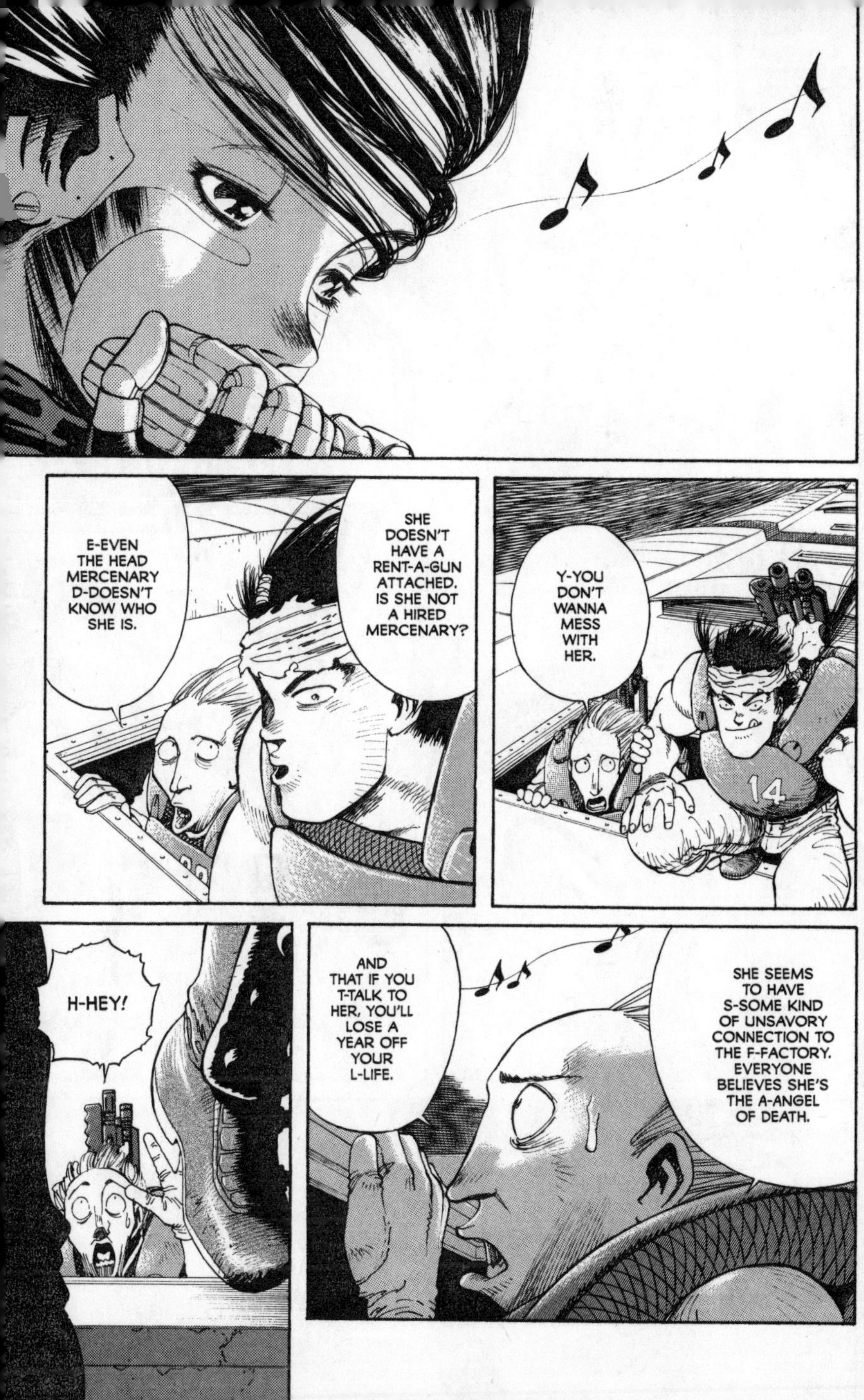
Y-YOU DON'T WANNA MESS WITH HER.
SHE DOESN'T HAVE A RENT-A-GUN ATTACHED. IS SHE NOT A HIRED MERCENARY?
E-EVEN THE HEAD MERCENARY D-DOESN'T KNOW WHO SHE IS.
SHE SEEMS TO HAVE S-SOME KIND OF UNSAVORY CONNECTION TO THE F-FACTORY. EVERYONE BELIEVES SHE'S THE A-ANGEL OF DEATH.
AND THAT IF YOU T-TALK TO HER, YOU'LL LOSE A YEAR OFF YOUR L-LIFE.
H-HEY!

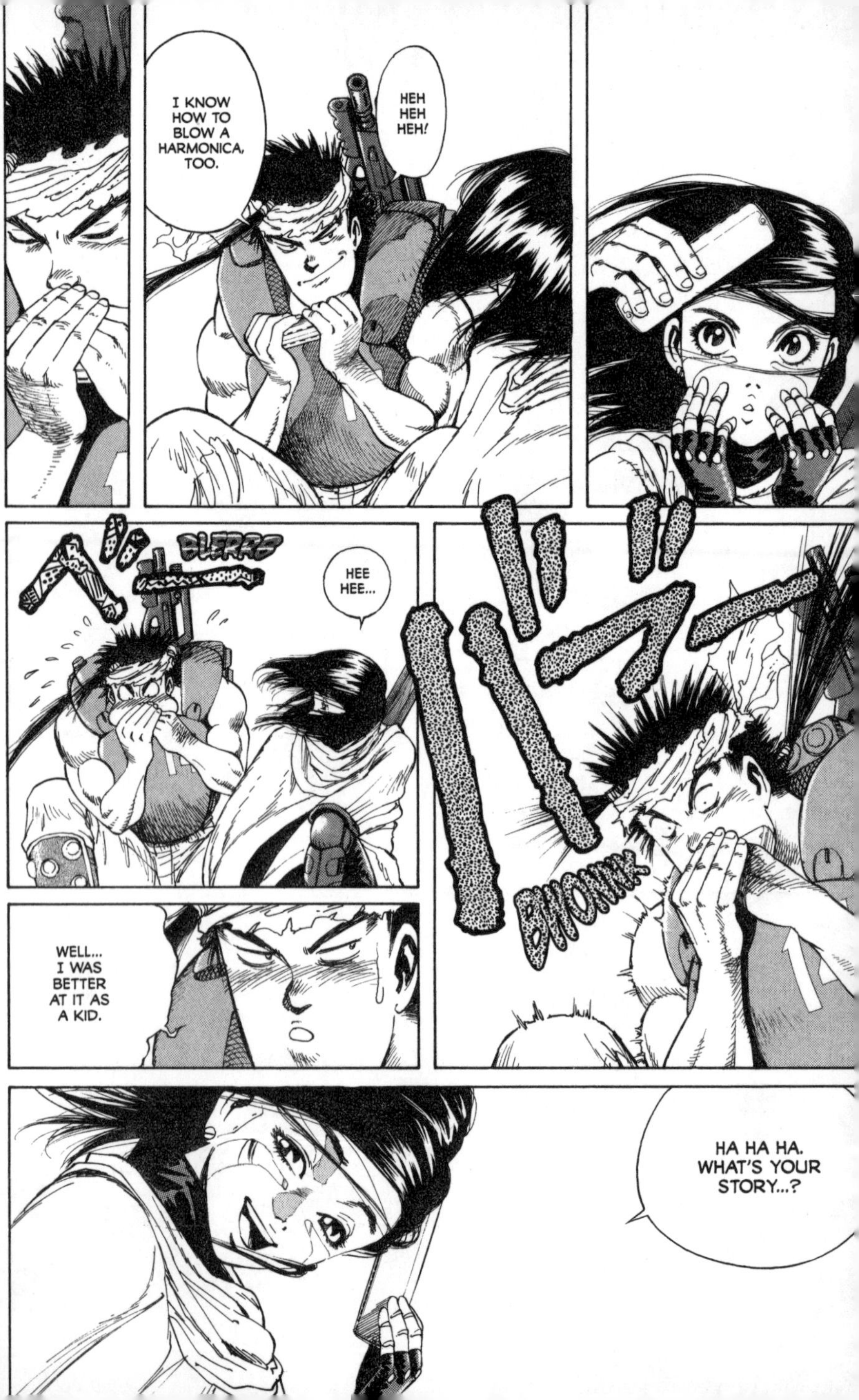
HEH HEH HEH!
I KNOW HOW TO BLOW A HARMONICA, TOO.
BWONKK
HEE HEE...
BLERRB
WELL... I WAS BETTER AT IT AS A KID.
HA HA HA. WHAT'S YOUR STORY...?

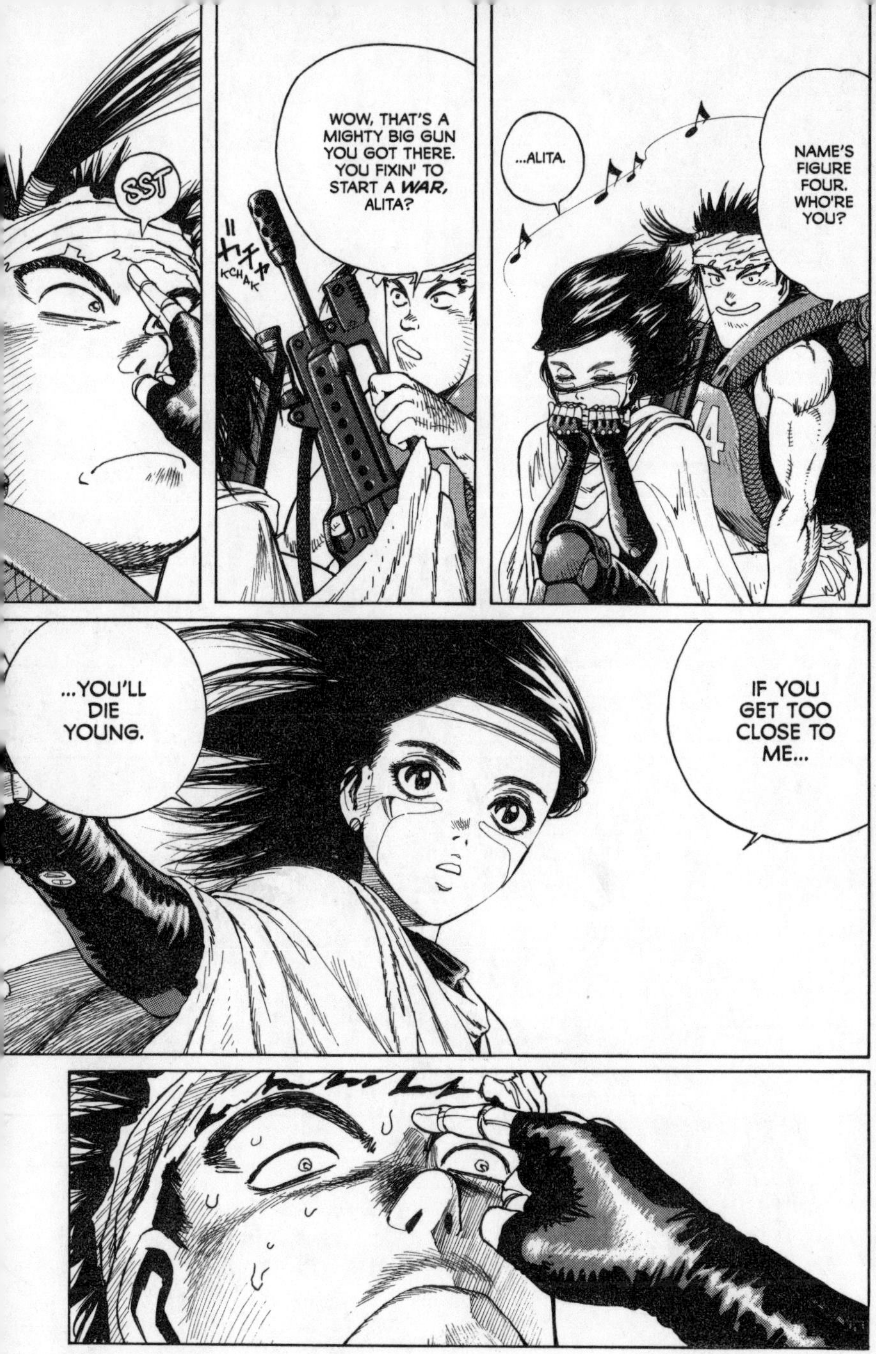
NAME'S FIGURE FOUR. WHO'RE YOU?
...ALITA.
WOW, THAT'S A MIGHTY BIG GUN YOU GOT THERE. YOU FIXIN' TO START A ***WAR,*** ALITA?
ガチャ
KCHAK
SST
IF YOU GET TOO CLOSE TO ME...
...YOU'LL DIE YOUNG.

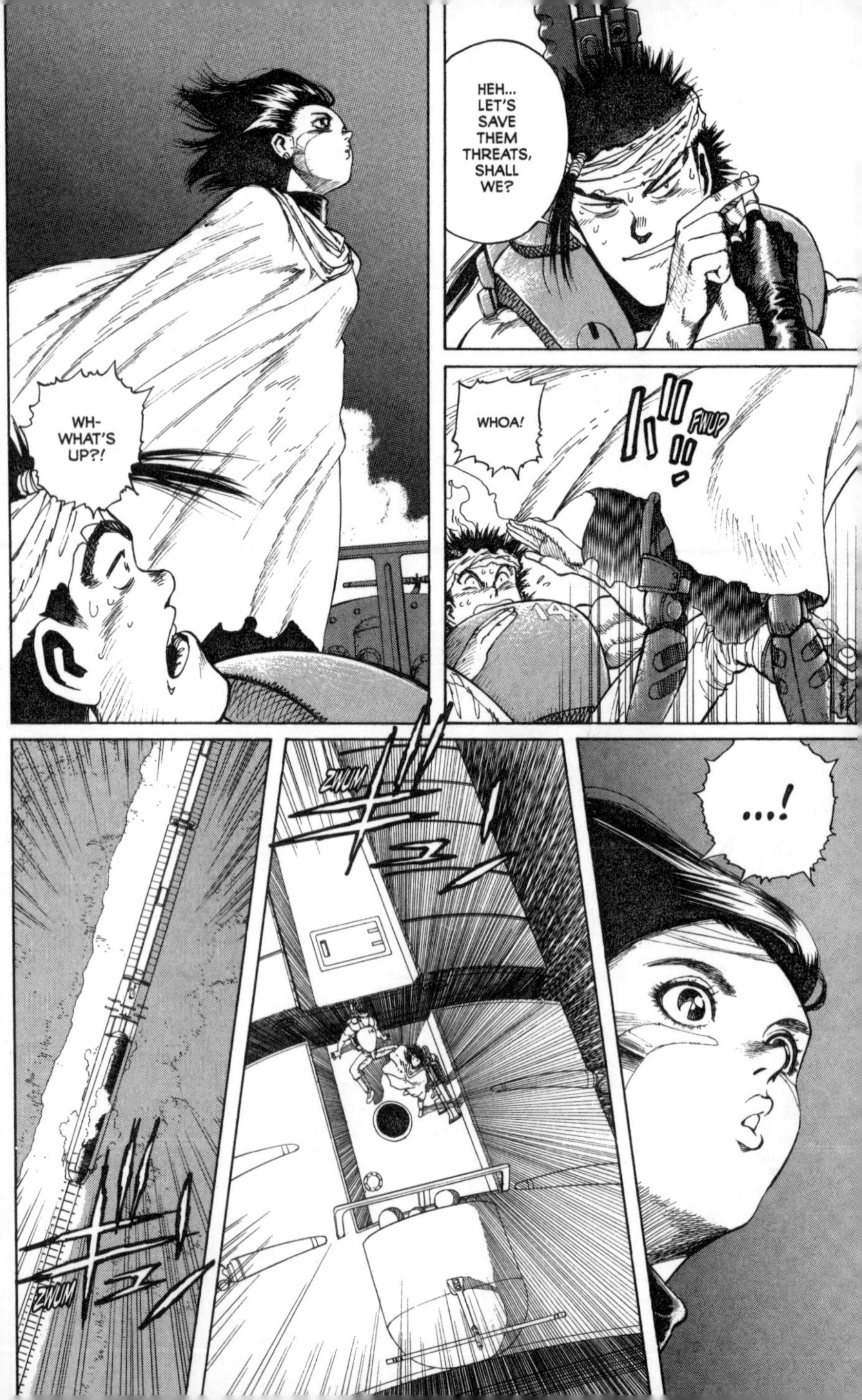
HEH... LET'S SAVE THEM THREATS, SHALL WE?
WHOA!
FWUP
WH- WHAT'S UP?!
...!
ZWUM
ZWUM

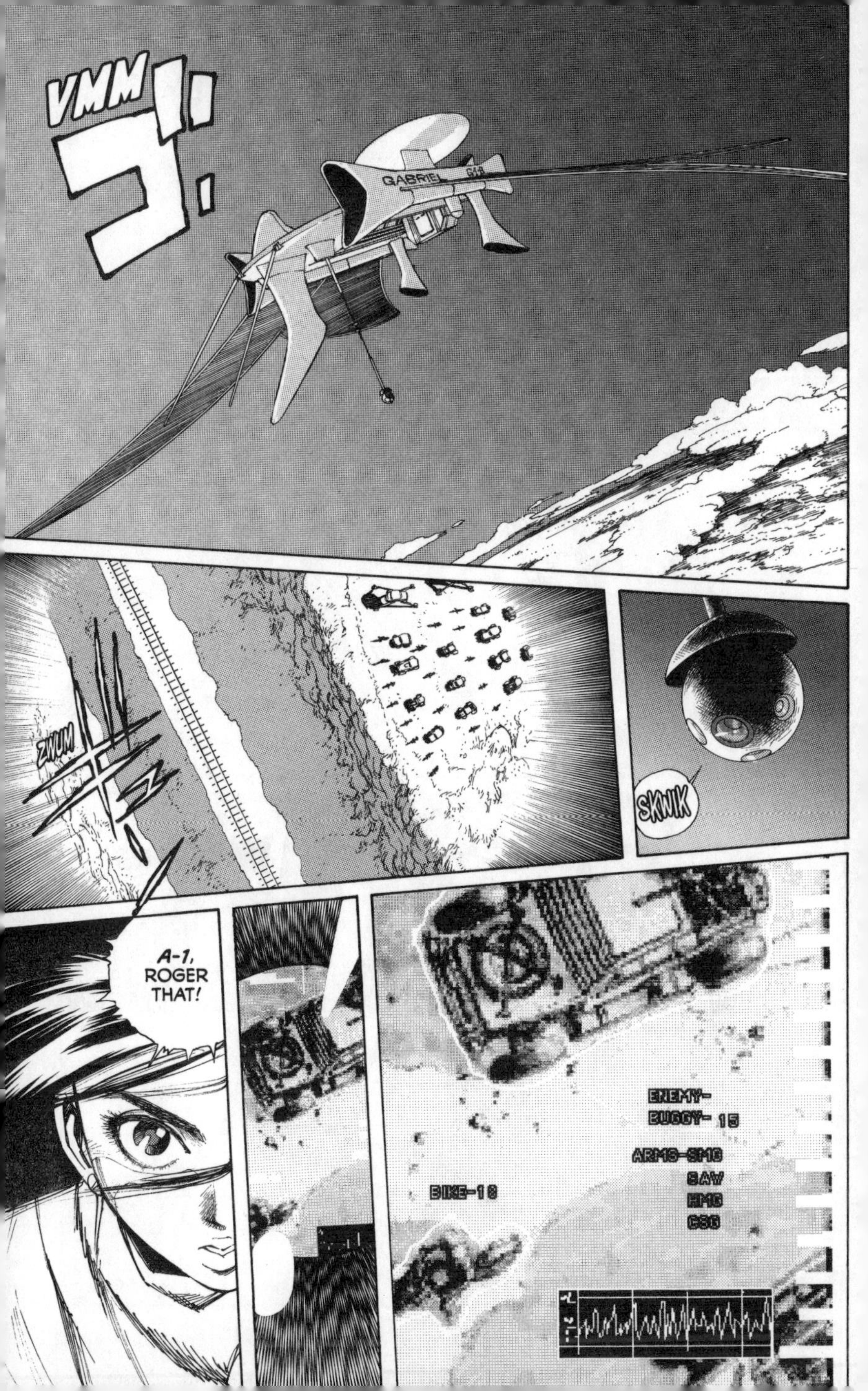
VMM
ゴ!!
GABRIEL
SKWIK
ZWUM
ENEMY-
BUGGY- 15
ARMS-SMG
SAW
HMG
CSG
BIKE-18
A-1, ROGER THAT!

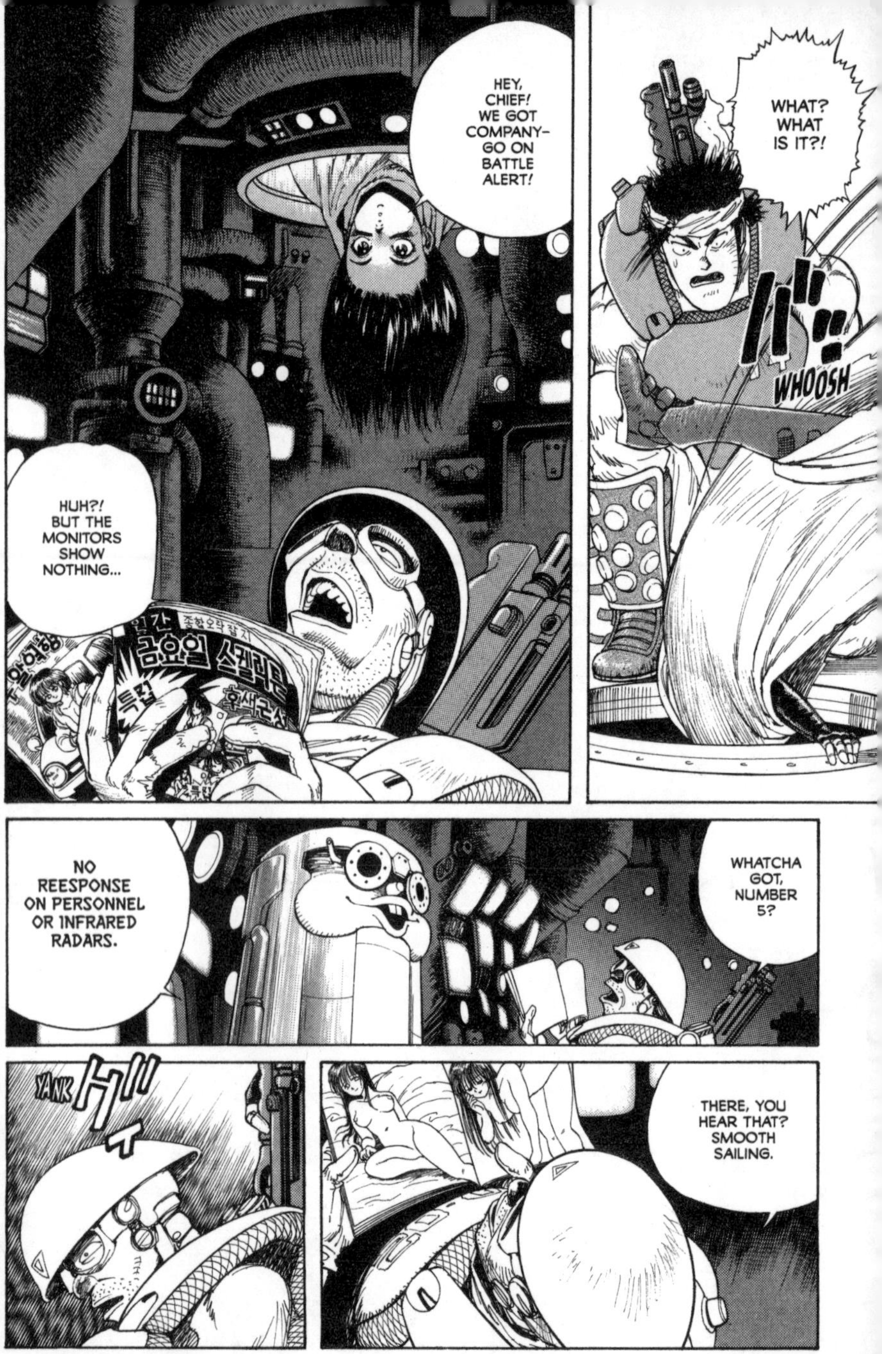
WHAT? WHAT IS IT?!
WHOOSH
HEY, CHIEF! WE GOT COMPANY-GO ON BATTLE ALERT!
HUH?! BUT THE MONITORS SHOW NOTHING...
WHATCHA GOT, NUMBER 5?
NO REESPONSE ON PERSONNEL OR INFRARED RADARS.
THERE, YOU HEAR THAT? SMOOTH SAILING.
YANK

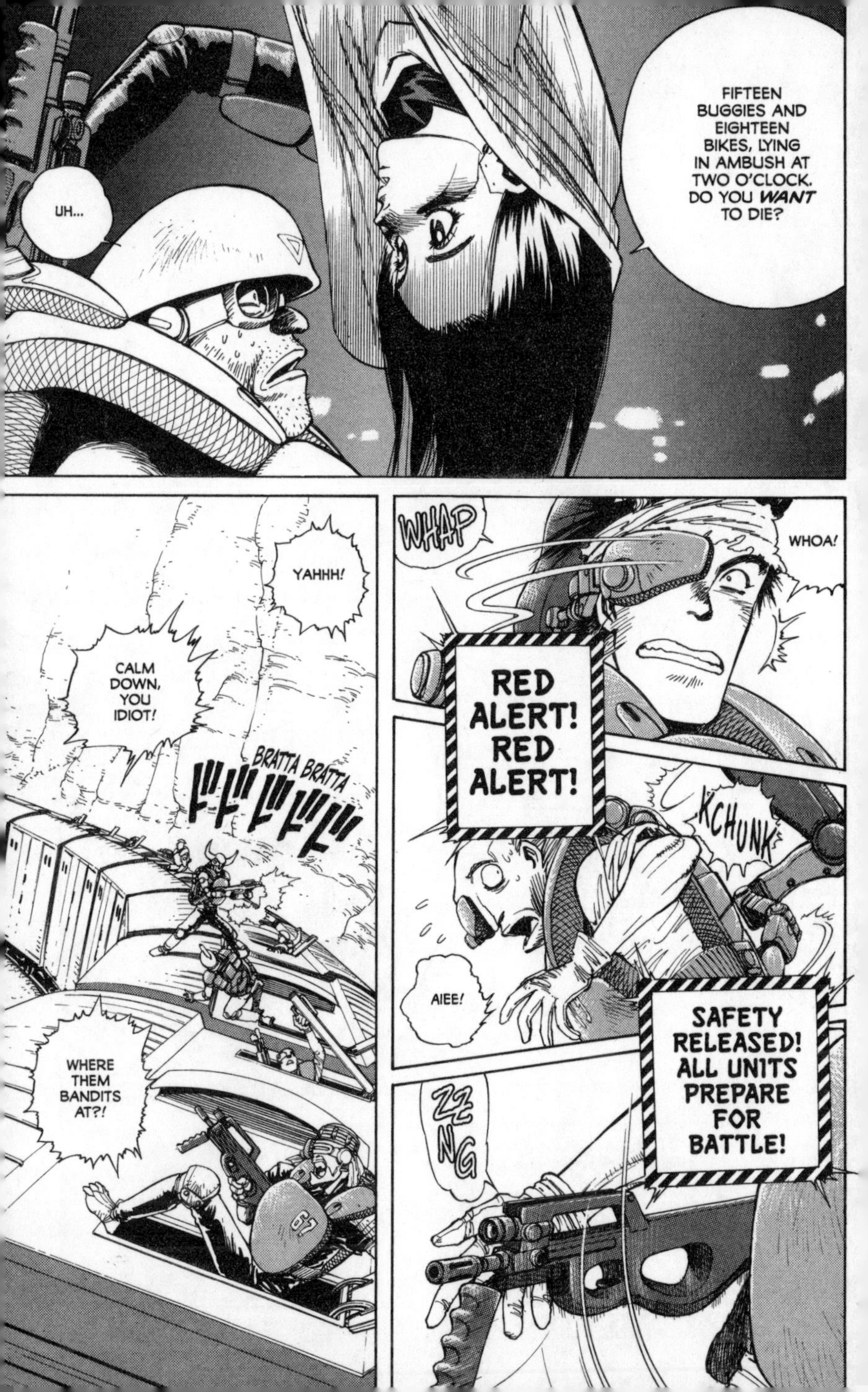
FIFTEEN BUGGIES AND EIGHTEEN BIKES, LYING IN AMBUSH AT TWO O'CLOCK. DO YOU *WANT* TO DIE?
UH...
WHOA!
WHAP
RED ALERT! RED ALERT!
KCHUNK
AIEE!
SAFETY RELEASED! ALL UNITS PREPARE FOR BATTLE!
ZZNG
YAHHH!
CALM DOWN, YOU IDIOT!
BRATTA BRATTA
WHERE THEM BANDITS AT?!

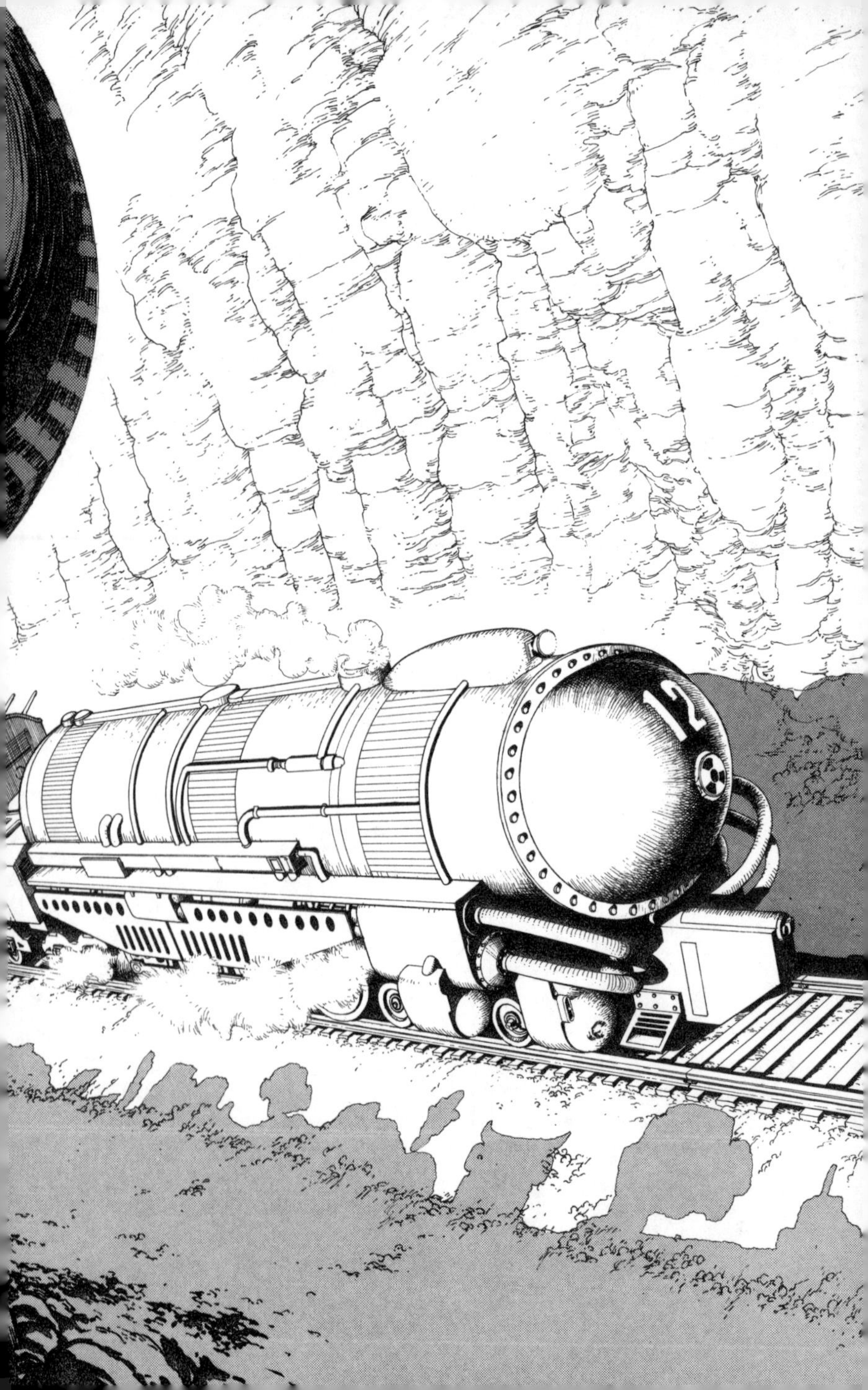
12

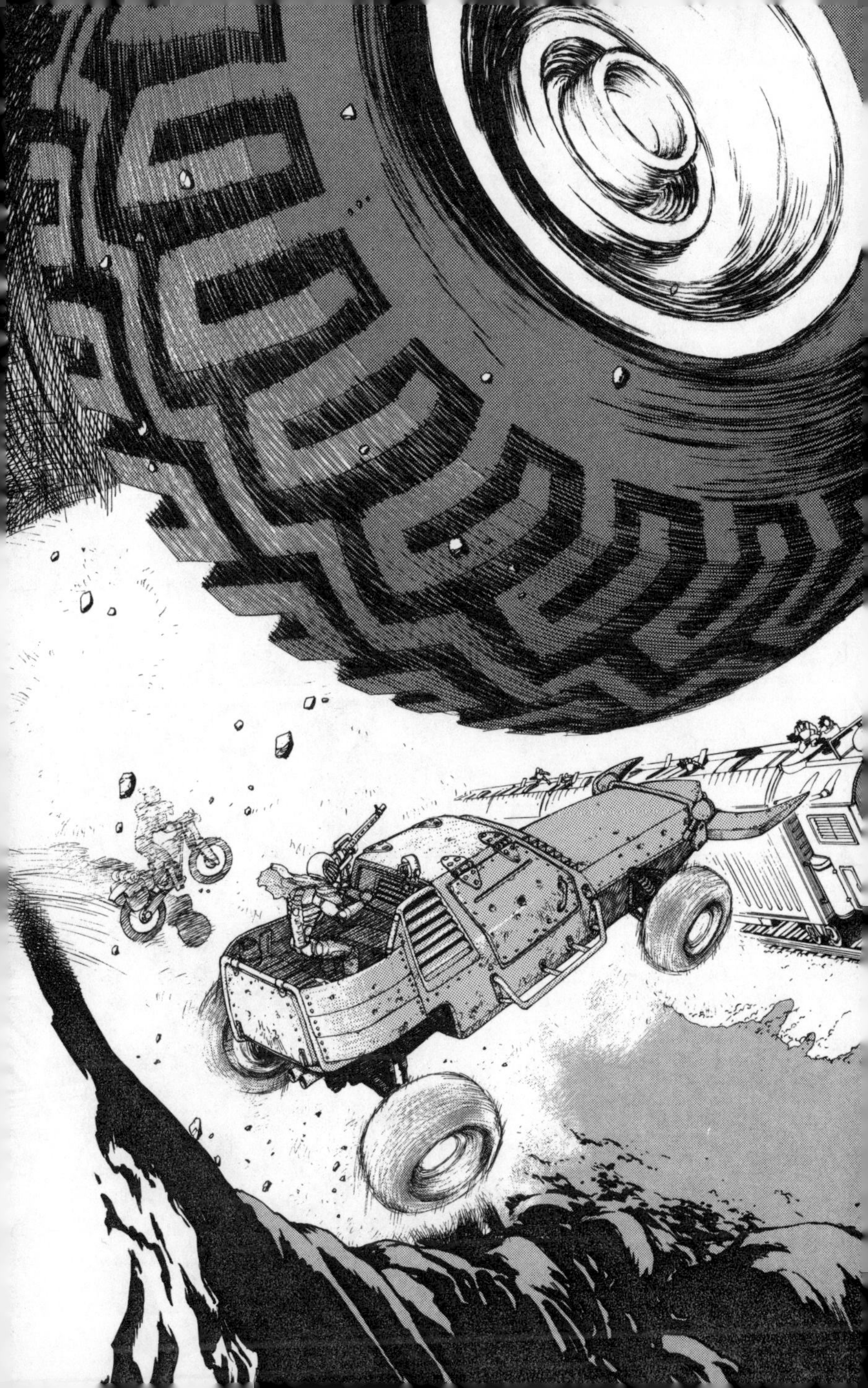

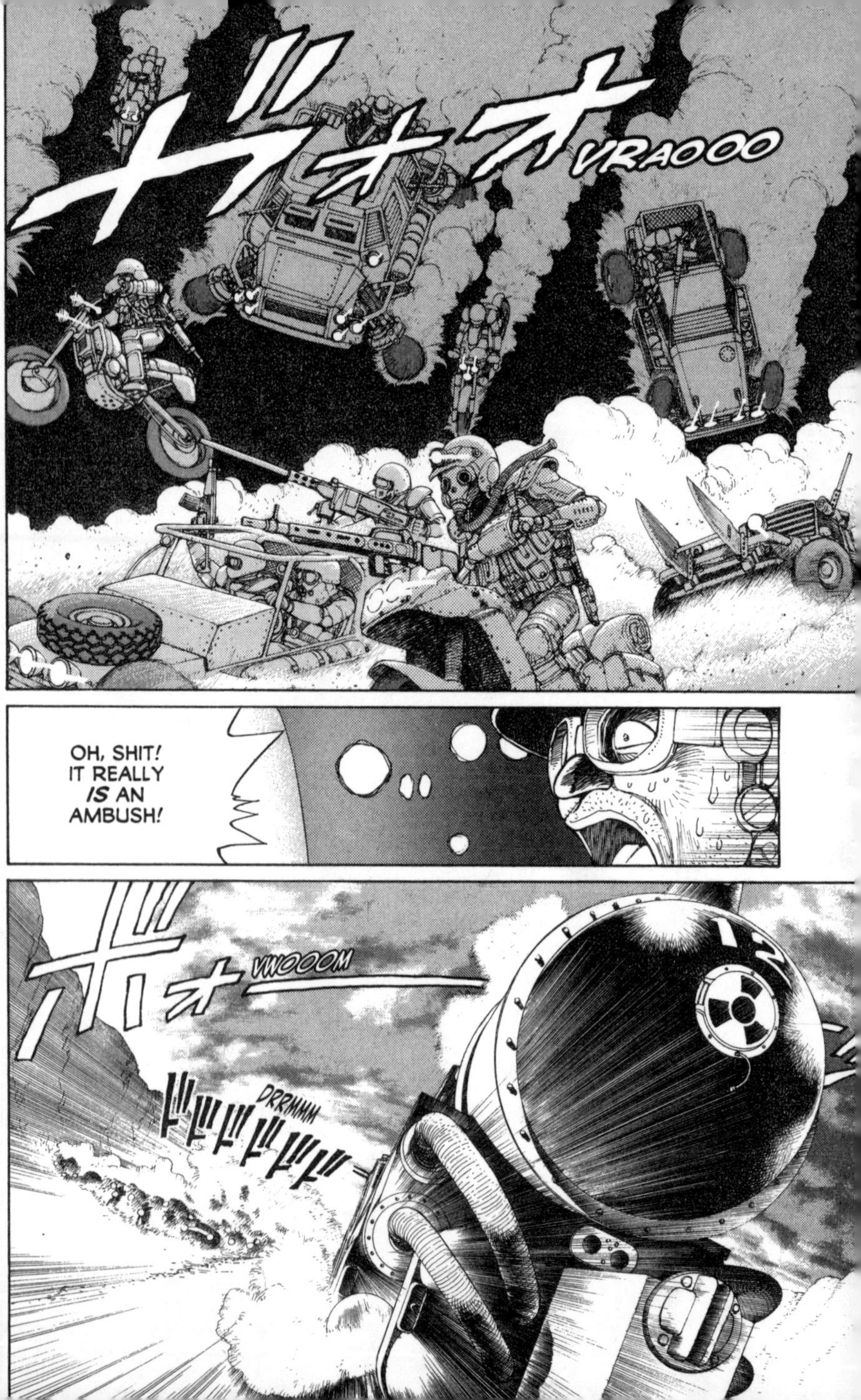
VRAOOO
OH, SHIT! IT REALLY *IS* AN AMBUSH!
VWOOOM
DRRMMM

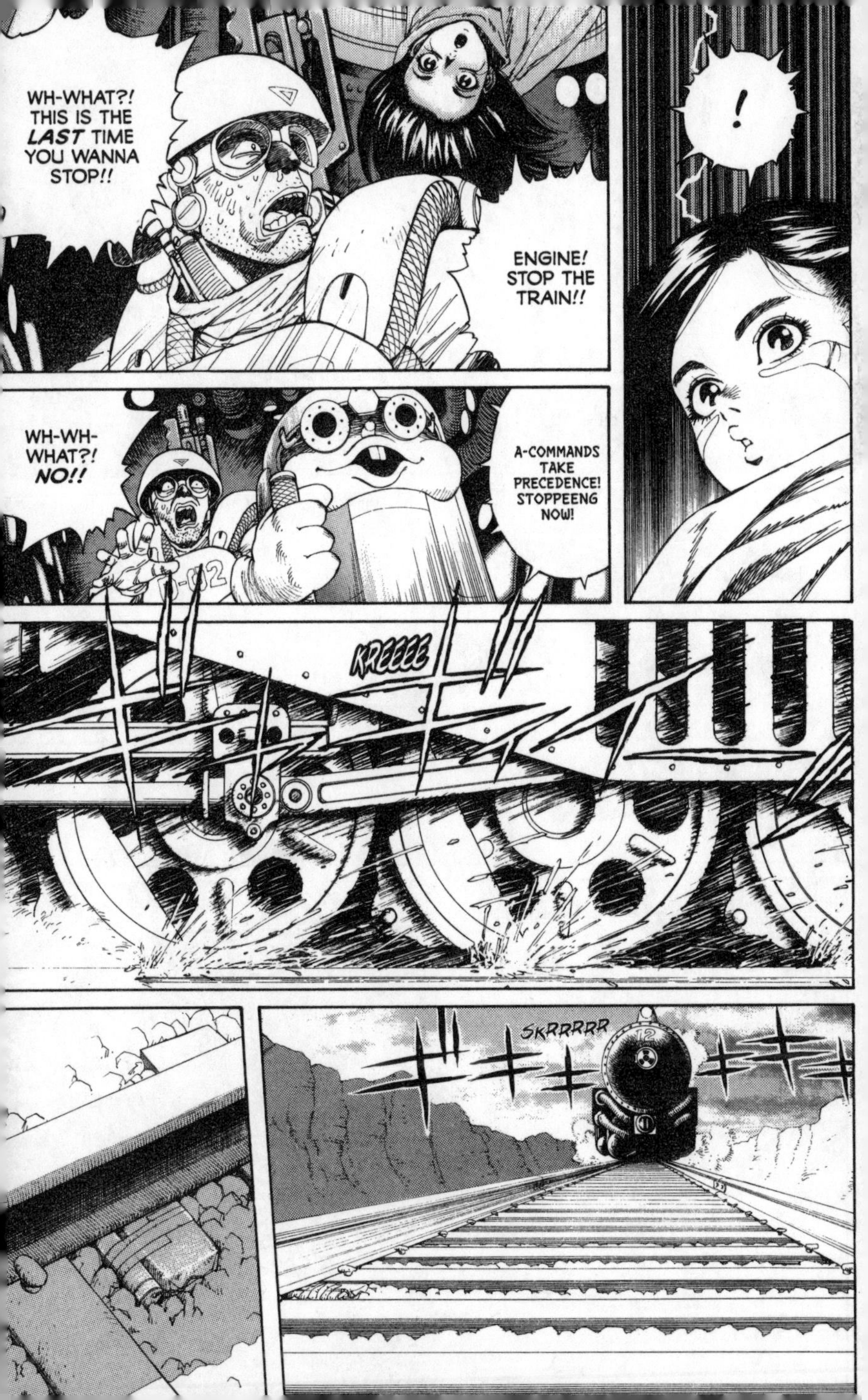
!
ENGINE! STOP THE TRAIN!!
WH-WHAT?! THIS IS THE LAST TIME YOU WANNA STOP!!
A-COMMANDS TAKE PRECEDENCE! STOPPEENG NOW!
WH-WH- WHAT?! NO!!
KREEEE
SKRRRRR

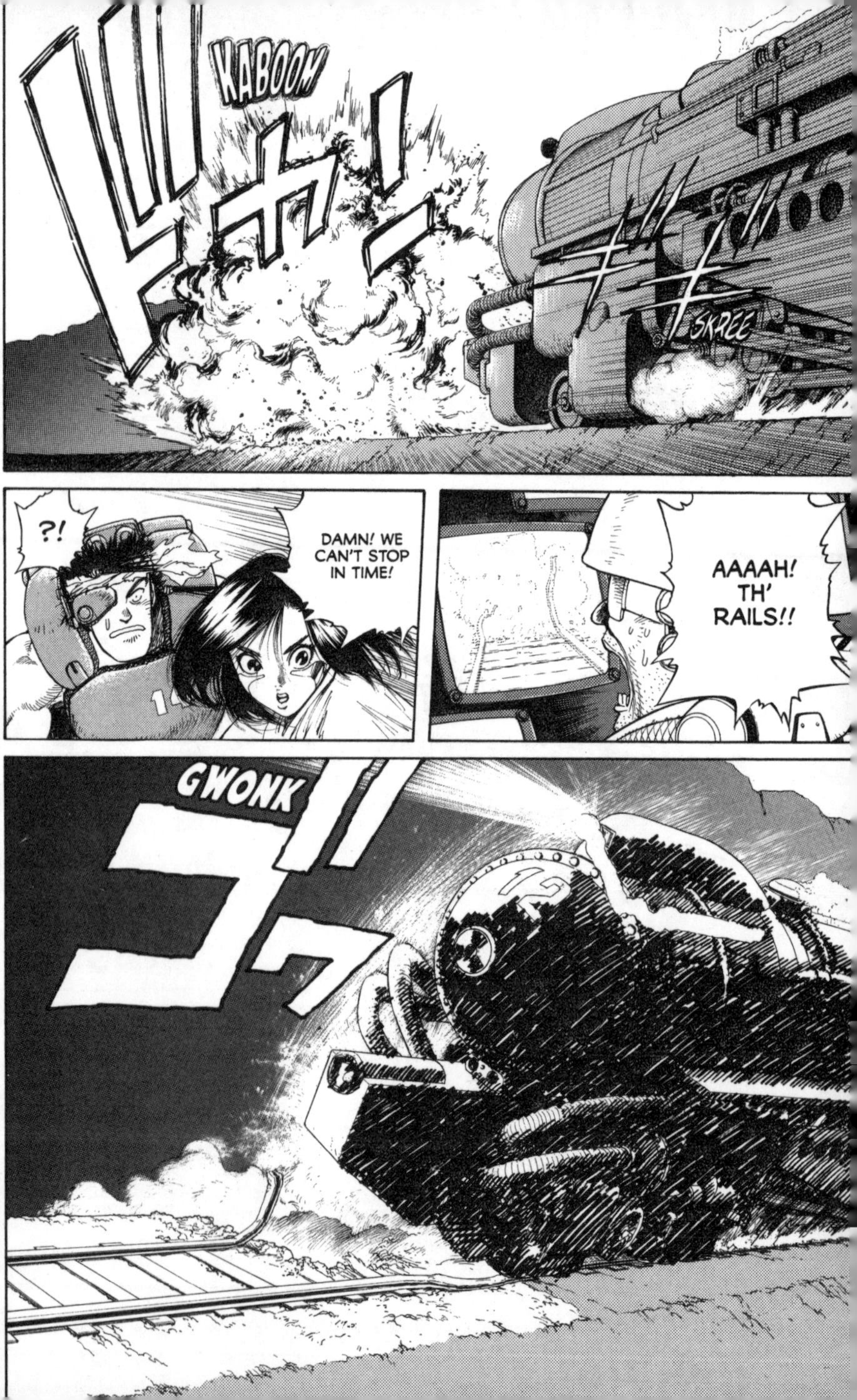
KABOOM
SKREE
AAAAH! TH' RAILS!!
DAMN! WE CAN'T STOP IN TIME!
?!
GWONK

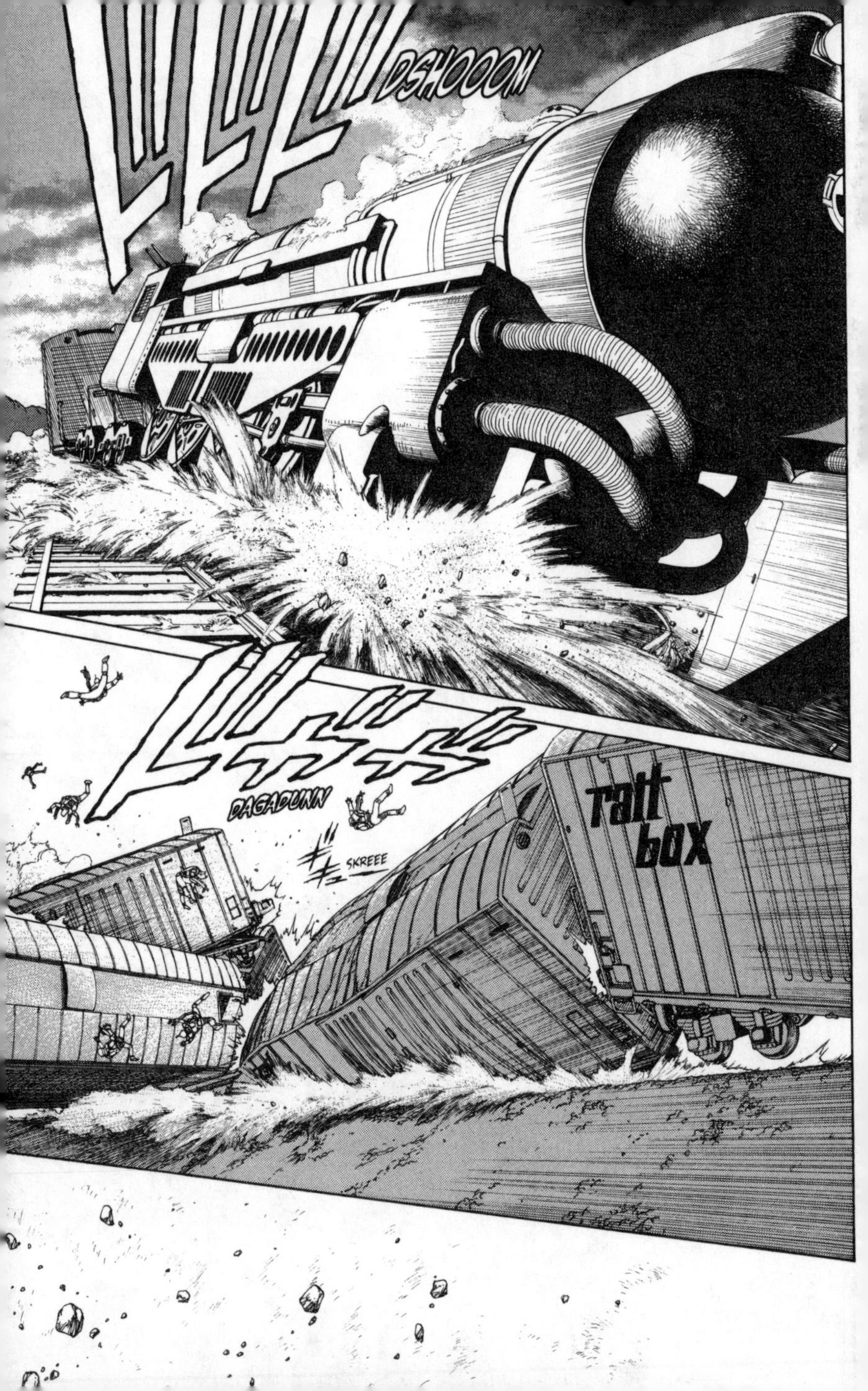
DSHOOOM
DAGADUNN
SKREEE
rail box

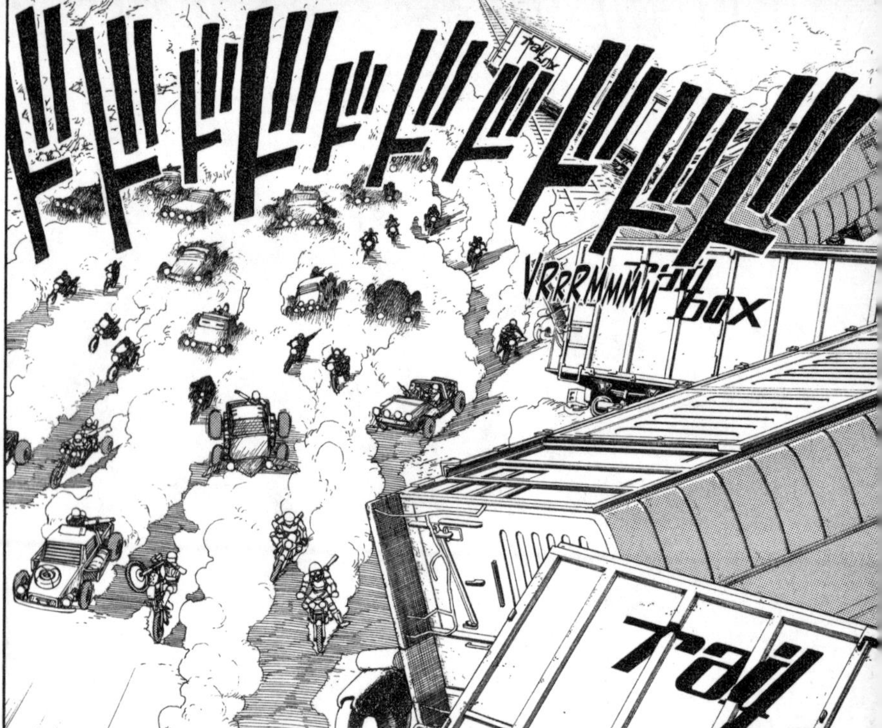
VRRRMMMM
trail box
trail box

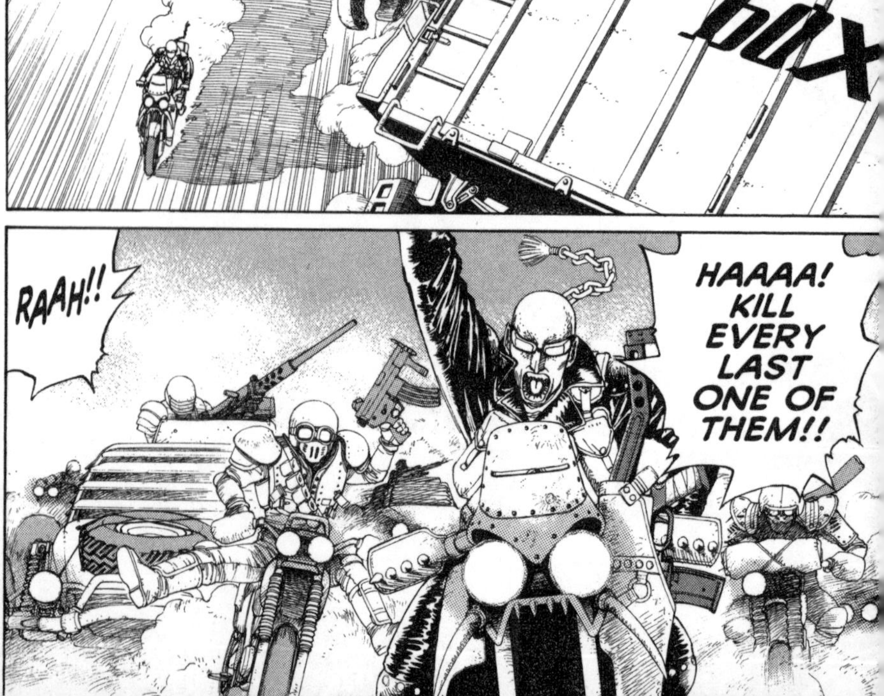
HAAAA! KILL EVERY LAST ONE OF THEM!!
RAAH!!

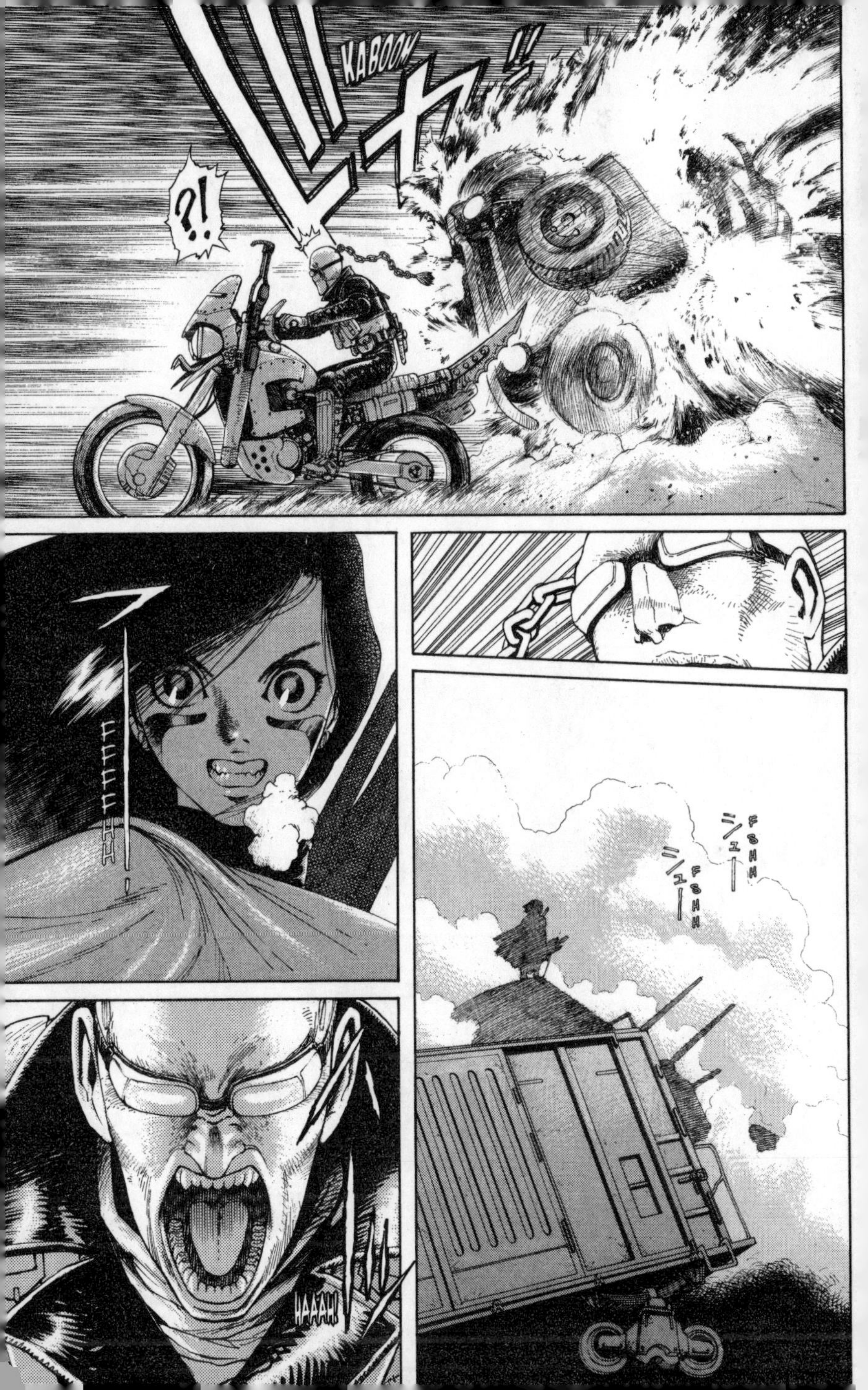
KABOOM
?!
FSHH
FSHH
FFFFHH
HAAAH!

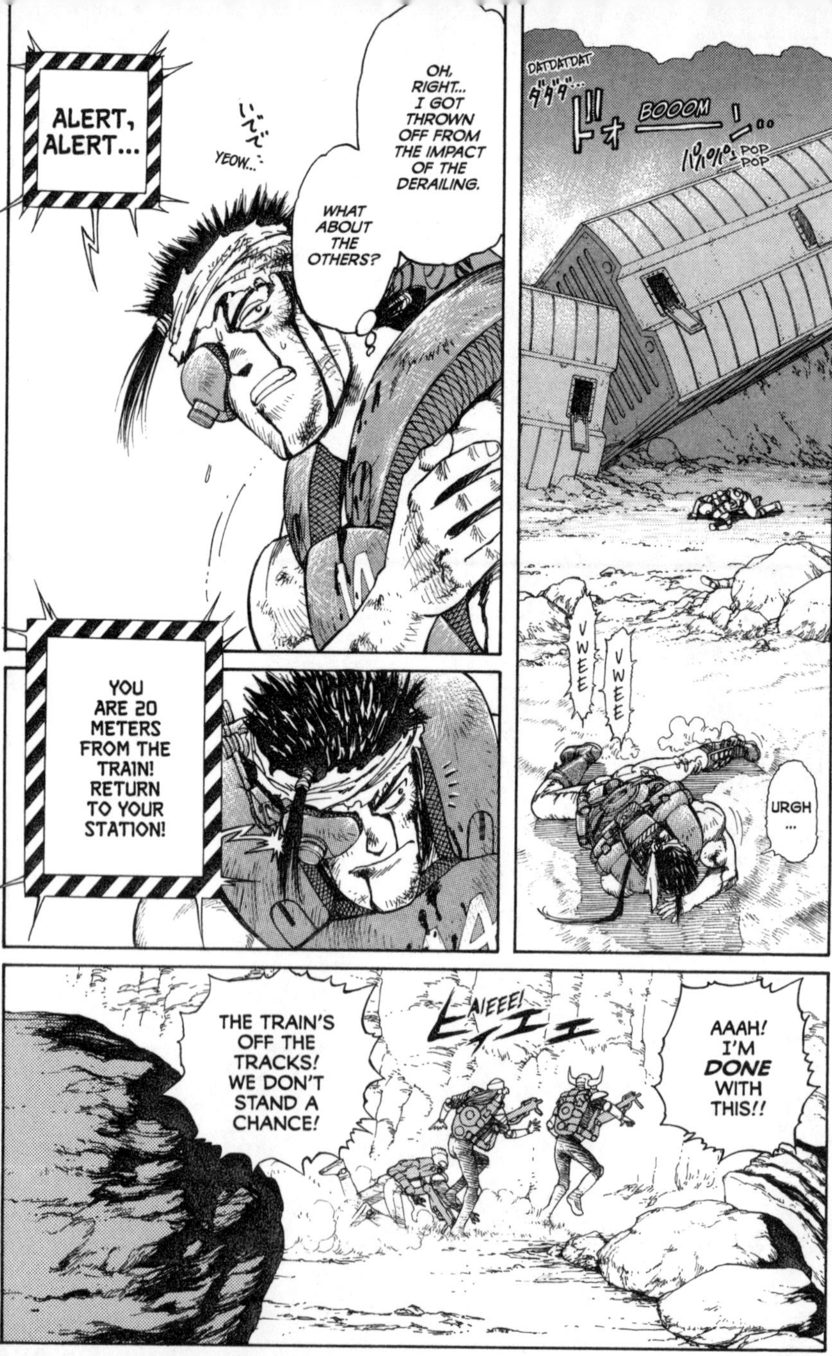
DATDATDAT
BOOOM
POP POP
VWEE
VWEE
URGH ...
OH, RIGHT... I GOT THROWN OFF FROM THE IMPACT OF THE DERAILING.
WHAT ABOUT THE OTHERS?
YEOW...
ALERT, ALERT...
YOU ARE 20 METERS FROM THE TRAIN! RETURN TO YOUR STATION!
AAAH! I'M DONE WITH THIS!!
AIEEE!
THE TRAIN'S OFF THE TRACKS! WE DON'T STAND A CHANCE!

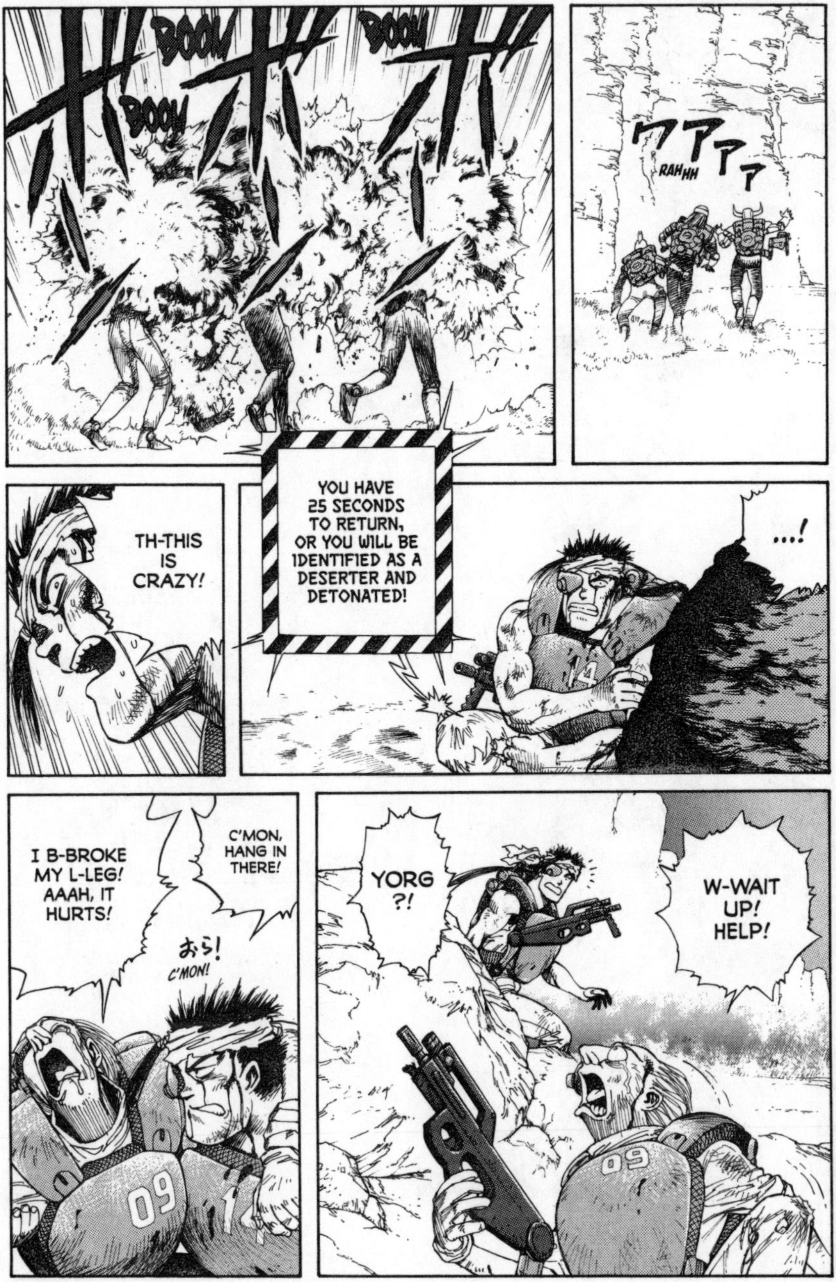
ワアアア
RAHHH
BOOM
BOOM
BOOM
...!
YOU HAVE 25 SECONDS TO RETURN, OR YOU WILL BE IDENTIFIED AS A DESERTER AND DETONATED!
TH-THIS IS CRAZY!
W-WAIT UP! HELP!
YORG ?!
C'MON, HANG IN THERE!
I B-BROKE MY L-LEG! AAAH, IT HURTS!
おら!
C'MON!

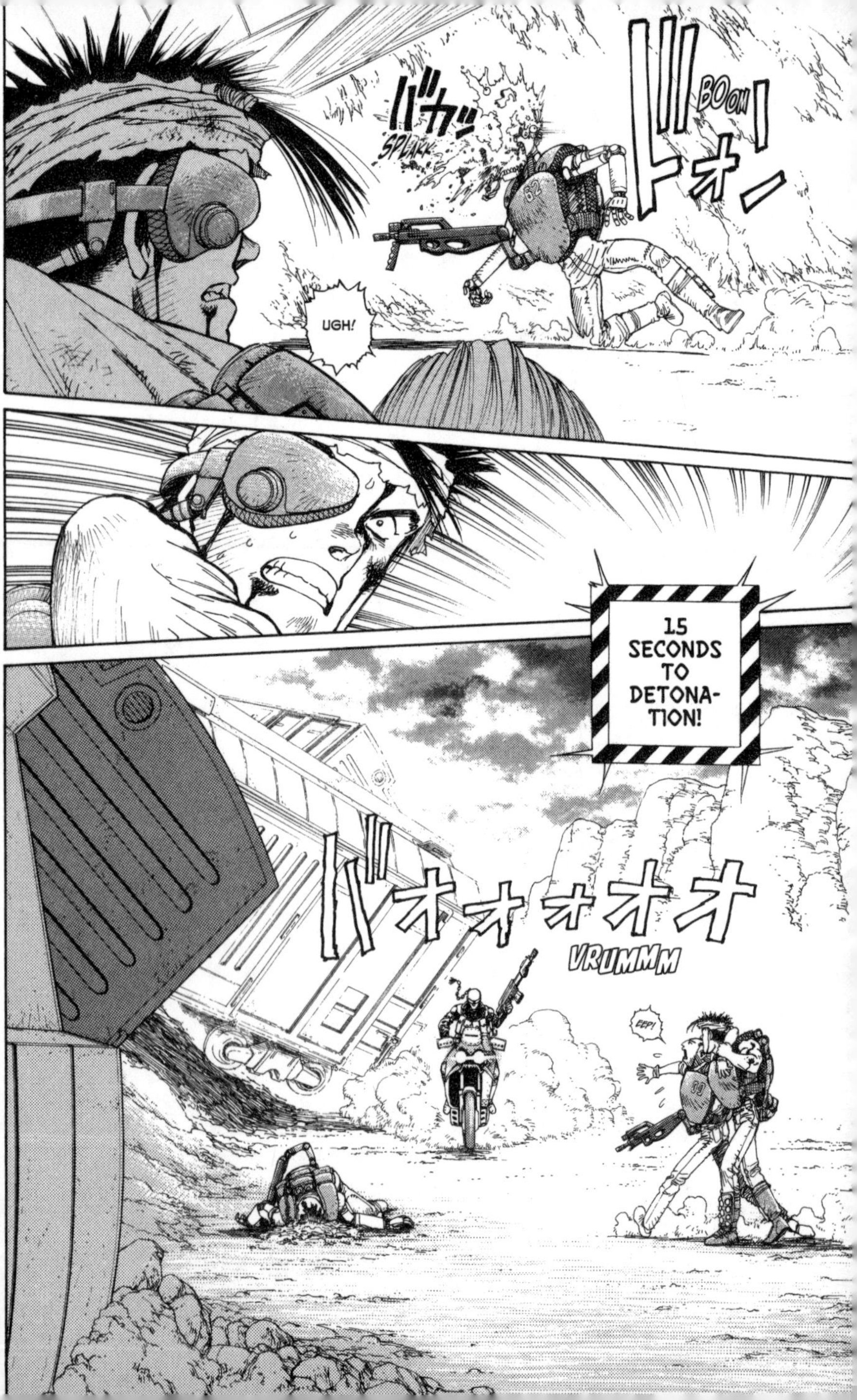
ドォー
BOOM
バガッ
SPLAKK
UGH!
15 SECONDS TO DETONATION!
ドオォォオオ
VRUMMM
EEP!

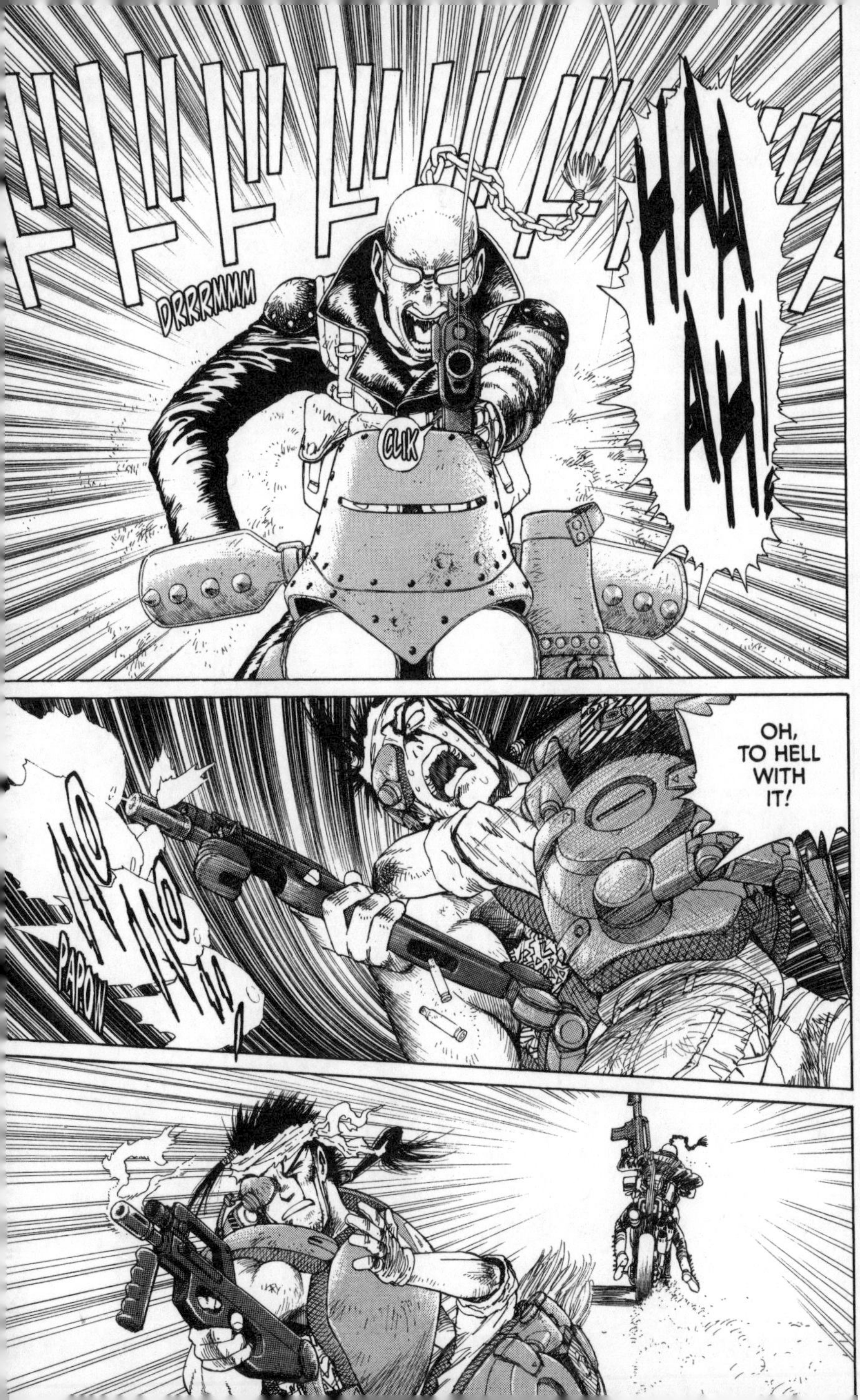
HAA AH!
DRRRMMM
CLIK
OH, TO HELL WITH IT!
PAPOW

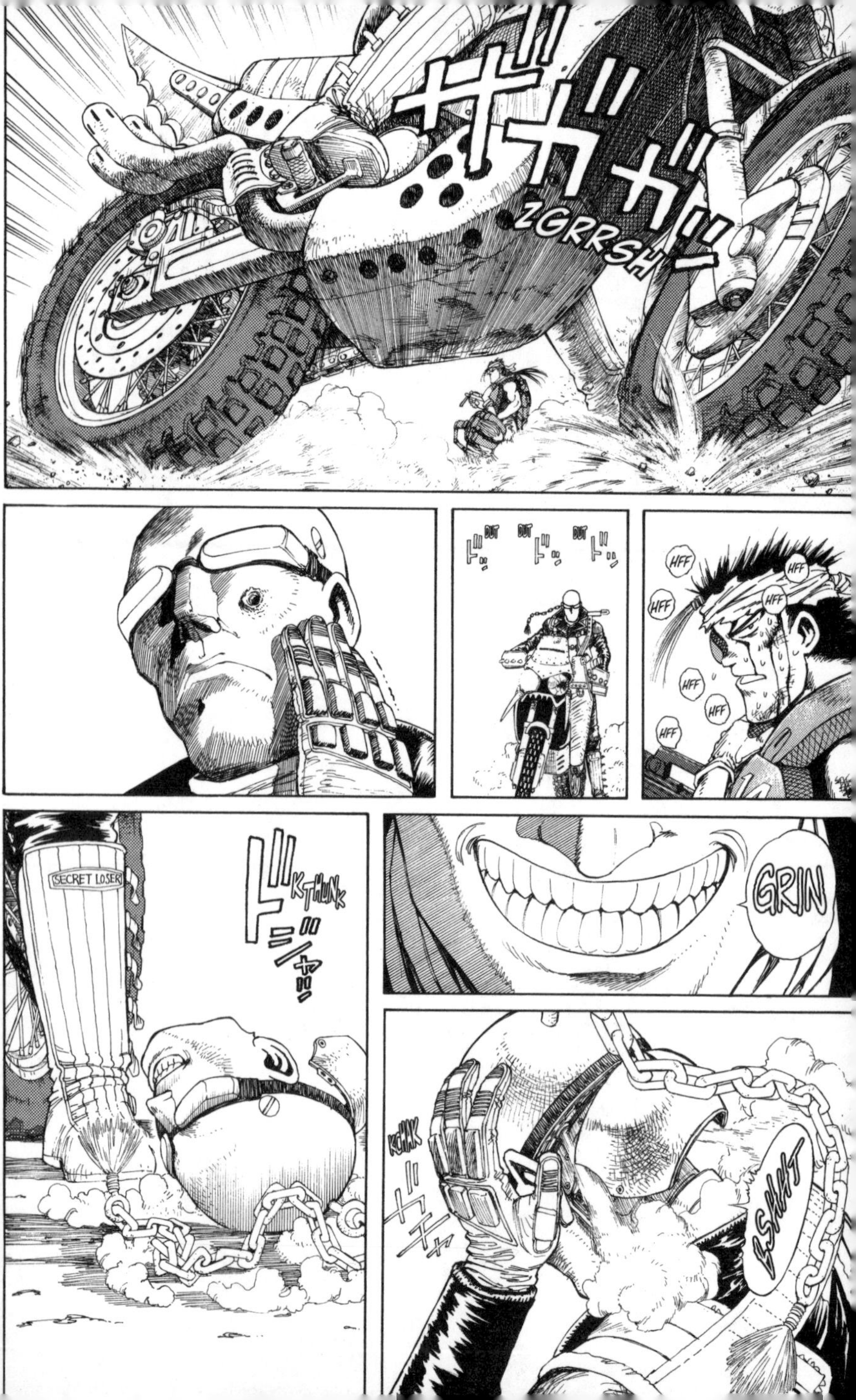
ZGRRSH
DUT DUT DUT
HFF HFF HFF HFF HFF HFF HFF
GRIN
SHAKT
KCHAK
KTHUNK
SECRET LOSER

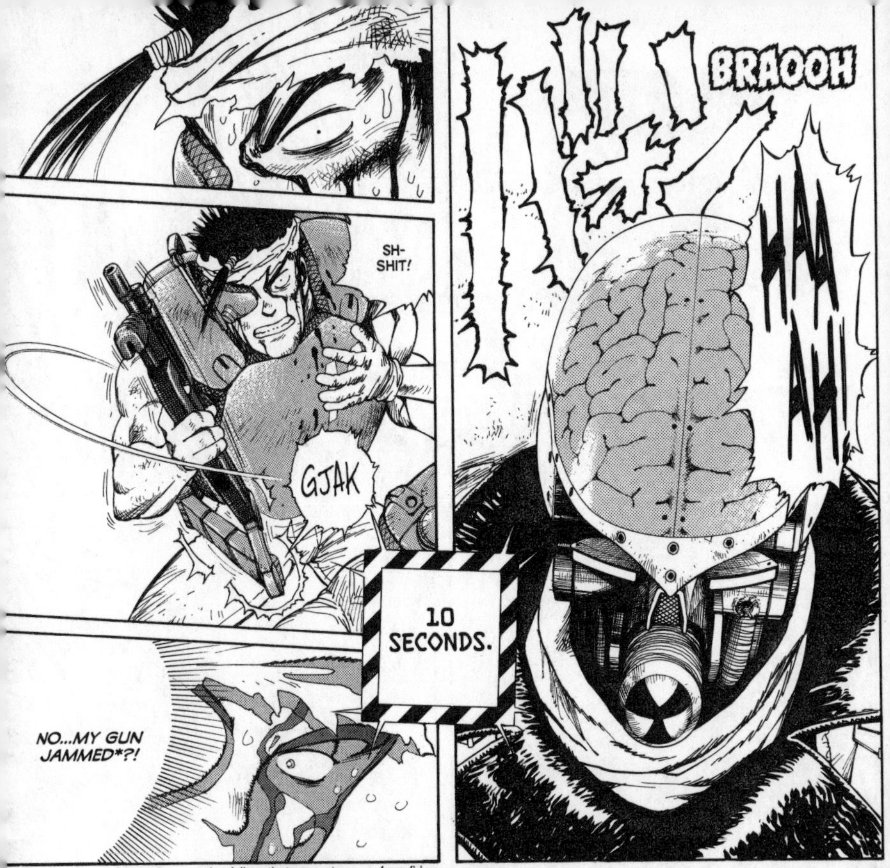
BRAOOH
HAA AAH!
10 SECONDS.
SH-SHIT!
GJAK
NO...MY GUN JAMMED*?!

***Jam:** An operation failure that prevents a gun from firing.

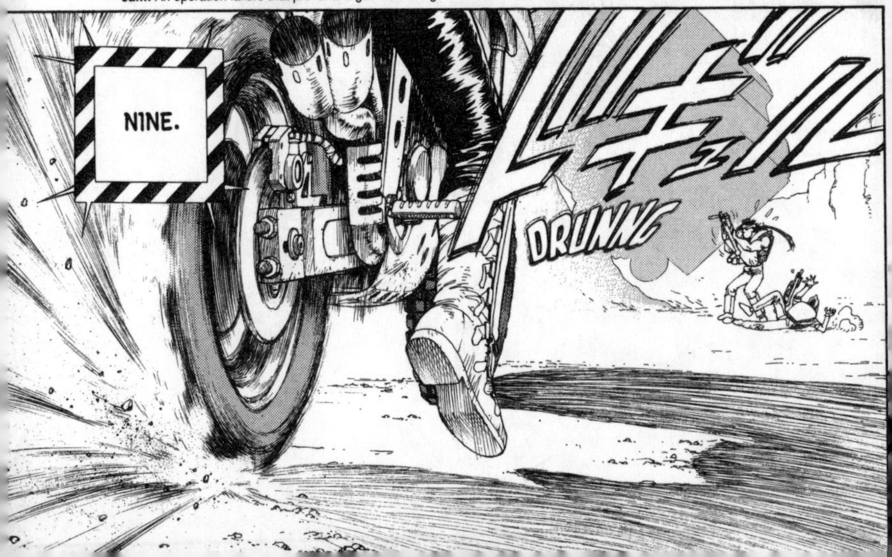
NINE.
DRUNNG

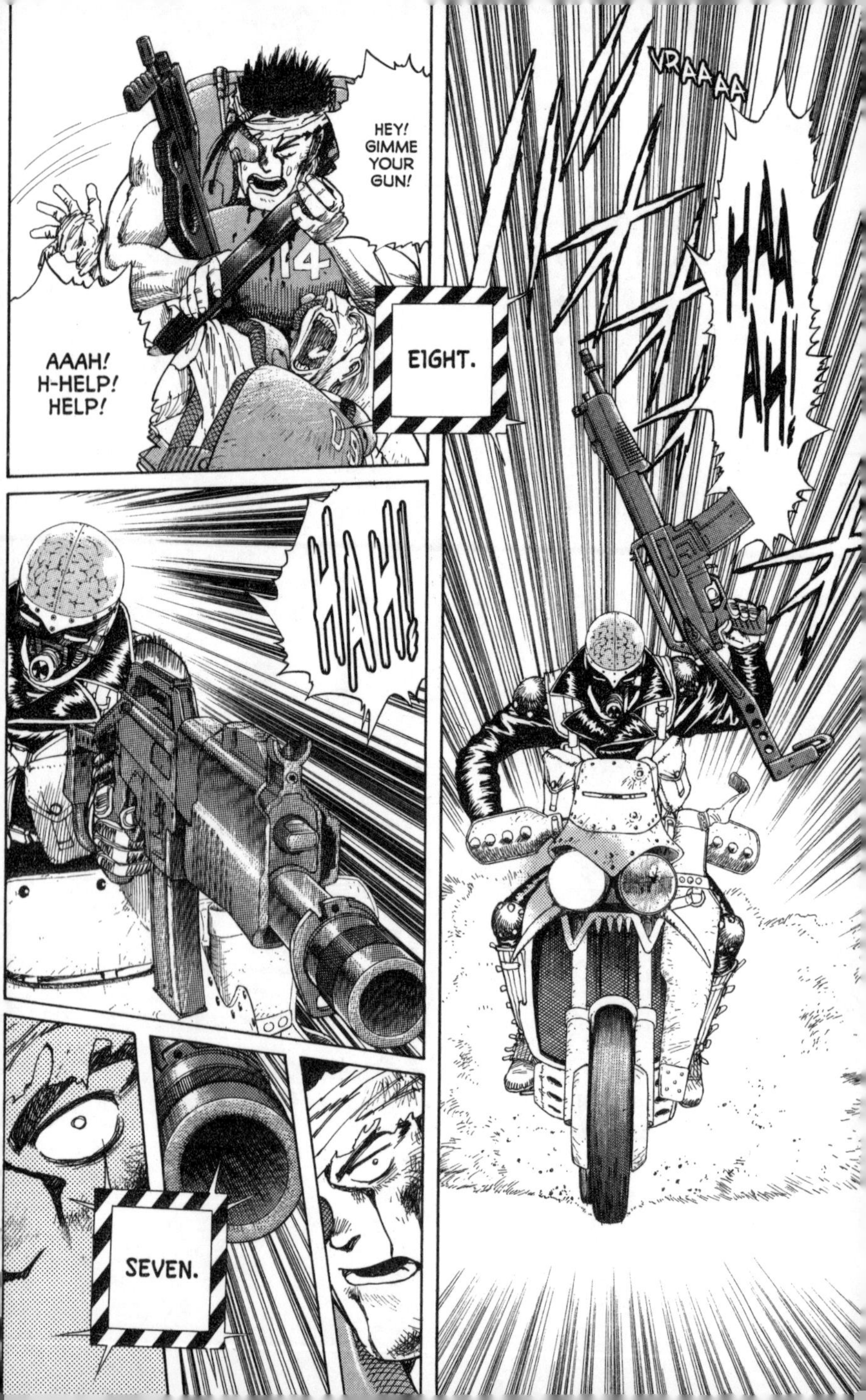
VRAAAAA
HAA AH!
HEY! GIMME YOUR GUN!
EIGHT.
AAAH! H-HELP! HELP!
HAH!
SEVEN.

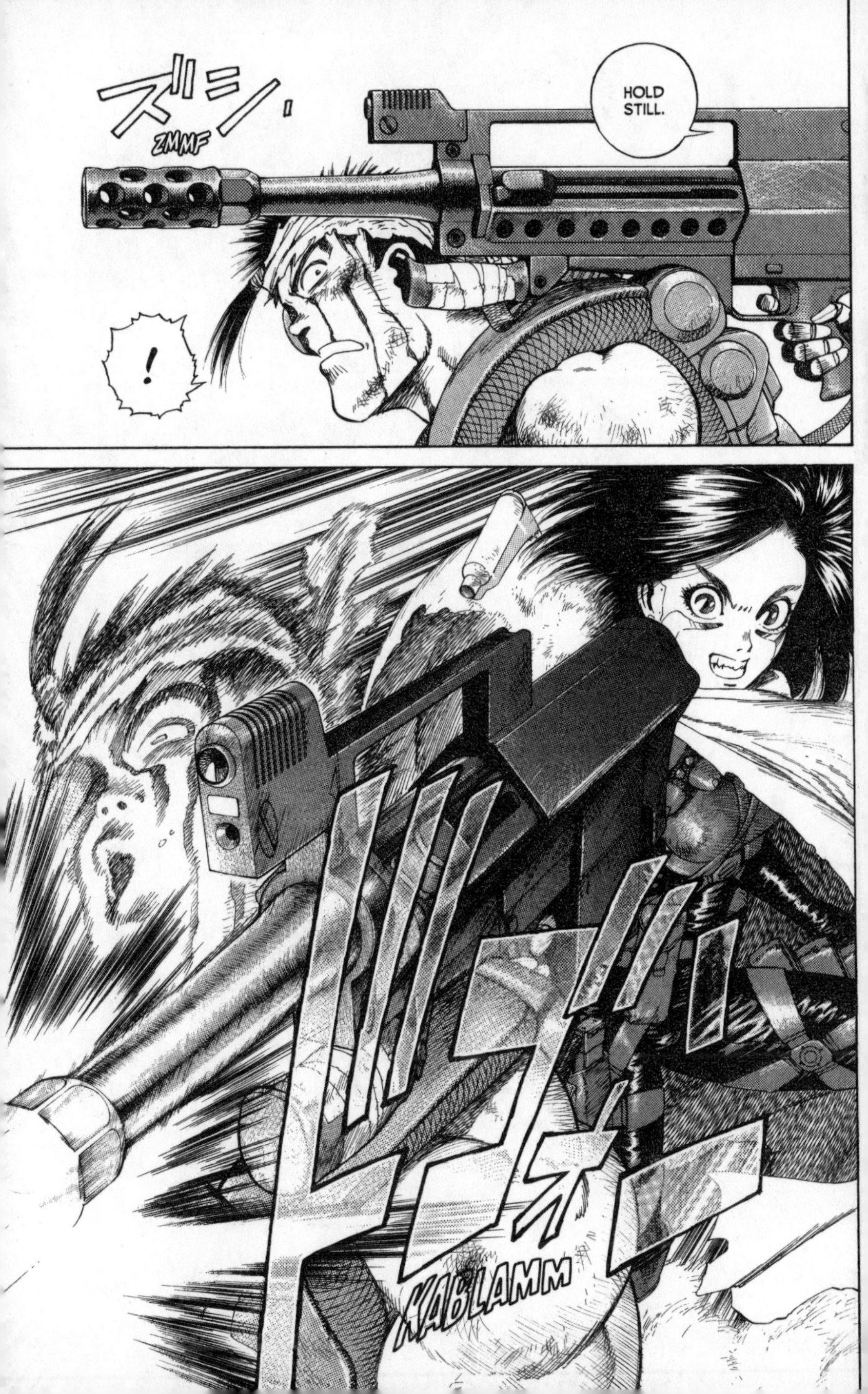
HOLD STILL.
ZMMF
!
KABLAMM

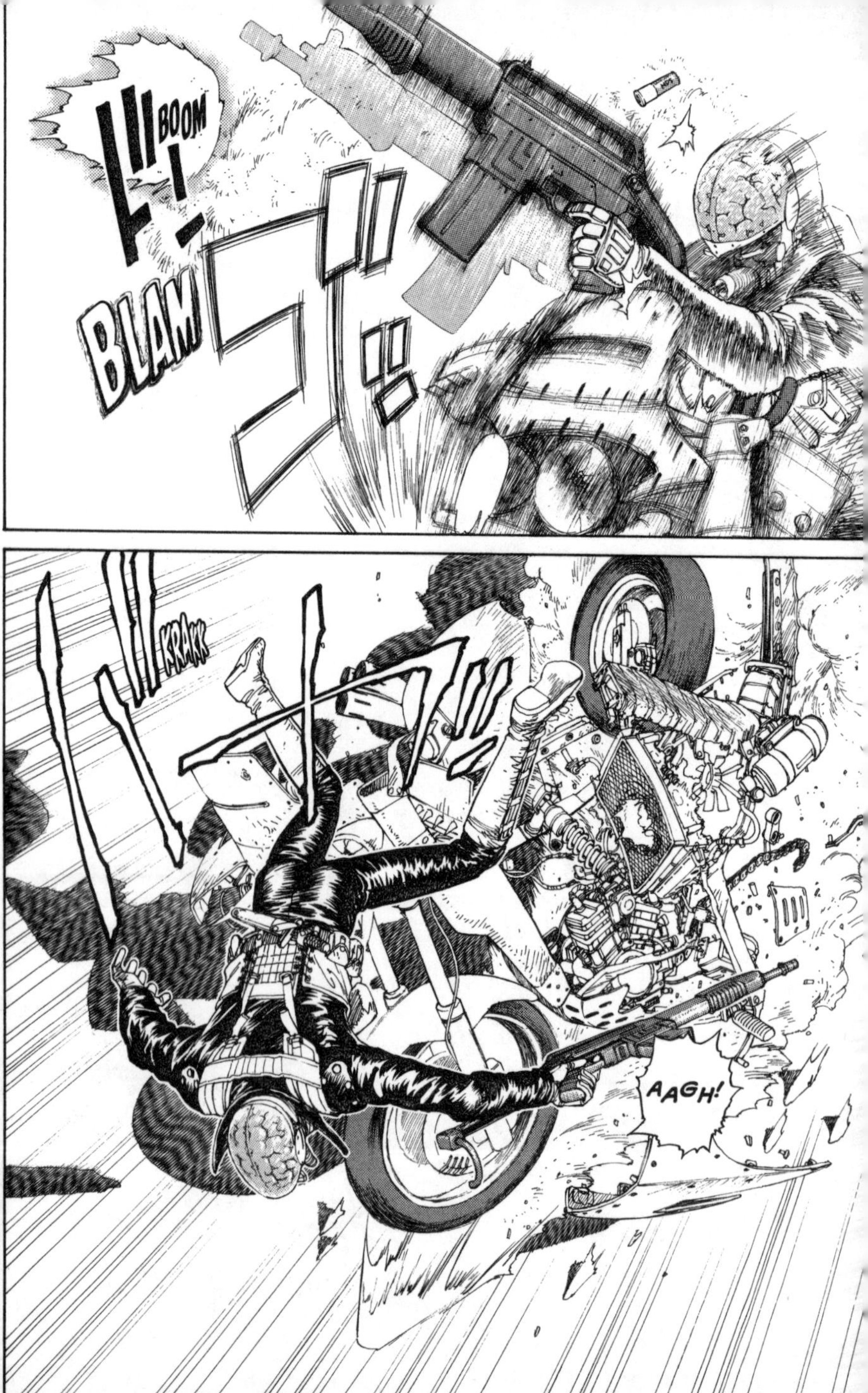
BOOM
BLAM
KRAKK
AAGH!

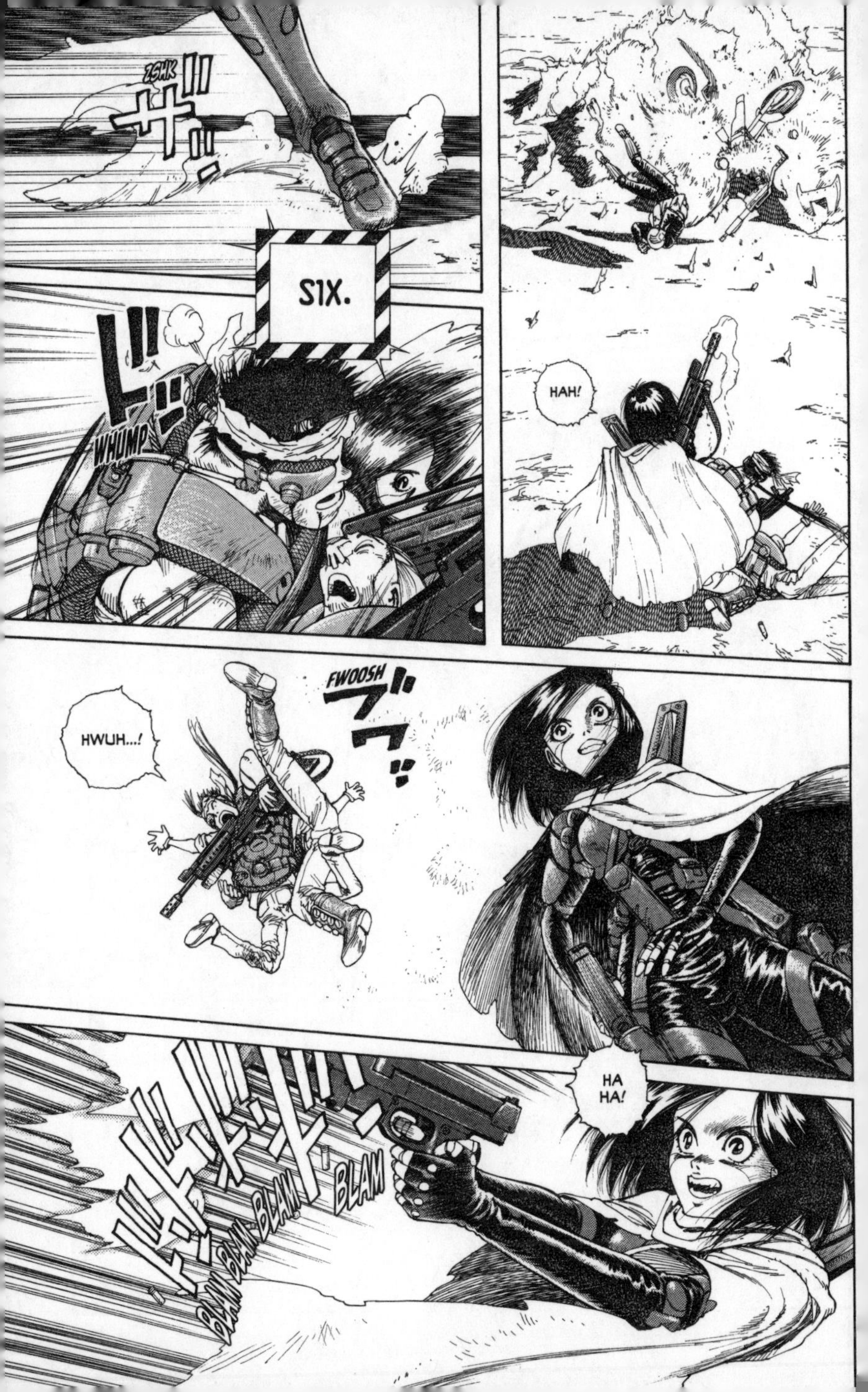
HAH!
ZSHK
SIX.
WHUMP
FWOOSH
HWUH...!
HA HA!
BLAM BLAM BLAM BLAM

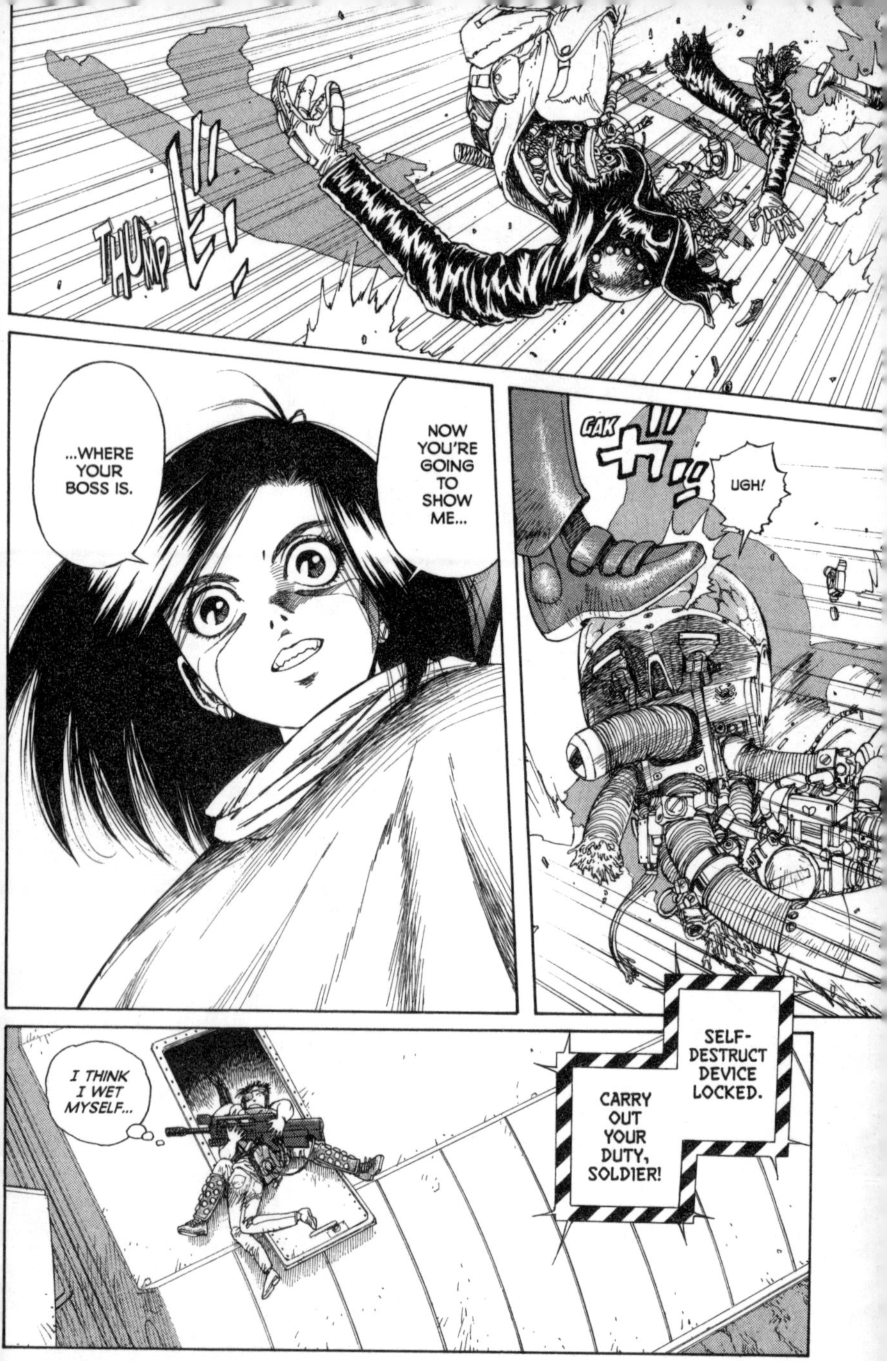
THUMP
GAK
UGH!
NOW YOU'RE GOING TO SHOW ME...
...WHERE YOUR BOSS IS.
SELF-DESTRUCT DEVICE LOCKED.
CARRY OUT YOUR DUTY, SOLDIER!
I THINK I WET MYSELF...

FIGHT_032 Wild West Heroes

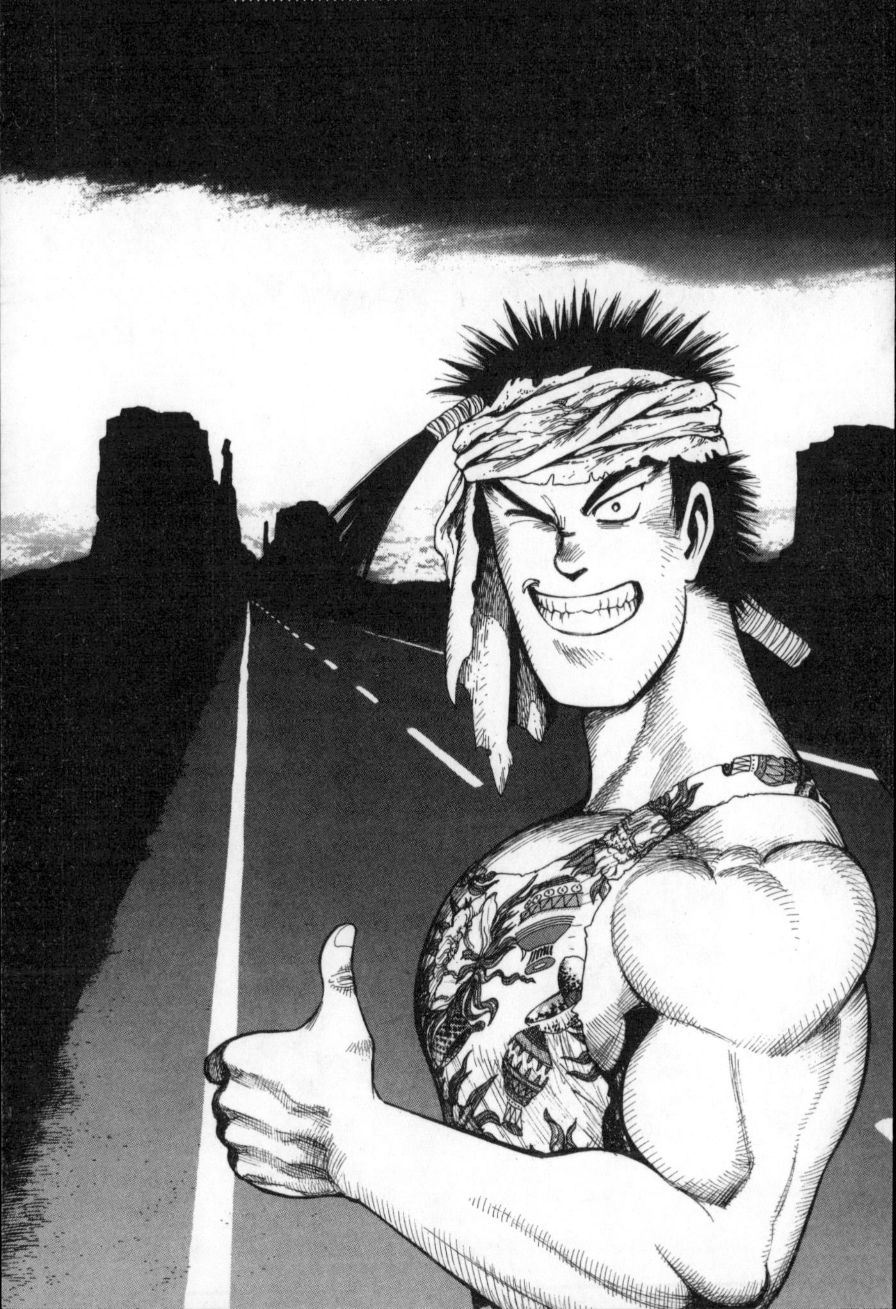

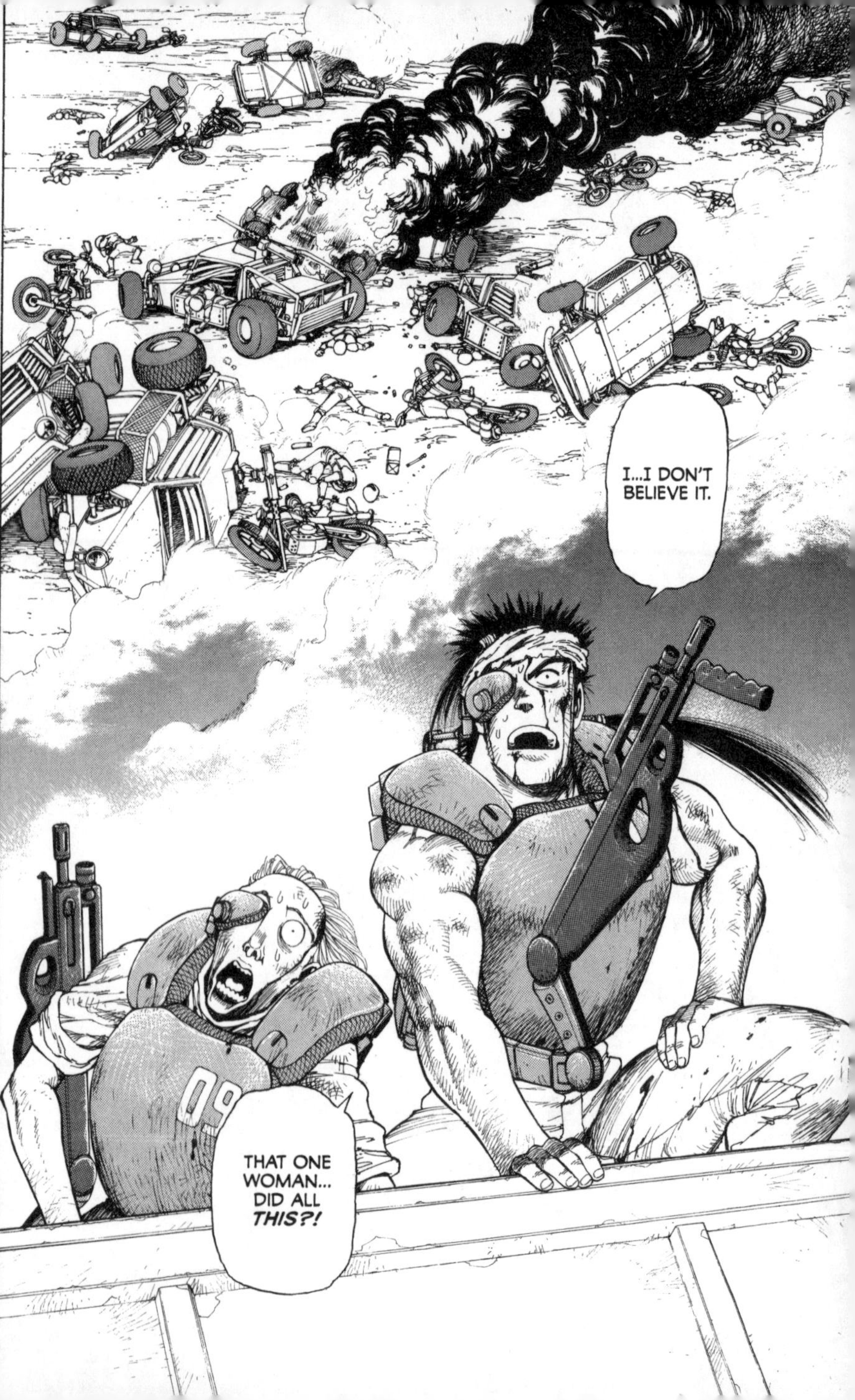
I...I DON'T BELIEVE IT.
THAT ONE WOMAN... DID ALL *THIS?!*

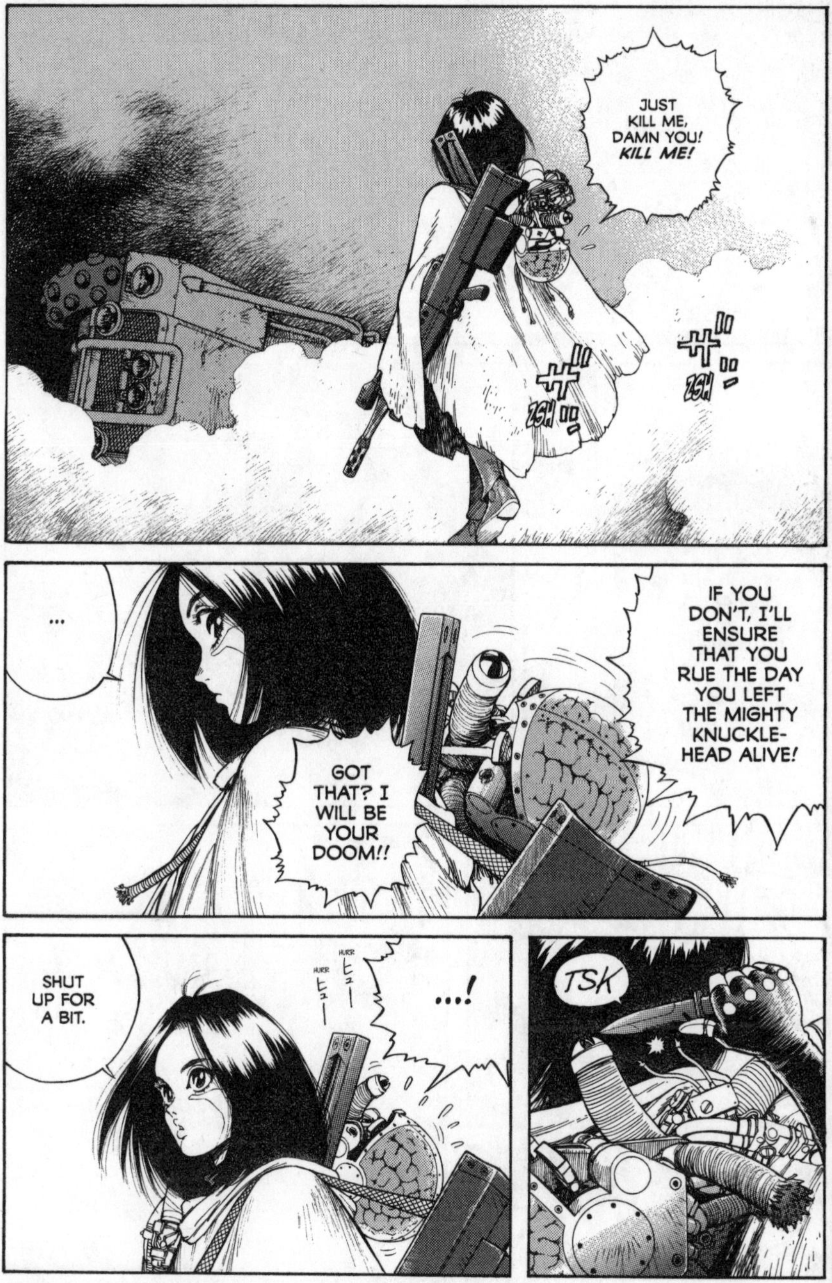
JUST KILL ME, DAMN YOU! *KILL ME!*
ZSH
ZSH
IF YOU DON'T, I'LL ENSURE THAT YOU RUE THE DAY YOU LEFT THE MIGHTY KNUCKLE-HEAD ALIVE!
GOT THAT? I WILL BE YOUR DOOM!!
...
TSK
...!
HURR
HURR
SHUT UP FOR A BIT.

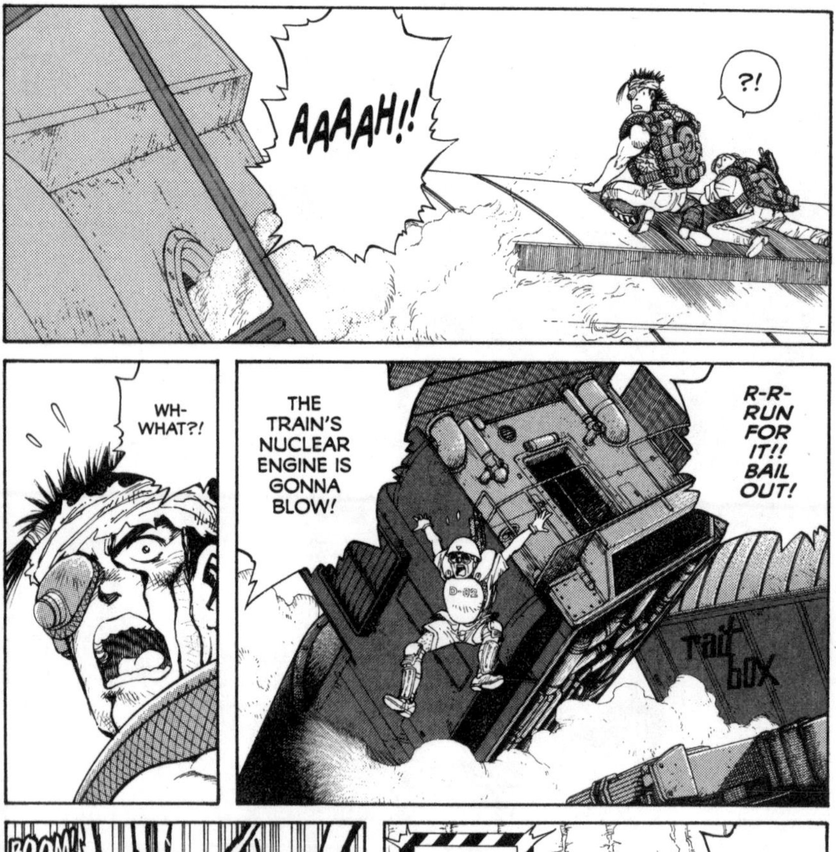
?!
AAAAH!!
R-R-RUN FOR IT!! BAIL OUT!
THE TRAIN'S NUCLEAR ENGINE IS GONNA BLOW!
rail box
WH-WHAT?!
TAKE MY ADVICE: RUN FOR YOUR LIVES!!
ALERT, ALERT...
BOOM!
EEP!

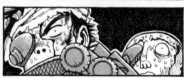

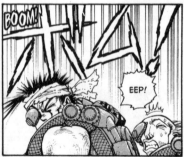

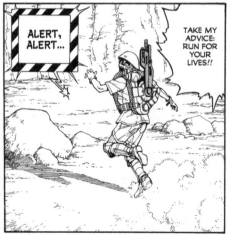

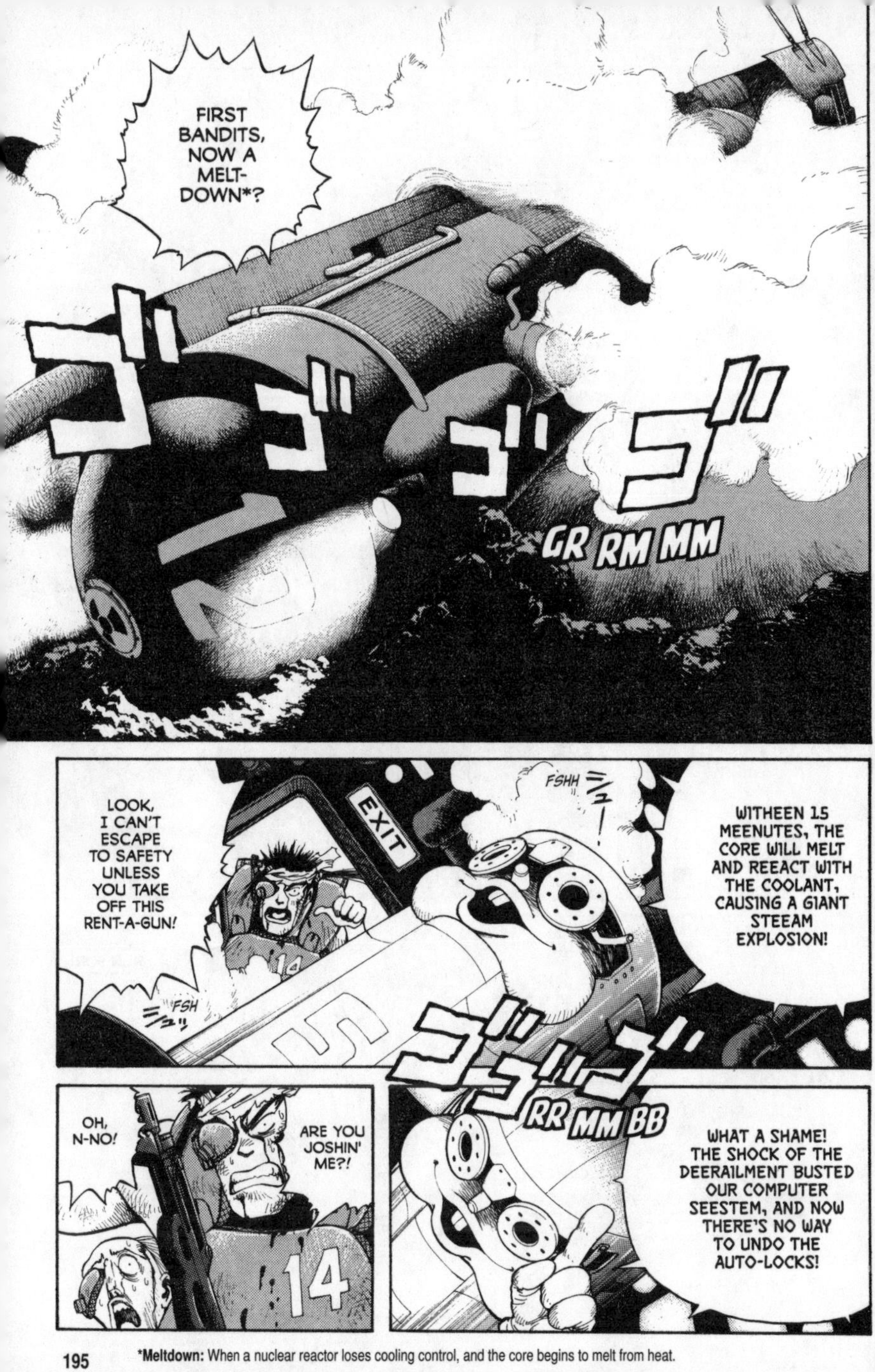
FIRST BANDITS, NOW A MELT-DOWN*?
ゴゴゴゴ
GR RM MM
FSHH
WITHEEN 15 MEENUTES, THE CORE WILL MELT AND REEACT WITH THE COOLANT, CAUSING A GIANT STEEAM EXPLOSION!
EXIT
LOOK, I CAN'T ESCAPE TO SAFETY UNLESS YOU TAKE OFF THIS RENT-A-GUN!
14
FSH
RR MM BB
WHAT A SHAME! THE SHOCK OF THE DEERAILMENT BUSTED OUR COMPUTER SEESTEM, AND NOW THERE'S NO WAY TO UNDO THE AUTO-LOCKS!
ARE YOU JOSHIN' ME?!
OH, N-NO!
14

***Meltdown:** When a nuclear reactor loses cooling control, and the core begins to melt from heat.

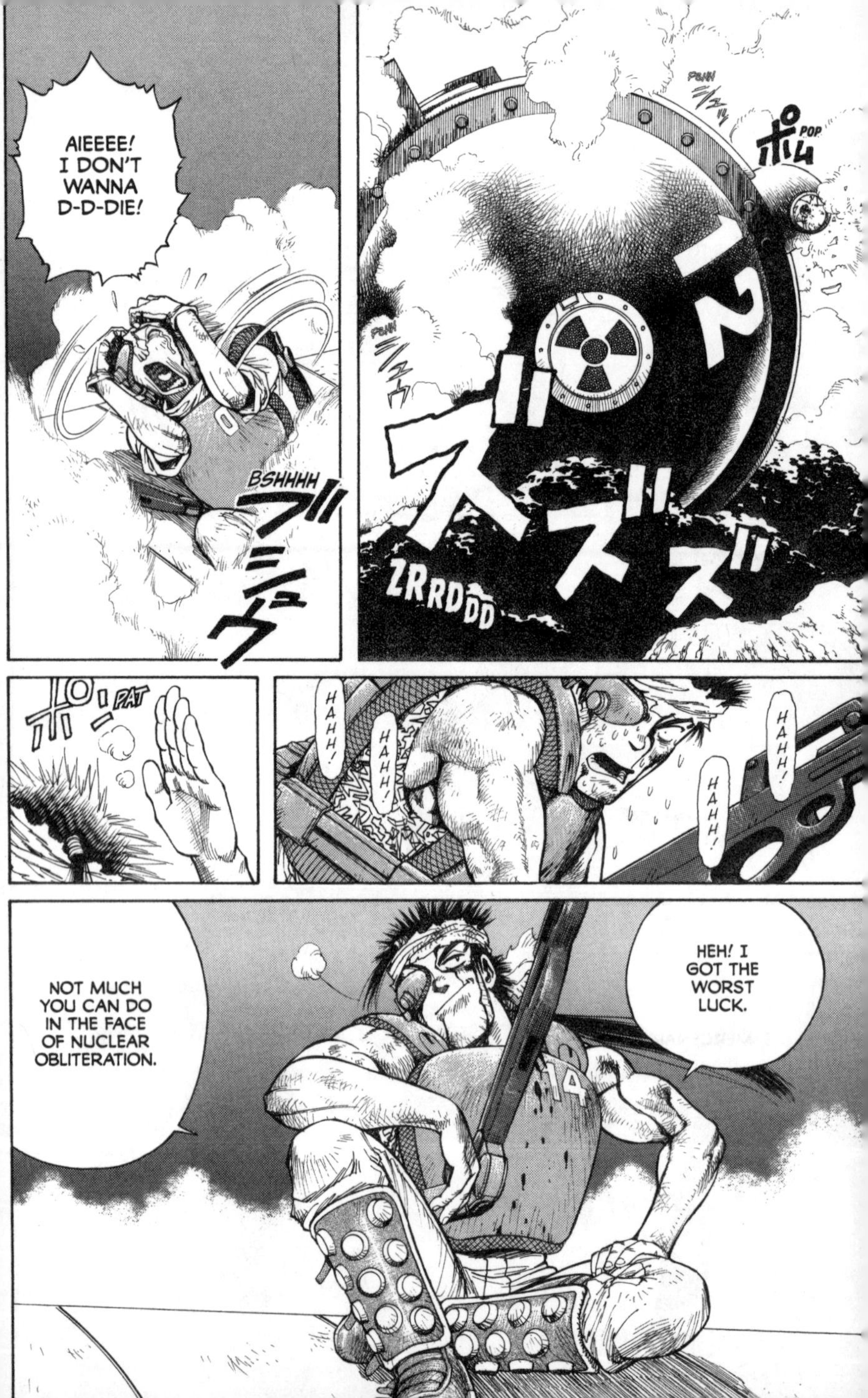
PSHH
ポム POP
PSHH
ズズズ
ZRRDDD
AIEEEE! I DON'T WANNA D-D-DIE!
BSHHHH
HAHH!
HAHH!
HAHH!
HAHH!
PAT
HEH! I GOT THE WORST LUCK.
NOT MUCH YOU CAN DO IN THE FACE OF NUCLEAR OBLITERATION.

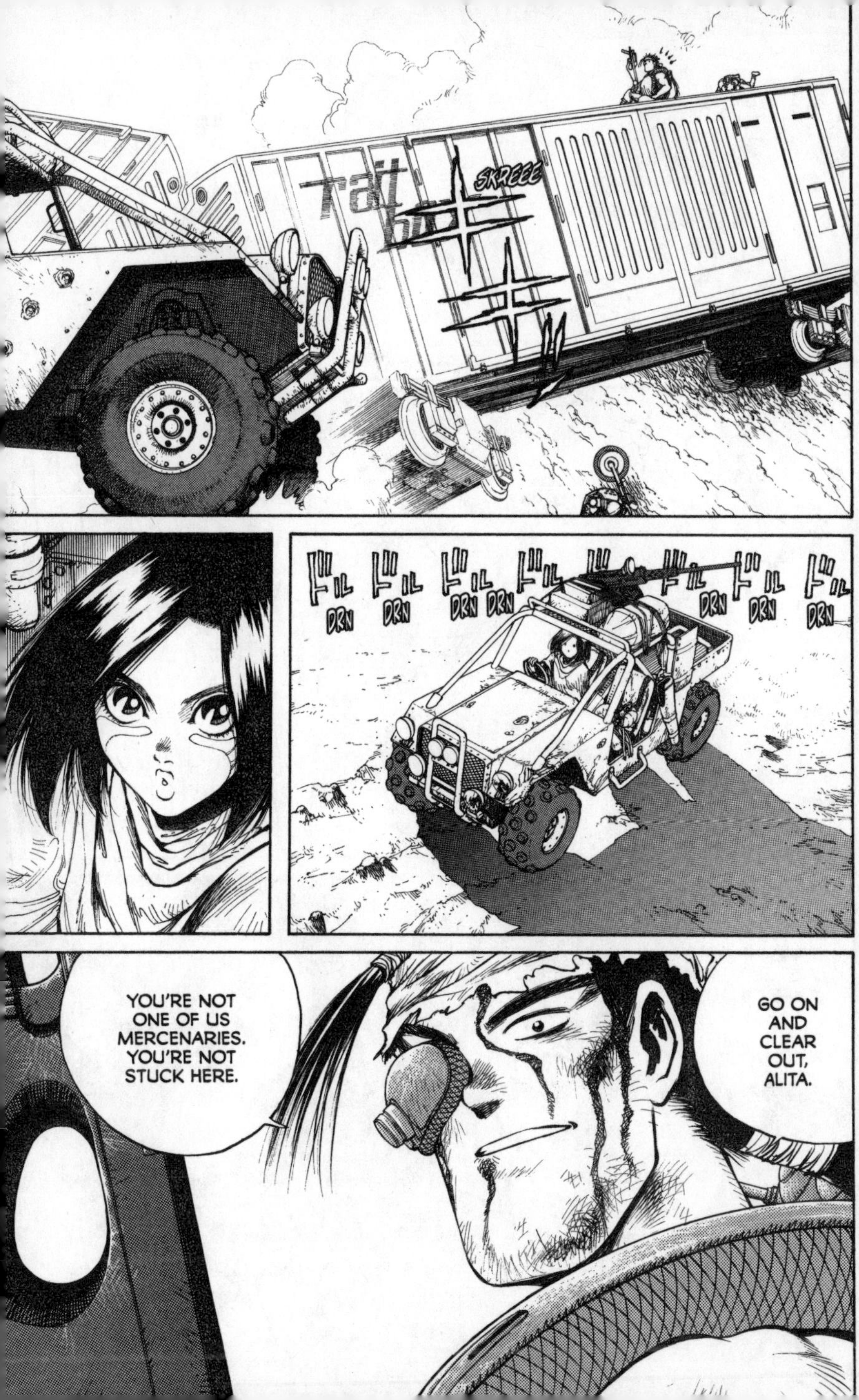
SKREEE
ドル DRN
ドル DRN
ドル DRN
ドル DRN
ドル DRN
ドル DRN
ドル DRN
ドル DRN
GO ON AND CLEAR OUT, ALITA.
YOU'RE NOT ONE OF US MERCENARIES. YOU'RE NOT STUCK HERE.

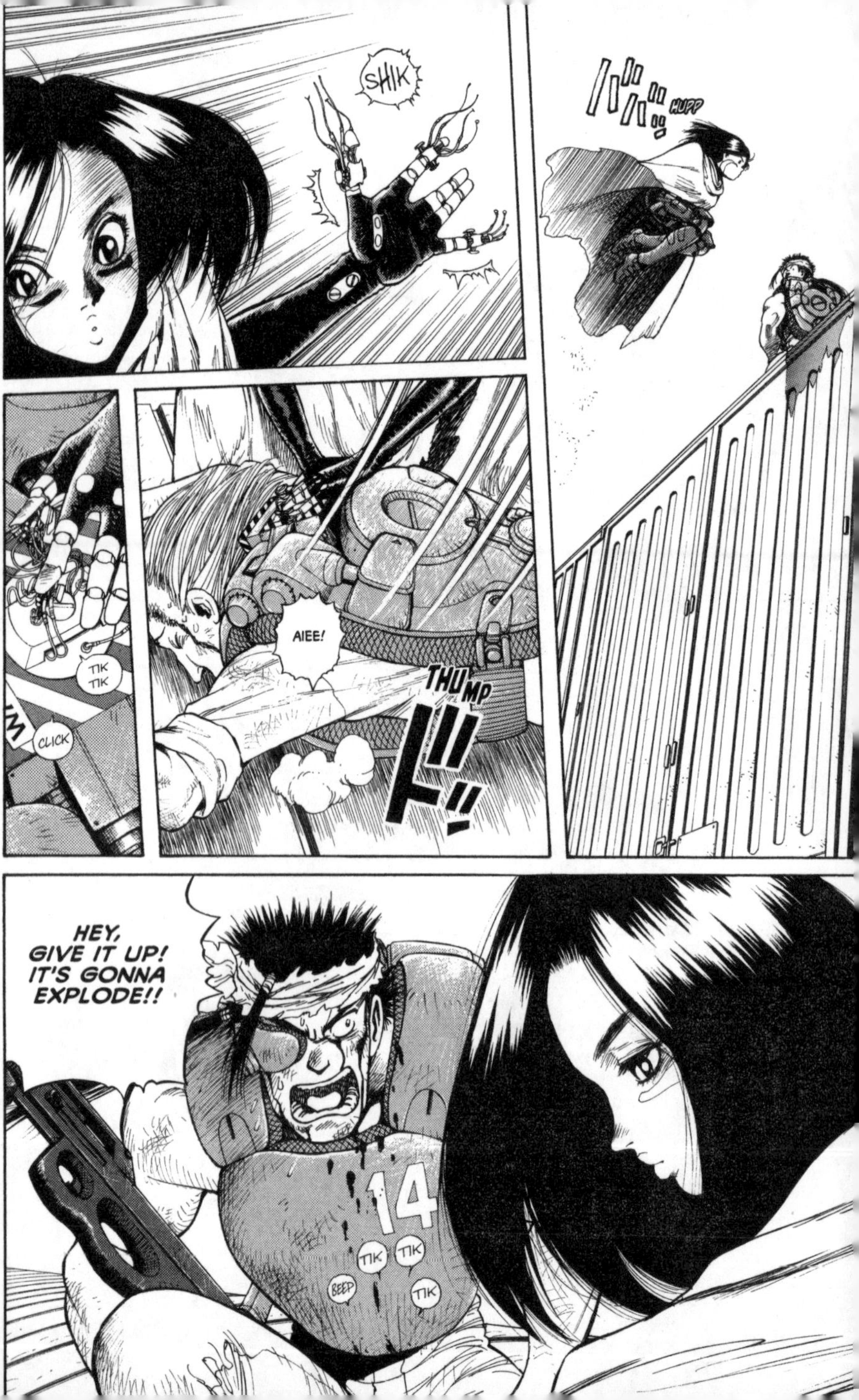

HUPP
SHIK
AIEE!
THUMP
TIK TIK
CLICK
HEY, GIVE IT UP! IT'S GONNA EXPLODE!!
TIK
TIK
BEEP
TIK

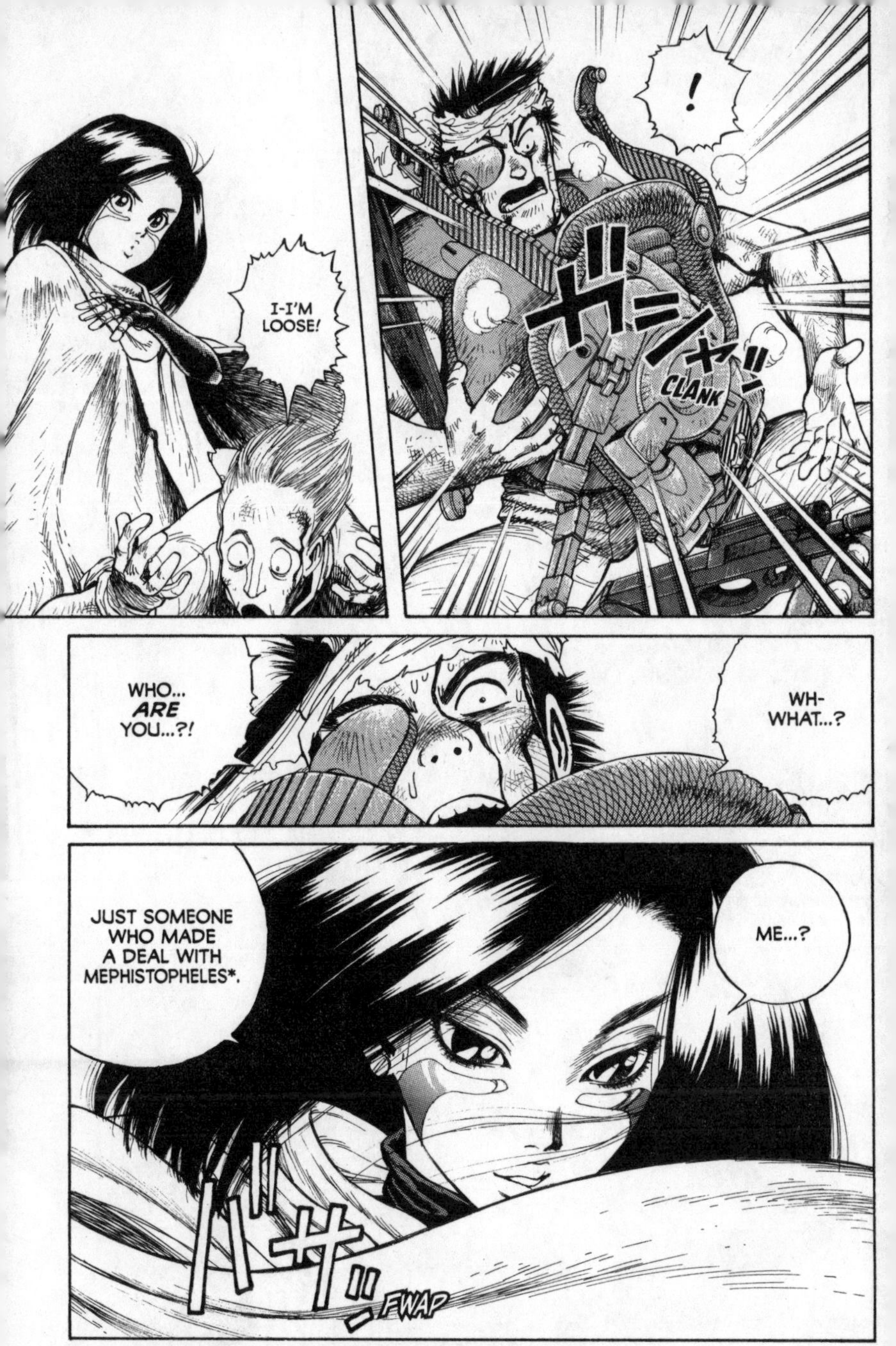
!
CLANK
I-I'M LOOSE!
WH- WHAT...?
WHO... *ARE* YOU...?!
ME...?
JUST SOMEONE WHO MADE A DEAL WITH MEPHISTOPHELES*.
FWAP

***Mephistopheles:** A capricious demon from Goethe's *Faust*. By making a deal with the demon, Dr. Faust gains youth and the ability to travel throughout time on a grand adventure.

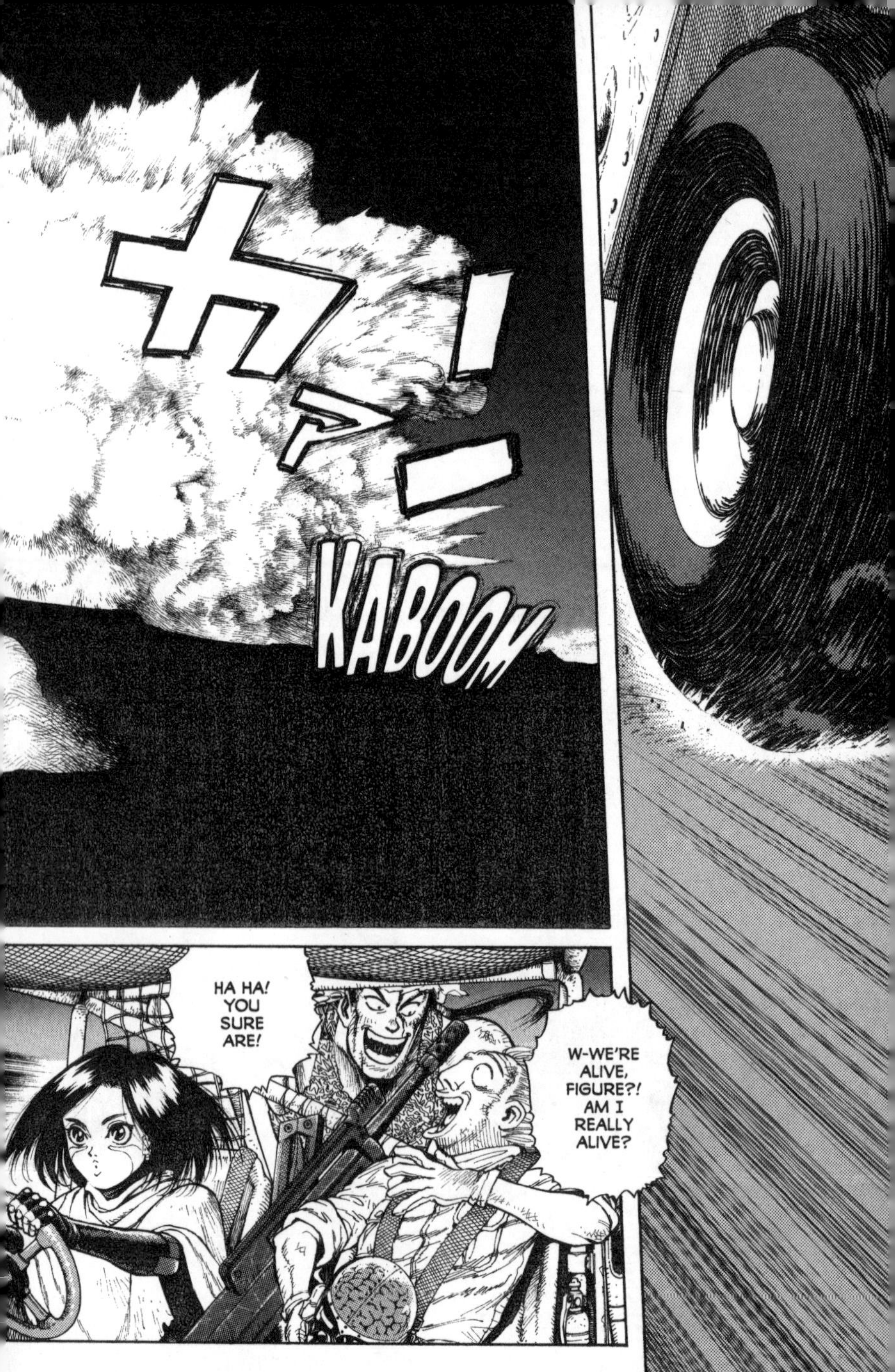
KABOOM
W-WE'RE ALIVE, FIGURE?! AM I REALLY ALIVE?
HA HA! YOU SURE ARE!

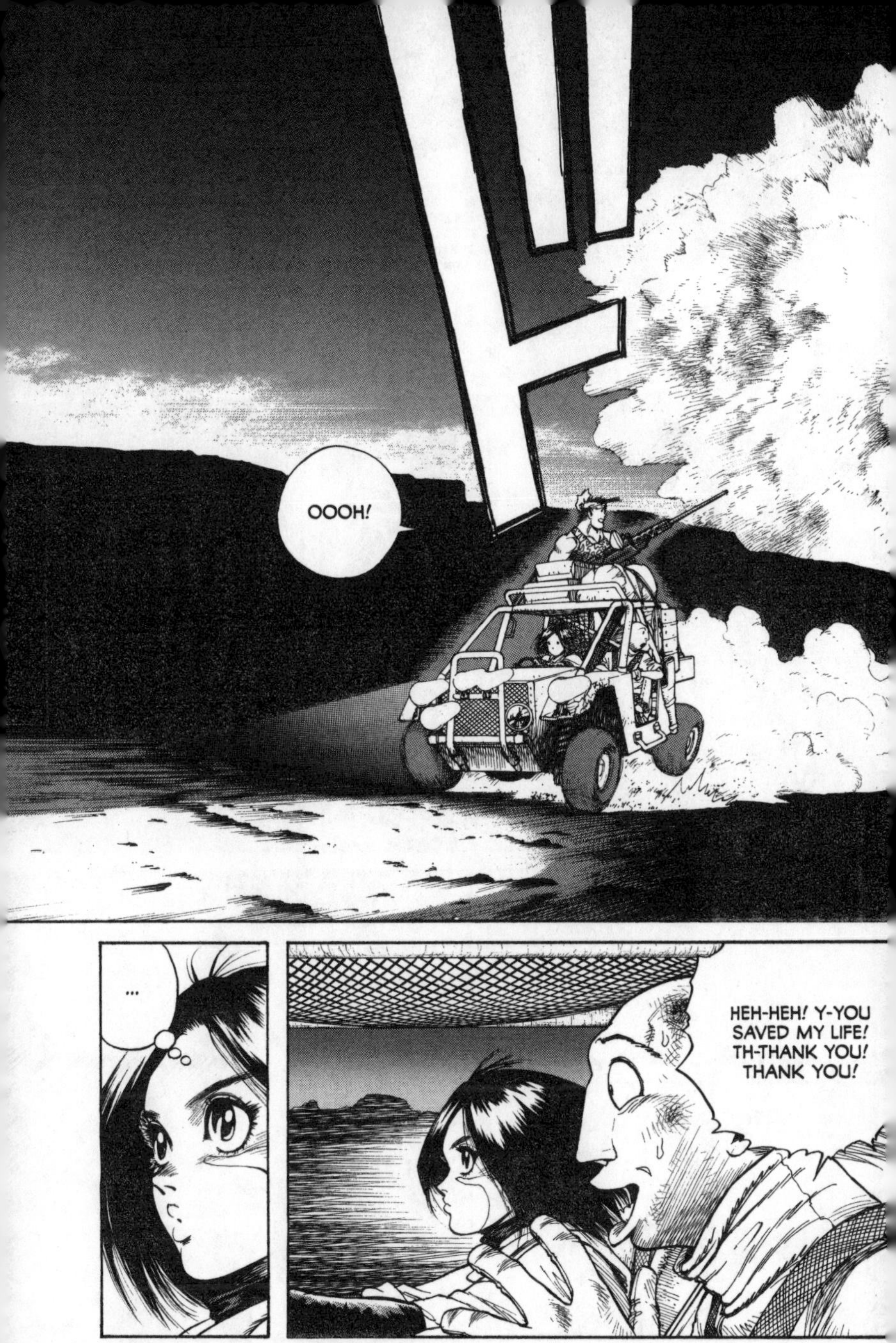
OOOH!
HEH-HEH! Y-YOU SAVED MY LIFE! TH-THANK YOU! THANK YOU!
...

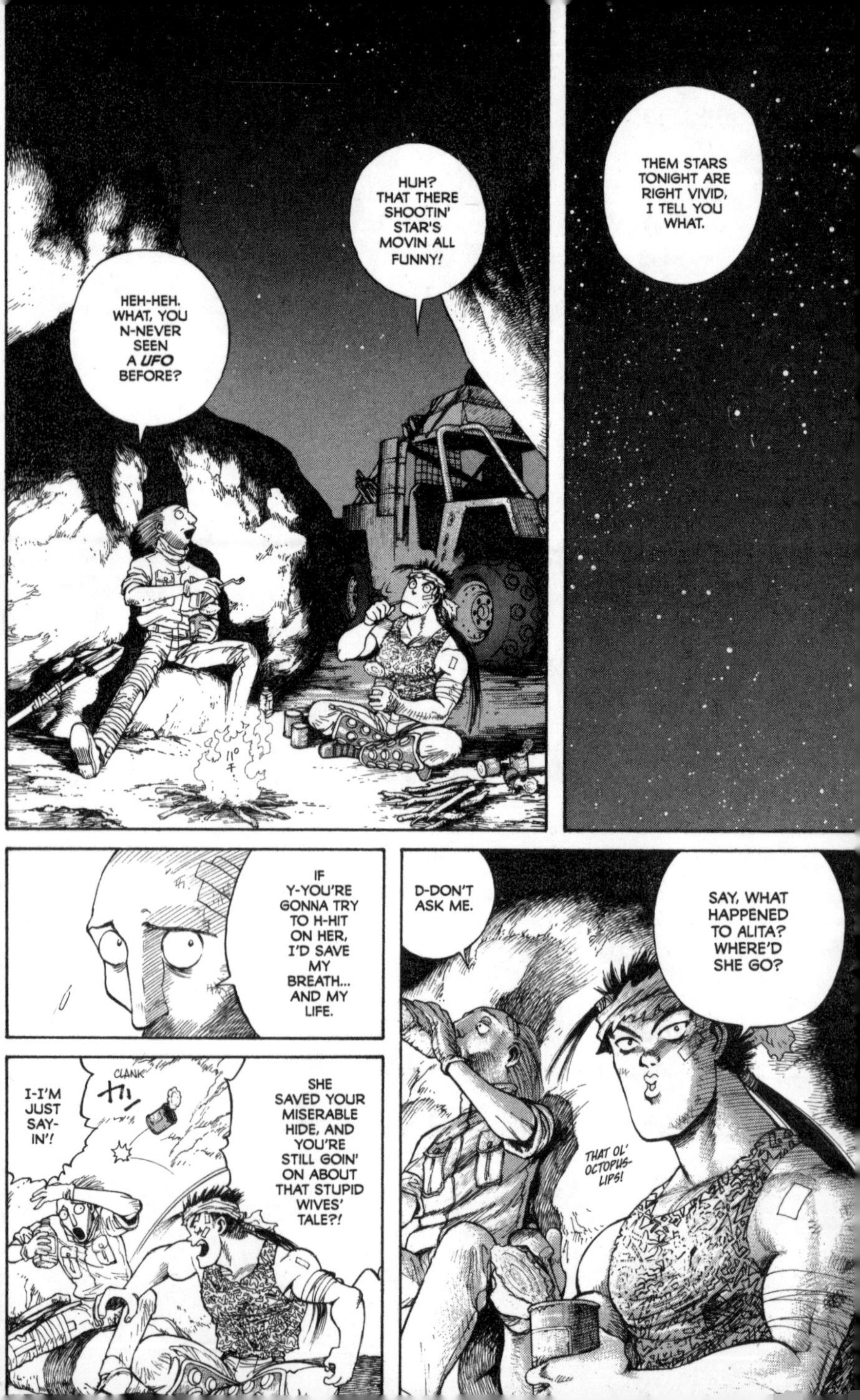
THEM STARS TONIGHT ARE RIGHT VIVID, I TELL YOU WHAT.
HUH? THAT THERE SHOOTIN' STAR'S MOVIN ALL FUNNY!
HEH-HEH. WHAT, YOU N-NEVER SEEN A *UFO* BEFORE?
SAY, WHAT HAPPENED TO ALITA? WHERE'D SHE GO?
D-DON'T ASK ME.
THAT OL' OCTOPUS-LIPS!
IF Y-YOU'RE GONNA TRY TO H-HIT ON HER, I'D SAVE MY BREATH... AND MY LIFE.
SHE SAVED YOUR MISERABLE HIDE, AND YOU'RE STILL GOIN' ON ABOUT THAT STUPID WIVES' TALE?!
CLANK
I-I'M JUST SAY-IN'!

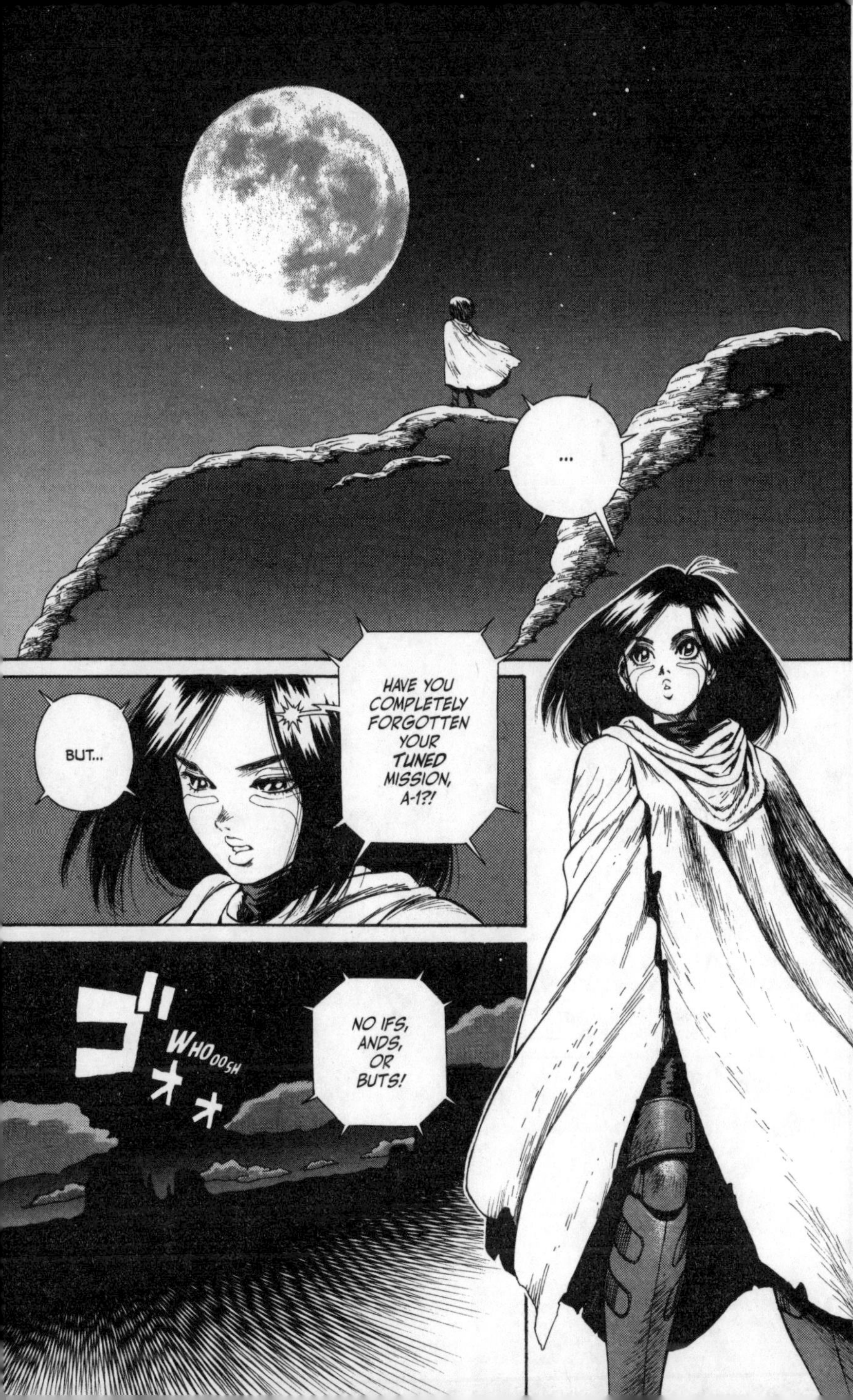
...
HAVE YOU COMPLETELY FORGOTTEN YOUR TUNED MISSION, A-1?!
BUT...
NO IFS, ANDS, OR BUTS!
ゴオォ
WHOOOSH

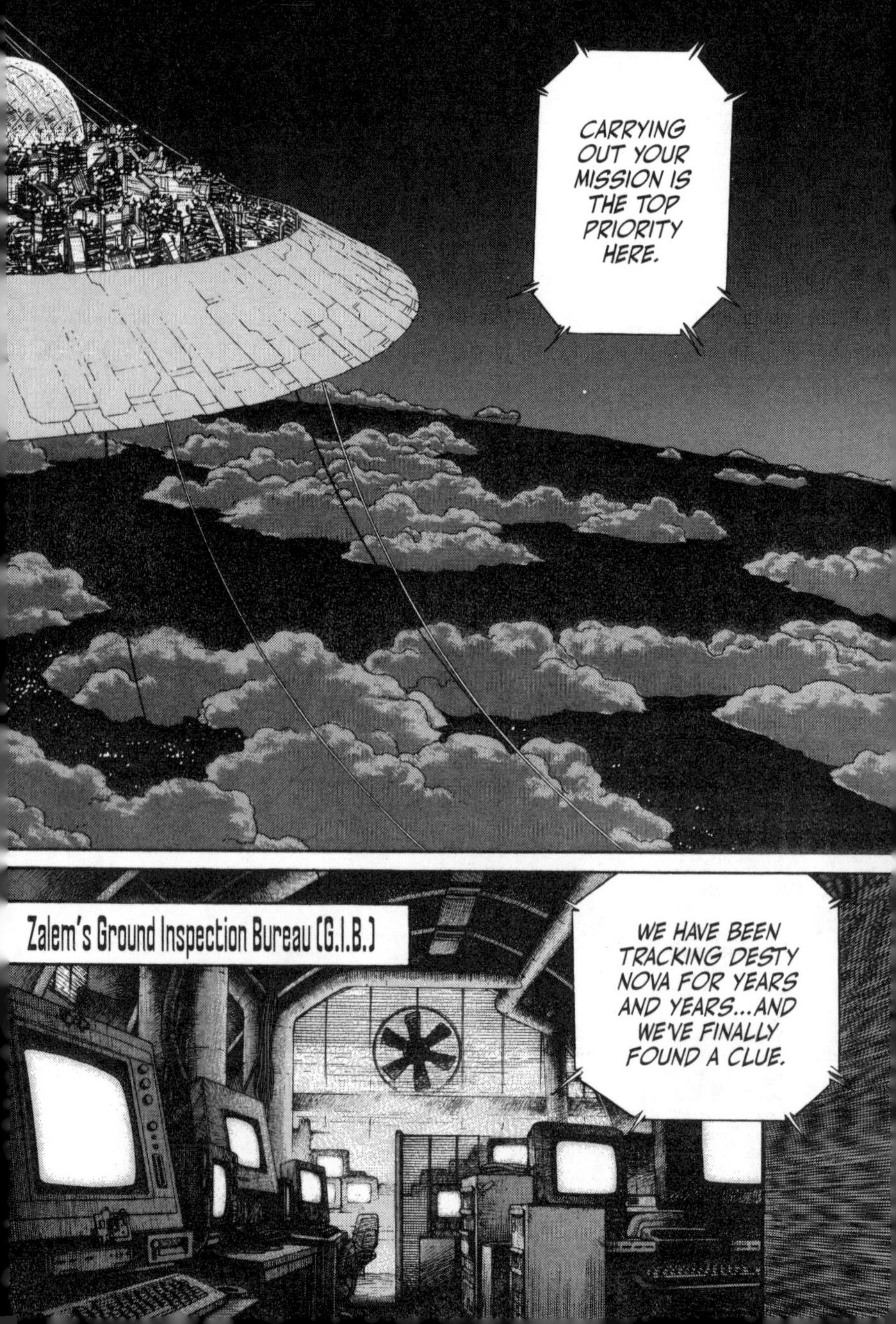
CARRYING OUT YOUR MISSION IS THE TOP PRIORITY HERE.
WE HAVE BEEN TRACKING DESTY NOVA FOR YEARS AND YEARS...AND WE'VE FINALLY FOUND A CLUE.
Zalem's Ground Inspection Bureau (G.I.B.)

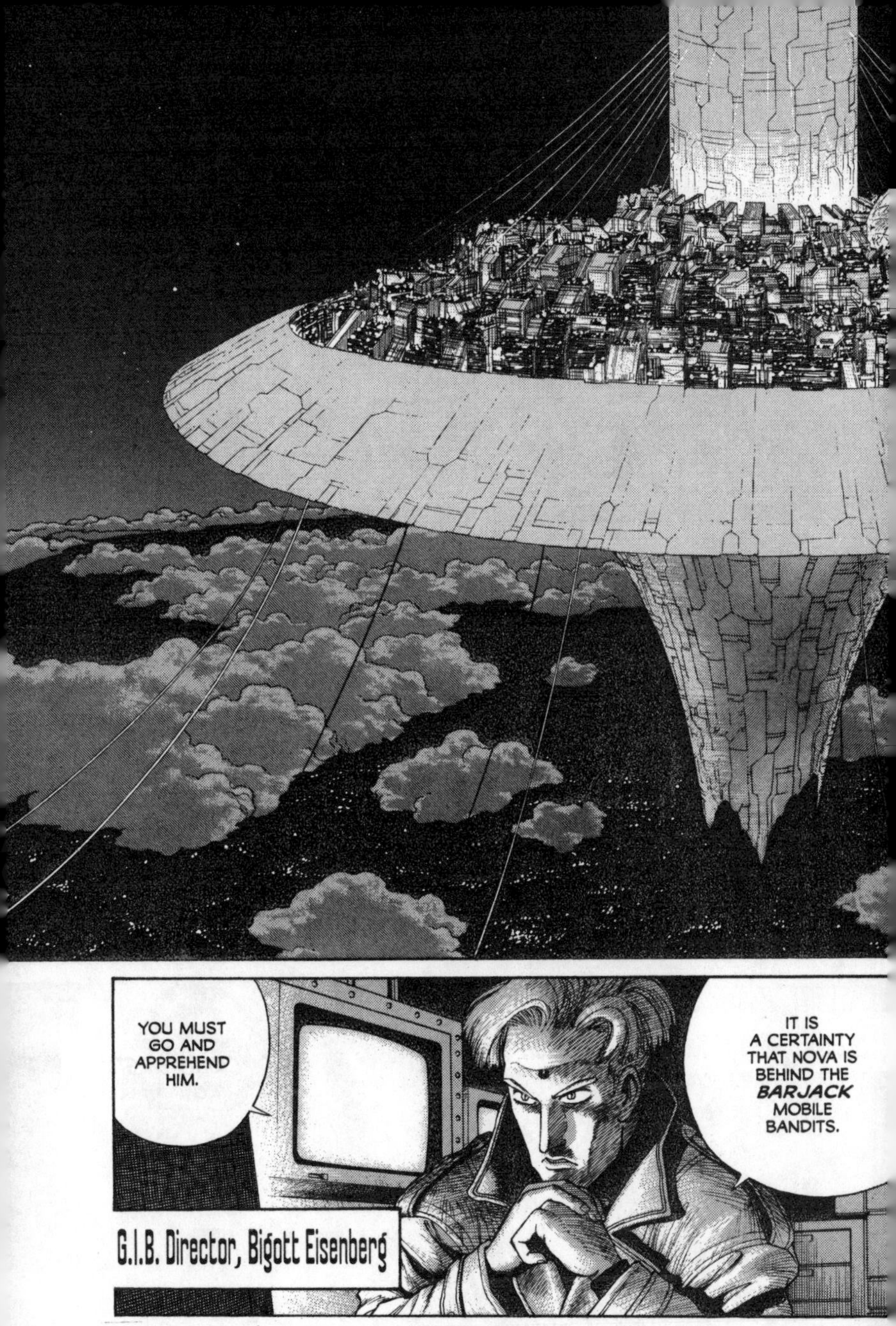
IT IS A CERTAINTY THAT NOVA IS BEHIND THE *BARJACK* MOBILE BANDITS.
YOU MUST GO AND APPREHEND HIM.
G.I.B. Director, Bigott Eisenberg

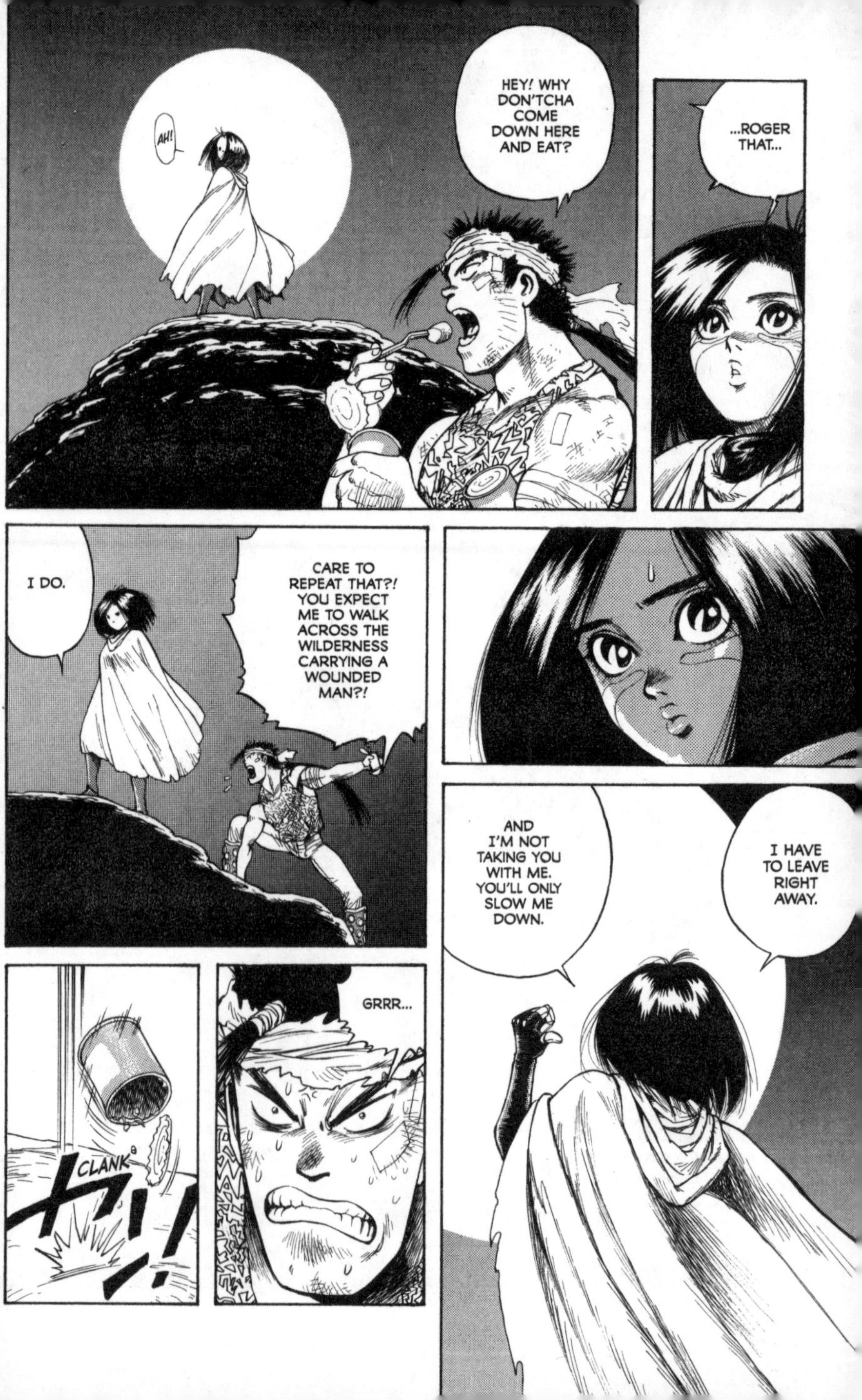
...ROGER THAT...
HEY! WHY DON'TCHA COME DOWN HERE AND EAT?
AH!
CARE TO REPEAT THAT?! YOU EXPECT ME TO WALK ACROSS THE WILDERNESS CARRYING A WOUNDED MAN?!
I DO.
I HAVE TO LEAVE RIGHT AWAY.
AND I'M NOT TAKING YOU WITH ME. YOU'LL ONLY SLOW ME DOWN.
GRRR...
CLANK

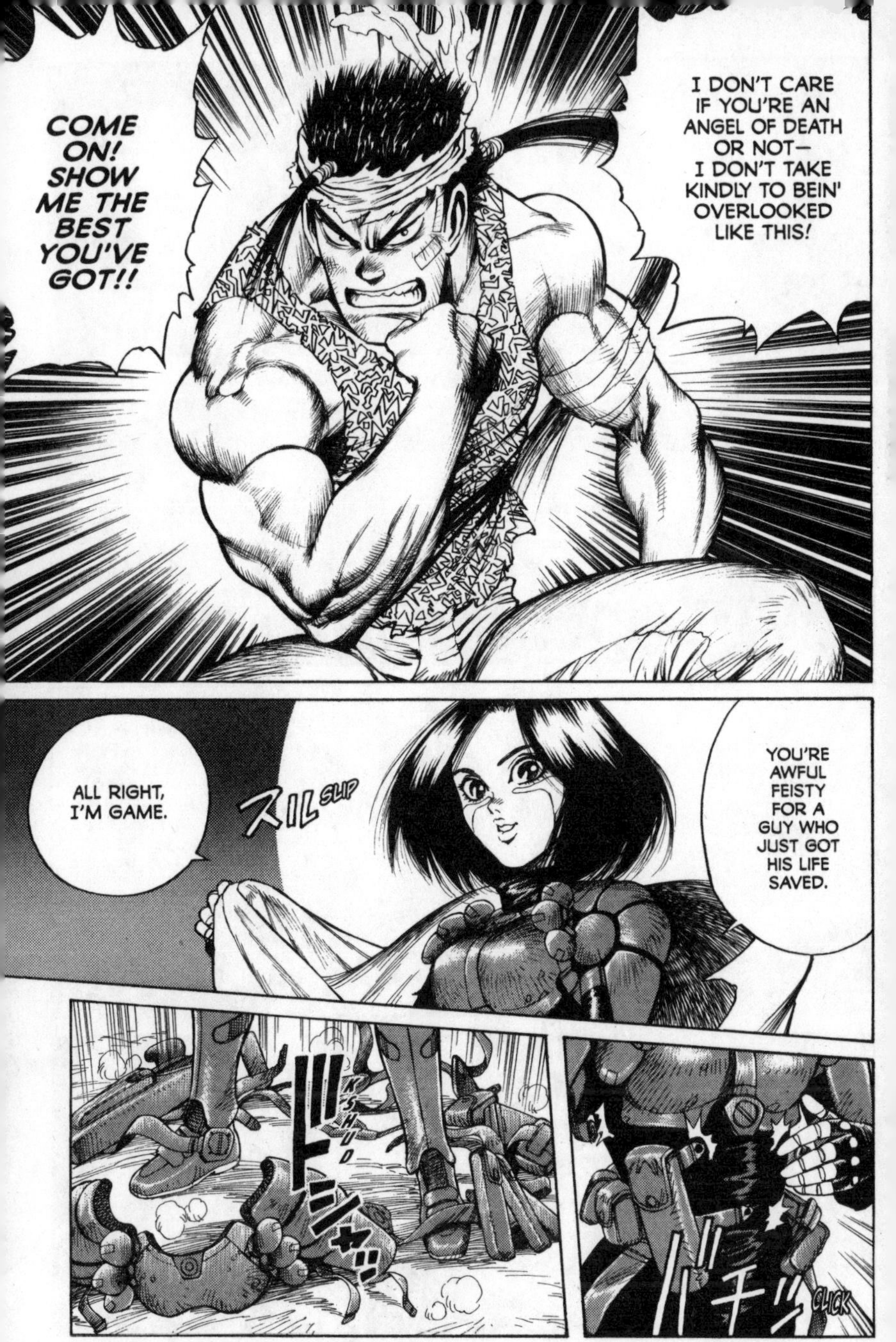
I DON'T CARE IF YOU'RE AN ANGEL OF DEATH OR NOT— I DON'T TAKE KINDLY TO BEIN' OVERLOOKED LIKE THIS!
COME ON! SHOW ME THE BEST YOU'VE GOT!!
YOU'RE AWFUL FEISTY FOR A GUY WHO JUST GOT HIS LIFE SAVED.
スル SLIP
ALL RIGHT, I'M GAME.
CLICK
KSHUD

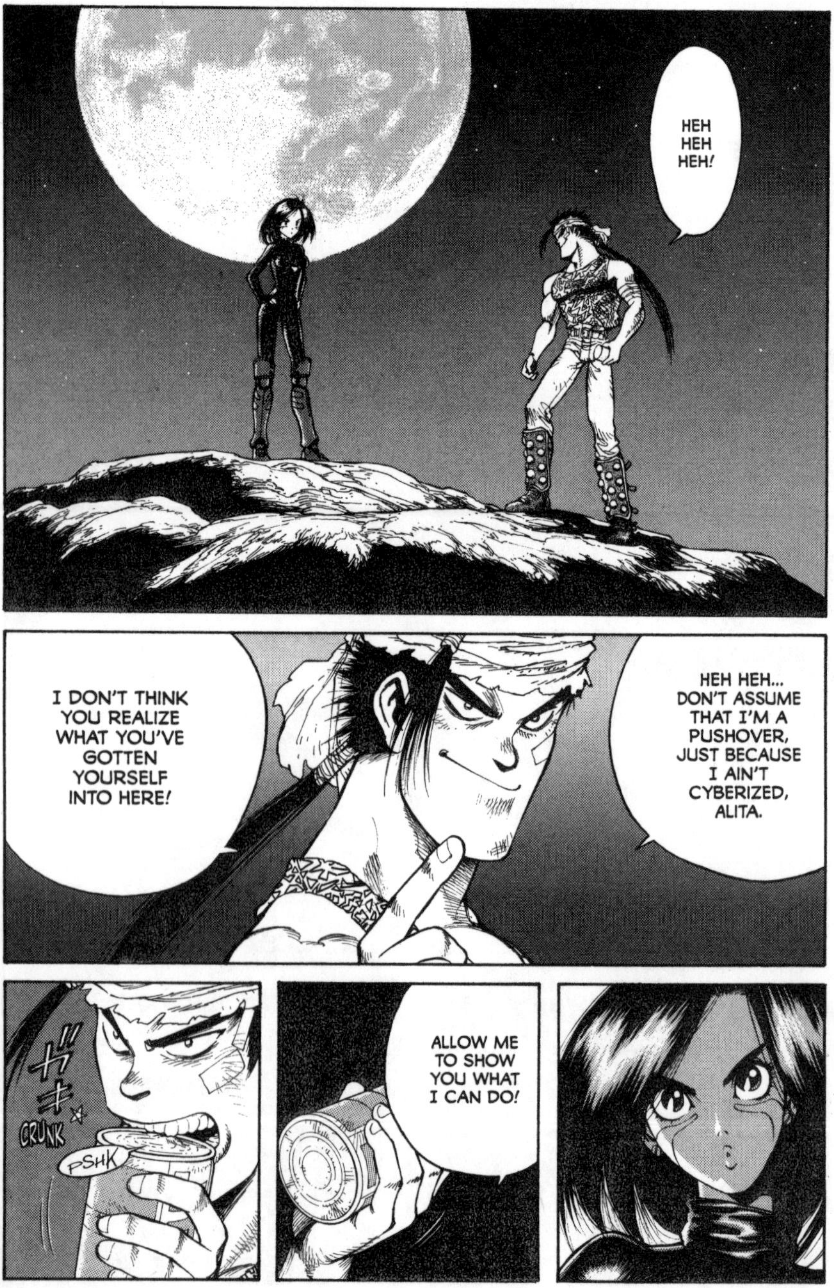
HEH HEH HEH!
HEH HEH... DON'T ASSUME THAT I'M A PUSHOVER, JUST BECAUSE I AIN'T CYBERIZED, ALITA.
I DON'T THINK YOU REALIZE WHAT YOU'VE GOTTEN YOURSELF INTO HERE!
ALLOW ME TO SHOW YOU WHAT I CAN DO!
CRUNK
PSHK

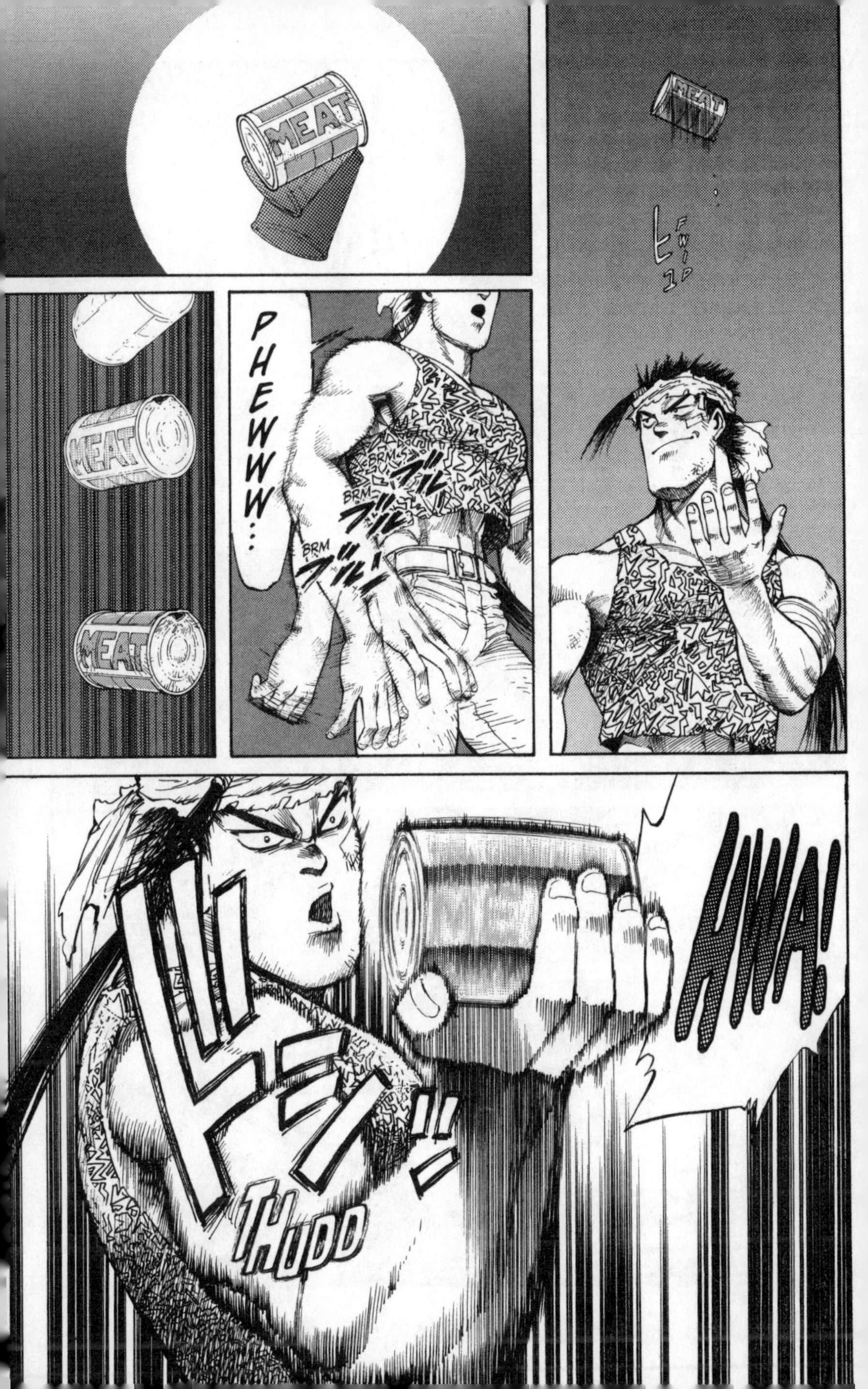
MEAT
FWIP
MEAT
PHEWWW...
BRM
BRM
MEAT
MEAT
HWA!
THUDD

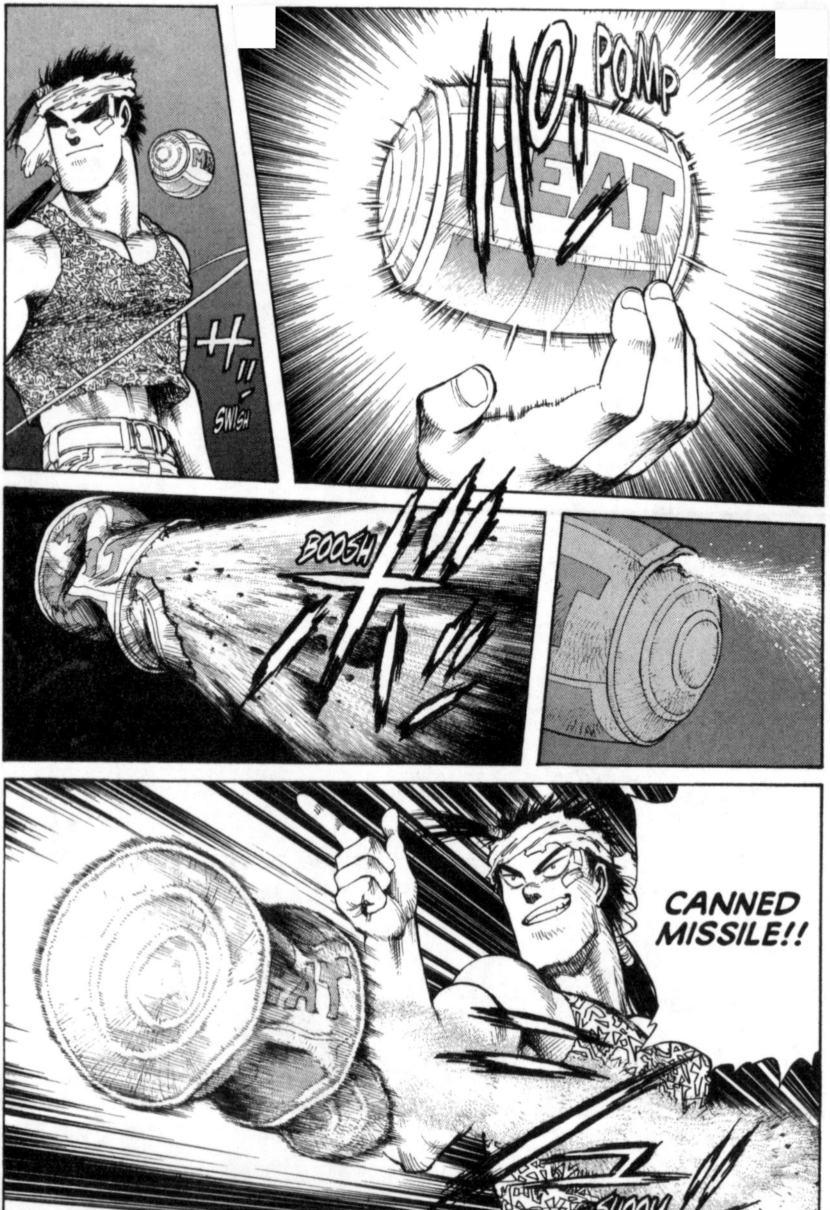
POMP
SWISH
BOOSH
CANNED MISSILE!!
SHOOM

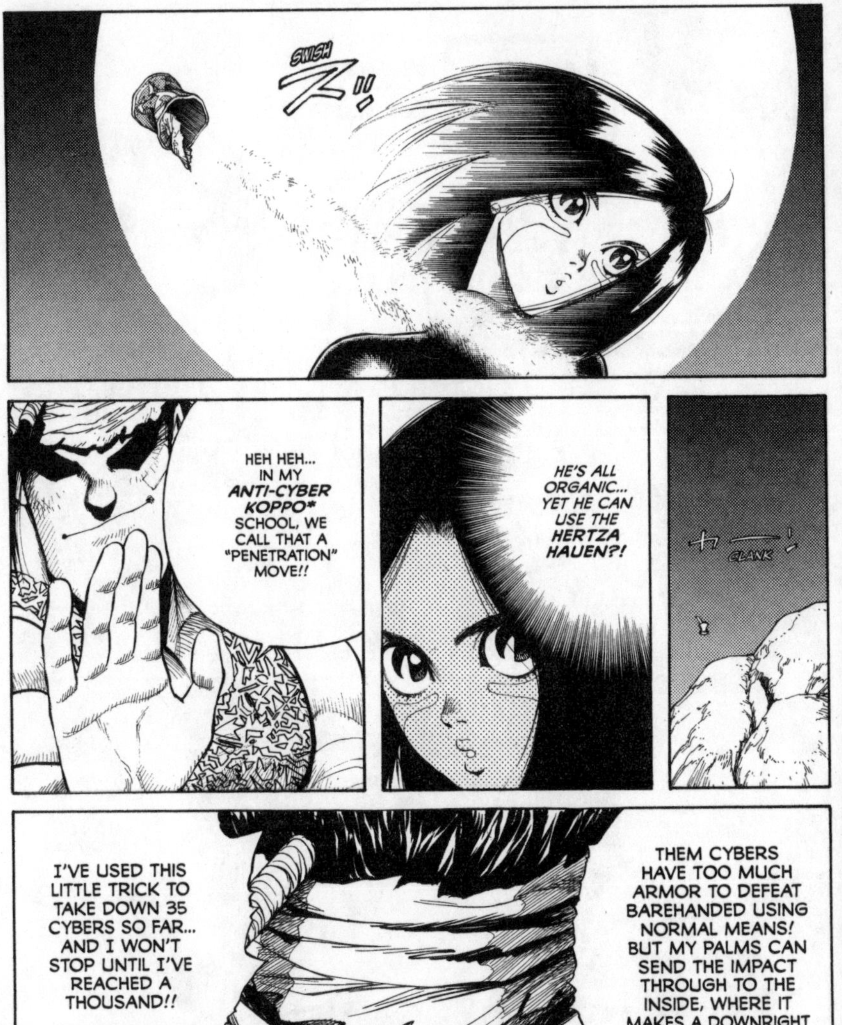
SWISH
CLANK
HE'S ALL ORGANIC... YET HE CAN USE THE HERTZA HAUEN?!
HEH HEH... IN MY ANTI-CYBER KOPPO* SCHOOL, WE CALL THAT A "PENETRATION" MOVE!!
THEM CYBERS HAVE TOO MUCH ARMOR TO DEFEAT BAREHANDED USING NORMAL MEANS! BUT MY PALMS CAN SEND THE IMPACT THROUGH TO THE INSIDE, WHERE IT MAKES A DOWNRIGHT MESS OF THAT SOFT, JUICY BRAIN!!
I'VE USED THIS LITTLE TRICK TO TAKE DOWN 35 CYBERS SO FAR... AND I WON'T STOP UNTIL I'VE REACHED A THOUSAND!!

***Anti-Cyber Koppo:** A type of Asian Art. While *koppo* is said to be one of the oldest forms of martial arts in Japan, going back to Otomo-no-Komaro in the Nara Period (8th century), it was later co-opted and revived by Seiji Horibe for his "Fighting-style Koppo." The word literally means "bone method," but in this case the word "bone" means more like "trick" or "knack," as in, "to have the knack for."

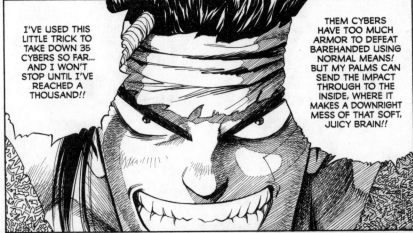

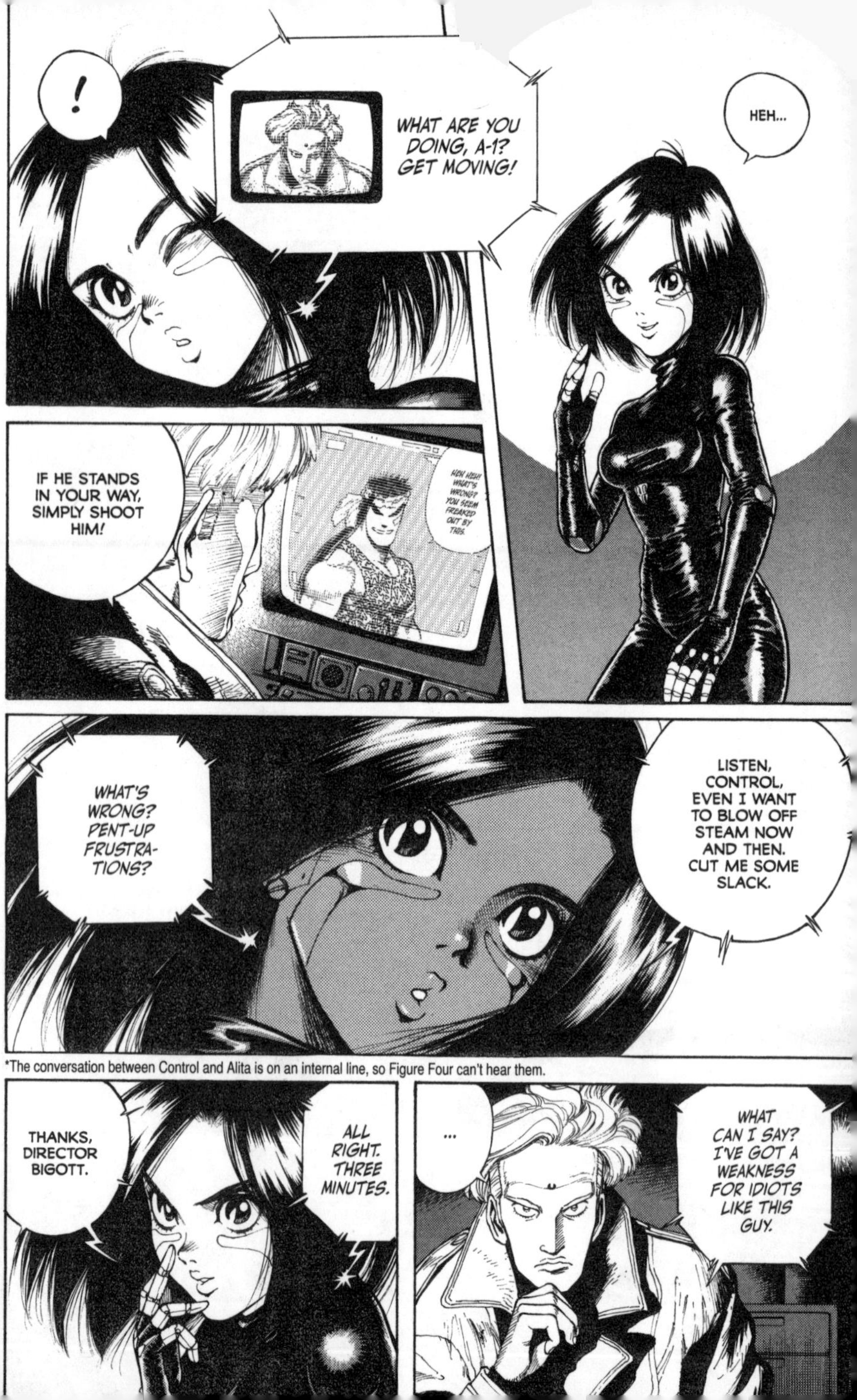
HEH...
WHAT ARE YOU DOING, A-1? GET MOVING!
!
HEH HEH! WHAT'S WRONG? YOU SEEM FREAKED OUT BY THIS.
IF HE STANDS IN YOUR WAY, SIMPLY SHOOT HIM!
LISTEN, CONTROL, EVEN I WANT TO BLOW OFF STEAM NOW AND THEN. CUT ME SOME SLACK.
WHAT'S WRONG? PENT-UP FRUSTRATIONS?
WHAT CAN I SAY? I'VE GOT A WEAKNESS FOR IDIOTS LIKE THIS GUY.
...
ALL RIGHT. THREE MINUTES.
THANKS, DIRECTOR BIGOTT.

*The conversation between Control and Alita is on an internal line, so Figure Four can't hear them.

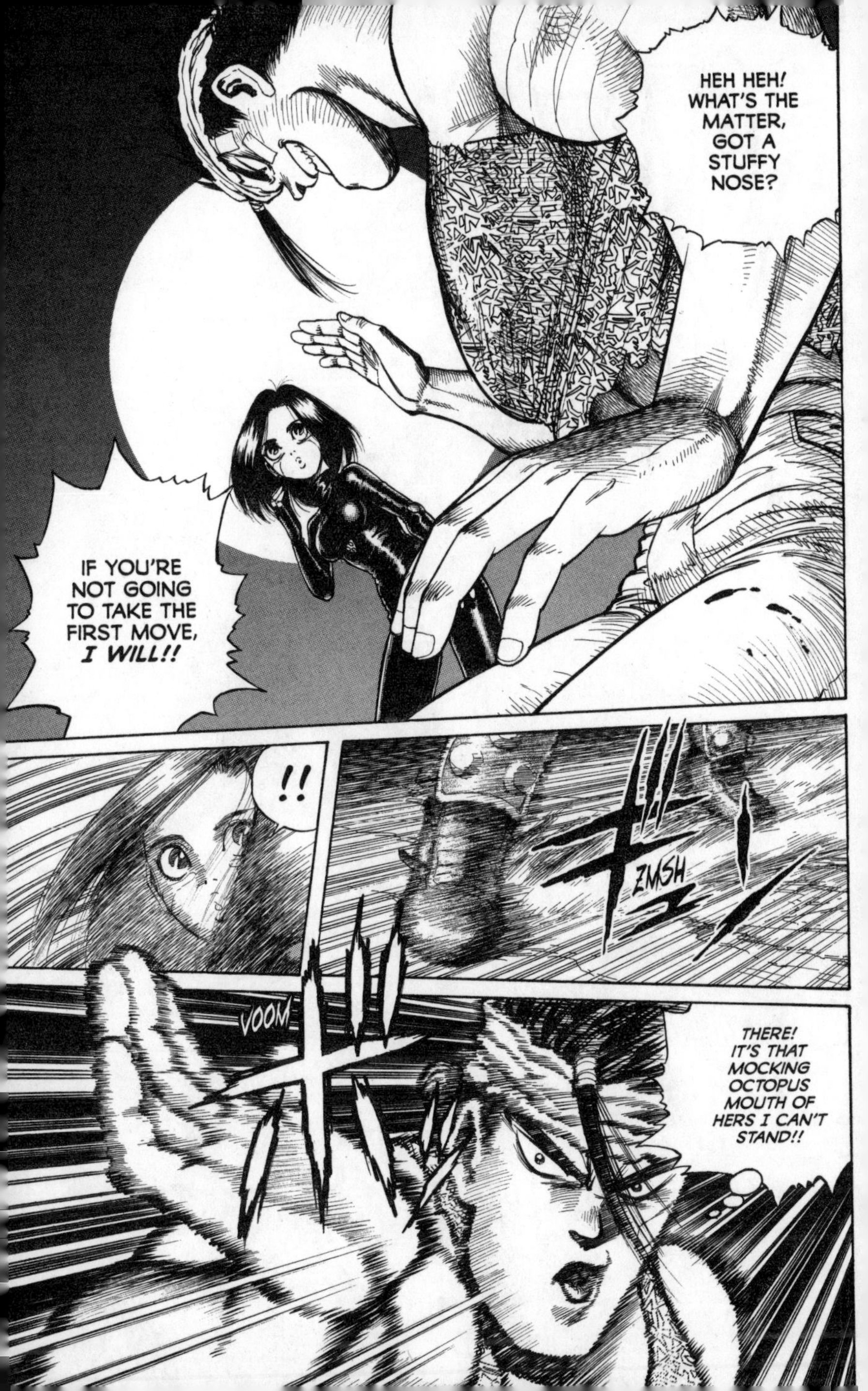
HEH HEH! WHAT'S THE MATTER, GOT A STUFFY NOSE?
IF YOU'RE NOT GOING TO TAKE THE FIRST MOVE, I WILL!!
ZMSH
!!
THERE! IT'S THAT MOCKING OCTOPUS MOUTH OF HERS I CAN'T STAND!!
VOOM

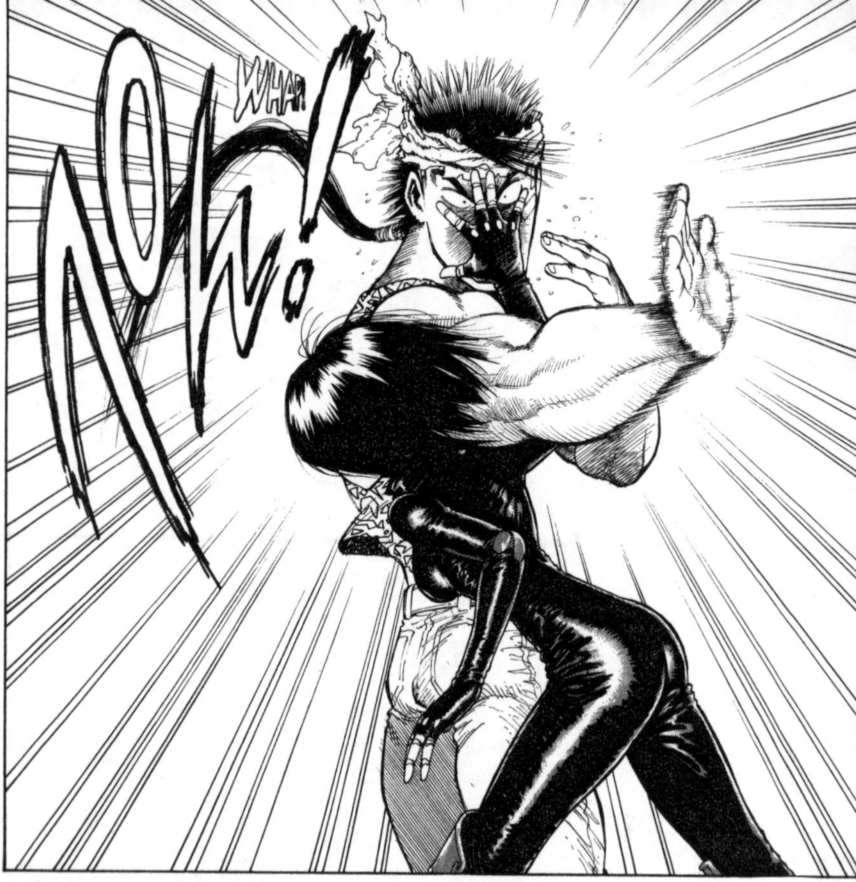
WHAP!

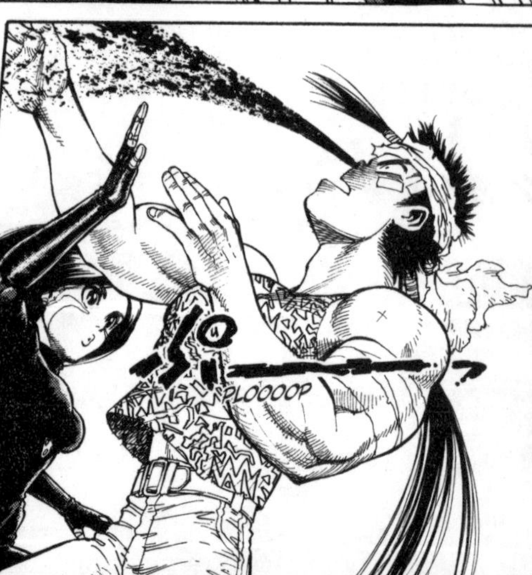
PLOOOOP

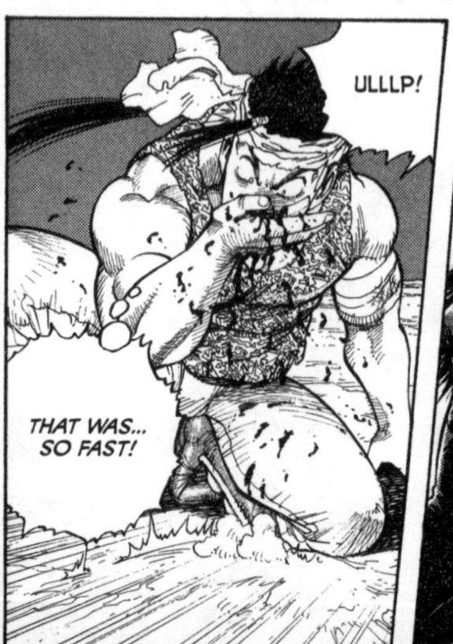
ULLLP!
THAT WAS... SO FAST!

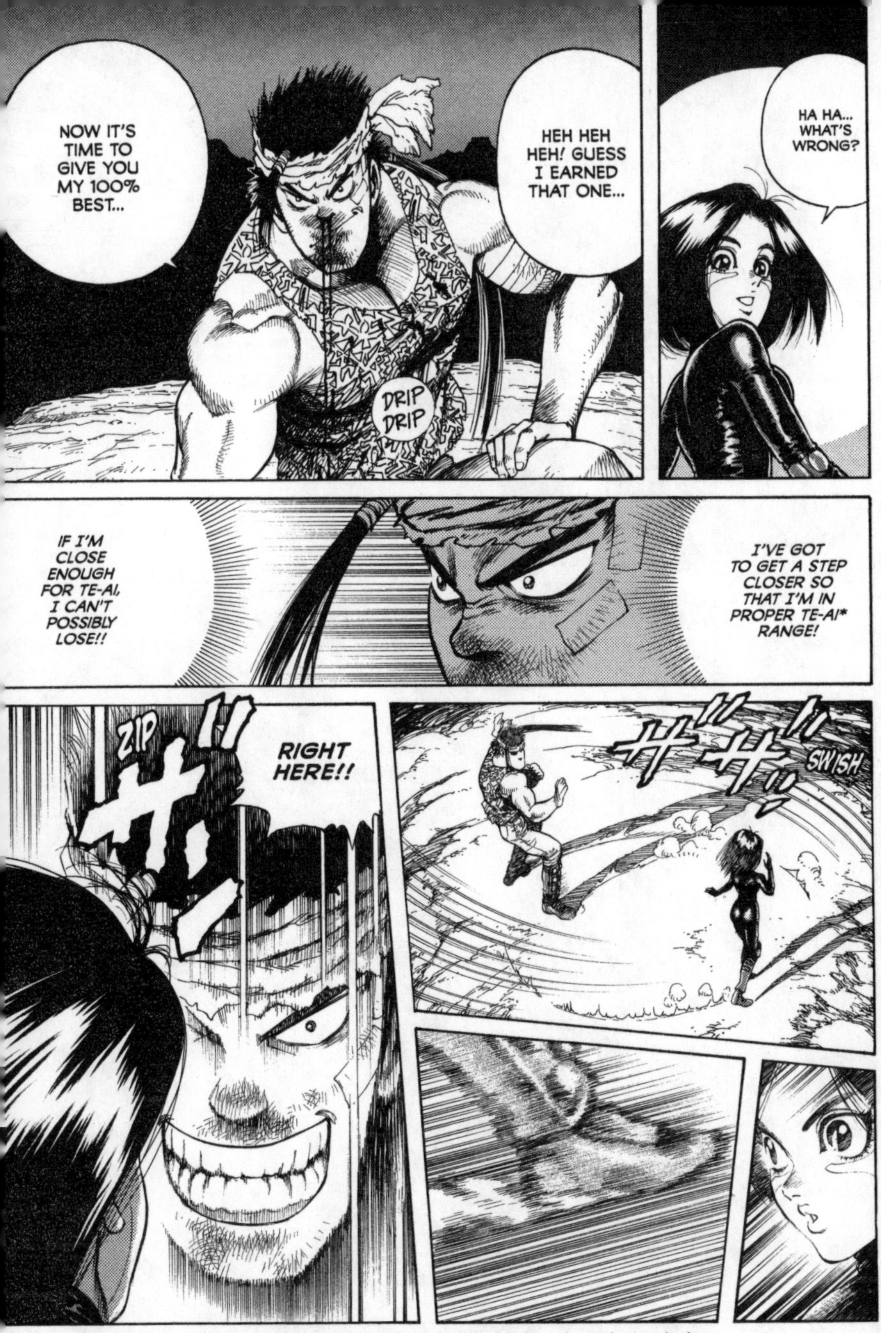
HA HA... WHAT'S WRONG?
HEH HEH HEH! GUESS I EARNED THAT ONE...
NOW IT'S TIME TO GIVE YOU MY 100% BEST...
DRIP DRIP
I'VE GOT TO GET A STEP CLOSER SO THAT I'M IN PROPER TE-AI* RANGE!
IF I'M CLOSE ENOUGH FOR TE-AI, I CAN'T POSSIBLY LOSE!!
SWISH
RIGHT HERE!!
ZIP

***Te-ai:** The effective range between combatants for a palm strike. In Koppo, palm attacks stemming from the elbow are effective at an extremely close range. Te-ai range is too close for punches, which originate from the shoulder and cannot reach full power when the target is so close.

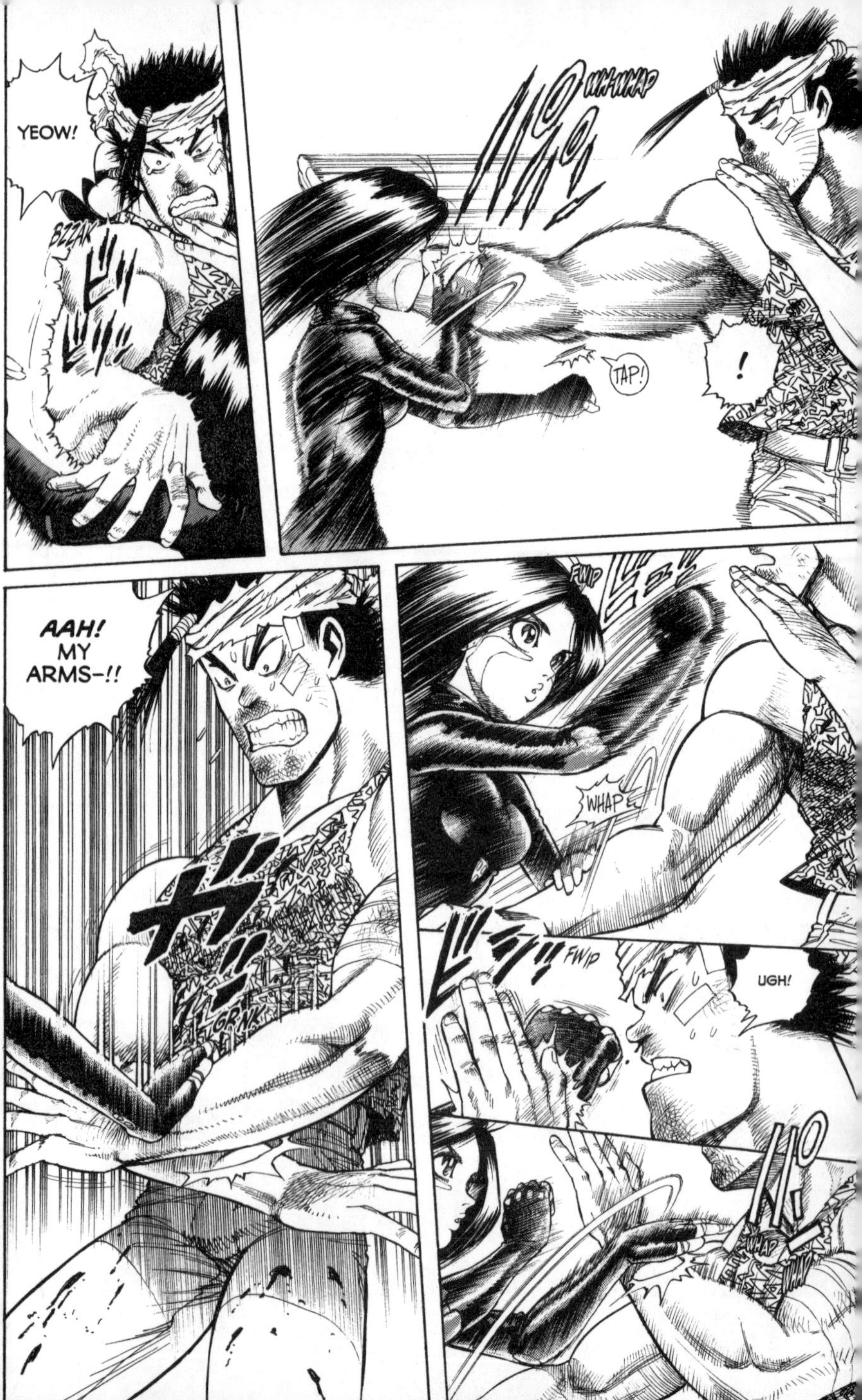
WH-WHAP
TAP!
!
YEOW!
BZZAK
FWIP
WHAP
FWIP
UGH!
AAH! MY ARMS-!!
GRNK

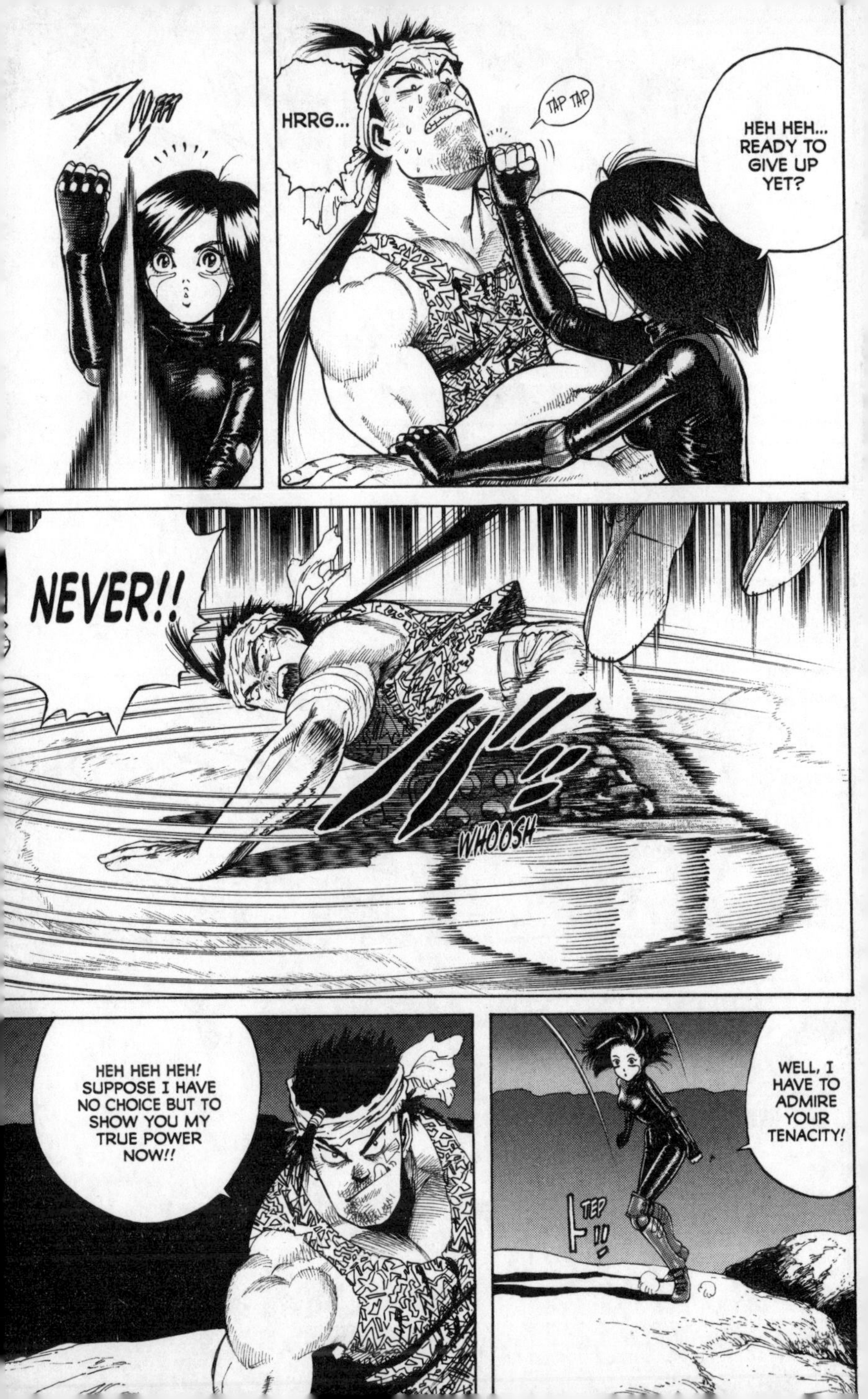
HEH HEH... READY TO GIVE UP YET?
TAP TAP
HRRG...
NEVER!!
WHOOSH
WELL, I HAVE TO ADMIRE YOUR TENACITY!
TEP !!
HEH HEH HEH! SUPPOSE I HAVE NO CHOICE BUT TO SHOW YOU MY TRUE POWER NOW!!

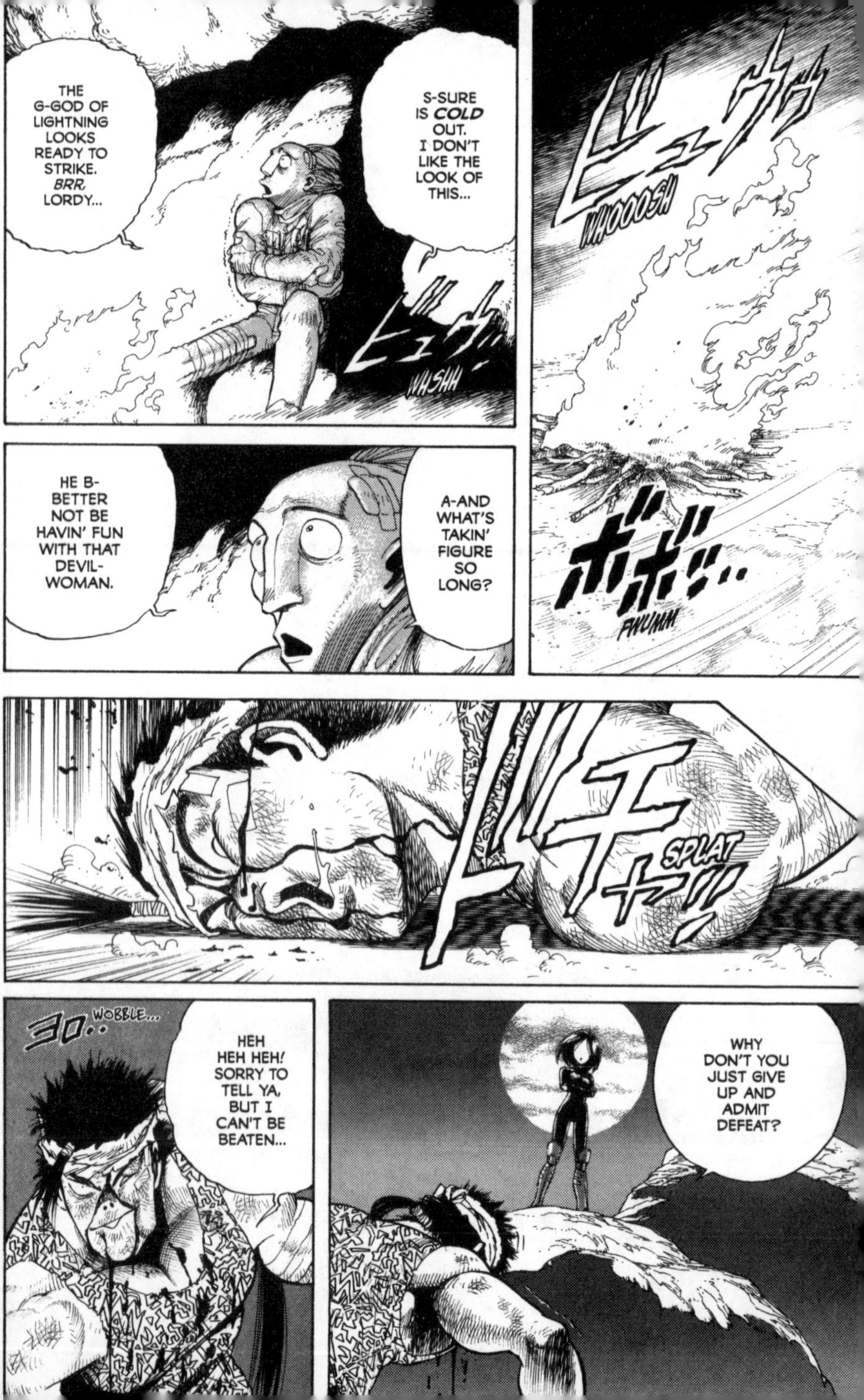
WHOOOSH
FWUMM
S-SURE IS *COLD* OUT. I DON'T LIKE THE LOOK OF THIS...
THE G-GOD OF LIGHTNING LOOKS READY TO STRIKE. *BRR,* LORDY...
WHSHH
A-AND WHAT'S TAKIN' FIGURE SO LONG?
HE B-BETTER NOT BE HAVIN' FUN WITH THAT DEVIL-WOMAN.
SPLAT
WHY DON'T YOU JUST GIVE UP AND ADMIT DEFEAT?
WOBBLE...
HEH HEH HEH! SORRY TO TELL YA, BUT I CAN'T BE BEATEN...

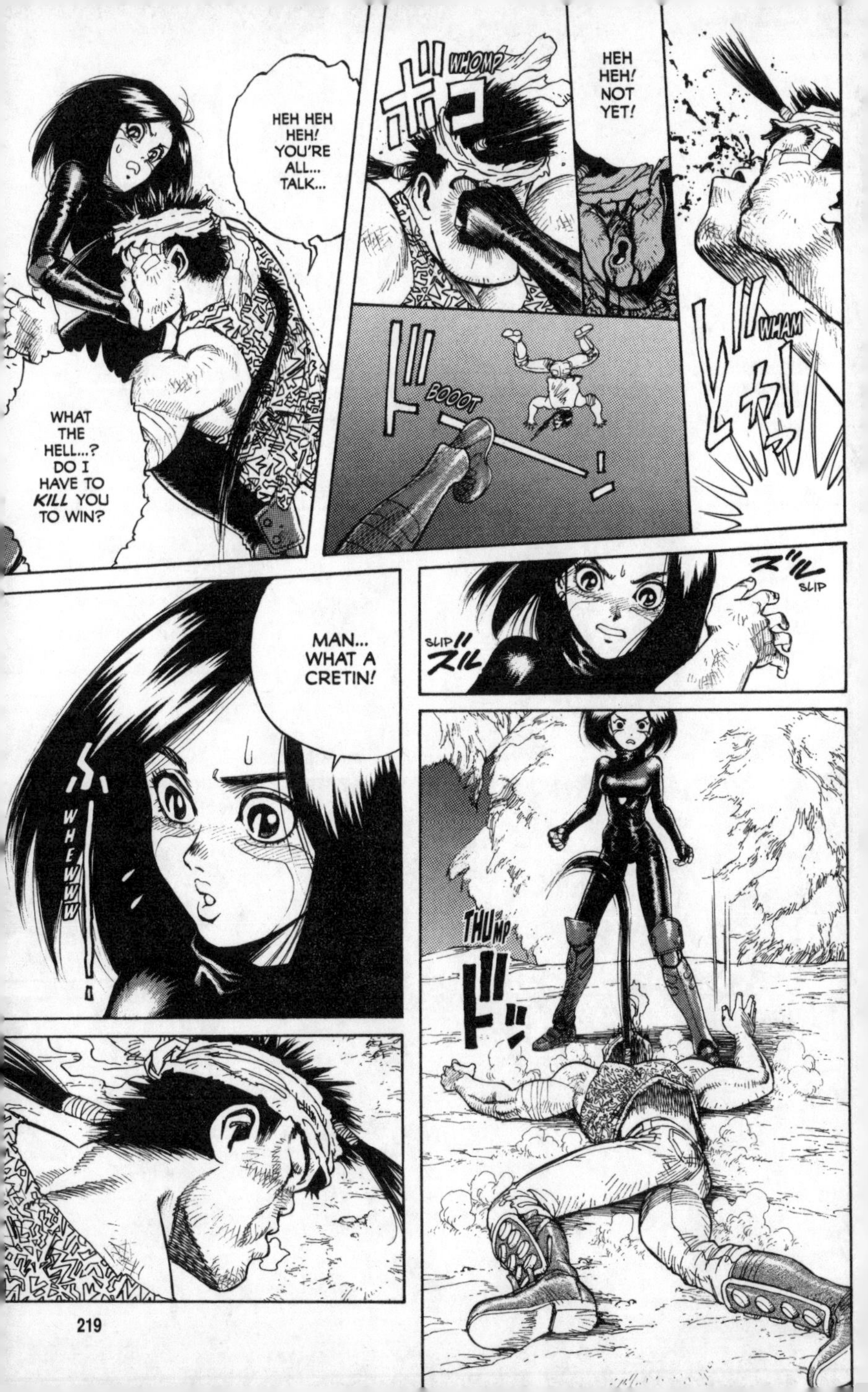
WHAM
HEH HEH! NOT YET!
WHOMP
BOOOT
HEH HEH HEH! YOU'RE ALL... TALK...
WHAT THE HELL...? DO I HAVE TO *KILL* YOU TO WIN?
ズル SLIP
SLIP!! ズル
MAN... WHAT A CRETIN!
WHEWWWW
THUMP

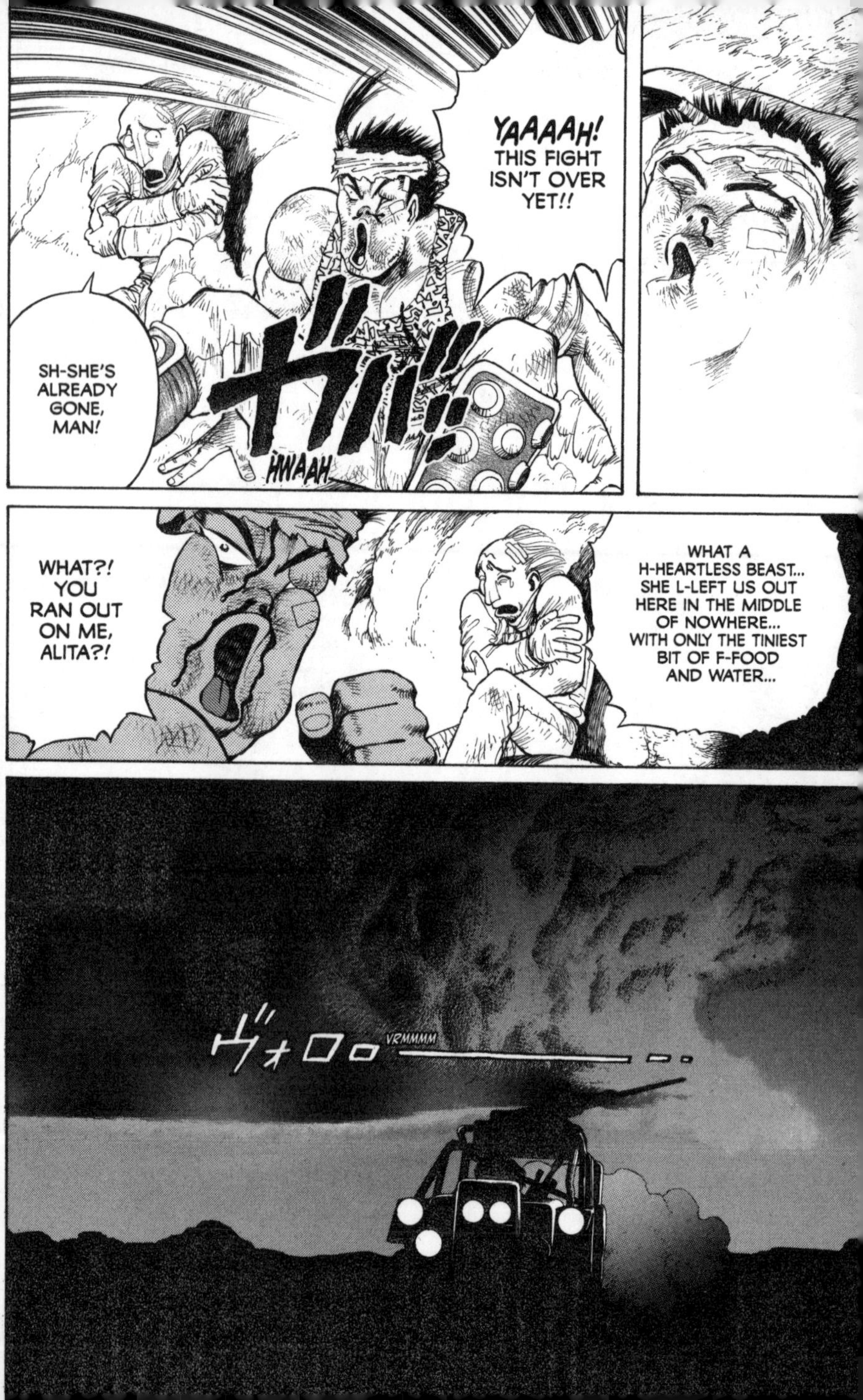
YAAAAH! THIS FIGHT ISN'T OVER YET!!
HWAAH
SH-SHE'S ALREADY GONE, MAN!
WHAT A H-HEARTLESS BEAST... SHE L-LEFT US OUT HERE IN THE MIDDLE OF NOWHERE... WITH ONLY THE TINIEST BIT OF F-FOOD AND WATER...
WHAT?! YOU RAN OUT ON ME, ALITA?!
ヴォロロ
VRMMMM

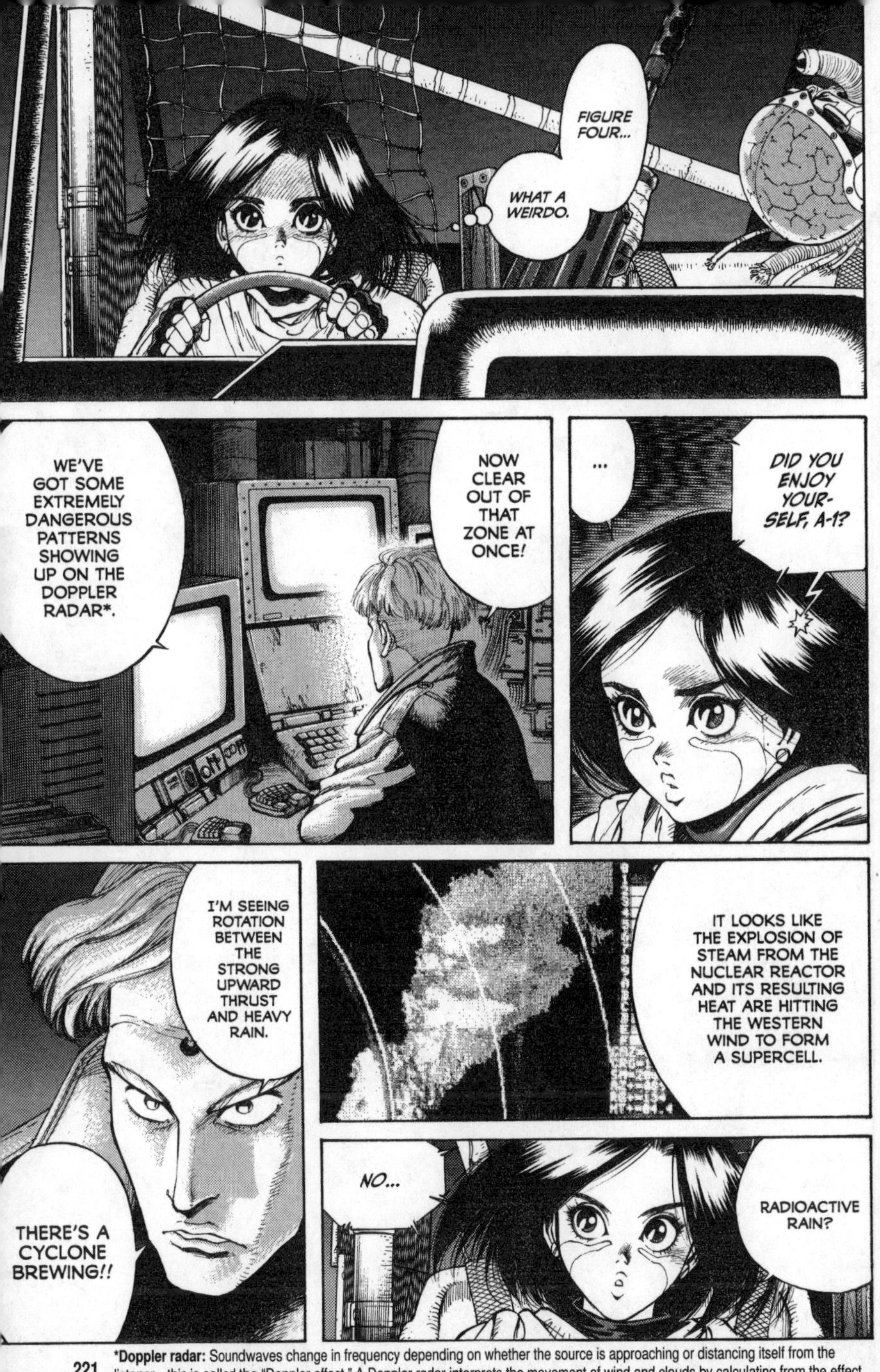
FIGURE FOUR...
WHAT A WEIRDO.
DID YOU ENJOY YOURSELF, A-1?
...
NOW CLEAR OUT OF THAT ZONE AT ONCE!
WE'VE GOT SOME EXTREMELY DANGEROUS PATTERNS SHOWING UP ON THE DOPPLER RADAR*.
IT LOOKS LIKE THE EXPLOSION OF STEAM FROM THE NUCLEAR REACTOR AND ITS RESULTING HEAT ARE HITTING THE WESTERN WIND TO FORM A SUPERCELL.
RADIOACTIVE RAIN?
NO...
I'M SEEING ROTATION BETWEEN THE STRONG UPWARD THRUST AND HEAVY RAIN.
THERE'S A CYCLONE BREWING!!

***Doppler radar:** Soundwaves change in frequency depending on whether the source is approaching or distancing itself from the listener—this is called the "Doppler effect." A Doppler radar interprets the movement of wind and clouds by calculating from the effect.

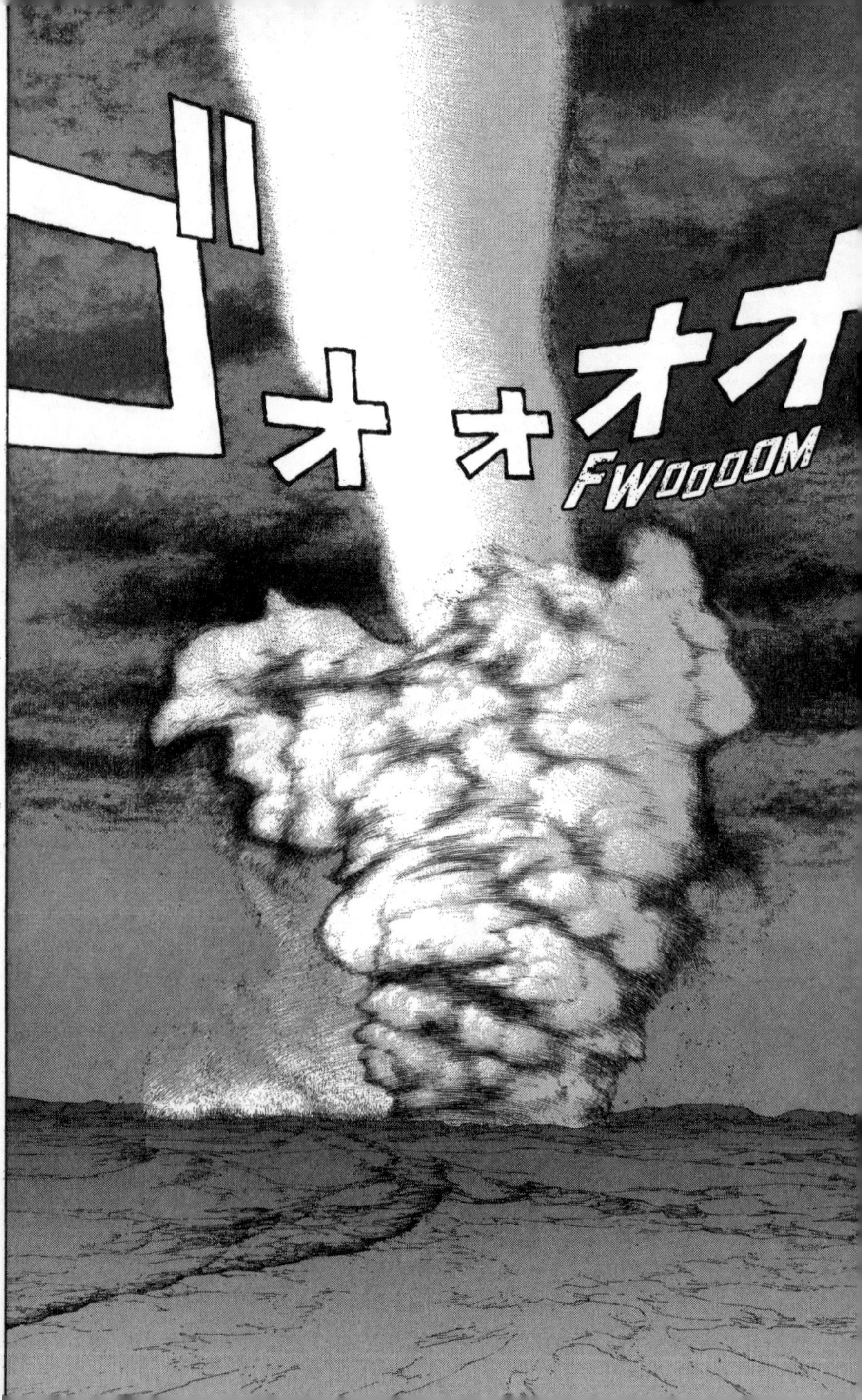
ゴォォオオ
FWOOOOOM

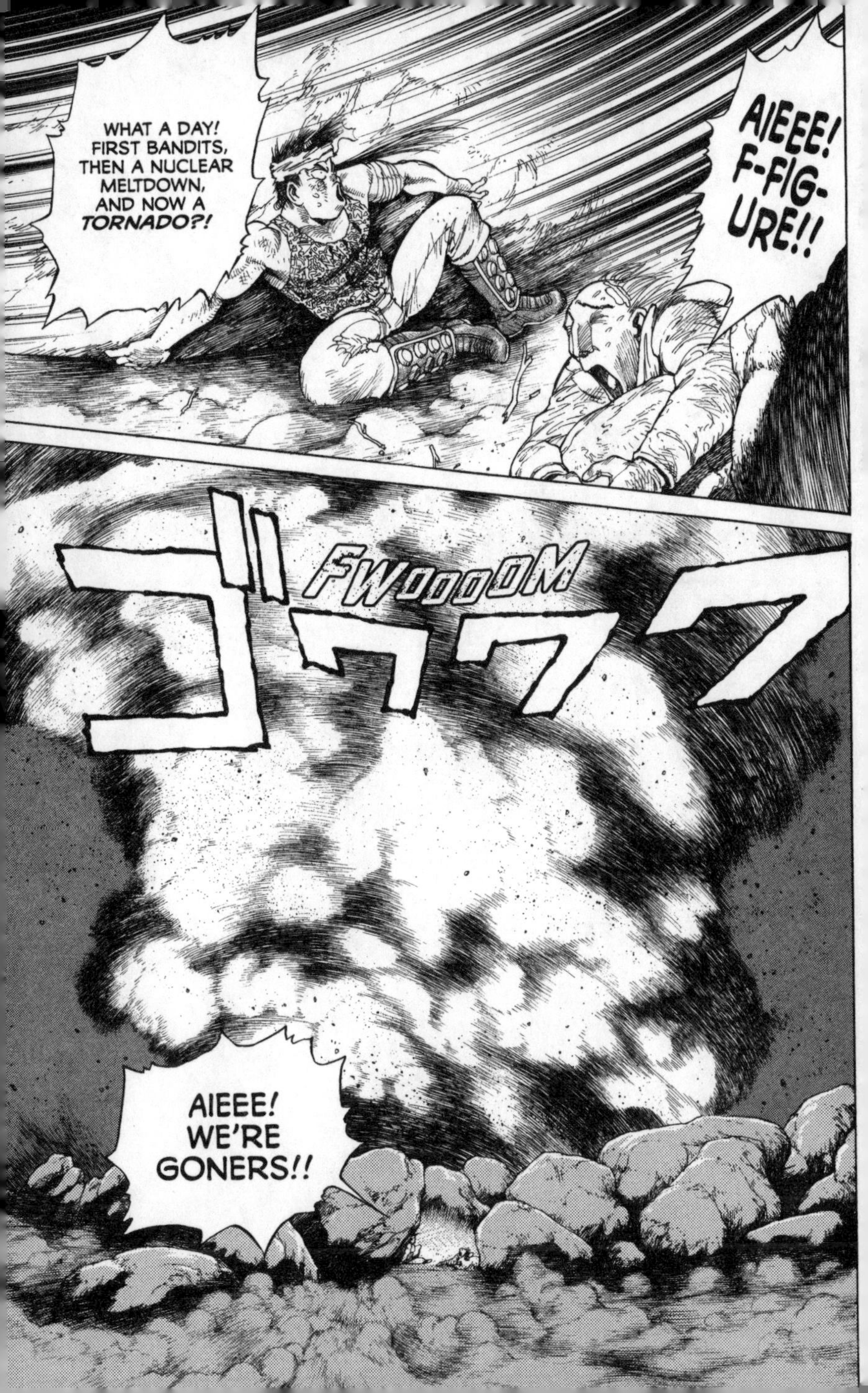
AIEEE! F-FIG-URE!!
WHAT A DAY! FIRST BANDITS, THEN A NUCLEAR MELTDOWN, AND NOW A *TORNADO?!*
FWOOOOOM
ゴワァ
AIEEE! WE'RE GONERS!!

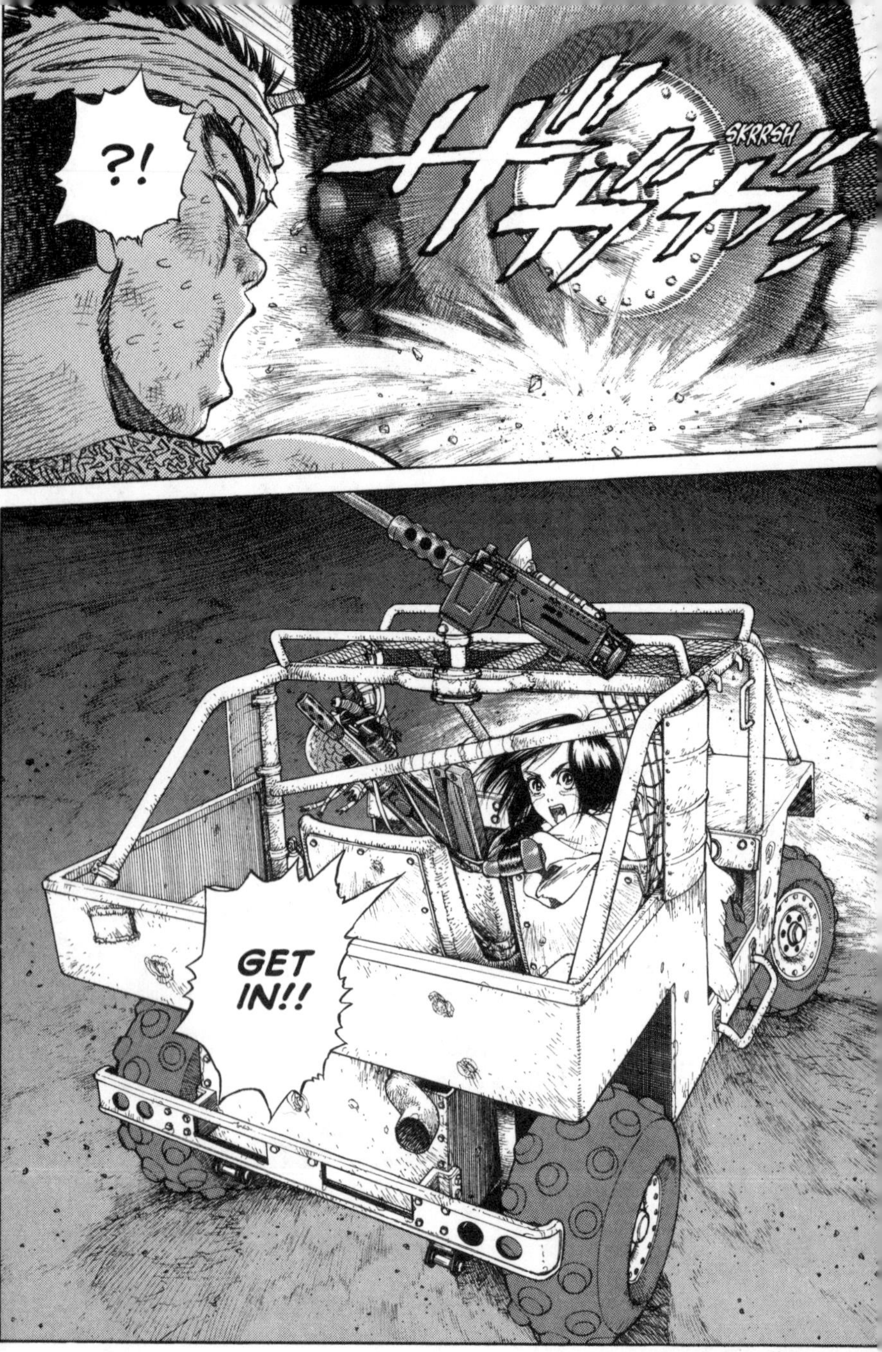
?!
SKRRSH
GET IN!!

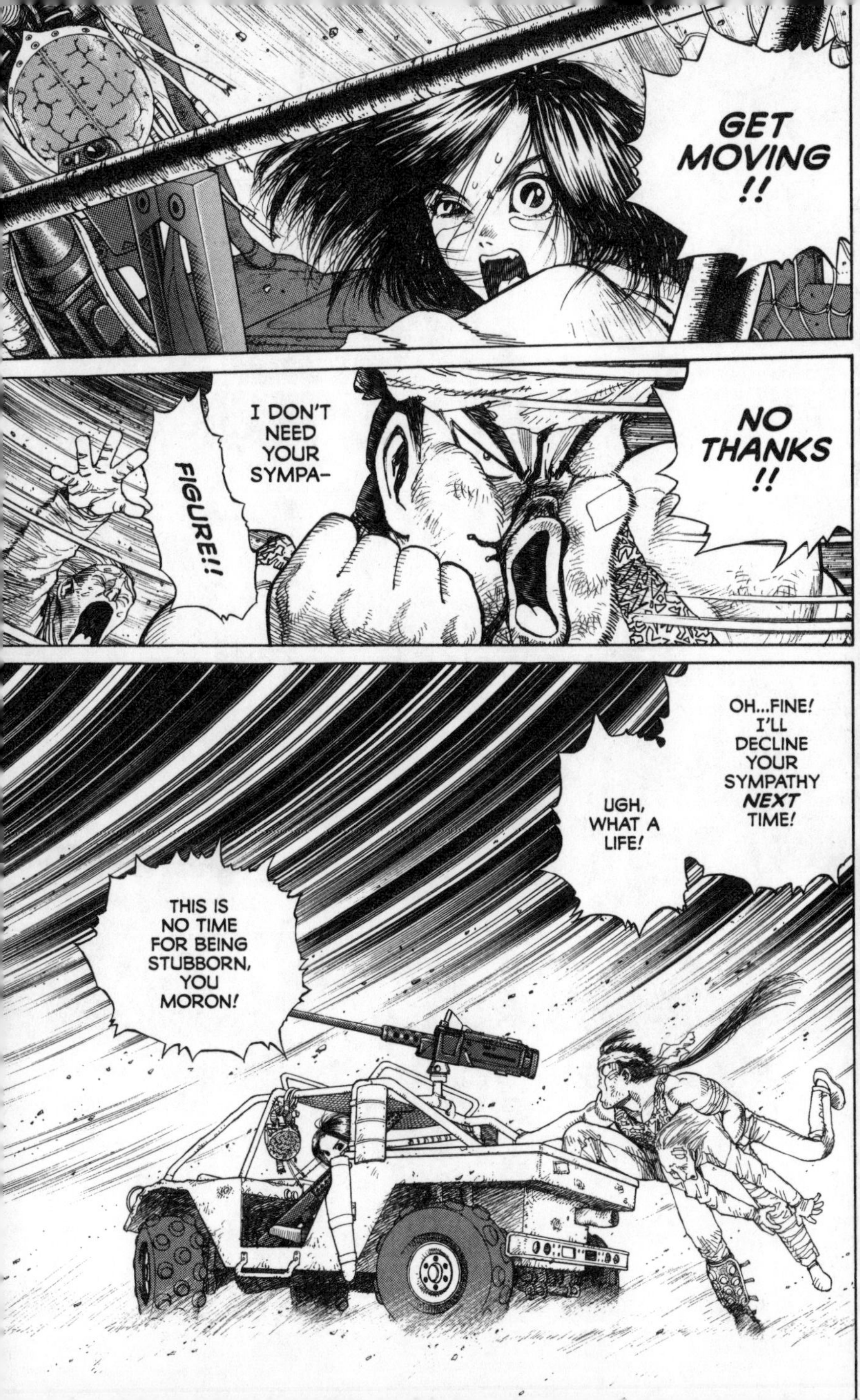
GET MOVING !!
NO THANKS !!
I DON'T NEED YOUR SYMPA-
FIGURE!!
OH...FINE! I'LL DECLINE YOUR SYMPATHY *NEXT* TIME!
UGH, WHAT A LIFE!
THIS IS NO TIME FOR BEING STUBBORN, YOU MORON!

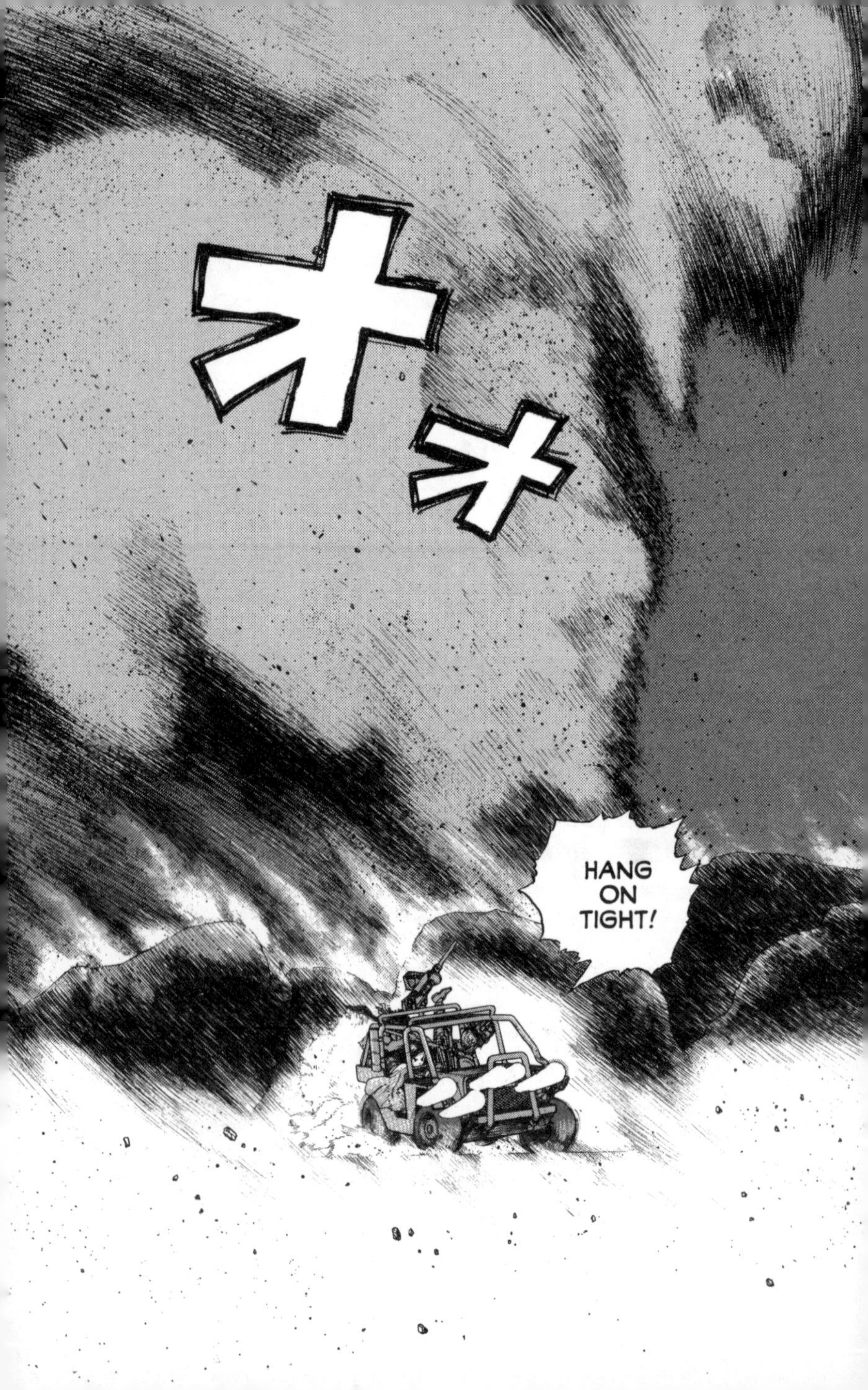
オォ
HANG ON TIGHT!

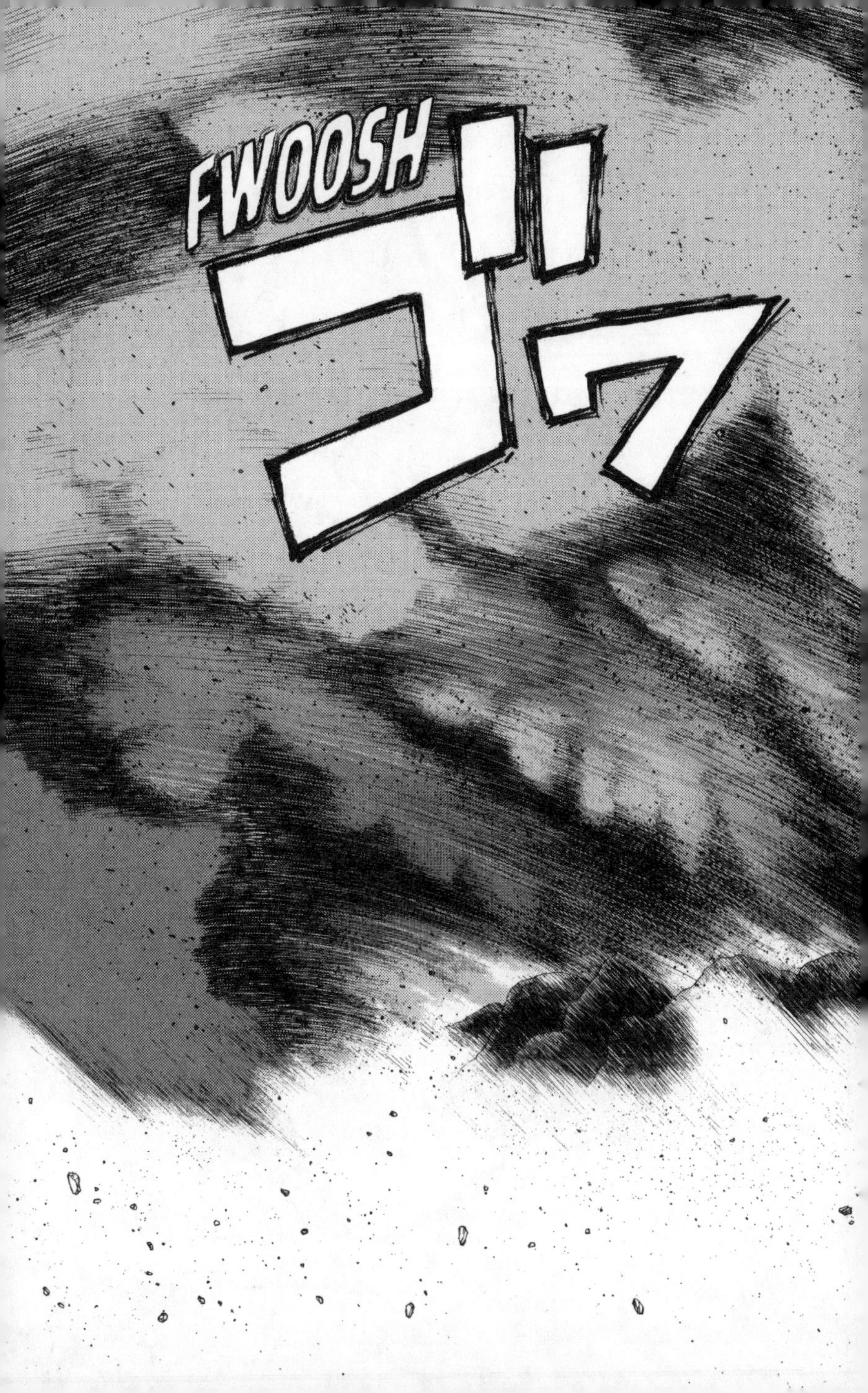
FWOOSH
ゴワ

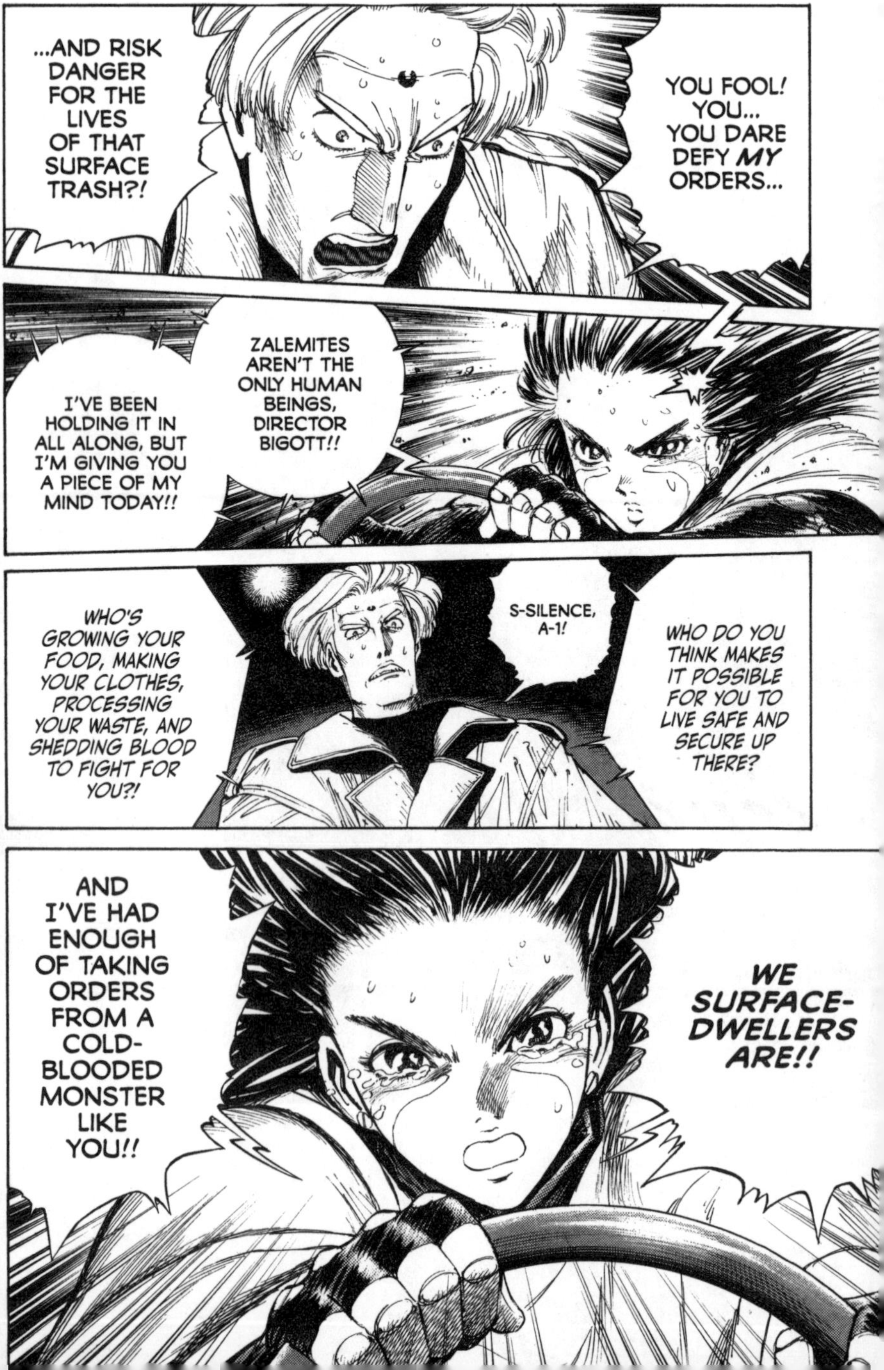
YOU FOOL! YOU... YOU DARE DEFY *MY* ORDERS...
...AND RISK DANGER FOR THE LIVES OF THAT SURFACE TRASH?!
ZALEMITES AREN'T THE ONLY HUMAN BEINGS, DIRECTOR BIGOTT!!
I'VE BEEN HOLDING IT IN ALL ALONG, BUT I'M GIVING YOU A PIECE OF MY MIND TODAY!!
WHO DO YOU THINK MAKES IT POSSIBLE FOR YOU TO LIVE SAFE AND SECURE UP THERE?
S-SILENCE, A-1!
WHO'S GROWING YOUR FOOD, MAKING YOUR CLOTHES, PROCESSING YOUR WASTE, AND SHEDDING BLOOD TO FIGHT FOR YOU?!
WE SURFACE-DWELLERS ARE!!
AND I'VE HAD ENOUGH OF TAKING ORDERS FROM A COLD-BLOODED MONSTER LIKE YOU!!

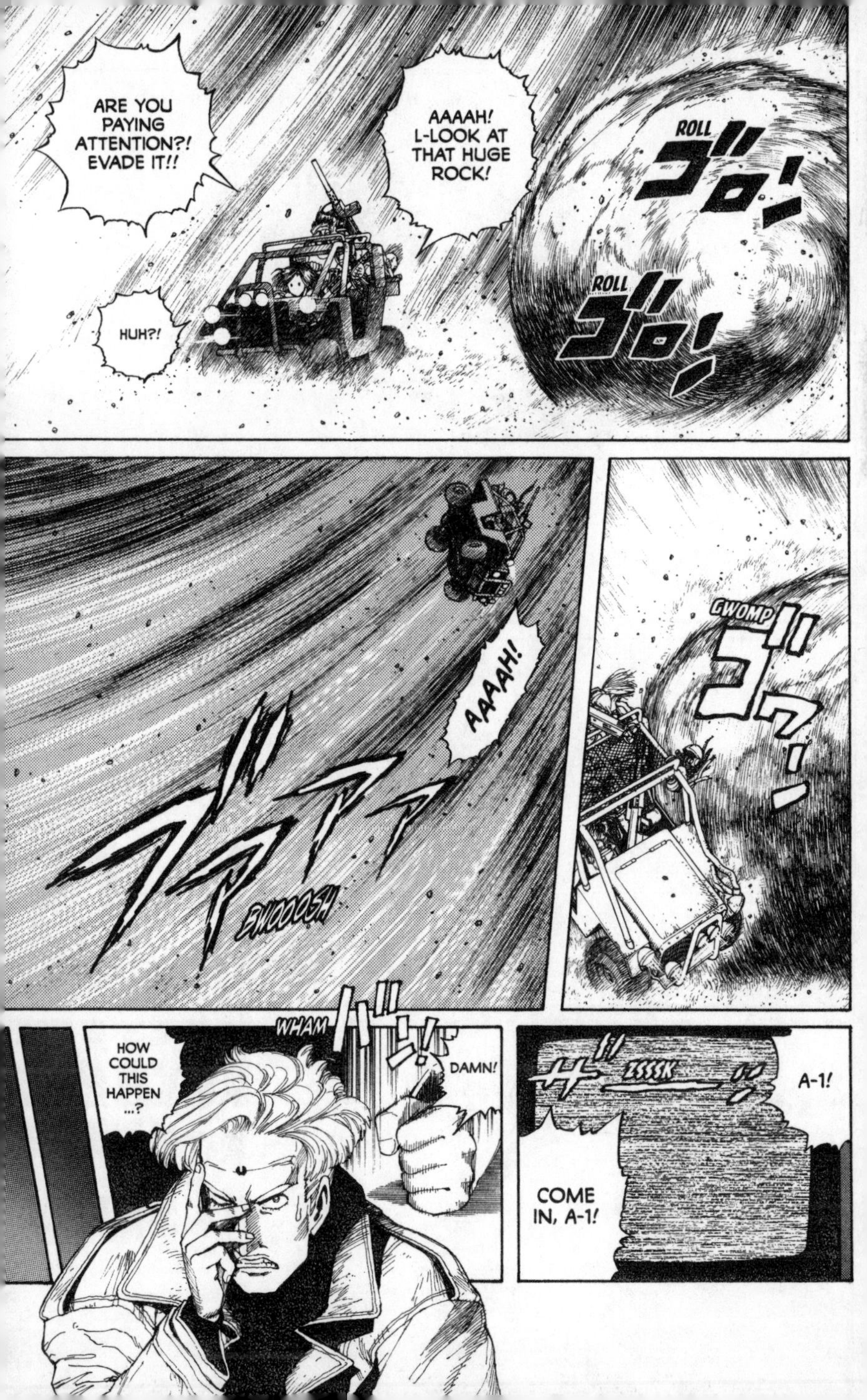
ROLL
ROLL
AAAAH! L-LOOK AT THAT HUGE ROCK!
ARE YOU PAYING ATTENTION?! EVADE IT!!
HUH?!
GWOMP
AAAAH!
BWOOOSH
ZSSSK
A-1!
COME IN, A-1!
WHAM
DAMN!
HOW COULD THIS HAPPEN ...?

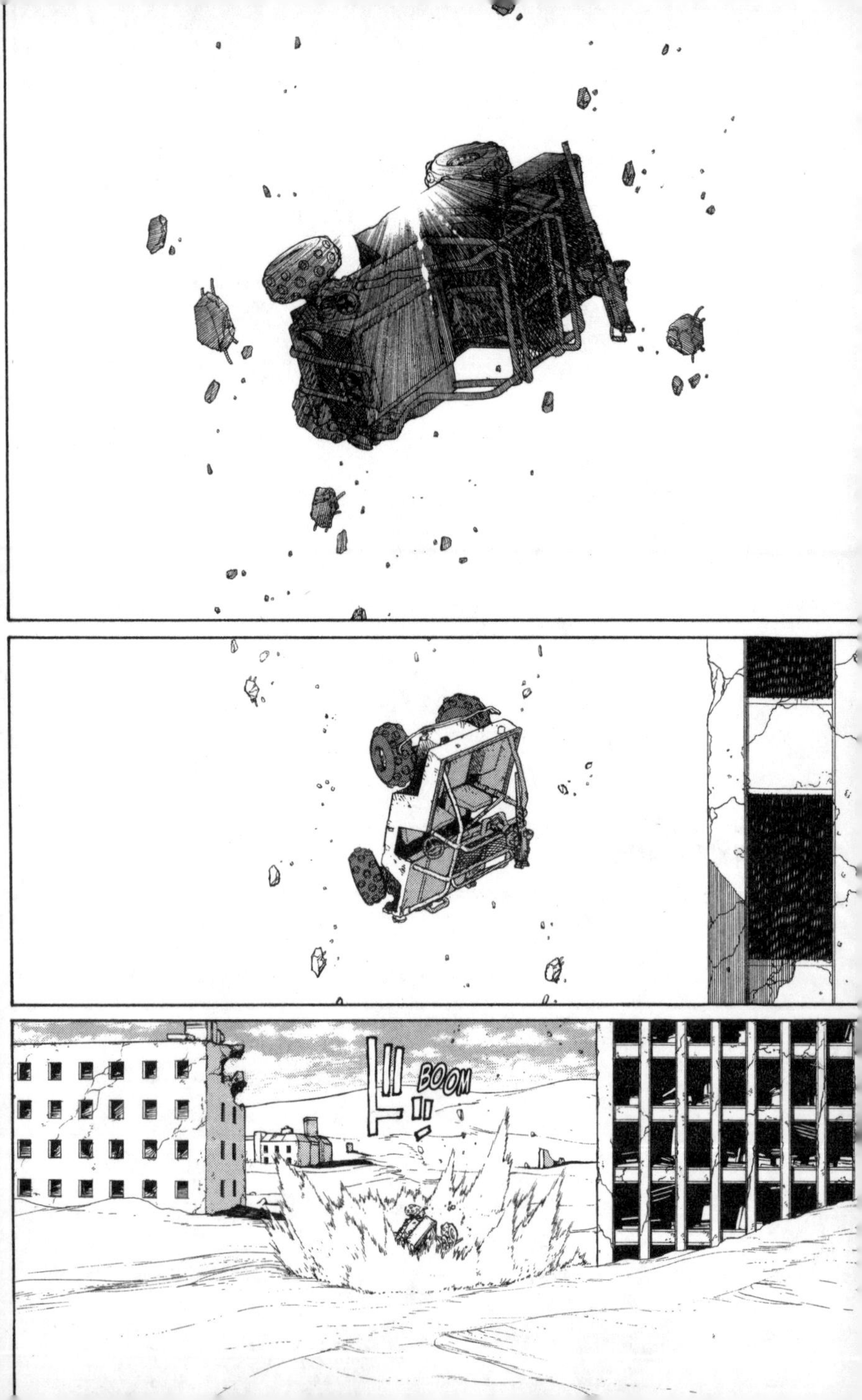
BOOM

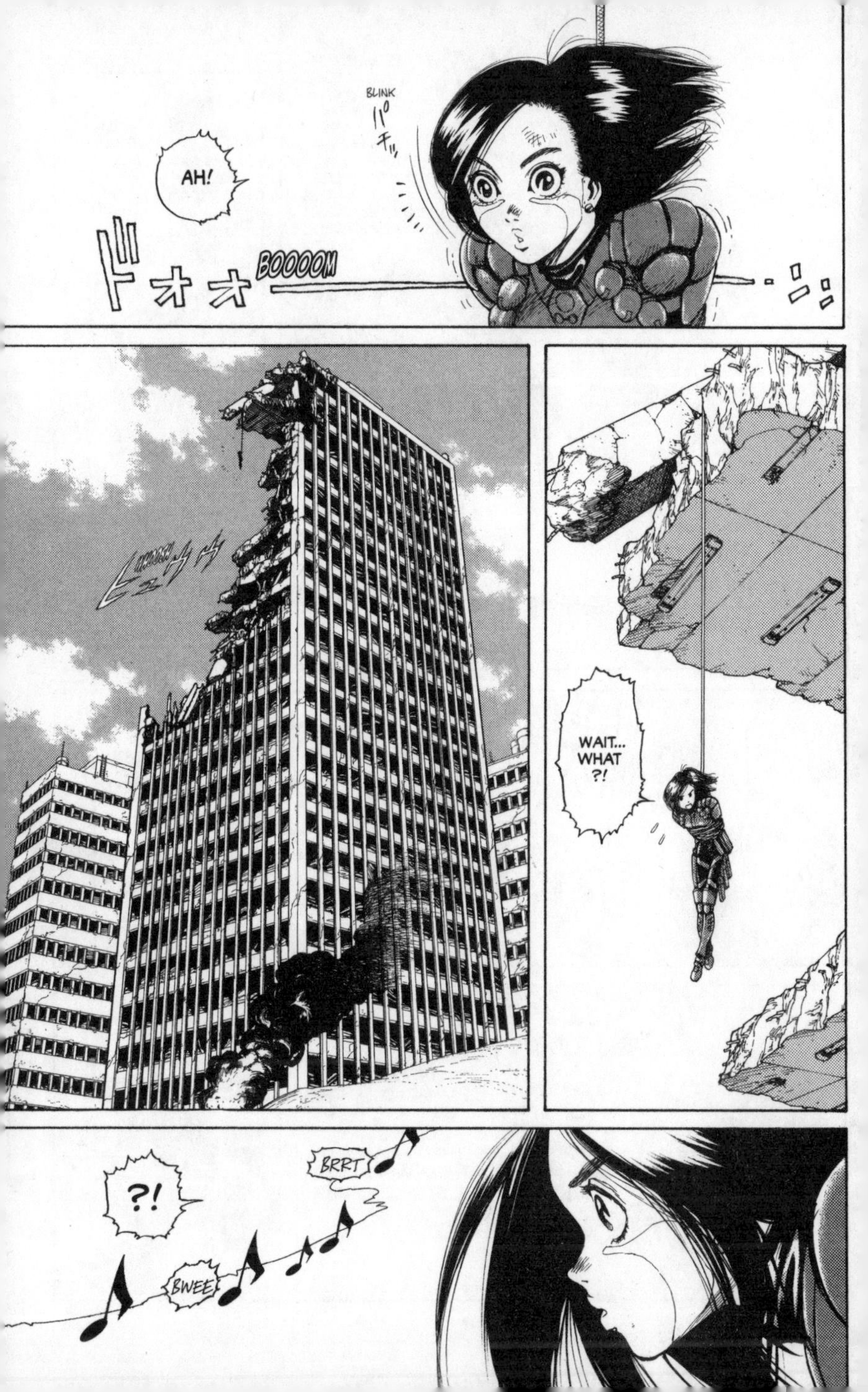
BLINK
パチッ
AH!
ドオオ
BOOOOM
WAIT... WHAT ?!
ヒュウウ
?!
BRRT
BWEE

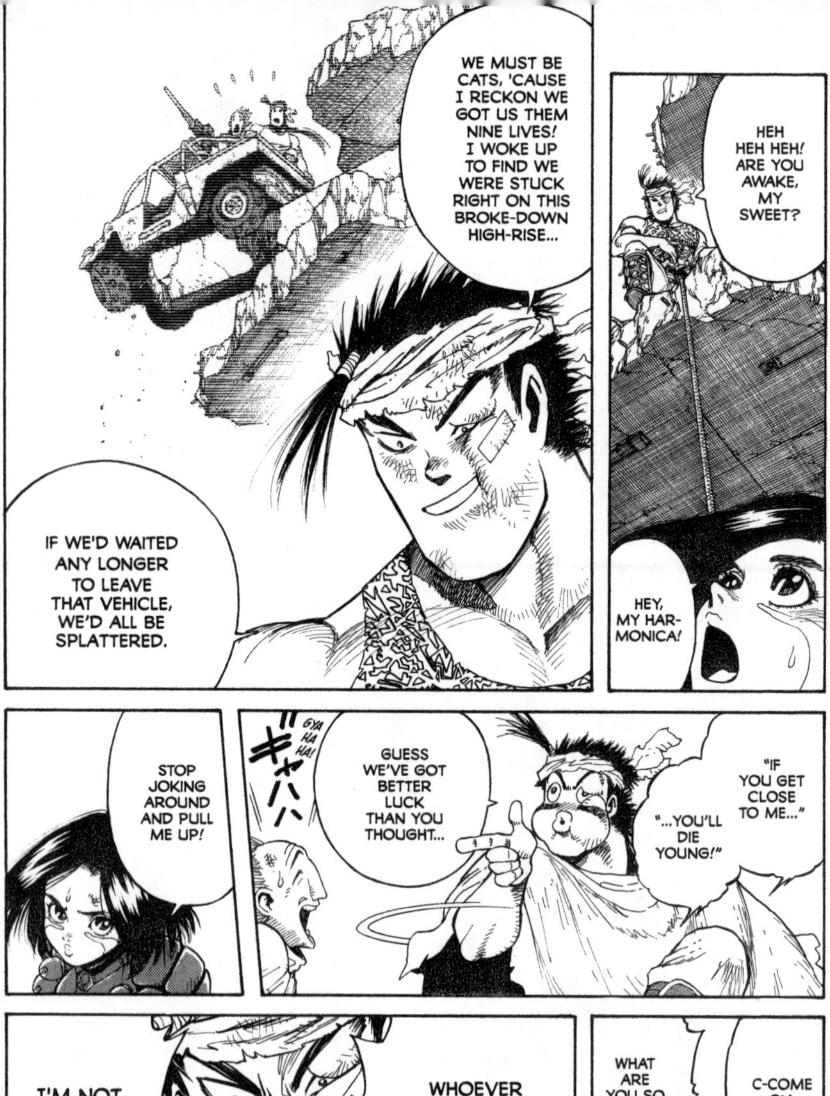
HEH HEH HEH! ARE YOU AWAKE, MY SWEET?
HEY, MY HARMONICA!
WE MUST BE CATS, 'CAUSE I RECKON WE GOT US THEM NINE LIVES! I WOKE UP TO FIND WE WERE STUCK RIGHT ON THIS BROKE-DOWN HIGH-RISE...
IF WE'D WAITED ANY LONGER TO LEAVE THAT VEHICLE, WE'D ALL BE SPLATTERED.
"IF YOU GET CLOSE TO ME..."
"...YOU'LL DIE YOUNG!"
GUESS WE'VE GOT BETTER LUCK THAN YOU THOUGHT...
GYA HA HA!
STOP JOKING AROUND AND PULL ME UP!
C-COME ON, FIGURE...
WHAT ARE YOU SO AFRAID OF?!
WHOEVER YOU REALLY ARE, I'M TIRED OF THE WAY YOU HELP PEOPLE AND THEN ABANDON THEM WHENEVER IT STRIKES YOUR FANCY!
I'M NOT GONNA BE YOUR PLAYTHING! YOU UNDER-STAND ME?!

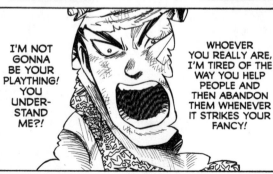

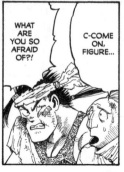

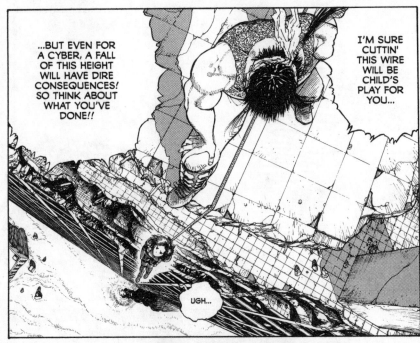

I'M SURE CUTTIN' THIS WIRE WILL BE CHILD'S PLAY FOR YOU...
...BUT EVEN FOR A CYBER, A FALL OF THIS HEIGHT WILL HAVE DIRE CONSEQUENCES! SO THINK ABOUT WHAT YOU'VE DONE!!
UGH...
UNGRATEFUL PUNK... HE HAS NO IDEA WHAT I JUST DID FOR HIM!
CONTROL! COME IN, CONTROL!
DAMN, NO SIGNAL...
HEY! IS ***KNUCKLE-HEAD***, THE LEADER OF THOSE BANDITS, STILL INTACT?!
HMM? NOW THAT YOU MEN-TION IT...
H-HE WASN'T IN THE CAR.
TOO BAD! LOOKS LIKE HIS BRAIN MUST HAVE FALLEN OUT AT SOME POINT!

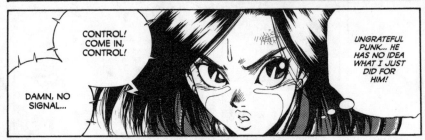

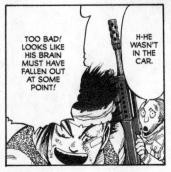

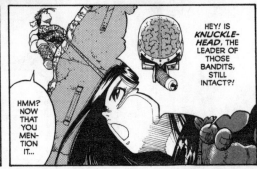

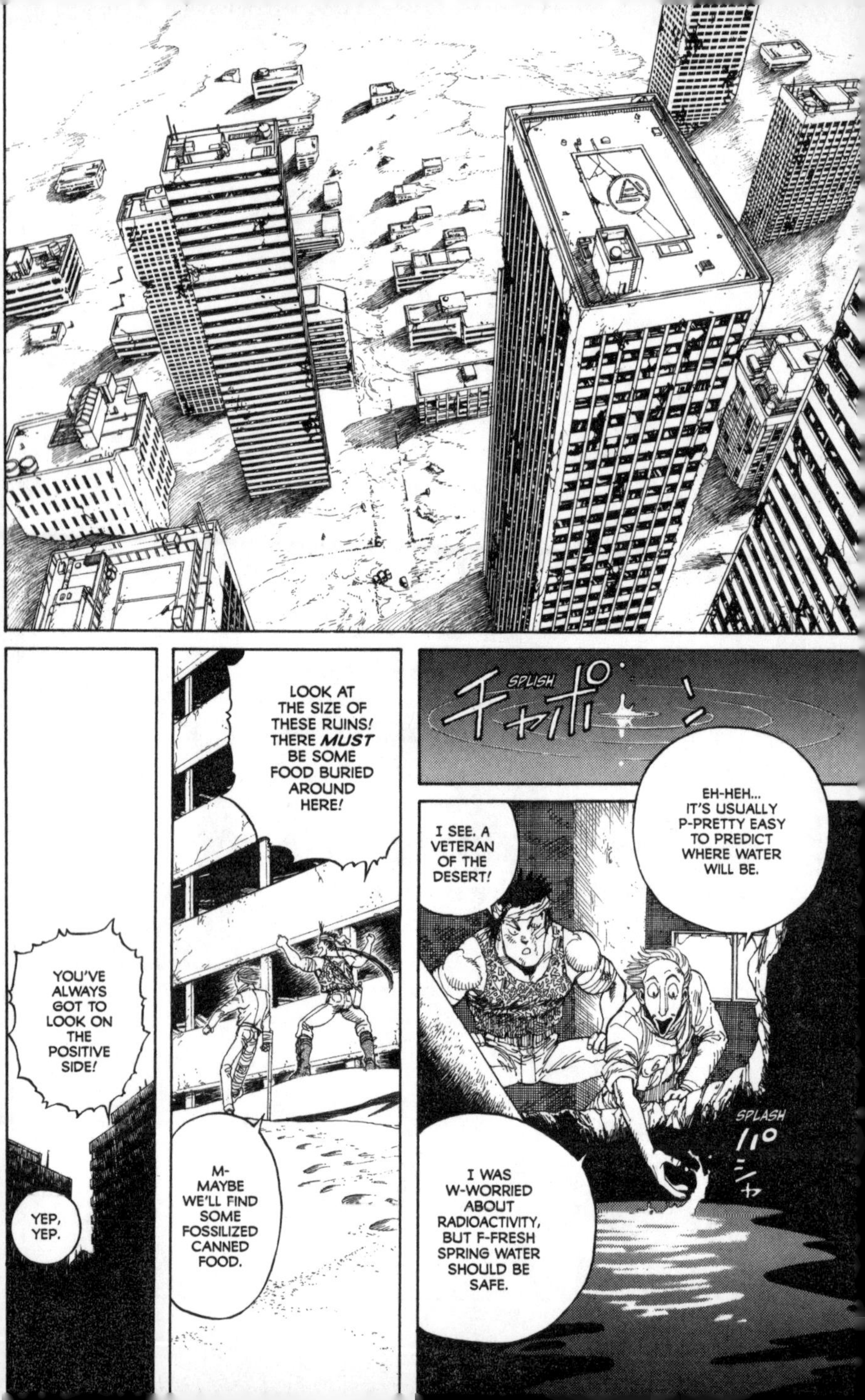
SPLISH
チャポーン
EH-HEH... IT'S USUALLY P-PRETTY EASY TO PREDICT WHERE WATER WILL BE.
I SEE. A VETERAN OF THE DESERT!
I WAS W-WORRIED ABOUT RADIOACTIVITY, BUT F-FRESH SPRING WATER SHOULD BE SAFE.
SPLASH
パシャ
LOOK AT THE SIZE OF THESE RUINS! THERE *MUST* BE SOME FOOD BURIED AROUND HERE!
M-MAYBE WE'LL FIND SOME FOSSILIZED CANNED FOOD.
YOU'VE ALWAYS GOT TO LOOK ON THE POSITIVE SIDE!
YEP, YEP.

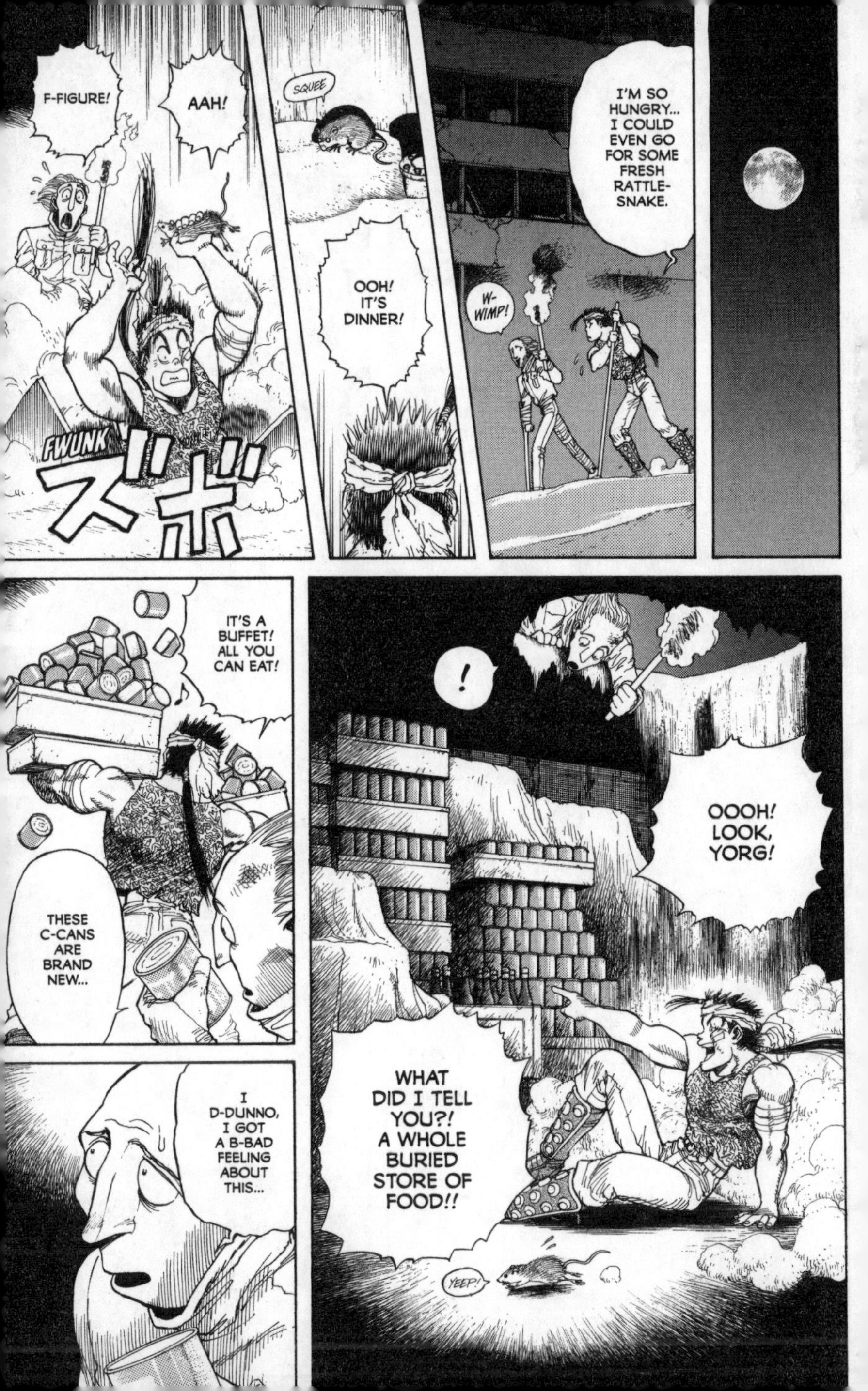
I'M SO HUNGRY... I COULD EVEN GO FOR SOME FRESH RATTLE-SNAKE.
W-WIMP!
SQUEE
OOH! IT'S DINNER!
AAH!
F-FIGURE!
FWUNK
ズボ
!
OOOH! LOOK, YORG!
WHAT DID I TELL YOU?! A WHOLE BURIED STORE OF FOOD!!
YEEP!
IT'S A BUFFET! ALL YOU CAN EAT!
THESE C-CANS ARE BRAND NEW...
I D-DUNNO, I GOT A B-BAD FEELING ABOUT THIS...

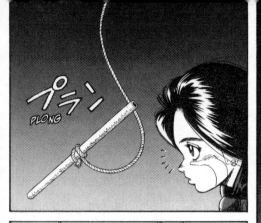

プラン
PLONG

WHOOOSH

WELL? FEELING APOLOGETIC YET?

ズル
SHLIP

ズル
SHLIP

EVEN A CYBER'S GOTTA GET HUNGRY, RIGHT?

HERE, GOT SOME YUMMY CORNED BEEF FOR YA.

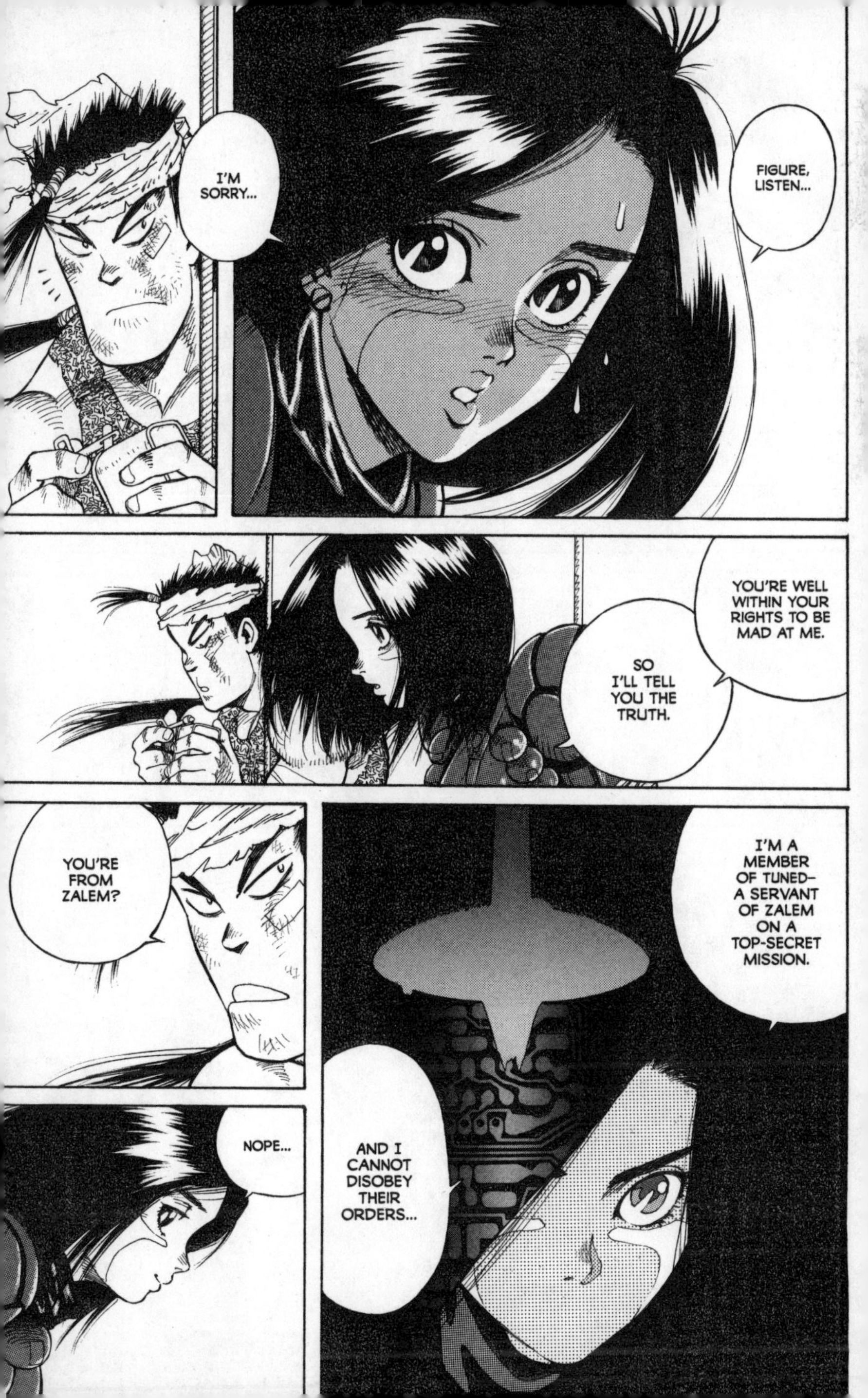
FIGURE, LISTEN...
I'M SORRY...
YOU'RE WELL WITHIN YOUR RIGHTS TO BE MAD AT ME.
SO I'LL TELL YOU THE TRUTH.
I'M A MEMBER OF TUNED– A SERVANT OF ZALEM ON A TOP-SECRET MISSION.
AND I CANNOT DISOBEY THEIR ORDERS...
YOU'RE FROM ZALEM?
NOPE...

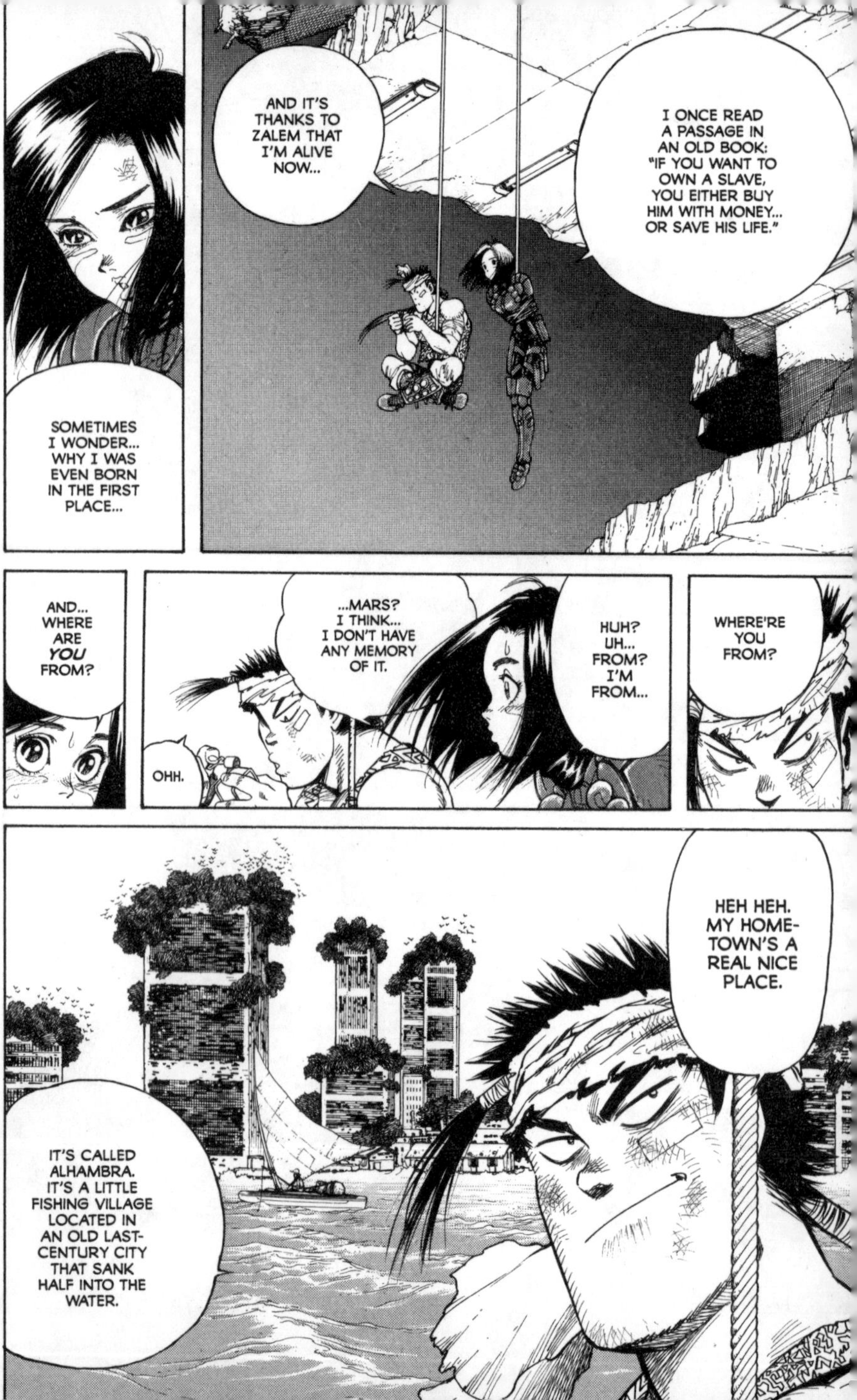
I ONCE READ A PASSAGE IN AN OLD BOOK: "IF YOU WANT TO OWN A SLAVE, YOU EITHER BUY HIM WITH MONEY... OR SAVE HIS LIFE."
AND IT'S THANKS TO ZALEM THAT I'M ALIVE NOW...
SOMETIMES I WONDER... WHY I WAS EVEN BORN IN THE FIRST PLACE...
WHERE'RE YOU FROM?
HUH? UH... FROM? I'M FROM...
...MARS? I THINK... I DON'T HAVE ANY MEMORY OF IT.
OHH.
AND... WHERE ARE *YOU* FROM?
HEH HEH. MY HOME-TOWN'S A REAL NICE PLACE.
IT'S CALLED ALHAMBRA. IT'S A LITTLE FISHING VILLAGE LOCATED IN AN OLD LAST-CENTURY CITY THAT SANK HALF INTO THE WATER.

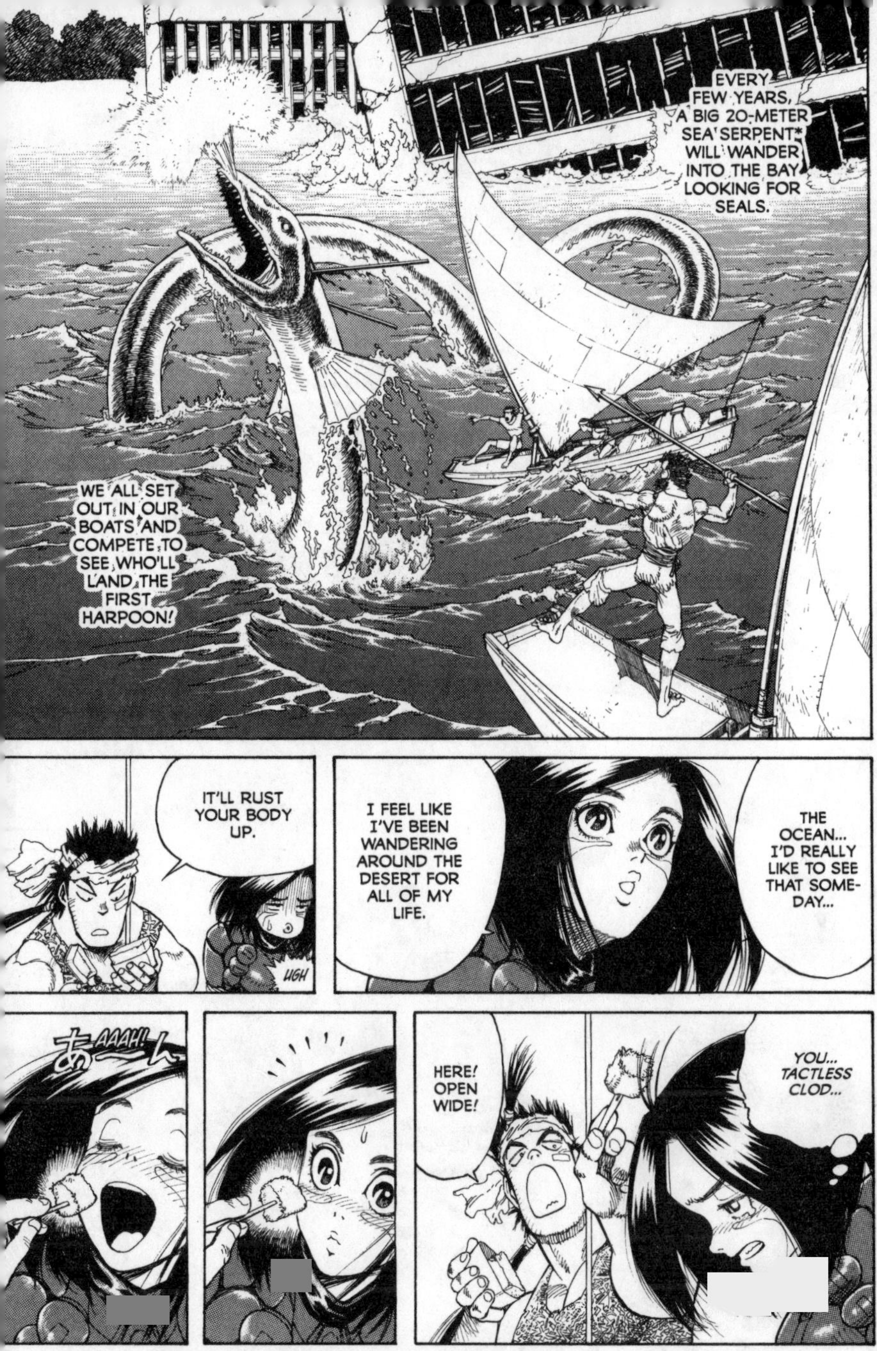
EVERY FEW YEARS, A BIG 20-METER SEA SERPENT* WILL WANDER INTO THE BAY LOOKING FOR SEALS.
WE ALL SET OUT IN OUR BOATS AND COMPETE TO SEE WHO'LL LAND THE FIRST HARPOON!
THE OCEAN... I'D REALLY LIKE TO SEE THAT SOME-DAY...
I FEEL LIKE I'VE BEEN WANDERING AROUND THE DESERT FOR ALL OF MY LIFE.
IT'LL RUST YOUR BODY UP.
UGH
YOU... TACTLESS CLOD...
HERE! OPEN WIDE!
あ〜ん
AAAAH!

***Sea serpent:** A marine animal often witnessed, but never scientifically observed. It's said that one once provided as much meat and oil as an entire whale.

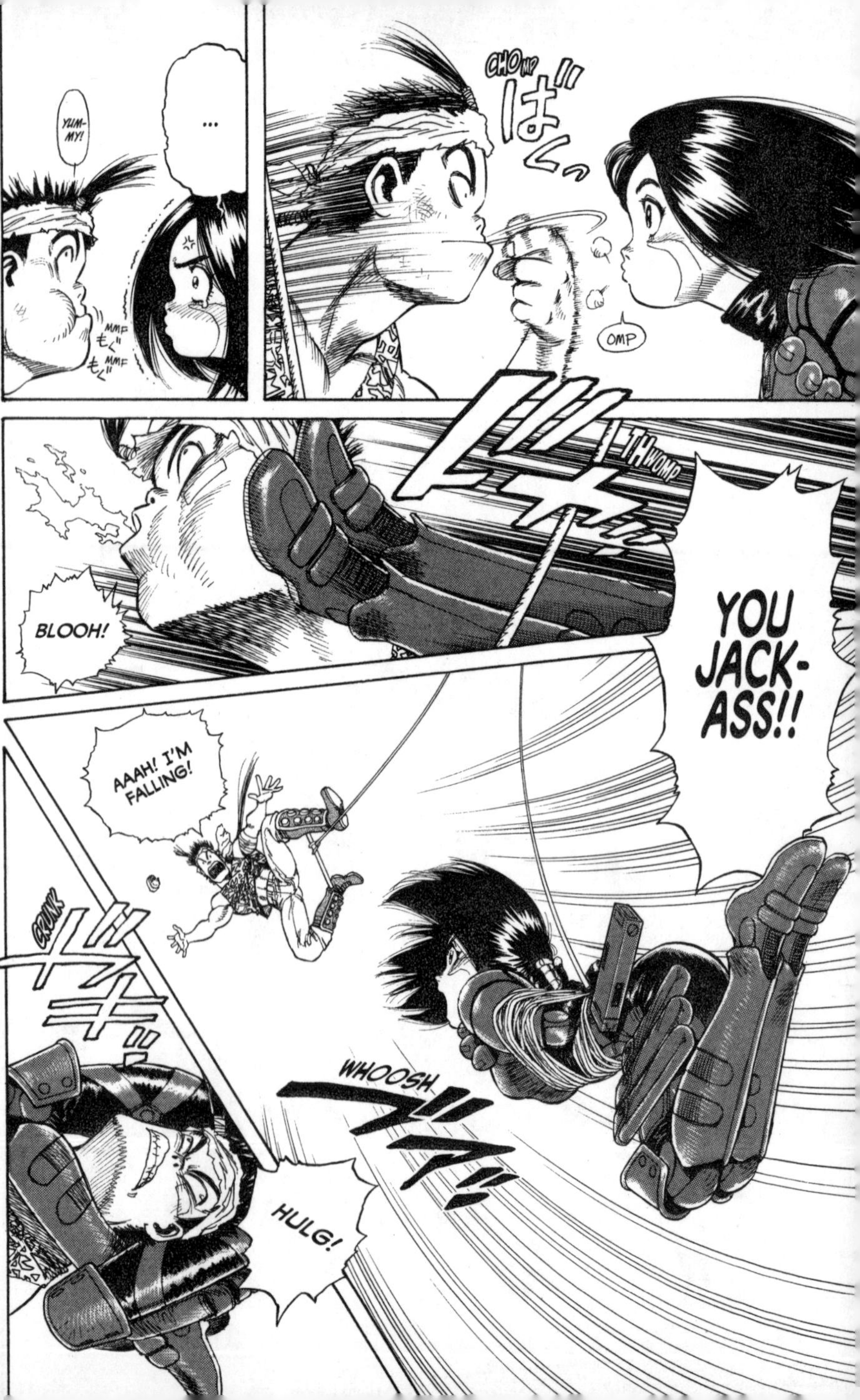
CHOMP
ばくっ
OMP
...
YUM-MY!
MMF もぐ
MMF もぐ
THWOMP
YOU JACK-ASS!!
BLOOH!
AAAH! I'M FALLING!
WHOOSH
GRUNK
HULG!

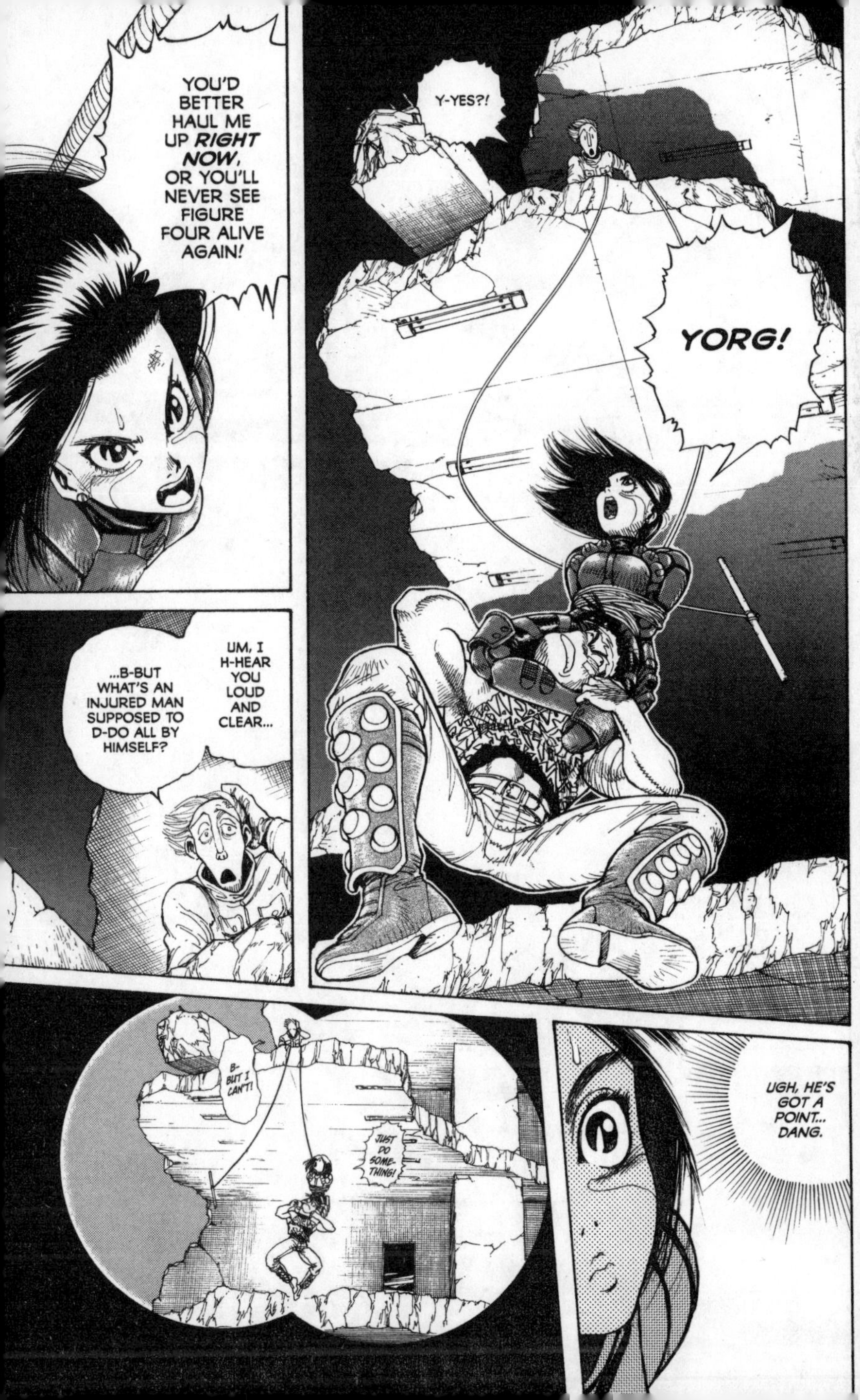
YORG!
Y-YES?!
YOU'D BETTER HAUL ME UP ***RIGHT NOW***, OR YOU'LL NEVER SEE FIGURE FOUR ALIVE AGAIN!
UM, I H-HEAR YOU LOUD AND CLEAR...
...B-BUT WHAT'S AN INJURED MAN SUPPOSED TO D-DO ALL BY HIMSELF?
UGH, HE'S GOT A POINT... DANG.
JUST DO SOME-THING!
B-BUT I CAN'T!

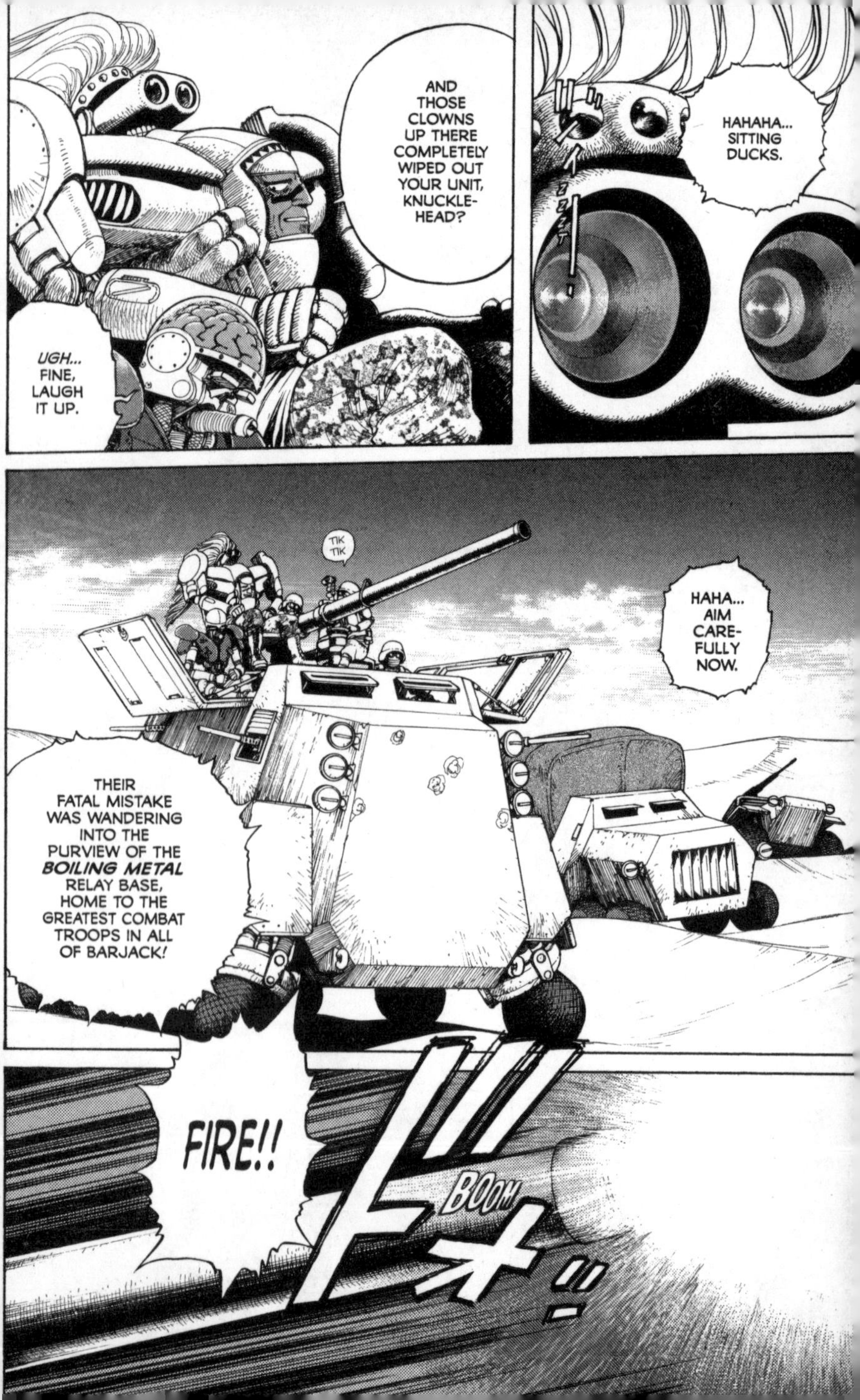
HAHAHA... SITTING DUCKS.
ZZZT
AND THOSE CLOWNS UP THERE COMPLETELY WIPED OUT YOUR UNIT, KNUCKLE-HEAD?
UGH... FINE, LAUGH IT UP.
HAHA... AIM CARE-FULLY NOW.
TIK TIK
THEIR FATAL MISTAKE WAS WANDERING INTO THE PURVIEW OF THE BOILING METAL RELAY BASE, HOME TO THE GREATEST COMBAT TROOPS IN ALL OF BARJACK!
FIRE!!
BOOM

FIGHT_033 Dog Eat Dog

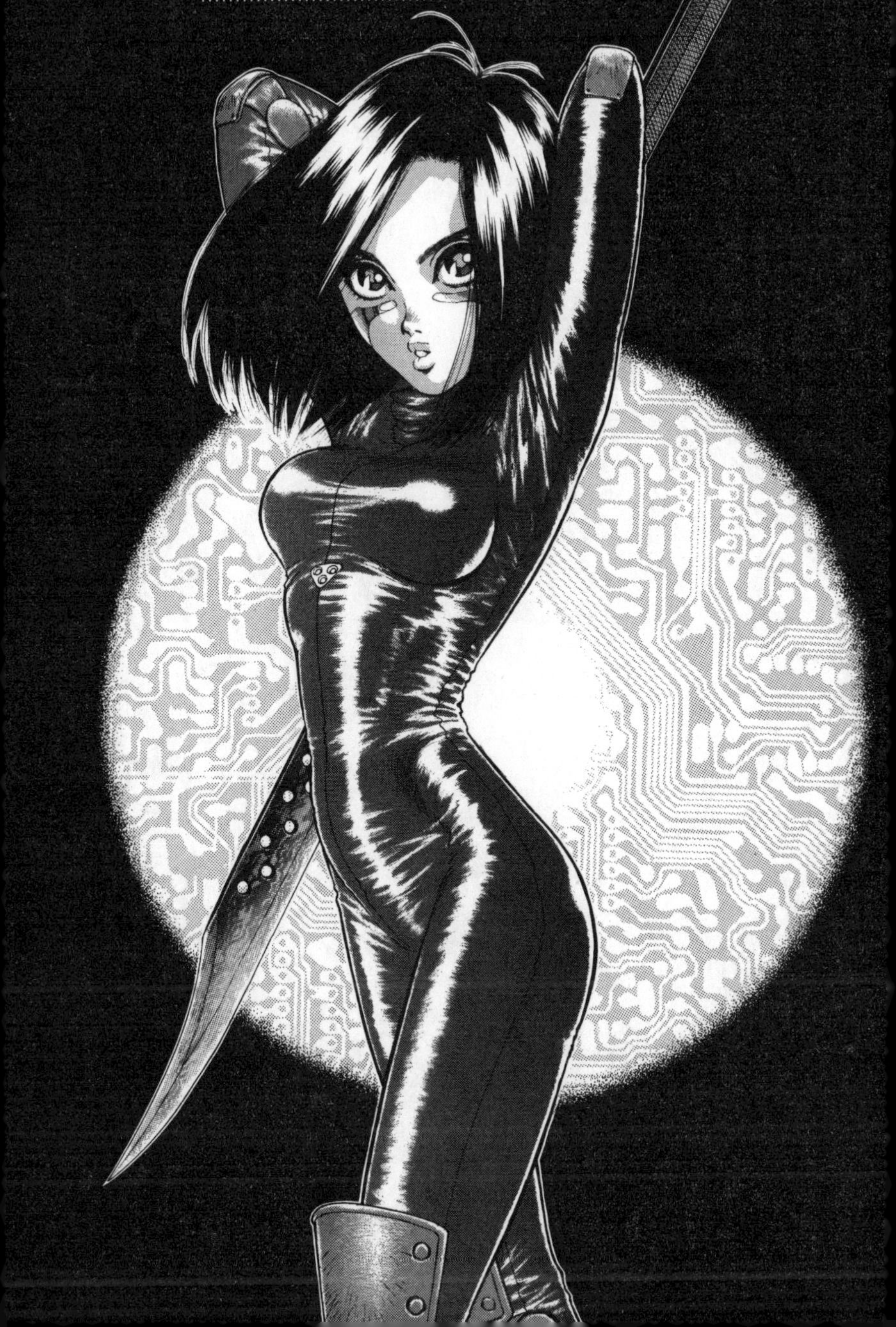

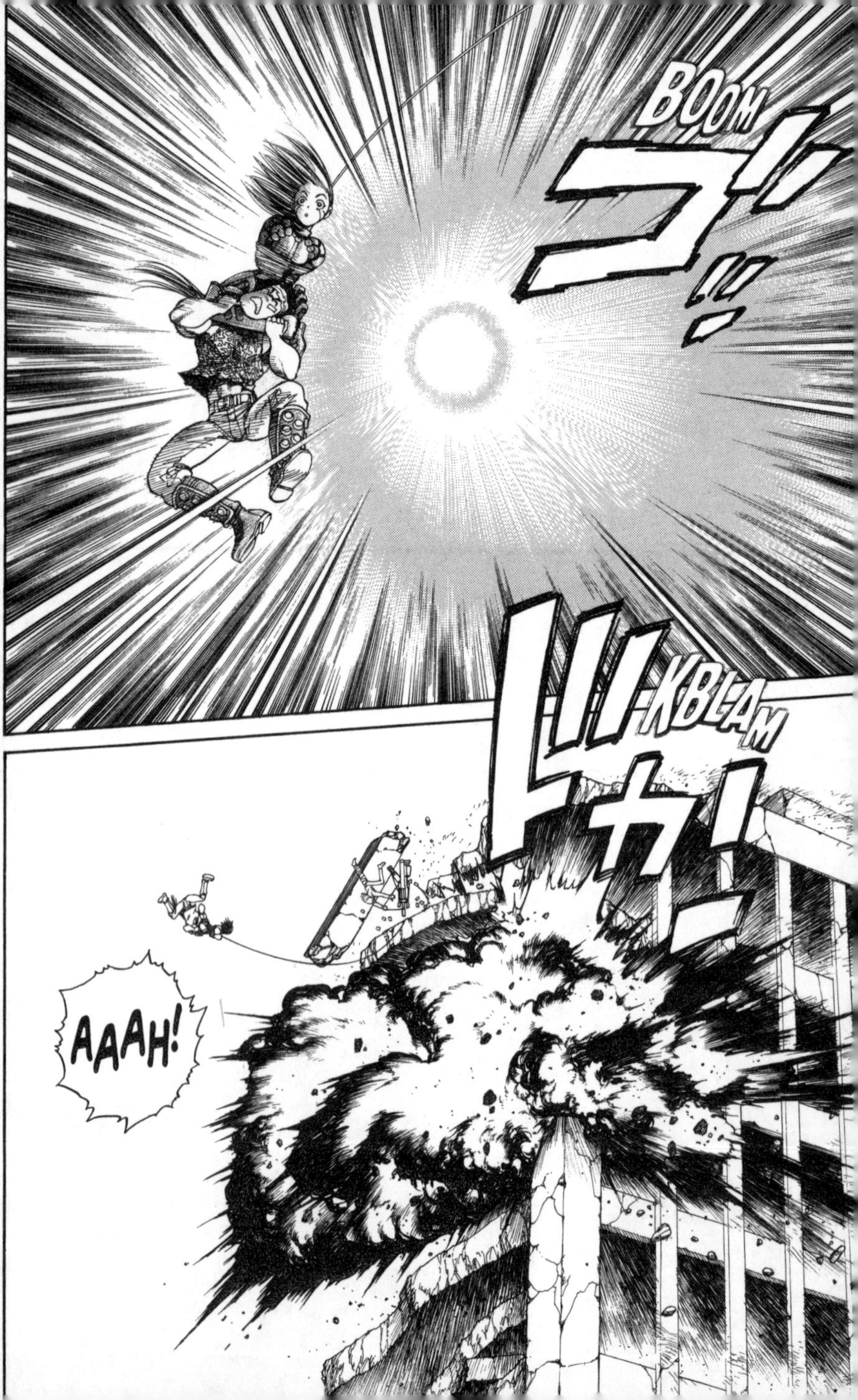
BOOM
KBLAM
AAAH!

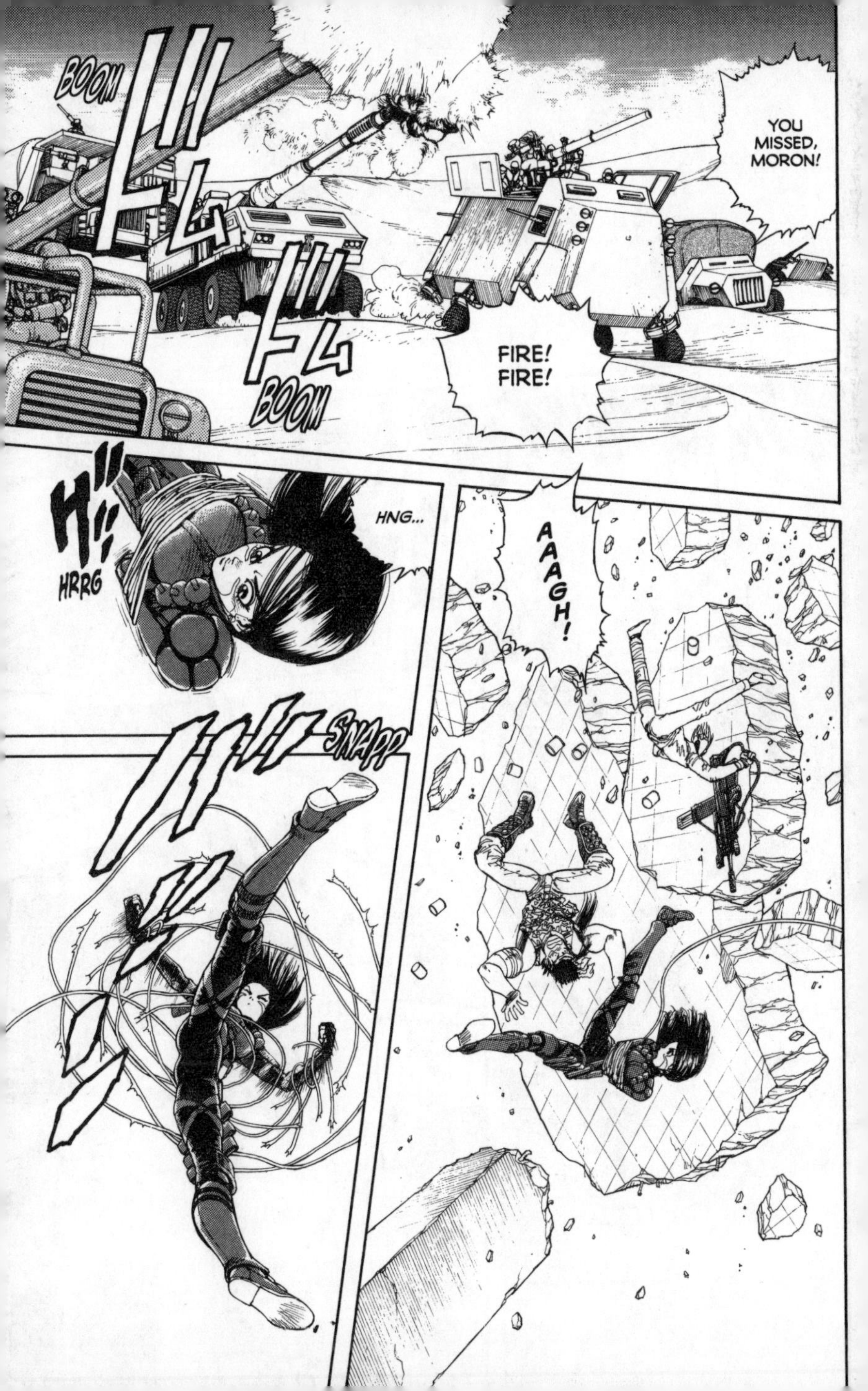
YOU MISSED, MORON!
BOOM
FIRE! FIRE!
BOOM
AAAAGH!
HNG...
HRRG
SNAPP

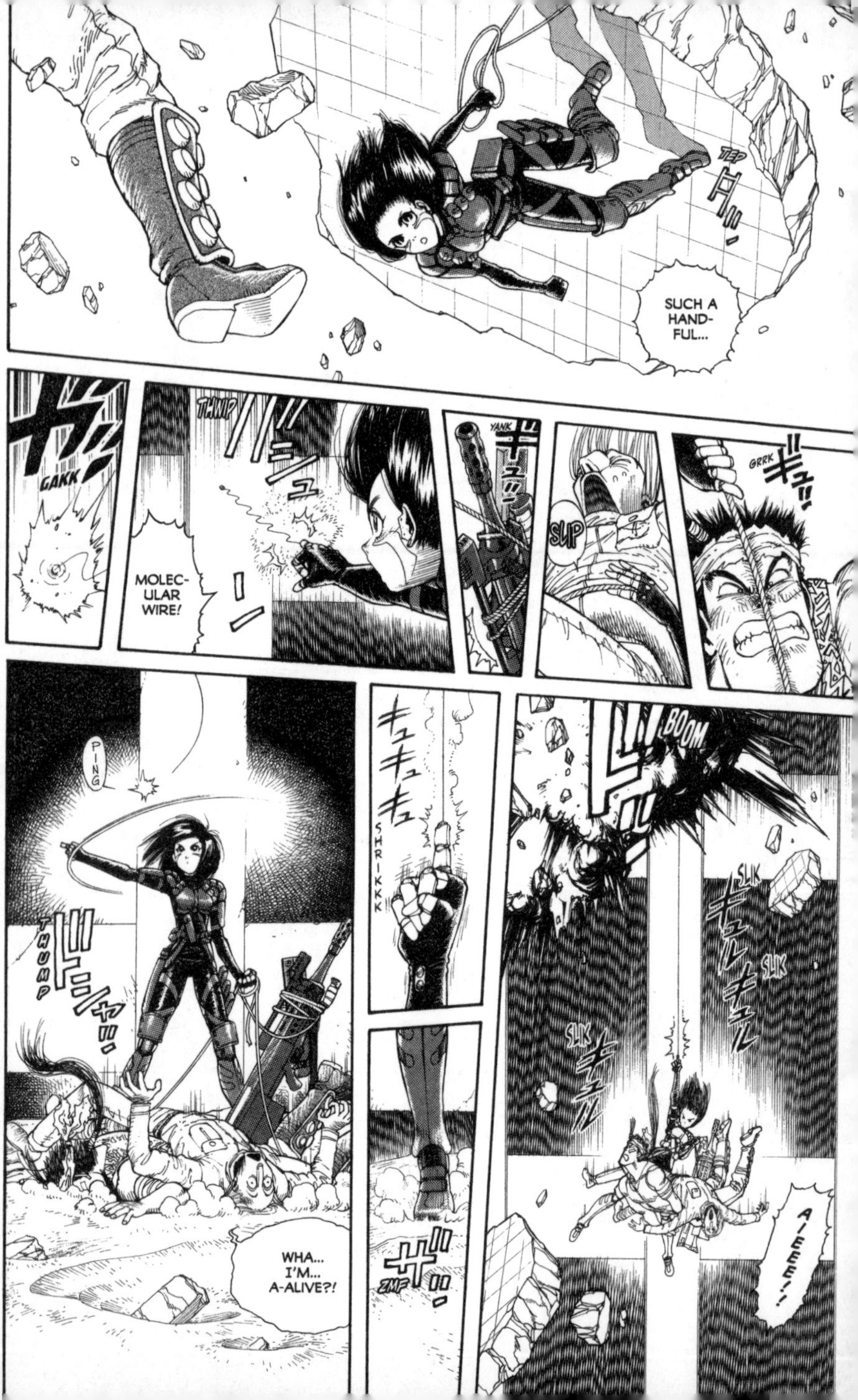

TEP
SUCH A HAND-FUL...
GRRK
SLIP
YANK
THWIP
MOLECULAR WIRE!
GAKK
BOOM
SLIK
SLIK
SLIK
AIEEE...!
SHRIKKK
ZMF
PING
THUMP
WHA... I'M... A-ALIVE?!

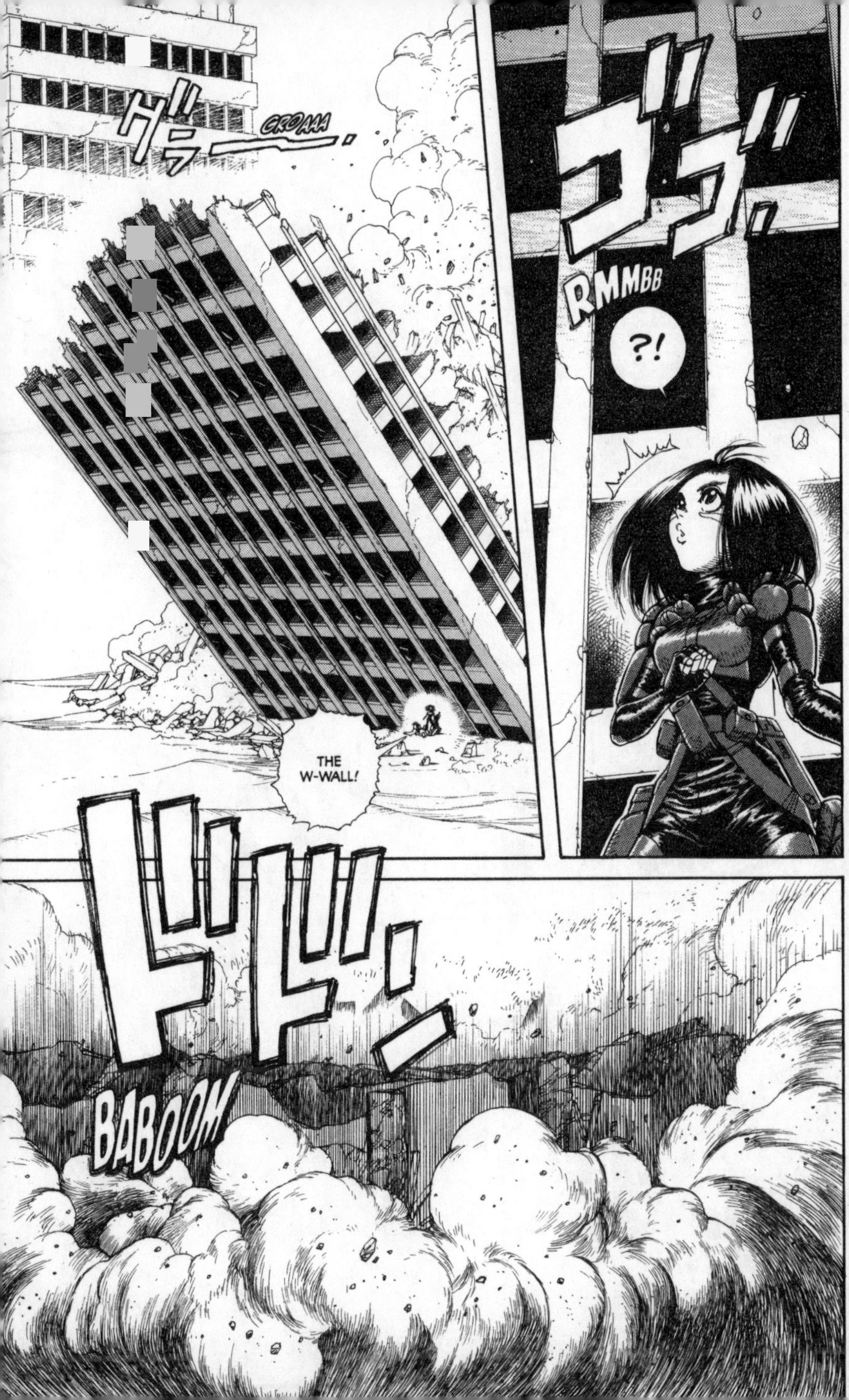
RMMBB
?!
GROAAA
THE W-WALL!
BABOOM

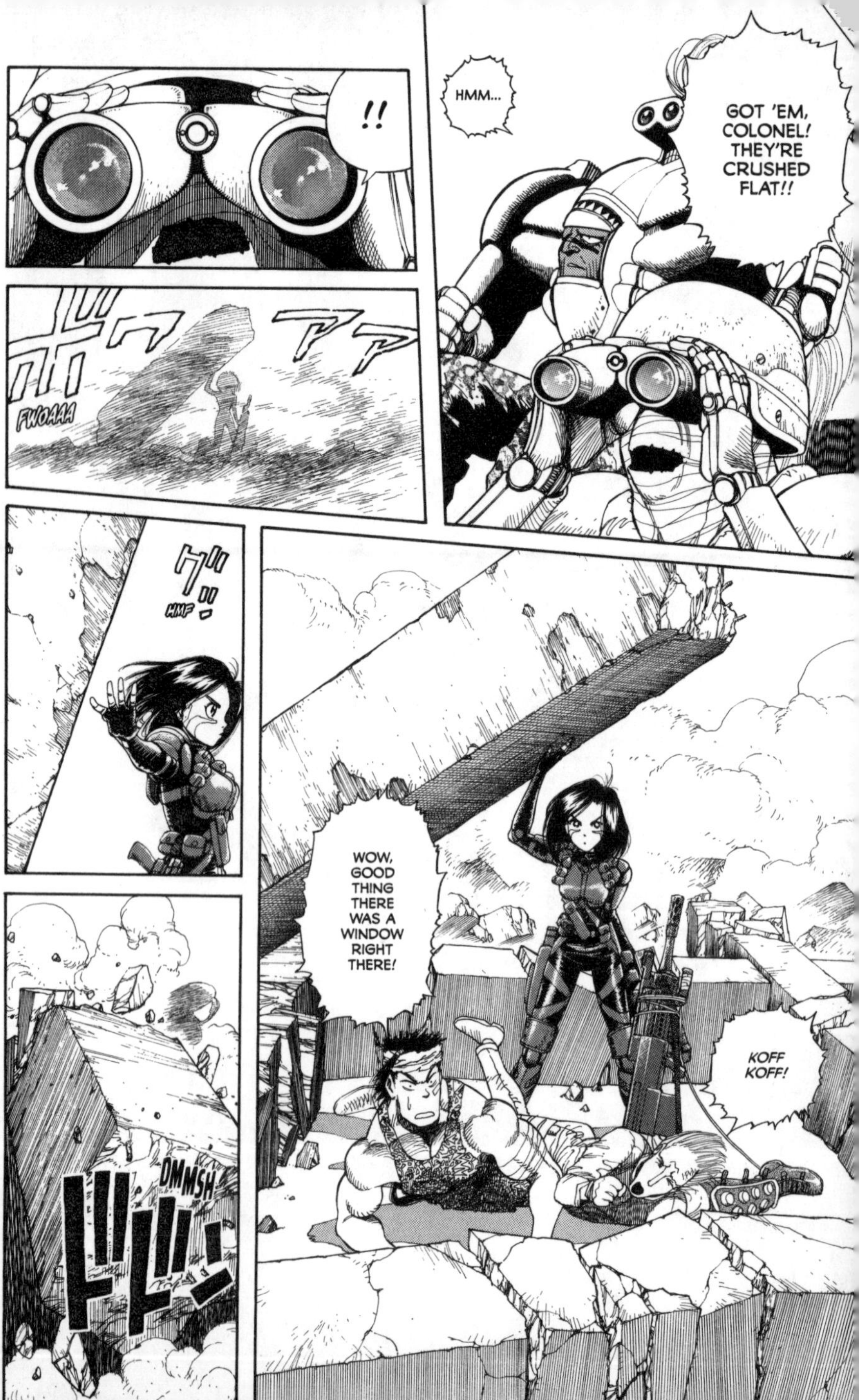
GOT 'EM, COLONEL! THEY'RE CRUSHED FLAT!!
HMM...
!!
FWOAAA
WOW, GOOD THING THERE WAS A WINDOW RIGHT THERE!
KOFF KOFF!
HMF
DMMSH

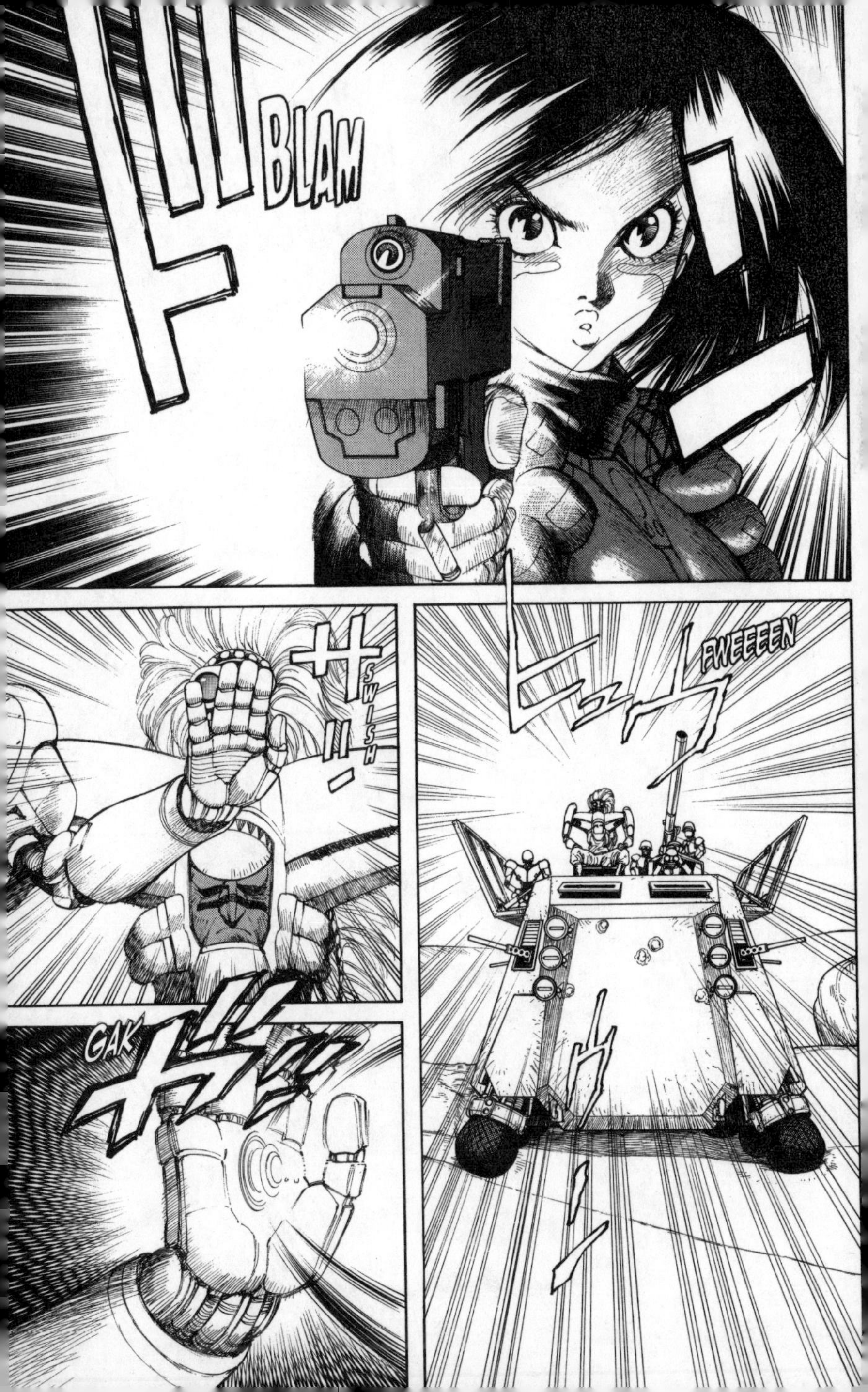
BLAM
FWEEEEN
SWISH
GAK

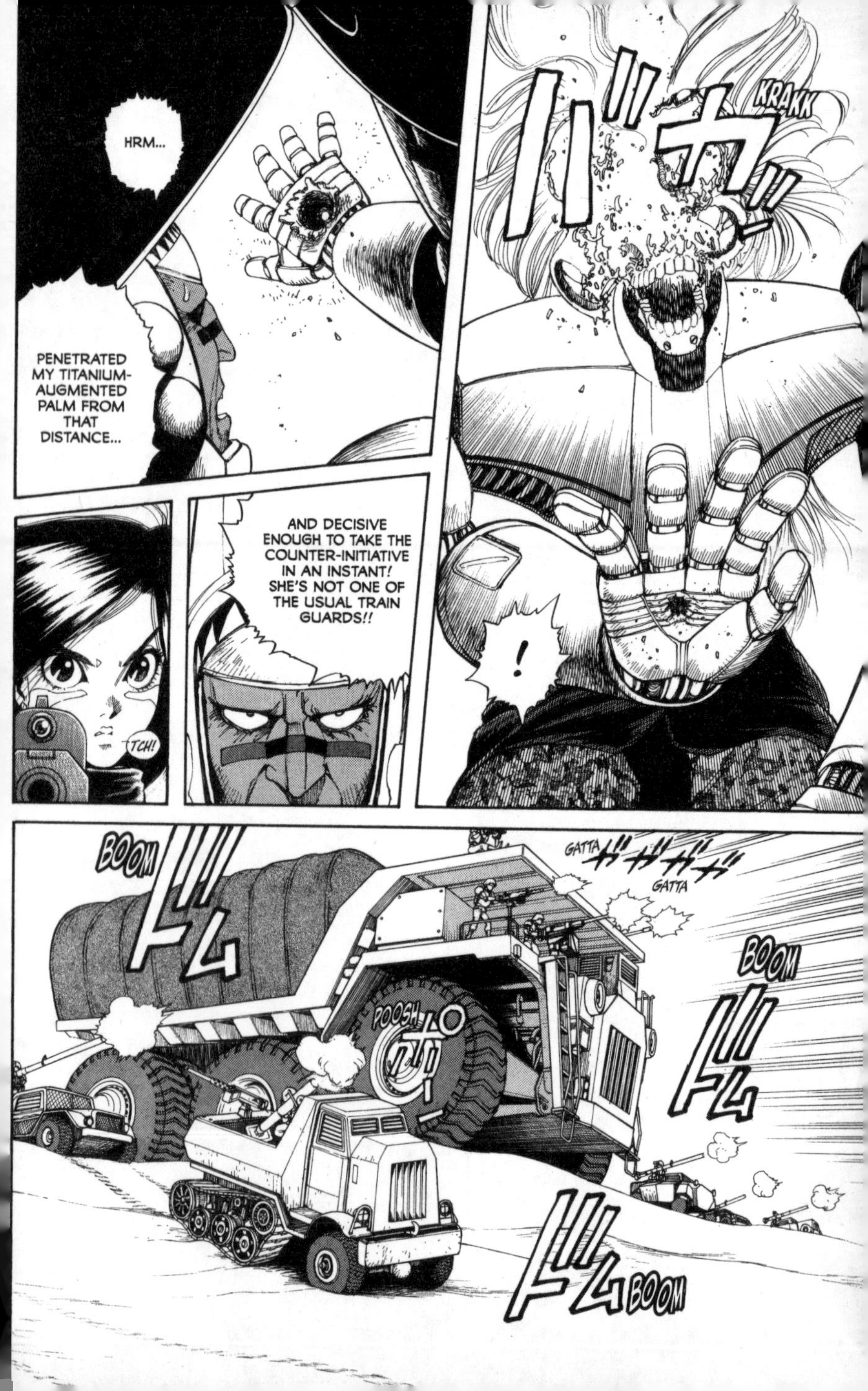
KRAKK
!
HRM...
PENETRATED MY TITANIUM-AUGMENTED PALM FROM THAT DISTANCE...
AND DECISIVE ENOUGH TO TAKE THE COUNTER-INITIATIVE IN AN INSTANT! SHE'S NOT ONE OF THE USUAL TRAIN GUARDS!!
TCH!
GATTA
GATTA
BOOM
POOSH
BOOM
BOOM

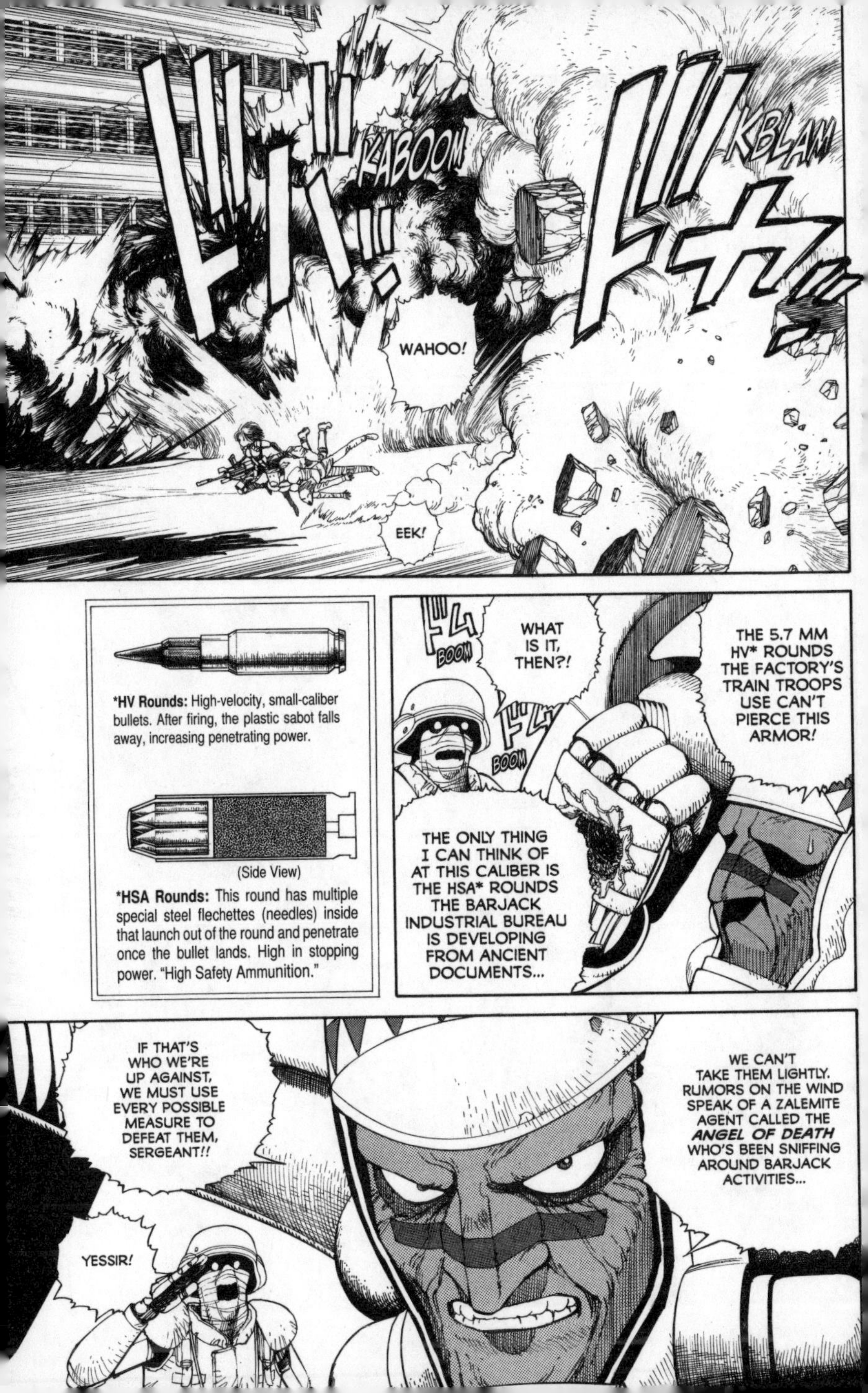
KBLAM
KABOOM
WAHOO!
EEK!
THE 5.7 MM HV* ROUNDS THE FACTORY'S TRAIN TROOPS USE CAN'T PIERCE THIS ARMOR!
WHAT IS IT, THEN?!
BOOM
BOOM
THE ONLY THING I CAN THINK OF AT THIS CALIBER IS THE HSA* ROUNDS THE BARJACK INDUSTRIAL BUREAU IS DEVELOPING FROM ANCIENT DOCUMENTS...
*HV Rounds: High-velocity, small-caliber bullets. After firing, the plastic sabot falls away, increasing penetrating power.
(Side View)
*HSA Rounds: This round has multiple special steel flechettes (needles) inside that launch out of the round and penetrate once the bullet lands. High in stopping power. "High Safety Ammunition."
WE CAN'T TAKE THEM LIGHTLY. RUMORS ON THE WIND SPEAK OF A ZALEMITE AGENT CALLED THE ANGEL OF DEATH WHO'S BEEN SNIFFING AROUND BARJACK ACTIVITIES...
IF THAT'S WHO WE'RE UP AGAINST, WE MUST USE EVERY POSSIBLE MEASURE TO DEFEAT THEM, SERGEANT!!
YESSIR!

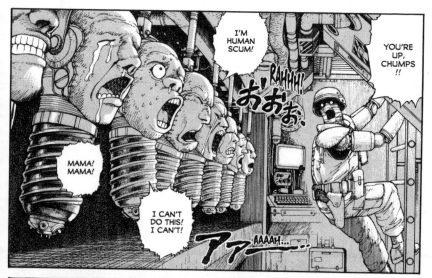

I'M HUMAN SCUM!

YOU'RE UP, CHUMPS!!

RAHHH! おおお、

MAMA! MAMA!

I CAN'T DO THIS! I CAN'T!

アアーAAAAH...

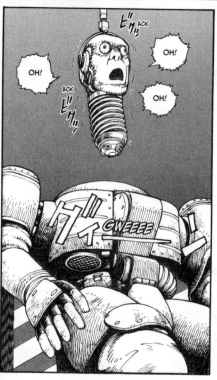

OH!

OH!

ビ"リ"ACK

ACK ビ"リ"

OH!

GWEEEE

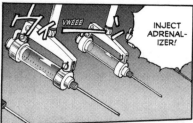

VWEEE

INJECT ADRENALIZER!

PSSSST

ビギ!! GRIK

SHNNNK

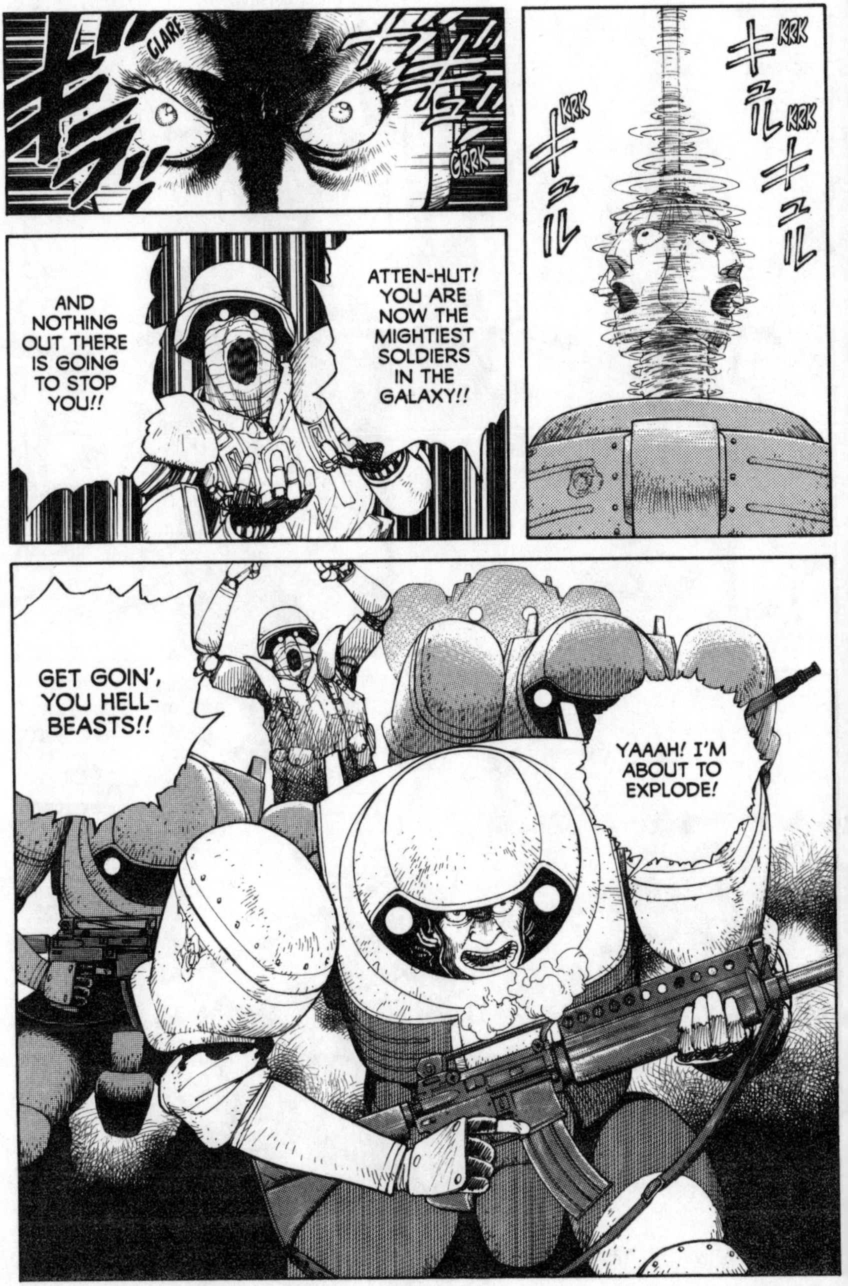
キュル KRK
キュル KRK
キュル KRK
GLARE
GRRK
ATTEN-HUT! YOU ARE NOW THE MIGHTIEST SOLDIERS IN THE GALAXY!!
AND NOTHING OUT THERE IS GOING TO STOP YOU!!
YAAAH! I'M ABOUT TO EXPLODE!
GET GOIN', YOU HELL-BEASTS!!

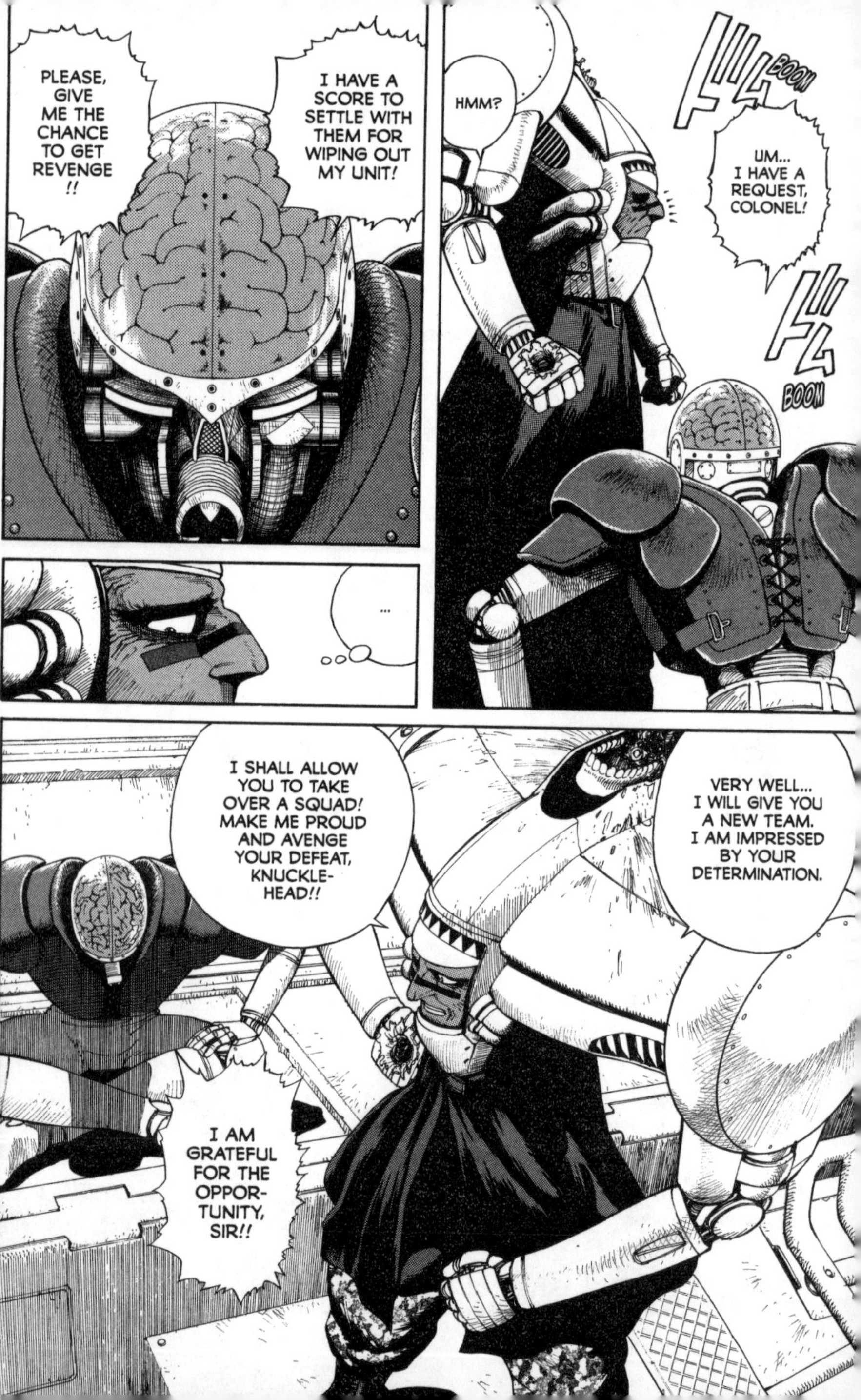
BOOM
UM... I HAVE A REQUEST, COLONEL!
BOOM
HMM?
I HAVE A SCORE TO SETTLE WITH THEM FOR WIPING OUT MY UNIT!
PLEASE, GIVE ME THE CHANCE TO GET REVENGE!!
...
VERY WELL... I WILL GIVE YOU A NEW TEAM. I AM IMPRESSED BY YOUR DETERMINATION.
I SHALL ALLOW YOU TO TAKE OVER A SQUAD! MAKE ME PROUD AND AVENGE YOUR DEFEAT, KNUCKLE-HEAD!!
I AM GRATEFUL FOR THE OPPOR-TUNITY, SIR!!

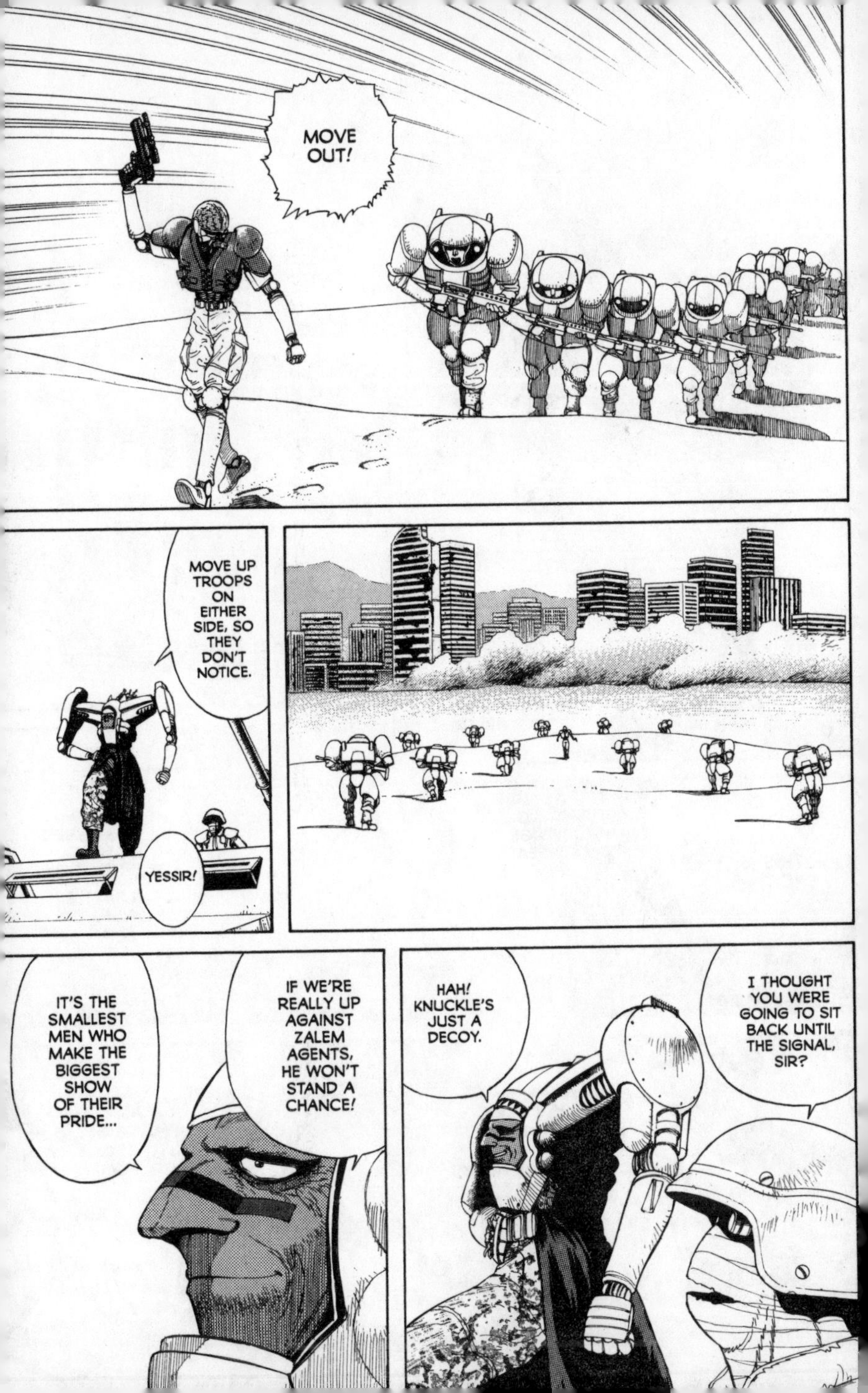
MOVE OUT!
MOVE UP TROOPS ON EITHER SIDE, SO THEY DON'T NOTICE.
YESSIR!
I THOUGHT YOU WERE GOING TO SIT BACK UNTIL THE SIGNAL, SIR?
HAH! KNUCKLE'S JUST A DECOY.
IF WE'RE REALLY UP AGAINST ZALEM AGENTS, HE WON'T STAND A CHANCE!
IT'S THE SMALLEST MEN WHO MAKE THE BIGGEST SHOW OF THEIR PRIDE...

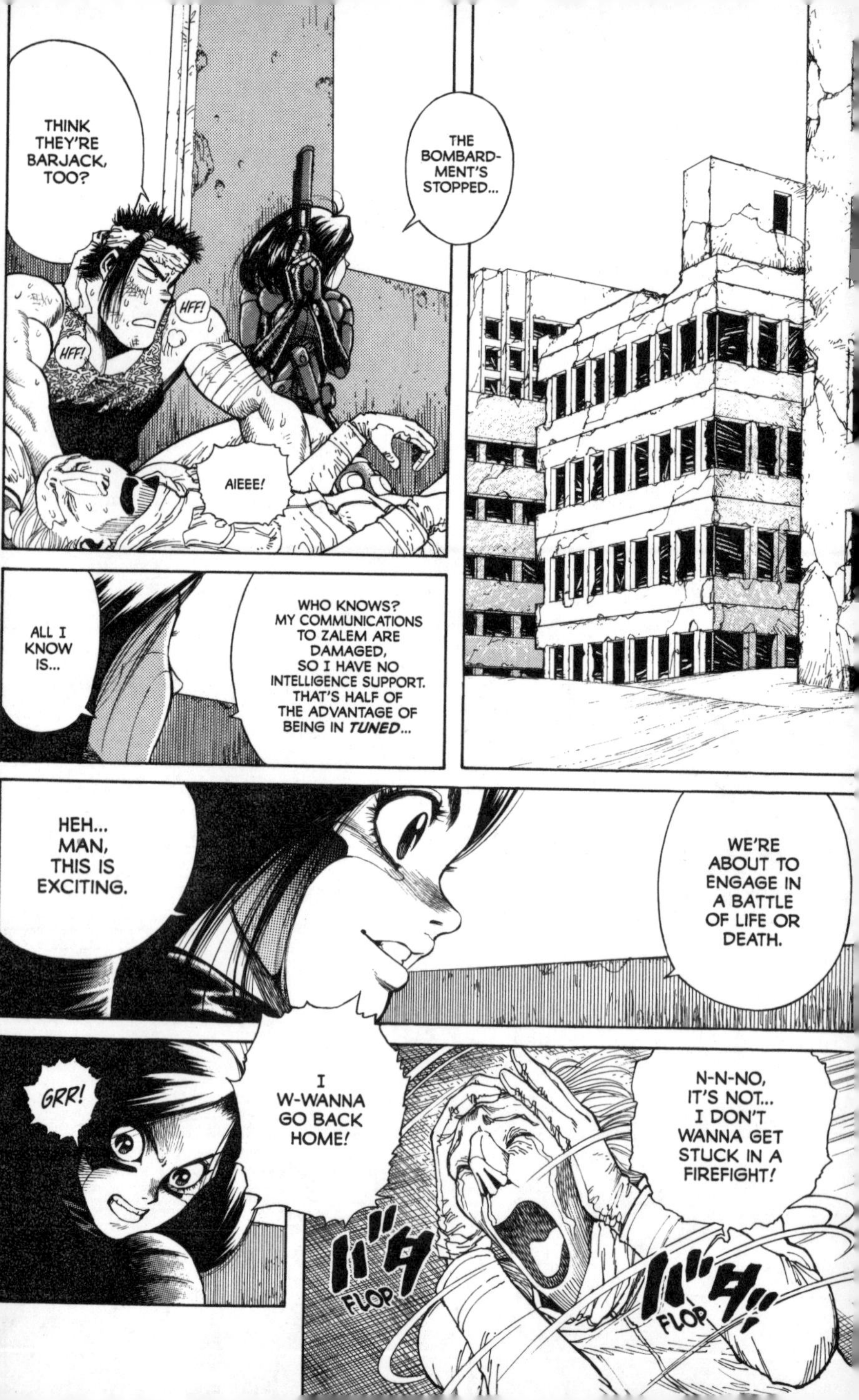
THE BOMBARD-MENT'S STOPPED...
THINK THEY'RE BARJACK, TOO?
HFF!
HFF!
AIEEE!
WHO KNOWS? MY COMMUNICATIONS TO ZALEM ARE DAMAGED, SO I HAVE NO INTELLIGENCE SUPPORT. THAT'S HALF OF THE ADVANTAGE OF BEING IN *TUNED*...
ALL I KNOW IS...
WE'RE ABOUT TO ENGAGE IN A BATTLE OF LIFE OR DEATH.
HEH... MAN, THIS IS EXCITING.
N-N-NO, IT'S NOT... I DON'T WANNA GET STUCK IN A FIREFIGHT!
FLOP
FLOP
I W-WANNA GO BACK HOME!
GRR!

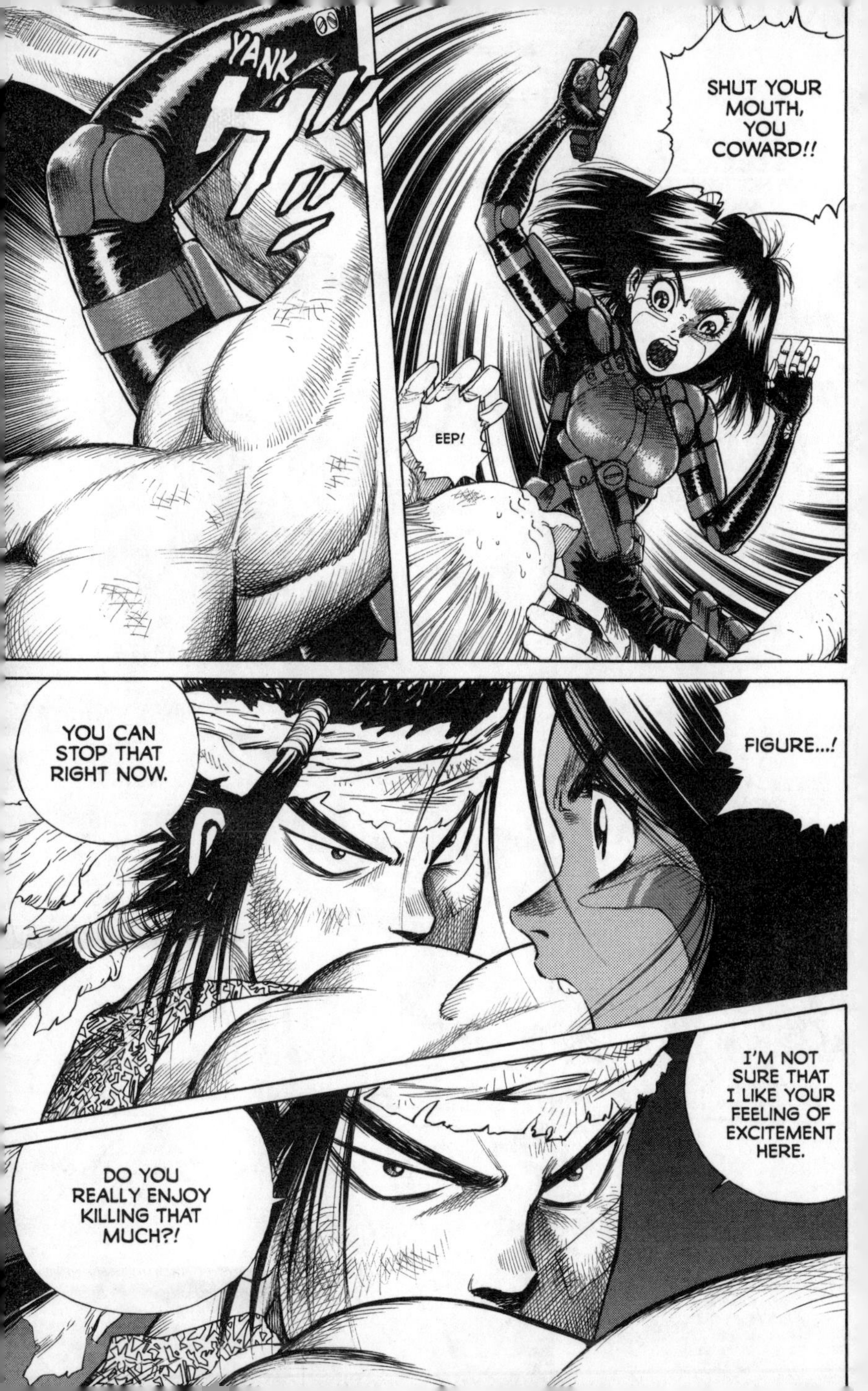
SHUT YOUR MOUTH, YOU COWARD!!
EEP!
YANK
FIGURE...!
YOU CAN STOP THAT RIGHT NOW.
I'M NOT SURE THAT I LIKE YOUR FEELING OF EXCITEMENT HERE.
DO YOU REALLY ENJOY KILLING THAT MUCH?!

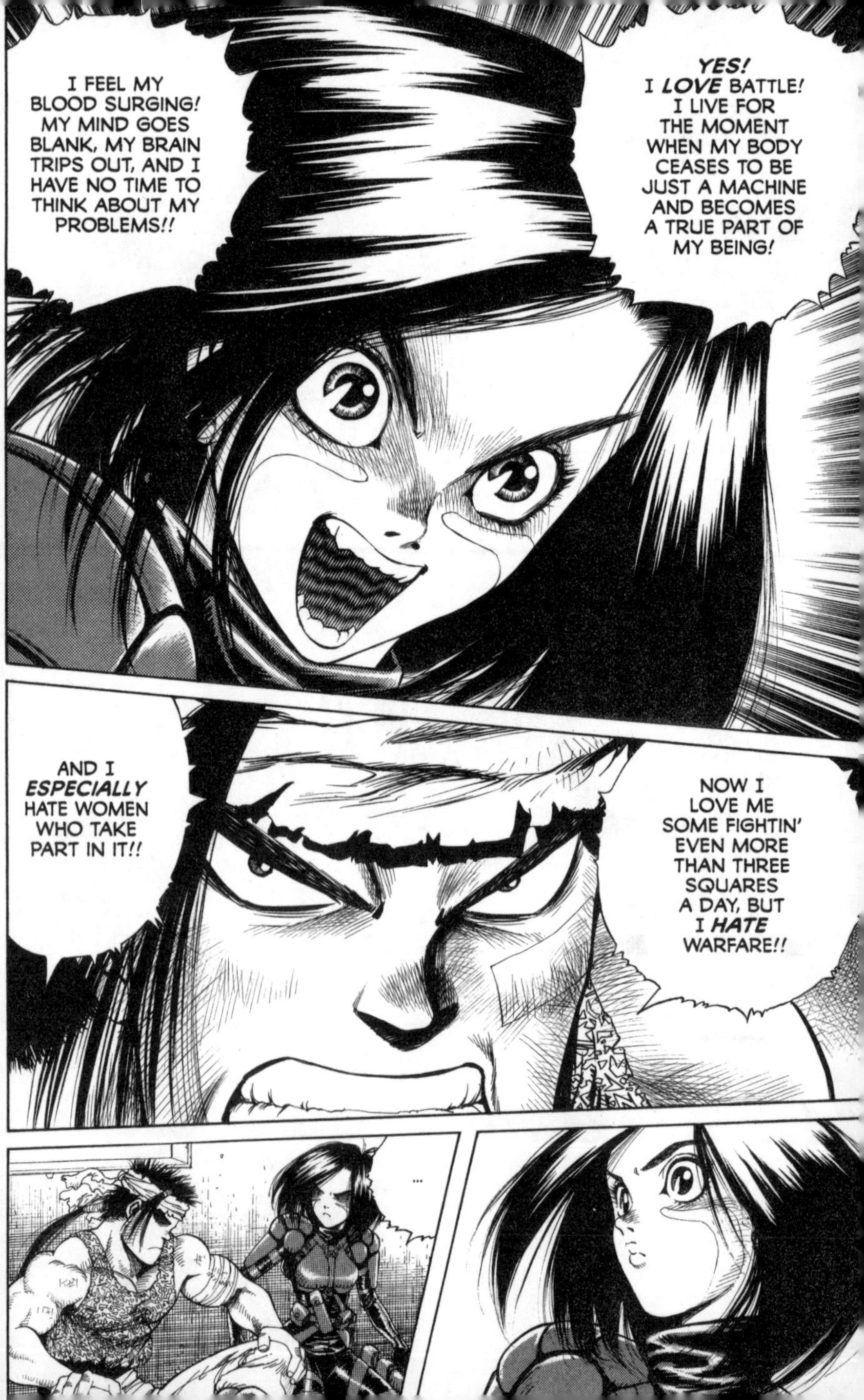
YES! I LOVE BATTLE! I LIVE FOR THE MOMENT WHEN MY BODY CEASES TO BE JUST A MACHINE AND BECOMES A TRUE PART OF MY BEING!
I FEEL MY BLOOD SURGING! MY MIND GOES BLANK, MY BRAIN TRIPS OUT, AND I HAVE NO TIME TO THINK ABOUT MY PROBLEMS!!
NOW I LOVE ME SOME FIGHTIN' EVEN MORE THAN THREE SQUARES A DAY, BUT I HATE WARFARE!!
AND I ESPECIALLY HATE WOMEN WHO TAKE PART IN IT!!
...

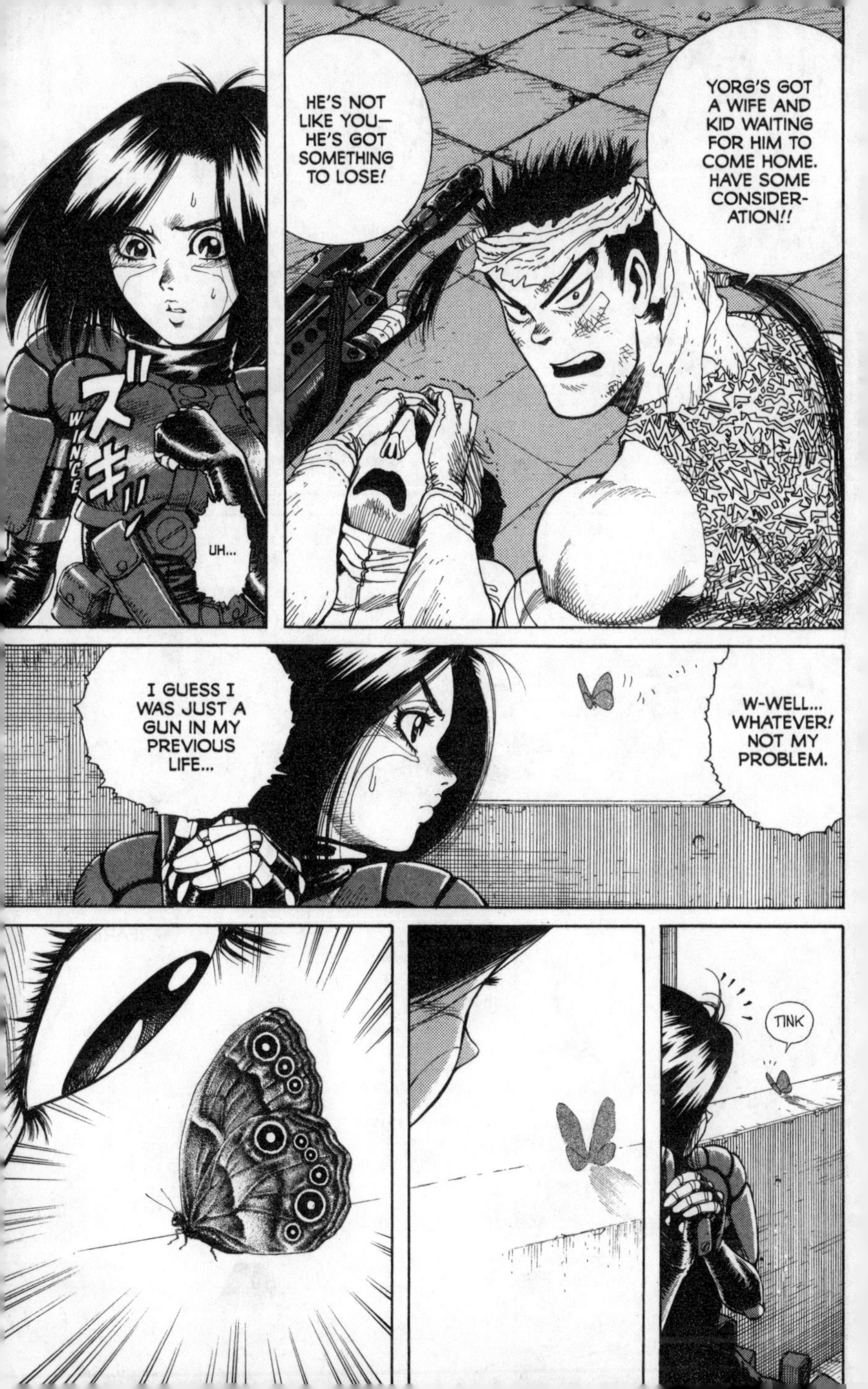
YORG'S GOT A WIFE AND KID WAITING FOR HIM TO COME HOME. HAVE SOME CONSIDER-ATION!!
HE'S NOT LIKE YOU— HE'S GOT SOMETHING TO LOSE!
ズキ
WINCE
UH...
W-WELL... WHATEVER! NOT MY PROBLEM.
I GUESS I WAS JUST A GUN IN MY PREVIOUS LIFE...
TINK

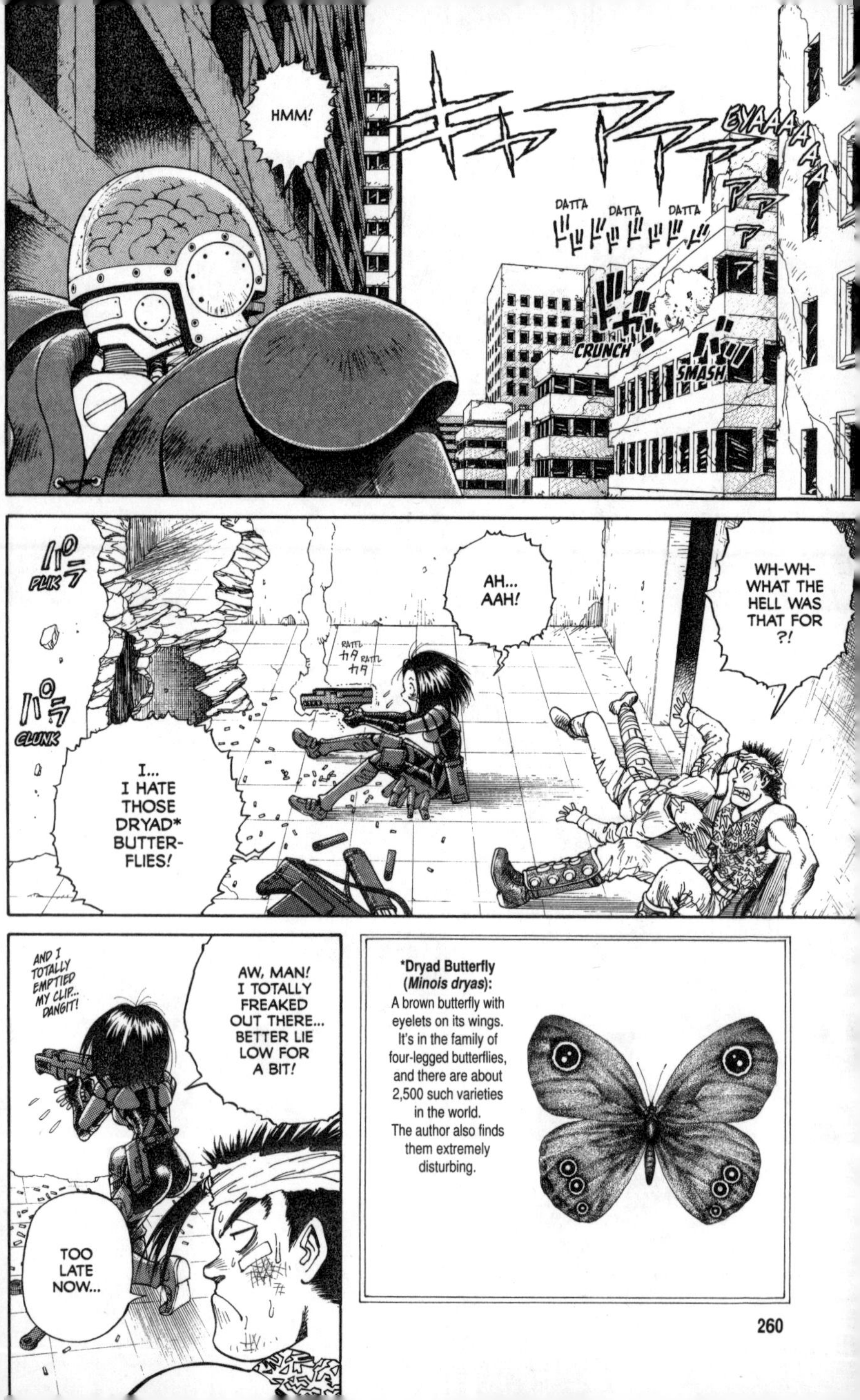
EYAAAAAA
DATTA DATTA DATTA
CRUNCH
SMASH
HMM!
WH-WH-WHAT THE HELL WAS THAT FOR ?!
AH... AAH!
RATTL RATTL
PLIK
CLUNK
I... I HATE THOSE DRYAD* BUTTERFLIES!
*Dryad Butterfly (*Minois dryas*): A brown butterfly with eyelets on its wings. It's in the family of four-legged butterflies, and there are about 2,500 such varieties in the world. The author also finds them extremely disturbing.
AW, MAN! I TOTALLY FREAKED OUT THERE... BETTER LIE LOW FOR A BIT!
AND I TOTALLY EMPTIED MY CLIP... DANGIT!
TOO LATE NOW...

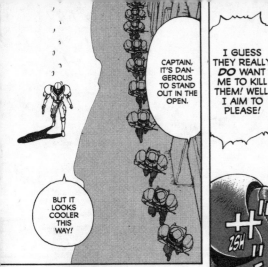

HAH! WHAT IDIOTS! THEY GAVE AWAY THEIR POSITION!
I GUESS THEY REALLY *DO* WANT ME TO KILL THEM! WELL, I AIM TO PLEASE!
ZSH
ZSH
CAPTAIN, IT'S DAN-GEROUS TO STAND OUT IN THE OPEN.
BUT IT LOOKS COOLER THIS WAY!
PSH! AMATEUR... FORGET HIM.
YEAH, LET'S GO.
HEY! I DIDN'T GIVE YOU THOSE ORDERS!!
SWISH
IGNORE HIM.
FWIP
BOOM

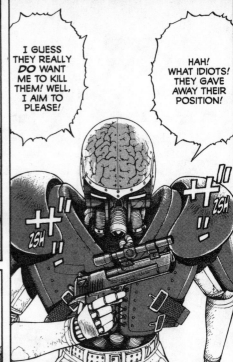

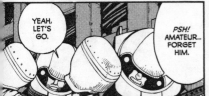

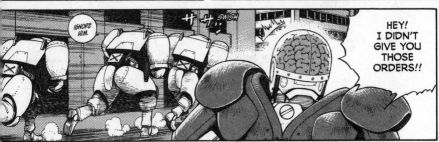

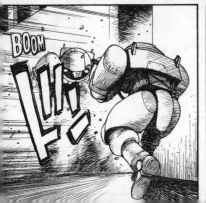

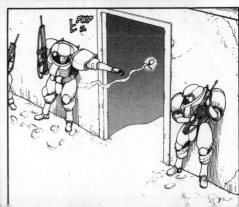

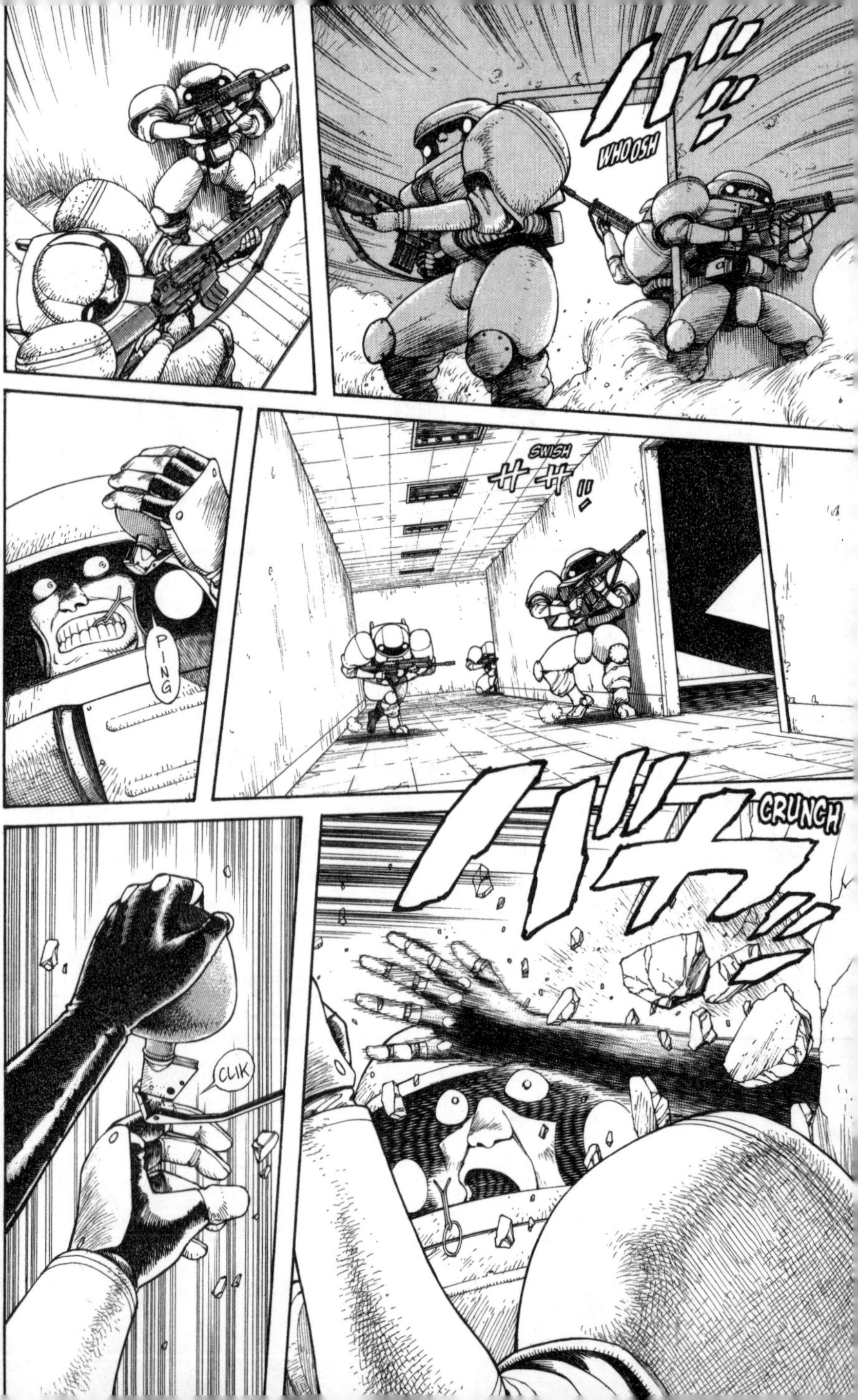
WHOOSH
SWISH
PING
CRUNCH
CLIK

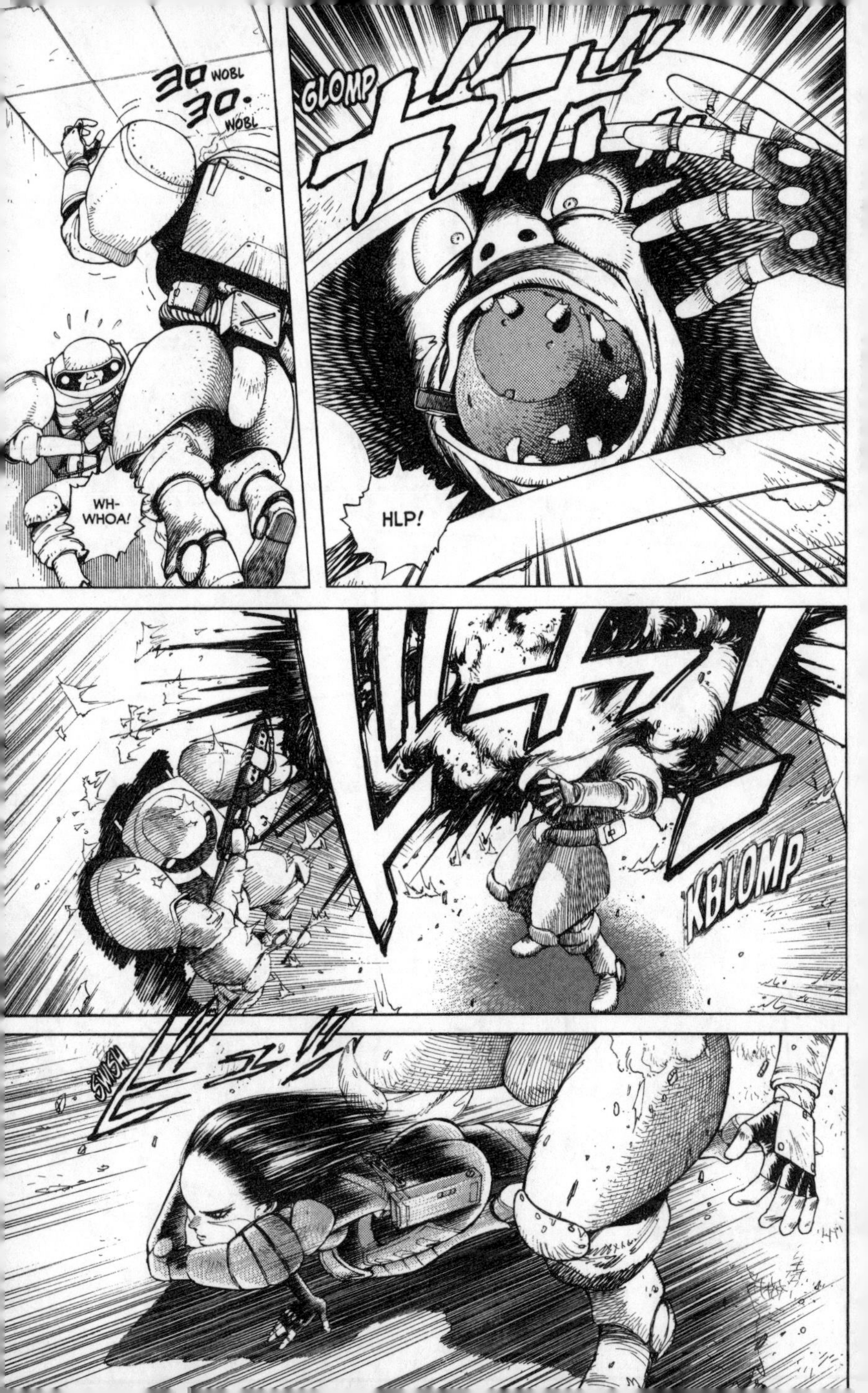
GLOMP
HLP!
ヨロ WOBL
ヨロ WOBL
WH- WHOA!
KBLOMP
SWISH

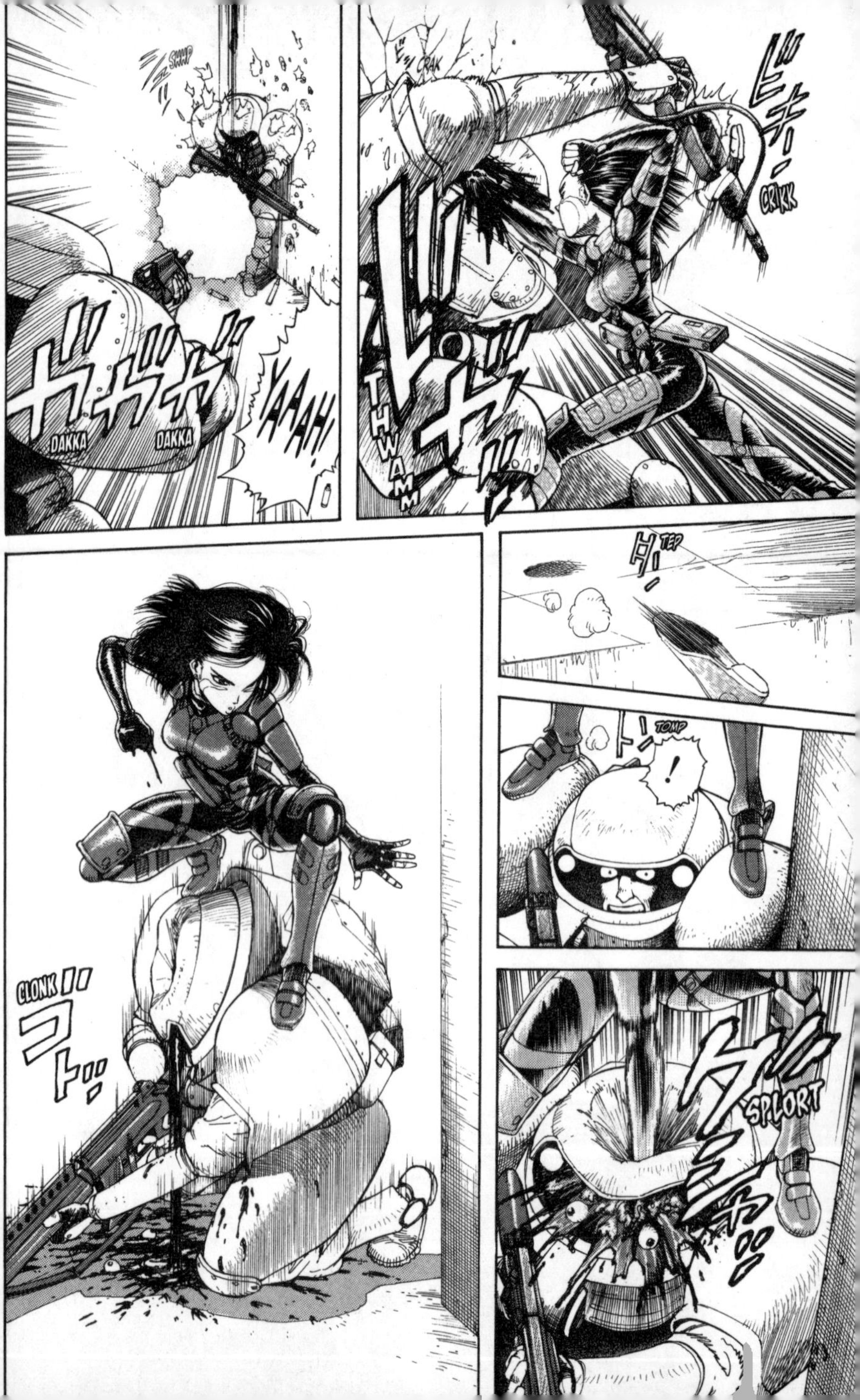
ビシ CRAK
ビキィ CRIKK
ドゴォ THWAMM
シュ SHMP
ダダダ DAKKA DAKKA
YAAAH!
タン TEP
トン TOMP
!
グシュ SPLORT
ゴト CLONK

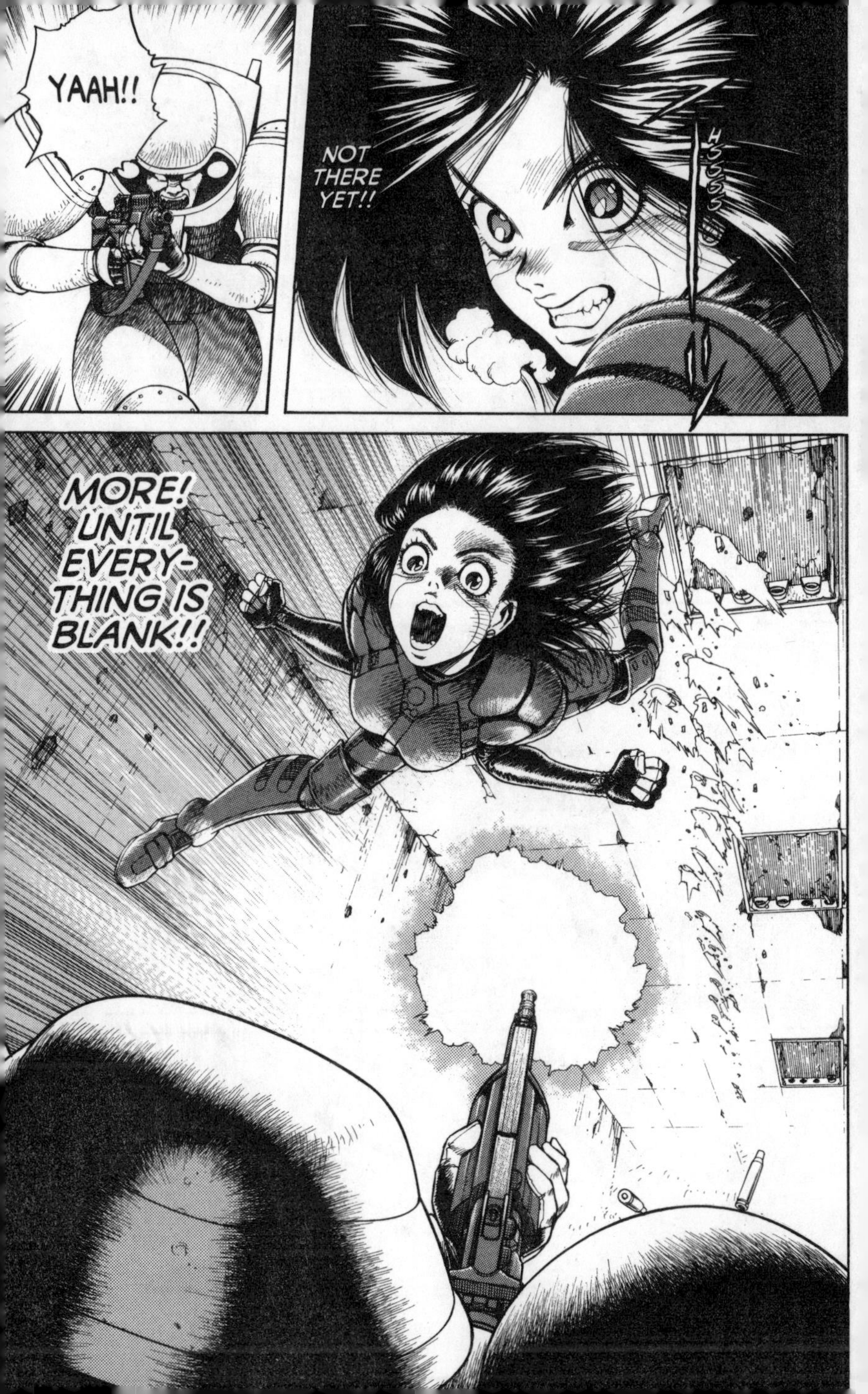
NOT THERE YET!!
HSSSS
YAAH!!
MORE! UNTIL EVERY-THING IS BLANK!!

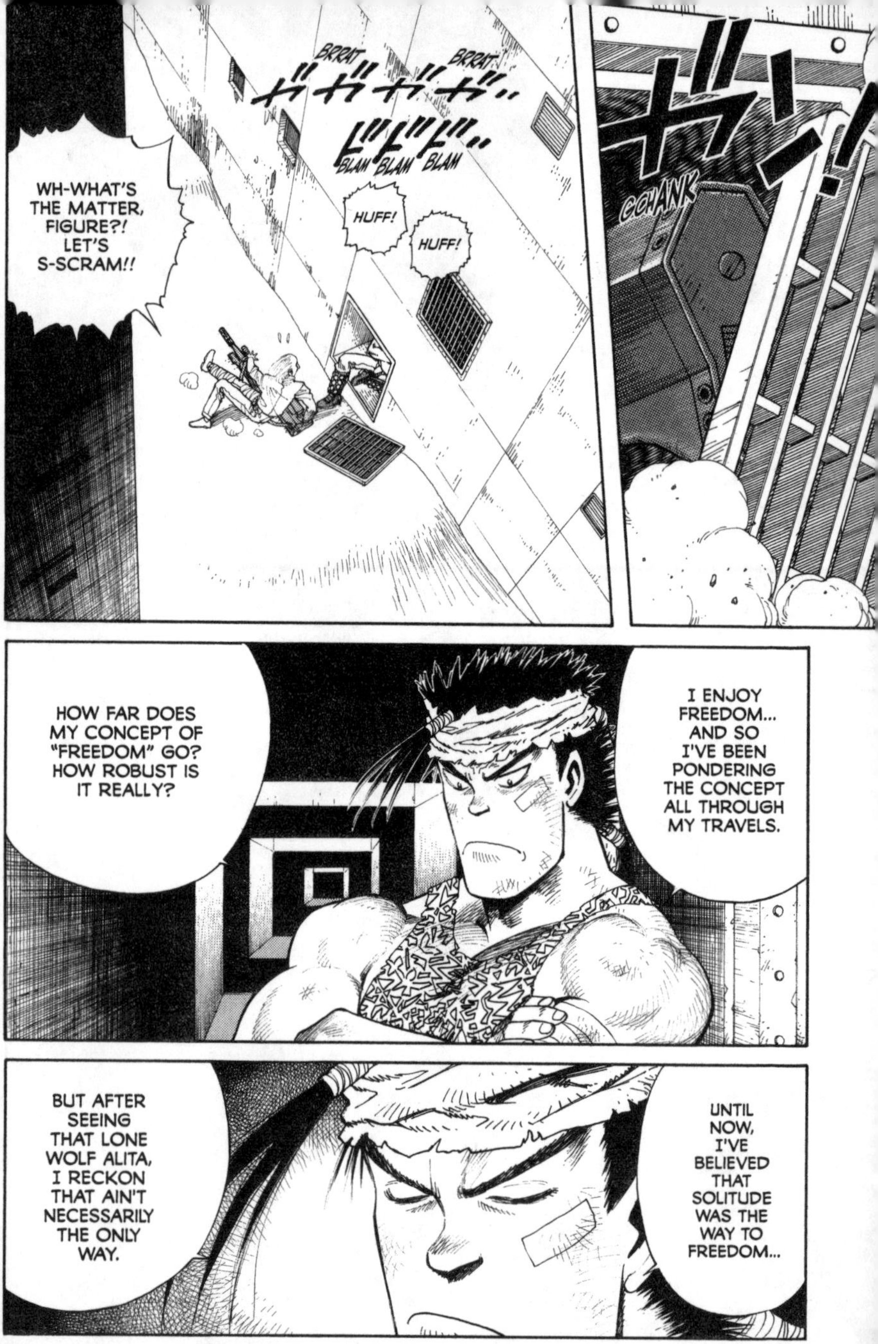
GCHANK
BRRAT
BRRAT
BLAM BLAM BLAM
HUFF!
HUFF!
WH-WHAT'S THE MATTER, FIGURE?! LET'S S-SCRAM!!
I ENJOY FREEDOM... AND SO I'VE BEEN PONDERING THE CONCEPT ALL THROUGH MY TRAVELS.
HOW FAR DOES MY CONCEPT OF "FREEDOM" GO? HOW ROBUST IS IT REALLY?
UNTIL NOW, I'VE BELIEVED THAT SOLITUDE WAS THE WAY TO FREEDOM...
BUT AFTER SEEING THAT LONE WOLF ALITA, I RECKON THAT AIN'T NECESSARILY THE ONLY WAY.

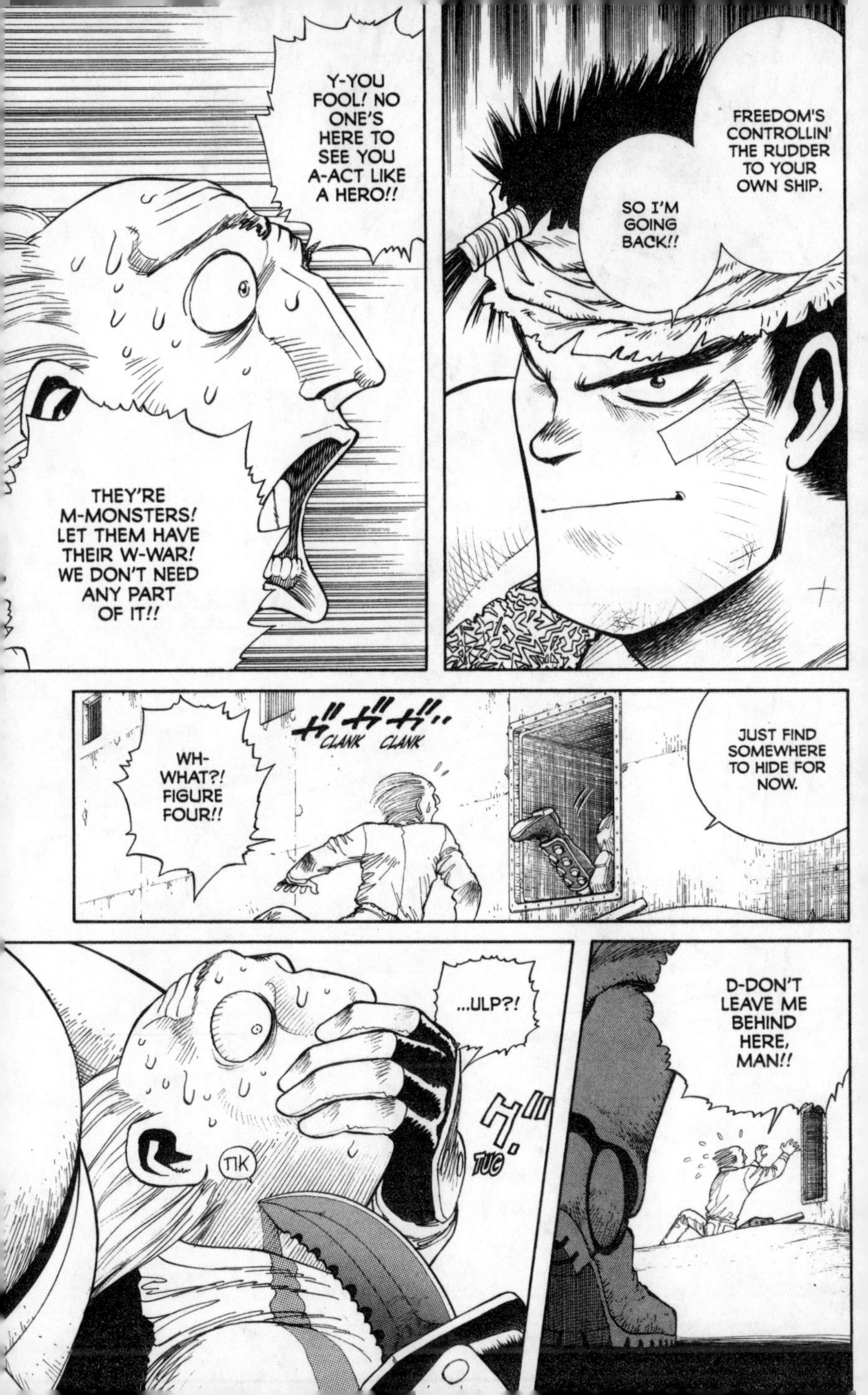
FREEDOM'S CONTROLLIN' THE RUDDER TO YOUR OWN SHIP.
SO I'M GOING BACK!!
Y-YOU FOOL! NO ONE'S HERE TO SEE YOU A-ACT LIKE A HERO!!
THEY'RE M-MONSTERS! LET THEM HAVE THEIR W-WAR! WE DON'T NEED ANY PART OF IT!!
JUST FIND SOMEWHERE TO HIDE FOR NOW.
CLANK CLANK
WH- WHAT?! FIGURE FOUR!!
D-DON'T LEAVE ME BEHIND HERE, MAN!!
...ULP?!
TUG
TIK

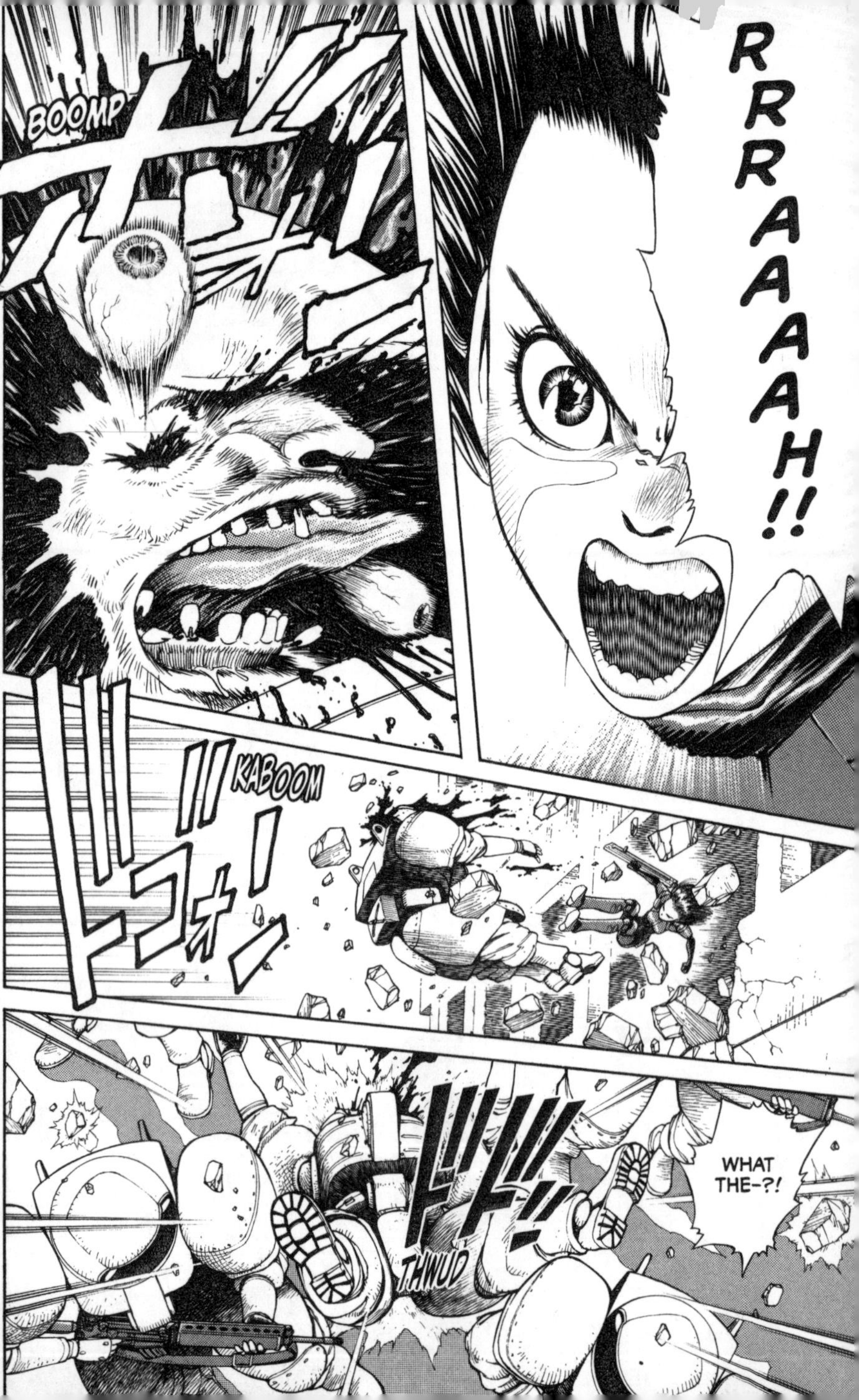
RRRAAAAAH!!
BOOMP
KABOOM
WHAT THE-?!
THWUD

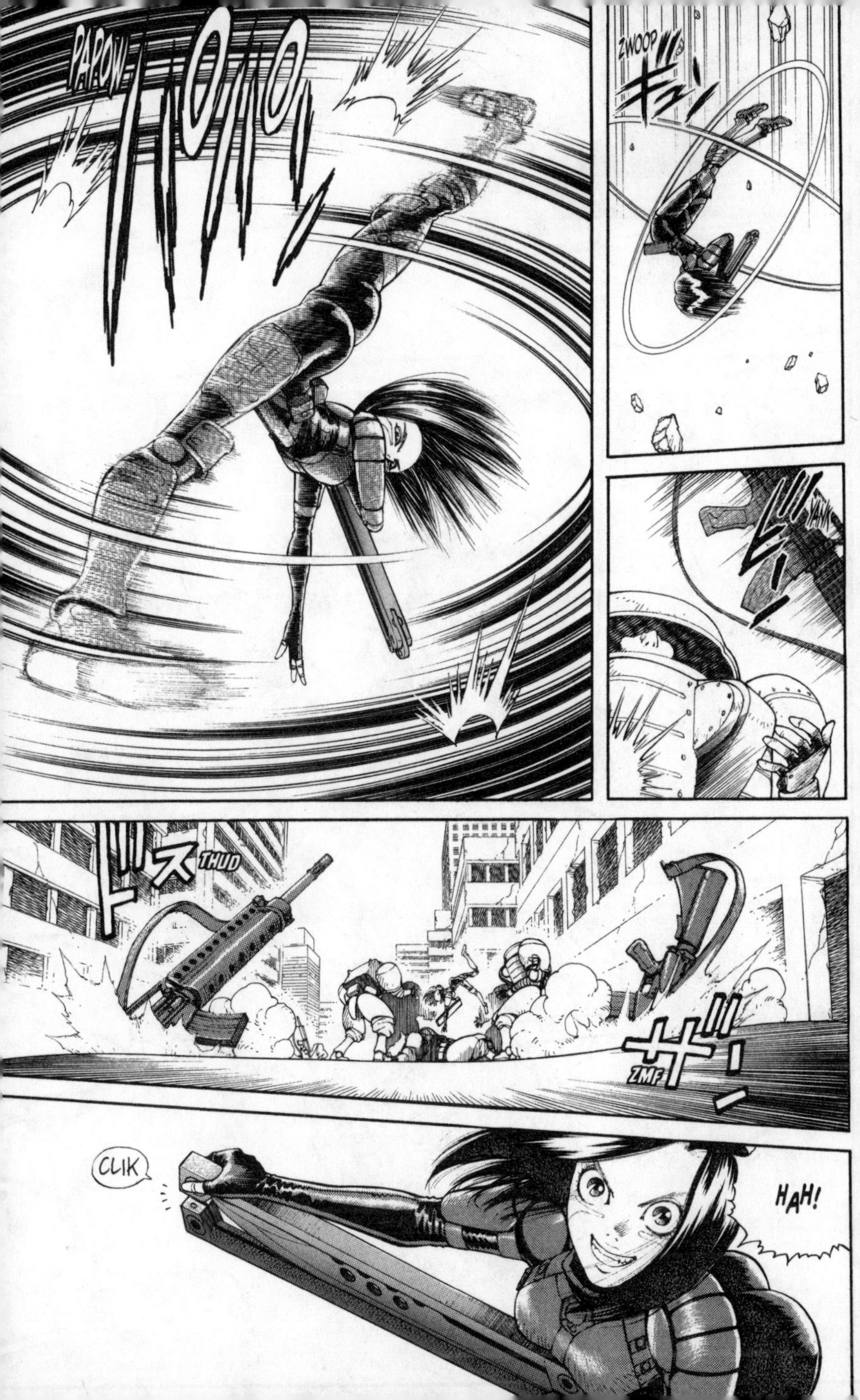
ZWOOP
YANK
PAROW
ZMF
THUD
HAH!
CLIK

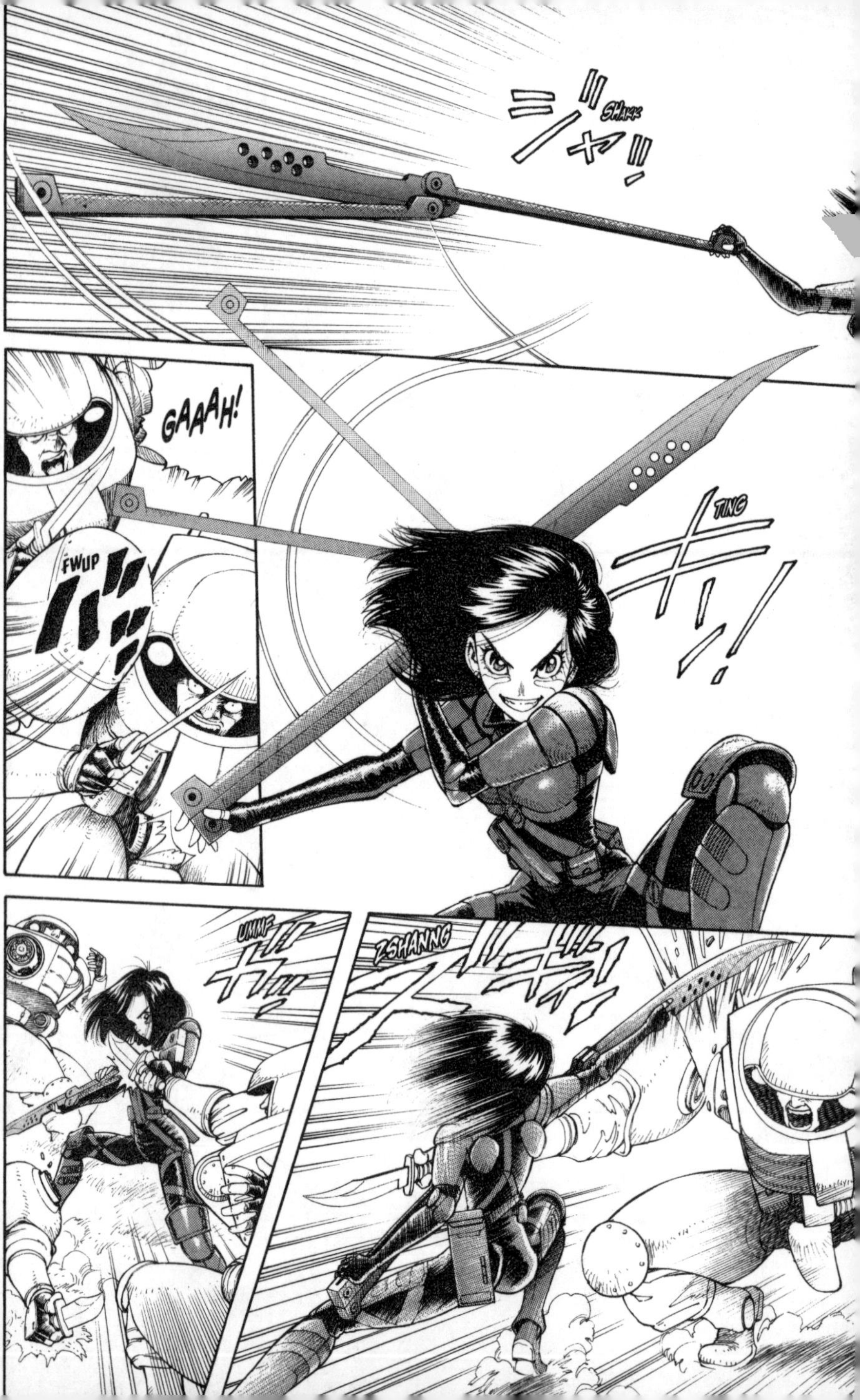

SHAKK
TING
GAAAH!
FWUP
ZSHANNG
UMMF

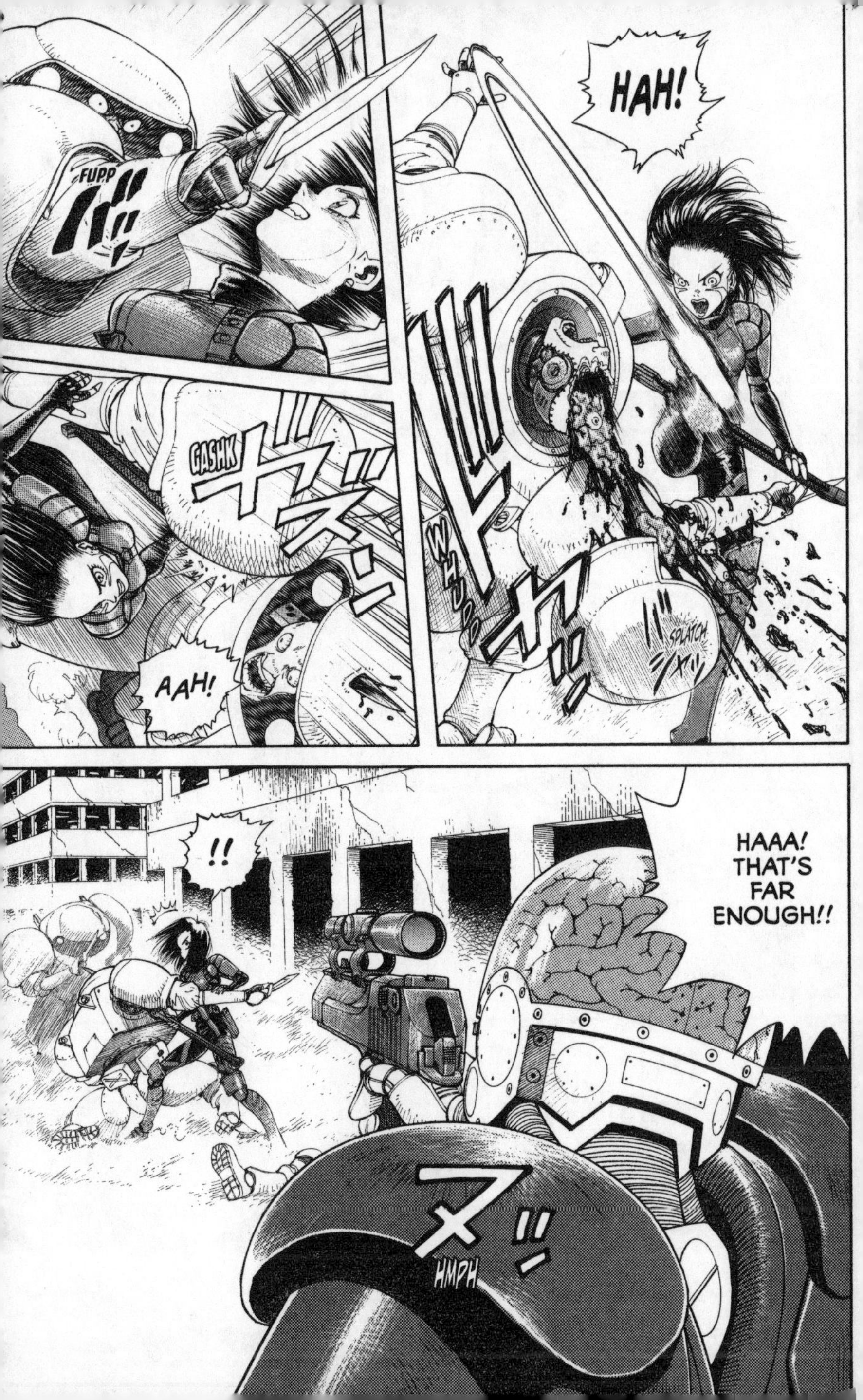
HAH!
WHUDDD
SPLATCH
FUPP
GASHK
AAH!
HAAA! THAT'S FAR ENOUGH!!
!!
HMPH

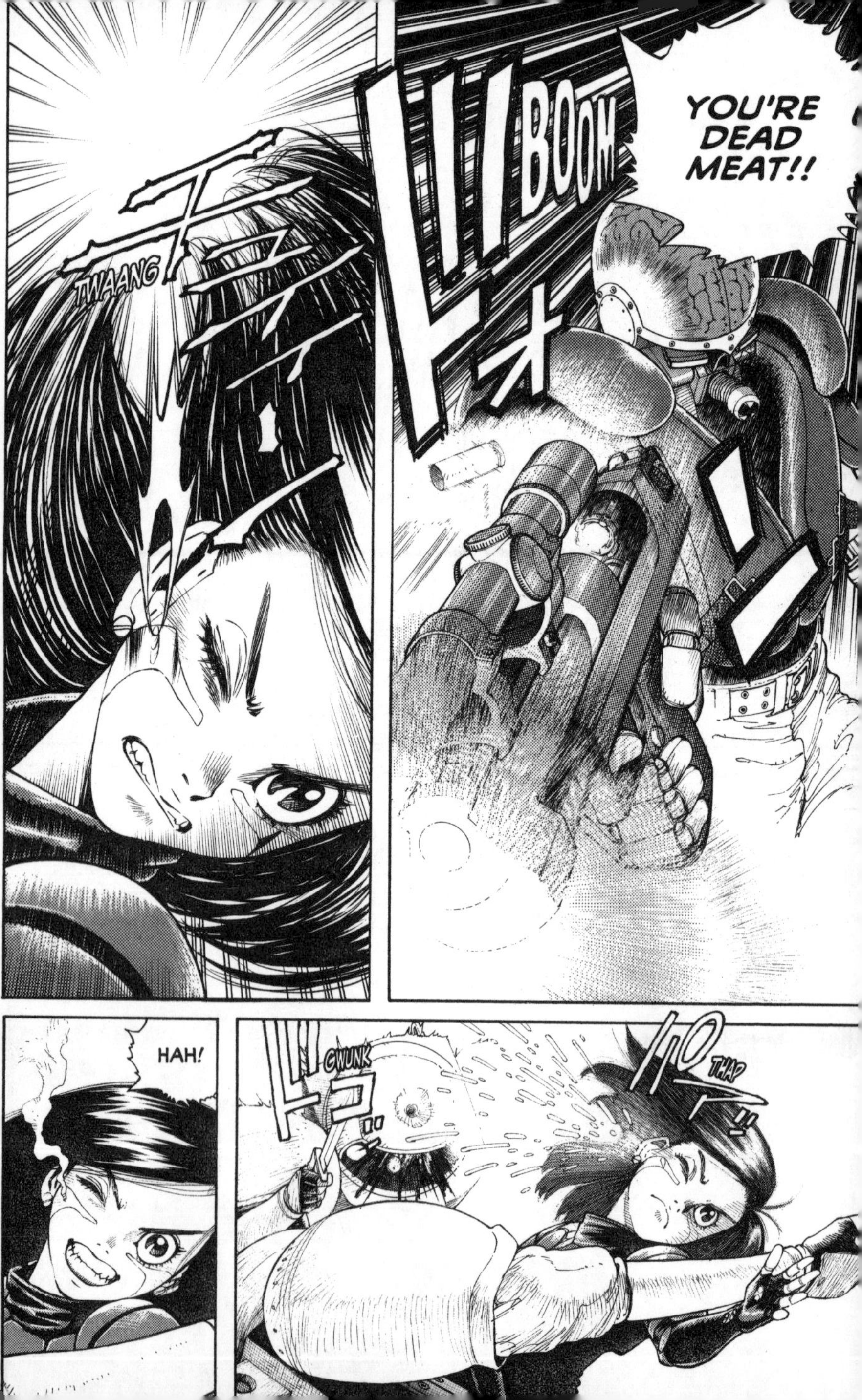
BOOM
YOU'RE DEAD MEAT!!
TWAANG
THAP
CWUNK
HAH!

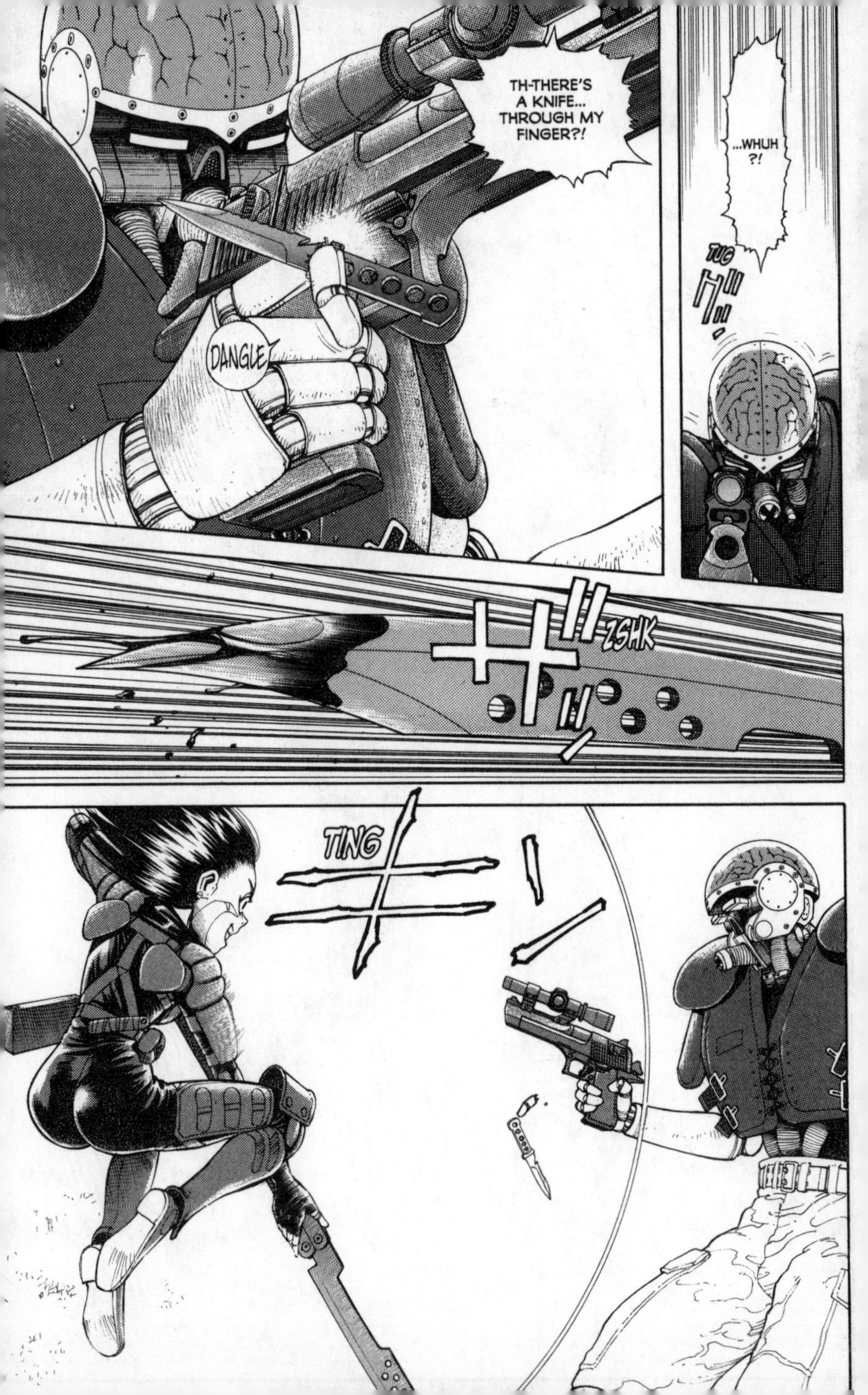
...WHUH ?!
TUG
TH-THERE'S A KNIFE... THROUGH MY FINGER?!
DANGLE
ZSHK
TING

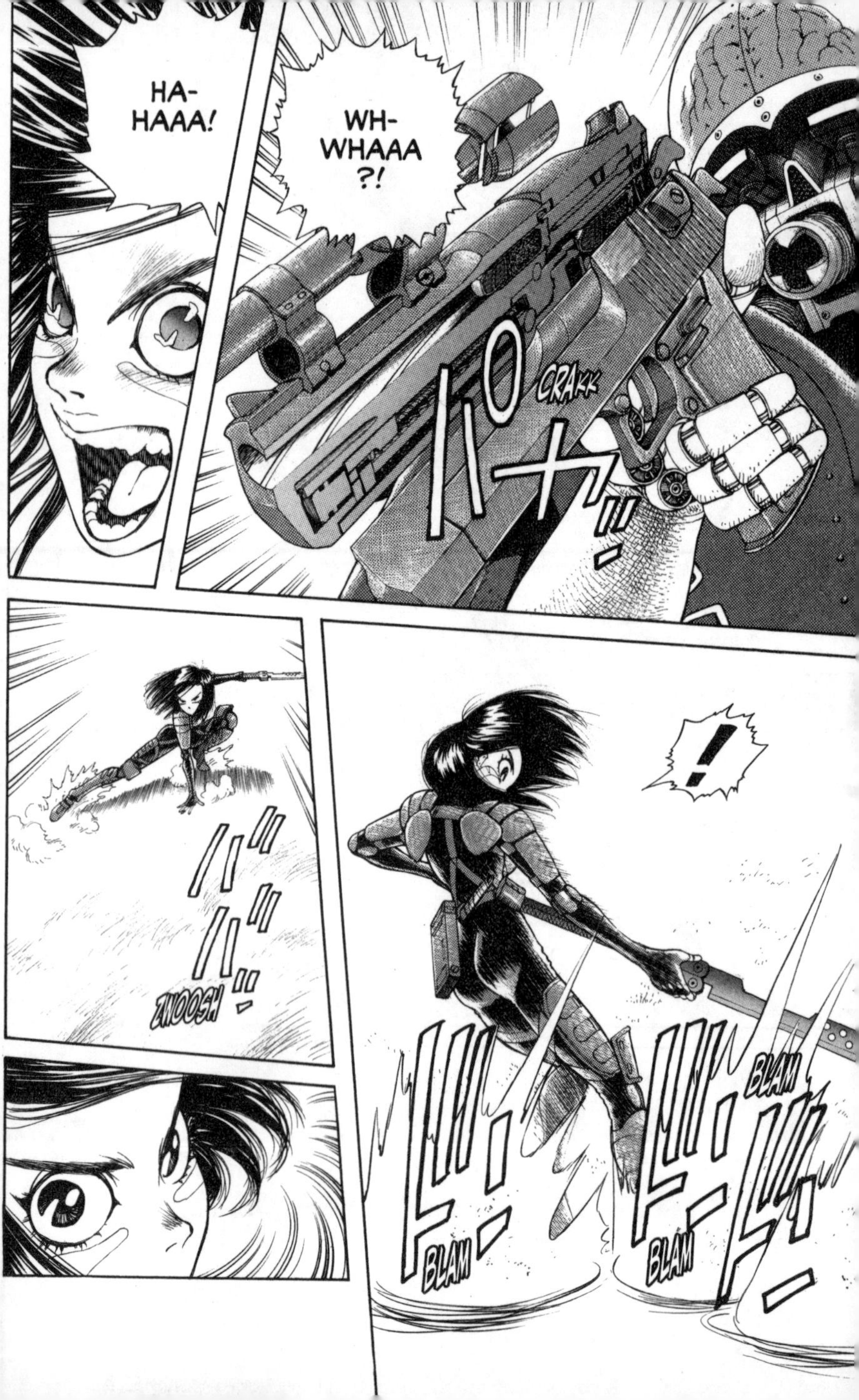
WH-WHAAA?!
CRAKK
HA-HAAA!
!
BLAM
BLAM
BLAM
ZWOOSH

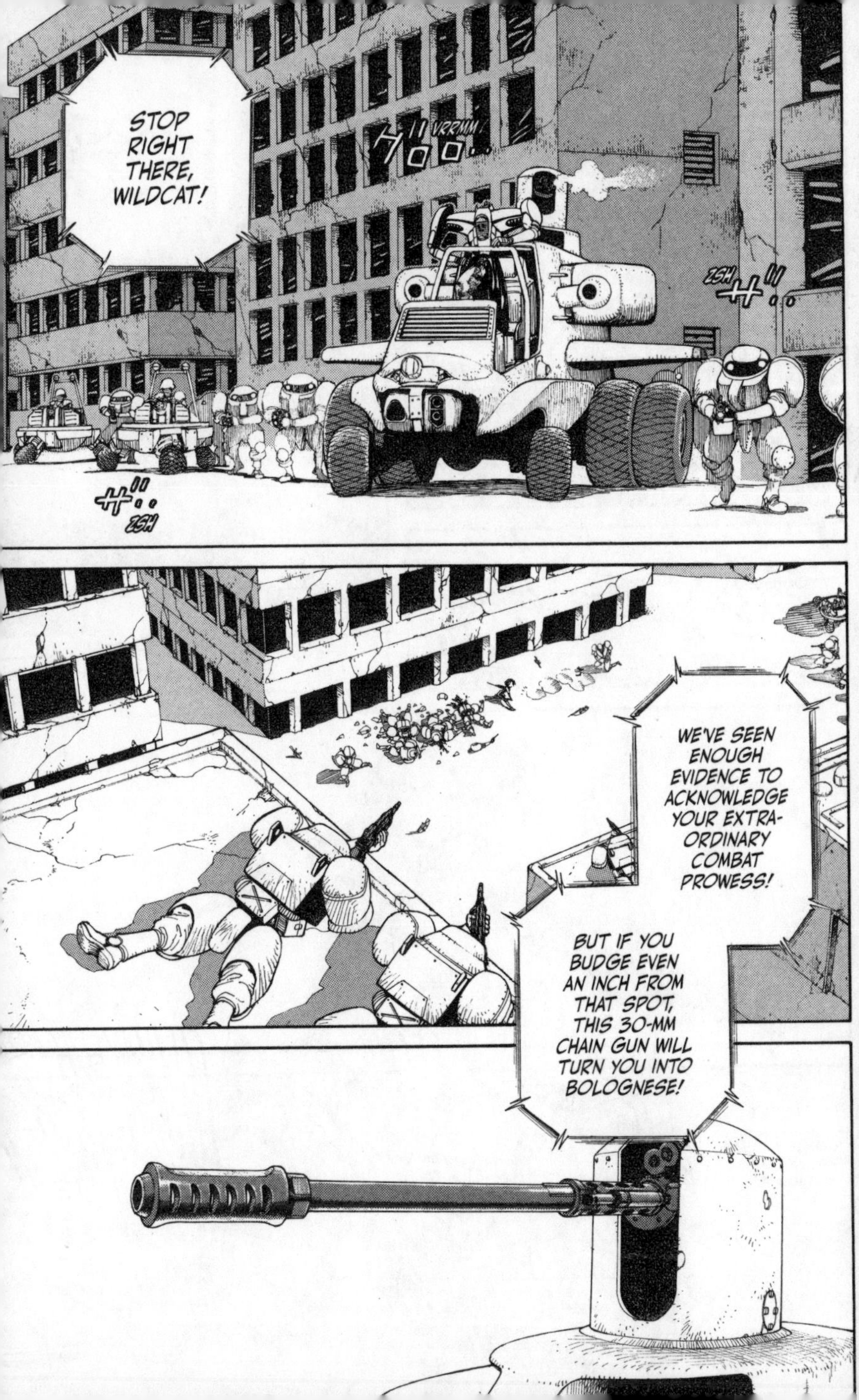
VRRMM
ZSH
STOP RIGHT THERE, WILDCAT!
ZSH
WE'VE SEEN ENOUGH EVIDENCE TO ACKNOWLEDGE YOUR EXTRA-ORDINARY COMBAT PROWESS!
BUT IF YOU BUDGE EVEN AN INCH FROM THAT SPOT, THIS 30-MM CHAIN GUN WILL TURN YOU INTO BOLOGNESE!

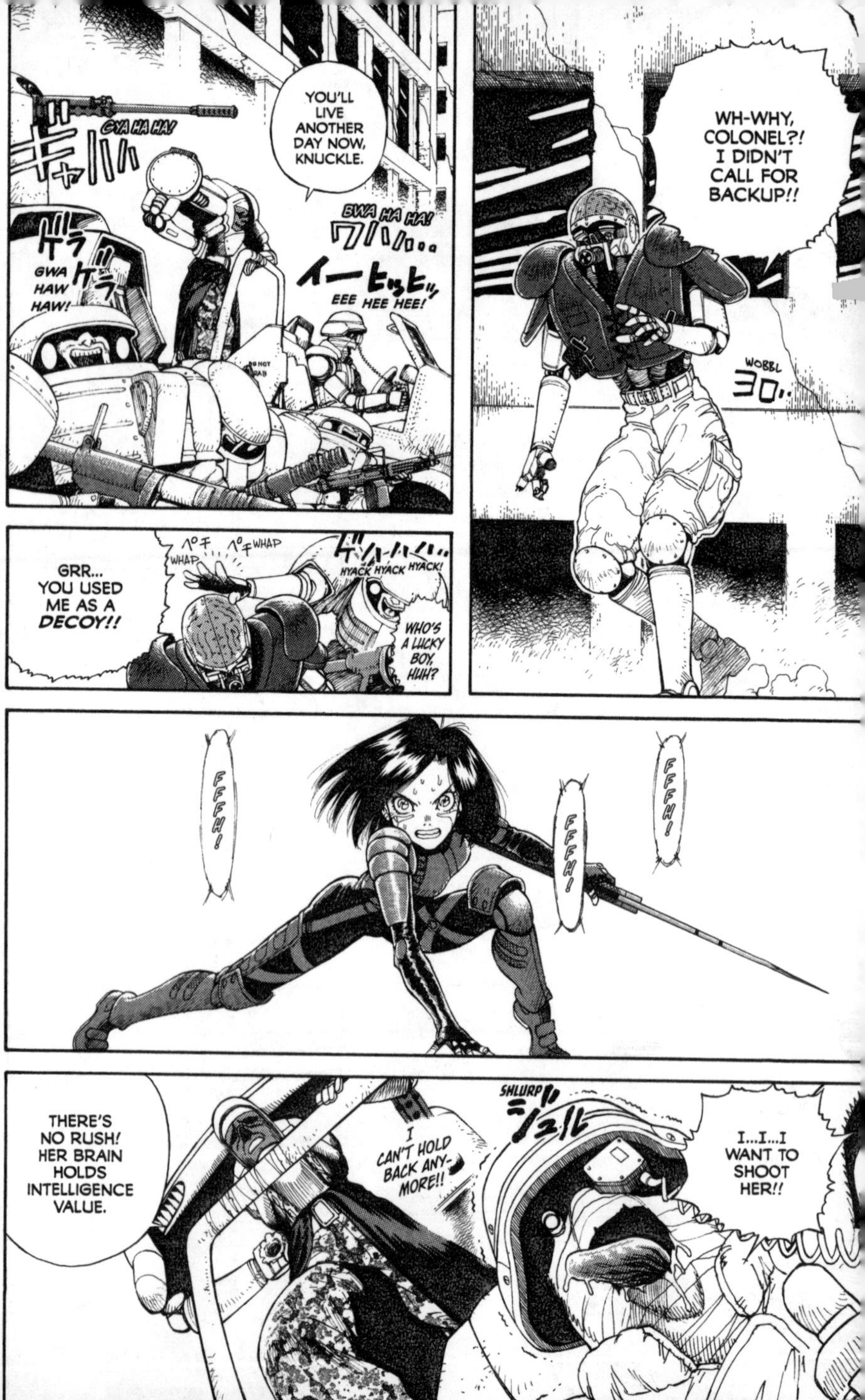

WH-WHY, COLONEL?! I DIDN'T CALL FOR BACKUP!!
WOBBL
ヨロ‥
BWA HA HA!
ワハハ‥
YOU'LL LIVE ANOTHER DAY NOW, KNUCKLE.
EEE HEE HEE!
イーヒッヒッ
GYA HA HA!
ギャハハ
GWA HAW HAW!
ゲラゲラ
HYACK HYACK HYACK!
WHO'S A LUCKY BOY, HUH?
WHAP WHAP
ペチ ペチ
GRR... YOU USED ME AS A DECOY!!
FFFH!
FFFH!
FFFH!
I...I...I WANT TO SHOOT HER!!
SHLURP
ジュル
I CAN'T HOLD BACK ANY-MORE!!
THERE'S NO RUSH! HER BRAIN HOLDS INTELLIGENCE VALUE.

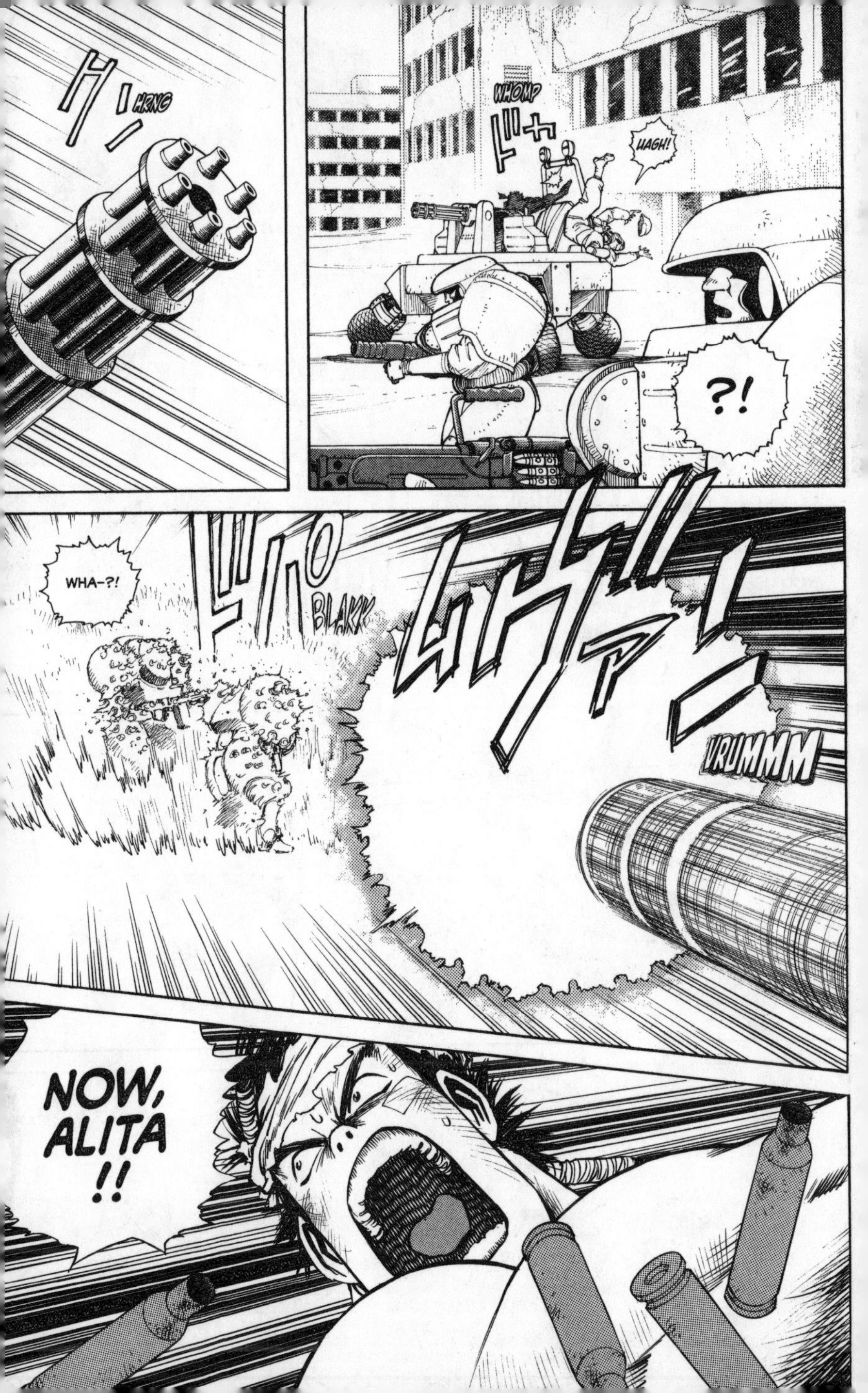
WHOMP
UAGH!
?!
HRNG
VRUMMM
BLAKK
WHA-?!
NOW, ALITA!!

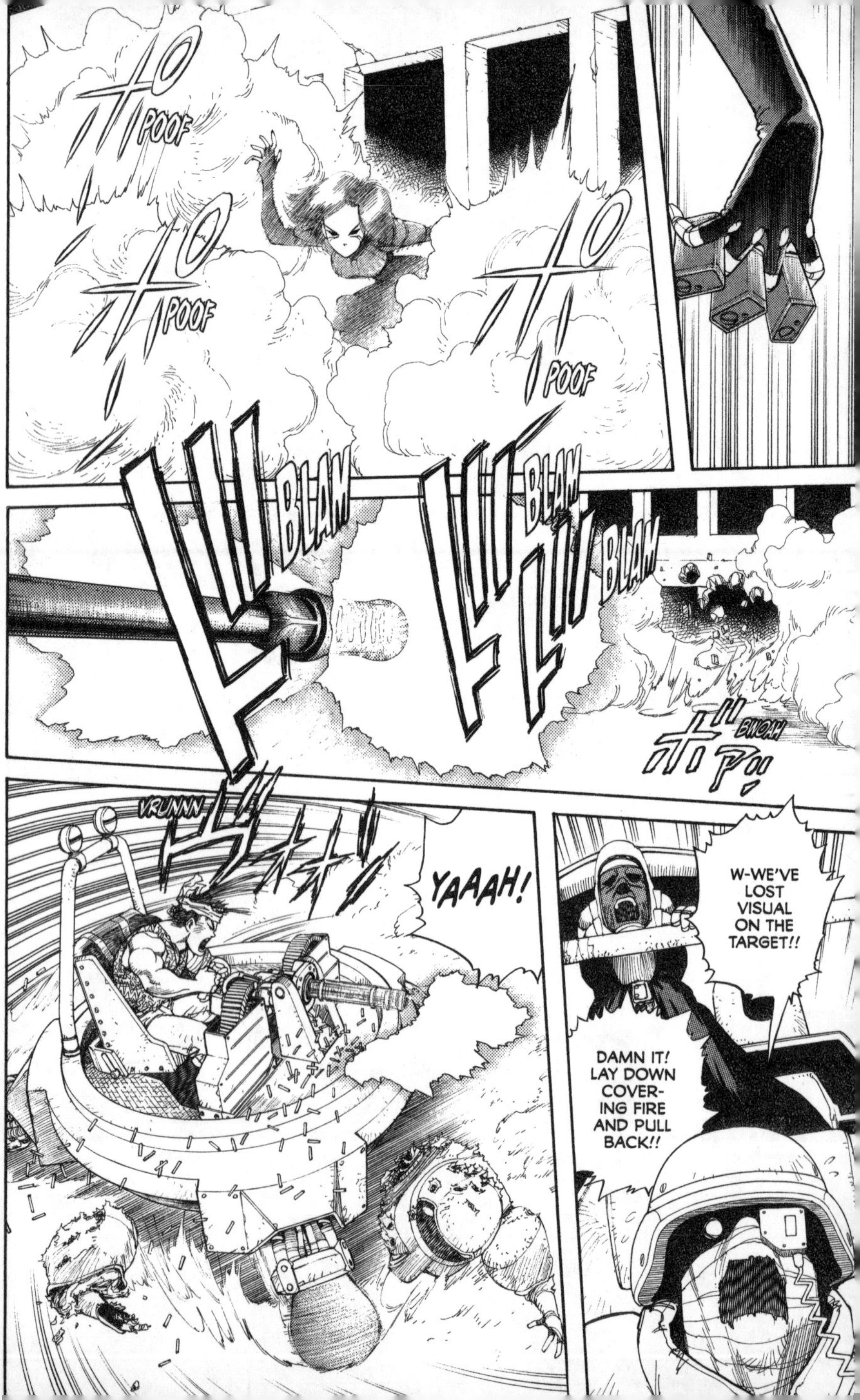
POOF
POOF
POOF
BWOAH
BLAM
BLAM
BLAM
W-WE'VE LOST VISUAL ON THE TARGET!!
DAMN IT! LAY DOWN COVER-ING FIRE AND PULL BACK!!
YAAAH!
VRUNNN

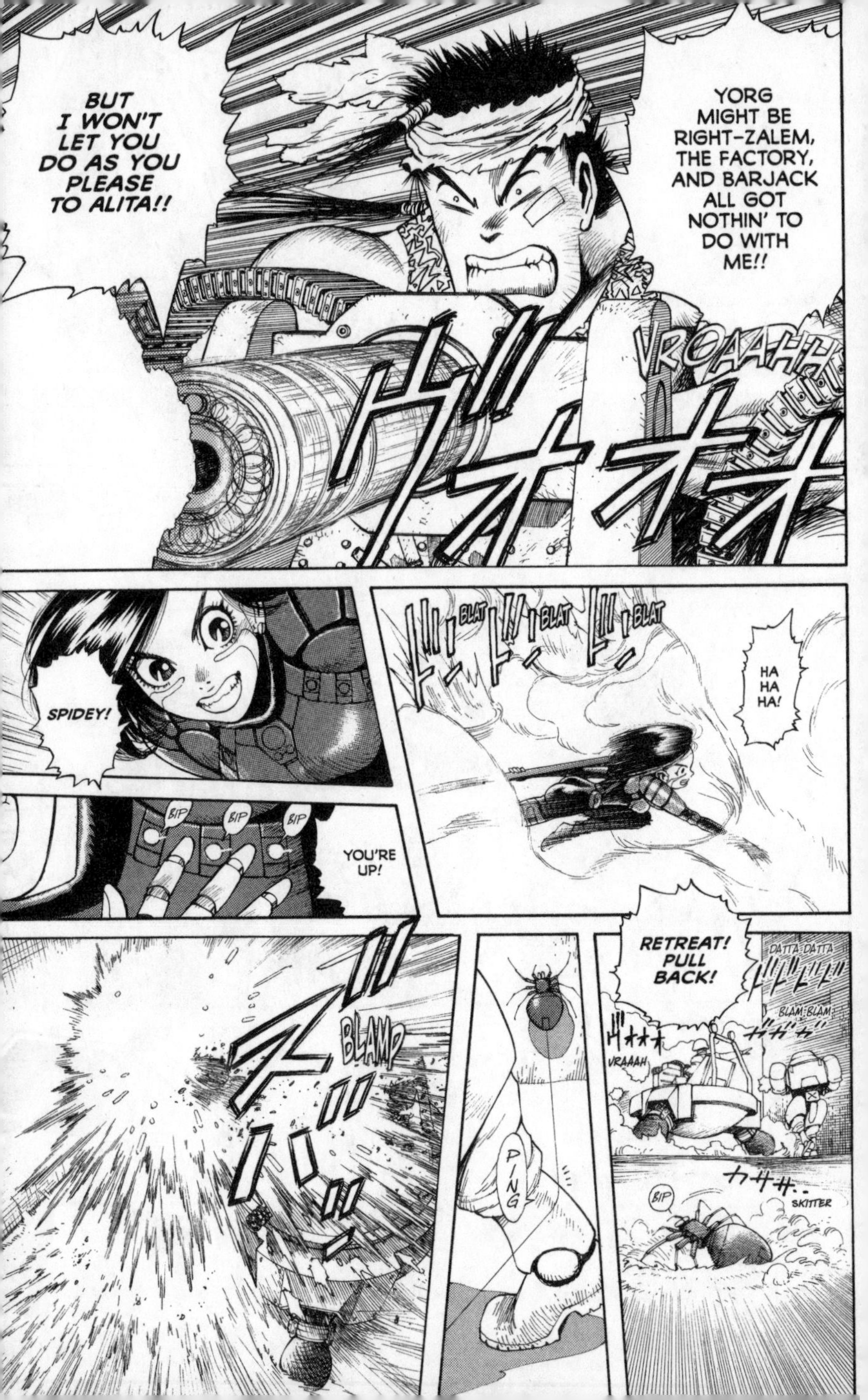
YORG MIGHT BE RIGHT–ZALEM, THE FACTORY, AND BARJACK ALL GOT NOTHIN' TO DO WITH ME!!
BUT I WON'T LET YOU DO AS YOU PLEASE TO ALITA!!
VROAAHH
BLAT
BLAT
BLAT
HA HA HA HA!
SPIDEY!
BIP
BIP
BIP
YOU'RE UP!
RETREAT! PULL BACK!
DATTA DATTA
BLAM BLAM
VRAAAH
BIP
SKITTER
PING
BLAMP

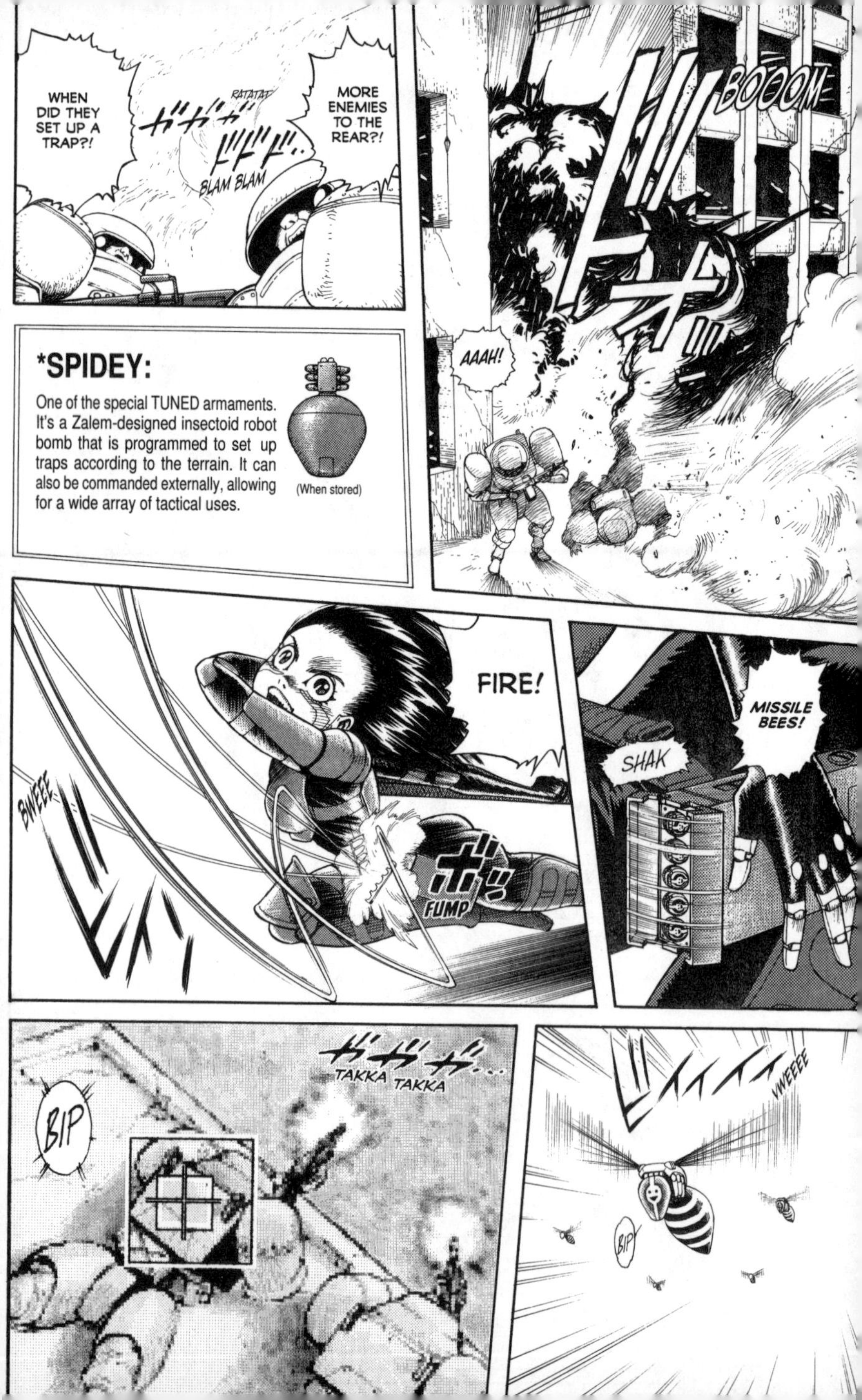
BOOOM
AAAH!
MORE ENEMIES TO THE REAR?!
RATATAT
BLAM BLAM
WHEN DID THEY SET UP A TRAP?!
*SPIDEY:
One of the special TUNED armaments. It's a Zalem-designed insectoid robot bomb that is programmed to set up traps according to the terrain. It can also be commanded externally, allowing for a wide array of tactical uses.
(When stored)
MISSILE BEES!
SHAK
FIRE!
BWEEE
FUMP
VWEEEE
BIP
TAKKA TAKKA
BIP

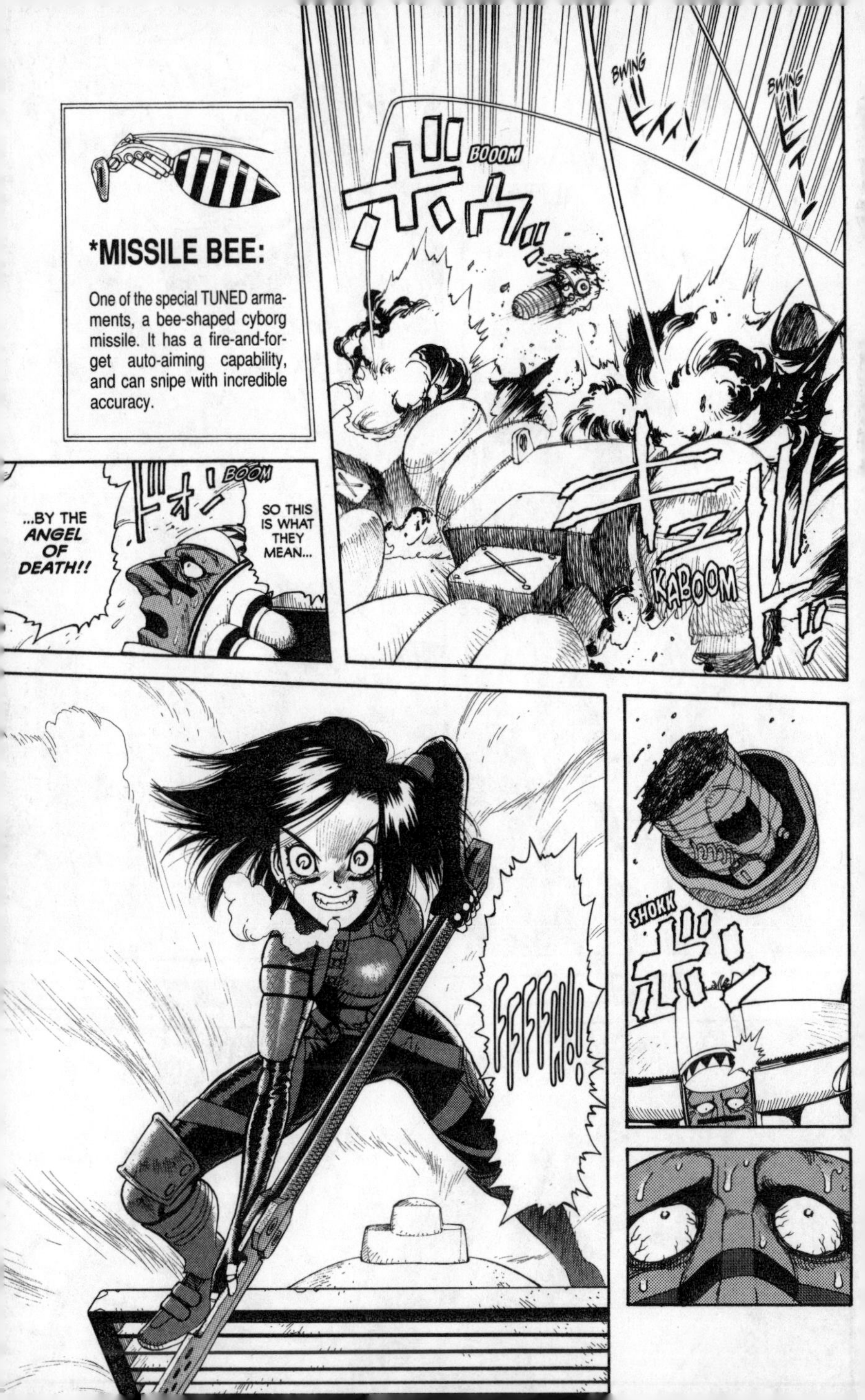

BWING
BWING
BOOOM
KABOOM
*MISSILE BEE:
One of the special TUNED armaments, a bee-shaped cyborg missile. It has a fire-and-forget auto-aiming capability, and can snipe with incredible accuracy.
BOOM
SO THIS IS WHAT THEY MEAN...
...BY THE ANGEL OF DEATH!!
SHOKK
FFFF!!

W-WAIT, ALITA!

HAAAA!

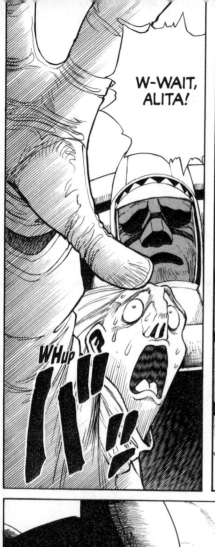

WHup

TWITCH

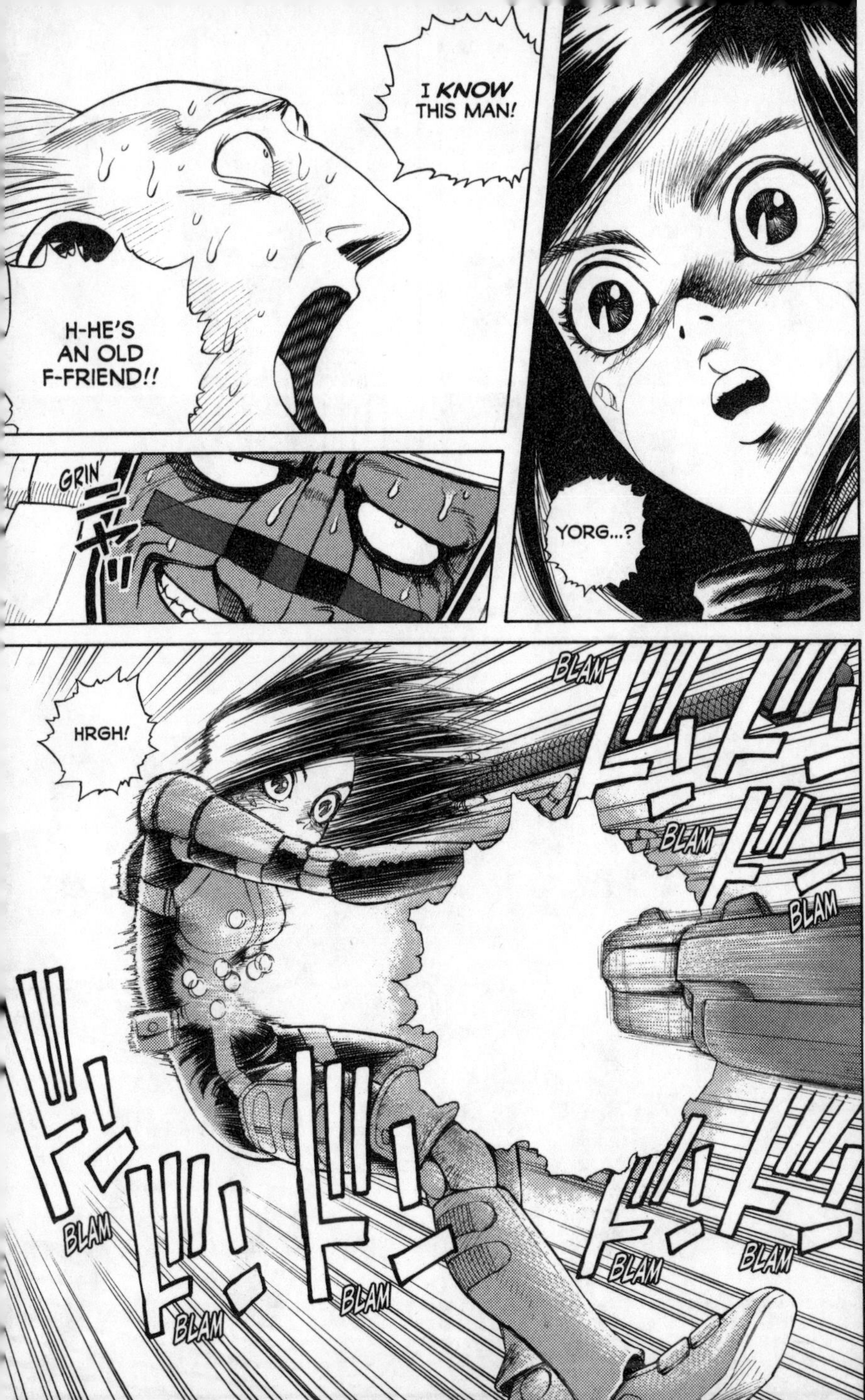
YORG...?
I KNOW THIS MAN!
H-HE'S AN OLD F-FRIEND!!
GRIN
ニヤッ
BLAM
HRGH!
BLAM
BLAM
BLAM
BLAM
BLAM
BLAM
BLAM

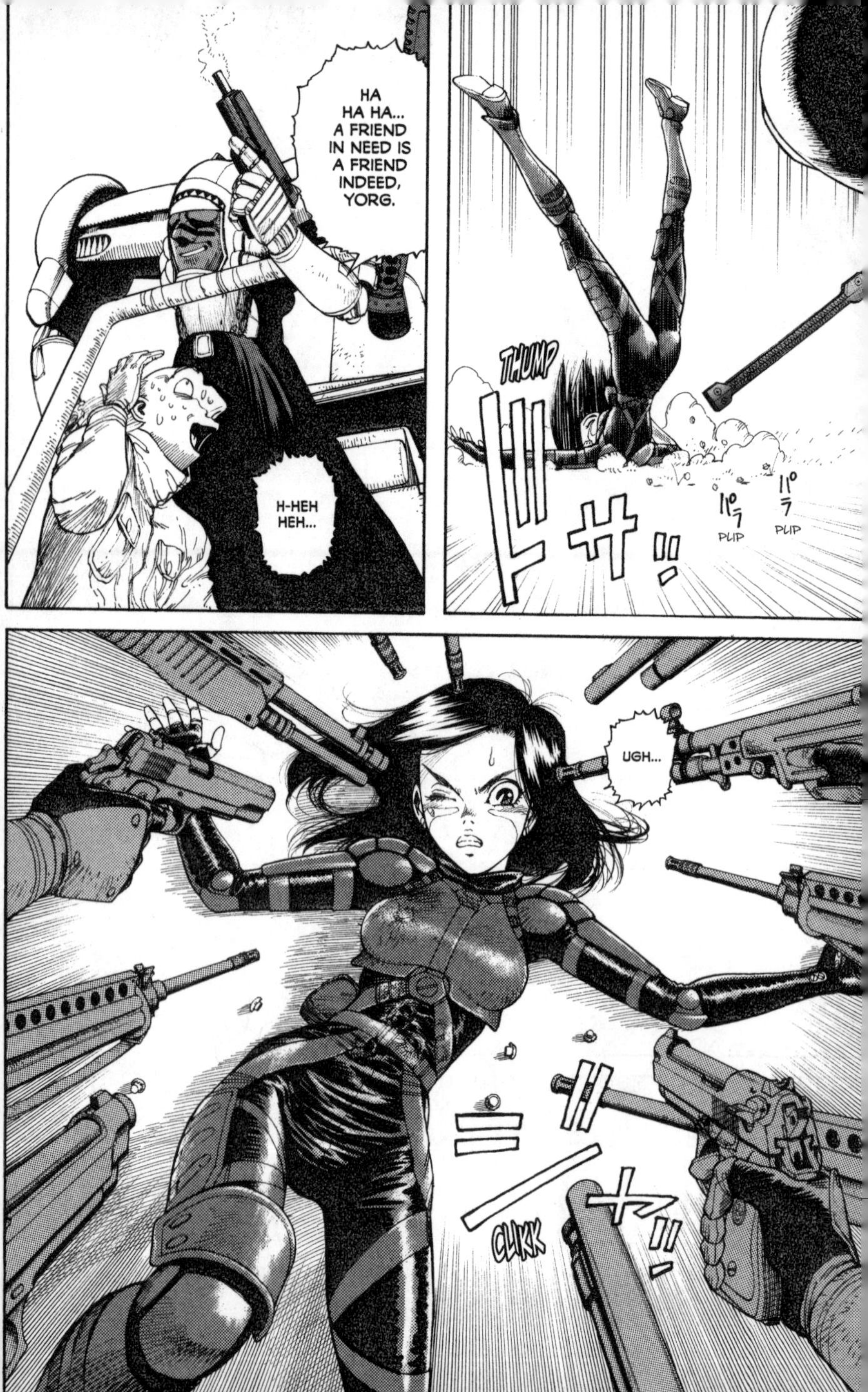
THUMP
ドサッ
パラ
PLIP
パラ
PLIP
HA HA HA... A FRIEND IN NEED IS A FRIEND INDEED, YORG.
H-HEH HEH...
UGH...
CLIKK

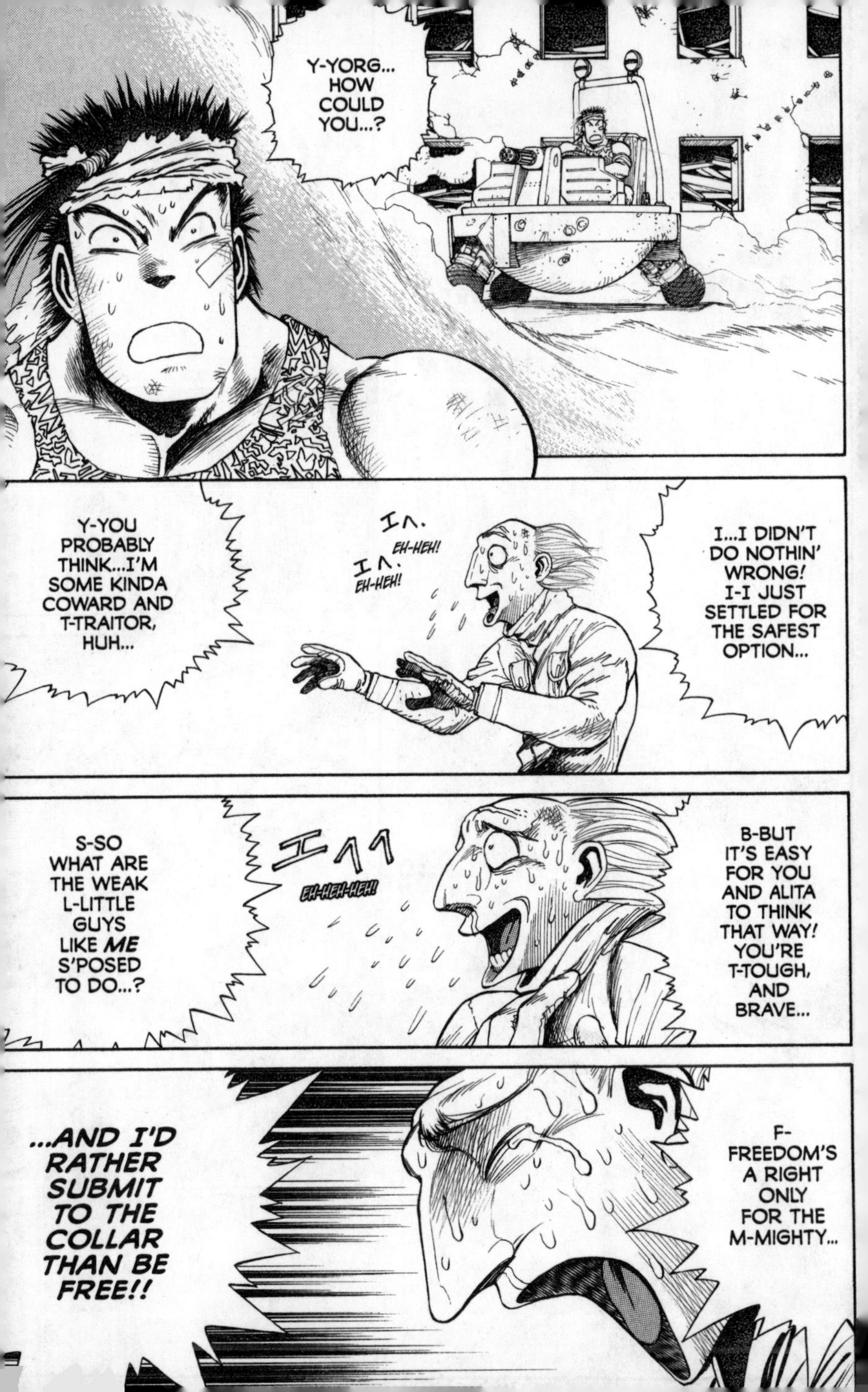
Y-YORG... HOW COULD YOU...?
I...I DIDN'T DO NOTHIN' WRONG! I-I JUST SETTLED FOR THE SAFEST OPTION...
エヘ EH-HEH!
エヘ EH-HEH!
Y-YOU PROBABLY THINK...I'M SOME KINDA COWARD AND T-TRAITOR, HUH...
B-BUT IT'S EASY FOR YOU AND ALITA TO THINK THAT WAY! YOU'RE T-TOUGH, AND BRAVE...
エヘヘ EH-HEH-HEH!
S-SO WHAT ARE THE WEAK L-LITTLE GUYS LIKE *ME* S'POSED TO DO...?
F- FREEDOM'S A RIGHT ONLY FOR THE M-MIGHTY...
...AND I'D RATHER SUBMIT TO THE COLLAR THAN BE FREE!!

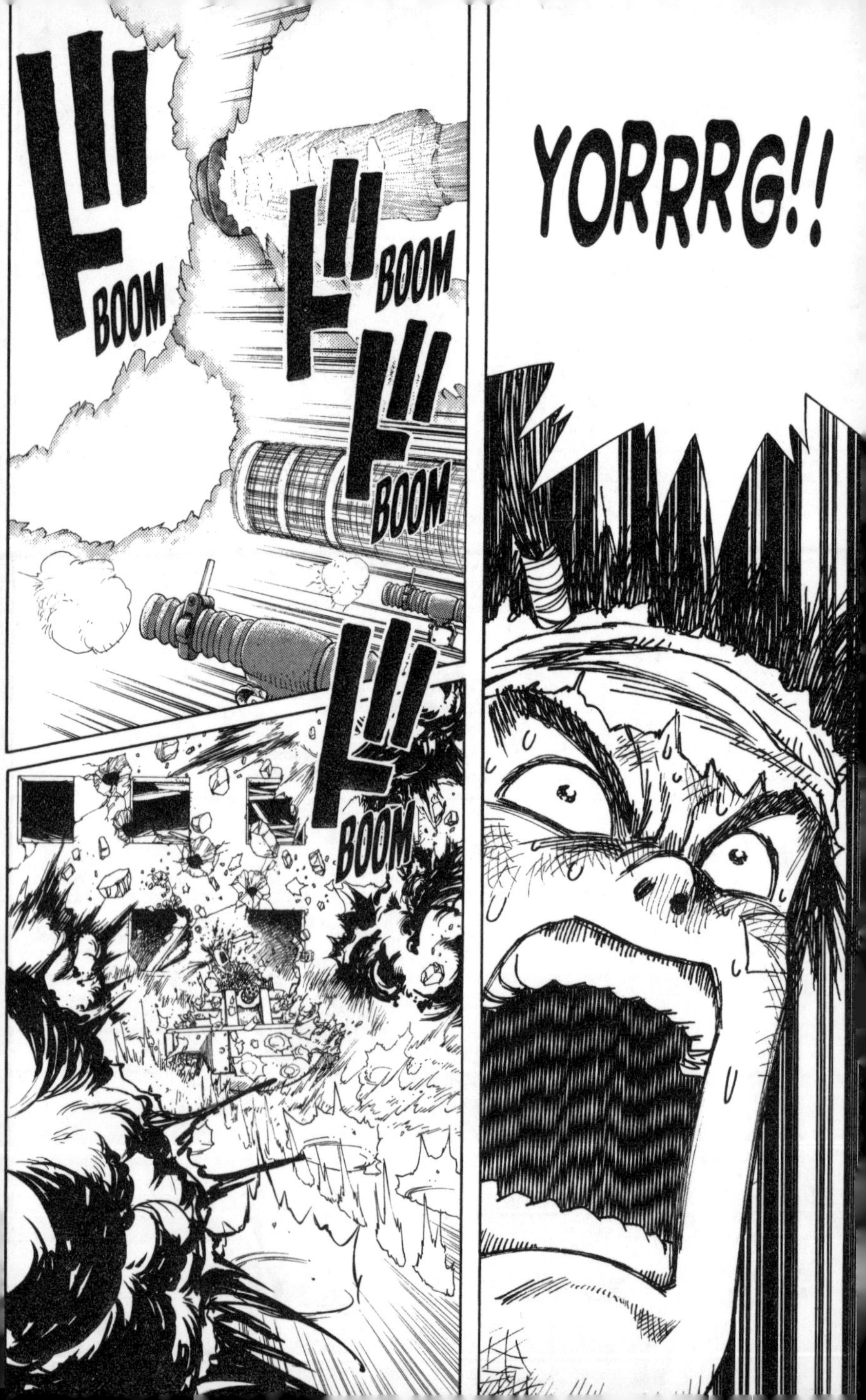
YORRRG!!
BOOM
BOOM
BOOM
BOOM

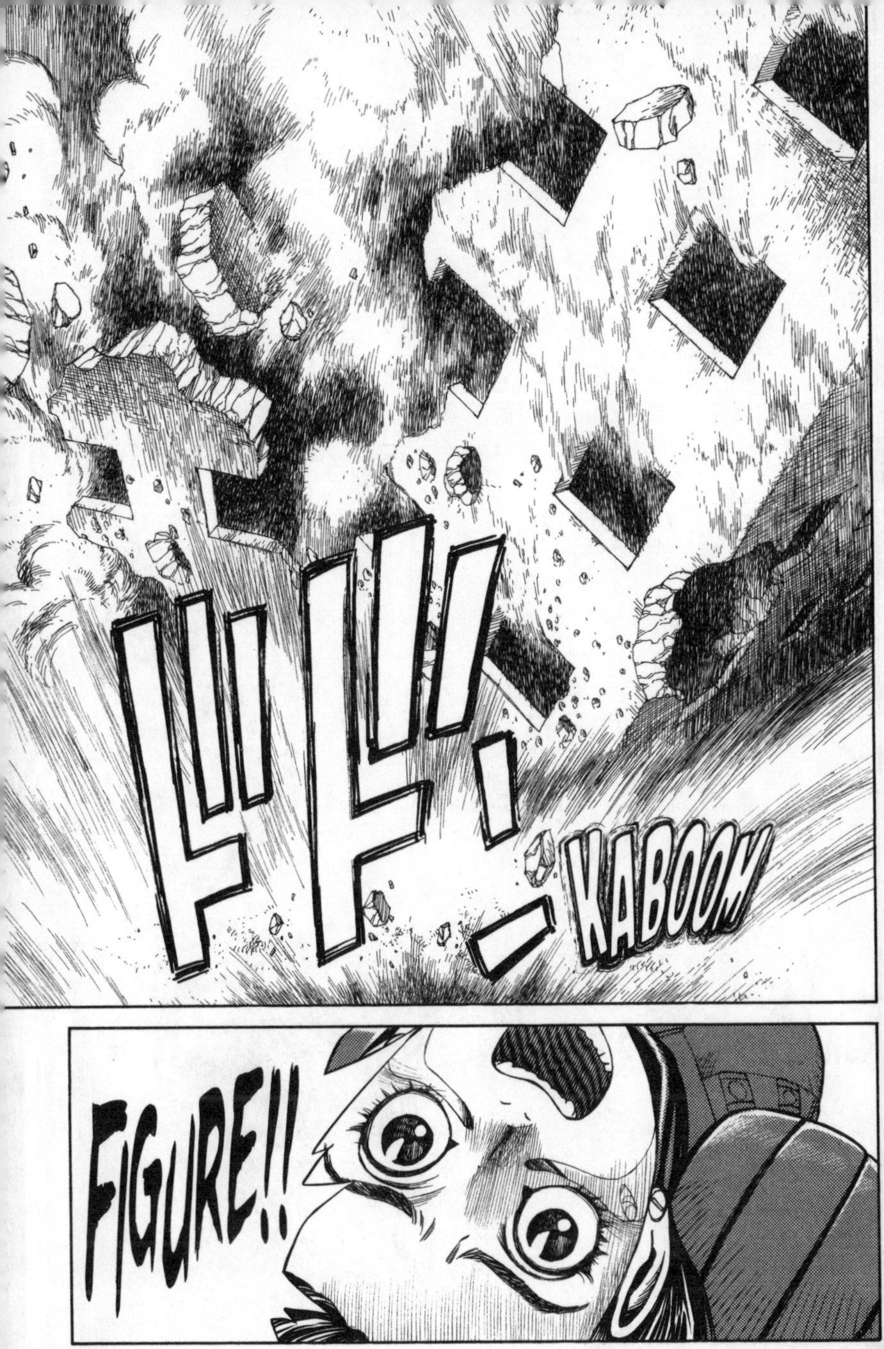
KABOOM
FIGURE!!

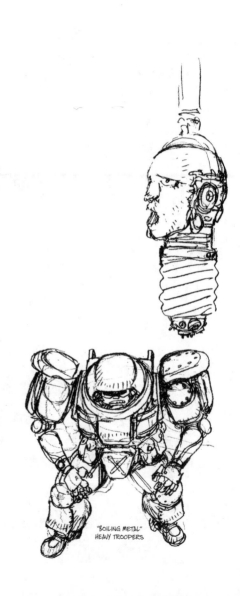

"BOILING METAL"
HEAVY TROOPERS

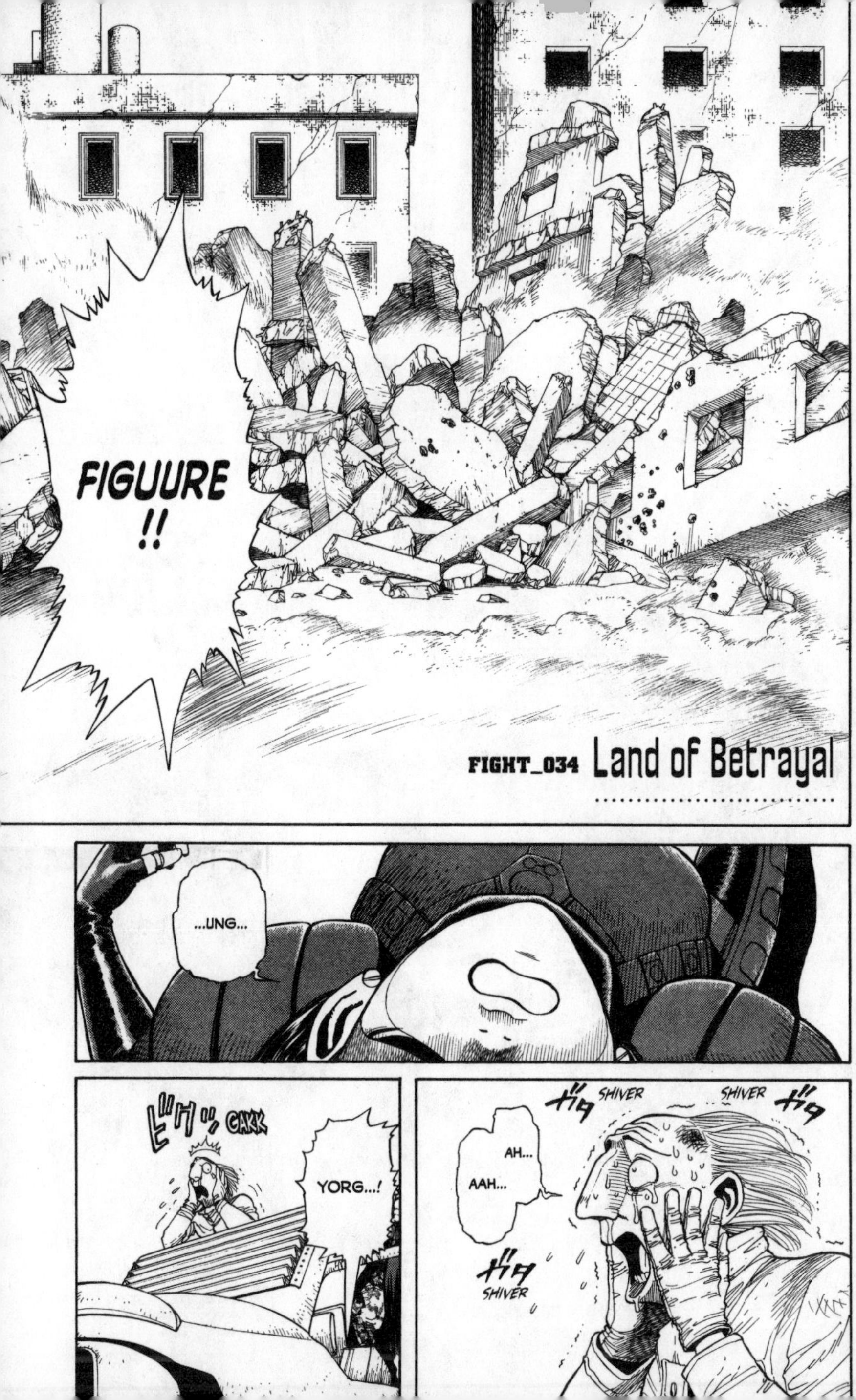
FIGUURE !!
FIGHT_034 Land of Betrayal
...UNG...
ガタ SHIVER
SHIVER ガタ
AH... AAH...
ガタ SHIVER
ビクッ GAKK
YORG...!

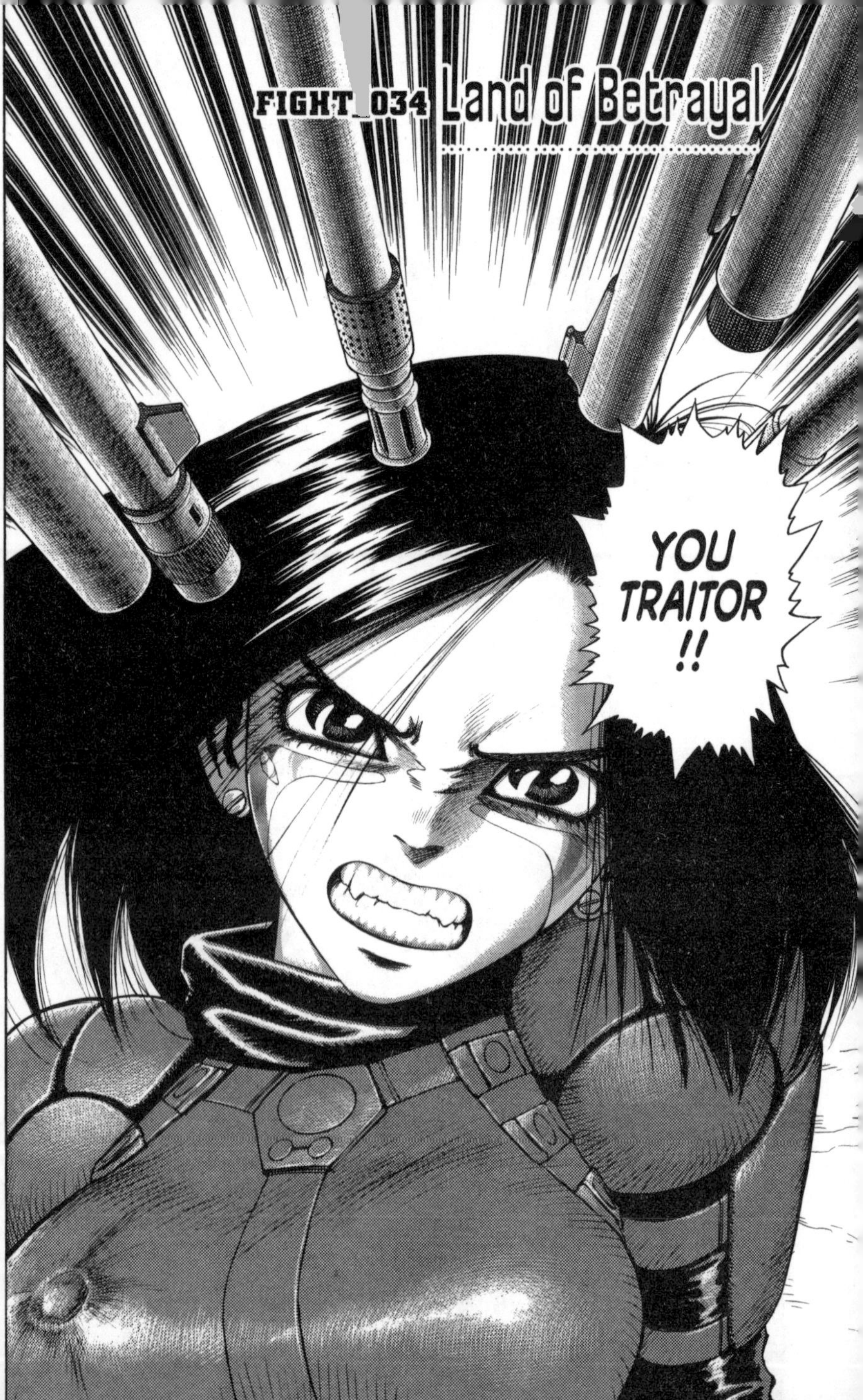
FIGHT_034 Land of Betrayal
YOU TRAITOR !!

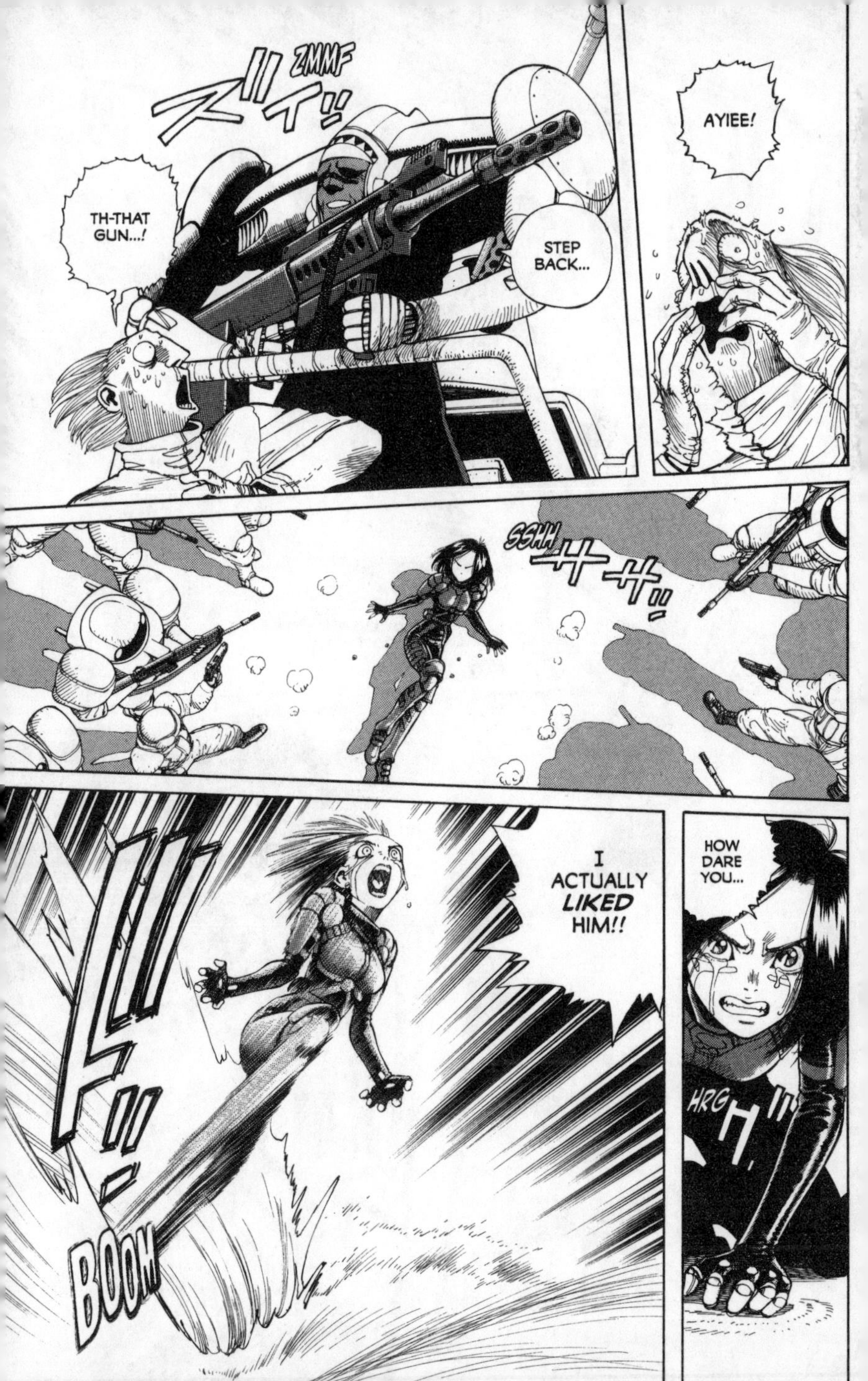
AYIEE!
ZMMF
STEP BACK...
TH-THAT GUN...!
SSHH
HOW DARE YOU...
HRG
I ACTUALLY *LIKED* HIM!!
BOOM

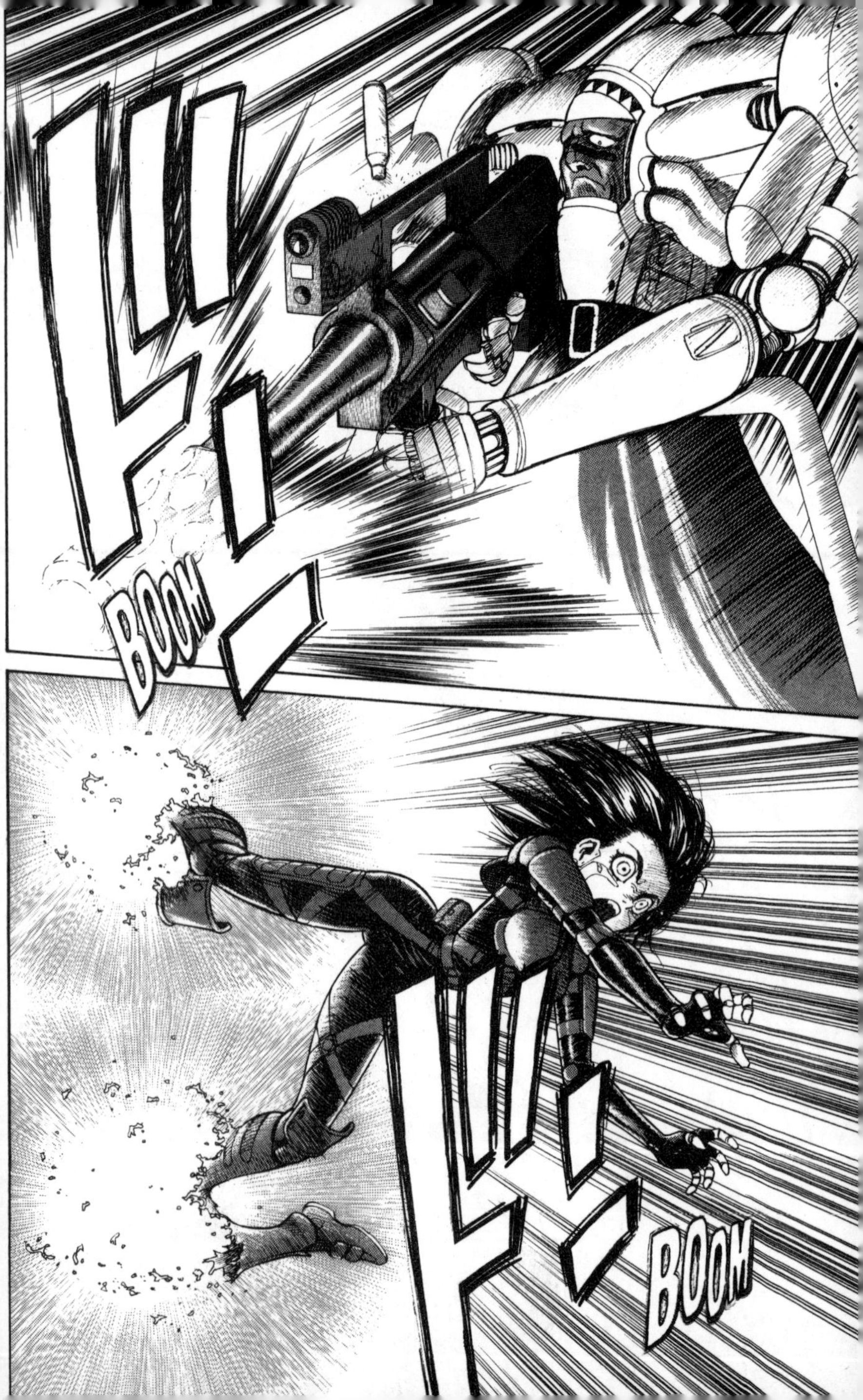
BOOM
BOOM

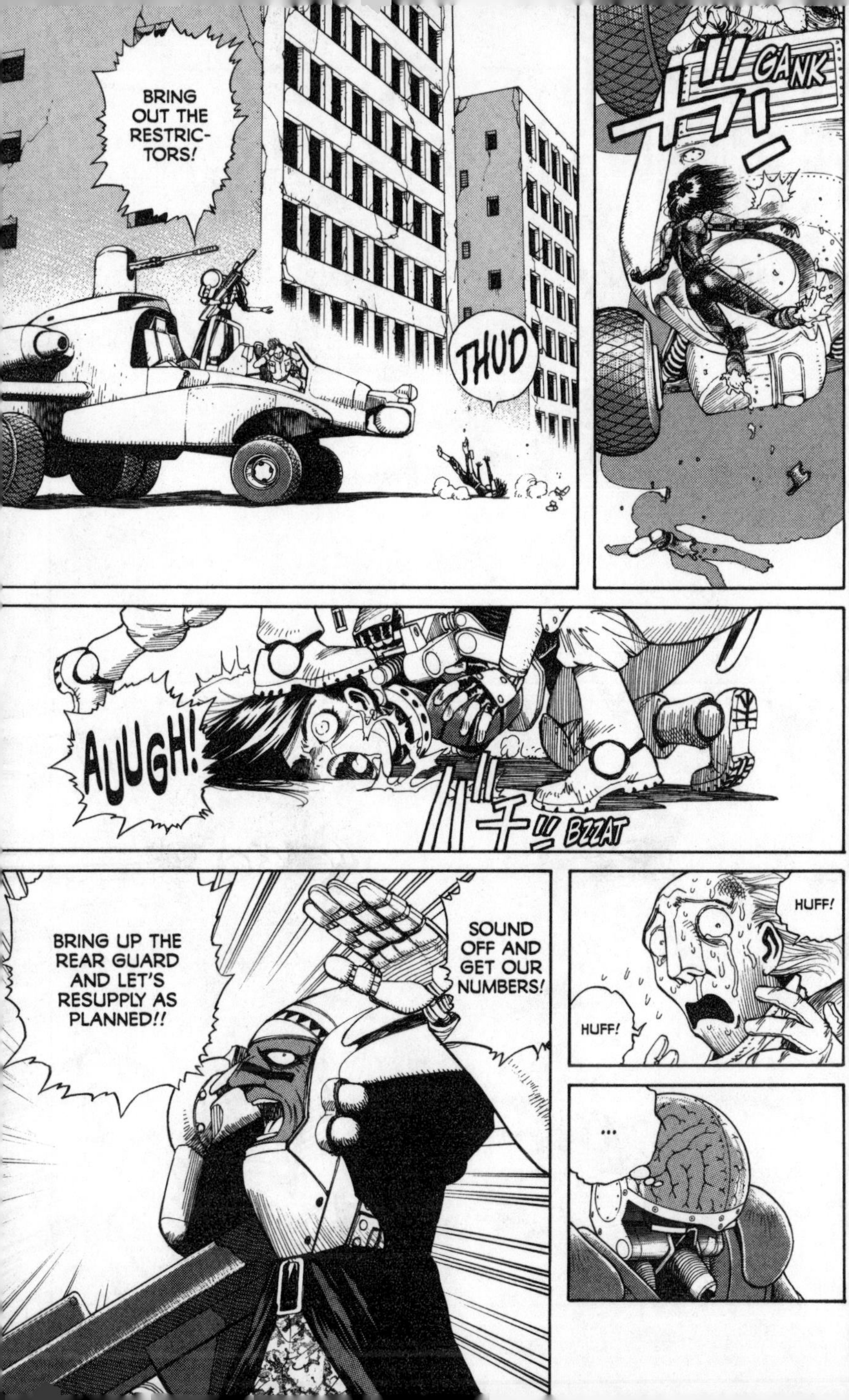
GANK
BRING OUT THE RESTRIC-TORS!
THUD
AUUGH!
BZZAT
HUFF!
HUFF!
...
SOUND OFF AND GET OUR NUMBERS!
BRING UP THE REAR GUARD AND LET'S RESUPPLY AS PLANNED!!

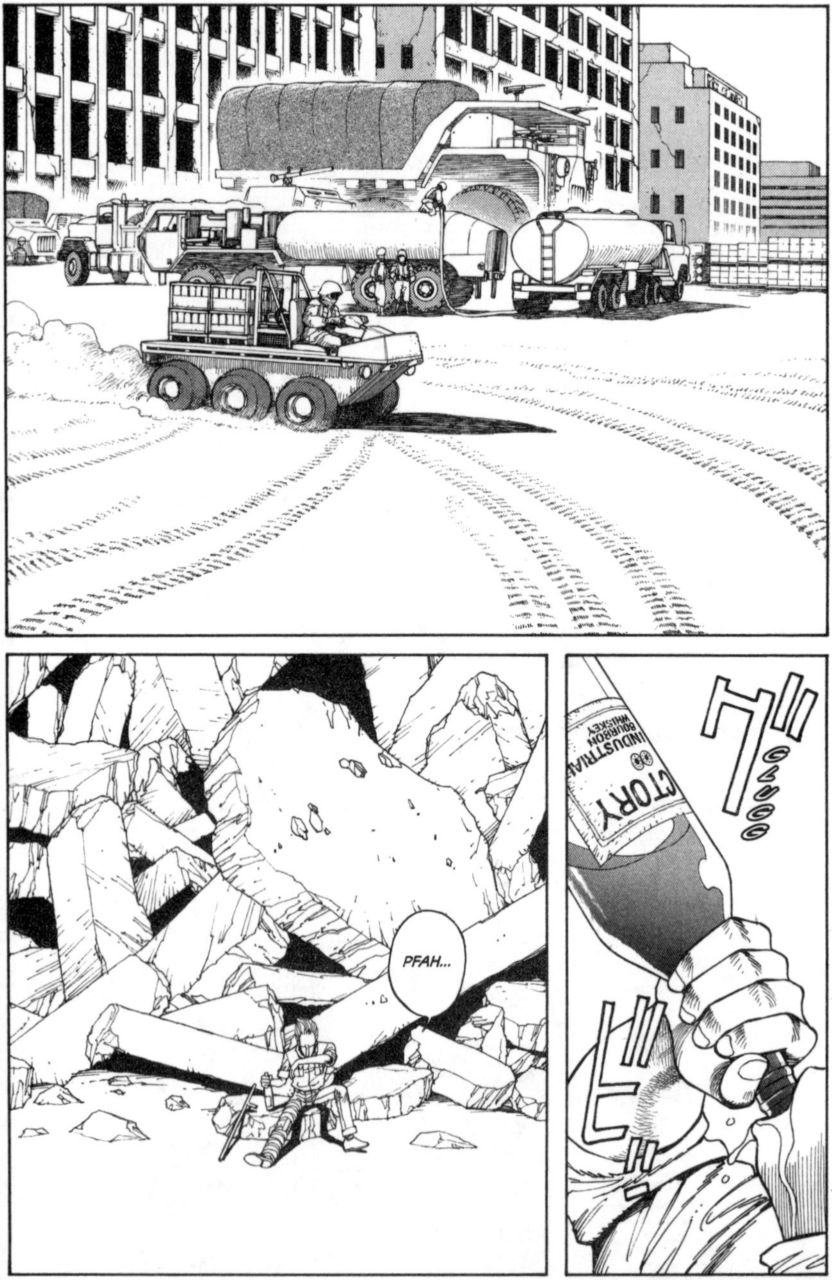
CTORY
INDUSTRIAL
BOURBON
WHISKEY
GLUGGG
PFAH...

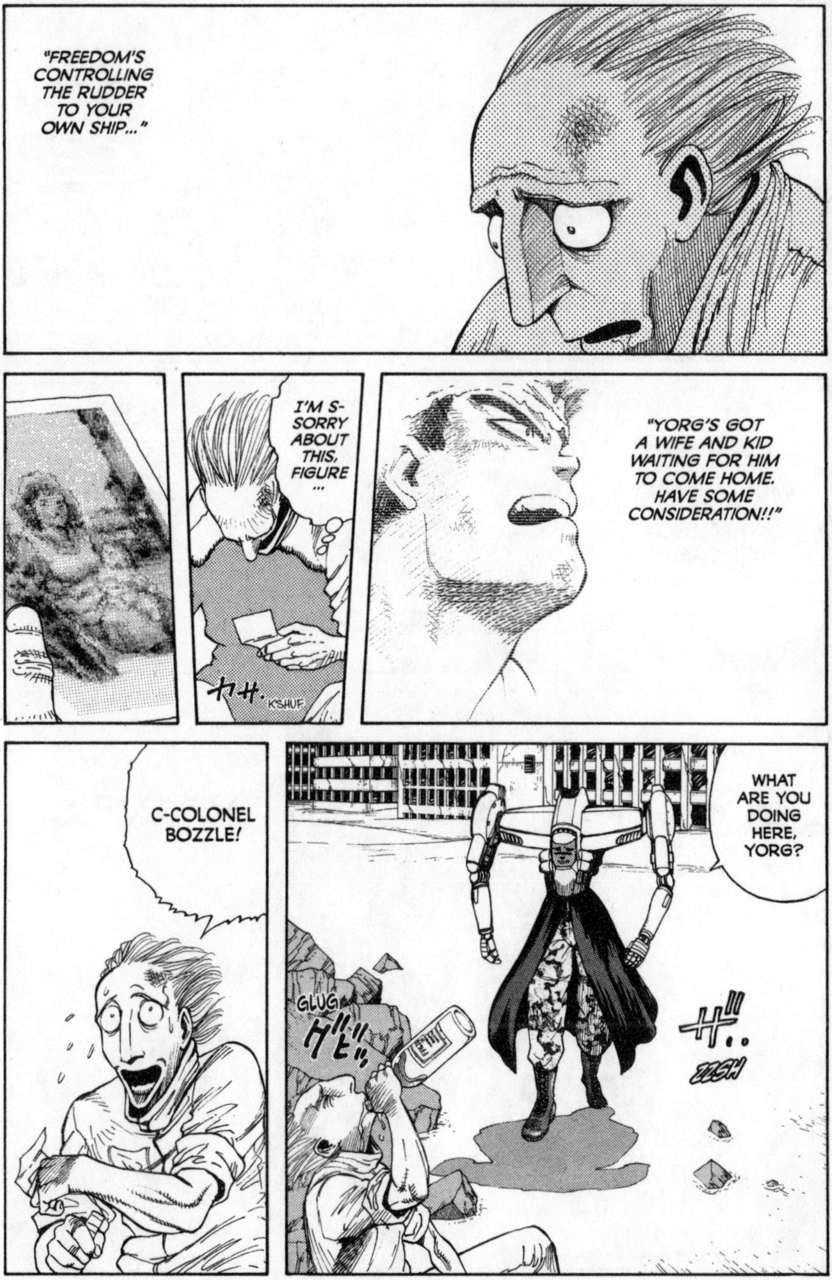
"FREEDOM'S CONTROLLING THE RUDDER TO YOUR OWN SHIP..."
"YORG'S GOT A WIFE AND KID WAITING FOR HIM TO COME HOME. HAVE SOME CONSIDERATION!!"
I'M S-SORRY ABOUT THIS, FIGURE...
KSHUF
WHAT ARE YOU DOING HERE, YORG?
ZZSH
GLUG
C-COLONEL BOZZLE!

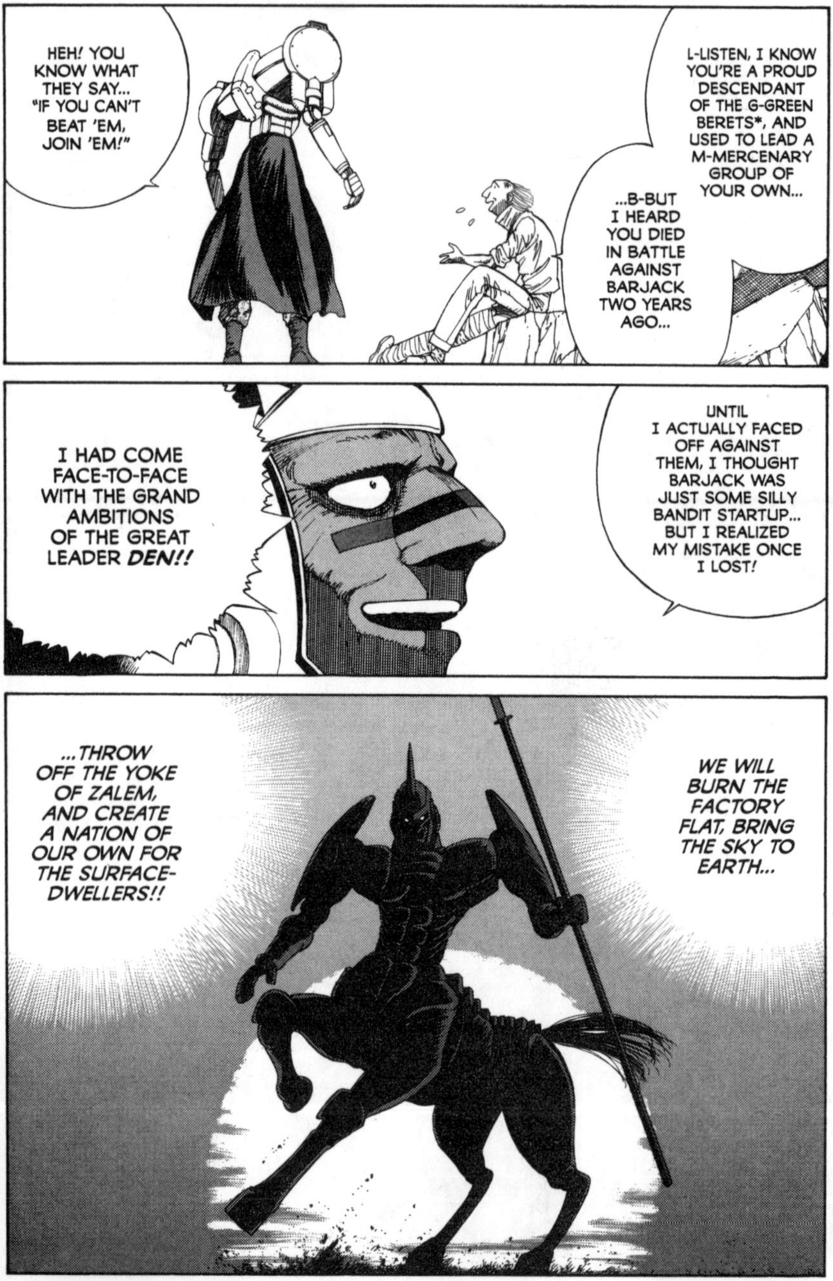
L-LISTEN, I KNOW YOU'RE A PROUD DESCENDANT OF THE G-GREEN BERETS*, AND USED TO LEAD A M-MERCENARY GROUP OF YOUR OWN...
...B-BUT I HEARD YOU DIED IN BATTLE AGAINST BARJACK TWO YEARS AGO...
HEH! YOU KNOW WHAT THEY SAY... "IF YOU CAN'T BEAT 'EM, JOIN 'EM!"
UNTIL I ACTUALLY FACED OFF AGAINST THEM, I THOUGHT BARJACK WAS JUST SOME SILLY BANDIT STARTUP... BUT I REALIZED MY MISTAKE ONCE I LOST!
I HAD COME FACE-TO-FACE WITH THE GRAND AMBITIONS OF THE GREAT LEADER DEN!!
WE WILL BURN THE FACTORY FLAT, BRING THE SKY TO EARTH...
...THROW OFF THE YOKE OF ZALEM, AND CREATE A NATION OF OUR OWN FOR THE SURFACE-DWELLERS!!

***Green Berets:** Referring to the special elite force of the American military.
In this era, it seems to be considered the name of some powerful tribe of ancient warriors.

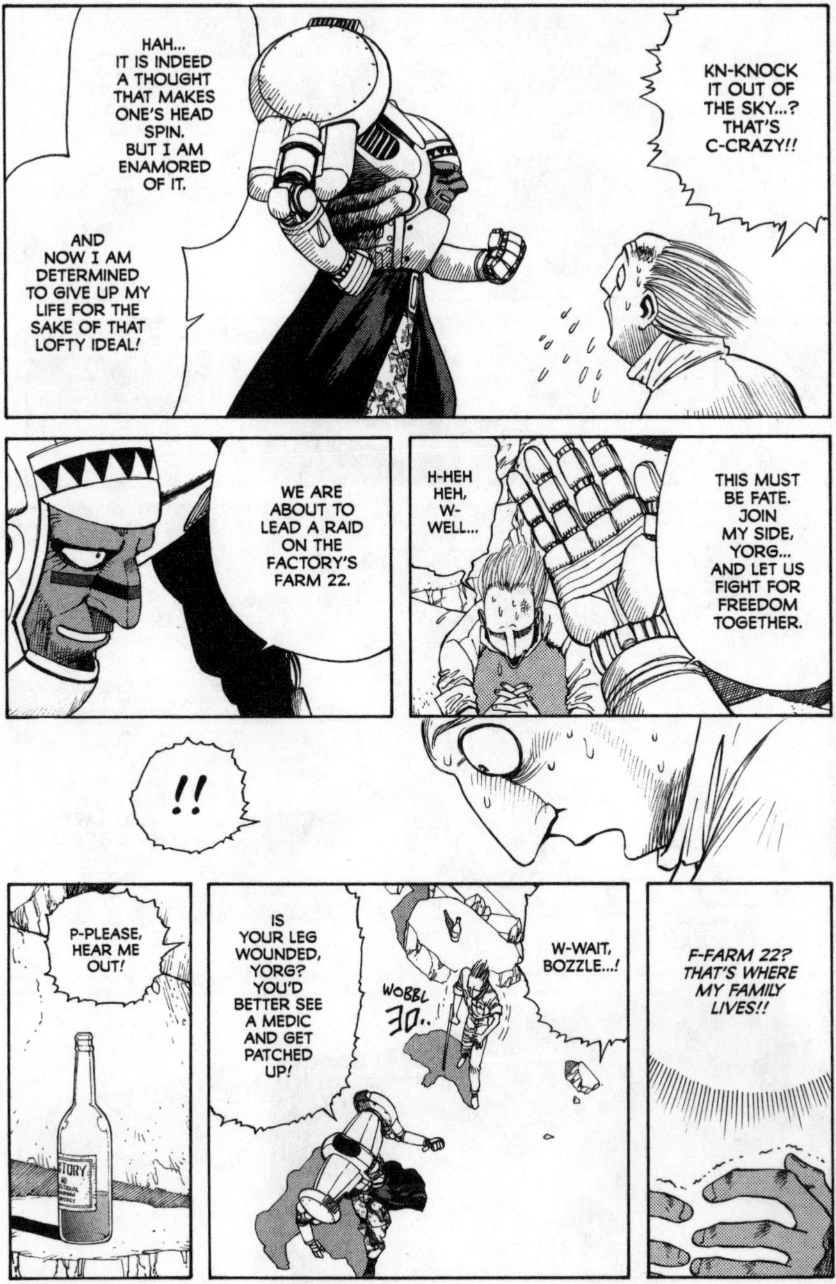
KN-KNOCK IT OUT OF THE SKY...? THAT'S C-CRAZY!!
HAH... IT IS INDEED A THOUGHT THAT MAKES ONE'S HEAD SPIN. BUT I AM ENAMORED OF IT.
AND NOW I AM DETERMINED TO GIVE UP MY LIFE FOR THE SAKE OF THAT LOFTY IDEAL!
THIS MUST BE FATE. JOIN MY SIDE, YORG... AND LET US FIGHT FOR FREEDOM TOGETHER.
H-HEH HEH, W-WELL...
WE ARE ABOUT TO LEAD A RAID ON THE FACTORY'S FARM 22.
!!
F-FARM 22? THAT'S WHERE MY FAMILY LIVES!!
IS YOUR LEG WOUNDED, YORG? YOU'D BETTER SEE A MEDIC AND GET PATCHED UP!
WOBBL
W-WAIT, BOZZLE...!
P-PLEASE, HEAR ME OUT!

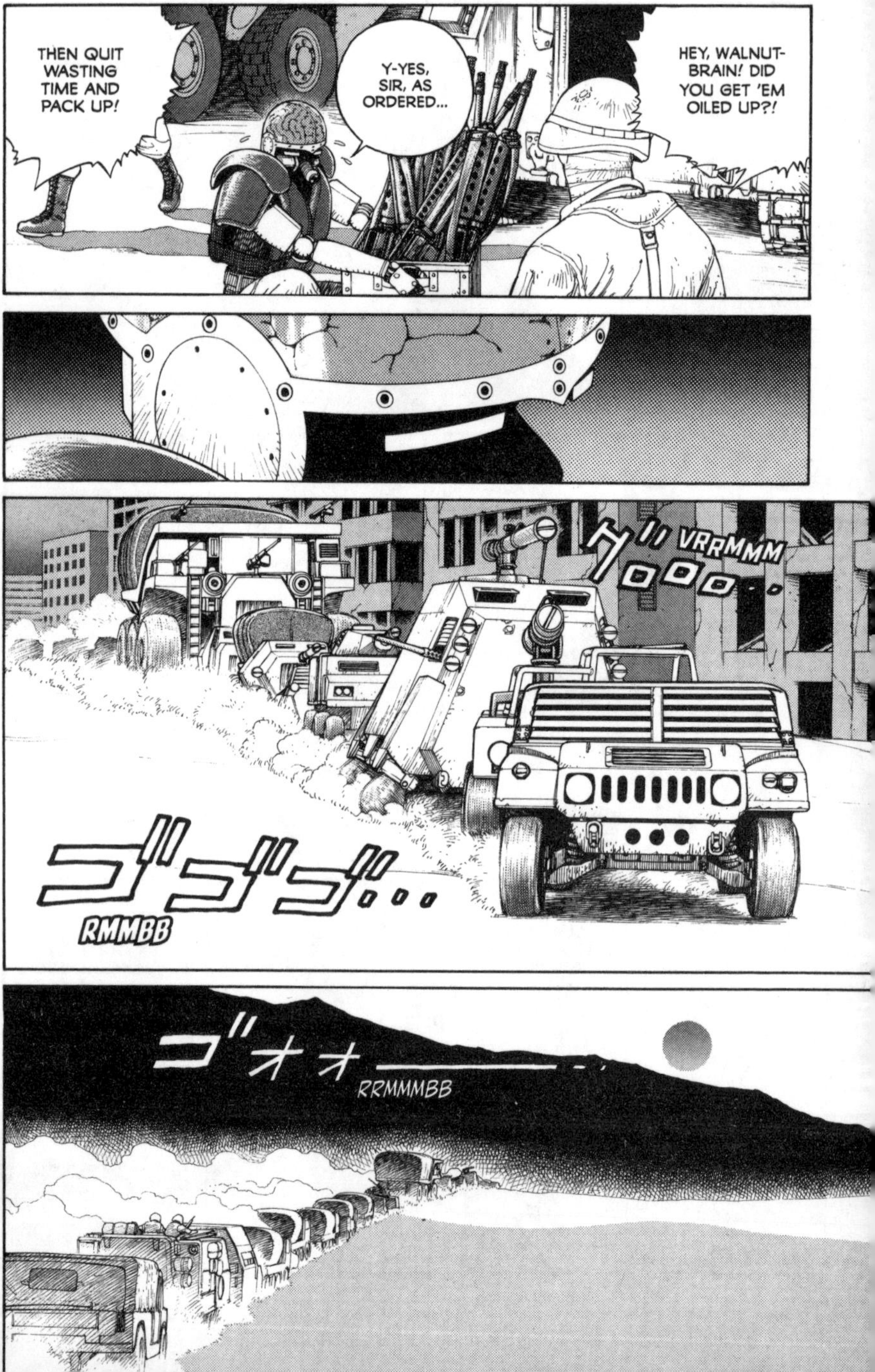
HEY, WALNUT-BRAIN! DID YOU GET 'EM OILED UP?!
Y-YES, SIR, AS ORDERED...
THEN QUIT WASTING TIME AND PACK UP!
VRRMMM
ゴゴゴ...
RMMBB
ゴオオ——
RRMMMBB

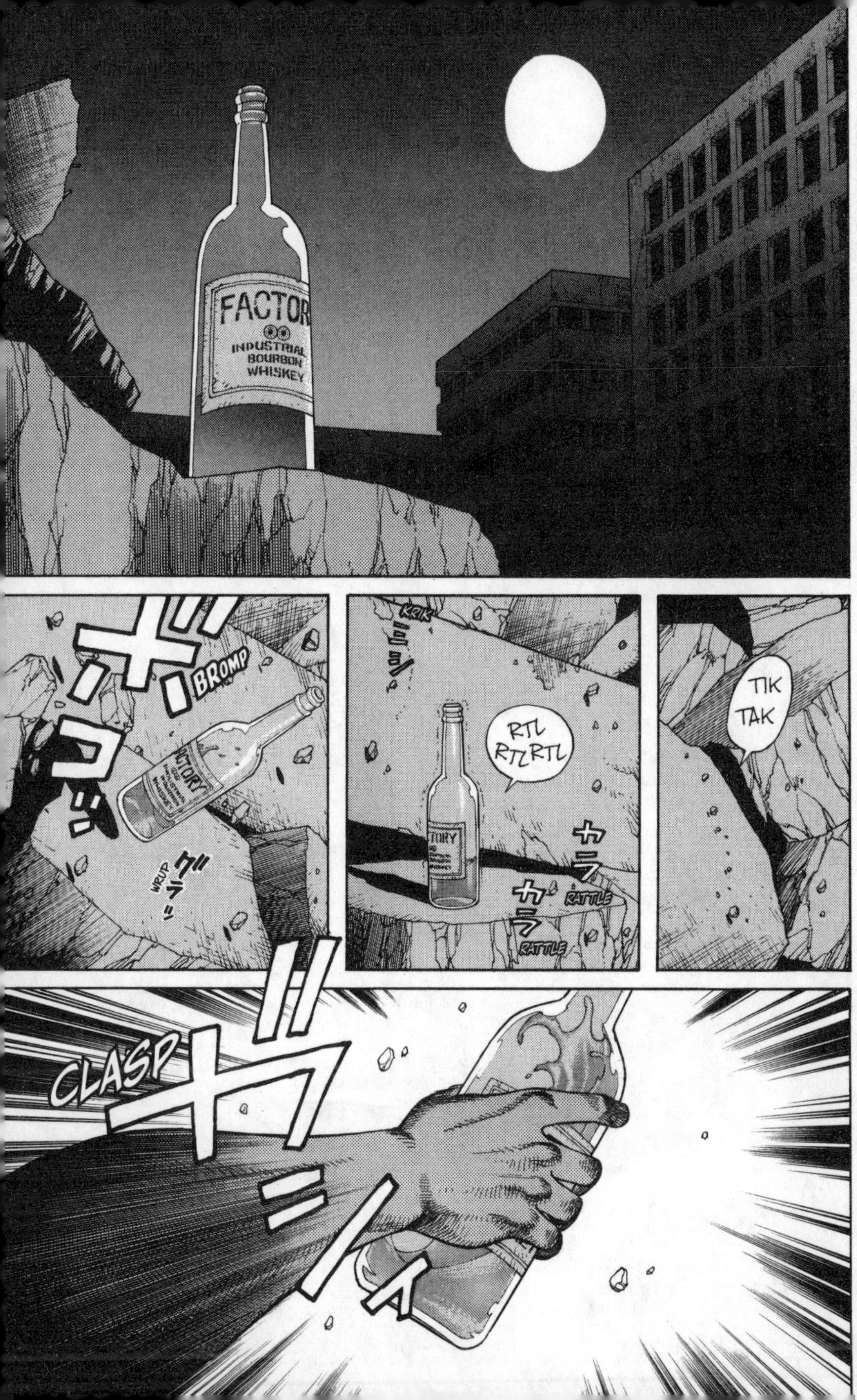
FACTOR
INDUSTRIAL
BOURBON
WHISKEY
TIK
TAK
KRIK
RTL
RTLRTL
RATTLE
RATTLE
BROMP
WRUP
CLASP

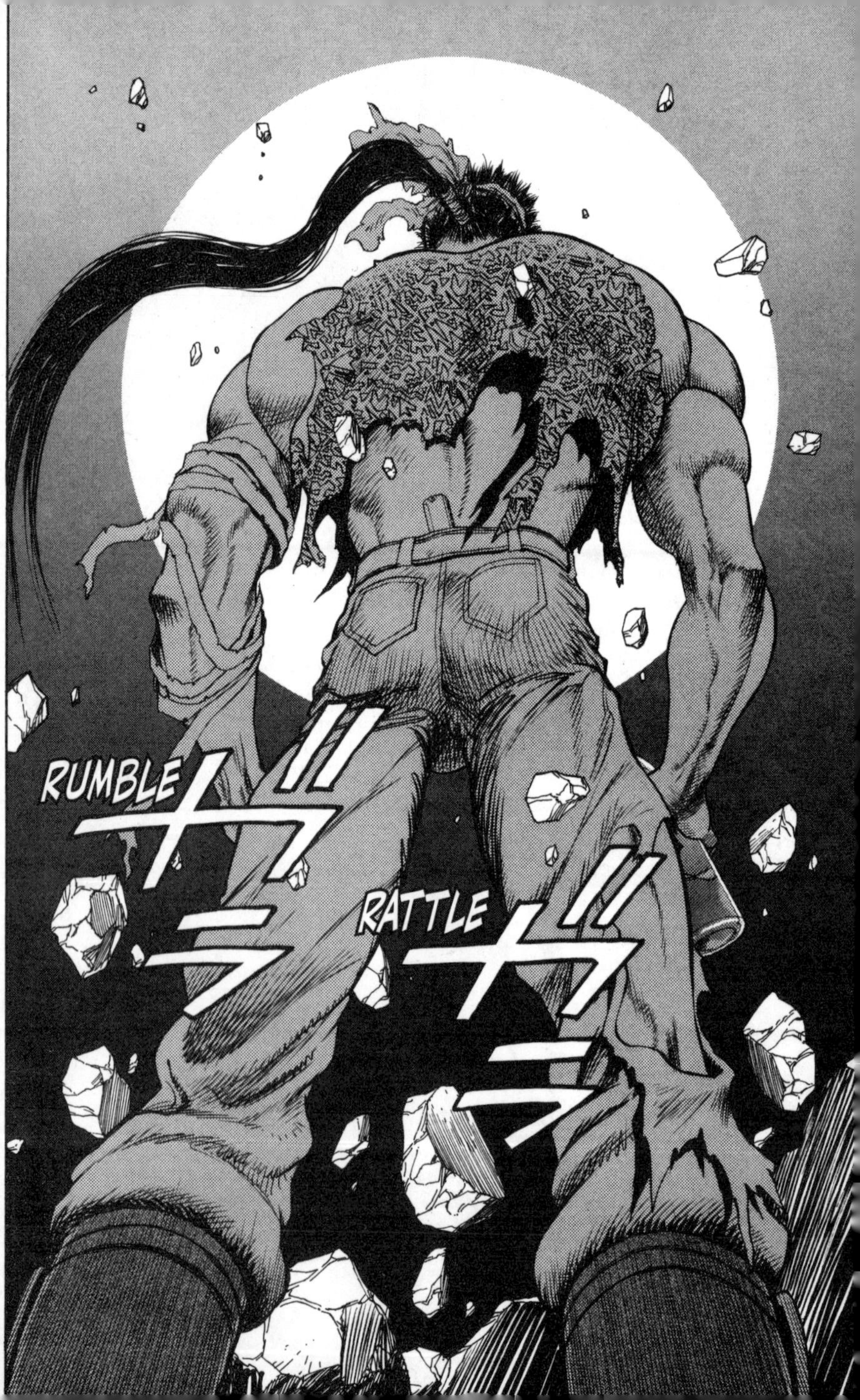
RUMBLE
ゴゴ
RATTLE
ゴゴ

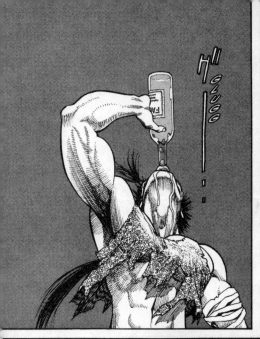

ゴキュッ
GULK
ゴキュッ
GULK
GLUGG
BWAAH! BACK TO LIFE!
EVEN BULLETS ARE SO SCARED THAT THEY AVOID ME!!

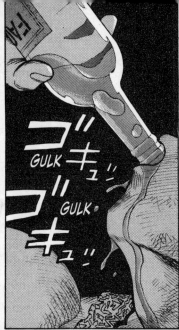

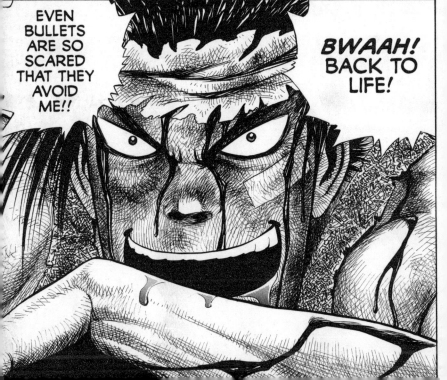

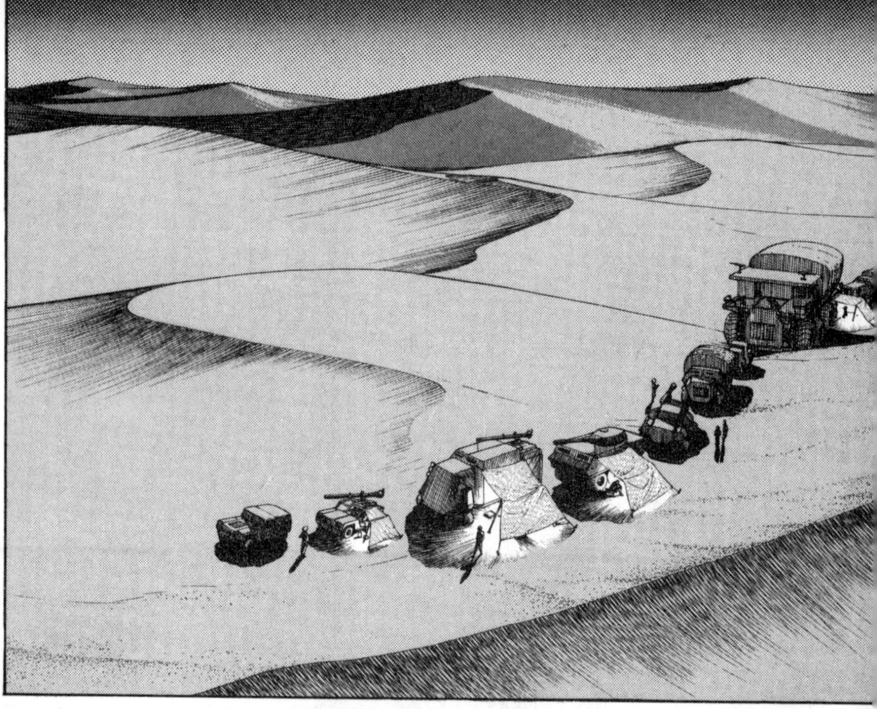

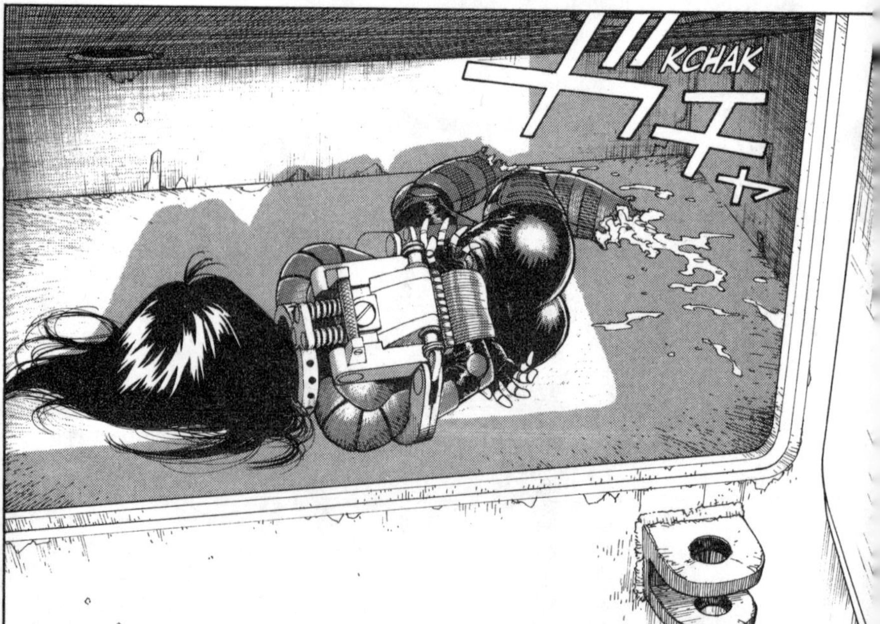
KCHAK

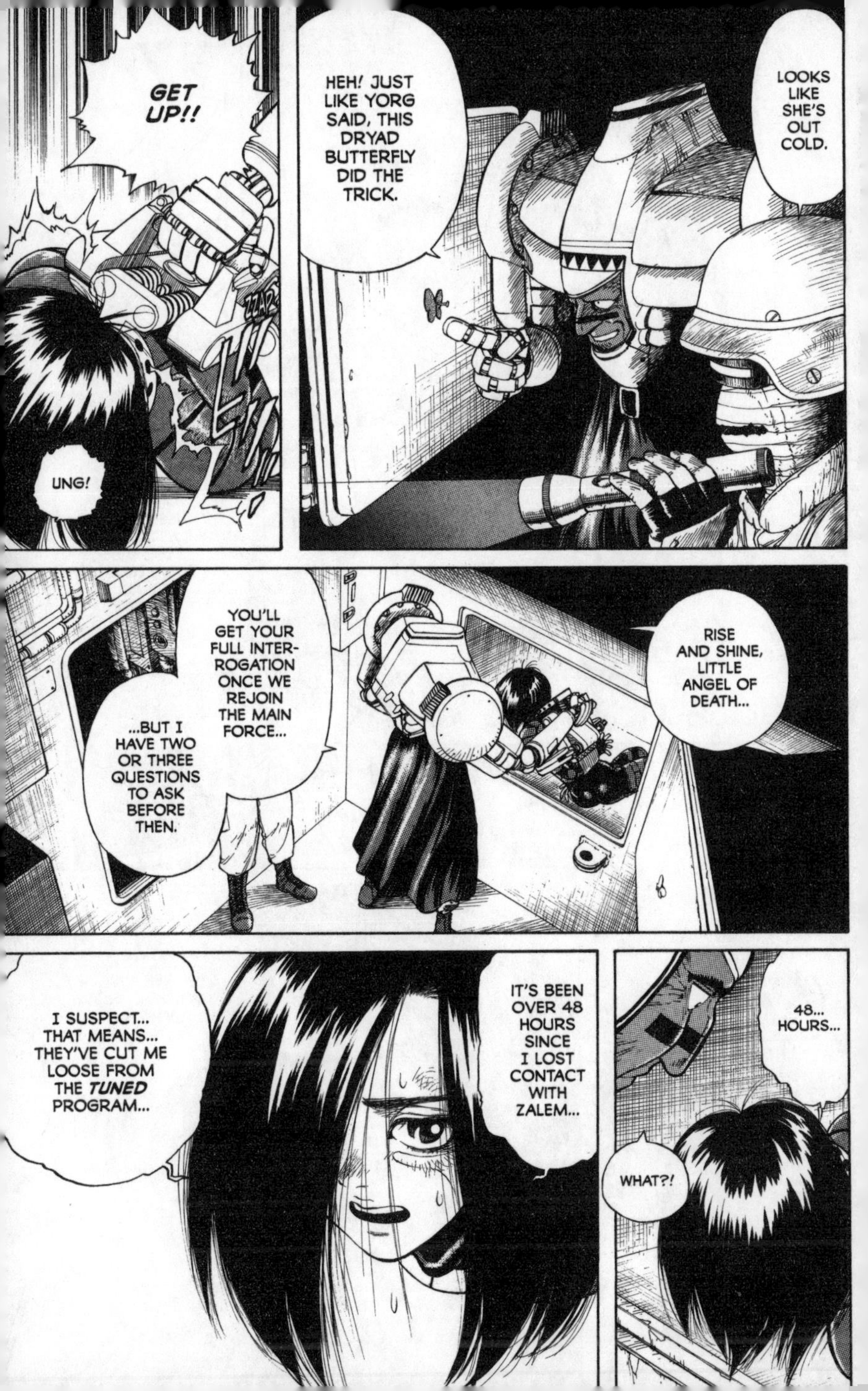
LOOKS LIKE SHE'S OUT COLD.
HEH! JUST LIKE YORG SAID, THIS DRYAD BUTTERFLY DID THE TRICK.
GET UP!!
UNG!
RISE AND SHINE, LITTLE ANGEL OF DEATH...
YOU'LL GET YOUR FULL INTER-ROGATION ONCE WE REJOIN THE MAIN FORCE...
...BUT I HAVE TWO OR THREE QUESTIONS TO ASK BEFORE THEN.
48... HOURS...
WHAT?!
IT'S BEEN OVER 48 HOURS SINCE I LOST CONTACT WITH ZALEM...
I SUSPECT... THAT MEANS... THEY'VE CUT ME LOOSE FROM THE *TUNED* PROGRAM...

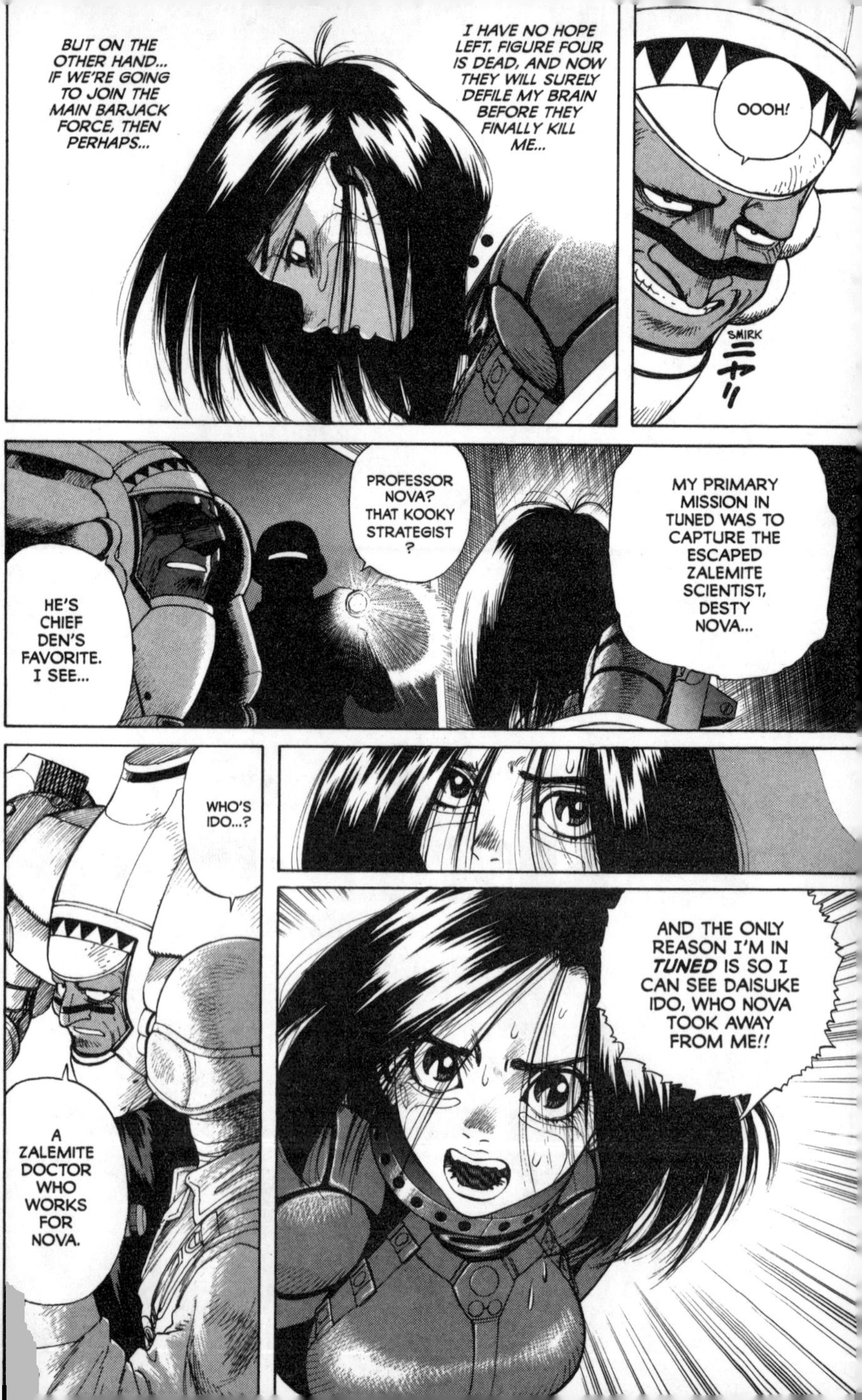
OOOH!
SMIRK
ニヤリ
I HAVE NO HOPE LEFT. FIGURE FOUR IS DEAD, AND NOW THEY WILL SURELY DEFILE MY BRAIN BEFORE THEY FINALLY KILL ME...
BUT ON THE OTHER HAND... IF WE'RE GOING TO JOIN THE MAIN BARJACK FORCE, THEN PERHAPS...
MY PRIMARY MISSION IN TUNED WAS TO CAPTURE THE ESCAPED ZALEMITE SCIENTIST, DESTY NOVA...
PROFESSOR NOVA? THAT KOOKY STRATEGIST?
HE'S CHIEF DEN'S FAVORITE. I SEE...
AND THE ONLY REASON I'M IN ***TUNED*** IS SO I CAN SEE DAISUKE IDO, WHO NOVA TOOK AWAY FROM ME!!
WHO'S IDO...?
A ZALEMITE DOCTOR WHO WORKS FOR NOVA.

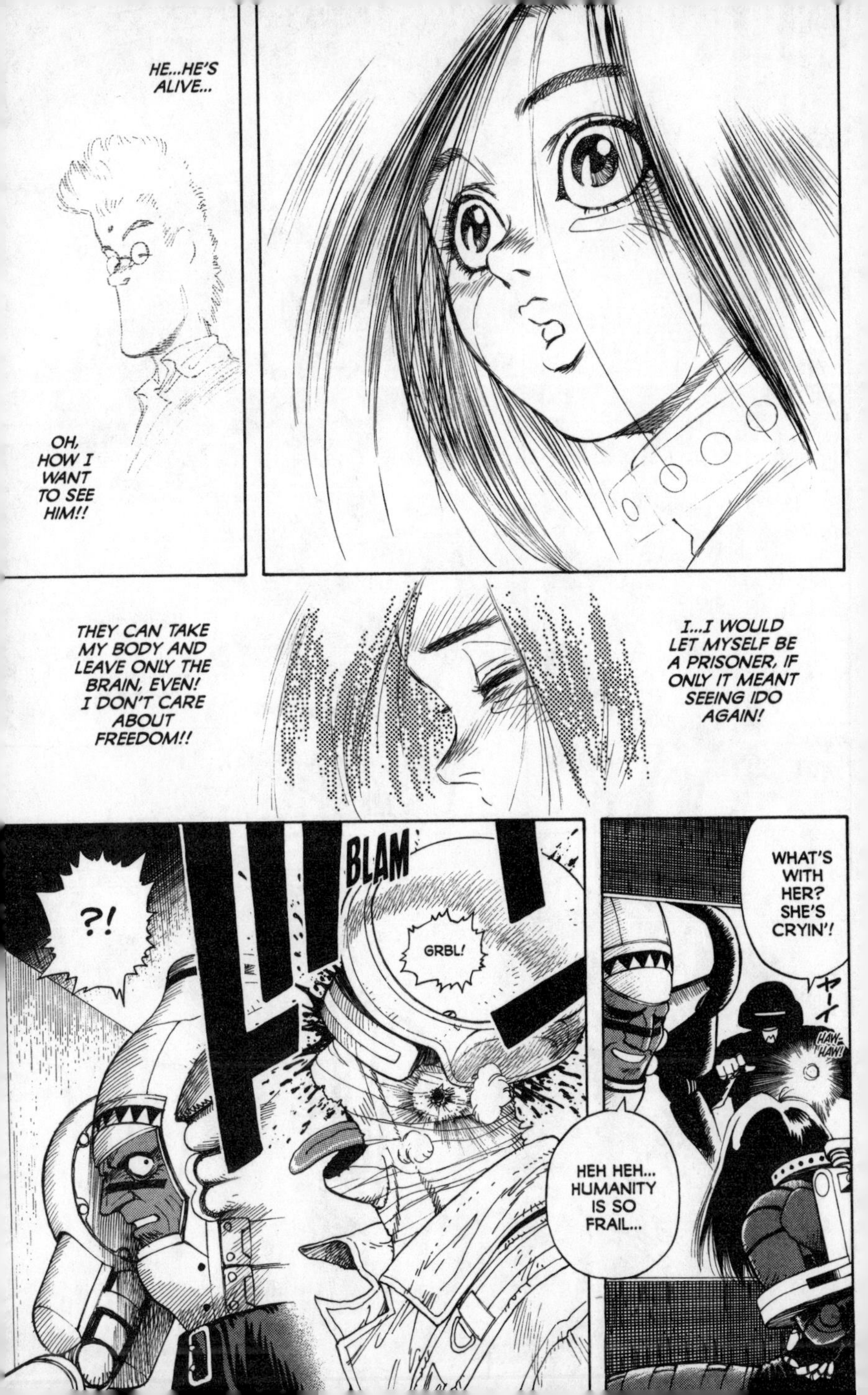
HE...HE'S ALIVE...
OH, HOW I WANT TO SEE HIM!!
I...I WOULD LET MYSELF BE A PRISONER, IF ONLY IT MEANT SEEING IDO AGAIN!
THEY CAN TAKE MY BODY AND LEAVE ONLY THE BRAIN, EVEN! I DON'T CARE ABOUT FREEDOM!!
WHAT'S WITH HER? SHE'S CRYIN'!
ヤーイ
HAW-HAW!
HEH HEH... HUMANITY IS SO FRAIL...
BLAM
GRBL!
?!

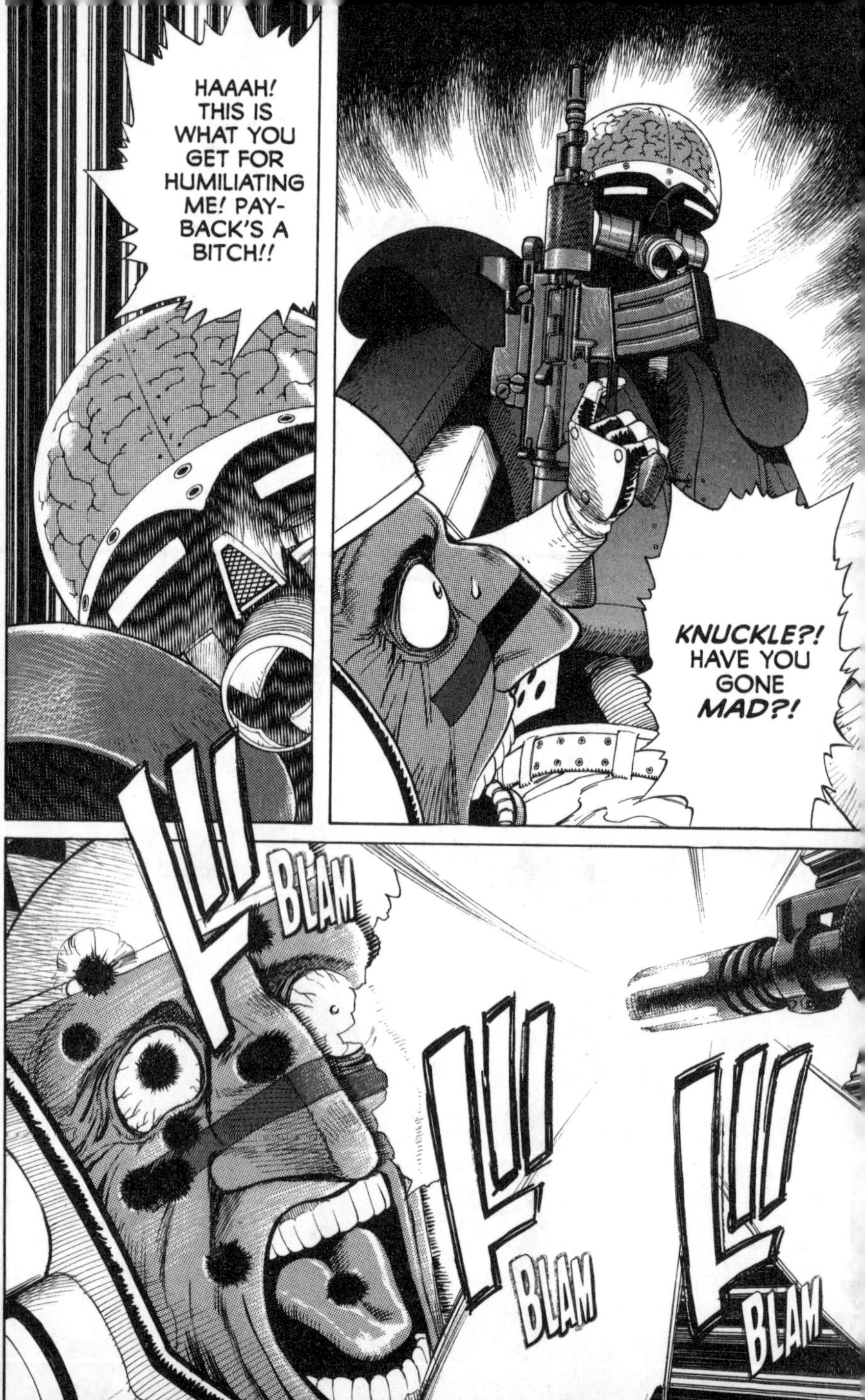
KNUCKLE?! HAVE YOU GONE MAD?!
HAAAH! THIS IS WHAT YOU GET FOR HUMILIATING ME! PAY-BACK'S A BITCH!!
BLAM
BLAM
BLAM

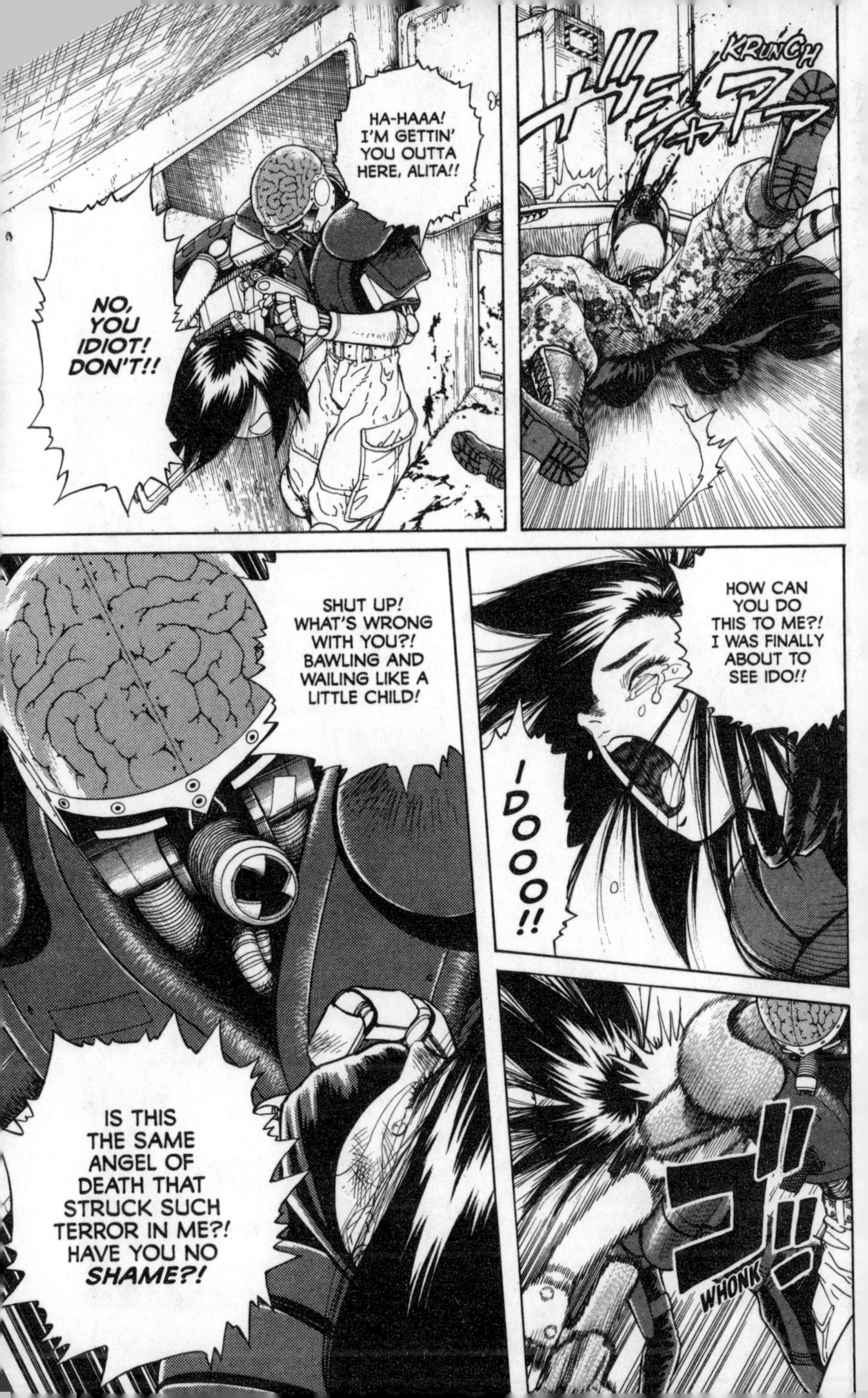
KRUNCH
HA-HAAA! I'M GETTIN' YOU OUTTA HERE, ALITA!!
NO, YOU IDIOT! DON'T!!
HOW CAN YOU DO THIS TO ME?! I WAS FINALLY ABOUT TO SEE IDO!!
IDOOOO!!
WHONK
SHUT UP! WHAT'S WRONG WITH YOU?! BAWLING AND WAILING LIKE A LITTLE CHILD!
IS THIS THE SAME ANGEL OF DEATH THAT STRUCK SUCH TERROR IN ME?! HAVE YOU NO SHAME?!

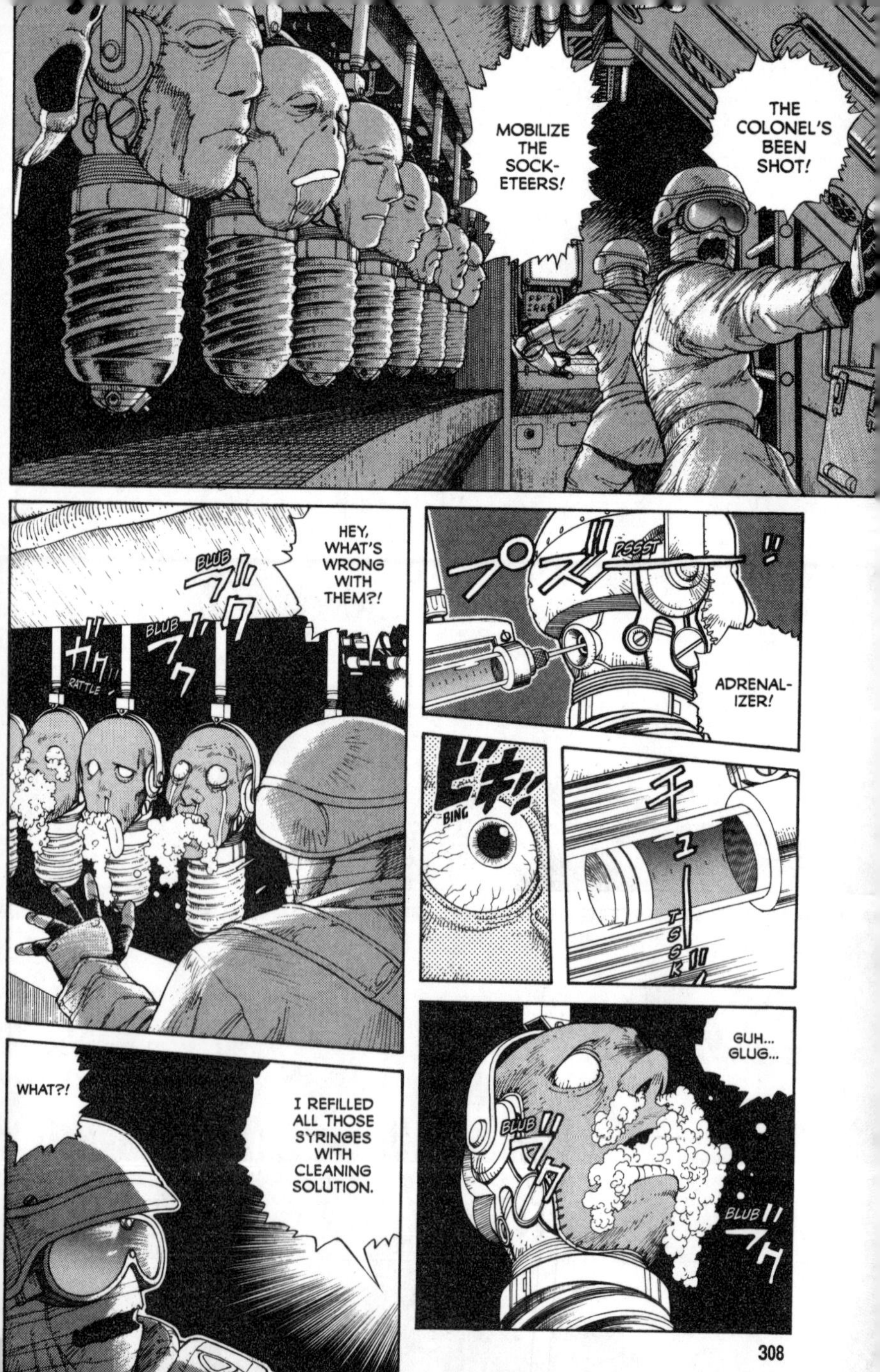
THE COLONEL'S BEEN SHOT!
MOBILIZE THE SOCK-ETEERS!
PSSST
ADRENAL-IZER!
TSSK
BING
HEY, WHAT'S WRONG WITH THEM?!
BLUB
BLUB
RATTLE
GUH... GLUG...
BLUB
BLUB
I REFILLED ALL THOSE SYRINGES WITH CLEANING SOLUTION.
WHAT?!

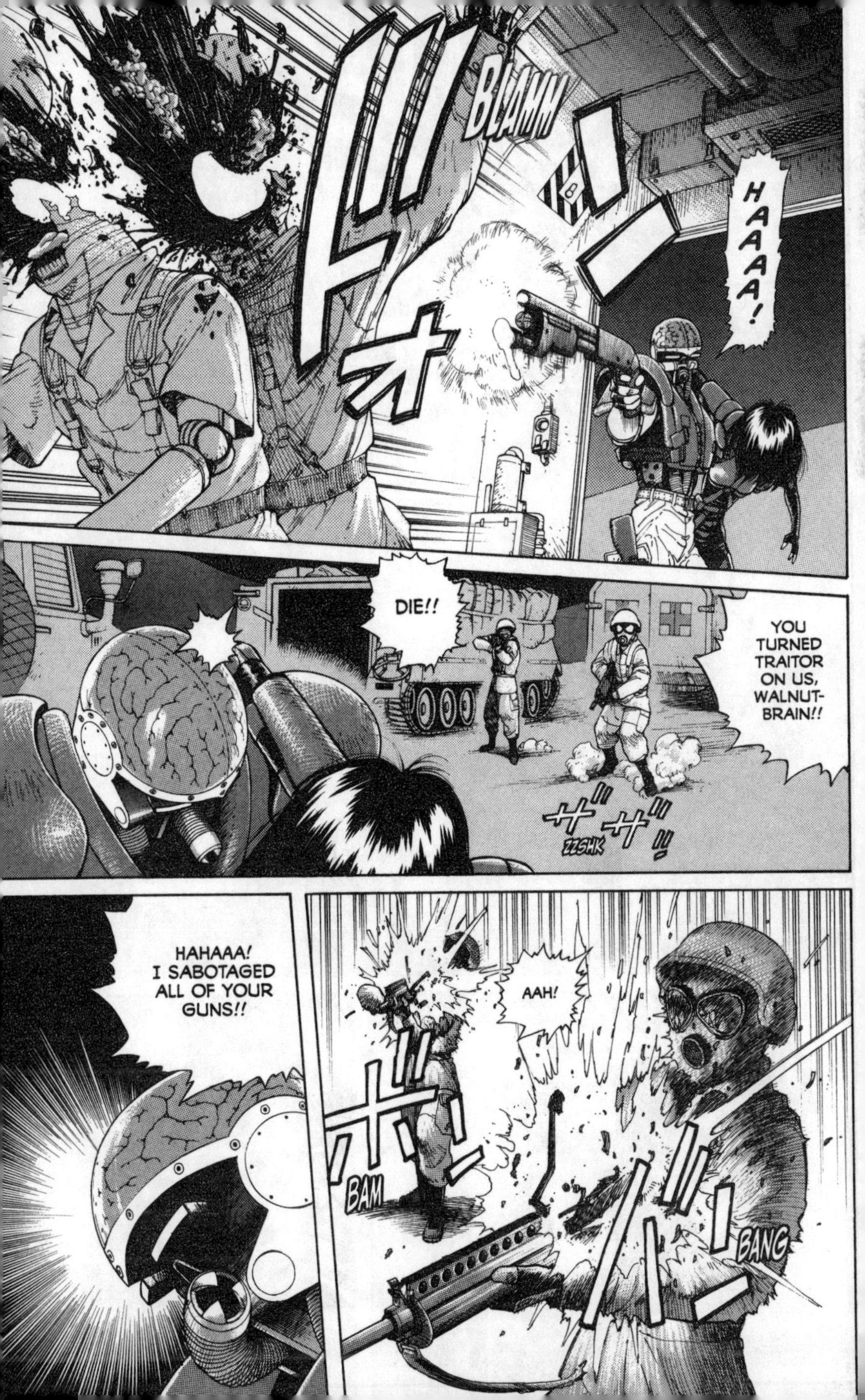
HAAAA!
BLAMM
YOU TURNED TRAITOR ON US, WALNUT-BRAIN!!
DIE!!
ZZSHK
AAH!
BANG
BAM
HAHAAA! I SABOTAGED ALL OF YOUR GUNS!!

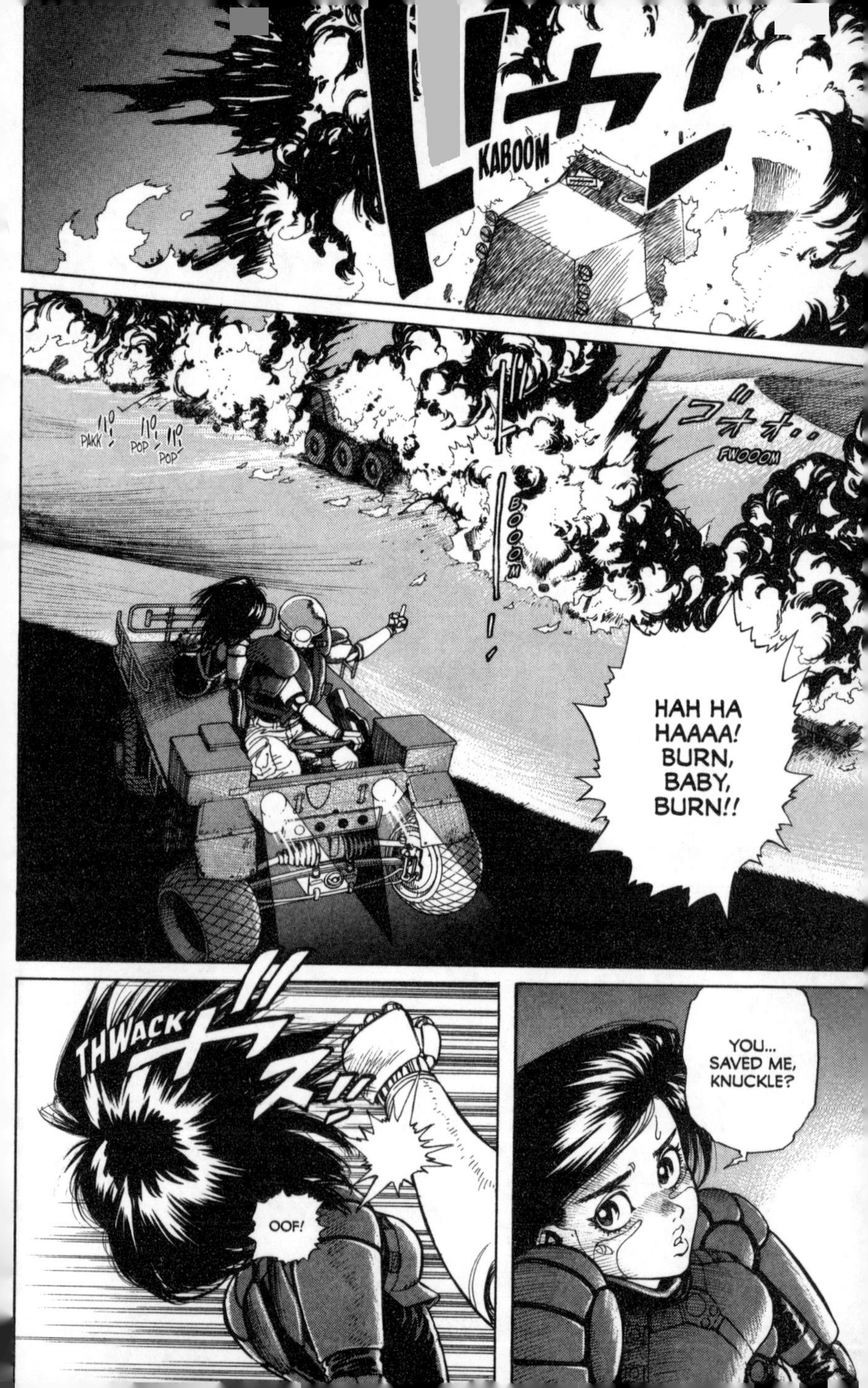
KABOOM
FWOOOM
PAKK POP POP
BOOOOM
HAH HA HAAAA! BURN, BABY, BURN!!
YOU... SAVED ME, KNUCKLE?
THWACK
OOF!

DON'T BE MISTAKEN... I JUST DIDN'T WANT THOSE OTHER SCUMBAGS TO KILL YOU *FIRST*...

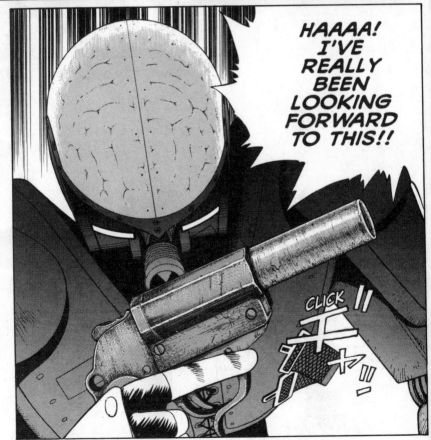

HAAAA! I'VE REALLY BEEN LOOKING FORWARD TO THIS!!

CLICK

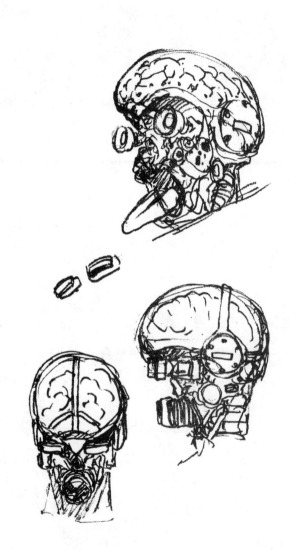

Young characters and steampunk setting, like *Howl's Moving Castle* and *Battle Angel Alita*

A boy with a talent for machines and a mysterious girl whose wings he's fixed will take you beyond the clouds! In the tradition of the high-flying, resonant adventure stories of Studio Ghibli comes a gorgeous tale about the longing of young hearts for adventure and friendship!

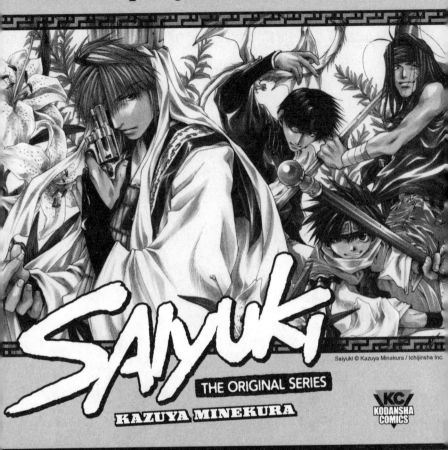

THE SWEET SCENT OF LOVE IS IN THE AIR! FOR FANS OF OFFBEAT ROMANCES LIKE *WOTAKOI*

Sweat and Soap © Kintetsu Yamada / Kodansha Ltd.

In an office romance, there's a fine line between sexy and awkward... and that line is where Asako — a woman who sweats copiously — meets Koutarou — a perfume developer who can't get enough of Asako's, er, scent. Don't miss a romcom manga like no other!

The adorable new odd-couple cat comedy manga from the creator of the beloved *Chi's Sweet Home*, in full color!

Sue & Tai-chan

Konami Kanata

Sue is an aging housecat who's looking forward to living out her life in peace... but her plans change when the mischievous black tomcat Tai-chan enters the picture! Hey! Sue never signed up to be a catsitter! *Sue & Tai-chan* is the latest from the reigning meow-narch of cute kitty comics, Konami Kanata.

PERFECT WORLD

Rie Aruga

A TOUCHING NEW SERIES ABOUT LOVE AND COPING WITH DISABILITY

An office party reunites Tsugumi with her high school crush Itsuki. He's realized his dream of becoming an architect, but along the way, he experienced a spinal injury that put him in a wheelchair. Now Tsugumi's rekindled feelings will butt up against prejudices she never considered — and Itsuki will have to decide if he's ready to let someone into his heart...

"Depicts with great delicacy and courage the difficulties some with disabilities experience getting involved in romantic relationships... Rie Aruga refuses to romanticize, pushing her heroine to face the reality of disability. She invites her readers to the same tasks of empathy, knowledge and recognition."
—Slate.fr

"An important entry [in manga romance]... The emotional core of both plot and characters indicates thoughtfulness... [Aruga's] research is readily apparent in the text and artwork, making this feel like a real story."
—Anime News Network

KC KODANSHA COMICS

A Kodansha Comics Trade Paperback Original
Battle Angel Alita Paperback volume 4 copyright © 2016 Yukito Kishiro
English translation copyright © 2021 Yukito Kishiro

Published in the United States by Kodansha Comics, an imprint of Kodansha USA Publishing, LLC, New York.

Publication rights for this English edition arranged through Kodansha Ltd., Tokyo.

First published in Japan in 2016 by Kodansha Ltd., Tokyo,
as *Battle Angel Alita*...

1st Printing
Translation: Stephen Paul
Lettering: Scott O. Brown, Evan Hayden
Editing: Ajani Oloye, Maggie Le
Kodansha Comics edition cover design by My Truong

Publisher: Kiichiro Sugawara

Director of publishing services: Ben Applegate
Associate director of publishing operations: Stephen Pakula
Publishing services managing editors: Alanna Ruse, Madison Salters
Production managers: Emi Lotto, Angela Zurlo
Logo © Kodansha USA Publishing, LLC